LINCOM Studies in
Indo-European Linguistics

LINCOM Studies in
Indo-European Linguistics

In this series

Welsh dictionaries in the twentieth century: a critical analysis

Sabine Heinz

2003
LINCOM EUROPA

Published by LINCOM GmbH 2003. 2nd edition.

All correspondence concerning *LINCOM Studies in Indo-European Linguistics* should be addressed to:

LINCOM GmbH
Freibadstr. 3
D-81543 Muenchen

LINCOM.EUROPA@t-online.de
http://home.t-online.de/home/LINCOM.EUROPA
www.lincom-europa.com

Printed in E.C.
Printed on chlorine-free paper

Die Deutsche Bibliothek - CIP Cataloguing-in-Publication-Data

A catalogue record for this publication is available from Die Deutsche Bibliothek (http://www.ddb.de)

ISBN 3 89586 750 0

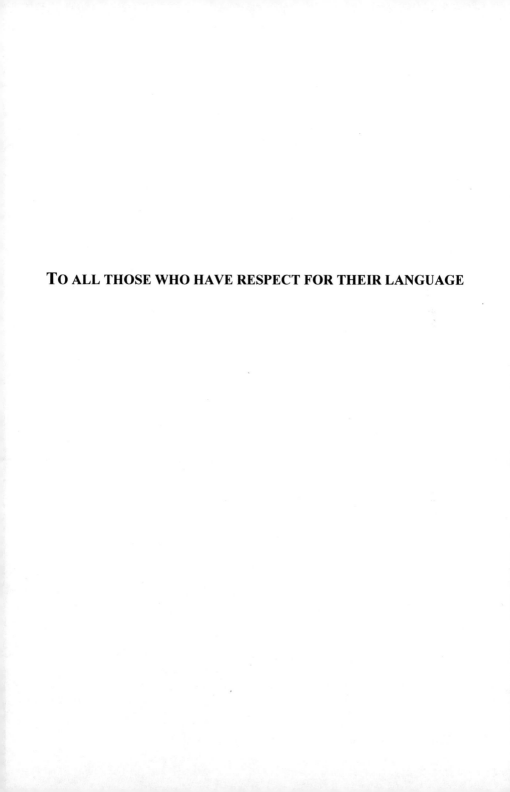

TO ALL THOSE WHO HAVE RESPECT FOR THEIR LANGUAGE

Acknowledgements

This book would not have been begun (or finished) without the constant encouragement of Professor Hildegard L.C. Tristram, University of Potsdam. I am indebted to her for valuable comments and stimulating suggestions on the most various aspects of this work. Professor Erich Poppe, University of Marburg, also deserves my deepest thanks for advising me on theoretical approaches and on the subtleties of the Welsh language. Both have saved me from numerous infelicities.

Many others scholars have also assisted in the progress of this investigation. Dr Habil. George Broderick, Humboldt-University of Berlin, was a permanent consultant. Dr Bryan Jenner, University of Vienna/Austria, smoothed out much of clumsiness in the English as did Dr Orin Gensler, Max Planck Institute for Evolutionary Anthropology/Leipzig and Wendy Großkopf, Thousand Oaks/USA.

Siôn Williams, University of Cardiff/Wales, kept me up-to-date with the latest information regarding Welsh language and language politics and was a critical reader of a number of sections of this book. The same holds for Dr Iwan Wmffre, Tregaron/Wales. Both also provided me with valuable material.

I am also grateful for the chance to discuss selected aspects of this work with Emeritus Professor Achim Hoffmann, University of Potsdam; Professor Seamus MacMathúna, University of Ulster Coleraine/Northern Ireland; Professor Ruaraidh MacThòmais, University of Glasgow/Scotland; Dr Graham Isaac, University of Wales/Aberystwyth; Dr Seán Ó Riain, Embassy of Ireland/Berlin; Jil Boucherit, librarian in the Bibliothèque du departement de Breton et Celtique Rennes/Brittany; Phylip Brake, Senior Tutor-organiser at the Welsh Teaching Centre of the University of Wales Llanbedr Pont Steffan/Wales; Aled Llion Jones, lecturer of Welsh at the Catholic University of Lublin/Poland; Sophie Francis Kidd Pont-hir-waun/Wales; Andrew Hawks, *Geiriadur Prifysgol Cymru*/Wales; and Mag Theresa Illés, Vienna/Austria.

I would also like to express my deep thanks to Professor Helmut Birkhan for inviting me to Vienna/Austria, and thereby giving me the opportunity to interact with the staff of the Institute for Indoeuropean Studies, Professor Heiner Eichner, Dr Hans C. Luschützky, Mag David Stifter, and to take full advantage of the excellent libraries there.

In this context, I would also like to thank the students in Berlin and Vienna, who were the first to be confronted with my latest ideas and discoveries, to provide me with the opportunity to discuss various matters.

I should not forget to thank my teacher of Celtic Studies, Hon. Professor Martin Rockel, who first drew my attention to Welsh studies and whose greatest wish it has been to see this work come to light.

I must also mention Family and friends who kept faith in me and continued to believe that I would, despite all circumstances, not give up before having finished this book. Special support came from my elder son, André, who proofread the work and from Carsten Heinz, who provided technical support. I also owe my younger son, René, a debt of gratitude for being patient with his mother.

2

I would like to thank the newspapers (*Golwg, The Daily Post, Y Cymro, Western Mail & Echo Ltd*) who have made available the archive material, the staff of the *National Library of Wales* and of *Welsh University Press* for providing me with the necessary photocopies. In addition, I take this opportunity to express my appreciation that I was granted permission to use figures from John Osmond's book *The National Assembly Agenda. A Handbook for the First Four Years* and from *Let's Do our Best for the Ancient Tongue. The Welsh Language in the Twentieth Century*. The latter is a book compiled by Professor Geraint H. Jenkins and Dr Maria A. Williams and includes the valuable maps of Professor John W. Aitchison and Emeritus Professor Harold Carter.

The reader will undoubtedly come across shortcomings and insufficiencies in this work, for which I alone take full responsibility. With all of its failings, however, it is the sincere wish of the author that this book may encourage all those who love their native language to make full use of it.

Welsh dictionaries in the twentieth century:
a critical analysis

Table of Contents:

I. Introduction
1.1. Introduction: Aim of the investigation

In 1995, shortly after *Geiriadur yr Academi. The Welsh Academy English-Welsh Dictionary* (Griffiths, B. & D.G. Jones: 1995) was published, a friend - a fluent Welsh speaker - told me that the first Welsh dictionary had recently come out. However, the first known Welsh dictionary, that is, *A Dictionary in Englyshe and Welshe* was compiled by William Salesbury and published in 1547. Given that, I began to give serious consideration about what my friend had said and started investigating aspects of Welsh lexicography.

Since human communication is primarily based on language, most misunderstandings can be traced to language problems. The room for misunderstanding is even larger when more than one language is involved. As soon as languages were committed to writing, therefore, attempts were made to create special tools to help achieve unambiguous communication and efficient language acquisition. One of the basic tools was the dictionary, the oldest self-instructional learning aid. The dictionary has since been used for language acquisition, for the improvement of communication skills, for professional translating and second-language teaching, as well as for linguistic research and personal perfection.

Since the Western world has become increasingly specialised and society has become highly mobile, the mastery of languages is a necessary qualification in professional life. In addition, it is important at a personal level and generally considered indispensable for the assimilation of knowledge.

Dictionaries, therefore, are still highly popular. Today, however, they are produced either in book form, or they are digitally recorded and available on electronic or optical data carriers, or they are analogously recorded on magnetic data carriers.

Dictionaries are used from school or even pre-school age onwards (cf. picture dictionaries in section 1.3.2.1.3. or chapter III). As comprehensive sources of linguistic information dictionaries can thereby make available essential structures of the languages described in them to their speakers. As a result, dictionaries are tools which may efficiently support language maintenance.

In this function they also serve the interests of the communities whose language they record, or those of the interest groups who commission them. Dictionaries supply the information required by these groups on subjects that are of foremost interest. They also promote that group's position and social status both at home and abroad. In light of this, it becomes clear that the compilation of dictionaries has always been part of social developments and has been carried out in the interest of particular cultural or political groups. There are many driving interests behind this. Some of them are: the spread of religious beliefs, the promotion of commerce, the strengthening of national consciousness or group consciousness, the prevention of language decline, the purification of a language, the establishment of a unified written language, the development of a variety into a standard variety, the establishment of linguistic norms and conventions, culture and pedagogy, the support of language politics, language planning with regard to the political lexicon,[1] the promotion of science, and the social integration of people by reducing linguistic barriers. All in all,

> "[d]ictionaries always tell us something about the characteristics of their compilers, about the characteristics of their intended users and about the characteristics of the society and culture in which their compilers intend them to be used" (Fishman 1995: 29).

Consequently, dictionaries are important repositories of information about both the languages presented in them and the social attitudes and expectations of their speakers and their compilers. In addition, morphological, syntactic and discourse structures are not only components of the respective language system, but also the devices that bind the reality we perceive. Since they, therefore, contribute - at least in part - to the construction of identity, the importance of adequately compiled dictionaries as

- instructional,
- translational and
- research tools, but also as
- devices for language maintenance and
- the construction of cultural identity

beomes apparent. Adequacy in this respect refers to the description of a language presented in a dictionary in relation to its grammatical system, its intended users and special purposes defined for the particular work. Therefore, if the compilations of dictionaries are deficient in this sense, they are reduced in their functions.

The encoding function of dictionaries has been widely accepted in the Western world and is a commonplace for well established languages. Encoding here is understood as a linguistic activity involving productive skills, such as writing, speaking or translating from the native into a foreign language. It is the opposite of decoding, which is a linguistic activity involving receptive skills such as reading, listening or translating from a foreign into a native language (Hartmann & James 1998: 35, 48).

However, the encoding function is of particular social relevance for regional or minority languages in order to develop, disseminate, stabilise and normalise them as genuine means of communication in present day society.

---

[1] Lexicon here is understood as "the totality of a language's vocabulary, seen either as a list or as a structured whole. The view of vocabulary as a list of words has led to the development of glossaries, dictionaries and other works of reference, while the structural view has encouraged such linguistic disciplines as grammar, lexicology and semantics" (Hartmann & James 1998: 86). The terms glossary and dictionary are defined in sections 1.3.2.1.1. and 2.1.3.

The term vocabulary is understood in two ways in this investigation; first, as "the sum total of the words used in a language [...]. The specialisation of vocabulary for different uses is potentially infinite, e.g. politics, religion, or sex, are often singled out for lexical treatment in reference works" and, second, as "a list of words or phrases, with or without definitions" (Hartmann & James 1998: 154). For further explanations, see section 1.3.2.1.1.

The term regional or minority language is understood here in the sense given in the *European Charter for Regional or Minority Languages*,[2] which formulates:

"Article 1 - Definition

[...]

a "regional or minority languages" means languages that are:

    i "traditionally used within a given territory of a State by nationals of that State who form a group numerically smaller than the rest of the State's population; and

    ii different from the official language(s) of that State;

    it does not include either dialects of the official language(s) of the State or the languages of migrants;

b "territory in which the regional or minority language is used" means the geographical area in which the said language is the mode of expression of a number of people justifying the adoption of the various protective and promotional measures provided for this Charter;

c "non-territorial languages" means languages used by nationals of the State which differ from the language or languages used by the rest of the State's population but which, although traditionally used within the territory of the State, cannot be identified with a particluar area thereof" (Council of Europe/Conseil de l'Europe 1992: 2).[3]

Normalisation is a term introduced by Catalan sociolinguists which describes one possible result of a linguistic conflict between dominated and dominant languages (cf. Vetter 1997: 25f., http://www.eape.es/publications/RLD/rld29abs.htm, 4.6.2001, C.H. Williams 2000: 677ff. and section 4.1.1.). It includes the implementation of the standard language by at least fifty per cent. Normalisation's counterpart is substitution. All changes in the use of the language by a group of people in a situation characterised by linguistic conflict move between these two possibilities; i.e. substitution, which means the elimination of the dominated language, and normalisation, i.e. the codification and social spread of the use of the dominated language in any social and functional domain. The language is normalised, therefore, when its usage as a common and natural means of communication at any time and in any sphere of life is realised (cf. Gruffudd 1999a: 3).

The compilation of a dictionary as a data pool of language material and a guide for appropriate language use thus frequently enjoys the highest priority for linguistic research in such minority language groups. Some languages are exclusively recorded in dictionaries (cf. Ickler 1985: 360).

---

[2] I would like to take the opportunity of thanking Dr Seán Ó Riain, Embassy or Ireland/Berlin, for bringing this matter to my attention.

[3] The term 'minority language', however, is misleading, since minority languages are predominantly indigenous tongues which have suffered minor status only recently and because of historical factors which often involve political suppression. Other terms employed in this context are 'lesser used languages' or 'languages of limited diffusion'. None of them is neutral and, therefore, none is satisfactory.

Nevertheless, the European institution which deals with minority languages is called *Bureau for Lesser Used Languages*, a fact that gives the term 'lesser used languages' a somewhat official status. Since there is no other term available, the terms 'minority languages' and 'lesser used languages' are used synonymously in this investigation as well as the term language of 'limited social influence' created by the author.

The Welsh language became a minority language as the result of the incorporation of Wales into England in 1536/42 (cf. S. Heinz 1998b). As early as 1536, English was granted official status[4] (cf. H. Thomas 1972: 45-55) while the Welsh language was excluded from certain areas of communication and lost gradually its prestige.[5] With emerging industrial capitalism at the end of the nineteenth century, the English language finally gained ground both socially and territorially. This was the language of a new social system and its political, economic and social institutions which consequently spread internationally on an enormous scale. The biggest blow hit the Welsh language in the twentieth century: two world wars not only depopulated some areas, but gave way to new social developments which further destabilised Welsh society. Among these were an increasing mobility of individuals, the creation of white-collar jobs, new occupations for women, the advent of electronic media and newspapers, and the decay of traditional industry. In addition, new leisure time activities became popular, which were no longer dominated by religious institutions, but predominantly by the emerging modern Anglo-American way of life, e.g. travelling by car and plane, new kinds of sports and so on. These developments promoted individualisation and the breaking up of close-knit language communities. The number of monolingual English speakers rose from 45% in 1891 to 81% in 1991, leaving almost only bilingual Welsh speakers.[6]

In this context, the compiling of dictionaries has been regarded as a linguistic priority in Wales since the 1950s. Although the country can look back on a long tradition of dictionary production, the second half of the twentieth century has seen the most remarkable growth in lexicographical work. Referring back to the statement at the beginning of this introduction, however, there are obvious gaps which could be improved in order to serve the functions of dictionaries mentioned above in a more efficient manner.

To give an outline of such gaps, the following investigation, first of all, looks at selected aspects of Welsh lexicography[7] particularly relevant to this problem area. Second, modern dictionaries with the highest impact on the Welsh speaking community are analysed in detail in order to comment on the present state of language description at end of the twentieth century. Third, conclusions are drawn as to the social role of these tools at the end of the second and the beginning of the third millennium.

All in all, this study focuses on the description of lexicographical gaps arising from a particular cultural context and the difficulties caused by them for the Welsh language at the beginning of the twenty-first century. It is hoped that the investigation will contribute to the filling of these gaps in the future.

---

[4]   The 'official status' of a language in this investigation is understood as its legally defined range of usage for communication in the respective society, such as done in the Irish constitution (cf. Bunreacht na hÉireann. Constitution of Ireland http://www.irlgov.ie/taoiseach/publication/constitution/english, 1.1.2002). Its actual status reflects the extent of the implementation of the language policy in society.

[5]   The 'prestige of a language' in this investigation is understood as the recognition and acceptance of a language among the population.

[6]   The number of monolingual speakers was about 1% in 1951. For further details, see S. Heinz (1998b).

[7]   For a definition of lexicography, see section 1.3.1.

1.2.   Methods

This investigation presents the achievements and the weaknesses of contemporary Welsh lexicography and details how dictionaries in this language are to face the challenges of twenty-first century society.

Welsh lexicography is - compared with its sister languages - well advanced in the development of general lexis and terminology (cf. chapter III and Ternes 1991a: 2345). However, other aspects of Welsh lexicography seem to be less prosperous. Therefore, this investigation, focuses primarily on the analysis of the grammatical information contained in modern Welsh dictionaries. This aspect is of highest priority, since grammatical information provides basic knowledge of how to use lexical items in context and how to make them applicable in speech (cf. section 1.3.2.2.). In addition, adequate grammatical description of a given language in a dictionary supports language maintenance and identity (cf. sections 1.1., 4.1.1. and 4.1.2.). Closely related to the analysis of grammatical information in Welsh dictionaries is a discussion on the inclusion of phonetic transcription into these reference works.

(A)   The corpus

The corpus of dictionaries analysed here consists of the most popular bi-directional bilingual general-purpose dictionaries. This type of dictionaries presents predominantly a non-specialist lexicon for anybody interested in the particular language (cf. section 1.3.2.1.), but especially for the advanced learner. Given the bilingual linguistic situation[1] in Wales and the lack of a modern Standard Welsh-Welsh and other dictionaries (cf. section 4.1.1.), they are, however, also essential for native speakers, mainly for written, but also for oral communication.

Learners are defined as people speaking Welsh as a second language (cf. sections 1.3.2.2., 1.3.2.3., 1.3.2.2.5. and McCorduck 1993: 5). These people form a high percentage of Welsh speakers (cf. section 4.1.1.).

Since bi-directional general-purpose dictionaries serve both the native speaker and the learner, this type of dictionaries is by far the most frequently used and thereby has the greatest impact on language acquisition and use. As such it is very important to the maintenance, stabilisation, and normalisation of the language (cf. sections 1.1. and 4.1.1.).

My own inquiries among teachers, lecturers, students and staff of public offices turned out that *Y Geiriadur Mawr* (cf. Ternes 1991: 2347), *Y Geiriadur Bach, Y Geiriadur Newydd* and *Geiriadur yr Academi. The Welsh Academy English-Welsh Dictionary*[2] are the ones which are

---

[1]   A linguistic situation is the: "ethnical and/or regional as well as the social and functional distribution and hierarchy of languages and/or varieties of such, which, at a given moment and in a certain (usually politically/administratively defined) territory, are in communicative use according to the prevalent ethnical, political, socio-economical, and cultural conditions" (Hansen & Carls et al. 1996: 13-21).

[2]   The entire corpus of Welsh dictionaries is presented in chapter III.

12

used most.[3] This is confirmed by the number of editions of these dictionaries printed so far (cf. section 3.1.).

The emphasis of the analysis in this investigation is placed on the Welsh-to-English sections of the dictionaries in order to discover as to whether the Welsh language is described adequately for decoding purposes. The question of how the language is explained in the English-to-Welsh sections, i.e. mainly for encoding purposes, is dealt with predominantly by back-referring to these sections. The inclusion of the uni-directional general-purpose English-Welsh dictionary *Geiriadur yr Academi. The Welsh Academy English-Welsh Dictionary* (*Geiriadur yr Academi* henceforth) supplements the demonstration as to how far the encoding function of Welsh dictionaries is met.

In order to adequately illustrate tendencies in modern Welsh lexicography, other popular reference books, such as learners' dictionaries, have also been considered. This has been found necessary, since a high percentage of Welsh speakers are learners and cannot be excluded from this investigation.

Because of English cultural influences in Wales over the centuries, and in view of the fact that English lexicography is the most advanced in this field (cf. section 1.3.2.2.) English dictionaries have also been looked at.

Comparing dictionaries of other Celtic languages, which are structurally similar to Welsh, with their Welsh counterparts reveals some of the weaknesses of lexicography in Wales. As a result, general demands on Welsh lexicography are formulated more accurately at the end of this investigation.

The dictionaries analysed here are predominantly printed books. Only when investigating lexicographical developments during the period of the Renaissance, at a time when the printing press was still difficult to employ, are dictionaries in manuscript form included. The analysis of reference books on electronic media is referred to when necessary in order to illustrate tendencies in Welsh lexicography.

Electronic reference books are not considered as objects of investigation in their own right here, since most of them are versions of dictionaries in print. Therefore, they, avail themselves of the possibilities offered by computer technology. The few dictionaries on electronic media specifically designed for use on computers are still in their infancy and are of varying standard in concept and quality. Their analysis, therefore, falls outside the scope of the present discussion and requires a separate investigation.

The same is true for system-bound machine dictionaries which form an integral part of translating software, of software for information acquisition, of question/answer-software, of data bases, etc. (Wiegand 1998: 242ff.). Examples for the English language are META, CONDOR, and BACON. A multilingual terminological data bank for the work in European institutions is EURODICAUTOM which includes Danish, Dutch, English, French, German, Greek, Italian, Portuguese, and Spanish (http://www.acad.bg/echo/eu92.html, 15.11.2000). For the Welsh *The*

National Welsh Assembly Agenda. A Handbook for the first four years (C.H. Williams 1998: 112) clearly says that the field of information technology for linguistic purposes is not sufficiently developed:

> "The current potential of [information technology] is not fully developed. It might consist of constructing databases of standard and specialist terms so that one Welsh term would correspond to one English term and vice versa; the upgrading of *CySill* and *CysGair*; the licencing of Welsh versions of standard computer packages and office systems; the development of speech to text procedures [...]."

A critical investigation into a scientific field still in its infancy, however, is not intended in this study. Second, system-bound machine dictionaries cater for a restricted number of specialist users only. Third, since their compilation follows different lexicographical processes (cf. section 1.3.), these tools do not fall within the field of lexicography as defined in section 1.3.1. (cf. also Wiegand 1998: 254ff.).

(B) Preliminary steps of the investigation

As is true for any analysis, a theoretical approach has to be formulated. The theoretical lexicographical basis of this investigation is the most recent research in the field of critical and historical lexicography relevant to the problem area.

With regard to critical lexicography (cf. section 1.3.2.), an apparatus of clearly defined terms has been established in sections 1.3.2.1.1. and 1.3.2.1.2. Second, a typology of dictionaries which establishes the basis to present the actual range of contemporary Welsh dictionaries has been developed in section 1.3.2.1.3. In a third step, parameters for the linguistic investigation of Welsh dictionaries have been set up in two stages: First, guided by critical lexicographical investigations of English-language dictionaries, generally useful parameters have been formulated in section 1.3.2.2. This approach is justified, since English dictionaries are not only used in Wales as part of the United Kingdom, but have generally attracted major scientific attention.

Second, based on the structure of the Welsh language, those parameters have finally been selected which are considered necessary in order to reflect adequately the properties of Welsh in dictionaries and to promote the correct usage of Welsh in daily communication (cf. section 1.3.2.3.).

(C) Historical perspective

The historical dimension is required in order to make a plea for the achievements and shortcomings of Welsh lexicography at the beginning of the twenty first century. Contemporary developments cannot be fully understood without considering their past. Therefore, major stages of historical lexicography, such as glossary and vocabulary production, are illustrated in the context of social developments in Wales. The discussion will confine itself to basic social events and processes which have influenced language usage and policy, and which are inextricably linked with developments in linguistics as an academic discipline. In a similar brief way, the historical linguistic works of major influence on lexicographical developments are introduced. Such an approach is justified, since most of these have already been studied in considerable detail (cf. chapter II).

In the context of the historical perspective, the investigation also includes (a) a survey of the entire corpus of Welsh dictionaries so far produced and (b) comparative considerations of dictionary production in the other Celtic languages (cf. chapter III).

In addition, essential to the investigation of Welsh lexicography is the inter-relationship between (a) dictionaries and language maintenance and (b) dictionaries and identity (cf. section 4.1.). The discussion of language maintenance is grounded on socio-linguistic approaches as introduced by Dressler (1977) and Fishman (1991). Questions with regard to the construction of cultural identity are dealt with by relying on socio-ethnological approaches as illustrated by Tovey & Hannan et al. (1989) and M. Heinz (1993). The investigation of both subjects refers to the linguistic situation of the Celtic sister languages of Welsh.

Before the linguistic analysis of selected reference books is entered into, however, the individual Welsh dictionaries selected for analysis are presented in detail and put in a comparative Celtic context (cf. section 4.2.).

(D)   Linguistic approaches resorted to

Before an analysis of the grammatical information contained in modern Welsh dictionaries can be carried out, the linguistic method to be used requires clarification. This is advocated, since first, there are different concepts of grammar. None of the models, however, has yet been able to describe principles and rules of word, sentence, or text formation comprehensively and exhaustively for any language.

Second, if not clearly stated, the grammatical approach of dictionary compilers often remains hidden behind the reduced or formulaic presentation of grammatical information.[4]

Third, the approaches identified in this investigation reveal that the individual lexicographers draw on various grammatical models, depending on their linguistic background.

In light of these facts, an integrated grammatical concept has been adopted for this study, which is purpose-orientated towards grammatical information, and is predominantly to serve the purposes of lexicography. Because of this, the following pre-conditions have to be established: first, a dependence on highly abstract grammatical theories should not be entertained in order to avoid unattainable tasks of the dictionaries under review. Second, a grammatical concept is needed to concentrate on the analysis of single lexical items. However, when definitions, collocations, idioms or simple phrases and sentences exemplify the use of single lexical items grammatical description takes in larger lexical units and phrases, sentences, or text production.

The concept favoured in this investigation, therefore, is an integrated one which (a) draws on traditional grammar, (b) is adapted to the peculiarities of the Welsh language, and (c) is open to

---

[4]   There is only one Welsh dictionary which is clearly based on a definite grammar, i.e. the *Pocket Modern Welsh Dictionary* by Gareth King.

elements of structural and functional grammatical theories and valency theory. Such an approach is justified in view of the aim of this investigation and of latest linguistic theories, such as that of *Basic Linguistic Theory*[5] (cf. Dixon 1997). Dixon claims that:

> "Over the last forty years or so the discipline of linguistics has been knocked off balance [...] The major development has been the invention of a number of restricted sets of formalisms, that have been called 'theories'. Each is based on some part of Basic Linguistic Theory. Each is useful for describing certain kinds of linguistic relationships, but it is put forward as if it were a complete theory of language. The word 'theory' is being used in a novel way [...] It is said that one shouldn't mix theories (just like one shouldn't mix religions) but in fact each [theory] is founded on a different part of Basic Theory, and it can be profitable in describing different parts of a language" (ibid.: 130f.).

A similar theoretical orientation is used by Dryer who states:

> "Instead of insisting on some detailed theoretical framework or precise formalism, it is good instead to discuss linguistics in terms of minimal, universally accepted linguistic notions" (Dryer http://wings.buffalo.edu/soc-sci/linguistics/dryer/dryer.htm, 20.10.2001).

Linguistic concepts of the same kind are adopted by Stassen (1985), when speaking of a 'common stock of traditional grammatical theory', and by Foley when describing his theoretical orientation as follows:

> "I wanted the organisation of the grammar to reflect the structure of the language as closely as possible. Hence, I have deliberately chosen to be eclectic, choosing various ideas from different theories when these seem to elucidate the structure of the language best" (Foley 1991: vii).

Such an orientation means, for instance, that the definition of the word class numeral is predominantly based on semantic-structural aspects. The definition of one of the non-inflecting word classes of functional words, in this case the particle, however, is mainly based on functional aspects.

Such an eclectic approach includes the development of alternative theoretical descriptions of linguistic properties of Welsh where found limitedely elucidated in current grammar books. The reference book primarily used for the analysis is *Gramadeg y Gymraeg* (P.W. Thomas 1995), the leading grammar of modern Welsh.

The kind of codification of the grammatical information is briefly discussed when found insufficient. Codification, derived from the term code,[6] is here understood as

---

[5]   I would like to take this opportunity of thanking Emeritus Prof. Achim Hoffmann and Dr Orin Gensler, Max Planck Institute for Evolutionary Anthropology/Leipzig, for their helpful discussions on this subject.

[6]   Code here is understood as "an abbreviated term or symbol used in reference works as a label to mark the provenance of a word or phrase" (Hartmann & James 1998: 22).

"the presentation of linguistic information about usage in reference works. There is no unified framework for this process, but the activity has a long tradition in the fields of pronunciation (orthoepy), spelling (orthography), vocabulary (lexicography), and technical terminology (terminography) [...] General dictionaries [...] fulfil an important role in codifying linguistic facts" (Hartmann & James 1998: 22).

However, a systematic investigation of grammatical codification found in Welsh dictionaries merits separate consideration.

The disussion on the phonetic description of the Welsh language in dictionaries is based on information drawn from *Welsh Phonology. Selected Readings* (Ball & G.E. Jones 1984). The phonetic model favoured in this investigation is that of the Prague School (cf. Trubetzkoy 1939, Arnold & Hansen 1975).

Problems with regard to the choice of lexical items included in Welsh dictionaries form a peripheral issue in this study. Some of them, however, are illustrated briefly where appropriate in order to underline the need for further research in this field.

The whole investigation is broadly descriptive. Some prescriptive elements are suggested as part of the discussion and analysis of selected linguistic phenomena[7] in Welsh which are to be included in dictionaries.

Finally, the conclusion summarises, based on the theoretical outlines of the first chapter, the present state of Welsh dictionary production in its historical and cultural context. This includes, first, comments on the adequacy of Welsh dictionaries in order to meet their functions as in-structional and translational tools. Second, some light is shed on the consequences the linguistic description contained in the dictionaries has on the use and maintenance of the Welsh language. Third, the social role of modern Welsh dictionaries, e.g. for the construction of identity, is mentioned.

---

[7] Phenomenon here is not to be understood in the sense as it is used in systemic grammar. In this investigation, the word is employed in its philosophical sense, i.e. as an object as it is perceived by the senses or even more general as an occurrence, circumstance, or fact that is perceptible by the senses.

1.3. Recent developments in general lexicography
1.3.1. Preliminary remarks

Lexicography as seen by Wiegand (1998), who is currently seeking to outline a general theory of lexicography (cf. ibid.: 6ff.), is divided into lexicography dealing with dictionaries (Wörterbuchforschung), lexicography dealing with encyclopaedias (Lexikonforschung), and lexicography dealing with other kinds of reference works (Allbuchforschung). Of predominant interest for this investigation is lexicography dealing with dictionaries, which will, following Wiegand (cf. ibid.: 120), henceforth be referred to simply as lexicography.

Lexicography in this respect is not yet a science in its own right, but is a scientific field of research with the potential to develop into a proper science. It is the scientific metafield of any practical and theoretical processes in relation to dictionary planning, compiling, production, and description excluding computer-lexicographical processes (cf. ibid.: 254ff.). It investigates and provides the principles necessary for documenting the lexicon of a language, a dialect, a sociolect or other lexicon by drawing not only on lexicology[1] with its theoretical bases and materials for lexicographic codification, but also on other branches of linguistics, and by taking practical concerns such as marketability, user-friendliness, and so on into consideration.

A guide to different aspects of lexicography is established by the three parts of Volume 5 of the series *Handbücher zur Sprach- und Kommunikationswissenschaft* (Hausmann & Wiegand et al. 1989), which is called *Wörterbücher. Dictionaries. Dictionnaires. Ein internationales Handbuch zur Lexikographie*. Most recent developments in lexicography are continuously reflected in the *International Journal of Lexicography*,[2] in the international yearbook *Lexicographica*[3] and its related series *Lexicographica. Series Maior*.[4] There are also lexicographical journals which are regionally based, such as *Dictionaries* in the USA, *Lexicographical Studies* in China, *Lexique* in France, *Lexikos* in South Africa, *LexikoNordica* in Scandinavia, and *Revista de Lexicographica* for Spanish-speaking countries. Since it is not possible to give a detailed account of the present state of lexicographical research here, I refer the reader to Wiegand (1998). He presents a comprehensive report on the state of research and discusses the most important trends, including those which are relevant to this work.

In order to meet the theoretical and practical demands, lexicography has to investigate theoretical, methodological, terminological, historical, documentary, didactic, cultural, and pedagogical problem areas. Four main branches of this scientific field have thus developed: research into the use of dictionaries, critical lexicography, historical lexicography and systematic lexicography (ibid.: 255f.). In particular, historical and critical lexicography are of major interest for this investigation.

---

[1] Lexicology in this study is defined as a discipline which deals with the lexicon of a language and its development. It comprises etymology, semantics and phraseology (see also page 34).

[2] Edited by A.P. Cowie, T. Fontenelle, C. Marello, T. Piotowski in Oxford.

[3] Edited by F.M. Dolezal, Alain Rey, Thorsten Roelcke, Herbert Ernst Wiegand, Werner Wolski, Ladislav Zgusta, Andrea Lehr in Tübingen.

[4] Edited by Sture Allén, Pierre Corbin, Reinhard R.K. Hartmann, Franz Josef Hausmann, Ulrich Heid, Oskar Reichmann, Ladislav Zgusta in Tübingen.

Historical lexicography deals with lexicographical processes in their historical context and relationship to cultural processes as part of which they have to be defined (ibid.: 10). Critical lexicography establishes the parameters for the evaluation of dictionaries. Some aspects and terms of these two fields of lexicography which are relevant for this examination are discussed in the following sections.

1.3.2. Critical lexicography
1.3.2.1. Typology of modern dictionaries
1.3.2.1.1. Defining the term dictionary

The definition of the term *dictionary* from a synchronic standpoint is somewhat complicated, since the term has, in the first place, been applied to different kinds of reference works. Second, there are different terms which denote what traditionally might have been called a *dictionary*, e.g. *vocabulary, lexicon, glossary, thesaurus, concordance, index, gazetter, encyclopedia, linguistic atlas*. The loose application of these and other terms, which is often guided by marketing strategies - such as the attracting of as many buyers as possible - and the difficulties resulting from this in defining the term *dictionary* are discussed in Wiegand (1998: 66ff.). As a result, Read (1971: 713) gives a rather vague definition:

> "The word 'dictionary' is used to describe a wide variety of reference works. Basically, a dictionary lists a set of words with information about them. The list may attempt to be a complete inventory of a language or may be only a small segment of it. A short list, sometimes at the back of a book, is often called a glossary. When a word list is an index to a limited body of writing, with reference to each passage, it is called concordance."

Third, there are lexicographical works which go beyond the functions commonly ascribed to dictionaries, if we think of them as a set of lexical items and information about them. They also include features of encyclopaedias, if we define these as reference works explaining objects and ideas of nature and human society (cf. Ternes 1991b: 98). In addition, there are reference works which cross the boundaries between dictionaries and grammar books, or dictionaries, encyclopaedias and grammar books, e.g. the *Power Wörterbuch Englisch*[1] by Langenscheidt. Apart from lexical items listed alphabetically and their grammatical and semantic explanation, whole paragraphs on special grammatical issues may be suddenly included as well as explanations on particular natural phenomena or certain social events.

Fourth, statistical data on the use of the various terms and accurate definitions deduced from such data, however, are lacking. This is the reason why Wiegand (1998: 69) employs the term *dictionary* as a hyperonym for any kind of linguistic lexicographical work.

Because of the vague application of the term dictionary and the fact that I can in no way investigate all linguistic lexicographical works produced in Wales, a definition which serves the purpose of this study is necessary. A dictionary here is defined as a reference work in which lexically relevant units,[2] i.e. words or phrases, are displayed in a specific structure, that is, as a succession of independent paragraphs or entries.[3] The latter are so ordered that they may be found through an explicitly statable search procedure, an algorithm, such as alphabetical order. The entries contain lexically relevant information, i.e. meaning, pronunciation and/or a varying

---

[1] For bibliographical notes of the works mentioned henceforth, see the references (section 6.2.).
[2] Units here are understood as elements (segments) forming classes, which can then be given seperate names. Units are distinguished and described by means of segmentation and classification.
[3] For a definition of the term entry, see section 1.3.2.1.2.

content of grammatical or other information, for the selected lexical units which are interpreted into the same or one or more different languages.

In order to express clearly what is not subject of this investigation, a definition of the term vocabulary from a synchronic standpoint is also recommended. However, when comparing Irish and Welsh lexicographical works, this proves nearly impossible. Most Welsh dictionaries would rather be called vocabularies if one looks at them in an Irish or English context, since they generally exhibit limited grammatical or even semantic information (cf. analysis in chapter IV). Considering these circumstances, the following definition for the term vocabulary was found appropriate: in the context of historical and contemporary lexicographical production of a particular country, a vocabulary appears to be a reference work in which lexically relevant units are displayed in a particular macrostructure, but which as a whole is - compared with existing dictionaries - purposefully reduced in both content and size. That means that a combination of reductions (a) in grammatical information, (b) in semantic variation, (c) in the selection of headwords[4] included, and (d) in the variety of the macrostructure[5] can be expected. The extent of such restrictions, however, is dependent on standards generally established for dictionaries in the given lexicographical context.

---

[4]   For a definition of the term headword, see section 1.3.2.1.2.
[5]   For a definition of the term macrostructure, see 1.3.2.1.2.

1.3.2.1.2.   Components of the dictionary structure

Some major components of the dictionary structure are: entry, macrostructure, headword, and microstructure. They are briefly defined in the following section.

(A)   The entry

As mentioned in the definition of *dictionary*, the entire paragraph containing the lexically relevant unit which is to be interpreted, and all information that concerns it is called an entry. As such it is also a significant component part for the constitution of the macrostructure of a given lexicographical work. Further features of the entry are described as follows:

> "A wide range of formats [...] is possible. In the dictionary, depending on its content and purpose, these component parts are common: the lemma[1] (which allows the compiler to locate and the user to find the entry within the overall word-list); the formal comment on the 'topic' introduced by the lemma (spelling, pronunciation, grammar); and the semantic 'comment' (definition, usage, etymology). In case of multiple meanings of the lemma, the entry is subdivided into (ususally numbered or otherwise marked) sections called 'sub-entries' or 'sub-senses', each of which provides the same basic information categories" (Hartmann & James 1998: 50).

(B)   The macrostructure

The term macrostructure has been variously and extensively described (cf. amongst others Wiegand 1989a: 371-409). Since the definitions proposed so far do not really further this investigation, a personal attempt was made. Following the idea expressed in Wiegand (ibid.: 372) and adapting it to the purpose of this study, a macrostructure can be defined as follows: it generally comprises those major elements of a lexicographical work which arrange the content to be displayed. The macrostructre mostly consists of sub-structures, e.g. that which organises the introduction of the dictionary, that which offers a search procedure for finding individual lexical items and related information, and that which arranges the appendices of a given work (ibid.: 395). Sub-structures organising the introduction or appendices or explanatory sections in the middle of a lexicographical work are also called outside matters (Hartmann & James 1998: 91).

The macrostructure which organsises the lexicon presented in such a way that it becomes accessible to the user can synonymously be called access structure (Zugriffsstruktur, Wiegand 1989a: 373, 393). It is that which is referred to in this investigation when discussing 'the macrostructure'.

There are various kinds of this particular type of structure:

1. A very common access structure, which is predominant in Welsh dictionaries, is the strict alphabetical one without grouping (glattalphabetisch, ibid.: 385). It is reflected, for instance, in *Y Geiriadur Cymraeg Cyfoes. The Modern Welsh Dictionary* (sic, H.M. Evans 1982, cf. section 4.2.):

---

[1]   In this investigation, the term 'headword' is favoured (cf. below).

dibynadwyedd   **di-flas**

dibynadwyedd, *n.m.* RELIABILITY	**di-ddadl,** *a.* UNQUESTIONABLE, SURE
dibynfentro, *n.m.* BRINKMANSHIP	**diddan,** *a.* AMUSING, INTERESTING
dibyniad, (-au), *n.m.* DEPENDENCY	**diddanion,** *n.pl.* JOKES
dibynnedd, *n.m.* DEPENDENCE	**diddanu,** *v.* AMUSE, DIVERT, COMFORT

2. The monolingual dictionary *Yr Odliadur* 'The Rhyming Dictionary' (R. Stephens 1978) exhibits a strict alphabetical macrostructure with grouping, in this case, with a niche-alphabetical one (Wiegand 1989a: 388). Here the lexical items are listed alphabetically under syllables which also follow the alphabetical order, e.g. *ab, abl, abr, ac, acl:*

ellt		**em**	*116*
cawsellt	eg[2]	oeddem	bf
crawcwellt	ell	petasem	cys
crydwellt	eg	problem	eb
dellt	ell	rhuddem	eb
glaswellt	ell	seldrem	eb
irwellt	ell	stem	eb
marchwellt	ell	trem	eb
mellt	ell	ucheldrem	a
		eml	
em		seml	ab
adnapem	bf	teml	eb
aethem	bf		
aflem	a		
anthem	eb		
berem	eg		
brem	eg	**emp**	
buasem	bf	gwemp	ab
byddem	bf	rhemp	eb
cawsem	bf		
cipdrem	eb		
clem	eb		
crygynnem	ebg		
daethem	bf	**en**	
delem	bf	absen	ebg
deuem	bf	absolfen	eb
di-glem	a	acen	eb
dylasem	bf	adacen	eb
dylem	bf	aden	eb
eitem	eb	adfresychen	eb
elem	bf	adwen	bf
elsem	bf	addien	a

[2] The abbreviations employed here are the following: eg = enw gwrywaidd 'masculine noun', ell = enw lluosog 'plural noun', bf = berf 'verb', cys = cysylltair 'conjunction', eb = enw benywaidd 'feminine noun', a = ansoddair 'adjective', ab = ansoddair benywaidd 'feminine adjective'.

A similar structure is exhibited in *Y Cleciadur* 'The Clatter Dictionary' (M. Jones 1996), in which the lexical items are listed according to clusters of consonants in alphabetical order, e.g. *mpr-, -nfr-, -rgr-*:

stampiau	cymryd	mawnbwll
stampio	emrallt	penben
stompio	Emrys	penboeth
swmpo	llymru	penbwl
swmpus	llymru	rhanbarth
Trwmped	limrig	tanbaid
twmpath	memrwn	tanboeth
twmpan	mymryn	tinben
	ymgymryd	trwynbwl
mpr		unben
	ms	
emprwr		**nbl**
llamprai	amser	
llemprog	cyfamser	coronbleth
llimpryn	damsang	gweunblu
pompren	llamsach	manblu
tampro	llymsur	penbleth
tempru	simsan	
ympryd	ymson	**nbr**
	ymswyn	
mr		addfwynbryd
		blaenbrawf
amrant		diheinbraw

44

3. A strict alphabetical macrostructure with niche-alphabetical grouping in a bilingual dictionary is displayed in *Geiriadur yr Academi* (Griffiths, B. & D.G. Jones 1995) when presenting nouns:

> **dove**[1] *n. & a.* **1.** *n.* colomen(-nod) *f*; **Barbary** ~, *(Streptopelia risoria):* colomen B|arbari; **collared** ~, *(S. decaoto):* turtur dorchog (turturod torchog) *f*, colomen dorchog (colomennod torchog *f*; **ground** ~, *(Columbigallina terrestris):* colomen y ddaear; **mourning** ~, *(Zenaidaura macroura):* colomen alarus [...]

The macrostructure used for the presentation of other word classes[3] follows the alphabetical access structure with non-alphabetical nest order (Wiegand 1989a: 391, 384):

---

[3] For a definition of the term word class, see sections 1.3.2.2.2. and 1.3.2.2.7.

at *prep.* **1.** *(position): usu:* yn + nasal mut.; ~ **the centre,** yn y canol; ~ **Oxford,** yn Rhydychen; ~ **Bristol,** ym Mryste; ~ **Bala,** yn y Bala; ~ **the centre of the room,** ynghanol yr ystafell, yng [...]

That means that the lexicon contained in a dictionary may be displayed by varying macrostructures.

4. The reverse alphabetical access structure is exhibited in *Geiriadur Gwrthdroadol Cymraeg Diweddar* 'A Reverse Dictionary of Modern Welsh' (S. Zimmer 1987):

bad	4	trychiad
bad	mablygad	tybiad
abad	llygad	chwinciad
rabad	pyngad	llynciad
diasbad	had	tociad
cad	sancteiddhad	benthyciad
nacâd	boddhad	bachiad
ymwacâd	ymfoddhad	fflachiad
arwyddocâd	rhyddhad	brechiad
blocâd	chwyddhad	ymdrechiad
iachâd	lleihad	trechiad
mandad	ffiwdalhad	breichiad
hendad	cwblhad	meichiad
cyndad	amlhad	gwichiad

5. More types of macrostructures have been developed in English lexicography, e.g. an access structure which runs vertically parallel in the *Collins COBUILD English Language Dictionary* dictionary (J. Sinclair 1987):

attendance   **81**   **attract**

attendance /ə'tendəns/, **attendances. 1** The attendance at a meeting or gathering is the number of people who are present at it. EG *There have been heavy attendances at recent conferences... At Easter, attendances at churches rose.* **2** Attendance at an event or an institution is the act of being present at the event or of going regularly to the institution. EG *He decided to improve himself by attendance at evening classes.* **3** If you are **in attendance** in a place or with a person, you are present in that place or with that person, a formal expression. EG *Proposals were placed before the people in attendance*

N COUNT
UNCOUNT : LP
PREP THEN *at*

audience, ◊ **attentively.** EG *He was listening attentively to a senior colleague... I could see he was following the play attentively.* **2** is very helpful and polite to someone else, often because they like them very much. EG *He was unfailingly attentive... ...a habit of not being too attentive to women.* ◊ **attentively.** EG *They circled attentively with drinks and olivs.*
attenuate /ə'tenju:eɪt/, **attenuates, attenuating, attenuated.** To **attenuate** something means to reduce it or weaken it; a formal...

◊ ADV WITH VB
= CAREFULLY
ADJ QUALIT
1 CARING
= SOLICITOUS
≠ OFFHANDE ◊ ADV WITH VB

There are, of course, many more types of macrostrcutures. Any further description of them, however, would fall beyond the scope of this investigation. I therefore refer the reader to Wiegand (1989a: 384) who made an attempt to establish a classification of some access structures in monolingual lexicographical works.

It is apparently also possible that the macrostructure remains unclear. This seems to be the case in *Cymraeg i'r Werin* 'Welsh for the people' (E.C. Rees 1932). Here the lexicon is arranged thematically but under each headline introducing a new theme, the lexical units, which may consist of single lexical items or phrases, are freely compiled:

UPSTAIRS
(LAN LLOFFT - I FYNY'R GRISIAU).

bedroom, hunystafell, ystafell wely
staircase, grisiau
step, gris, step
rug, hugan, -au, *f.*, cwrlid
bed, gwely, -au, m.
bedside, erchwyn gwely
feather bed, gwely plu
sleep, cysgu, huno
sheet, llen, sît
quilt, cwilt
counterpane, cwrlid, cwilt
blanket, planced, -i, *f.*, gwrthban
pillow, gobennydd, -iau, *m.*
bolster, gobennydd, clustog, -au, *f.*
pillow-case, tudded
mattres, matras
valance, cylchedlen
bedclothes, bedding, dillad gwely
bedridden, gorweiddiog
overlay, gorchudd
chest, cist
wardrobe, dilladfa
drawer, trôr
to draw, tynnu

strop, strap, hogi
to strop, hogi, minio
hone, hogalen
to hone, honio, hogi
lather, trochioni
cut, torri, naddu
tooth, dant, dannedd, f.
to clean, glanhau
dentifrice, deintolch
attic, crogloff, nenlofft, atig
ridge, coping, truman, m.f.
He is building a new house on the border of the village. There is no grate in the scullery, so it is very cold there in the winter. Let us go into the parlour ; it is more comfortable there.
Y mae (ef) yn codi tŷ newydd ar fin y pentref. Nid oes grat yn y gegin gefn, felly y mae hi'n oer iawn yno yn y gaeaf. Awn i'r parlwr ; y mae'n fwy cysurus yno.

WORK IN THE HOME
(GWAITH YN Y TŶ).

set the table, gosod y ford
clear the table, clirio'r ford
wash up, golchi'r llestri
skewer, gwaell, gweill, bêr, gwachell, gwechyll

(C)   The lemma

The term lemma derives from Greek in the sense of 'theme, headline' (Wolski 1989: 360). Some authors, therefore, "use the term as a synonym for headword or even the whole entry" (Hartmann & James 1998: 83). The definition of the term as used in this investagtion follows roughly that found in Hartmann & James (1998). They define a lemma as:

> "[t]he position at which an entry can be located and found in the structure of a reference work [... W]ithin the overall (e.g. alphabetical) macrostructure it constitutes the point of access where the compiler can place and the user can find the information listed" (ibid.: 83).

26

(D) The headword

The definition of headword here follows that of Wolski (ibid.: 362ff.). A headword is that representative of a lexically relevant unit for which lexical, linguistic and general information is given, i.e. which is lexicographically to be described. It is normally highlighted and part of the lexicographical discourse. It may be discontinuous, e.g. in *dic tion ar y*, thus reflecting primary descriptive elements. Lexicographical markers[4] (cf. Markierungsangaben in Wiegand 1989b: 429-36) or indications of intonation, hyphenation, stress or others, however, do not form part of the headword. As such, it is not part of the microstructure (cf. below). Nevertheless, the headword may consist of more than one lexical item, thus forming a multiple headword:

Verkäufer(in *f*) *m* **s**, - seller;
solid(e) *adj. Haus, Möbel etc* solid, sturdy; [...] (*Pons Collins Großwörterbuch für Experten und Universität. Deutsch-Englisch, Englisch-Deutsch*, Terrel, P. & V. Schnorr et al. 1997)

It is also possible that two headwords fill the position of one. In this case, a main headword and a subsidiary one or several subsidiary ones can be distinguished:

gwyring, gwyryng, gwyrin[1], gwyrn
[amr. ar gweryn[2]] *e.ll.* neu *e.tf.* a hefyd fel
eg. Math o lyngyr neu bryfed, sef larfa
Gastrophilus equi [...] (*Geiriadur Prifysgol Cymru* 'Dictionary of the University of Wales', R.J. Thomas et al. 1950-2002)

The choice of the form of the headword varies from one language to another, sometimes even within one language. Latin verb entries, for instance, regularly display the first person singular as the headword. This form can also occur in Welsh (cf. *Geiriadur Prifysgol Cymru*), although the commonly employed form for the lemma would be the verbal noun.

There are, of course, different types of headwords. If the alphabetical macrostructure is broken up, for instance, *nest headwords* are introduced, particularly for compound words. They in turn, however, may set up a secondary alphabetical structure (Wolski 1989: 365):

rühmenswert *adj* praiseworthy, laudable.
Ruhmes-: **~blatt** *nt (fig)* glorious chapter; **~halle** *f* hall of fame; **~tag** *m* glorious day; **~tat** *f* glorious deed.
Rühmlich *adj* praiseworthy, laudable; *Ausnahme* notable ♦ **kein ~es Ende finden** *or* **nehmen** to meet a bad end; sich rühmlich hervortun to distinguish oneself.
Ruhm-: **r~los** *adj* inglorious; **r~reich** *adj (liter)* glorious; **~sucht** *f* thirst for glory; **r~süchtig** *adj* thirsting for glory; **r~voll** adj glorious.
Ruhr[1] f - *(Geog)* Ruhr (*Pons Collins Großwörterbuch für Experten und Universität. Deutsch-Englisch, Englisch-Deutsch*, Terrel, P. & V. Schnorr et al. 1997).

---

[4]   Most important markers are the field or subject labels. They are used to indicate the technical discipline with which a word or phrase is associated (cf. Hartmann & James 1998: 57).

Another headword type is that of *reference headword*, which is intended to solve location problems of lexical items:

halaf²: halu, gw. **alaf : alu**⁵ (*Geiriadur Prifysgol Cymru*).

The description of other types can be found in Wolski (1989: 365), but exceeds the theoretical basis of this investigation.

(E)   The microstructure

The term microstructure has also predominantly been explained in the context of monolingual dictionaries (cf. Wiegand 1989b, c). It needs, therefore, to be adapted to the purposes of this investigation. The microstructure here is defined as that part of the entry which contains all the information provided for the related headword (cf. above), i.e. grammatical or other systematic information, one or several translations etc.

> "It, therefore, provides detailed information about the headword, with comments on its formal and semantic properties (spelling, pronunciation, grammar, definition, usage, etymology). If the headword has more than one sense, the information is given for each of these (sub-lemma)" (Hartmann & James 1998: 94).

The microstructure, therefore, is the internal design of an entry.

---

⁵   gw. = gweler 'see'

1.3.2.1.3.   Types of Welsh dictionaries

As a result of the various languages used for communication, many different types of dictionaries have developed. They have been created, for instance, on the basis of the chosen range and
register of the lexicon, or of the linguistic intentions of the producers, their facilities and authority, or their approaches or the purpose of dictionary compilation. Few attempts have been made,
however, to construct a general typology of dictionaries.[1]

In this section, therefore, some basic criteria for defining different types of dictionaries in the
context of this investigation are supplied. They are followed by a proposed type-classification.
A diagrammatic summary is provided at the end of the section (cf. below).

Different types of dictionaries are defined according to the following criteria:

(a)   criteria dominated by pre-conditions, circumstances and intentions which
         are called *circumstantial criteria* and comprise, for instance, the *funding,
         intended user, purpose, size,* and *media* used for the compilation;

(b)   the *conceptual criteria,* that is, whether the work is *onomasiologically*[2] or
         semasiologically arranged; and

(c)   *mainly linguistically based criteria.*

According to the first set of criteria, academic dictionaries can be distinguished from com-
mercially produced ones, e.g. *Geiriadur yr Academi* as opposed to the *Collins-Spurrell Welsh
Dictionary* (Thorne, D. & A. Convery 1991).

Dictionaries in different media are, for instance, those published on paper and those produced
on electronic, optical, or magnetic data carriers, e.g. *CysGair* (C. Ó Dohartaigh 1996) which is
available on CD-Rom. Another dictionary using modern media is *GaelDict 98* (C. Ó Duibhún
1998), which can be installed on hard disc. In addition, there are online dictionaries, which are
produced on data carriers individually and locally inaccessible, that is, they are stored on servers
on the internet (cf. corpus of dictionaries in chapter III).

Considering the second type of criteria, there are onomasiological dictionaries with microstructure, such as thesauri, e.g. *Y Thesawrws Cymraeg* (Gwasg Pobl Cymru 1993). Examples for
onomasiological dictionaries without a microstructure are picture dictionaries, i.e. *Geiriadur
Lluniau* (R.M. Jones 1969).

The third set of criteria, which are mainly linguistically based, are resorted to when the dictionary exhibits a semasiological approach. In some dictionary typologies the *linguistic criteria*
distinguish between the description of the macro- and microstructure (cf. Ternes 1991b: 109).
Here, however, other criteria are selected in order to feature different dictionary types, i.e. the

---

[1]   For aspects related to this problem, see Ternes (1991b).

[2]   An onomasiological approach studies "sets of associated concepts in relation to the linguistic
         forms which designate them; for example, the study of the ways lexical items can be organised
         conceptually in a section of an encyclopedia" (Crystal 1992: 277). "The onomasiological
         approach is associated with the solution of word-finding problems and the creation of terminolo-
         gy" (Hartmann & James 1998: 102). "This direction of study, from concepts to items (as in a
         typical thesaurus) is sometimes contrasted with semasiology, where the direction of study is
         from items to concepts" (Crystal 1992: 277).

language criteria. They allow the distinction between monolingual dictionaries and non-monolingual dictionaries.

The latter category can be sub-divided into bi- or multilingual dictionaries on the one hand and uni- or bi-directional dictionaries on the other. An example of a multilingual dictionary is *The Pan-Celtic Phrasebook* (W. Knox 1998) which provides equivalents in all six Celtic languages currently spoken.[3] A uni-directional dictionary is *Geiriadur yr Academi*. One of the most popular bi-directional dictionaries is, for instance, *Y Geiriadur Cyfoes. The Modern Welsh Dictionary* (sic).

Both monolingual and non-monolingual dictionaries can either reflect general language usage or they can focus on *special linguistic* or *lexical criteria*. In this case, they are called restricted or specialist dictionaries.

According to the *special linguistic criteria*, a large variety of dictionaries may be distinguished, e.g. etymological dictionaries, pronouncing dictionaries, dictionaries of orthography, e.g. *Orgraff yr Iaith Gymraeg* 'The Orthography of the Welsh language' (C. Lewis 1987),[4] dictionaries of slang, of style, of dialects, e.g. *Welsh Vocabulary of the Bangor District* (O.H. Fynes-Clinton 1913), of valency, dictionaries of abbreviations and others (cf. Ternes 1991b: 97). Unless a contrastive investigation of selected linguistic aspects is intended, linguistically restricted dictionaries would mostly be monolingual. The application of *linguistic criteria* has, therefore, to be seen within the context of the *language criteria*.

According to the particular sector of the lexicon that is being described (*lexical criteria*) the following types of dictionaries can be distinguished: e.g. *Y Geiriadur Termau* 'The Dictionary of terms' (J.L. Williams 1973) ; or dictionaries of jurisdictional terms, e.g. *Geiriadur y Gyfraith* 'The Dictionary of the Law' (R. Léwis 1992); of medical terms, e.g. *Termau Meddygol* 'Medical Terms' (University of Wales Press 1993) and many other terminological dictionaries, or those for new and for loanwords.

In some typologies, dictionaries of slang or dialects are assigned to the *lexical criteria*. Different registers of the language, however, are not restricted to lexical variation, but also include differing grammatical structures (cf. Thomas, B. & P.W. Thomas 1989).

Another type of restricted dictionaries is represented by historical dictionaries which reflect diachronic language usage (cf. also section 3.3.). Sometimes, however, they form very comprehensive lexicographical works, such as the *Geiriadur Prifysgol Cymru*. Here the linguistically related *time criterion* can be mentioned.

The time criterion, however, is a general problem in lexicography, since the production of comprehensive dictionaries usually takes a considerable amount of time. Strictly speaking, therefore, dictionaries cannot be really synchronic, as their entries will always lag behind the development of real language.

---

[3] Cornish and Manx are normally defined as dead languages which is true with regard to their function as a language of the community. In light of the fact, however, that there are about 1000 Cornish speakers and about 600 Manx speakers, that language courses are offered, and that A levels in Cornish and Manx can be taken, they are often refered to as living tongues.

[4] For comments on this reference book, see section 4.3.9.

As for the *access or algorithm criterion*, which is a description of the macrostructure, most dictionaries follow a strict initial-alphabetical order.[5] Some dictionaries, however, show a reverse alphabetical order, e.g. *Geiriadur Gwrthdroadol Cymraeg Diweddar* (cf. section 1.3.2.1.2. (B)). They would mainly be used for linguistic or metrical purposes. The same applies to dictionaries exhibiting rhyming syllables, e.g. *Yr Odliadur* (cf. section 1.3.2.1.2. (B)) or to dictionaries displaying homophonic consonantal clusters, e.g. *Y Cleciadur* (cf. section 1.3.2.1.2. (B)).

According to the linguistic and pragmatic peculiarities of various other languages, other algorithms or their combinations can be described (cf. Chinese language dictionaries Ternes 1991b: 97, 109). They do not, however, form part of this investigation and consequently do not need to be discussed here.

There are, of course, other options for setting up typologies of dictionaries (Hausmann 1989: 986). A typology of dictionaries based on their uses is described in Kühn (1989: 11-128). Its categories, for instance, include dictionaries as an aid in philological research, in linguistic research, in terminology, in various types of translation or into an aid to foreign-language teaching. Since Welsh lexicography, however, has not yet produced a range of dictionaries as comprehensive and as specialised as can be found in major world languages, e.g. English, French, Russian, Spanish, German and so on, further investigations into other dictionary typologies fall beyond the scope of this investigation. A list displaying the potential range of dictionary types can be found in Hausmann & Wiegand et al. (1989: XLII-XLV).

The following diagram summarises the preceding paragraphs and suggests a classification of different types of dictionaries, particularly applicable to this investigation:[6]

---

5   For discussions related to alphabetically arranged dictionaries, see Ternes (1991b: 95ff.).

6   For further definitions or examples of particular types of dictionaries, see section 3.3.

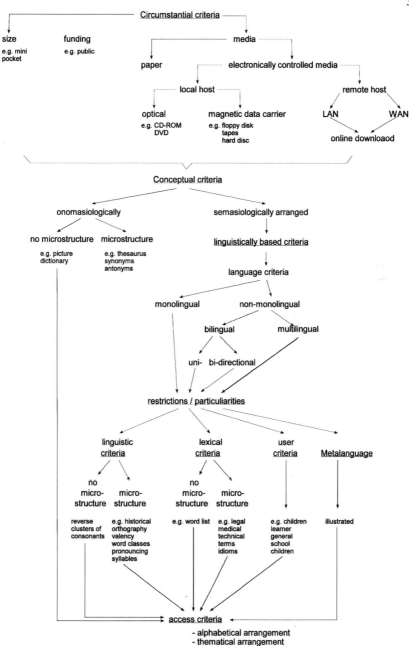

In conclusion, three general points need to be emphasised: first, as is true for all complex phenomena, most criteria on which a classification of dictionaries can be based are closely related to each other (cf. *linguistic* and *lexical* criteria). Second, dictionaries may fit in more than one category, since each category focuses on one chosen aspect out of a range of information provided by the compiled material and its arrangement. Third, the actual title of a dictionary does not necessarily reflect its theoretical approach, content or type. Denotations of reference works follow different rules, mostly those of the market. Since those are hardly restricted, various aspects of the whole complex of dictionary planning, compiling, selling and using offer a wide range of motivation for the denotation of dictionaries.

Considering the goal of this investigation and applying the diagram to existing Welsh dictionaries, it becomes immediately apparent that the range of monolingual and linguistic lexicographical works for the Welsh language is limited. There is neither a Standard Welsh-Welsh dictionary nor are there etymological, pronouncing, and spelling dictionaries of the modern language (cf. sections 3.3., 4.1.1. and 4.1.2.). Because of a prominent literary tradition, however, bound to traditional metres linguistic dictionaries, which support such metres, are common.

The following sections set up parameters for the critical investigation of some of the modern Welsh dictionaries, that is, of popular bi-directional bilingual general-purpose dictionaries.

1.3.2.2.   Possible parameters for the critical investigation of dictionaries
1.3.2.2.1.   General remarks

In order to pursue a critical investigation of dictionaries, some parameters of what to analyse should be defined. Such parameters can be derived from the maximum amount of information which a dictionary should contain with regard to its intended user and purpose. Ilson (1991: 294f.) presents a list of such information. Some of its points are:

- information about etymology,
- phonetic information (e.g. pronunciation),
- morphological information (e.g. number, gender),
- syntactic information (e.g. indication of word classes, government of the verb),
- paradigmatic information (e.g. synonyms, antonyms, converses, confusables and others),
- diasystematic information (e.g. indications of standard, technical, frequent, or other usage).

Disregarding particular specialist types of dictionaries, however, the range of information actually provided in them mainly depends on the peculiarities of the languages concerned and the standard of available linguistic description, but also on the purpose of the dictionary, the intended user, financiers and other factors (cf. section 1.3.2.1.).

Out of the range of information listed above, this investigation primarily focuses - as explained before (cf. section 1.2.) - on the analysis of the grammatical information contained in modern bi-directional general-purpose dictionaries. In the following sections, therefore, parameters as a guideline for the grammatical analysis need to be established.

1.3.2.2.2.   Defining the term grammar and related fields of linguistics

Because many meanings exist which may be and have been applied to the term *grammar* it is, necessary to clarify what is meant by the term in this investigation.

> "Even in linguistics, where a more specialized use of the term is employed, there is still variation in its precise usage; some linguists refer by "grammar" to all of the structural aspects of language, including not only morphological and syntactic but also phonological rules, while others may apply it only to the set of syntactic rules that are believed to generate grammatical sentences" (McCorduck 1993: 8).

Grammar, in this investigation, is understood as a system of structural phenomena of a language by which lexical items of a language are organised to form larger units, i.e. as a kind of skeleton for the lexis, which is determined by the regional, social and stylistic use of the language, all subject to historical development. This skeleton in turn, however, is described in a set of regulations which are conventionally assigned to the linguistic sub-disciplines morphology[1] and syntax, for which the hyperonym *grammar* is employed. Those are the two senses in which *grammar* is used here.

Morphology in this investigation is understood as the study of form, inner structure, function and occurrence of a morpheme as the smallest meaningful unit of a language. Goals of morphological analysis are: (a) the description of the morpheme inventory and morpheme combinations, (b) the development of criteria that determine word classes, (c) the description of regularities in inflection (declension, conjugation and comparison), and (d) the study of grammatical categories like tense and mood, and their linguistic correlates (cf. Bussmann 1996: 314f.). Word formation is not considered part of morphological analysis here.

Syntax is understood as the description of the way of how units of sound and writing and their meanings combine to form sentences (cf. Graustein & Hoffmann 1982: 24).

In light of the aforementioned definition, the analysis of grammatical information generally excludes semantics, i.e. the investigation of features which determine the range of conventions in which lexical items may occur in actual usage.

Since a set of regulations, however, is an artificial construct which is meant to make existing systems understandable and usable, they may split up phenomena into categories which cannot really be considered separately. This becomes apparent, for instance, when discussing the number category of the Welsh noun, which reaches into the field of lexicology[2] (cf. 4.3.2.2.2.).

---

[1]   Morphology is defined as a part of grammar which studies the formal variation of lexical items. It comprises the establishment of grammatical paradigms and the word class division. For other definitions, see Bussmann (280: 314).

[2]   Lexicology here is understood as a sub-discipline of linguistics or, more specifically, semantics that investigates and describes the structure of the lexicon of a language. Lexicology also examines linguistic expressions for their internal semantic structure and the relationships between individual words or lexical units. "The findings of lexicology may be codified by lexicography [...], although the relationship between both areas is not necessarily close" (Bussmann 1996: 280).

The same applies to the description of valency, e.g. of the verb (cf. below, see also the term complementation). The principle feature of valency theory is the specification of grammatical information in terms of 'valences' that specify the syntactic and semantic arguments which a verb, adjective, noun, or another word class may take (cf. McCorduck 1993: 119). For the purpose of this investigation, valency (also valence according to Bussmann 1996: 510) is defined as the ability of lexical items or word classes to predetermine their syntactic and semantic environment in that they place certain requirements on the surrounding constituents with reference to their grammatical and semantic characteristics. Certain lexical items, therefore, require a particular number and particular types of other lexical items. These are called dependents or complements. The number and types of complements may be unpredictable and are sometimes outside grammatical or semantic description (cf. Herbst 1983: 320-334, Ickler 1985: 372).

The concept of valency has two main dimensions (cf. Buchholz/Beyrer 1977: 1, Helbig/Schenkel 1973: 24ff.). One of these is primarily syntactically based, i.e. the relation between the verb and its objects and adverbials, which is also called the *government* of a particular word class. Following Bussmann (1996: 193), the term government is here understood as

> "a lexeme-specific property of verbs, adjectives, prepositions, nouns[, or other word classes] that determines the morphological realization [...] of dependent elements. Government can be subsumed under valence in so far as elements with valence govern the morphological form of their 'governed' (dependent) elements. The term 'government' is used especially with verbs whose differing valence is the primary criterion for distinguishing between transitive and intransitive verbs [cf. section 1.3.2.3.1., Bussmann 1996: 510]. The syntactic functions of the elements accompanying[, for example,] the verb are based on the various governing cases,"

or prepositions, or other governing phenomena, e.g. mutations[3] in Welsh.

The other dimension of valency predominantly describes semantically based preferences and restrictions on the selection of the linking of different lexical items and is also known as *collocation*.[4] However, in examples like *Widerstand leisten* 'offer resistance' it becomes clear that collocations may exceed the field of semantics, since a potential equivalent *Widerstand bieten* for 'offer resistance' does not really harm any semantic rules, but rather normatives and codes of the German language (cf. also Ickler 1985: 369). This is the reason why Carter (1987: 54) formulates:

> "The examination of collocational ranges of items begins where semantic analysis of selection restrictions leaves off".

Although drastically formulated, the sentence explains clearly the difficulties with collocations, i.e. that their discussion often exceeds both the field of grammar and that of semantics. It reaches, for example, into the discussion of register and *Sprachgefühl* of a language. In view of this situation, the term collocation is defined as follows in this investigation:

---

[3]   Mutation in this investigation is understood as morpho-syntactically motivated sound change at the beginning of a word.

[4]   I would like to take the opportunity of thanking Dr Orin Gensler, Max Planck Institute for Evolutionary Anthropology/Leipzig, for helpful discussion on this matter.

"Collocation typically denotes frequently repeated or statistically significant co-occurrences, whether or not there are any special semantic bonds between collocating items" (Moon 1998: 26, 20).

This definition encompasses larger units which are

"syntagmatically or paradigmatically aberrant: they cannot therefore be decoded purely compositionally nor encoded freely [...] either because a component item has a meaning not found in other collocations or contexts, although it has other compositional meanings, or because one or more of the component items is semantically depleted, [e.g.] *beg the question* [...], *foot the bill*, [and] *toe the line*" (ibid.: 21).

Grammatically ill-formed units are not subsumed under the term collocation. This is an important feature which helps to keep collocations apart from idioms. An idiom is defined as a

"particular kind of unit: one that is fixed and semantically opaque or metaphorical, or, traditional, 'not the sum of its parts', for example, *kick the bucket* or *spill the beans*" (Moon 1998: 4).

The definition comprises grammatically ill-formed items such as *by and large*, as well as

"transparent metaphors such as *skate on thin ice* and strings such as *move heaven and earth* which have no possible literal meaning" (ibid.: 4).

Although the border between different types of collocations (ibid.: 26f.) and idioms is not easy to draw, there are four features which keep both phenomena apart: first, grammatically ill-formed lexical units are assigned to idioms. Second, those units which predominantly serve stylistic purposes are called idioms. Third, there is a tendency according to which larger lexical units of a certain length belong to idioms. This means that when their constituent parts exceed the number of three or four items, as in *skate on thin ice* or *move heaven and earth*, they form an idiom. Fourth, because of the possibility of being grammatically ill-formed, idioms have not been investigated in the context of valency theory and do not form a regular part of this study. Both idioms and collocations, however, can themselves act in a way single lexical units may perform within a syntagm.[5]

Even within valency theory syntactic valency is seized within grammatical concepts. Semantic valency, however, i.e. collocations, is preferably dealt within the context of semantics. It is this situation, as well as the notion that collocations are mostly discussed in the context of a particular word class, which prompts lexicographers to include both government and collocations by grammatical coding in dictionaries.

Looking at other grammatical concepts, the difficulty of seizing semantic or other linguistic problems which are not conventionally assigned to morphology and syntax, or which cannot be restricted to one of the linguistic sub-disciplines, remains. Traditional grammar, for instance, also called school grammar (cf. Bussmann 1996: 416), can roughly be characterised as follows: (a) it provides a classification of data into formal categories, e.g. word classes[6] (cf. below), (b)

---

[5]   The term syntagm is understood here as a structured syntactic sequence of linguistic elements, which can consist of phrases, clauses, or entire sentences (cf. Bussmann 1996: 472).

[6]   In this investigation, the term 'word class' is given preference to the term 'part of speech' in order to refer to the classification of words in the languages under review (Quirk 1990: 11f.).

this classification is based on logical, semantic, syntactic, and extralinguistic criteria, (c) it is primarily prescriptive, and (d) it pays little attention to functional aspects of communication and tends to obscure larger speech patterns (cf. Allen & Corder 1975: 51). In addition, school grammar focuses on the written rather than the spoken language as a subject.

Approaches of structural grammar investigate (a) the language use as part of a more extensive social process; (b) this process takes place in situations, i.e. each linguistic expression is determined by its situational context as well as by its linguistic context (i.e. its distribution or co-occurrence); (c) meaning is understood to be a complex relation in the context of situations. Fundamental to structuralism is the analysis of language data based on the segmentation and classification of utterances, without reference to the 'deeper', more abstract levels of linguistic organisation. Structural grammar shifts

> "from an item-centred view of language to one which is structure-centred. According to the structuralists, individual sounds, words or parts of sentences have no linguistic significance in themselves; they have significance only as they contrast and combine with other items in the patterns of a linguistic system. Language elements are [therefore] related to one another in a system (or network of systems) rather than being mere collections of individual items" (Allen & Corder 1975: 51f.).

The term 'structural' is used more generally, with reference to all grammars which emphasise the phonological and grammatical structure, in contrast to the semantic.

Transformational-generative grammar refers to the ability of competent speakers and to the linguistic intuitions which a competent speaker can make explicit about his/her language.

> "A generative grammar is one which aims to specify the nature of a speaker's knowledge about his language, but with such accuracy and in such detail that someone who does not know the language will be able to produce its forms simply by following the rules of the grammar, and without having to refer to any source of information outside grammar. A transformational grammar is one which incorporates two aspects of syntactic description, a surface structure and a more abstract deep structure, together with a set of transformational rules relating deep and surface structure" (Allen & Corder 1975: 58).

The development of competence is explained by the innate language acquisition device on the basis of grammar universals. The formulation of the theory, therefore, takes precedence over the analysis of data. Transformational grammar proceeds deductively by laying down hypotheses about the linguistic generation mechanism. The theory is expanded to a general theory of grammar which includes phonology and semantics. In this case, grammar is understood as a comprehensive linguistic theory, which consists of a generative, syntactic component as well as interpretive, semantic, and phonological components (cf. Chomsky 1965).

The basic assumption of functional grammar, as the last major theoretical model mentioned here, is that linguistic phenomena cannot be explained without examining their functions. It

---

Both terms can be used synonymously. The term 'part of speech' (cf. Jackson 1985: 54; 'part of speech' is also written 'part-of-speech', ibid.), however, is only applied to constituents of the sentence, such as subjects, objects, predicates, and adverbials.

touches on the question of how far our view of reality is in correspondence with the structure of the language. Certain areas of grammar, therefore,

> "can be put into correspondence with certain interpersonal functions and can be said to reflect the operation of language as a means of social interaction" (Allen & Corder 1975: 74f.)

and questions as to how language patterns perform different communicative acts become central. Consequently, functional grammar offers an alternative to structural attempts at describing linguistic phenomena formally. Functional descriptions are preferred in the empirically orientated research on universals, since the formal means of marking syntactic function vary across languages, while their functions are universal (cf. Halliday 1985).

Contemporary linguistic theory is far from being a single monolithic system; rather, it is a combination of different approaches, all of which are subject to constant development and change. None of the various grammatical concepts, however, has yet succeeded in describing principles and rules of word, sentence, or text formation comprehensively and exhaustively for any language. An example illustrating some difficulties in this respect is the formation of Welsh diminutives. When formed by the singulative suffix[7] (lexicology), as in *corffyn* 'little body' or *diawlyn* 'little devil', the diminutive formation can easily be mistaken as pure singularisation (morphology), as it happens in words like *eirinen* 'one plum' (< *eirin* 'plums') or *mochyn* 'one pig' (< *moch* 'pigs'). Confusion occurs in particular when words like *hadyn, hedyn* (< *had* 'seed') are described with *un. bach.* (unigol bachigol) 'singular diminutive' in *Geiriadur Prifysgol Cymru*, suggesting that the lexical items can be used in the sense 'a corn of seed' or 'little seed'. There is apparently a close relation between the concept of diminishing in Welsh and that of particularisation. The derivational suffixes *-yn/-en*, which serve for systematic semantic differentiation, are in this case also inflectional suffixes for singularisation. They can, in addition, serve for the determining of word classes, e.g. *symud + -yn -> symudyn* 'mobile' (verb -> noun).

The phenomenon 'diminutive', therefore, the function of which may be universal to languages, although not generally linked to singularisation, has to be described in Welsh by formal means assigned to both morphology and semantics.

The example of the diminutive illustrates that an integrated grammatical concept which is purpose-orientated on the goal of this investigation is needed in this study. It is outlined in the next section. Generally, however, when dealing with intricate linguistic phenomena, the analysis of grammatical description to be included in dictionary entries is extended by discussions which fall into other fields of linguistics. Issues of such sister disciplines, however, are not central to this investigation. An exception is the discipline of phonology with which is dealt with when discussing phonetic transcription in section 4.4.

---

7   The term suffix is understood here as a "morphological element that is attached finally to free morpheme constructions, but does not occur as a rule as a free morpheme. In regard to morpho-syntactic function, a distinction is drawn between inflectional suffixes [...] and derivational suffixes" [...] (Bussmann 1996: 464).

1.3.2.2.3. Choice of grammatical concept

As explained in the preceding section, the choice of grammatical concept in this investagtion has to be purpose-orientated. In this study, the grammatical approach needs to serve the grammatical analysis of a lexicographical work, i.e. grammatical phenomena have to be seen in the function they fulfil in a dictionary. Second, general-purpose dictionaries belong to the group of reference books which present the language to an audience which is predominantly not linguistically trained (cf. below). McCorduck (1993: 39), therefore, states that the most frequent and trouble-some linguistic phenomena have to be listed in them with a certain degree of pedagogically based simplification. Third, dictionaries explain first of all single lexical items rather than texts. This is particularly apparent in Welsh dictionaries (cf. chapter IV). Fourth, dictionaries are, at least, partly prescriptive (cf. section 4.2.). Fifth, general-purpose dictionaries focus rather on the written than on the spoken language.

In view of this, it is apparent that the analysis of the presentation of grammatical features in general-purpose dictionaries should, first, avoid a dependence on highly abstract grammatical theories in order not to ask for unattainable tasks in lexicographical works. Second, a gram-matical concept has been chosen that concentrates on the analysis of single lexical items. This task is supported by the school type of grammar (cf. Bussmann 1996: 416). School, or traditional, grammar also promotes the description of the written language which is pre-dominantly compiled in dictionaries. A problem with regard to more recent linguistic theories in this context is illustrated as follows:

> "Whereas the traditional handbooks provided descriptions of wide areas of surface structure, a typical paper or book written by a contemporary linguist discusses theoretical issues and presents only as much of the data as is necessary to support the hypotheses advanced. In filling out the details, we find ourselves drawing more and more upon the work of the scholarly traditional grammarians [...]. The current trend in linguistic studies, involving an attempt to describe the abstract system of rules that underlies the surface forms of utterances, has led to a marked revival of interest in the methods of traditional grammar" (Allen & Corder 1975: 47, 51).

Being essentially prescriptive in its approach, the school type grammar provides to a large extent also a useful apparatus to demonstrate adequacy of dictionaries, i.e. as to what degree these works meet their functions as instructional tools and establish norms, or as translational devices for encoding purposes, or as factors of language maintenance.

In addition, leaving aside the methodological restrictions, there is no doubt that all modern linguistic approaches are based on categories, data and results of school grammar or, at least, draw on the knowledge it is to provide potential dictionary users with (cf. below).

However, more comprehensive dictionaries include contexts in which the lexical item may be used, e.g. definitions, collocations, idioms or simple phrases and sentences. Questions of co-oc-currence, e.g. when presenting collocations, or particular linguistic functions within the lan-guage, e.g. the function of Welsh particles, then become part of the investigation. Their gram-matical description reaches into the fields of the formation of larger lexical units and of phrase, sentence, or text production. In such cases, the analysis draws on descriptions of structural and functional grammar and valency theory.

In short, the concept favoured in this investigation is, therefore, an integrated one (cf. approaches of grammatical description in Graustein & Hoffmann et al. 1982) which (a) draws on traditional grammar (b) is adapted to the peculiarities of the Welsh language and which (c) is open to elements of structural and functional grammatical theories and valency theory. Such an approach includes the development of alternative theoretical descriptions where former analyses were found wanting (cf. categorisation of Welsh verbs in section 1.3.2.3.1.).

1.3.2.2.4.   Necessity for grammar in dictionaries

There are five main reasons why grammatical information is of importance in dictionaries and consequently increasingly apparent in them (cf. Herbst 1985: 308):

(a)   Dictionaries aim to list the lexical items in a language and to give a description of their meaning and usage; within 'usage' is included the part a lexical item plays in the grammatical system of a language. In this context, it is, according to H. Jackson (1985: 57), an important - and by the user expected - feature of dictionaries that they provide information on the grammatical functions and operations of the lexical items displayed. Syntactic information about a word, for instance, is for learners often the most essential information in their production of the second language (cf. McCorduck 1993: 84).

(b)   Grammatical functions and operations which characterise individual words cannot be deduced with certainty and ease from a simple grammatical rule, e.g. the prepositions by which verbs are connected with the words they govern.

(c)   As bilingual dictionaries are mostly polyfunctional in their aim, addressing themselves to native speakers of either of the two languages involved, they are mainly used for text production. Without linguistic information they can only be used to a limited extent for their intended purpose (cf. Bergenholz/Tarp 1995: 111, 114).

(d)   Language users have more recourse to the dictionary - a necessary tool in any school class - than to the grammar, whether they are first-language or second-language users (cf. Jackson 1985: 53).

(e)   A dictionary depends on a grammatical description, either explicitly or implicitly, since all dictionaries use grammatical terms, e.g. noun, verb, which have their characterisation in the grammar.

1.3.2.2.5.   Experience of the provision of grammatical information in dictionaries

In light of the facts mentioned above, there can be no doubt that grammatical information must be included in dictionaries. The question to be addressed, therefore, is what information is regarded essential and to what extent it ought to be described.

Unfortunately very little has been written on the question of which aspects of grammatical description should be contained in dictionaries. There are some analyses which investigate dictionaries with regard to their provision of grammatical information,[1] but generalisations of suggestions or parameters of what should be entered are lacking.

Most studies pursued by different scholars on grammar in dictionary entries deal with learners' reference books, that means with monolingual dictionaries which devote more space to grammatical information than bilingual dictionaries do (cf. Herbst 1985: 329) and consequently economise on the number of entries (cf. Heath 1985: 333). In addition, these dictionaries predominantly discuss the English language.

One of the things, however, that one can learn from the investigations into general users' language needs and reference skills is that it cannot be taken for granted that learners are prepared to study all the introductory sections and their explanations, and to refer to tables provided by reference books (cf. Lemmens 11f.). On the other hand,

> "[t]he term Learners is meant to refer to a broad range of persons, including those who use English formally in an educational setting, those who use English as a second language in business, government or the like, and those who are simply not native speakers of English" (McCorduck 1993: 5).

Information for second-language learners, therefore, has to be much more comprehensive since even if they have acquired a full degree, they have not internalised all the grammatical rules nor do they normally have a full command of semantic rules and restrictions that govern the use of individual words.

Nevertheless, Bergenholtz/Tarp (1985: 114) maintain that grammatical information is important even for the native speaker, since "a user cannot be presumed to fully master the grammar of his own native language" (cf. also above and Herbst 1985: 329).

---

[1]   See, for instance:

Bergenholtz, Henning & Joachim Mugdan, 1985, *Lexicographie und Grammatik*, in: Lexicographica Series Maior 3, Tübingen.

Lemmens, Marcel & Herman Wekker, 1986, *Grammar in English Learners' Dictionaries*, in: Lexicographica Series Maior 16, Tübingen.

McCorduck, Edward Scott, 1993, *Grammatical Information in ESL Dictionaries*, in: Lexicographica 48, Tübingen.

Morán, María Teresa Fuentes, 1997, *Gramática en la lexicografía bilinge*, in: Lexicographica Series Maior 81, Tübingen.

Herbst, Thomas & Kerstin Popp, 1999, *The Perfect Learners' Dictionary (?)*, in: Lexicographica Maior 95, Tübingen.

Since, both learners' and bilingual dictionaries have in the end to serve the decoding and encoding functions (cf. Heath 1985: 333, Herbst 1985: 310), some major points about grammar found in learners' dictionaries serve as a guide to establish parameters for this investigation.

Together with the result of the few analyses of bilingual dictionaries, a possible model for the inclusion of grammatical information in bilingual general-purpose dictionaries is briefly outlined.

1.3.2.2.6. Principles on grammatical information in dictionaries

Four general principles on grammatical information can be formulated:

1. Grammatical information can either be provided directly, i.e. by abbreviations or codes (cf. McCorduck 1993: 13ff.), or indirectly by incorporating information into the definitions and examples or other parts of the entry. The latter, however, makes the information less accessible to the user and takes up far more space.

2. It has been suggested, therefore, to introduce transparent and self-explanatory descriptions. A full inventory of grammatical information should be given with the entries themselves. The grammar should not be presented in such a condensed form or complicated formula that frequent reference to explanatory notes elsewhere in the dictionary is required.

3. There should be little dependence on highly abstract theories but rather a recognisable link to some commonly used comprehensive grammatical system. A good instance of a learner's dictionary in this respect is the *Longman Dictionary of Contemporary English* (1978), which uses the system of the *Grammar of Contemporary English* (Quirk et al. 1972).[1] Grammatical information should be presented

    > "in traditional terminology with the assumption that [dictionary users] will already be familiar with such terminology[2] and with the customary means of presenting grammar in classroom and/or textbook instruction" (McCorduck 1993: 10f.),

    that is, in accordance with advances in language pedagogy rather than with the latest considerations of grammatical theory.

    > "The fact is [...] that the traditional [word class] approach to grammar is still one of the most widely taught and studied systems of linguistic methodology [...] The traditional handbooks provided the array of terms and distinctions which most of us used in learning to talk about our own language, and which many educated people continue to find serviceable throughout their lives" (Allen & Corder 1975: 47, 51).

    However, "[i]n some cases the presentation of grammar [...] in dictionaries is [...] perhaps too conservative" (McCorduck 1993: 11).

4. Based on contrastive studies, bilingual lexicography should pay particular attention to those areas of grammar and usage which are known to cause problems for learners from different linguistic backgrounds (cf. ibid.: 11).

---

[1] The first systematic inclusion of grammar into an English dictionary was done by Hornby in his *Oxford Advanced Learner's Dictionary* in 1942 which was based on Palmer's grammar (cf. Herbst 1985: 309).

[2] With regard to English-language instruction in Europe, Lemmens and Wecker state that
    > "users of [English] learner's dictionaries are also users of the well-known survey grammars of English (in particular those by Randolph Quirk and his associates)" (ibid.: 1986: 9)
    > "[B]ut the teaching of grammar (when it is done explicitly) in English language instruction in the United State is also carried out largely in traditional terms and categories" (McCorduck 1993: 11).

1.3.2.2.7.   Proposed parameters for grammatical information in dictionaries

As to the actual grammatical information which can be expected in bilingual general-purpose dictionaries, it is agreed in lexicographic literature that the *word class* label is the first information to be provided. Despite theoretical diversity of word class divisions, the recognition of word classes allows a close look at specific features of individual lexical items. The reason for this is that, according to the concept of grammar chosen above, word classes are groups of lexical items the division of which is established with regard to morphological, syntactic, semantic, logical, functional, and conceptual-categorial aspects. Nouns, adjectives and verbs are, for instance, based on the logical categories 'substance', 'property' and 'process'. Because they may inflect, as in the Germanic and Slavonic languages, morphological considerations can be added. Syntactic criteria are the abilities to take complements, or to modify nominal or verbal elements.

In general, word classes fulfil specific functions in a sentence which are closely connected to their distinctive properties described by grammatical categories. Only the linkage of these distinctive properties to the individual lexical item, however, will ultimately enable the dictionary user to apply the lexicon presented in the dictionary properly.

The word class label, therefore, is an instruction about the possibility of inflections of lexical items and types of their inflection. Recognising the word class with its particular features allows the dictionary user to pre-anaylse and pre-suppose potential functions and operations of individual lexical items concerning grammar and semantics on the basis of his passive knowledge of the language. To be told that an item is, for instance, a 'verb' is to be informed about the places at which it may occur in syntactic structure, for example (mostly inflected) in sentence initial position in most of the Celtic languages. To know that a lexical item belongs to conjunctions, prepositions, or pronouns is to be informed about its position in relation to other constituents of the sentence (cf. Kromann 1985: 348).[1]

The next step for establishing parameters for an analysis of the grammatical information contained in dictionary entries is to determine which particular grammatical features of each word class affect lexical rules and thus need to be described in them.

---

[1]   It is also suggested to attribute word class labels to idioms, since they are often used like single words (cf. ibid.: 31) and may function as individual constituents in sentences. As such they may have special syntactic or discourse properties (cf. ibid.: 114.). For differing views, see Standop (1985: 100).

(A)   The verb

First of all, the inflection expressing *number* and *person* is of interest for verbs in most European languages, i.e. also in Celtic tongues.[2] Inflection becomes even more significant when the categories *tense* and *mood* are also expressed by it.[3] Second, the *aspect* may be of interest, that is, whether or not a verb can be used in the progressive (cf. McCorduck 1993: 55).

Third, of importance, even for phrasal verbs, is the *voice* category, that is, whether a verb can be intransitive (cf. ibid.: 50, 61f.).

Fourth, the *complementation* should be referred to, that is,

> "the range of objects, subject complements, object complements or other elements, such as prepositional phrases, adverbials, and other adjuncts, that can or must be used with a particular [...] verb" (ibid.: 84).

Verb complementation is difficult, since a translation equivalent in one language may not take an identical range of complements in the other. In the case of English

> "[t]he need to supply the full range of complementation a verb can take has been long recognised yet often not realized; in the words of Országh (1961: 219), [...] exhaustive answers should be given in dictionaries to these questions (in the case of verbs): *where, what, of / for what, when, how?* Without these, all but the most literate users of English, native and foreigners, will often be at loss when trying to measure the perimeter of the living range of English words. [...] The importance of verb complementation may be ascribed in part to the fact that many schools of linguistics hold that the verb is the central, *sine qua non* of a sentence, and the complementation features of verbs determine the overall syntactic structure of any sentence" (McCorduck 1993: 84f.).

Verb complementation thus reaches far into the field of semantics and cannot be restricted to syntactic rules:

> "As decades of research on grammar have shown, the role of semantic factors in the choice of and/or restrictions on syntactic phenomena must also be taken into consideration. Perhaps in the selection of potential subjects, objects and other clause elements is the role of semantic information most obvious. Most verbs in English (and in other languages) can be used only with a restricted set of subjects, objects, namely those with appropriate semantic features" (McCorduck 1993: 118).

Although valency (cf. section 1.3.2.2.3.), seen in this way, clearly exceeds the word class level, it is always treated in relation to particular word classes, i.e. for verbs, nouns and adjectives separately. For practical reasons, therefore, it is proposed that syntactic constructions exceeding the word class level, or semantically motivated constructions, so called semantico-syntactic or semantico-grammatical constructions such as collocations, to be regularly included in discussions on the description of features of individual word classes.

---

[2]   This approach is adopted by Morán (1997: 130-151) with reference to the Spanish language.

[3]   Again, the indication is even demanded for idioms, when they are defined as functioning as verbs or when they contain verb indications (cf. McCorduck 1993: 57).

On the basis of, and in accordance with, latest valency grammars which deal with the matter of syntactic and semantic selectional features the incorporation of such grammatical information is also advocated.

(B)   The noun

First of all *gender, number* and/or *case inflection* are of interest for the display of nouns in dictionaries when they belong to the properties of this word class and affect lexical rules (cf. Heath 1985: 338f, 342). This is the case for nouns in German and the Slavonic languages. In the English language, only the number category affects lexical rules, and that only when irregular plurals need to be considered, e.g. *child - children*. In Welsh, the gender and number inflections deserve attention (cf. section 4.3.2.).[4]

Second, the *countability* or uncountability of nouns proves to be significant, a problem which occurs in most languages that show inflection for number; a common interlingual difficulty for a learner is that a specific noun may be countable in his or her language but uncountable in another, i.e. *die Information/die Informationen* in German and *information* in English, or vice versa (cf. ibid.: 39).[5] In relation to countability, guidance in *concord* or *agreement*, i.e. the selection of the morphological form of a verb to match the number of its subject noun or noun phrase, is needed. This is most true for polysem lexical items which can be used both in the plural and singular, e.g. *Statistics is a branch of mathematics/The road accident statistics are reliable* (McCorduck 1993: 109, Herbst 1985: 312).

Third, in cases where lexical rules apply for the use of *articles*, such rules ought to be indicated, as is even done in some dictionaries for native speakers (cf. McCorduck 1993: 44).

Fourth, the *complementation* of the noun is of interest when affecting lexical rules.

> "What is meant by complementation is the range of a word or word classes, or "complements," that accompany a word when it is used in a phrase or sentence, usually (but not always) following the word in syntactic position. In addition, complements may be obligatory or optional, and some complements when used with their headwords may affect the meaning of the headwords" (ibid.: 83),

thus having a strong influence on semantic features. Noun complementation in this sense is the range of structures, e.g. prepositions, prepositional phrases, clauses, and verb phrases, that may follow a noun. Lemmens (1985: 86), therefore, calls complementations, for which he uses the term collocations, "the best parts of the grammatical information".

Some of the rules governing the complementation of individual nouns seem particularly unpredictable (cf. McCorduck 1993: 92). Since they give exact and concrete realisation of clause and phrase elements, however, their inclusion in dictionary entries is strongly advocated.

---

[4]   The presentation of the number and gender inflection in entries of bilingual dictionaries for Spanish/German, for instance, is discussed by Morán (1997: 170-219).

[5]   Even in dictionaries such as idiom dictionaries, which concentrate on presenting lexical units of more than one word, the feature countability is indicated when phrases function as a noun (cf. Heath 1985: 42).

(C)   The adjective

First, if applicable, *case*, *gender* and *number* inflections of adjectives are to be indicated in dictionaries. This applies for German, Spanish, and the Slavonic languages. Number and gender inflections are also features of Welsh adjectives.[6]

Second, the *category of degree* is most important. Gradability, i.e. whether an adjective may take comparative or superlative forms, or whether it is always used in the positive degree, or whether or not an adjective may be modified by intensifiers, is an essential item of information for the dictionary user (cf. McCorduck 1993: 76). In Celtic languages, the equative has to be added. In view of the fact that the enthusiastic learner does not learn anything about this degree if relying on Welsh bi-directional general-purpose dictionaries[7] (cf. statement above that language users have more recourse to the dictionary as a necessary tool in any school class than to the grammar), the importance of introducing this feature of Welsh adjectives into dictionary entries becomes apparent.

Third, restrictions on *syntactic positions*, that is, their predicative and attributive use, are necessary for the productive application of adjectives, information which is not essential for the native speaker, but for the learner (McCorduck 1993: 71, Heath 1985: 338). In some languages, including in Welsh, the position before and after the referent also matters.

Fourth, the question whether the adjective needs a *complement* or not, obligatory or optional, is lexically relevant, too (cf. McCorduck 1993: 97).

In this context, one might think that rules governing the use of intensifiers with particular adjectives would be viewed as collocational matter. The only collocational dictionary for English, however, *The BBI Combinatory Dictionary of English* (Benson 1986), does not deal at all with collocations involving intensifiers. Their inclusion into general-purpose dictionaries is, therefore, to be considered.

Beyond the word class level is the question concerning the possible use or its restrictions of some *present* and *past participles* of verbs as attributive adjectives (cf. ibid.: 79). However, their inclusion in the dictionary needs to be considered. Even the rules governing the attributive use of individual nouns are largely lexical and should, therefore, be indicated (cf. ibid.: 81, Heath 1985: 338[8]).

(D)   Prepositions

Rules governing the *use of prepositions* are highly lexical, particularly in the case where nouns, verbs and adjectives require complementation by phrases headed by specific prepositions (McCorduck 1993: 82). In addition, prepositions themselves can impose a government on following lexical items (cf. Schaeder 1985: 278).

---

6   The number inflection of adjectives in Spanish presented in entries of bilingual lexicographical works is outlined in Morán (1997: 198-219).

7   The only exception is the uni-directional English-Welsh dictionary *Geiriadur yr Academi*.

8   Heath, however, discusses the attributive use of individual nouns under the word class noun.

In cases when prepositions inflect, e.g. in Celtic languages, their paradigms should be treated like that of adjectives, nouns and verbs and be reflected in dictionary entries.

(E) Numerals

Numerals in English form a word class on the basis of lexical features, i.e. they are terms for numbers and quantities. Syntactically, the individual members of that word class may act as nouns, e.g. *thousands of people*, adjectives, e.g. *one book*, pronouns, e.g. *many*, or adverbs, e.g. *call twice*. Therefore, they would usually be delt with under the respective word classes.

Nevertheless, for Welsh it seems practicable to define a word class 'numerals' on the basis of semantic, morphological and syntactic features. Apart from denoting numeric quantities, Welsh numerals exhibit traces of *gender inflection,* e.g. *dau - y ddau* 'two - the two' and of number inflection, e.g. *chwech - chwechau* 'six (singular and plural)'. Some also demand special *complementation,* e.g. ordinals are generally followed by nouns in the singular, unless the partitive particle *o* 'of' is placed between the numeral and the following noun. In addition, numerals may cause mutation in subsequent lexical items. Consequently, for Welsh numerals inflection and complementation need to be included into the grammatical information provided by the respective dictionary entry.

(F) Function words

Function words are lexical items which primarily carry grammatical, rather than lexical meaning and which mainly fulfil syntactic and structural functions. Function words may include articles, pronouns, conjunctions, and particles (cf. Bussmann 1996: 175). McCorduck and others do not discuss the analysis of these word classes. However, since grammar is regarded as highly important in dictionaries (cf. above), the description of lexically relevant features of these word classes should be carefully designed in dictionary entries.

Pronouns

In Celtic languages, pronouns show *gender* and *number inflection* as well as special *complementation* (cf. chapter IV). Both need to be indicated in dictionary entries.

Conjunctions and particles

Conjunctions or particles are also of interest when their usage affects lexical rules. This is certainly the case in Celtic languages, in which certain conjunctions and particles demand special *complementation* (cf. chapter IV).

1.3.2.2.8.   Summary

To conclude: first, the actual need to include comprehensive grammatical information in dictionary entries has been illustrated in the preceding sections.

Second, this illustration is based predominantly on the analysis of English-language dictionaries. However, it should be noted, that English is a dominant language in the world. Therefore, its acquisition is supported world-wide and furthered by trade, tourism and mass media. This is not the case with languages of limited diffusion, such as Welsh. In order to master lesser used languages, an equivalent or greater extent of detailed grammatical information in dictionaries (and other reference books) is required.

Third, the discussion of necessary grammatical features to be included in dictionary entries on the basis of a somewhat traditional word class division seems to provide a good foundation in order to establish which information is fundamental. Such an approach focuses on the most essential functions and operations of lexical items that need to be understood in order to make communication possible. However, comprehensive reflections on more complex phenomena (cf. valency, above) need to be presented, too.

Fourth, in order to deal with grammatical attributes of word classes comprehensively, inflection paradigms, syntactic restrictions and particular government or collocation must be contained in dictionary entries as these are features which affect lexical rules.

Fifth, the word class labels included need to be broadly comprehensible (cf. section 1.3.2.2.6.). McCorduck (ibid.: 29ff.) cites the *Collins COBUILD English Language Dictionary,* which overshoots the mark by listing intensifiers, partitive nouns, different types of adjectives, ergative verbs, and predeterminers. It thus violates the principle of presenting grammar for the non-linguistically trained dictionary user. Other dictionaries, however, show little discrimination and do not even distinguish between transitive and intransitive verbs, e.g. *The New Horizon Ladder Dictionary of the English Language* (Shaw, J.R. & S.J. Shaw 1990). Sixth, information on word order or grammatical rules in discourse, i.e. stylistic information as it affects the choice of a grammatical construction, or shift of focus, are often provided indirectly as soon as dictionaries exemplify the usage of their lexical items in examples and definitions. These are desirable but exceed the level of simple sentences and are, therefore, not considered a compulsory part of essential grammatical information in entries of bilingual general-purpose dictionaries.

With the basis provided above, the parameters for the analysis of Welsh dictionary entries are established in the next section.

1.3.2.3.   Parameters for the critical investigation of Welsh dictionaries

Comparing current bilingual general-purpose dictionaries of easy manageable size, that is, from about 30 000 headwords onwards,[1] some common practise of including grammatical and systematic information becomes apparent, at least, within Indoeuropean languages in Europe. Concerning grammatical information, these dictionaries always comprise various degrees of morphological and syntactic information. Most of them also include phonetic information in their entries, or at least, information on the word stress (cf. Russian dictionaries). Apart from the *phonetic information* or information on word stress, this is also true for Welsh general-purpose dictionaries. The decisive difference is the extent of the information provided in them.

Looking at *morphological information*, dictionaries generally exemplify special features of each inflected word class of a given language. Welsh dictionaries, however, orientating themselves on English-language description or French dictionaries,[2] present restricted details only. Even for verbs, which - in contrast to verbs in English - show comprehensive inflection, Welsh dictionaries offer less information than their English or French models, thus lacking basic grammatical information.

Syntactic information beyond the word class label, which is common to other bilingual general-purpose dictionaries, is often lacking in Welsh lexicographical works.

Hyphenation, on the other hand, presents special treatment of lexical items. Therefore, its inclusion in dictionary entries is optional.

Based on the preceding section and on the properties of the Welsh language, those grammatical categories are determined in this section which should ideally be reflected in Welsh bilingual general-purpose dictionaries in order to provide basic grammatical information of lexical items and consequently enable the dictionary user to make full use of the potential functions of a dictionary (cf. section 1.1.). This includes, for instance, both the decoding and encoding functions. Without grammatical information the encoding function of a dictionary, for example, cannot be comprehensively met, i.e. the active use of lexical items in texts and speech in order to perform effective communication.

The determination of parameters to be included into dictionary entries in the preceding sections has been partly drawn from monolingual learners' dictionaries. Although there are no current monolingual lexicographical works apart from *Y Thesawrws*, some aspects of their investigations are particularly useful in the Welsh context. This is due to the communicative situ-

---

[1]   *Langenscheidts Taschenwörterbuch Englisch, Französisch, Russisch* (ca. 52.000 headwords; estimated by the author, since the publisher counts more than the headwords, so called *Stichwörter*; cf. section 4.2.); *Foclóir Póca* (ca. 30.000 headwords), *Großes Wörterbuch Französisch, Spanisch, Englisch* (Juncker Verlag, ca. 30.000 headwords), but even some smaller ones, such as the *Elementary breton-english & english-breton dictionary* (9.000 headwords; counted by the publisher) and the *Wörterbuch Irisch-Deutsch* (ca. 14.000 headwords), *Dictionnaire Français-Russe* (ca. 51.000 headwords), *Handwörterbuch Französisch-Deutsch* (ca. 60.000 headwords).

[2]   This, for instance, is the case with *Geiriadur yr Academi* (cf. sections 4.2. and 4.5.) and *Geiriadur Almaeneg* (W. Greller 1996).

ation[3] in Wales, in which a high percentage of the Welsh speakers are learners (cf. section 4.1.1.).

As shown in the preceding section, the minimum grammatical information a dictionary should provide is, according to lexicographical practise, the indication to which word class a lexical item belongs. Although essential (cf. section 1.3.2.2.), such linguistic information is limited, since, first, the properties of some word classes may overlap each other. This becomes apparent in the following examples where the word *clo* appears first as a verb then as a noun and as an adjective (P.W. Thomas 1996: 17):

Clo'r drws! 'Close the door',
Mae'r siop ar glo. 'The shop is closed.'
Drws clo. 'The locked door.'

Second, the syntactic information provided by the word class label is insufficient, if the word order is not strictly fixed. In this case, further rules need to be given for the formation of interrogative, negative or passive sentences.

Third, the grammatical background of the individual user can vary and be based on different classifications of word classes or other grammatical categories.

Consequently, the word class label needs to be extended by basic properties of the respective word class. The following brief discussion on Welsh word classes, therefore, includes the presentation of features of them which are lexically relevant.

Current theories of grammar, based on individual languages, found it necessary to add new word classes to the eight traditional ones (cf. section 1.3.2.2.7.). According to the structure of a given language and the grammatical concept employed for its description, therefore, word class definitions also vary in languages which are genetically closely related. Following P.W. Thomas (ibid.: 16f.), who uses a structural grammar model, there are eleven word classes in the Welsh language;[4] verbs, nouns, adjectives, pronouns, prepositions, adverbs, conjunctions, the article,

---

[3]   Communicative situation is defined here as the ethnic or regional distribution, particularly the social and functional disposition and hierarchy of languages and/or language varieties which are commonly used for communication at a certain time and within a certain territory and according to the political, socio-economic, ethnic and cultural conditions found in it. Features of this socio-communicative setting are the attitude of the speakers towards the languages and/or language varieties used in communication as well as the character and goal of the respective language policy related to it.
A communicative situation is shaped by historical processes which caused its formation, i.e. it is historically restricted. It is characterised by the following factors:
−   the community of speakers of the respective language
−   the linguistic potential the community provides, including the status and social functions of the language and/or language varieties it employs
−   the linguistic potential that is to the speaker's disposal
−   the attitude of the speaker of the community towards the respective language and/or language varieties (Hansen 1987: 6).

[4]   Since comparisons are drawn with lexicography of the English, Breton, Irish and German languages, differing word classes in those languages are discussed as the need arises. This is also the case for Latin forms, since this language played an important part in history as the language of scientific and political communication in Wales and other European countries.

ategion berfol 'verb props', e.g. *yn, wedi,* adjective qualifiers, e.g. *iawn* 'very', *rhy* 'too' and particles, e.g. *nid* 'not'. His classification is debatable and differs from those in the other Welsh grammar books. Different attitudes occur among those word classes which exceed the traditional word class division. S.J. Williams (1980) lists numerals, for instance. However, he does not make clear whether he defines verbal adjectives and preverbal particles as separate word classes. The same approach can be found in Thorne (1993). King (1993) lists quantifiers, e.g *digon* 'enough', but does not make clear whether he counts them as a separate word class. In his dictionary, he defines them as adverbs.

P.W. Thomas is the only linguist who discusses the problem of word classes in his grammar book. Nevertheless, his adjective qualifiers can also be classified as adverbs and do not really need to be treated as a separate word class. The verb props (ibid.: 90f.) can be assigned to adverbs, adjectives or particles and act as such words. They form a very limited group of words and do not share any morphological features, but support the expression of temporal determination of the action in the sentence.

That there are words in the Welsh language which can best be assigned to a word class called particles is accepted in all grammars. Another arguable matter, however, is the assumption of a word class of numerals. As pointed out before (cf. section 1.3.2.2.7.), numerals draw their members from different word classes and P.W. Thomas (1996: 242, 271) assigns them to a sub-group of pronouns. However, some Welsh number words exhibit gender and number inflection. In addition, the complementation of number words is different to members of other word classes (cf. sections 1.3.2.2.7., 1.3.2.3.7., and 4.3.7.). In this investigation, therefore, they are defined as a word class in its own right.

In view of the facts presented above, the following word class division is proposed for the purposes of this investigation: verbs, nouns, adjectives, pronouns, prepositions, adverbs, conjunctions, the article, numerals and particles.

Following the discussion in previous sections, lexically relevant grammatical features are now discussed for each word class. No further discussion, however, is pursued for adverbs and the article. The article in Welsh is relatively easy to apply. First, there is only one article, namely the definite article *yr* 'the' (cf. P.W. Thomas 1996: 178f.) which may change its appearance according to the vowel environment to *y* and *'r*, e.g. *yr* + *bwrdd* -> *y bwrdd* 'the table', *a* + *yr* + *afal* -> *a'r afal* 'and the apple' (ibid.). Second, the only other relevant feature is that *yr* governs mutation in following feminine nouns in the singular apart from those beginning with *ll, rh,* and apart from English loanwords which commence with *g*, e.g. *grŵp* 'group'. These two rules can be easily remembered by anybody learning Welsh. Consequently, there is no need to investigate the general-purpose dictionaries to whether they mention the government of the article or not. In addition, it can be assumed that their government is similarly treated like that of the other word classes (cf. chapter IV).

The group of adverbs is limited to some predominantly temporal and local adverbs without eminent morphological or syntactic features which would deserve special attention in a dictionary entry. There are also some quantifiers, which belong to adverbs. Only four of them, e.g.

54

rhy 'too (much)', *cryn* 'considerable', *go* 'somewhat' and *hollol* 'entire(ly)', are lexically relevant, since they cause soft mutation[5] in the following lexical item. Another adverb which causes mutation is *na(c)* 'than', which is used for comparison.

The other adverbs are mostly identical in appearance with existing adjectives. The differentiation between both word classes is made by their application. Adverbs of the same appearance as adjectives are employed by placing the adverbial marker *yn*[6] in front of them. Adverbs beginning with *p, t, c, b, d, g,* and *m* are lenited. The local and temporal adverbs exhibit, apart from being mutated when used, no other lexically relevant grammatical features either.

For the other word classes listed previously, lexically relevant grammatical features which need to be reflected in entries of Welsh general-purpose dictionaries are discussed in the following sections.

---

[5]   Another term for soft mutation is *lenition*. When a lexical item is discussed which causes soft mutation in a following constituent of the sentence, an 'L' is used to indicate this kind of mutation. In this way, a differentiation from spirant mutation, which is indicated by 'S' is guaranteed.
Soft mutation is a sound change that leads to the reduction of sounds and, in some cases, to their loss (cf. table of mutations in any of the Welsh grammars mentioned in this investigation).
Aspirate mutation is the replacement of plosives through homorganic fricatives (cf. table of mutations in any of the Welsh grammars mentioned in this investigation).

[6]   *Yn* as an adverbial marker has no particular semantic meaning.

1.3.2.3.1.   The Welsh verb
(A)   Morphological categories of the Welsh verb relevant for dictionary purposes

The Welsh verb has three *moods*; the indicative, the subjunctive and the imperative. According to P.W. Thomas (ibid.: 27), there are six *tenses* in the indicative: the present, the future, the past, the *amhenodol* 'the indefinite', the imperfect, and the pluperfect. Since this categorisation is unusual to traditional grammatical descriptions, it needs to be explained. Paradigms for present and future tense can only be distinguished for the verbs *bod* 'to be', *gwybod* 'to know (things)', and *adnabod* 'to know (people)'. The other verbs exhibit only one paradigm for both tenses. Depending on the linguistic point of view, this is explained either as future (Uned Iaith Genedlaethol Cymru, 1976: 44ff., P.W. Thomas 1996: 56ff.) or as present tense (cf. Thorne 1993: 271ff.). In any case, periphrastic constructions using the two paradigms of *bod* can be used to complement tenses: '*wyf*[1]+ yn + verb' the present tense and '*byddaf* + yn + verb' the future.

For the imperfect tense, traditional grammars again list two paradigms, but only for the verb *bod* and its compounds (cf. S.J. Williams 1990: 119f., Thorne 1993: 248f.). P.W. Thomas (1996: 55), however, defines one of them as imperfect, i.e. the *oeddwn*-forms of the verb *bod*. The *byddwn*-paradigm is called *amhenodol*, thereby claiming an imperfect tense exclusively for the verb *bod*.

Nevertheless, looking at synthetic verb inflection and speaking in traditional terms, four tenses would normally be listed (cf. S.J. Williams 1990, Thorne 1993). The additional paradigms in the present and imperfect tense are called the habitual and can fulfil other grammatical functions, such as the expression of future tense, as seen in the *byddaf*-paradigm, and that of the subjunctive mood, as found in the *byddwn*-paradigm. There are two tenses in the subjunctive mood: the present and the imperfect tense; according to P.W. Thomas (1996: 35, 59ff.), the future and the *amhenodol* (cf. above).

In all tenses, the inflection of the Welsh verb distinguishes between three *persons* plus one, that is, three in the singular, three in the plural, and one impersonal. The information denoting *person, number, mood*, and *tense* is contained in the suffixes attached to the verbal stem, the verb endings.

The Welsh verb has no inflected forms which indicate the *genus verbi* passive. Passive meaning can only be expressed by periphrastic constructions. Consequently, grammatical coding like 'transitive' and 'intransitive' in Welsh refer to syntactic rules, e.g. the government of the verb.

Apart from fossilised forms, such as *agored* 'open, opened', which now count as adjectives, there are no special forms for the participle either. The construction 'wedi + (pronoun) + verb' can be used for the present participle. Alternatively, adjectives ending in the suffixes *-edig* and *-adwy* may express the past participle. Therefore, these forms are often called verbal adjectives (cf. S.J. Williams 1990).

---

[1]   For variation with regard to the first person singular, see S.J. Williams (1980: 119, Thorne 1993: 248, 250, P.W. Thomas 1996: 37 and others).

There is only a limited number of modal verbs in the Welsh language, e.g. *gorfod* 'to be ob-liged'. Modality is consequently often expressed syntactically, e.g. by constructions like *bod am* 'want', or *bod* + noun + preposition (*mae rhaid i* 'must'). This is a phenomenon which should be lemmatised in the dictionaries.

Welsh features both regular and irregular verbs. When inflected, the Welsh verb may undergo various changes (cf. P.W. Thomas 1996: 29ff.), which dictionary producers need to be aware of: (a) some verbs ending in *-o* and *-i* keep these endings, since *-o* and *-i* form part of the stem and not a verbal ending, e.g. *addo* 'to promise' -> *addaw-*, *deffro* 'to wake up' -> *deffro-*; (b) some verbs exhibit stem extension, e.g. *atal* 'to stop' -> *atali-*; (c) others undergo stem contraction, e.g. *troi* 'to turn' -> *tro-*; (d) a number of verbs use different stems, e.g. *aredig* 'to plough' -> *ardd-*, irregular verbs might even employ more than one stem, e.g. *cael* 'to get' -> *caff-*, *ca(h)-*, *caw-* (ibid.: 50); (e) vowel affection occurs under certain circumstances either on its own or in connection with some of the changes mentioned (above), e.g. *arwain* 'lead'-> *arweini-* (stem ex-tension by *i* + vowel affection). Further vowel affection is common to many verbs used in the third person singular present, e.g. *colli* 'to loose' -> *cyll*.

Some Welsh verbs are defective, e.g. *dylwn* 'I should' and exhibit reduced paradigms. Other verbs show no inflection at all, e.g. *byw* 'to live' (Griffiths, B. & D.G. Jones 1995: lxv).

This brief exemplification of the Welsh verb inflection suggests that comprehensive knowledge is necessary in order to apply it correctly. With reference to the key role of the in-flected verb for sentence construction, the provision of guidelines on the inflection peculiarities should be a basic requirement of any Welsh dictionary. For a discussion of this matter, see section 4.3.1.1.

(B)   Syntactic categories of the verb relevant for dictionary purposes

According to how the verb can influence the sentence structure, P.W. Thomas (1996: 401) de-fines three main categories of verbs: (a) verbs which do not take an object or other complements are called 'intransitive verbs' *berf gyflawn*, e.g. *marw* 'to die' (ibid.: 402); (b) those which are followed by an object are referred to as 'transitive verbs' *berfau anghyflawn*, e.g. *adnabod* 'to know'; (c) those which need a complement, henceforth labelled 'to be complemented', are called 'complemented verbs' *berfau dibeniadol*, e.g. *aros yn glerc* 'to remain a clerk' (ibid.: 410ff.). The category of transitive verbs has a sub-category, that is, a group of verbs which govern spe-cific prepositions. P.W. Thomas (ibid.: 403, 560) terms them *berfau arddodiadol* 'prepositional verbs', e.g. *methu â* 'to fail', *siarad â ... am* 'to talk to ... about', *edrych ar* 'to look at'. The com-plement, which is introduced by such a preposition, is called *gwrthrych traws* 'oblique object' (cf. also A.R. Thomas 1992: 309). The prepositions chosen can vary according to stylistic or dialectal variation.

For the category of verbs 'to be complemented', P.W. Thomas (ibid.: 410) defines two sub-groups: one is called 'complemented intransitive verbs' *berfau dibeniadol cyflawn*, and the other 'complemented transitive verbs' *berfau dibeniadol anghyflawn*. The first sub-group of verbs lacks an object and refers back to the subject, e.g. *Arhosodd Ifan yn glerc* 'Ifan remained a clerc', and the latter takes an object and refers to it, e.g. *Galwodd Ifan Siân yn angel.* 'Ifan called Siân an angel.'

In a footnote, P.W. Thomas (ibid.: 560f.) mentions *berfau ymadroddol* 'phrasal verbs'; i.e. verbs which often take adverbials (ibid.: 560), e.g. *cymryd yn ôl* 'take back'. He assigns them to transitive and intransitive verbs or to adoptions from English, e.g. *eistedd i lawr*,[2] the meaning of which can be fully covered by existing Welsh words, e.g. *eistedd*.

Following Thomas' examples, *yn*-complements are possible with these verbs as well (cf. berfau dibeniadol above), e.g. *dod yn ôl yn feddyg* 'to come back as a doctor'. Since they are apparently complemented in correspondence with their base verbs, they form a semantic, rather than a separate syntactic, verb group (cf. semantics of the verb). This view is in accordance with Aarts (1999: 15-33),[3] although there are syntactic difficulties with English phrasal verbs, e.g. the position of the object. This, however, is a problem of English.

Phrasal verbs in Welsh have not yet been examined. Consequently, since there is no reliable definition for phrasal verbs in the Welsh language and their existence is arguable - by some academics they would be recognised as being wrong in Welsh (cf. Sorlin 1999: 335) - a discussion of this issue is beyond the immediate scope of this study.

Referring back to P.W. Thomas, it remains unclear whether he is speaking of the same phrasal verbs in his footnotes on pages 560f. and 402. In the latter, he mentions the fact that very few verbs take adverbials as complements, e.g. *bod* if it does not mean 'existing'. Since there are only three examples provided, further consideration on this group becomes impossible here.

Although the phenomenon is known to the Welsh language, the term government (*rheolaeth*, Evans 1987: 40) is not itself used by P.W. Thomas to categorise the Welsh verb on the basis of its complementation. His groups of verbs are somewhat tenuously defined and exemplified, thereby causing difficulties in differentiating between the verb groups proposed by him (ibid.: 402-410ff., 560ff.).

---

[2]   In this discussion, the influence of the English language becomes markedly apparent. First, also because of the high percentage of learners among Welsh speakers (cf. section 4.1.1.), there is a tendency to introduce English structures into the Welsh language and second, many linguistic terms denoting grammatical features of the English language are adopted to characterise properties of the Welsh language. This, however, is a problem, since English is basically different from Welsh. The latter still belongs predominantly to languages which inflect, whereas English has lost most inflections, a phenomenon which affects other spheres of the language, too, for instance, the syntax. Whenever the Welsh language is described, therefore, other languages than English should also be taken into consideration for comparison and contrastive investigations or the search for linguistic terms.

[3]   McCorduck (1993) discusses phrasal verbs in English dictionaries under 'morphological and word class information'.

As a result, the grammar of P.W. Thomas hardly offers useful criteria to distinguish between the syntactic categories of verbs; information which is essential to the dictionary user in order to apply verbs comprehensibly in speech. The most important questions for the user are, first, whether a verb has to have a complement, and second, what kind of complement it takes. The answers to these questions, therefore, form the decisive criteria for the classification of the verbs in this investigation. Optional complements are certainly also of interest for the dictionary user. Since they are of secondary importance, however, they are left for further discussion.

In the following, a basic categorisation of verbs on the basis of their obligatory complements is proposed. It would need to be refined in separate comprehensive and corpus-based studies on the complementation of verbs. There is, of course, an optional element even in this catgeorisation; if, for instance, a verb takes more than one complement, e.g. *aros* 'to wait', then the choice of the complement is left to the dictionary user and his communicative intentions. A categorisation of Welsh verbs based on their syntactic complementation may be presented as follows:

    (a)   intransitive verbs, which take no complement, e.g. *marw* 'to die',

    (b)   transitive verbs, which take a direct object, e.g. *adnabod* 'to know',

    (c)   prepositional verbs, which take prepositions as connectors to the complements, e.g. *mynd at* 'to go to somebody', *dal i* 'to keep',

    (d)   verbs 'to be complemented', which take *yn*[4] as a connector; after taking *yn* they can be complemented in accordance with their base verb,

    (e)   verbs which take adverbials, e.g. *dodi yma* 'to place here',

    (f)   verbs which take verbs as a complement, e.g. *ymarfer nofio* 'to practise swimming',

    (g)   reflexive verbs, e.g. *ymolchi* 'to wash oneself'.

Prepositional verbs and those 'to be complemented' could traditionally be assigned to the category of intransitive verbs (cf. prepositional objects in German, Helbig/Buscha 1981: 56). For easy understanding and application in speech acts by the dictionary user, however, the maintenance of separate categories would appear advisable.

The group of verbs which take other verbs as complements has, to the best of my knowledge, not yet been mentioned anywhere with regard to the Welsh language.

Looking at the categorisation of the Welsh verbs, it is strikingly similar, although not exactly the same, to that which can be found in Schumacher (1985: 167) when suggesting a categorisation of German verbs for a dictionary of valency.

There is also a group of reflexive verbs (P.W. Thomas 1996: 403), mostly prefixed by *ym-*, e.g. *ymolchi* 'to wash oneself'. This group is limited, since reflexivity can also be expressed syntactically.

For a discussion on the presentation of the syntactic complementation of verbs in Welsh dictionaries, see section 4.3.1.2.

---

[4]   Looking at *yn* as a syntactic connector, it has no particular semantic meaning.

(C)   Semantics of the verb relevant for dictionaries

As far as I am aware, there are no systematic theoretical treatments available concerning the semantics of the Welsh verb except *The Semantics of the Welsh Verbs* by Fife (1990). Some reference books exist on idioms which also subsume different categories of verb complementation e.g. C. Davies (1990, 1987, 1980), R.E. Jones (1987), Cownie (2001). Syntactic verb complementation may be found under the headline 'idiom', for example in C. Davies *Torri'r Garw. Idioms for Welsh Learners based on the verb noun* (1996) when listing *mynd at* 'to go to (a person)'. Apart from syntactic complementation, such reference books predominantly reflect the following three categories of semantic aspects of the Welsh verb:

(a)   idiomatic verbs, e.g. *bod am* 'to want',
(b)   collocations based on verbs, e.g. *clywed arogl* 'to smell',
(c)   idioms based on verbs, e.g. *canu ar ei fwyd ei hun* 'not behoven to any benefactor',
[(d)   phrasal verbs or verbs which take adverbials as their complement, e.g. *cymryd yn ôl* 'to take back'[5]].

If taken as existing (cf. above), phrasal verbs could form a fourth category. They do, however, follow the syntactic complementation of their base verb.

The other three categories exhibit syntactic interaction independent of that of their apparent base verb. Idiomatic verbs are a sub-group of verbs which do not belong to those which take prepositions as connectors to complements, e.g. *mynd i* 'to go to somewhere' and *mynd at* 'to go to someone'. According to P.W. Thomas, they form a sub-group of transitive verbs (cf. syntactic categories of the verb). Prepositions of verbs, as in *bod am* 'want' *bod â/ag* 'to have', *bod gan* 'to have', *bod ar* 'to have', *dod o hyd i* 'to find', *dod i ben* 'to expire', *dod i oed* 'to reach maturity', *gweld eisiau* 'to miss (the presence of someone/something)' form a constituent part of the verb. Consequently, they cannot be separated from it or substituted as is the case with prepositions acting as connectors to syntactic complements, as for instance in *mynd at* 'to go to someone' or *mynd i* 'to go to somewhere'.

As a result, I define idiomatic verbs, which are not discussed by P.W. Thomas, as verbs the meaning of which cannot necessarily be predicted from the meanings of their constituent parts, and whose individual items are only separable by the subject, e.g. *dod o hyd i* 'to find' -> *daeth Alan o hyd i* 'Alan found'. Looking at various examples, idiomatic verbs may be composed as follows: '(base) verb + preposition (+ noun)', e.g. *dod â* 'to bring', *dod dros ben* 'to overcome', and '(base) verb + noun', e.g. *troi llygaid* 'to goggle'.

Idiomatic verbs remain either without a complement, e.g. *mynd am dro* 'to stroll', thereby behaving[6] like intransitive verbs; or they take a genitive construction, e.g. *bod ag angen (bwyd)* 'to have the need of (food)', or they require a prepositional connector to the complement, e.g.

---

5   These verbs can mostly be replaced by other Welsh verbs.
6   The usage of 'behave' in this investigation does not refer to linguistic behaviourism (cf. Bussmann 1996: 50), instead it is used in its unmarked general sense.

cael gafael ar 'to get hold of'; or *yn* + complements, e.g. *bod wrthi yn* 'to be busy with', as do other verbs.

The semantic functioning of idiomatic verbs is comparable with prefixed verbs in German. Both kinds of verbs share the same base verb but change their meaning and government clearly by taking other constituent parts, i.e. prepositions and/or nouns in Welsh (cf. above) and prefixes[7] in German. Examples of the prefixation of *gehen* 'to go' (+ preposition *zu, nach* 'to') are: *eingehen* 'to die, to shrink' (no complementation), *weggehen* 'to leave' (no complementation), *zugehen* 'to close' (no complementation), *aufgehen* 'to open, to rise' (no complementation), *abgehen* 'to depart, to send, to come off' (no complementation).[8] As the German language has a rich pattern of prefixation, the Welsh language also has plenty of idiomatic verbs.

Their distinctive features from phrasal verbs are that idiomatic verbs (a) do not take adverbials and (b) show a different syntactic complementation to that of their apparent base verb (cf. list of verbs: Syntactic and semantic valency of the Welsh verb in selection - Falensi'r ferf Gymraeg, section 4.3.1.2.).

The question of distinguishing idiomatic verbs from idioms is more problematic, since idioms can also participate in syntactic processes. The basic distinctive feature is the stylistic value which is characteristic of idioms. In addition, there is a tendency for larger units of a certain length to belong to idioms (cf. section 1.3.2.2.2.).

In light of these features of idiomatic verbs, their description should be assigned to word formation rather than to complementation and, therefore, ought to be reflected in dictionary entries. Idiomatic verbs need to be treated as independent lexical items and listed in separate dictionary entries, assigned to the above listed syntactic categories of Welsh verbs. Phrasal verbs (as in English), however, should be compiled under their base verb (cf. McCorduck 1993: 58-71, Aarts 1999: 15-33).

A kind of semantic complementation is reflected in collocations. The emphasis of collocations is on "frequently repeated or statistically significant co-occurrences" whether or not there are apparent semantic bonds (cf. section 1.3.2.2.2.) between their constituent parts. The lexical items thereby linked form a semantic unit, which may impose a different government on a subsequently placed complement to that of its base verb, e.g. *cael* (transitive) 'to get, have' -> *cael hwyl* (am) 'to have fun'. Since their individual constituent parts are linked within the syntactic pattern of their base verb but with unpredictable semantic linkage, they need to be listed under their base verb, plus the government they impose on a subsequently placed complement.

Within an idiom, however, the verb does not have to be linked to its complement within the governing rules of the apparent base verb, that is to say, idioms may be grammatically ill-formed, as in *siarad wrth y pwys a byw* 'to talk much and do little' (< *siarad â ... am* 'to talk to ... about'). Consequently, idioms are larger units the individual constituent parts of which are often

---

[7]   It is notable that these prefixes are placed as separate prepositions at the end of a sentence when the verb is inflected, e.g. *Ich ging von zu Hause weg* 'I left home'.

[8]   More examples could be added.

unpredictably put together (cf. section 1.3.2.2.2.). Like idiomatic verbs and collocations, they form their own semantic unit and as such can participate in the syntactic processes and can themselves impose a government on other parts of speech.

Since most idioms, however, show a specific stylistic value, they require particular communicative pre-conditions for their application and usage. Emphasising specific expressions and taking part in syntactic processes make this category fall under syntactic and semantic valency and stylistics. Idioms could consequently form a separate dictionary entry. Since it is customary, however, to have mainly one-word headwords in bilingual general-purpose dictionaries, idioms are best compiled under their base word.

The distinction between the semantic sub-categories of the verb is extremely difficult at times. The three semantic verbal sub-categories illustrated above form lexical units which distinguish them semantically from their base verb but which still need to be complemented. Therefore, their grammatical description in dictionaries, i.e. their inflection, and the assignment to syntactic categories exemplified above is advocated to make them applicable in context.

In addition, semantic relations between the verb and its surrounding lexical items express culturally based language usage and mark off the language under discussion as distinct from others. In the same way as grammatical structures, they add linguistically to the unique component parts which make up the conception of the language, thereby arousing particular feelings and associations among its speakers. Contributing to the constitution of identity, they should form an integral part of bilingual general-purpose dictionaries. For a discussion of the semantic complementation of verbs, see section 4.3.1.2.

1.3.2.3.2.   The Welsh noun

The Welsh noun distinguishes between two *genders*, masculine and feminine. The grammatical gender normally corresponds to the biological. In the number category, there is no gender distinction. The gender of some nouns can vary, either dialectally, e.g. *angladd* 'funeral' and *nifer* 'number' which are feminine in the South and masculine in the North (cf. P.W. Thomas 1996: 141f.), according to the context (cf. ibid.: 139ff.), or in order to indicate different semantic meaning, e.g. *ewyllys* <u>eg</u>[1] 'will, ability to choose' vs. <u>eb</u> 'testament, last will' (ibid.: 137). Without such distinctions, the dictionary user is able to apply correctly neither this part of the lexicon, nor the lexical or syntactic constructions that depend upon it. For a discussion of what is called gender-coupled semantic variation (cf. ibid.: *Enwau y mae eu cenedl a'u hystyr yn cyd-amrywio*) in dictionaries, see section 4.3.2.1.

Regarding the category *number* of the Welsh noun, there are two main categories which can be distinguished according to P.W. Thomas (1996: 150); (a) the *plural* and (b) the *singular* for countable nouns.

There are nouns, however, which are not countable. They are called *enwau cynnull* 'collected, assembled' (cf. ibid: 150). In this investigation, they are called non-countable nouns, since they can only be counted when preceded by a *rhanolyn* 'partitive' *o* 'of', e.g. *torf o fara* 'loaf of bread'. Some nouns belong both to countable and non-countable nouns and change their semantic meaning with the number, e.g. *dau haearn smwddio* 'two irons' vs. *Oes yr Haearn* 'Iron time'. Just as a shift in gender may be linked to semantic variation, a shift in number can also cause semantic variation. This phenomenon is referred to here as number-coupled semantic variation.

Non-countable nouns can in some instances behave like nouns in the singular and in others like nouns in the plural. On the one hand, therefore, it is possible to use a demonstrative construction to refer to a particular bread, e.g. *y bara hwn* 'this bread', or to replace such a noun by a singular pronoun. On the other hand, non-countable nouns are preceded by phrases which would normally come before nouns in the plural, e.g. *llawer o fara* 'much bread'.

A third group in the category of number is, according to P.W. Thomas (1996: 154), formed by *enwau torfol* 'collective nouns'. They refer to groups of people, creatures or inanimate objects, e.g. *byddin* 'army', *haid* 'flock'. Only when they do not refer to a particular group can they be counted.

On pages 166f. P.W. Thomas (1996) describes briefly a fourth group, that is, 'plural nouns' *enwau lluosog*. He defines them as nouns which refer to things where distinctions between them are not easy to detect (*enwau lluosog* [... *sy'n*] *cyfeirio at bethau nad hawdd canfod gwahaniaeth rhyngddynt*), e.g. *ceirios* 'cherries', *madarch* 'mushrooms'. However, the differences between the individuals groups of nouns as defined by P.W. Thomas remain somewhat unclear. For lexi-

---

[1]   *Eg* is the abbreviation for *enw gwrywaidd* 'masculine noun' and *eb* is the abbreviation for *enw benywaidd* 'feminine noun'.

cographical purposes, therefore, an alternative classification of Welsh nouns based on their morphology has been developed in section 4.3.2.2.

The number category dual is not mentioned by P.W. Thomas. Since there are only some traces of it left, e.g. *yr efeilliaid* 'twins' < *gefell* 'twin', *Yr Eifl* (the name of two mountains in *Llŷn*) < *gafl* 'fork' (S.J. Williams 1990: 21f.), no further attention is paid to this category here either.

Looking at how the number inflection works, P.W. Thomas (1996: 155) distinguishes between two main methods of this inflection; exchange and extending. Both of them can be sub-divided into two other methods; the former in consisting of a vowel change, e.g. *ffon* 'stick' -> *ffyn* 'sticks', and an exchange of endings, e.g. *athronydd* 'philosopher' -> *athronwyr* 'philosophers', and the latter of extending a plural ending, e.g. *gwrach* 'hag' -> *gwrachod* 'hags' or extending a singular ending, e.g. *moch* 'pigs' -> *mochyn* 'pig'. The nouns which may form a singulative are called *enwau lluosog* 'plural nouns' by P.W. Thomas (1996: 166). This problem area has also been dealt with in section 4.3.2.2.

The Welsh noun exhibits no *case inflection*, apart from a few attested fossilised examples in mediaeval Welsh poetry. No further attention is, therefore, paid to this category here.

64

1.3.2.3.3.   The Welsh adjective

Some Welsh adjectives exhibit *gender* and *number* inflection, e.g. *gwyrdd* - *gwerdd* 'green' (masculine, feminine); *balch* - *beilchion* 'proud' (singular, plural). Most of them, however, feature only one category, few both of them, e.g. *gwyn* 'white' - *gwen* - *gwynion* (masculine, feminine, plural for both genders; cf. P.W. Thomas 1996: 191). Since the adjectives which do inflect are relatively frequently used, their forms should be provided in dictionaries. This requirement is supported by the fact that the plural forms of a number of adjectives are regularly used as a plural noun (cf. section 1.3.2.3.2.), thereby emphasising the close relation between adjectives and nouns (ibid.: 194ff.).

What is important and different from Germanic languages is the fact that the *category of degree* distinguishes four levels in Welsh; the positive, the equative, the comparative and the superlative, e.g. *da* - *cystal* - *gwell* - *gorau* 'good - as good - better - best' (suppletion), *byr* - *cyn byrred/mor fyr* - *byrrach* - *byrraf* 'short - so short - shorter - shortest' (suffixation).

The comparison of adjectives can be carried out morphologically, periphrastically or lexically, that is, synthetically by suffixation, analytically by employing the comparative forms of intensifying adjectives, or by suppletion. The equative uses a combination of suffixation and employing the adverb *cyn* 'so' or *mor* 'so' (cf. examples above). Regular and irregular comparisons can be distinguished, the latter employing suppletives as shown in the comparison of *da* (cf. above).

There are two ways of forming regular comparisons in Welsh; (a) adding the suffixes *-ed*, *-ach*, *-af* and (b) employing the degrees of *mawr* 'big' or *bach* 'small' for periphrastic comparison. The adjective *agos* is quite exceptional in that it is comparable in all three ways; the comparison *agos* - *agosed* - *agosach* - *agosaf* 'near - so near - nearer - nearest' represents synthetic comparison, *agos* - *mor agos* - *mwy agos* - *mwyaf agos* illustrate analytic comparison, and *nesed* - *nes* - *nesach* - *nesaf* comparison by suppletion. The forms *cynted*, *cynt*, and *cyntaf*, however, may be the forms of comparison of two adjectives, i.e. *cynnar* 'early' and *buan* 'swift'.

In comparing, vowel affection, e.g. *tlawd* -> *tlotach*, and change of the final or penultimate consonants, e.g. *budr* -> *butred* 'dirty, so dirty' and *teg* -> *teced* 'fair, so fair', may occur, as well as the doubling of <r, n> (cf. Thorne 1993: 136, P.W. Thomas 1996: 224ff.).

There is a small group of adjectives which exhibit defective comparison, e.g. *trech* - *trechaf* 'dominant - most dominant' (P.W. Thomas 1996: 228). Some adjectives do not compare at all, e.g. *blynyddol* 'annual', *priod* 'married' (ibid.: 216). There is, however, a group of nouns which can take affixes of comparison; e.g. *blaen* - *blaenaf* 'point front - foremost'; *gwerth* - *cyfwerth* 'value - of the same value, equivalent' (ibid.: 228f.), thereby again reflecting the close relation between adjectives and nouns (cf. above).

To sum up: the comparison of Welsh adjectives can apparently be somewhat unusual, for instance, because of the equative. It may also be somewhat tricky, since it is not as regular as in the sister language Breton. Because of this, an appropriate presentation of the above peculiarities of the comparison of Welsh adjectives in dictionary entries is recommended. The same is true for the close relation between adjectives and nouns which reflects word formation patterns. In section 4.3.3. the current situation of entries in bilingual Welsh general-purpose dictionaries with regard to the presentation of the morphology and semantics of Welsh adjectives is discussed.

1.3.2.3.4.   The Welsh pronoun[1]

P.W. Thomas (ibid.: 242) divides the word class of pronouns into (a) *rhagenwau canolog* 'central pronouns' and (b) *rhagenwolion* 'pronominals'. The former sub-group comprises *rhagenwau personol* 'personal pronouns', *rhagenwau perthynol* 'relative pronouns' and *rhagenwau holiadol* 'interrogative pronouns'. The latter is defined as:

> "Elfen a chanddi swyddogaeth rhagenw er bod ganddi o leiaf un swyddogaeth arall."
> 'An element which is characterised by the function of a pronoun but features, at least, one other function' (ibid.: 271[2]).

This sub-group is divided into *rhagenwau cyffredinol* 'general pronouns', *mesurau* 'measurements', *dangosolion* 'demonstratives' and *rhifeiriau* 'number words'.

What P.W. Thomas calls *rhagenwau cyffredinol* 'general pronouns', e.g. *un* 'one', *rhai* 'some' (ibid.: 272ff.), is otherwise defined as the sub-group 'indefinite pronoun' (cf. Bussmann 1996: 223). 'Demonstratives', e.g. *hon* 'this (feminine)', *yma* 'here' (cf. ibid.: 286ff.), however, do not cause many difficulties in their application and are, therefore, not discussed in this investigation. 'Number words', e.g. *dau* 'two' (cf. ibid.: 294ff.), are being dealt with separately as was explained in the discussion of the classification of Welsh word classes (cf. 1.3.2.3.). Measurements are not regarded as pronouns here.

Some pronouns assigned to *rhagenwau perthynol* 'relative pronouns', e.g. *a* 'which, who, whom', na(d) 'which, who, whom ... not', *rhagenwau holiadol* 'interrogative pronouns', e.g. *pa* 'which, what', *rhagenwau cyffredinol* 'general pronouns', e.g. *rhyw* 'some', and *dangosolion* 'demonstratives', e.g. *dyma* 'this here', impose a government on their subsequent referent. Together with the dependent pronouns (cf. below), the presentation of their government in Welsh dictionary entries is investigated in section 4.3.4.

The only possessive pronoun in Welsh, i.e. *eiddo* 'possession, some, to him...' (cf. ibid.: 279) exhibits the same inflection as prepositions (cf. following section). It is shown in section 4.3.4. whether *eiddo* is adequately introduced in Welsh general-purpose dictionaries.

Of major interest for the dictionary user is the application of, in terms of P.W. Thomas (cf. above), the 'central pronouns', especially of their sub-group 'personal pronouns'. Under this term, P.W. Thomas also subsumes possessive pronouns (ibid.: 252ff.) because of the special functioning of mainly the dependent Welsh 'personal pronouns' (cf. below).

The actual function of a Welsh pronoun, that is, whether it is used as a possessive, a personal, or an object pronoun, however, predominantly depends on its position as to its referent and the referent's function in the sentence. Consequently, a given set of pronoun forms can perform various functions in differing contexts. Since the classification of P.W. Thomas obscures these facts, an alternative classification of pronouns is proposed in the following table:

---

[1]   I would like to take this opportunity of thanking Siôn Williams, Cardiff/Wales, for his helpful comments on this section.

[2]   Although P.W. Thomas assignes four sub-groups to 'pronominals' at page 242, he lists only three at page 271. However, in his detailed description of the different types of 'pronominals' on the following pages he includes 'measurements' again.

Person	Independent Pronouns			Dependent Pronouns		
	simple	double[3]	conjunctive[4]	prefixed	infixed	suffixed[5]
1. Sg.	mi	myfi	m-/finnau	fy^{N}[6]	'm^{H}	i, fi
2. Sg.	chd-/ti	chd-/tyfi	chd-/tithau	dy^{L}	'th^{L}	di
3. Sg. m.	(f)o/e(f)	(e)fo, (e)fe	yntau	ei^{L}	'i^{L}, 'w^{L}, -s	(f)o/(e)f
3. Sg. f.	hi	hyhi	hithau	ei$^{S/H}$	'i$^{S/H}$, 'w$^{S/H}$, -s	hi
1. Pl.	ni	nyni	ninnau	ein^{H}	'n^{H}	ni
2. Pl.	ch(w)i	chwychwi	chwithau	eich	'ch	ch(w)i
3. Pl.	hwy(nt) nhw	hwynt-hwy	hwythau nwthau	eu^{H}	'u^{H}, 'w^{H}, -s	hwy(nt) nhw

The table displays a set of forms of Welsh pronouns which may be used in different contexts. The dependence of their functions on the position with respect to their referent, the word class of their referent and their referent's function in the sentence is illustrated by the following examples:

1. When the dependent pronoun precedes a verb, a noun, or when it splits a preposition, it functions as an object or possessive pronoun: *Mae 'r mam wedi fy ngweld (i)* 'My mother has seen me' (object pronoun); *Fe 'i sgrifennwyd* 'Him was written' (object pronoun); *fy nhŷ (i)* 'my house', *ei char (hi)* 'her car', *ein hafalau (ni)* 'our apples', *uwch fy mhen (i)* (< *uwchben* 'above') 'above me' (possessive pronoun).

   As a possessive pronoun, it can, according to the register of the language and stylistic implication (a) stand on its own (cf. below) or (b) co-occur with suffixed pronouns following the referent and thereby forming a frame (cf. above).

2. Preceding a verb, the pronoun can be the resumption of an object and act as an independent pronoun: *Beth (y) mae 'n ei wneud.* 'What is he/she doing?'

3. Preceding a verbal noun, the pronoun either indicates an object or possession. Its actual function depends on the function of the entire phrase it is in within the sentence:

   (a) *Yr oedd difaterwch wedi ein llyncu (ni)* 'Indifference had swallowed us' (object pronoun in complement).

   (b) *Yr oedd fy narllen yn wael* 'My reading was bad' (possessive marker in subject).

4. Pronouns suffixed to a verb function as personal pronouns emphasising the formers' number and person: *A glywaist di?* 'Did you hear?'

---

3   This sub-group of pronouns is called 'reduplicated' by Thorne (1993: 155).
4   Conjunctive pronouns can be used as suffixed pronouns, too (cf. Thorne 1993: 166).
5   Thorne (1993: 166) uses the term 'affixed or auxiliary' for them. The term 'auxiliary' is supported by the functions of suffixed pronouns explained in 1., 3., and 4.
6   The superior letters indicate the government the pronoun imposes on its referent.

5. Pronouns suffixed to a noun perform like possessive pronouns: *Dyma dy gi **di***. 'Here is your dog.' As possessive pronouns, they can, according to the register and style, co-occur with a prefixed pronoun or stand on their own (cf. above).

6. When suffixed to prepositions, pronouns mark their person, number and genus: *Es i ato.* 'I went to him.' *Meddyliais amdani* 'I thought of her'

To sum up: considering the various functions particularly of dependent personal pronouns and thinking of them as headwords, they cannot simply be described as 'possessive' or 'personal pronouns'. Their definition should be 'pronoun', unless the dictionary provides enough space to exemplify their usage comprehensively.

In addition, important for the dictionary user with regard to their usage, is also the government the prefixed and infixed pronouns impose on their referents (cf. small letters in the table above). Making a gender distinction between masculine and feminine referents *ei* 'she/her - he/his - it/its', for instance, causes different shifts of inital consonants. When the referent is feminine, *ei* governs aspirate mutation or h-prefixation in it, e.g. *ei chi (hi)* (< ci) 'her dog', *ei hafal (hi)* (< afal) 'her apple', *ei theipio* (< teipio) 'her typing' whereas *ei* causes lenition when the referent is masculine, e.g. *ei gadno (fe)* (< cadno) 'his fox'.

The presentation of features of Welsh pronouns is analysed in section 4.3.4.

1.3.2.3.5.   The Welsh preposition

Welsh prepositions are certainly troublesome for dictionary users, since they behave morphologically and syntactically in a different way from those in non-Celtic Indoeuropean languages. This becomes clear in the following brief discussion of them:

First, Welsh prepositions can, according to P.W. Thomas (1996: 339), be sub-divided into (a) simple prepositions, e.g. *dros* 'over', and (b) compound ones, e.g. *ar ôl* 'after'. Some of the simple prepositions he presents are themselves compound words, or nominal prepositions, that is, they contain a noun, e.g. *gerllaw* (< *ger* + *llaw*) 'beside'. What P.W. Thomas (ibid.) defines as simple and compound prepositions, therefore, should rather be described as prepositions which consist of one item and those which consist of more than one constituent part. Since dictionaries normally concentrate on one-word headwords, however, it is interesting to see how Welsh lexicographers handle compound prepositions in their dictionaries (cf. section 4.3.5.).

Second, unlike English prepositions, for instance, most Welsh prepositions inflect and thereby form parts of speech and may, for example, act as prepositional objects, e.g. *Es i ato.* 'I went to him'. In addition, they are essential for the formation of complex sentences when constructed by relative clauses, e.g. *Y garreg yr wyf yn eistedd arni* 'The stone I am sitting on' or *Y llythyr yr wyf yn ysgrifennu ato* 'The letter I am writing to him' (cf. also section 1.3.2.3.8.).

Welsh prepositions can be assigned to four classes of inflection indicating person, number and gender (P.W. Thomas 1996: 346ff.). These are exemplified in the following table with *at* 'to', *tros* 'over' and *i* 'to, for':

Person	I	II	III	IV
1. Sg.	ataf	trosof	wrthyf	imi, i mi
2. Sg.	atat	trosot	wrthyt	iti, i ti
3. Sg. m.	ato	trosto	wrtho	iddo
3. Sg. f.	ati	trosti	wrthi	iddi
1. Pl.	atom	trostom	wrthym	inni, i ni
2. Pl.	atoch	trostoch	wrthych	ich(w)i, i chi
3. Pl.	atynt	trostynt	wrthynt	iddynt

Compound prepositions also inflect, but analytically, e.g. *uwchben* 'above' -> *uwch fy mhen (i)* 'above my head', *uwch dy ben di* 'above your head' etc. Some non-inflectable prepositions are, for instance, *â(ag)* 'with', *cyn* 'before'.

Since Welsh prepositions can form major sentence components, such as prepositional objects (cf. above), or establish relations between sentence constituents, their correct use is essential. I discuss in section 4.3.5.3. how far the Welsh bi-directional general-purpose dictionaries provide guidelines in this respect.

Third, most Welsh prepositions share with those in other languages the potential to impose a government on the following lexical item, i.e. they cause mutations in them. Three kinds of government can be distinguished (cf. ibid.: 349f.); lenition caused, for example by *am* 'at', spirant mutation, e.g. provoked by *gyda* 'with', and nasal mutation,[1] e.g. *yn* 'in'.

Since government also causes difficulties in the application of Welsh prepositions, it requires further explanation in dictionaries. Guidance with regard to this problem area in Welsh dictionary entries is reviewed in section 4.3.5.2.

---

[1]   In q-Celtic languages this phenomenon is known as *eclipsis.*

1.3.2.3.6.   The Welsh conjunction[1]

Welsh conjunctions are also troublesome for dictionary users, since they may perform syntactically in a different way from those in Standard Average European languages (SAE). In addition, some of them resemble lexical items of other word classes. Items such as *ar ôl* 'after', for instance, can be used as a conjunction or a preposition depending on their context (cf. below and section 4.3.6.). However, if lexical items cannot be correctly classified, their accurate use in speech is not guaranteed. Some brief remarks on Welsh conjunctions are necessary, therefore, in order to provide a basis for their analysis in dictionary entries.

P.W. Thomas (1996: 461-478) distinguishes between coordinating and sub-ordinating conjunction. In both groups, there are correlative conjunctions (*cysyllteiriau dibynnol* in *Gramadeg y Gymraeg* ibid.: 462, 473), e.g. *naill ai... neu...* 'either... or...', *os... yna...* 'if... then...', as well as those which consist of more than one constituent part, e.g. *ar ôl* 'after', *yn ystod* 'during'. Since dictionaries normally concentrate on one-word headwords, it is interesting to see how Welsh lexicographers handle correlative conjunctions or those consisting of more than one constitutent part in their dictionaries (cf. section 4.3.6.).

Both coordinating and sub-ordinating simple or correlative conjunctions can express various semantic relations: Coordinating conjunctions establish the following relations: (a) copulative, e.g. with *a/ac* 'and', *nid yn unig... ond hefyd* 'not only... but also...' (affirmative), *nac*[2] 'not' (negative); (b) disjunctive, e.g. with *neu* 'or', *naill ai... neu...* 'either... or...'; (c) adversative, e.g. with *ond* 'but', *nid... ond...* 'not... but...'; and (d) causal relations, e.g. with *canys* 'for' (cf. P.W. Thomas 1996: 461).

Sub-ordinating conjunctions can also include causal relations, e.g. with *am* 'because', *gan* 'because', *o achos* 'because'. Other semantic links they set up are the following: (a) conditional, e.g. with *os* 'if', *pe* 'though', *os... yna...* 'if... then'; (b) temporal, e.g. with *hyd* 'until', *pryd* 'when', *tra* 'as', *cyn* 'before', *wrth* 'while', *tan* 'until', *ar ôl* 'after'; (c) final, e.g. with *er mwyn* 'for the sake of'; (d) consecutive, e.g. with *fel* 'so', (e) concessive, e.g. with *er* 'although'; (f) modal, e.g. *megis* 'as'.

In particular the sub-ordinating conjunctions can cause problems as when to be applied, since many lexical items used to relate words, phrases, or sentences syntactically, while characterising semantic relations between those elements, can also occur in other word classes. The following examples illustrate this situation:

---

[1]   I would like to take this opportunity of thanking William Ll. Griffith, Dinbych/Wales, for his helpful comments on this section.

[2]   As part of the correlative conjunction *nac ... nac*, however, *nac* acts as a disjunctive conjunction, e.g. in *Nid oes gennyf nac aur nac arian.* 'I have neither gold nor money'.

Lexical items used as conjunctions and preposition (*cysyllteiriau arddodiadol*):

> *Deuthum adref am nad oedd gwaith i'w gael.* 'I came home, since there was no work to be found' (conjunction; S.J. Williams 1990: 205).
>
> *Arhosais yn y cysgod am (y) gwyddwn y deuai'r lleidr yn ôl.* 'I stayed in the shadow, since I knew the thief would come back' (conjunction; ibid.: 205).
>
> *Aeth ef adref am ei fod yn flinedig.* 'He went home because he was tired' (conjunction).[3]
>
> *Arhosais amdano am^L ddwy awr.* 'I waited for him for two hours' (preposition).

> *Ar ôl i mi ddod siaradom yn hir.* 'After I came we had a long talk' (conjunction).
>
> *Cyrhaeddodd ar ôl crwydro'r pentref...* 'He arrived after wandering through the village...' (conjunction; P.W. Thomas 1996: 475).
>
> *Ar ôl pump o'r gloch yr oedd hi'n dawel.* 'It was quiet after five o'clock/It was after five o'clock that it became quiet'[4] (preposition).
>
> *Daeth ef ar fy ôl i.* 'He followed me' (preposition).

> *Arhoswn yma tan (y) canu.* 'We shall remain here until the singing' (conjunction; cf. P.W. Thomas 1996: 478, S.J. Williams 1990: 206).
>
> *Tan y ceni.* 'Until you sing' (conjunction; ibid.).
>
> *Tan bod pawb yn canu.* 'Until everybody sings' (conjunction; ibid.).
>
> *Yr wyf yn aros tan^L ddeg o'r gloch.* 'I wait till ten o'clock' (preposition).

> *Aethom dan ganu.* 'We were singing as we went' (conjunction).
>
> *Gweithgareddau dan do.* 'Indoor activities' (preposition; D.G. Lewis 1993: 18).

> *Gellwch aros yma hyd (y) mynnoch.* 'You can wait here as long as you want' (conjunction; S.J. Williams 1990: 206).
>
> *Eisteddwch hyd^L ddiwedd y wers.* 'Sit here until the end of the lesson' (preposition; D.G. Lewis 1993: 22).

Lexical items used as conjunctions and adverbs:

> *Tra pery'r iaith Gymraeg.* 'For as long as Welsh survives' (conjunction; D.G. Lewis 1993: 35).
>
> *Tra bu hi oddi cartref, bu lladron yn ei thŷ.* 'Whilst she was away from home, her house was burgled' (conjunction; P.W. Thomas 1996: 484).
>
> *Mae Huw yn berson tra^S charedig.* 'Huw is quite a (very) kind person' (adverb; D.G. Lewis 1993: 35).

Lexical items used as conjunctions and nouns (*cysyllteiriau enwol*):

> *Nid oedd dim gwell na dianc i'r cwm dros y Sul, pryd (y) gallai ymgolli yn y tawelwch.* 'There was nothing better than escaping to the valley on Sunday, when he became immersed in tranquility' (conjunction; P.W. Thomas 1996: 483, 476).

---

[3]   Examples without a reference are constructed by the author.
[4]   The actual translation of the example depends on the emphasis of the sentence.

Dyna <u>pryd y sylweddolwyd</u> y camgymeriad. 'This was when they realised the
  mistake' (<u>conjunction</u>; ibid.).
Dyna <u>bryd</u> i ddechrau. 'It's time to start' (<u>noun</u>).

Lexical items used as conjunctions and adjectives:

  <u>cyhyd ag y</u> ceni 'As soon as you sing' (<u>conjunction</u>; ibid.: 477).
  <u>cyhyd â bod</u> pawb yn canu. 'As soon as everybody sings' (<u>conjunction</u>; ibid.).
  Mae'r stryd <u>cyhyd â</u>^{S} <u>choed</u> y fferm. 'The street is as long as the wood of the
  farm' (<u>adjective</u> in the equative).

It is apparent that dictionaries have to provide guidelines for the usage of such lexical items.
Looking at the examples above, the following properties, apart from differing semantic meanings (cf. examples above), distinguish sub-ordinating conjunctions from other word classes:

First, the difference in the complementation of lexical items used as conjunctions may
separate them from those of other word classes. This difference in turn, however, depends on the
word class the lexical item employed as a conjunction can otherwise be assigned to: most lexical
items which can also perform as prepositions, or adverbs, or adjectives predominantly do not
cause mutation in the following sentence constituent when used as a conjunction and preceding
an inflected verb, e.g. the conjunctions and prepositions *am, cyn,*[5] *gan, hyd,*[6] *tan,* the adverb *tra,*
the adjective *cyhyd â* (cf. examples above). The reason for this is the affirmative particle *y/yr* or
its negative pendant *na/nad* which are mostly placed as connectors between the conjunction and
the following sentence constituent (cf. section 1.3.2.3.8.), i.e. the inflected verb.[7]

A small number of the lexical items which can act both as prepositions or conjunctions,
nevertheless, causes mutation when used as a conjunction before a verbal noun including *bod* 'to
be', e.g. *dan, gan, am* (cf. P.W. Thomas 1996: 477f.).

Second, when these sub-ordinating conjunctions are used in a nominal phrase, they often need
the preposition *i* as a connector to the following constituent, e.g. *wrth i mi sgrifennu* 'whilst I
am/was writing', *cyn i mi ddod* 'before I am coming' (cf. ibid.: 475).

Third, lexical items which behave as nouns or conjunctions cannot be distinguished by the
mutation they induce in the following constituent, e.g. *hyd.* They are, however, connected to it
by the particle *y* or its negation *na/nad.*

Fourth, conjunctions cannot be inflected as many prepositions can (cf. section 1.3.2.3.5.).

---

[5]   As a particle of comparison, *cyn* causes mutation. In this function it is defined as an adverb in
       Geiriadur yr Academi.
[6]   *Hyd* can also be a noun (cf. below).
[7]   The particle *y,* however, is often omitted in speech, a reason why it is difficult for learners to
       understand the different sentence structures and the use of their constituents accurately.

To sum up: Welsh conjunctions demand a different syntactic structure from words which look the same but can be assigned to the word classes noun, preposition, or adverb. In addition, they mostly express other semantic relations and cannot act as a part of speech. Moreover, the indication of their complementation is important, since, depending on their context, it differs significantly among sub-ordinating conjunctions.

In section 4.3.6., the extent of the presentation of the properties of Welsh conjunctions as well as the inclusion of correlative conjunctions and those consisting of more than one constituent part is analysed.

1.3.2.3.7.   The Welsh numeral[1]

In this study, Welsh numerals are treated as a word class in its own right as discussed in section
1.3.2.3. There are three major types of numerals in Welsh; cardinals, ordinals, and fractions as
well as some quantifiers. The ordinals in turn are of two types, which relate (a) to a decimal
system, e.g. *deg* 'ten', *dau ddeg* 'twenty', *tri deg* 'thirty', *pedwar deg* 'fourty', *chwe deg* 'sixty',
and (b) to a vigesimal system, e.g. *deg* 'ten', *ugain* 'twenty', *deg ar hugain* 'thirty', *deugain*
'fourty', *trigain* 'sixty' (P.W. Thomas 1996: 294f.). The former was first introduced in the
middle of the nineteenth century when the numbers of the hymns had to be announced to the non-
conformist audience. Its usage was enforced when Welsh became a medium of scientific
teaching. Its advantage lies in its correspondence to contemporary counting of money and measurements. The decimal system has, however, up to the present day not developed ordinals. For
that reason, it is essential for everybody to be acquainted with the vigesimal system as well (cf.
below and ibid.: 299).

There are four fractions which are particularly denoted in Welsh: *chwarter* 'a quarter', *traean*
'a third' *hanner* 'half' and *deuparth* 'two thirds'.[2]

All types of numerals can take nouns in the singular or prepositional clauses as defined by
P.W. Thomas (ibid.: 314ff.) as complements, e.g. *un deg tri o blant* 'thirteen children' (decimal
system) *tri ar ddeg o blant* 'thirteen children' (vigesimal system),[3] *traean o 'r deisen* 'a third of
a cake' (fraction). This complementation is also required for the quantifiers *digon* 'enough',
gormod 'too many/much', *tipyn* 'sufficient(ly)', and *llawer* 'many/much'. Since they denote
quantities - although somewhat vaguely - as do the other numerals, they are also assigned to this
word class (cf. also section 4.3.7.).

In particular the first three groups of numerals can also be characterised by other properties,
which are discussed below.

(A)   Gender distinction

The cardinals 'zero' to 'ten' are shared by both the decimal and the vigesimal systems. The
numerals *dau, tri, pedwar* 'two, three, four' have feminine forms, i.e. *dwy, tair, pedair*. The
ordinals for the last two have also feminine and masculine forms, namely *trydydd - trydedd*
'third' (masculine, feminine), *pedwerydd - pedwaredd* 'fourth' (masculine, feminine). When the
vigesimal system is used, compound numerals containing 'two, three, four' have also to make
the gender distinction, e.g. *tair merch ar hugain* 'twenty three girls', *pedair mam ar ddeg ar
hugain* 'thirty four mothers', *dwy goeden a deugain* 'fourty two trees'. The numeral *un* 'one' distinguishes the gender by the mutation it causes in its referent, e.g. *un mab* 'one son' - *un ferch*
'one daughter'.

---

[1]   I would like to take this opportunity of thanking William Ll. Griffith, Dinbych/Wales, for his
helpful comments on this section.

[2]   P.W. Thomas mentions only the first three (1996: 315). S.J. Williams mentions more (1990: 55).

[3]   However, the following sentence is also possible: *tri phlentyn ar ddeg.*

Four cardinal numerals exhibit mutation when used with an article, namely *dwy - y ddwy* 'two (feminine) - the two', *dau - y ddau* 'two (masculine) - the two', *mil - y fil* 'thousand - the thousand', *miliwn - y filiwn* 'million - the million'. The last two, however, can also behave like a masculine noun when followed by a noun, e.g. *y mil blynyddoedd*[4] 'the thousand years', *y miliwn punnoedd* 'the million pounds' (cf. ibid.: 308).

Ordinals, however, generally undergo mutation when following an article and preceding a feminine noun, i.e. they behave like feminine nouns themselves, e.g. *y filfed babell* 'the thousandth tent' (ibid.: 311). The same happens when they are used as pronouns representing a female, e.g. in *Sian yw 'r drydedd i ennill eleni* 'Jane is the third to win this year'.

(B)   Number inflection

Some cardinals also exhibit number inflection, e.g. *chwech - chwechau* 'six (singular - plural)', *deg - degau* 'ten - tens', *ugain - ugeiniau* 'twenty (singular - plural)'.

(C)   Complementation

Cardinals are generally followed by nouns in the singular, a property henceforth called direct complementation. Some cardinal numbers govern mutation in their following referents as well as the ordinal *ail* 'second', e.g. *un*[L] 'one', *dau*[L] 'two (masculine)',[5] *dwy*[L] 'two (feminine)', *tri*[S] 'three (masculine)' and *chwech*[S] 'six', *yr ail ddyn* 'the second man', *yr ail ferch* 'the second girl'. *Saith*[L] 'seven', *wyth*[L] 'eight' cause relatively regular mutation in *cant* 'hundred' and *punt* 'pound' and *pump*[N], *chwech*[N] and *deg*[N] in the words *blwydd* 'year', *blynedd* 'years' and *diwrnod* 'day' (cf. also section 4.3.7.). Any other mutations induced by cardinals are rather historical or due to style and dialect and are not subject of this investigation.[6] Ordinals, except *ail*, however, cause lenition in their feminine referents, e.g. *y drigeinfed gaer* 'the sixtieth castle'.

If the referent of the numeral is an adjective which itself refers to a feminine noun, it also undergoes mutation, e.g. *y pedair fygythiol* 'the four threatening (females)', *y bumed dderbyniol* 'the fifth acceptable (female)'. An exception is the ordinal *cyntaf* 'first', which performs syntactically like an adjective and follows the referent, e.g. *y dyn cyntaf* 'the first man', *y ferch gyntaf* 'the first girl'.

Another way of complementation is the use of the partitive particle *o* 'of', which is placed between the numeral and its referent in the plural, e.g. *naw o ferched* 'nine girls'. This kind of

---

4   It should be noted that the cardinals in this case are followed by a referent in the plural.

5   Some nouns, however, can for semantic reasons follow the numerals *dau* unmutated (for further explanation, see Morgan 1989: 131, P.W. Thomas 1996: 306).

6   The government of the cardinals as exemplified here is a rather recent one as is illustrated by P.W. Thomas (1996: 309). A study of Morgan (1989: 129-146, cf. also P.W. Thomas 1996: 310) shows that mutations originally caused by cardinals could vary considerably; *saith* and *wyth*, for instance, can still induce nasal mutation. For the purpose of this investigation, the 'reduced' system of governmental constraints may serve as an indicator as to how far the government of cardinals is included in entries of Welsh general-purpose dictionaries.

complementation is called prepositional clause by P.W. Thomas (ibid.: 314 and above), but is here referred to as indirect complementation.

Although both systems of complementation can be used with any numeral, there may be semantic differences by using the one or the other, e.g. the difference between a set of things denoted by direct complementation and a definite number of items indicated by indirect complementation as in *Y Deg Gorchymyn* 'The ten Commandments' and *deg o orchmynion* 'ten commands', or *y deuddeng apostol* 'the twelve apostles' and *deuddeg o apostolion* 'twelve apostles'.

In addition, some numerals may follow their referent when the latter is in the plural or is a non-countable noun as defined by P.W. Thomas (1996: 150f.), e.g. *digon, llawer, tri, mil* as in *gwin lawer* 'much wine', *brenhinoedd dri* 'three kings'. In these cases, the numerals are mutated (cf. ibid.: 1996: 334).

Compound numerals, e.g. *tri ar ddeg ar hugain* 'thirty three', take the referent after its first element: *tri dyn ar ddeg ar hugain* 'thirty three men'. Some numerals have conjuncted forms, i.e. their form changes according to whether their referent begins with a vowel or consonant. These numerals are: *pump afal* 'five apples' - *pum sach* 'five sacks', *chwech ogof* 'six caves' - *chwe llyn* 'six lakes', *cant arth* 'a hundred oranges'- *can merch* 'a hundred girls', *deg/deng arth* 'ten bears' - *deg/deng mis* 'ten month', *pymtheg afal* 'fifteen apples' - *pymtheng mam* 'fifteen mothers'.[7]

The last properties mentioned above are quite regular. They, therefore, do not necessarily need to be illustrated in the individual dictionary entries but rather in a paragraph in a grammatical introduction at the beginning of a dictionary.

(D)   Compounds consisting of a numeral and an appelativum

Compounds consisting of a numeral and an appelativum are interesting, since the government of the numerals used as constituents is somewhat irregular and differs from that of the cardinals when employed as single lexical items. The following variation can be found:

- no mutation after *dau*: *deucorn* 'two horns', *deuparth* 'two portions', *deutu* 'two sides',
- mutation as is usual after *dau, dwy*: *deuddyn* 'two persons (a couple)', *deuddarn* 'two pieces',
- inconsistent mutations: *deuben* - *deupen* 'both ends', *deubeth* - *deupeth* 'two things', *deublyg* - *deuplyg* 'twofold', *deudroed* - *deutroed* 'two feet',
- mutation is caused when *dau* occurs in compound words denoting things which naturally come in pairs, e.g. *deulin* 'two knees', *deuddwrn* 'two fists', *dwyael* 'two eyebrows', *deurudd* 'two cheeks', *dwyglust* 'two ears',

---

[7]   The last two numerals do not strictly follow the constraints displayed in the example (P.W. Thomas 1996: 303).

dwyfron 'brest'. These compounds are often recognised as duals, since they themselves undergo mutation after the article (cf. *dau*, *dwy* above).[8]

All in all, there seems to be significant uncertainty as to when and how to mutate or whether to mutate at all. Since there is a considerable amount of compound words with numerals from 'one' to 'ten' and also with 'hundred' (Morgan 1989: 133), e.g. *tridiau* 'three days', *deufis* 'two months', *deuddydd* 'two days', *canmlwyddiant* 'centenary', such words should ideally form individual dictionary entries.

To sum up: normally numerals are listed in the back of dictionaries. Since some of the Welsh numerals, however, exhibit gender and/or number inflection and/or govern mutation in their referent or are mutated themselves, those numerals should form individual entries in Welsh general-purpose dictionaries. Whereas the complementation by the partitive particle *o* only needs to be exemplified when semantically different from the direct complementation of numerals, the constraints causing mutation in the referent or the numeral itself are rather intricate.

The Welsh number system seems to undergo rapid change. This became apparent to me when consulting native speakers. They disagreed on some points with P.W. Thomas in the matter of the usage of individual numerals (cf. also the grammar books of J. Morris-Jones and P.W. Thomas on this matter). It is, therefore, advocated that mutations caused in or by numerals be fully illustrated in individual dictionary entries. To what extent the properties of the numerals are reflected in entries of Welsh general-purpose dictionaries, is analysed in section 4.3.7.

---

[8] *Dwylo* 'hands', however, is not recognised as a dual, since it is a plural noun and does not mutate when following the article. This rule, nevertheless, does not work with *deupen* and *deutu*, which also mutate when preceded by an article (for further details, see Morgan 1989: 130-133).

1.3.2.3.8.   The Welsh particle[1]

The last word class to discuss is that of the particles. Comprising only a small number of lexical items, it is, nevertheless, frequently used. In this study, particles are defined as non-inflectable words which have lost their own semantic meaning (semantic bleaching, cf. in particular the particles *fe*, *mi* below). Instead, Welsh particles introduce specific syntactic structures, i.e. they have a grammatical function and could, except one (cf. *yn* below), as well be called syntactic markers. P.W. Thomas (1996: 84) introduces the following classification of particles:

(a)   affirmative particles, i.e. *y(r)* as in *Yr wyf* 'I am', *fe*[L] and *mi*[L2] as in *Fe'i lladdwyd* 'He was killed' and *Mi gei di boen bol* 'You will have stomach-ache',

(b)   negative particles, i.e. *ni*[L/S]*(d)*, as in *Nid arhosodd* 'He did not wait', *Nid fi ydy'r person yn y llun* 'I'm not the person who is in the picture' and *na*[L]*(g)* in dialects as in *Nag ych chi'n dod?* 'Aren't you coming?' (P.W. Thomas 1996: 521),

(c)   interrogative particles, i.e. *a*[L], as in *A arwyddwyd?* 'Did one sign?' and *ai* as in *Ai gwyn yw ei liw?* 'Is its colour white?' or *Pa un bynnag yr ydym ai byw ai marw...* 'What ever we be, whether alive or dead...' (S.J. Williams 1990: 196),

(d)   the negative answering particle, i.e. *na*[L/S]*(c)*, as in *Nac oes* 'There is not', which can also indicate a command as in *Nac ysmygwch!* 'Don't smoke!',

(e)   the exclamational particle or that which introduces questions which expect an affirmative answer, i.e. *oni*[L/S]*(d)*, as in *Onid edrychodd?* 'Didn't he look?',

(f)   relative particles need to be added, i.e. *na*[L/S]*(d)* as in *Y bwthyn na ellir ei adfer* 'The cottage which cannot be restored' and its very formal compound *nas* which includes the object pronoun -*s*[3] as in *Y plentyn nas gwelais* 'The child whom I did not see' (P.W. Thomas 1996: 499f.), the back-referring particle *a* as in *Y llew a laddodd y carw* 'The lion that killed the deer', and the forward-referring *y(r)*[4] as in *Y llew y gwelsoch ei ffau* 'The lion whose lair you saw' or *Y llew yr edrychodd yr heliwr arno* 'The lion the hunter looked at'[5] (ibid.: 270).

---

[1]   I would like to take this opportunity of thanking William Ll. Griffith, Dinbych/Wales, for his helpful comments on this section.

[2]   *Fe* and *mi* are originally personal pronouns which have lost their semantic meaning. They are now used irrespective of number and person of the verb they precede, unless they represent a sentence-initial subject which has the relative particle placed before the inflected verb, e.g. in *Ti (a) addewaist* 'You promised', *Tydi a anfonaist* 'It was you who sent...' (cf. P.W. Thomas 1996: 89).

[3]   '*s* represents the third person singular or plural.

[4]   Both *a* and *y(r)* as relative particles are of different origin to the sentence-initial particles looking alike. Relative *y(r)*, for instance, derives from *ry/yr* whereas the sentence-initial particle has developed from *y(dd)/yd* (D.S. Evans 1992: 112-115).

[5]   There is another indicator for relative clauses, i.e. *sydd* 'which, who, that is' (and its variants *y sydd*, *sy*, *y sy*, cf. S.J. Williams 1990: 66), the relative form of the verb *bod* 'to be'.

Apart from *ai*, which is only used in emphatic questions or those which introduce an alternative in indirect questions, and *ni(d)* and *na(d)*, which may also introduce emphatic negative sentences, or *yn* (cf. below) Welsh particles always precede the inflected verb. Based on a structural approach, they are mostly called preverbal particles (cf. S.J. Williams 1990: 192-199, Thorne 1993: 345-56). Such denotation, however, obscures their functions; particles in sentence-initial position (cf. examples above) indicate the sentence type and could be called sentence-initial marker. Relative particles either introduce relative clauses and can, therefore, also be called relative pronouns (cf. P.W. Thomas ibid.: 494-501, Thorne 1993: 369-373, S.J. Williams 1990: 62), or they perform as markers of change in word order. After all, any of the constituents of a Welsh sentence can be topicalised or emphasised by fronting of that constituent to precede the inflected verb. The topicalised or emphasised constituent is followed by a relative clause (cf. A.R. Thomas 1992: 273, 286f., Thorne 1993: 369-373), which is introduced by a relative particle. In this case, the relative particle can also be called marker of word order transformation. The following sentences exemplify the particle in this function:

1. Ysgrifennodd Gwilym lythyr at ei frawd ddoe.[6] V-S-O-Pr-A[7]
   [unmarked sentence]
2. Gwilym *a* ysgrifennodd lythyr at ei frawd ddoe. S-(a)[8]-V-O-Pr-A
   [subject topicalised]
3. Llythyr *a* ysgrifenodd Gwilym at ei frawd ddoe. O-(a)-V-S-Pr-A
   [object topicalised]
4. At ei frawd *yr* ysgrifennodd Gwilym lythyr ddoe. Pr-(y/yr)-V-S-O-A
   [prepositional complement topicalised]
5. Ddoe *yr* ysgrifennodd Gwilym lythyr. A-(y/yr)-V-S-O
   [adverbial topicalised]
6. Ysgrifennu llythyr at ei frawd *a* *w*naeth Gwilym ddoe. VN-O-Pr-(a)-V-S-A
   [emphasis of process]
7. Ysgrifennu llythyr at ei frawd *y* bu Gwilym ddoe. VN-O-Pr-(y/yr)-V-S-A
   [emphasis of duration of process]

Another particle in Welsh is *yn*, which has the following functions: causing mutation in its subsequent constituent, it can (a) perform as an adverbial marker, e.g. *Rhedodd yn gyflym* 'He ran fast' or (b) as a marker of descriptions and identifications (predicate marker), e.g. *Mae llyfr yn fawr* 'The book is big', *Yr wyf yn ddarlithydd* 'I am a lecturer'. In the latter function it contrasts the expression of actions (King 2000: 244) for which *yn*$^{\theta}$ is employed, e.g. in *Yr wyf yn darlithio*

---

[6]   The translations of the following sentences are:
        Gwilym wrote a letter to his brother yesterday. - (It was) Gwilym (who) wrote a letter to his brother yesterday. - It was a letter that Gwilym wrote to his brother yesterday. - It was to his brother that Gwilym wrote a letter yesterday. - It was yesterday that Gwilym wrote a letter to his brother. - What Gwilym did yesterday was to write a letter to his brother. - Gwilym occupied himself yesterday writing a letter to his brother.
[7]   S = subject, V = inflected verb, O = direct object, Pr = prepositional complement, A = adverbial phrase, VN = verbal noun.
[8]   The particle is often omitted, particularly in speech. The mutation it causes in the following constituent, however, remains.

'I lecture'. In such periphrastic verbal constructions *yn* acts as (c) an aspectual marker. In this function it marks the verbal noun for the sake of aspectual distinction.

In the case of *yn*, its government is significant. As illustrated above, the adverbial marker causes lenition. The distinction between aspectual marker and marker of predicative noun is made by absence and presence of this type of government (cf. examples above). Only when *yn* causes nasal mutation, however, it is not a particle but a preposition, e.g. *Bues yn Nhregaron.* 'I was in Tregaron.'[9] (cf. government as word class indicator with some conjunctions in section 1.3.2.3.6.).

As illustrated by the examples of *yn*, the government of particles is of considerable importance and needs to be displayed in dictionary entries, as well as their sentence-indicating and sentence-constructing properties. As to which extent these properties of particles are presented in general-purpose dictionaries, is analysed in section 4.3.8.

Having created the theoretical basis for the linguistic analysis of popular modern bi-directional, bilingual Welsh general-purpose dictionaries, a critical analysis of these reference books is made in chapter IV. Before that, however, a look at the history of Welsh lexicography is desirable (cf. chapter II), in order to understand contemporary developments more fully.

Of significance in this context is also the presentation of the whole corpus of Welsh dictionaries on the one hand and the comparison of dictionary production in the other Celtic languages on the other hand (cf. chapter III).

After illustrating the importance of adequately compiled dictionaries for language maintenance and cultural identity, the linguistic analysis states to what extent Welsh dictionaries meet their functions in Wales at the end of the twentieth and the beginning of the twenty first century.

---

[9]   Recent research has shown that the preposition *yn* must be clearly kept apart from the predicate, adverbial and periphrastic *yn*, although there is yet no agreement on their actual origin (cf. Isaac 1994, Gensler 1999).

II. Historical lexicography
2.1. Early stages of lexicography
2.1.1. General developments[1]

As soon as an alphabet and materials to write on were sufficiently available, the production of tools for teaching, learning, and translating languages became popular (cf. Green 1977: 39ff.): about 2600 BC, a monolingual Sumerian dictionary and some word lists were produced, around 2340 BC also a Sumerian-Akkadian dictionary (cf. Pohling 1971: 155, J.A. Halloran) after the semitic tribes of Akkad had conquered the Sumerians. From 1900 BC onwards, glossaries and a quadri-lingual dictionary (Sumerian, Akkadic, Hurrian, Ugarit) were at hand (cf. also J.E. Caerwyn Williams 1983: 6). Greek lexicography, however, emerged to take on a specific task:

> "the interpretation of the first ever works of Classical Greek literature, Homers's *Iliad* and *Odyssey*, which are believed to have appeared during the eighth century BC. Homer, as Plato noted in *The Republic* 'educated Greece', but for that education to take effect, it was necessary that his vocabulary, much of which had grown unintelligible in the intervening four hundred years, should be made accessible [...] As would re-emerge 1500 years later, with the accretion of explanatory translations written above the less comprehensible words in a variety of Latin manuscripts, this early Greek lexicography took the form of elucidating the opaque words, or γλῶσσαι 'glossai' [...] Classical Greece had no one, all-encompassing language and a range of specific dialects were used [...] Once again, this gave rise to the νεεδφορ *glossai* [...] A third source of analysis was ancient law, the language of which was invariably obscure [...]
>
> Unsurprisingly, the history of these early *glossai* is virtually lost. The names of a few authors and of a number of their works reappear in later books, but of the originals there are but fragments. One knows only that there existed glossaries dealing with Homer, with the medical pioneer Hippocrates, with various dialects, with half-forgotten plays and with the long-dead, but still renowned speeches of great orators. Most of these early works were produced at the philological school of Alexandria, which flourished between the fourth and third centuries BC.
>
> The Alexandrian glossaries were of various types: some alphabetical (a technique that cannot have lasted long, since it had to be re-invented for the glossaries of the eighth and ninth centuries AD), some based on the appearance of the glossed words in the text under consideration, some by semantic fields and so on. The first dictionary proper would appear to be that compiled by Aristophanes of Byzantium (257-180 BC), head of the Library *c.* 200 BC and the most famous philologist of his era. His dictionary, entitled *Lexeis* (Words), was part of a literary oeuvre which included the first critical editions of Homer, Hesiod, Pindar, the regularisation of Greek accents [...]
>
> The *Lexeis* was organised in several ways, typical of which is a section ordered by related classes, rather as a modern thesaurus is compiled" (Green 1977: 42f.).

One of his pupils was Dionysios Thrax (ca. 170 - ca. 90 BC). As author of *Techne Grammatike* or 'The Art of Letters', he is responsible for compiling the earliest surviving authoritative work on Greek grammar. Thrax may have been acquainted with L. Aelius Stilo (ca. 100 BC), the first of the great Roman grammarians. He and his pupil Varro (116-27 BC) interpreted 'hard words' (ibid.: 44). Varro dedicated his major work *De Lingua Latina*, pimarily a detailed study of

[1]   I would like to take this opportunity of thanking William Ll. Griffith, Dinbych/Wales, for providing me with material and assistance with translation.

grammar which includes notes on many etymologies, to Cicero (106-43 BC). He, in turn, dedicated the second edition of his *Academica* to Varro.

Another Roman absorbed into the works of later lexicographers was Verrius Flaccus (ca. 14 AD) with his book *De significatione verborum* 'On the meaning of words' (ibid.: 45). Julius Pollux's (180-238) contribution was the *Onomasticon*. It offered an extensive Greek vocabulary, including many synonyms and antonyms. His contemporary Phrynichus compiled expressions which should be avoided.

Hesychius of Alexandria (ca. fifth century AD) compiled a list of uncommon words and technical terms. A supreme example of Byzantine dictionary production is the *Suda*, which appeared around the end of the tenth century. The *Suda* was prepared by a group of scholars and is a mixture of both dictionary and encyclopedia (ibid.: 49).

The first well-known scholar to pay tribute to the shift away from Latin to the vernacular was Isidore of Seville (ca. 570-636). His major work *Originum sive etymologiarum libri* is essentially an encyclopedic rather than a pure lexicographical one

> "designed as a wide-ranging vademecum by which the newly concerted people of Spain might gain access to every aspect of their new, Catholic faith" (ibid.: 50).

After this brief overview on early stages of lexicography the actual developments in Wales are more extensively outlined in the following sections.

2.1.2.   Glosses

Welsh lexicography also started with the production of glosses. *Glosses* are notes explaining, translating, amending, or supplementing linguistically or contentwise problematic passages in a text. They can also form independent notes to texts. Depending on the place of an explication, a distinction can be made between interlinear glosses, marginal glosses and context glosses (cf. Ó Cuiv 1961: 60f., J.E. Caerwyn Williams 1983: 8). The glosses can consist of single lexical items, phrases or even poetic verses (cf. below).[1] The importance of glossing as a specialised work which introduces explanations necessary for understanding texts is stressed by Lapidge (1986: 98). Particularly, interlinear and marginal glosses could be added by a glossator other than the copyist (cf. ibid.).

The earliest Welsh glosses, which are text related and important for its understanding can be dated to the ninth century.[2] They are contained in the *Liber Commonei* (K.H. Jackson 1994: 47ff.).[3] In this manuscript, there are, first, Welsh names for the letters of the Latin alphabet, second, calculations on the moon and, third, glosses on measures[4] and weights which are called *De Mensuris et Ponderibus* (cf. I. Williams 1931: 226ff.). The following reconstruction by I. Williams (ibid.: 230ff.) illustrates the type of glosses (underlined) employed in the text:

> Duo ·u· int dou pimp. In libra ·iii· u· ir tri ·u· IN libra mellis ·i· trean cant mel.
> semper sex ·i· u· hint tri pimp. in sextario ·i· hi hestaur mel. ·i· is xxx ha
> guorennieu. guotig ·iiii· u· ir petguar pimp ad libram olei ·i· ir hestoriou oleu. is
> trimuceint hestaur mel uerbigratia. uas in quo mensurantur xx uñc de oleo usque
> dum plenum fuerit. in ipso iterum remensurantur xxx uñc mellis usque dum
> plenum fuerit sed distat in grauitate et in multitudine unciarum quam uis si melle
> uas impleat non tertia pars numeri sextariorum olei in mellis sextaris.
> continentur:

Glosses, interlinear and marginal, are also contained in the *Cambridge Juvencus* manuscript.[5] One part of them can be defined as plain glosses. They date from the ninth century, whilst most of them date from the tenth century (cf. K.H. Jackson 1994: 48-53, see also Falileyev 2000: xv). The other part of the glosses forms the oldest Welsh poetry in the form of *englynion* (abbreviated Juv. 3, Juv. 9)[6] and is dated to the first half of the ninth century (Juv. 3) and "ninth or tenth century, the former being taken as a good deal more likely than the latter" (K.H. Jackson 1994: 53, cf. also M. Stephens 1997: 450, Lapidge 1986: 98ff., see also Falileyev 2000:

---

[1]   With regard to the construction of glosses and their content, see Gneuss (1992: 115f.) and Strachan (1900).

[2]   An earlier Old Welsh text is the *Surexit*-Memorandum in the *Book of St. Chad* (*Lichfield Gospels*). This, however, is an independent text and does not count as a gloss (cf. K.H. Jackson 1994: 40ff. and Falileyev 2000: xiv).

[3]   It is also called *Codex Oxoniensis Prior* and edited by I. Williams in BBCS 7 (1933-5).

[4]   As for instance for honey, oil and money.

[5]   For the latest complete facsimile of the Cambridge *Juvencus*, see McKee (2000).

[6]   *Englynion* (Sg. *englyn*) form a genre in Welsh literature. Early *englynion* merely consist of three lines. There are different types of *englynion*. For further details with regard to this genre, see Morris-Jones (1925).

xvf.).[7] The plain glosses serve as an explanation for Hebrew names, difficult words from Isidore's *Etymologiae,* and some grammatical matter (cf. Lindsay 1912: 16), or elucidate points of *Juvencus*'s narrative. At least, one of them is assumed to be an etymological explanation (I. Williams 1932: 116f.).

Proxima roboreis (MS. arboreis) iam iam radicibus instat	steria ·i· pi
Cunctorum ante oculos acie[sque] leuata securis	penn reu
Caeduntur siluae stiriles ignemque fouebunt.	laun . ca
	d endens
	de domu
	sterilis asē.

The Latin text on the left provides the context for the gloss on the right, which was identified as an amendment elucidating the etymology of the word *steria* (ibid.).

Such glosses reflect an early kind of lexicographical work. Taken as a whole, Lapidge (1998: 99f.) defines the glosses in the *Juvencus* manuscript as a kind of *commentary*. Commentaries in the form of glosses were partly produced for the purpose of supporting and facilitating the reading of Latin texts.

The glosses which form the *englynion,* however, do not belong to the explanatory category of glosses. Juv. 3 perhaps reflects the intentions and emotions of their composer[8] and Juv. 9 praises God. A rough translation by me, disregarding the rhyme and metres indicated in bold and italics below, are to give an impression of the content of the glosses:[9]

Juv. 3

niguorcosam nemheun**aur** henoid	I shall not talk even for one hour tonight,
mitelu nit gurm**aur**	my family/retinue is not too big,
mi *am* [fr*am*][10] d*am* ancal**aur**	I and my servant round our cauldron.[11]

Juv. 9

dicones ihesu dielim**lu** pbetid	You Jesus, you created for the many peoples of the world
aguirdou pan di**bu**	miracles when he came
guotiapaur oimer di**du**	after the meal he gave mirth to them

---

7   The oldest Welsh poetry is, of course, attributed to Taliesin and Aneirin who composed in the sixth century. Potential texts of the authors, however, which are handed down to us in the *Llyfr Taliesin* (fourteenth century) and *Llyfr Aneirin* (1250/1265) are difficult to date and to attribute to them. For further discussion on this matter, see Isaac (1996) and Koch (1997).

8   Jarman (1976: 82) defines them as saga poetry.

9   For details with regard to the translations, see I. Williams (1932a, 1932b).

10   *Fram* is according to I. Williams (1932a: 102) an interpolation by Lhuyd. The meaning of *fram,* however, is not totally clear. It may mean 'mercenary soldier' or denote a weapon, a spear or lance. I would like to take this opportunity of thanking Dr Iwan Wmffre, Tregaron/Wales, for assistance with the translation. - In the manuscript, the glosses form one line.

11   The translation follows roughly that of Jarmen (in: Jarmen, A.O.H. & G.R. Hughes 1976: 82).

A third example of explanatory glosses can be found in *De Nuptiis Philologiae et Mercuri* by Martianus Capella from the ninth century (cf. K.H. Jackson 1994: 53). Two examples illustrate the type of glosses:

Quicquid *agentes* Stoici praescia dant futuris ·ī· ardomaul[12]
Semper anhelis docilis fomitibus tulisti.

quo uiso phi
lais[13] lologia consurgens totaque ue
neratione supplicans

Glosses of a similar type are also contained in Ovid's *Ars Amatoria* which dates from the ninth or tenth centuries (cf. K.H. Jackson 1994: 54).

Lastly, there are Old Welsh glosses in the colloquium *De raris fabulis* from the *Codex Oxoniensis Posterior* (abbreviated Ox 2) dated to the tenth century (cf. K.H. Jackson 1994: 54ff.).[14]

> "Colloquies were a form of literature widely studied in schools of the early middle ages. Having their origin in the bilingual phrase-books of the late antiquity (such as the *Hermeneumata* of pseudo-Dositheus) their purpose was to impart the vocabulary and phraseology of everyday life to young novices who were being taught to converse in Latin, either within the confines of their own monastery, or as visitors in foreign monasteries. Hence the colloquies usually take the form of simple conversation, into which items of useful alternative vocabulary may easily be introduced: 'Good morning students: go to the river, or: to the spring, or: to the well, and bring back, or: carry back pure water [...]' One sees that infinite permutations of the one simple sentence are possible [...] I should argue that *De raris fabulis* as we have it is composite, and that various layers of accretion can be recognised and then removed. The uppermost layer is most easily identified: the Latin text has embedded in it numerous Old Welsh and Old Cornish words which stand outside the syntax and clearly originated as interlinear glosses subsequently incorporated into the text itself" (Lapidge 1986: 94).

The type of glosses found in the colloquium is illustrated by the following examples taken from Stevenson (1929: 3ff.). The glosses form part of the (Latin) text unless otherwise stated:

'Non dificile ; date nobís panem triticum et ordinatium, loleum, secalium, *spelticum, millicum, butyrum, lardum uel larda, atque lác et *colomaticus*, et iterum *cipius*, galmula, *lucani(c)a*, *spumaticum*, *fordalium*, *pultum*, *lacticula*, caseum, *babtuta*, colestrum, *ius*.'
'Audi, pincerna ! da nobis potum de celea (i. ceruisa), uinum, siccera, medus, *mulsum*, uel melligratum.'

---

[12]   For notes on the location of the gloss and the word glossed by it, see H. Lewis (1932: 111).
[13]   For notes on the location of the gloss and the word glossed by it, see H. Lewis (1932: 112).
[14]   Further material exhibiting Old Welsh language use, other than proper names, is the *Computus-Fragment*. This text, however, can hardly be defined as tools for language teaching and learning (cf. W. Davies 1989: 213, K.H. Jackson 1974: 49ff.). For further Old Welsh notes, see K.H. Jackson (1994: 40ff.).

Glossemata Celtica: colomaticus i. barr, cipius i. cennin, lucani⟨c⟩a i. selsic (1 *supra versum addita*), spumaticum, i. bloteit, fordalium i. leflet, pultum i. iot,[15] lacticula i. laiðper, babtuta i. emmeni, ius i. iotum, mulsum i. bracaut

Together with glossaries colloquies were the tools used in language teaching and learning by that time (cf. H. Lewis 1921: vf.). The production of colloquies required work prior to and essential for lexicographical work, the glossing, which provided the lexicon to be learned and practised. It is the question, however, as to whether the existence of one colloquium written in Britain and including Welsh (cf. K.H. Jackson 1994: 56) is sufficient to assume the successful compilation of Welsh glosses in form of glossaries. At least, it does not exclude their potential existence.

A continuum in lexicography can, therefore, not be attested for Wales as is illustrated in the following two sections, although, first, glossing - a work prior to lexicography - was practised.

Second, Welsh learning was of a high standard at that time (cf. C. Davies 1995: 12-17), although classified as conservative by Lapidge (1998: 102). The best proof for its reputation is the Welsh scholar Asser († 909). He was called to the court of King Alfred (849-901) as a personal advisor. Asser - together with two scholars from Mercia and two from the continent - was asked to re-establish Christian learning in Wessex after its decline following Danish destruction (cf. Brown 1991: 14). Asser is generally believed to have written the *Annales rerum gestarum Alfredi Magni* (cf. C. Davies 1995: 13), a fact disputed up to the present day.[16] Asser read texts out to Alfred, explained them to him and helped him to translate them into Old English (cf. Keynes & Lapidge 1983: 28, 126). He practised translating himself and was Alfred's 'teacher of translation'. It is possible that Asser had acted as an interpreter for *Hywel ap Rhys* and *Hyfaidd of Dyfed* during their submission talks with Alfred (ibid.: 52) and thus caught Alfred's attention.

Third, as was previously illustrated, translating and language teaching was succesfully practised by Welsh scholars. Fourth, there are references to the existence of a Welsh ecclesiastical library (cf. Lapidge 1986: 98) and to Welsh book production. It is said that Welsh, Cornish and Breton books went to England in the tenth century to be translated there in order to help to re-establish the English centres of learning after their destruction by the Vikings (cf. W. Davies 1990: 79). It is assumed that the scholars, Asser amongst them, called at Alfred's court, brought manuscripts and teaching material with them (cf. also Keynes & Lapidge 1983: 214).

To sum up: as illustrated above, Welsh learning had apparently reached a stage which may have allowed the compilation of glossaries. In addition, there is at last one text, which has glossing as a pre-condition for its production, the colloquium *De raris fabulis*. Although it does not form reliable evidence for the compilation of glossaries, it, however, supports its potential existence.

---

[15]   *iot* and *laiðper* look rather Cornish (cf. K.H. Jackson 1994: 55).

[16]   Doubts concerning the authorship still exist. As far as is known, it was not very common to write *vitae* about secular rulers. It is suggested that Alfred's *vita* was composed following Einhard's *Vita Caroli* and the *Vita Alcuini* (Keynes & Lapidge 1983: 54f., 222) and following the *Vita Hludowici Imperatoris*. Einhard himself was a scholar at Charlemagne's court.
Another example of a *vita* of a non-saint is the *Historia Gruffudd ap Cynan* (for details with regards to the dating, see S. Evans 1977). Its author was also familiar with other *vitae*, e.g. the one of *Caesar*.

2.1.3.   Glossaries

An early stage of lexicography evolved when the first glossaries were compiled. As a starting point, they can be roughly defined as:

> "merely (or mainly) collections of marginalia from some MS" (Lindsay 1929: vii).

Based on different kinds of glosses, early simple glossaries were created as is described in the following quotation:

> "[One has to] extract from a given text the phrase or sentence in which a lemma with an interlinear[, contextual,] or marginal gloss was found, and [to] put these phrases together in the order in which they follow in the text" (Meyer 1907: 138).

Accordingly, the headwords[1] of what Russell (1999: 88) calls *glossae collectae* could invariably be presented in the form they appeared in the text from which they derived (cf. ibid., Murray 1900: 11).

Later glossaries, or according to Russell (cf. below) real glossaries, arranged the words or phrases glossed according to the alphabet or according to other guidelines (cf. J.E. Caerwyn Williams 1983: 8, Meyer 1907: 138-44), thus creating a headword which was followed by the gloss, the latter forming the microstructure.[2] The headword now usually exhibited a restored nominative of a noun or a verbal noun. The alphabetic order was started with the 'first-letter order', i.e. by gathering together all words beginning with the same letter, as for instance *A*. It was followed by the 'second-letter order', i.e. by the *AB*-order (cf. below). Russell describes this next step in glossary compiling as follows:

> "The subsequent stage seems to have been the application of alphabetical order, usually by the first letter only [...] The implications of alphabetisation are worth pursuing, for it suggests first a separation of the glossary from the text and second its possible incorporation into some larger enterprise. If the glossary was to remain firmly attached to its text, there would be no points in changing the order" (Russell 1998: 27).

More comprehensive glossaries drew material from smaller text-bound glossaries. With every copying, the content of the former glosses underwent changes, as for instance by shortening, dropping, or adding explanations, in order to serve explanatory needs. Lindsay described the practice with the following words:

> "[...] we must remember that our 'stemma codicum' is not like the 'stemma codicum' of a text of Vergil or Horace. Our glossaries were not full and conscientious transcriptions of the archetype and never pretended to be. They are extract glossaries. Each compiler selects, at his own caprice, some items of the mass that lies before him and passes over others. So no arrangement 'ex silentio' is possible. And the items selected are often recast at the compiler's caprice" (Lindsay 1921: 52).

---

[1]   For the definition of headword as lemma, see section 1.3.2.1.2.
[2]   For the definition of microstructure, see section 1.3.2.1.2.

Russell (1999) offers a brief summary of the complex process of glossary creation from its first steps to an advanced stage emphasising that not all stages mentioned are attested in every glossary:

"(a)   the first stage involves the addition to a text of interlinear or marginal glosses (usually one or two words only); [interlinear glosses tend to be context specific, but when the word is extracted from that context further explanation may be necessary[3]] the type of comment, whether grammatical (including construe marks), explanatory or etymological, will obviously depend on the concerns or interests of the reader(s). The source of the glosses can also be of interest; whether the glossator is himself making use of a commentary or glossary. The Old Irish glosses on biblical or grammatical texts may be instanced.

(b)   the second stage is the creation of an ancillary document in which lemmata and glosses are collected. At this stage they remain in textual order as *glossae collectae* [...]; as such, they are only of practical use in relation to the text from which they have been taken.

(c)   this stage comprises two developments:
either (i) *glossae collectae* from one text are alphabeticised and subsequently merged with other groups, also already alphabeticised;
or (ii) *glossae collectae* from different texts are merged and subsequently alphabeticised.

By the end of stage (c) we are dealing with a glossary. A further stage which is also attested in Irish is the versification of a glossary. [...] Moreover, glossaries did not smoothly develop through all these stages in a linear fashion. They might themselves be glossed or excerpted to produce fresh sets of *glossae collectae*. They can generate new entries within themselves; especially if a quotation in an entry is particularly obscure or contains unfamiliar words, those words might well be extracted and lemmatised" (ibid.: 88f).

In light of Russells's summary, glossaries may thus be defined as compilations of glosses which (a) follow an alphabetical order, (b) exhibit headwords in a basic grammatical form, and which (c) are of practical use independently from specific texts.

Leaving out several word classes, *glossae collectae* and simple glossaries were apparently partly still supplements for mnemotechnical aids (cf. Stevenson 1929: vi) in a predominantly oral situation of learning, in which translating was a method of teaching and learning. Their compilation, however, also had didactic functions for acquisition of the vernacular language (cf. below), since first grammatical variation of headwords was presented (cf. examples of English glossary entries below). Complex glossaries may already have served as comprehensive reference books for specialists (cf. Irish glossaries, below).

Whereas there are no Welsh glossaries, English and Irish glossaries are well attested. Some of them are briefly introduced here in order to illustrate the kind of lexicographical works produced at an early stage in West European lexicography.

---

[3]   This fact is well attested by the etymological gloss found in the *Juvencus* manuscript (cf. section 2.1.2.).

There are four related Old English-Latin glossaries: the first is the *Épinal glossary*, probably produced in England at the end of the seventh century.[4] One of its purposes was doubtlessly to help to teach Anglo-Saxon scribes to separate individual Old English lexical items from each other (cf. Bischoff et al. 1988: 15).

The glossary has three columns of headwords, each with a column of interpretations alongside it, and affords ample provision for two- or three-word interpretations, occasionally more. The headwords are listed within alphabetical sections in two groups. In the first group, the different collections of glosses have been arranged alphabetically according to the first letter of the headword, i.e. in *A*-order. In the second group, the glosses have been arranged alphabetically according to the first two letters of the headword, i.e. in *AB*-order.

The second is the *Erfurt manuscript*. It consists of three alphabetical glossaries, *Erfurt I, II, III*. They were produced at the beginning of the ninth century (cf. ibid.: 19) and kept in Erfurt. *Erfurt I* exhibits the same macrostructure as the *Épinal glossary*. In *Erfurt II* and *III*, all the headwords have been arranged within alphabetical sections in *AB*-order (cf. ibid.: 17).

The third glossary is the *Werden glossary*, which is contemporary with the *Erfurt glossaries*, and was copied at Werden (cf. ibid.: 22). The macrostructure is the same as in *Erfurt II* and *III* (cf. ibid.: 21).

Most interesting is the MS 144 of Corpus Christi College. It contains (a) a collection of names from the Bible, (b) Greek technical terms of grammar, metre, and rhetoric with interpretations, and (c) a fourth alphabetical Old English-Latin glossary known as *Corpus* (cf. ibid.: 22). The latter was produced in the second quarter of the ninth century (ibid.: 25). Its macrostructure is the same as in the glossaries *Erfurt II, III* and *Werden*. It exhibits some alternative grammatical forms and contains one headword in Greek characters.

Pheifer (in Bischoff et al. 1988: 49) states that the *Épinal* and *Erfurt I* compilations are closely related copies of the same glossaries. That is why they are commonly referred to as *Épinal-Erfurt*. However, since each contains entries not found in the other, neither can be the copy of the other. Nevertheless, relationships can also be established with the other glossaries (for details, see ibid.: 49ff.). The following example - for better reading hand-copied in the original format - illustrates the structure of the *Corpus glossary*:

---

[4] For problems with regard to its origin, see Bischoff et al. (1988: 16f.). It is really an early document considering the fact that the earliest text in English known to have been written down is the laws of Æthelbert of Kent. This was made sometime after the arrival of Augustine c. 597 and before Æthelbert's death c. 616. These laws are retained in a single twelfth-century copy preserved in the *Textus Roffensis* (cf. Bischoff et al. 1988: 16f.).

babigena ,[5]   stulta, ,

basiliscus,   fenpens ,   **b** ellicus . subauditum aliquidi sonum . aut tremor.[6]

[...]

banatnum ,   sepucrum   ber.   puteus meus.

bassancles ,   baccae ,   bennus ,   baan , ,

baubant ,   latr[?]nt.   bennuca. ,   ueante ,

banclus ,   stultus,   benna ,   senuus ,

basilla ,   regina ,   bellum , cibricum . gallicum cibiu

baccanalia ,   bachatio .   enim gallisunt. ,

banbenta. , [...]

The corpus of Irish glossaries exhibits a very wide range of different types of glossaries:

"Early Irish glossaries come in all shapes and sizes, ranging from short glossaries with brief, laconic two word entries to vast compendia of material which contain some entries which would easily do duty as complete narrative tales in their own right" (Russell 1999: 87).

They seem to reflect a longer period of early continuous lexicographical development.[7] Some of the Irish glossaries reflect a very advanced stage of lexicography and are, therefore, defined as forerunners of modern type dictionaries by Russell (1988: 16). Others exhibit "the more encyclopaedic type" (Russell 1999: 86). Altogether, Irish glossaries cover a wide range of subjects: legal,[8] mythological, historical, poetical, linguistic (cf. Russell 1988: 1). Metrical glossaries are known, too.[9]

Irish glossaries in general were used to interpret obsolete vernacular or Latin lexical items or to differentiate synonyms and homonyms (cf. Schmidt 1991: 2339). There was also an interest in etymology and in rare words. As glossary corpora grew and became less easy to use with a specific text, matters became more complicated (cf. Russell 1999: 96):

"It may be that a need had arisen by the 9th century for more general linguistic material for understanding old and difficult texts, but [...] it is difficult to believe that the creation of a huge encyclopaedic glossary in southern Ireland in the 9th century is unconnected to the influence of Isidore's *Etymologiae* (particularly Book X)" (Russell 1999: 110).

---

[5]   Readings tentative.

[6]   *R* in this example looks rather like an *n*. For difficulties with both letters, see Bischoff (1988: 23).

[7]   For the dating of different Irish glossaries between the ninth and fourteenth centuries, see Russell (1999).

[8]   For a detailed analysis of legal glossaries, see Russell (1999).

[9]   For a complex classification of Irish glossaries, see R. Hofman (1996).

The most famous Irish glossary is the *Sanas Cormaic* 'Cormac's Whisper/Secret Council'[10] by *Cormac Úa Cuilennáin*, Bishop of Cashel, who became King of Munster in 901.[11] It is kept in the *Book of Leinster*, a manuscript from the twelfth century. The work's purpose is apparently to elucidate difficult words and to etymologise individual Irish lexical items (cf. Russell 1998: 14f.) in form of a huge encyclopaedic glossary, which was probably influenced by Isidore's *Etymologiae* (cf. above). With regard to its composition, Russell states:

> "One source of material which has gone into the making of the Cormac group of glossaries derives from the process of explaining difficult words in various texts, hence the glossaries which relate to particular texts, such as the glossaries to the *Amra Choluim Chille* and the *Félire*" (Russell 1998: 27).[12]

In comparison to English glossaries, for instance, the *Cormac glossary group* exhibits a very comprehensive interpretation of headwords. Altogether, three different methods of explanation are employed in the *Cormac* compilations:[13]

1. Explanations by means of a gloss:

  sceng .i. imdæ, unde dicitur imsceng .i. both bec imma timchellæ imdæ. Inde dicitur: ferr imscing adbar il.

  '*sceng*, i.e. couch, from which is said imsceng, i.e. a small hut which surrounds a bed/beds. Thus it is said 'better a hut than much equipment'.'

  This type of explanation is used in the whole of *O'Clery's glossary*, which is, therefore, called a forerunner of the modern type dictionary by Russell (1998: 16).

2. Etymology by analysis into elements:

  lelup .i. lú-lep .i. lú cach mbecc. No lenab .i. lenis abbati .i. patri et matri .i. íarsindi lenas abbatim 7 matrem. Aliter: lelup .i. lú pell .i. lú cach mbeg, pell óndi is pellis .i. maoth.

  '*lelup* ('child') i.e. *lú lep*, i.e. every small thing is *lú*. Or *lenab*, i.e. gentle to an abbot, i.e. father and mother, i.e. on account of the fact that it follows an abbot and its mother. Alternatively: *lelup*, i.e. *lú pell*, i.e. every small thing is *lú*, *pell* from the fact that it is *pellis* ('skin'), i.e. soft.'

3. Etymology of complex and simple lexical items by comparison with Latin, Greek, and Hebrew words:

  Ab .i. ab eo quod est abbas; uel a nomine ebraeico quod est aba .i. pater.

---

[10] For discussions with regard to the interpretation of the title and the authorship, see Russell (1988: 11f., 1999). Russell also speaks of the *Cormac glossary group* because of the existence of seven different compilations of this glossary (1998: 2).

[11] For a detailed analysis of *Cormac's Glossary*, see Russell (1988, 1999), who also provides different facts and figures in relation to *Cormac*'s life.

[12] For more details, see Russell (1999: 111ff.).

[13] The examples and translations are taken from Russell (1998: 16ff.). They exemplify the glossary group better than the edition by Meyer (1913, cf. Russell ibid.: 4).

'*Ab* ('abbot'), i.e. from that which is abbas ('abbot'); or from the Hebrew noun, namely aba, i.e. pater ('father').'

itharnnae .i. ith 7 feorna .i. semend, ar it glaine 7 ith na cethra no téged isna cainnle [B no legdais isna simnib] apud veteress. Aliter: ith 7 ornnae .i. orn organ .i. orcuin itha.

'*itharnnae* ('candles'), i.e. *Íth* ('fat') and *feorna*', i.e. rushes, for they are clear and the fat of animals used to go into a candle [B 'which they used to melt into rushes'] in the old days. Alternatively: *íth* and *ornnae*, i.e. *orn* (means) destruction, i.e. destruction of fat.'

Some headwords in the *Cormac glossary group* are followed by multiple interpretations. An explanation for this phenomenon is again provided by Russell:

> "There is also evidence for re-editing of material within the glossary so that a single headword can incorporate a number of different explanations. The key words are ... déde/tréde/cethardae fordingair '... has two/three/four different meanings'" (Russell 1998: 29).

An excellent example for multiple interpretations because of re-editing is also illustrated by Russell (ibid.):

> Artt tréde fordingair .i. art úasal, unde dictitur art fine. Art .i. dia, unde dicitur Eochaid Find Fúath n-Airt .i. fúath déa fair ar a cháime. Item Cú Chulainn post mortem dicere perhibetur, 'Domemaid Art úsal' .i. día úasal. Art dono cloch no leac ligi, cuius diminutivum arténe .i. cloichéne .i. ainm disbecad, unde Gúaire Aidne dixit
>
> Do cealat mór n-amra ind airténi
> bíte for ligiu Marcáin maic Aedha maic Mairceni.

> '*Artt* means three things: *art* high, thus it is said *art fine* ('head of the kin')'. *Art*, i.e. god, thus Eochaid Find Fúath n-Airt, i.e. the likeness of a god upon him on account of his beauty. Similarly, Cú Chulainn is claimed to have said after his death, 'A high art has perished', i.e. a high god. Art, moreover, is a stone or gravestone, the diminutive of which is *arténe*, i.e. 'little' *cloch* ('stone'), i.e. diminutive noun, thus Gúaire Aidne said:
> The little stones conceal a great wonder, those which are upon Marcán mac Aedha maic Maircéni.'

In view of early Welsh, English and Irish lexicographical activities, it is somewhat surprising that there are no Welsh glossaries which have been handed down to us (cf. also J.E. Caerwyn Williams 1983: 10f.). Conditions for producing glossaries had certainly developed early enough in Wales as was illustrated previously (cf. section 2.1.2.) and as is re-affirmed by the following facts:

1. There are early Old English and Irish glossaries, and at about 1100 a Cornish vocabulary (cf. *Vocabularium Cornicum* below) was available. That is, all around Wales, there survives lexicographical material.

2. Old Welsh glosses reveal that intellectual relations were also close between Wales,

Cornwall, and Brittany (cf. Falileyev 2000: xii, K.H. Jackson 1994: 49ff.). A witness for mutual cultural exchange between Wales and Cornwall is, for instance, the compiler of the *Vocabularium Cornicum* (cf. ibid.: 49-62 and section 2.1.4.).

3. At the time when Old English and Irish glossaries and the Cornish vocabulary were compiled, Wales kept close political and intellectual relations with all three cultures:

    –   There have been early Welsh-English family relationships and permanent English raids to Wales between the eighth and eleventh centuries and from the eleventh century onwards also from Wales to England (cf. W. Davies 1990: 62, 67ff.). As a result, mutual 'relations' of submission or obedience developed, as well as alliances (cf. ibid.: 76, 78, 1989: 115).

    –   Intellectual relations between Wales and England, as illustrated in section 2.1.2., were part of the aforementioned processes.

    –   Welsh-Irish relations are traditional and go back at least to the Irish settlements in Wales between the fourth and the seventh centuries (cf. W. Davies 1990: 39), continue with Irish claims of power in Wales,[14] or the seeking for asylum there (cf. O'Rahilly 1924: 64ff.). Ireland, on the other hand, was a retreat area for Welsh people in difficulty.[15] Kinship relationships between Wales and Ireland were not broken up by the Scandinavians (cf. K.H. Jackson 1994: 155):

        > "For example, the court of some kings of Gwynedd, notably of the ninth-century Merfyn Frych and his son Rhodri Mawr, was an important meeting-point for Irish scholars on their way to the continent" (C. Davies 1995: 13).

        Resulting cultural, religious, political and personal contacts between Wales and Ireland were vital (cf. W. Davies 1990: 39f.). Well attested relations[16] in the tenth and eleventh centuries were probably essential for the survival of the Welsh aristocracy.[17]

    –   We also have to think of clerical British influence on Ireland between the fifth and eighth centuries leading to the mutual exchange of scholars up to the eleventh century (cf. Slover 1926: 52ff., Evans, S. 1977: lxi, Lapidge 1986: 102, and C. Davies 1995: 13), a time when Irish glossaries flourished:

    –   Long-established intellectual relations between Ireland and Wales (cf. Ó Cuiv 1961: 12, Lapidge 1986: 98) can be proved for the Welsh centres of learning,

---

[14]   Some of them were *Rhian* in South-West Wales, *Turchil*, killed in 1093 in Wales, *Brian Ború* (*Bóramha, Bóroime* 941-1014), *Diarmait mac Mael na mBó* (cf. W. Davies. 1990: 39).

[15]   Up to the twelfth century, we find Welsh inhabitants in Ireland (cf. Bullock-Davies 1966: 24). See also Slover (1926: 37).

[16]   For further details, see Heinz (1999b).

[17]   This assumption is confirmed in pre-Norman Welsh literature as in *Armes Prydein* where is said: "Gwyr gwychyr gwallt hiryon ergyr dofyd. o dihol Saesson o Iwerddon dybyd ... Dybi o Lydaw orydaw gyweithyd." 'Valiant long-haired warriors, adept in fighting, will come from Ireland to expel the Saxons... a brave company will come from Brittany' (I. Williams 1972: 13). Earlier in the text, there is a reference to the Scandinavians and the help the Welsh received from them (ibid.: 11), exactly as we know it from *Gruffudd ap Cynan* (cf. V.E. Davies 1959: 1, 11).

amongst others, Llanbadarn Fawr, a glossing centre, and St. David's (cf. C. Davies 1995: 12f.). They remained in close contact with Ireland (cf. S. Evans 1977: lxi, lxiiff.) and England in the tenth and eleventh centuries; Llanbadarn Fawr especially with Canterbury, a place known for early lexicographical productions, and St. David's with Oxford and others. St. David's is mentioned in Irish documents in the eighth and ninth centuries in relation to the Irish monastic reform (cf. J.W. Evans 1991: 4). The Welsh, Latin, Irish[18] and English languages were quite likely practised here.[19]

– One of the most famous early Welsh scholars was Sulien (1010/11-91), who ran the writing centre at Llanbadarn Fawr, received his first education in St. David's and then studied for several years in Scotland and Ireland (cf. J.E. Lloyd 1937: 29f.).

> "Under Sulien's inspiration Llanbadarn grew to become an immensely important centre of scholarship and of manuscript production" (C. Davies 1995: 16).

The works of Sulien and his sons suggest that Welsh, Latin, Irish, Hebrew and English were languages used in Llanbadarn Fawr.

– Although economic relations between Ireland and Wales cannot be proved, Slover (1926: 45f.) speculates that such connections existed, since Roman streets were still in existence at that time. Because of the close aristocratic relations (cf. above and Heinz 1999b), we can, at least, assume exchange of war goods as part of close kinship connections. Systematic trade other than family based trade, however, seems rather unlikely.

– Because of the relations between the Irish and Welsh on the one hand and the Welsh and the English on the other over centuries, Irish and English can perhaps be regarded as traditional second languages spoken in Wales.

4. Welsh scholars had a high reputation outside the country as was illustrated in section 2.1.2. (cf. also C. Davies 1995: 12ff.). Another famous scholar was Lifris (at the end of the eleventh century, cf. C. Davies 1995: 13), archdeacon and master of the monastery of Llancarfan.

5. Scholars in Welsh learning centres certainly worked lexicographically or pursued work prior to it. Sulien and his sons, for instance, copied manuscripts and illuminated them at Llanbadarn Fawr. They glossed texts in Latin, wrote the local chronicle (cf. Lloyd 1937: 25), composed literature, principally Rhygyfarch (1056?-99), and translated.

6. Although the body of evidence with regard to Welsh early book production is weak, there are some references to it as was illustrated previously (cf. section 2.1.2.).

---

[18] After the raiding of Irish monasteries and libraries, *Brian Ború* sent scholars abroad to study and to buy books.

[19] For other languages, see Heinz (1999b).

The question as to why there is virtually no evidence for glossaries and vocabularies can partly be answered by looking at the fate Welsh society faced in mediaeval times. Scandinavian raids, which certainly prepared the ground for the Norman invasion, began in the ninth century and mostly affected the monasteries, i.e. potential centres of learning.[20] Only at the beginning of the eleventh century, were the Scandinavians pushed back,[21] just before the Normans invaded the country following 1066. Later the latter dominated the *March,*[22] particularly in the twelfth and thirteenth centuries. In the wake of the Norman invasion, accompanied by re-settlements of the Welsh and their replacement by foreigners, the reform of the monasteries at the end of the eleventh and the beginning of the twelfth century saw a substitution of the Welsh elite by members of Latin orders.[23] Kinship and intellectual relations to Ireland were gradually interrupted. In the end, Wales was cut off from its vital link to Ireland. As a result of these processes, Welsh book 'production' must have decreased if not ceased.[24] It has to be borne in mind that the situation also led to an isolation and edging out of the Welsh book producers from socially relevant posts. Welsh book production was, therefore, in decline when important early Irish and English manuscripts were being compiled. Books produced earlier must have been susceptible to destruction, either by accident or because of them being regarded as worthless, or because of there being nobody to care for them.[25] The development of Wales, hindered from the outside, must have retarded the region-wide use of written Welsh.

D. Huws (2000: 3-7) goes even further in his assumption and maintains

> "that in Wales fewer than one in a hundred medieval manuscripts in Latin [have] survived; certainly a lower percentage than in England. On the other hand, an informed guess might be that one in five medieval manuscripts in Welsh [have] survived, perhaps more. In Wales, as elsewhere, the parchment of books was recycled as their content became outmoded, often as a consequence of legal or liturgical changes. But the main reasons for the scarcity in Wales of surviving books in Latin must have been the destruction of liturgical works during the Reformation [cf. section 2.2.] - not a dozen books survive - and the apathy and wanton destructiveness which led to the loss of the Welsh monastic and cathedral libraries (perhaps already badly neglected) after the Dissolution. Whereas fifteen medieval libraries in England are each represented by more than 100 surviving books, only one Welsh library, that of Llanthony Prima, is represented by more than four, and the books of this Augustinian priory had found

---

[20]   The Viking invasions started in 852 and mostly effected Anglesey. Chester was raided in 893. In the tenth century, the following monasteries were raided: Holyhead (961), Tywyn (963), Penmon (971), Clynnog (978), Llanbadarn (988), St. Dogmaels, Llantwit, Lancarfan (988) and St. David's. The Scandinavians also attacked the peninsulas in the South and North West, and later the Welsh Midlands and South Wales (cf. W. Davies, 1990: 50f., 54f.).

[21]   For instance by *Gruffudd ap Llywelyn* (cf. W. Davies 1990: 52).

[22]   *March* is the term for Norman dominated areas in the South and South-East of Wales (cf. Rees 1959: Plate 30ff.), particularly in Pembroke, Brycheiniog 'Brecknock' and Morgannwg 'Glamorgan'. Temporarily, the Normans also conquered parts of Gwynedd and Powys (cf. J.G. Jones 1994: 18, scheme of the conquest in T. Jones 1983: 17). At about 1135, nearly the whole Welsh south was in Norman hands (cf. Cowley 1977: 7f., J.E. Lloyd 1941: 1).

[23]   The first monastic foundations in South Wales were: 1087-1100 in Abergavenny by *Hamelin of Ballon*, 1074-86 in Monmouth by *Wihenoc*, 1098 in Pembroke by *Arnulf of Montgomery*. For more information, see Cowley (1977).

[24]   For the disastrous effects the Norman invasion had on English learning, see Murray (1900: 14f.).

[25]   See the statements of *Rhygyfarch* in Cowley (1977: 1f.).

shelter well before the Dissolution in Gloucestershire at Lanthony Secunda. Of 242 titles listed at the rich Cistercian abbey of Margram in the early fourteenth century not one book is known to survive.

Serious losses must have occurred even before the Dissolution. None of the few surviving pre-Norman books from Wales is likely to have been in its original home at the Dissolution, unless possibly at St David's. Few even of the post-Norman religious houses in Wales escaped damage in war, particularly in the rising of Owain Glyndŵr during the first decade of the fifteenth century when many monasteries were devastated."

In light of the facts presented here, I tend to assume that the lack of glossaries, which is paralleled by a general shortage of Welsh language material, particularly in the eleventh century (cf. K.H. Jackson 1994: 56), may be due to the social situation as briefly described above (cf. above, Heinz 1999b, and section 2.2.). The existence of more glosses than those passed down to us and the one or the other glossary can be assumed. Firm evidence, however, is as scarce as that for vocabulary production in mediaeval Wales. The first glossaries which are handed down to us date from the second half of the fourteenth century, e.g. a Latin-Welsh herbal list (cf. J.E. Caerwyn Williams 1983: 12), that is, from the Middle Welsh period (cf. section 2.1.4.).

2.1.4.   Vocabularies

Vocabularies reflect an advanced stage of early lexicography. They clearly go beyond the purpose of early glossaries in that they do not predominantly explain selected individual items, but describe a more comprehensive lexicon of one or more semantic fields, e.g. herbs (cf. below). Vocabularies may still leave out important parts of the lexicon. They are, however, already based upon a clear concept, taking into account intended groups of users, special purposes, thematic or logical arrangements. As a result, they often exhibit a macrostructure, which allows a first statable search procedure. In addition, some vocabularies may offer first systematic grammatical and other information.

Since lexicographical material including Welsh remains limited, a brief look at early English vocabulary production is advocated. Decades after the *De raris fabulis* (cf. section 2.1.2.), the Abbot of Eynsham (near Oxford), Ælfric (955-1020)[1] wrote colloquies for teaching purposes by substituting Greek words with English equivalents (cf. H. Lewis 1929: vi). He may have been in the position to draw material from English glossaries (cf. below). Æelfric also wrote a grammar based on Donatus (4th century) and Priscian (6th century, Green 1977: 59, cf. section 2.2.1.2.1.) and a glossary appended to it. Later (cf. below) he compiled a Latin-Old English vocabulary (the sample text for the *Vocabularium Cornicum*, cf. below). Green (1977: 59) defines his *Dictionarium Saxonico-Latino-Anglicum* as a dictionary. It was eventually printed in 1659 and consists of thirty groups of words, covering a variety of topics. Ælfric is, therefore, the one who best represents an early continuous English lexicographical tradition in mediaeval England.

He was, however, followed by others:

> "A vocabulary list of a century later works on very much the same basis, this time making its way through eighteen topics, each of which holds a number of sub-groups. These include God, heaven, the angels, sun, moon, earth and sea; man, woman and their bodies; blood relations, professional and trades people; diseases; such abstract terms as 'impious' and 'prudent'; fishes; beasts; household equipment and so on. [...]
> The list, of some 1,300 words, has been subject of some confusion [...] Current researchers, spearheaded by Gabriele Stein have given it a new name, the 'London Manuscript' (ibid.: 60).

Among other vocabularies which followed was a variety of anonymous Anglo-Saxon works. They reflected the gradual development of lexicographical technique. There are, however, two lexicographers who need to be mentioned. One is Alexander Neckham (1157-1217), abbot of Cirencester. His major lexicographical work is entitled *De Utensilibus*, 'a kind of vocabulary in

---

[1]   "Aelfric had been abbot for many years at Cernel Cloister (Cerne Abbas) near Dorchester, and a friend of Aethelmaer, Alderman of Devon. He wrote two series of English homilies, lives of Saints (996-997), a Hetateuch and Canons (998), but is most famous for his colloquies, or dialogues for the use of English school-boys learning Latin, in which the students spoke and construed in Latin the parts of various interlocutors, while the master's copy contained the Latin glosses." (Graves 1962: 13).

the form of a reading book' (ibid.: 61). Neckham deals with farming and its necessary implements, with navigation and ships, and the stores they carried and

> "the tools, qualifications, and duties of a medieval scribe, the operations of the goldsmith, and a copious enumeration of ecclesiastical furniture [... At] the time Neckham's listing of a relatively wide, but still specialised vocabulary, almost a list of dedicated jargon rather than mainstream English, is a relatively rare production" (ibid.: 61).

The other lexicographer to be introduced is Johannes de Garlandia (ca. 1180 - ca. 1250), known in England as John of Garland, a theologian, chronologist, alchemist, versifier and grammarian.

> "His two most important grammatical works are the *Cornutus*, or *Distigium* or *Scolarium Morale* and the *Dictionarius ad res explicandas* (1240?). The former (printed 1481) is [...] 'a vocabulary listing vocables associated with these topics: the names of animals; a house and furnishing of a house; the parts of the body; a mill and objects associated with it; a blacksmith's shop; instruments of the household and farm, including distaff, spindle, plow, and wagon; musical instruments; various artificers, such as cobbler, tailor, dyer, tanner, mason, and carpenter; species of trees, dress materials; and various classes of people'" (ibid.: 64).

Despite its title, the *Dictionarius ad res explicandas* is not a dictionary as such.

> "Like Neckham's *De Utensilibus*, and indeed like many such teaching vocabularies, it is more a piece of heavily glossed and annotated fictional prose. There are no headwords and definitions; rather the reader would read the text and refer where appropriate to the notes and interlinear glosses. The aim of the book, so Garland explains, is to help the young scholar amass a vocabulary of necessary words. Starting with those that cover parts of the human body [...]
> Garland's list gradually expand to create a promptorium, or treasure house of words, a concept that would be taken up, some two centuries later, both as a book and a title by the Norfolk monk who may or may not have been named 'Geoffrey the Grammarian'" (ibid.: 64).

The only vocabulary which contains Welsh lexical items is the *Vocabularium Cornicum*. At about 1000, the abbot Ælfric (cf. above) compiled a Latin-Anglo-Saxon vocabulary. The Anglo-Saxon entries were substituted by Cornish ones in the eleventh or twelfth centuries, perhaps around 1100 (cf. K.H. Jackson 1994: 60f., Graves 1962: 9). Although the language presented in the vocabulary is usually regarded as Old Cornish, it was edited at a stage which is transitional between Old and Middle Cornish (cf. K.H. Jackson 1994: 60). A few words in the vocabulary are Welsh amendments (cf. ibid.: 61). K.H. Jackson (ibid.:) offers the following explanation for this phenomenon:

> "The most satisfactory explanation of this is that the scribe of the Cotton MS. was a Welshman, who occasionally substituted or added his own forms in copying the OC. words" (for an example, see below).

The Welsh interpolations, however, justify looking at the *Vocabularium Cornicum* in a Welsh context.[2]

---

[2]   This is even more justified, since Falileyev (personal correspondence) affirms that new consideration concerning this vocabulary and its prehistory are necessary (cf. also Graves 1962: 11).

The vocabulary has 961 entries and is arranged thematically, i.e. in a manner typical of this time. The subjects are: God, Heaven, Earth, Man, birds, fish, animals, plants, trees, houses and furniture. The lexicon consists entirely of nouns and adjectives (cf. I. Williams 1941: 1). The following examples illustrate the macrostructure of the vocabulary:

[...] fili. [?][3]
mab.filia: m[?]ch.liberi: flechec.Soboles: ach.Familia: goscor pi teilu.
Frater: broder.ł braud[4] [...]

The first Welsh lexicographical work known to us dates from the second half of the fourteenth century and is Latin-Welsh. It is from an unknown author and confined to herbs (cf. J.E. Caerwyn Williams 1983: 12, 41).

The first known author who produced lexicogaphical material was Gwilym Tew (fl. ca. 1470).[5] He was the first bard proven to have copied manuscripts in Morgannwg (J.E. Caerwyn Williams 1983: 14). Copying manuscripts was a method to enlarge one's own vocabulary and flexibility in the language. The manuscripts were perhaps used as a kind of 'handbook' in bardic schools.

Tew's work reflects an interest in Welsh vocabulary and general grammar. He copied the manuscript Peniarth 51 in which there is a collection of poetry, a copy of the *Dwned*[6] and a list of old words from *Canu Aneirin*. In addition, he tried to explain them by providing synonyms. Tew can, therefore, be described as a vocabulary compiler.

There are hardly any other traces of early Welsh lexicographical activity (cf. sections 2.1.2. and 2.1.3.). The situation of material handed down to us only changes with the beginning of the sixteenth century. Apart from the linguistic need to produce lexicographical tools for teaching, learning, and translating, this has been one of the periods when, because of cultural needs and historical developments, lexicographical production was particularly intensive. Translating and language learning now became a social phenomenon, since writing was no longer the specialised craft of a restricted number of individuals and education no longer a monopoly of the Church (C. Davies 1995: 27f.), but regular communicational means of larger and socially dominating groups. More details as to this new era are given in the following section.

---

[3] Readings tentative. Where there is a question mark, correct reading was impossible.

[4] *Braud* is Old Welsh for Latin *frater*.

[5] The dating is not clear (cf. M. Stephens 1997: 303 and E.I. Rowlands 1976: vii). He was the brother or son of Rhys Brydydd (there is not much known about him either - cf. E.I. Rowlands 1976: vii). Both ascended from the noble Einion ap Gollwyn (there is no further data available) and were part of a famous bard's family (cf. Rhisiart ap Rhys, Lewys Morgannwg in the following sections).

[6] The word *Dwned*, derived from the name Donatus, was used from the fifteenth century onwards to denote bardic grammars. These were employed in bardic schools as a kind of framework deduced from the works of the classical grammarians Donatus and Priscian, i.e. *Artes* and *Institutiones* (C. Davies 1995: 40). For further details with regard to bardic grammars, see section 2.2.1.2.1.

2.2.   The Renaissance
2.2.1.   Pre-conditions for dictionary production
2.2.1.1.   General pre-conditions[1]

The time of the Renaissance was a period of changes in intellectual, cultural and economic ideas in Europe which - due to their nature - cannot be pinned down to an exact date, but influenced society some time between the fourteenth and seventeenth centuries.[2] For Wales, the years of the *Acts of Union* with England (1536/43) indicate the beginning of the Renaissance (cf. C. Davies 1995: 54). The Restoration period from 1660 to 1689,[3] which was characterised by a decline of social, cultural and economic achievements, marks the end of the Renaissance (cf. H. Thomas 1972).

During this period, new ideas developed in philosophy (cf. Schmitt, Ch.B. & Skinner et al. 1988, S. Collins 1989), education (cf. Ch.B. Schmitt 1984), the arts (cf. Gordon 1975, Letts 1981, Clark 1983), literature (cf. Bono 1984, Giamatti 1984, Mirollo 1984, Lepschy & Took et al. 1986), music (cf. Reese 1959, Palisca 1986), theatre (cf. Scott 1982, Cohen 1985), sciences and technology (cf. D. Lindsay 1971, Pagel 1986), and religion (cf. developments of the Reformation in Esteep 1986, G. Williams 1997b). In acquiring new ideologies, the striving new classes and their elite, the humanists, not only introduced a change away from the concentration on God (theocentrism), predominant in mediaeval times, to that on people (anthropocentrism), but eventually a period of transition in society, i.e. from feudalism to capitalism. Of particular importance for this investigation is the desire of the humanists

> "that ordinary people should be allowed to share in the new learning, both religious and secular, that they were working to promote. Much of their work therefore is, in a broad sense, educative in its nature and intent. William Salesbury [cf. below] expressed this desire to uplift ordinary people in words which have become famous as one of the keynote passages of the Renaissance thought: *oni fynnwch fyned yn waeth nag anifeiliaid, mynnwch ddysg yn eich iaith* (unless you wish to become worse than animals, insist on having learning in your language)" (Jarvis 1997: 128).

The *New Learning* was to be based

> "on the truths and glories of the past. In terms of biblical scholarship, this can be interpreted as a search for early sources and a sound knowledge of the language of original texts. In more general European terms, this meant a resurgence of respect for the languages, literatures and ideas of the Ancient World, in particular the culture embodied in Latin, Greek and Hebrew writings" (ibid.: 130).

To the humanists, therefore, the rediscovery of the Greek and Roman past was essential and classical antiquity became

---

[1]   I would like to take this opportunity of thanking Dr Iwan Wmffre, Tregaron/Wales, for helpful discussion on this subject.

[2]   The exact dates of the beginning and end of the Renaissance vary according to differing points of view. The dates given above are first of all related to essential social events, events which encouraged developments or made their end especially clear and thus roughly mark the period of the Renaissance (cf. Elton 1976, A. Brown 1988).

[3]   See also the dates 1530-1770 of volume III of *A guide to Welsh Literature* (R.G. Gruffydd 1997) or *Hanes Cymru yn y Cyfnod Modern Cynnar* 1530-1760 (G.H. Jenkins 1983).

"a touchstone against which cultural, moral and intellectual concern (*sapientia*) as well as literary and stylistic principles (*eloquentia*) [were] to be measured [...] As a philosopher and literary stylist who was not above putting his formidable oratorical skills at the disposal of the world of government and politics, Cicero represented the Renaissance ideal of civilized and civilizing statesman, a prototype of Castiglione's courtier or Thomas Elyot's governor. Cicero provided a pattern to which educated scholar-gentlemen might aspire to conform [...] The Ciceronian image of the engaged man, devoted both to the things of the mind and to the business of the state" (C. Davies 1995: 66)

was of much significance to humanists throughout Europe.

"In marked contrast to the way in which the rediscovery of the classics led in other countries to something of a rejection of much of the medieval heritage, in Wales many of the humanists were inspired by the New Learning to rediscover their own traditions more fully and more gloriously.[4] The renewal of interest in the Greek and Latin classics led them to search for the manuscripts of their own country, just as Petrarch and the early Italian humanists had avidly looked in monastery and cathedral libraries for classical manuscripts" (C. Davies 1995: 59).

As part of these developments, dictionaries became popular in Western Europe and early lexicographical discussions developed. In the preceding centuries, the production of lexicographical reference works was mainly the result of assisting in training and teaching (cf. Green 1977: 55-75) in a society where writing was confined to a small elitist scholarly class, since education was a monopoly of the Church (C. Davies 1995: 27). At the time of the Renaissance, however, dictionaries, vocabularies and other reference books developed because of the cultural and educational demands for new larger social groups (cf. above and below) which evolved during the basic social, economic, spiritual and conceptual changes in society. In addition, lexicographical productions which had so far been orientated on standards set by Latin lexicographical works received new impulses from the examination of the individual vernacular languages (cf. Green 1977: 105-122).

Before the production of dictionaries could eventually emerge in Wales, however, long-term basic social developments were necessary. In the twelfth and thirteenth centuries, for instance, Welsh society gradually stabilised. New forms of administration, mode of production, new techniques, and mobility evolved and resulted in new social conditions. Part of these developments were processes of intellectual integration of the different groups of peoples, who had made home in Wales in the wake of the Norman conquest, in order to level out the cultural differences between them. These changes in society, also referred to as the Renaissance of the twelfth century (S. Evans 1977: 1), saw a gradually growing assimilation of the new settlers. In the thirteenth century, important centres of learning were assimilated by the Welsh culture (ibid.: liii, cf. I. Thomas 1997: 154f.). The manuscript tradition (re?)started. The access of the Welsh to the newly developed, i.e. Norman dominated, society initiated new intellectual

---

[4]   The reason for this may be found in Welsh traditional history whereby Nennius (J. Morris 1980), Geoffrey of Monmouth (Thorpe 1983) and others later saw Wales' origins in Greek history (cf. C.W. Lewis 1997: 34).

activities including translating[5] and interpreting as part of the process of accepting and rejecting foreign cultures.

Translating, for instance, has over the centuries generally been recognised as a creative act for developing languages (cf. Gruffydd Robert below and in section 2.2.1.2.1. and the translation of the Bible, section 2.2.1.2.3.).[6] Especially in times of accelerating social developments verbalised in language, however, and in societies where access to media is restricted, translators and any other person able to write creatively promotes the development, codifying, and acceptance of the language. By translating into a language, the flexible usage of its lexicon, registers, and word formation is encouraged as well as the borrowing and/or inventing of new lexical items.

Particularly important for translating were the monasteries of the *Cistercians* and, from the fourteenth century onwards, *Mendicant* orders, which became important centres of learning. From 1350 on, therefore, a new impetus for translation can be observed (cf. I. Thomas 1997: 154ff.). The *Mendicants*, for instance, translated various literature into Welsh in order to preach to the local people. One example is *Y Bibyl yng Nghymraeg* (1350-1400), i.e. the translation of Petraus Pictaviensis' *Promptuarium* by an unknown person (cf. T. Jones 1940, I. Thomas 1997: 155). Other translations were *Gwassanaeth Meir* from 'Officium Pavum Beatae Mariae Virginis' (ca. 1440 by Dafydd Ddu o Hiraddug; cf. section 2.2.1.2.1.),[7] the Opening of the *Gospel of John* (cf. ibid.: 154), the ten Commandments, some 150 verses from the Old Testament, and parts of the New Testament in different essays in *Llyfr Ancr Llanddewi Brefi* (1346), the earliest and most abundant collection of religious texts. The *Ystorya Adaf ac Eua y Wreic* 'Vitae Adae et Euae' is handed down in eight versions, translated between ca. 1350 and 1500. The translation of 'Vita Santorum Amici et Amelii' *Kedymdeithyas Amlyn ac Amic* dates from the fourteenth century (cf. P. Williams 1982: xxxivff.).

Secular literature, however, was also translated, e.g. *Brut y Brenhinedd* from 'Historia Regum Britanniae' (ca. sixty translations between the thirteenth and fifteenth centuries, M. Stephens 1997: 65, H. Lewis 1974: xviii-xxx), its preface *Ystorya Dared* from 'Historia Daretis Phrygii de Excidio Troiae' ca. 1300 (cf. C. Davies 1995: 43), its continuation *Brut y Tywysogion* from the lost original 'Cronica Principum Wallie' between 1307-1350 (*Red Book of Hergest* version, cf. T. Jones 1955: lv and 1952), the *Ystorya Bown o Hamtwn* from 'Boeve de Haumtoun' perhaps before 1300 (M. Stephens 1997: 811) and others (cf. S.J. Williams 1968, H. Lewis 1967).

---

[5] Early translation was carried out by monks and/or bards providing material from which later the humanists drew (cf. following section). It seems rather unlikely, however, that translating had always formed a regular part of the bard's occupation.

[6] Still in the twentieth century, for instance, translating from other languages was used by Roparz Hemon to develop the Breton language. He demonstrated that translation itself is not only a means of transmission language, culture and knowledge, but is itself part of lexicographical work by asking for new words, expressions, realities, and processes to be denoted.

[7] For details concerning the contents of the translation, see B.F. Roberts (1961), I. Thomas (1997: 156), and B.R. Jones (1994: 43).

In this context, comprehensive oral and written usage of Welsh gained ground and the language itself became gradually a subject of research, as can be seen from the early *Gramadegau'r Penceirddiaid* 'The Grammars of the Chief bards' in the fourteenth century (cf. section 2.2.1.2.1.). In light of the fact that the bardic grammars were influenced by the works of the classical grammarians Donatus and Priscian, it seems likely that classical lexicography was also studied. This assumption may be supported by two facts: On the one hand, it has to be noted that various domains of research in applying the language, such as grammar, rhetoric, literature, and lexicography have hardly been dealt with separately until the sixteenth century (cf. early dictionaries and their authors in sections 2.1.1., 2.1.4., below and bardic grammars in section 2.2.1.2.1.). On the other hand, Varro's *De Lingua Latina* (cf. section 2.1.1.), for instance, was rediscovered by monks of the mother monastery of the Benedictines under their abbot Desiderius (1058-87). Probably before 1074, monks of this order settled in Llangua and in 1074 in Monmouth (cf. Cowley 1977: 270).

In addition, new lexicographical activities increased in the eleventh and twelfth centuries on the continent: Hugo of Pisa († 1212), for example, is the author of the *Derivationes magnae sive dictionarium etymologicum*. Giovanni Balbi († 1298) completed a book called *Catholicon* or *Summa* in 1286, which was first printed in 1460 by the pioneer printer Johannes Gutenberg.

> "The work is divided into four prefatory sections on 'Orthographia', 'Ethimologia', 'Diasintastica', 'Prosodia', or spelling, etymology, syntax and prosody or the study of versification. Then comes the dictionary itself, mixing words and proper names (of both places and people) in alphabetical order throughout the text. Basically an encyclopedic dictionary, and as such a repository of information both lexicographical and non-lexicographical, it was one of the most sought-after books of the fifteenth century and the pivotal medieval (rather than classical) dictionary" (Green 1977: 51).

In view of these developments, it can be said that essential developments for producing universally applicable teaching or learning aids, therefore, had commenced within and outside Wales already in the Middle Ages.

In light of the fact that it took another four hundred years before the actual breakthrough of dictionary production in Wales in the period of the Renaissance, the accumulation of more internal and external pre-conditions was apparently required. One of them was, first, the interest of a new social elite, the humanists, in classical antiquity (cf. above) and thereby in its lexicographical works (cf. section 2.1.1.).

Second, an external factor was the development of lexicography on the continent and in England.[8] Apart from re-publishing mediaeval and classical dictionaries (cf. above, Green 1977: 47, 51, 59, 63f.), many new were produced: The first English dictionary, the English-Latin *Promptorium parvulorum sive clericorum* 'A treasure-house for the young or for clerks',[9] was

---

[8] See also Green's comments on lexicography as being '*de facto* plagiaristic' (1977: 27-30, 53).

[9] Some scholars regard the English glossaries from the seventh and eighth centuries still in use in the fifteenth century as the first dictionaries (cf. section 2.1.3. and Lehnert 1956: 271).

written at about 1440 maybe by Giraldus Grammaticus[10] and printed in 1499. It was compiled in

AB- or ABC-order, without distinguishing *I* and *J* and *U* and *V*, but with separate listing of nouns and other word classes on the one hand and verbs on the other.

Three other lexicographical works followed in this century: first the Latin-English dictionary *Medulla Grammatice* (1460). It is in ABC-order with unknown authorship. Drawing from *glossae collectae*, glosses from classical texts, from the Bible and from *vocabularia*, it formed the basis of the first Latin-English dictionary ever printed (cf. ibid: 66f.), the *[H]ortus Vocabulorum* by Wynkyn de Worde 1500 (J.E. Caerwyn Williams 1983: 8, Green 1977: 67). A fourth dictionary was the *Catholicum Anglicum* 'The Universal Remedy', an English-Latin wordbook compiled in 1483.

By the turn of the fifteenth century alphabetical order had been properly established and there had been a regular flow of first Latin-English and then English-Latin lexicographical works, which were paralleled by similar compilations across Europe. In the sixteenth century the flow of major dictionaries increased and specialisation began, e.g. with John Withals *A Shorte Dictionarie for Yonge Beginners* (1553).[11] It was the best selling dictionary of the century running to thirteen editions (ibid.: 92). Another kind of lexicographical work developed with the *Pictorial Vocabulary*, produced at about 1500. Among its approximately 2,500 entries are seventy illustrative sketches (ibid.: 65).

In 1580 the first dictionary of synonyms *Synonymorium Sylva* was published by Simon Pelegromius and in 1604 the first monolingual dictionary *A Table Alphabeticall, conteyning and teaching the True Writing, and Understanding of Hard Usuall English Wordes...* compiled by Robert Cawdrey appeared.

Although not yet 'lexicographors' in the modern, professional sense of the term, there were emerging a number of linguistic authorities. One of them was Thomas Elyot. Leaving all other works aside, it is for his *Dictionnarie of Syr Thomas Eliot, knight* published in 1538 that he is best remembered. It was the first ever English reference work to employ the word 'Dictionary' in its title (ibid.: 85).

Vocabulary production did not cease either. Particularly from the sixteenth century onwards, it rather developed into a tool of supporting conversation in the vernacular and specialised topics, thereby contributing largely to the evolvement of monolingual dictionaries in the seventeenth century (cf. Green 1977: 62, 73, 77, 122-147).

Two continental lexicographers are of major intercultural importance. They both drew extensively on the past and in their turn had a substantial influence on English as well as European lexicography. One was Ambrosius Calepinus (1435-1511) whose *Dictionarium ex optimis quibusquam authoribus studiose collectum...* was first published in 1502. It has been re-published for two hundred years being constantly extended both in content and languages. The

---

For details with regard to the authorship and other background knowledge, see Green (1977: 39, 54,67-70, 85).

11   Without giving any explanation, Green provides two other dates of publication for this book: 1529 (1977: 224) and 1554 (ibid.: 56).

largest *Calepine*, as it became known, covered eleven languages (ibid: 52f.). The other famous lexicographer was Robert Estienne (1503-59) who published the *Thesaurus linguae latinae* in 1532 and the Hebrew text of the Old Testament 1539-44 (cf. I. Thomas 1997: 157).

Third, dictionary-making proved to be an adjunct to the education of scholars in the classical texts. Dictionaries were again regarded (cf. section 2.1.1.) as repositories of learning,

"offering the scholar a means of better understanding and appreciating the classical texts which he or his peers are rediscovering, preserving, criticising and above all handing on" (ibid.: 46).

Fourth, the needs of traders who had rather commercial than academic interests and spoke in the vernacular could only be met by bilingual and multilingual dictionaries, such as the three-language *Introito a porta*, originally published as an Italian-German dictionary by Adam von Rottweil in 1477 and expanded to three languages in 1513, the *Calepine* (cf. above), the *Introductio quaedam utilissima* printed in 1510 and many others (cf. ibid.: 105).

Altogether, the need for proper education and training (cf. ibid.: 93), foremost for the new specialised professions gradually developing, such as copyists, scientists, (translators),[12] tradesmen, and politicians, that is, for an audience longing for such material, prepared the ground for comprehensive lexicographical activities. Their training could neither be met by feudal clerical education nor by the training offered by the *Bardic Order* (cf. below) as an institution confined to and associated with the feudal Welsh aristocracy. Emerging scholarly specialists, and occasionally highly talented bards and clerics, working at English or foreign universities (cf. C. Davies 1985: 55) and other educational institutions, took over the new tasks. They developed new teaching and didactic methods, as well as specialist material for those who wished to use their own language and express themselves properly or those who desired to make their own knowledge available Europe-wide.

A fifth requirement was a pool of people who were similarly highly and comprehensively qualified and at the same time were specialists in linguistics. Some of them were the compilers, and copyists of bardic grammars (cf. below) and of manuscripts, others were translators, clerics, or humanist bards. They can best be subsumed under the term *New Learning*, this time denoting a movement of versatile educated rich people with a universal claim and orientated on classical education (cf. above).

The pool of adequately qualified intellectuals consequently established a sixth pre-condition for assembling lexic systematically and in book form, i.e. the possibility for co-operation. Much lexicographical work was done in co-operation (and still is), as can be proved for Gruffudd

---

[12]   Some specialist professions, foremost within the humanities, were for a while dominated by the ideal of a versatile educated personality and fully recognised somewhat delayed. Translating, for instance, was still not acknowledged as a separate profession, but was rather seen as being part of the abilities of skilled linguists and literats (cf. G.C.G. Thomas 1997: 254), clerics or physicians or other scientists who had to have English or Latin or other languages in order to obtain necessary knowledge. This might be a reason why James Howell (1593-1666), for instance, was not explicitly called an interpreter, although he certainly was an interpreter of Latin, as well as John Davies (1627-93, an interpreter of French-English, cf. M. Stephens 1997: 176) and others (cf. below).

Hiraethog's († 1564)[13] vocabulary (cf. J.E. Caerwyn Williams 1983: 15ff.). Maybe it is true for William Salesbury's (ca. 1520-1584?, cf. also sections 2.2.1.2.1., 2.2.1.2.2., 2.2.1.2.3., and 2.2.2.)[14] dictionary (cf. below), too? Being a friend of Hiraethog, he had already published the bard's proverbs and probably helped with the bardic grammar of Simwnt Fychan (ca. 1530-1606),[15] that is, he was a willing (although maybe difficult, cf. his controversy with Richard Davies in section 2.2.1.2.3.) collaborator and used to co-operate. Broad co-operation is even basic to major translation projects, as can be seen from the translation of the Bible (cf. also G. Williams 1997b: 338-361 and section 2.2.1.2.3.).

A seventh pre-condition was the availability of literature collected and copied and/or translated describing any aspects of life, thus introducing enough vocabulary to be listed and providing a linguistic data base which could be compared, sorted, extended and exploited. After having lost much material, which could have constituted a broad data base during the various wars, such as the *Wars of the Roses* (1455-1485, cf. Jarvis 1997: 149), even more vanished during the Dissolution of the monasteries (1536-1539),[16] which had considerably contributed to the growth of Welsh language material (cf. above). Despite political restrictions on the Welsh language, e.g. by the *Act of Uniformity* from 1549 which introduced English into the divine service, and economic disadvantages for its speakers and promoters in the decades following the incorporation of Wales into England (1536/43), some Welsh manuscripts were collected and copied by bards (cf. C. Davies 1995: 81), clerics and humanists. They were aware of the possible cultural loss and keen on training themselves and, therefore, safeguarded material, thus counter-balancing the onset of constriction in the use of the Welsh language and its later decline (cf. ibid.: 80, Green 1977: 108). By constituting a pool of language material, they contributed to a healthy level of published works to fix the meanings of certain words and make them applic-

---

[13] Hiraethog was a herald, herald bard, and pupil of Lewys Morgannwg (before 1520-65; *pencerdd 'drwy holl Gymru'* 'chief bard throughout Wales', and therefore a teacher of the bardic craft. He had close connections to W. Salesbury (cf. below and sections 2.2.1.2.1.-2.2.1.2.3, 2.2.2. and M. Stephens 1997: 292) and "was to be the link between [the] bardic learning and the new writing of the Renaissance [... Salesbury] was much obliged to his friend Gruffudd Hiraethog for communicating to him the secrets of bardic craft and the vocabulary of earlier Welsh writing" (B.R. Jones 1994: 4).

[14] He was born before 1520 (B.R. Jones 1994: 1). W. Salesbury, Welsh Wiliam Salsbri, a descendant of a family which had benefitted from the time of the Tudors (cf. H. Thomas 1972: 78, R.B. Jones 1994: 1-2), graduated from Oxford, and was a scholar, translator, and a versatile, highly productive and perhaps professional author. He published books treating linguistic, literary, philosophical, clerical and scientific questions (e.g. botanical, biological, astronomical in *The Description of the Sphere ... of the World*, 1550); coming very near the ideal of a humanist scholar. W. Salesbury also produced poetry and prose, and was interested in belief, law, politics, history, rhetoric, and languages (cf. Edgar 1977: xii, xxiv, cf. M. M. Stephens 1997: 657). Some of his works are still in manuscript form.

[15] Fychan was a bard and genealogist (cf. also sections 2.2.1.2.1. and 2.2.1.2.2.).

[16] The regular orders had at that time forty-seven religious houses, thirty-four monasteries, three nunneries, and ten friaries. The largest single monastic order was the *Cistercian* with thirteen houses while the *Benedictines* had eight and the *Augustinian Canons* had six. Half the friaries belonged to the *Dominicans*, three to the *Franciscans*. The *Carmelites* and *Austin Friars* had one each, mostly situated near the coast or in the rich river valleys.

able, habitual and familiar to others. An eventually sufficient number of translations, particularly in spheres of rapidly developing life, provided in the end an extensive lexicon applied and defined, as for instance, by synonyms, thus making comprehensive lexicographical compilation possible.

Although there was little direct translation of classical texts, e.g. part of Cicero's *De Senectute* by Gruffydd Robert (before 1532 - after 1598[17] cf. section 2.2.1.2.1.; Jarvis 1997: 131, G.C.G. Thomas 1997: 254f.), the literary production necessary for the provision of material to draw from for lexicographical purposes was, nevertheless, also promoted by the high demands of contemporary literature from foreign cultures. Its subsequent translation was enforced by the following developments during the Renaissance: (a) the need for gratification of individual humanists (cf. G.C.G. Thomas), (b) new beliefs were being pushed through, as for instance, the English Reformation in Wales, (c) there were competing cultural and religious trends, e.g. Catholics, Anglicans, Puritans,[18] (d) there were new trends in entertainment, which were strongly inspired by international trends (cf. Ciceronian competitions), and (e) there was a general search for markets for new products causing intensified international trading activities and politics. Altogether, there was an enforced Europe-wide cultural exchange inextricably linked with a new spiritual input, new technical possibilities for producing abundant material, and new standards in scholarship.

Basic linguistic description was an eighth essential. Some of it had been preserved in the form of the mediaeval bardic grammars (cf. above and section 2.2.1.2.1.). Other linguistic material was provided by glossaries (cf. section 2.1.3.) and later by vocabularies (cf. sections 2.1.4. and 2.2.1.2.2.).

A ninth pre-condition was the still vital Welsh language, which was for the first time after the *Acts of Union* 1536/43 officially supported in 1563 by an Act which demanded the translation of the Scriptures (cf. section 2.2.1.2.3.) and, therefore, provided the Welsh language with a semi-official status for preaching. As soon as the translation was made, the whole divine service in the Welsh speaking parts of the country was to be conducted in the Welsh language. English and Welsh versions of the Bible and the *Book of Common Prayer* were to be placed in every

---

[17] Gruffydd Robert was a Catholic, student of Oxford, a grammarian and competitor in Ciceronian prose in the Welsh language (Johnston 1994: 46). He was Archdeacon of Anglesey in 1558 and left the country after the introduction of the *Act of Uniformity* from 1549 (cf. M. Stephens 1997: 625). Robert made his way to Rome, "where he attracted the notice of the Archbishop of Milan, Cardinal Carlo Borromeo, nephew of Pope Pius IV and a leader of the Counter-Reformation. Borromeo invited the Welshman to Milan as his confessor and to be Canon Theologian at the Duomo" (C. Davies 1995: 71).

[18] "However great was the humanists' professed admiration for classical literature, however highly skilled they were as Latinists (and in some cases as scholars of Greek and Hebrew), the 'past' was for the Welsh humanists overwhelmingly a Welsh one. They were steeped in traditional Welsh learning. Their command of the Welsh language, the cornerstone of so much of their achievement, was the result of their immersion in their native linguistic and cultural inheritance. Thus many religious terms used by Williams Salesbury, for example, are not contemporary inventions, but can be traced back to the medieval text known as *Llyfr yr Ancr*, the Book of the Anchorite" (Jarvis 1997: 131, cf. above).

church throughout Wales. This was the first formal recognition by the government of the right to use the Welsh language in public worship (H. Thomas 1972: 104f.).

A tenth pre-condition was the possibility of producing materials by the latest technology, i.e. the printing press. The new technology provoked a new era of Bible translation (cf. I. Thomas 1997: 157ff. and section 2.2.1.2.3.). In England translation, copying and book production accelerated noticeably after the printing press was introduced there in 1476:

> "The entire print production throughout Europe in the years between Gutenberg's invention (c. 1436) and 1550 had been approximately 35,000 items. The bulk of them, unsurprisingly, were in Latin. The next 140 years would see 20,000 items printed in England alone, and these were all English-language works. The effect was twofold: the increased literacy offered by these books helped promote a rising middle class; and that same middle class made it clear that, unlike the denizens of academe, they wanted their reading in the vernacular" (Green 1977: 77).

Because of the ban on provincial printing until 1695, however, similar developments in Wales were made impossible and its intellectual potentials were oppressed. As a result Welsh intellectuals declared that many of the works they copied were available in print in England, but had to be handwritten in Wales (cf. H. Thomas 1972: 177). To have books printed in London, however, was awkward:

> "The London trade, on the one hand, was very loath to involve itself in ventures which were financially risky and, on the other hand, had a longstanding reputation for unreliability and fraudulent practices [...] Monoglot English printers also had difficulties with the Welsh alphabet with its additional letters such as *dd* and *ll* and its use of *w* and *y* as both consonants and vowels. These differences put a strain on type fonts never designed to accomodate the Welsh alphabet. There were not sufficient characters since their incidents in Welsh is quite different from that in English. Sixteenth-century authors moreover had varying theories on orthography. The reader is told that *c* is being used for *k* since the printers lack the number required by the Welsh. In some words *c* is used for *g*. A shortage of the letter *w* was often overcome by the use of two *vs*, especially in capitals" (Ch. Parry 1997: 269, 272).

Worried[19] about the delay of introducing the printing press into Wales, therefore, some Catholics tried to run a press illegally ca. 1585-7 in a cave on Rhiwledyn near Rhos-on-Sea (ibid.: 8f., 12ff.).[20] The second attempt was ca. 1586-87 in the house of Siôn Dafydd Rhys (1534?-1621?,

---

[19] The cleric of Dyffryn, Syr Lewys Gethin, expressed his concern in an *englyn* (cf. G.R. Gruffydd 1972: 21):

Pob gwlad aeth, o rad Un a Thri - a'u braint,	Each country went by the grace and priviledge of God,
I brintio mewn trefi;	To print in towns;
Nid anos, mewn daioni,	No more difficult, in goodness,
Fod yr un gwaith i'n hiaith ni.	Is this work for our language.

[20] One of them was William Davies who was executed as a martyr in 1593 (cf. M. Stephens 1997: 182, R.G. Gruffydd 1989: 45).

cf. also section 2.2.1.2.1.)[21] in Brecon (ibid.: 15ff.)[22] and the third about 1590.[23] As late as 1718, i.e. after a delay of 242 years, the first printing press was established in Wales (Isaac Carter in Atpar; cf. G.R. Gruffydd 1972: 5),[24] thereby reducing the chances for the country to develop its sciences in a similar progressive and lasting way as in England.

The lack of facilities in Wales and the differences in the development of both countries, however, were neither seen nor felt by officials and governing bodies, since Wales was part of England. Enlightened men, nevertheless, tried to get access to it (cf. the three attempts to establish the printing press illegally above) or found supporters in the English centres or abroad (cf. for instance Gruffydd Robert in section 2.2.1.2.1.), as for instance, from Welsh scholars teaching there, Welsh businessmen, etc. Other requirements were means of delivering the material and an economic basis to produce them.

To sum up: although the social pre-conditions for dictionary production, particularly the economic and juridical ones, were not ideal in Wales, a certain basis for a Welsh lexicographical tradition had evolved. Without going into too much detail, the major sources for Welsh dictionary production are briefly introduced in the following section in order to illustrate its linguistic basis in the time of the Renaissance.

---

[21] He was a physician and scholar who had graduated from Oxford and travelled the continent. He is also known as Dr John Davies of Brecon (Aberhonddu). With regard to his personal details, see G.R. Gruffydd (1972: 11-18). Despite being a Catholic, he nevertheless translated Protestant books and kept in contact with Protestant humanists (ibid.).

[22] It is neither known what was published nor the circumstances of the attempt nor its date.

[23] A certain William Hanmer is mentioned in this context. Whether he can be linked to the pro-Welsh family Hanmer (cf. below) in Fflint is not certain (cf. G.R. Gruffydd 1972: 20f.).

[24] In Switzerland it was introduced in 1466, in Italy in 1467, in France in 1470, in Spain in 1473, and in Brittany in 1484. The ban on provincial printing in Britain was removed in 1695 (Ch. Parry 1997: 268).

2.2.1.2. Linguistic sources
2.2.1.2.1. Grammars
(A) Bardic Grammars

The first Welsh bardic grammars[1] are distinctly mediaeval products, which present independent efforts to (a) describe peculiarities of Welsh linguistics and metrical systems for which there were no analogies in their Latin models, i.e. the popular Latin handbooks of Donatus and Priscian. The compilers of bardic grammars perhaps also tried to (b) introduce a number of general linguistic concepts and to exemplify these with reference to Welsh (cf. Poppe 1991: 104). While the grammars purport to be manuals of twelfth- and thirteenth century bardic usage,[2] supplemented by examples from an earlier period, they may (c) constitute an attempt to codify contemporary fourteenth century practice (cf. Matonis 1981: 144, C. Lewis 1995: 40). It has to be emphasised that the bard's training was still mainly oral. The 'grammars', therefore, might (d) have functioned as guidelines for testing the bard's mastership. Matonis, in summary, believes that

"There can be little doubt that the subject matter that most interested the compiler was Welsh poetry and not grammar per se (except insofar as a command of the syllables and diphthongs was essential in the composition of verse), and that the motivation behind the treatise was pedagogical" (Matonis 1991: 286f.).

Another significant aspect of the function of the bardic grammars is mentioned by C. Davies when saying:

"However unsuitable the classical structures of Donatus' *Artes* and Priscian's *Institutiones* were to meet the needs of Welsh poets, their work gave Welsh poetry the distinction of being one with medieval Latin culture" (C. Davies 1995: 40).

The presence of four extant fourteenth century corpora suggests that the grammars were widely circulated, copied, and therefore esteemed (cf. Matonis 1991: 286). They have to be put in the context of popular and influential teaching aids, such as the manuals of instructions, rhetorics, handbooks, and encyclopaedias.

"The grammars are throughout pedagogic, prescriptive, and proscriptive, so un-mistakably so that they look like primers and have, in fact, been taken for manuals of instruction" (Matonis 1990: 275; cf. C. Davies 1995: 40).

Although the framework and grammatical categories are borrowed from Latin grammars, the bardic compilations contained the earliest examples of a linguistic terminology in Welsh. The terminology was later cymricized ([sic], cf. Matonis 1990: 273) by substituting where possible Welsh terms for Latin loans employed in Middle Welsh texts.

Like the majority of grammars from the fourth century onwards, the Welsh ones included metrics as part of the grammatical *ars*. The explanations of Welsh metrics, however, seem to ex-

---

[1] It has to be stressed that there is no certainty with regard to the genealogical relationship of the different copies of grammatical texts (cf. Matonis 1991: 281ff.). Since a single original for all of them is rather unlikely, I will henceforth speak of grammars, i.e. suggesting the existence of grammatical compilations (cf. G.J. Williams & E.J. Jones 1934: xxiv).

[2] This, at least was their function in Ireland (cf. Ross 1996: 87).

ceed conventional proportions, as is also the case with the Irish bardic grammars,[3] in which the grammatical material can be so small that it constitutes less than one third of the corpus (cf. Ó Cuív 1973). In the four early Welsh grammars (for dates cf. below), the grammar section forms roughly a good third of the tract. The rest of the text is concerned with *metrica* (cf. Matonis 1981: 128).

> "The treatise as a whole represents an amalgam of three distinct traditions: the late Latin grammatical tradition, the native bardic tradition, and the ideological system of Roman Christianity. The grammar proper derives from a Latin model, which accounts for the peculiarities and shortcomings of the description of Welsh, the compiler's frequent presentation of language as a written system, and the linguistic terminology [...] It also contains interpolated material on the Welsh syllables and diphthongs in a discussion that not only departs from the Latin source but is on the whole a remarkably intelligent classification by a compiler alert to what he evidently regarded as inconsistencies between the written and spoken character of Welsh syllables. Native bardic tradition accounts for the discussion of the Welsh syllables and the larger account of the principles of bardic composition. In their different ways, both the *prydlyfr* [[4]] and the passage on *prydyddiaeth* [[5]] owe much to Roman Christian thought [...]" (Matonis 1990: 275).

Welsh grammars are handed down in different manuscripts (cf. G.J. Williams & E.J. Jones 1934: xiii-xvii, xlvii-lxi; Matonis 1981: 123), dating from the beginning of the fourteenth century (1382/1410, i.e. *Llyfr Coch Hergest* 'Red Book of Hergest' compiled by Hywel Fychan ap Hywel Goch o Fuellt)[6] up to 1832 when the last copy was produced (cf. Matonis 1990: 273). Altogether some seventy-eight grammars have been preserved. Most of them belong to the sixteenth and seventeenth centuries.

From the mid-fifteenth century, scribes and bards alike regarded these grammars as manuals of instruction (cf. Matonis 1981: 126). At this stage, the grammars reflected Early Modern Welsh, thus increasing their importance to what was now a broader audience.

Although much is disputed, e.g.

> "the dating and provenance of the manuscripts in which the grammars are located; the date and circumstances of the grammar's composition; the genealogical relationship of the early texts; and attribution [...;] questions of the grammar's bardic authority" (Matonis 1990: 275, cf. also Matonis 1981: 122ff.),

---

[3]   Bardic grammars are also known from Ireland (cf. Ó Cuív 1973). Irish bardic grammars reflect a sophisticated grasp of linguistic detail that was not drawn from Latin sources and is not apparent in the Welsh texts.

[4]   The explanation for *prydlyfr* in *Geiriadur Prifysgol Cymru* (R. J. Thomas et al. 1950-2002: 2918) reads as follows: section of traditional Welsh bardic grammar (esp. one setting out the principles of eulogistic poetry), ?book of poetry [sic].

[5]   The definition for *prydyddiaeth* in *Geiriadur Prifysgol Cymru* (ibid.: 2918) reads as follows: poetry, poem; profession and function of a 'prydydd', the highest of the three branches of traditional Welsh poetry.

[6]   No further details were available to me with regard to this person.

the earliest extant grammars[7] are commonly attributed to Einion Offeiriad, Einion the Priest (ca. 1330),[8] kept in MS Peniarth 20 and dated to before 1350[9] and to Dafydd Ddu o Hiraddug, Dafydd the Swarthy (ca. 1330-80)[10] dated to before 1330 (cf. M. Stephens 1997: 158f.).[11] In the middle of the fifteenth century, at the Carmarthen *Eisteddfod*[12] of about 1451 (cf. M. Stephens 1997: 76), another version was launched, introduced by the *Pencerdd* Dafydd ab Edmwnd (1450-97),[13] but prepared by his pupil Gutun Owain (1450-98).[14] The works of Gutun Owain and the *Pencerdd* 'chief bard' Simwnt Fychan (cf. section 2.2.1.1.) mark the climax of this grammar tradition. The grammar of the latter *Y Pum Llyfr Kerddwriaeth* 'The Five Books of Poetic Art', published around 1575, is one of the fullest and most interesting reference books, which also drew from additional or different sources (cf. Matonis 1981: 122). With regard to its content Matonis (1990) notes that it

> "increases the parts of speech to eight, expands the triads with additional bardic material, and "updates" the medieval texts to a Renaissance standard by adding commentary that pointedly draws the Welsh grammar into the tradition of classical and late medieval grammatical and rhetorical study" (Matonis 1990: 273).

It is believed that Simwnt's teacher Gruffudd Hiraethog (cf. section 2.2.1.1.) and W. Salesbury (cf. sections 2.2.1.1., 2.2.1.2.2., 2.2.1.2.3., and 2.2.2.) helped with some sections, the former with mutations and the latter with syntax. An interesting facet of the book, however, is that it illustrates some of the elements of the instruction given by the master-poets to their pupils in the bardic schools (cf. Gruffydd Robert's complaint below).

The Middle Welsh and Early Modern Welsh bardic grammars are similar with regard to their contents, their organisation and style (cf. G.J. Williams & E.J. Jones 1934: xxix-xlii, lxi-lxxxviii, Matonis 1990: 273-5). They consist of discrete essays dealing with individual subjects. They can also contain a glossary (cf. early classical lexicography in section 2.1.1., Ælfric's grammar and glossary and the work of Gwilym Tew in section 2.1.4.). An outline of the organisation of the grammars reads as follows:

---

[7] For problems of dating the grammars or identifying their authors, see G.J. Williams & E.J. Jones (1934: xvii-xxix).

[8] He was a clerk and perhaps bard and compiled the bardic grammar at the request of his sponsor Rhys ap Gruffudd (there are no further details with regard to the latter).

[9] For problems of dating the whole or parts of the grammar, see Matonis (1990: 276ff.).

[10] Hiraddug was a bard, scholar, and translator (cf. G.J. Williams & E.J. Jones 1934: xviiif.). He translated the Dominican *Officium Parvum Beatae Marie Virginis* under the title *Gwassanaeth Meir* into Middle Welsh (cf. B.F. Roberts 1961). It is the earliest Welsh version of psalms and liturgical prayers written in verse, thus being an early example of free composition (B.F. Roberts ibid., see also above). It was one of the most popular services.

[11] For a detailed discussion on the possible authorship of the bardic grammars, see Matonis (1990: 283-286).

[12] The *Eisteddfod* is originally a bardic competition. The first recorded *Eisteddfod* was held in Aberteifi/Cardigan in 1176. For further information, see H.T. Edwards (1976).

[13] He was a noble and bard from the Hanmer family, which had foreign antecedents and settled in Wales as officials of Edward I and later supported Owain Glyndŵr (cf. M. Stephens 1997: 155).

[14] Owain was a noble, bard, genealogist, and also a copyist of astronomical, medical and religious texts (cf. M. Stephens 1997: 296).

"The grammatical tract divides into two major units: (a) the grammar proper, or *ars grammatica*, which is thoroughly normative and based on a Latin model; and (b) a far larger unit on *cerdd dafod*, based on native bardic tradition. The *cerdd dafod* (or *ars versificatoria* [i.e., the poetic art[15]...]) comprises several subsections: an *ars metrica* on Welsh meter; the metrical faults to be avoided; a *prydlyfr*; a brief passage on *prydyddiaeth* (found in Peniarth 20 and Llanstephan 3 but lacking in Llyfr Coch Hergest); and the *trioedd cerdd* [the manner in which to praise each thing: that which pertains to poetry]" (Matonis 1990: 275).

The grammatical tracts reflect the major linguistic categories perceived by mediaeval grammarians, that is, *orthographia, etymologia,* and *oratio.* Although the grammar part is mainly based on Latin models, the discussion of the alphabet indicates a bardic context (cf. Matonis 1981: 131). The extensive and distinctive treatment of the Welsh syllable constitutes a notable contribution to early vernacular grammatical descriptions (cf. ibid.: 133) and goes beyond Ælfric's Grammar.[16] The parts on bardic principles almost certainly represent an older, native tradition of bardic usage.

Taken as a whole, the Welsh bardic grammars can briefly be characterised as follows:

"Like Ælfric's grammar, the Welsh grammars derive from Latin sources and are equally pedagogic in purpose; unlike Ælfric's, they attempt principally to tutor the student in the grammatical principles of his own language [...They are] normative, descriptive, pedagogical treatises firmly rooted in the tradition of the Latin grammars [...] They are attempts at a systematic disciplining of complex grammatical and poetic materials, the former almost entirely dependent on Latin sources [and largely deviant from the actual linguistic system of Welsh], the latter a curious amalgam of older bardic usage and the compiler's sometimes eccentric perception of contemporary bardic practice." (Matonis 1981: 121, 124, 145).

---

[15] *Cerdd Dafod* are official - i.e. accepted at the *Eisteddfodau* - linguistic metrical and philosophical principles of the bards' craft. The question arises as to whether there is any connection between the twenty-four metres in *Cerdd Dafod*, the twenty-four letters of the alphabet in the bardic grammars, the twenty-four officials at the court in the law of Hywel Dda (cf. D. Jenkins 1970), the twenty-four knights of Arthur's court (cf. Bromwich 1978), the twenty-four knights of Osla (cf. the tale of *Breuddwyd Rhonabwy*), the twenty-four wonders of Britain, the twenty-four strongest kings (cf. M. Stephens 1997: 575f.), and the twenty-four sons of *Llywarch Hen* (cf. I. Williams 1955).

Does the numbering have anything to do with manuscript tradition and alignment whilst copying and collecting? The twenty-four letters, for instance, neither properly reflect Welsh orthography nor Welsh pronunciation (cf. Matonis 1981: 129). The metres were officially introduced at the beginning of the fourteenth century (cf. dating of grammars in Matonis 1981, 1990: 273, 276ff.). In addition, there are no versions of the laws earlier than the thirteenth century.

Or does the number twenty-four refer to post-Norman structures in mediaeval Welsh society? In the agreement of Woodstock (1247) between King Henry III and Owain and Llywelyn ap Gruffudd, the Welsh have to pay twenty-four horsemen to the King (J. Davies 1990: 139) and in 1198 Hywel Sais "son of Rhys, late prince of South Wales, confirms to Llanfihangel Abercywyn, and its chaplain, the grant made by Hywel ab Iduard of twenty-four acres of arable land [...]" (Maund 1996: 8).

[16] For details with regard to Ælfric, see section 2.1.4. It has to be stressed, however, that the intention of his grammar was different. He wrote the book in order to describe Latin and provided English forms alongside it primarily to illustrate the Latin system.

Apart from presenting linguistic and literary material, the bardic grammars also yield a picture of literary tradition resisting cultural threat. Their later compilers might have been antiquarians sensitive to the very real threat to Welsh bardic tradition and keen to see it surviving as part of Welsh culture and learning. They might have attempted to make the traditional learning fit for survival under the conditions of a new period in human society, i.e. the Renaissance.

A brief outline of major problems facing Welsh bardic learning institutionalised in the *Bardic Order* in the sixteenth and seventeeth centuries, however, proves this attempt to be a difficult task: the climax of the *Bardic Order* was in the fifteenth and sixteenth centuries, in particular from 1435 to 1535 (cf. J.E. Caerwyn Williams 1983: 13, S. Lewis 1932, vol I.). This period of time was characterised by a decline in Welsh society (cf. section 2.2.1.1.). Troublesome social periods, however, often produce the best pieces of literature reflecting conflicts and changes in society.[17]

Although the decline of the monasteries had caused difficulties for bards closely associated with them, the *Wars of the Roses* offered a new stage to perfom in the traditional bardic way, that is, to praise and promote nobles engaged in the struggle, to support them in the name of the coming liberation, to underline their national task, and to praise and to develop the language as a unifying and identifying symbol.

With the reign of the Tudor descendant Henry VII (1485-1509, crowned by the King of Man), these tasks seemed to have been achieved. With the accession to the throne of Henry VIII (1509-1553) and the Dissolution of the monasteries, the number of possible asylums or places of employment or education for bards was drastically reduced. The call for national identity be-came silent after the *Acts of Union* and was now, if necessary, formulated by humanists for the new state. The need to promote wars for Wales no longer existed and the propaganda for the new state was taken over by its officials. Genealogies were not as important as in pre-Tudor and mediaeval times, since social advancement was now merely based on fortunes made in the professions or in industry. If they became necessary, genealogies were written by trained scholars, that is, new specialised professions took over these formerly bardic tasks. Eulogistic poetry was criticised, since literature was now to be mainly religious and moral in purpose (cf. C.W. Lewis 1997: 41). The language could be more comprehensively and systematically de-veloped by scholars, and education was now provided by the first educational system. The enter-tainment of the bards might still have pleased Welshmen firmly anchored in tradition. On the whole, however, the search for new spiritual challenge gave preference to new forms of literature from abroad (cf. Welsh authors competing in Ciceronian literature), promoted also by increasing mobility and subsequent individualism. The introduction of the printing press demonstrated to the wealthy, educated class that literature could be produced and disseminated more easily than by keeping a bard in the home.

Facing a lack of interest in their services, bards could only survive as long as some of the re-presentatives of the old classes continued in society. This was the case after the *Wars of the*

---

[17] See also poetry satirising the church of the time or the literature of Athens during the Peloponne-sian War 431-04 BC.

Roses in the wake of which a number of Welsh families joined the new rising gentry, especially those who headed for London. This gentry, however, suffered decline during the Dissolution of the monasteries and the Reformation. The remaining or newly developing gentry in turn, suffered decline during the *Civil Wars* (1642-48), adding severely to the fatal wasting away of the *Bardic Order* witnessed particularly in the years following the *Civil Wars* (cf. C.W. Lewis 1997: 49ff.). New acceptance among the higher classes was bound to fail, since the bards were the representatives not only of an old social system, but also of a language and literature with low prestige (cf. above) now being merely connected and restricted to the people of a remote part of Britain. In addition,

> "It is extremely doubtful whether there existed in Wales at this time a sufficiently large audience of patrons prepared to reward the bards in the time-honoured manner of poems composed on themes advocated by the humanists [...] Furthermore, the new-style poetry favoured by the humanists would have had to be published in books, not disseminated by means of manuscripts, or by declamation in the mansions[18] of the gentry, and it is extremely doubtful, bearing in mind the comparatively poor economic state of the country at this time, whether there were enough enlightened patrons in Wales, or whether it contained a sufficiently large and adequately literate book-buying public, to support this new type of verse. [...]
> Renaissance culture and patronage [...] was unmistakably courtly, aristocratic, and urban, whereas Welsh society in the sixteenth and seventeenth centuries was predominantly agricultural, pastoral and kin-based, and was unable, as a result, to create a sufficient number of literate patrons interested in books [...] Nor was there an independent Welsh state [nor a university] to support a thriving indigenous humanist culture" (C.W. Lewis 1997: 47f.)

into which the bards might have developed. Some individual bards, however, found a place in the new environment, those who belonged to the rising classes themselves, e.g. Siôn Tudur (before 1522-1602)[19] and Edmwnd Prys (1543/44-1632),[20] or those who succeeded in co-operating with members of the new classes, above all with humanists, such as Gruffudd Hiraethog (cf. above and sections 2.2.1.1. and 2.2.1.2.2.). Others continued under new conditions of production as scholars or clerics or in other professions serving the concepts of the new time and, at least partly, new audiences and themes. They may have kept a special interest in Welsh poetry and history or practised "the composition of poetry as a pleasantly diverting cultural hobby" (ibid.: 57).

---

[18] "Even contemporary developments in domestic architecture proved to be inimical to the continuance of some long-established bardic practises. For example, it had long been the custom for *awdlau* and *cywyddau* to be ceremoniously declaimed at the high-table, before the family, in the hall of the mansion, but during the sixteenth century first-floor hall and hall-house became obsolete" (C.W. Davies 1997: 52).

[19] He was one of the last *beirdd yr uchelwyr* 'bards of the nobles', yeoman and sponsor of bards (cf. M. Stephens 1997: 672).

[20] He was a bard and humanist. Together with William Morgan (cf. section 2.2.1.2.3.), Prys studied at Cambridge university where he later became a preacher. He learnt eight languages including Hebrew and was a distinguished bard. Prys was an outstanding figure among the bards in that he composed in strict and free metres and was very close to the ideas of the humanists. He became particularly famous for his dispute with the bard Wiliam Cynwal (cf. section 2.2.1.2.2.), but also with other bards (cf. M. Stephens 1997: 605).

As a feudal institution, however, the *Bardic Order* could not survive under the new social conditions, and the late seventeenth century saw its final deplacement. Its decline, which increased according to the gradual establishment of the new society with its new demands in philosophy, learning, educational, cultural and religious activities and new techniques, was therefore not a personal failure by its individual members but part of the general social changes taking place.

> "Indeed, it has been suggested that the humanists, rather than arresting the steep decline of professional poetry in their days, as they genuinely attempted to do, may have unwittingly accelerated by means of their criticism, however constructive and well intentioned those were, that process of artistic degeneration and, as a natural corollary, may have involuntarily precipitated the eventual extinction of the Welsh Bardic Order" (ibid.: 48).

As in any fundamental social change, it became impossible for major institutions of the fading type of society, such as the *Bardic Order*, to continue in the new society as before, since the structures formerly constituing the feudal system had been broken away. Nevertheless, the bards left behind a rich heritage without which the *New Learning* would not have succeeded in the way it did. In part, the bards passed it on themselves, but to a considerable extent it was taken up by the scholars. The passing on of knowledge was the only process where individual commitment or failure could really have any import.

Just as the Welsh elite had been replaced by Normans in the eleventh century enforcing feudal development in Wales with new dominating classes, so the Welsh elite was edged out or assimilated by the English introducing capitalist development with new dominant classes. The spiritual ideals of the Renaissance and the involvement of self-confident native Welsh in the social changes diminished the extent of possible Welsh cultural replacements considerably and allowed the Welsh scholarly heritage to survive as described.

To return to the linguistic material produced by the Welsh bardic learning: the corpora of the bardic grammars, nevertheless, contain essential linguistic material, such as the word class division, which is fundamental to compiling the lexicon of a language systematically in a dictionary. They did, however, also provide material for humanist grammatical writing as can be seen in the next section.

(B)   Grammars of the Humanists

Without going into too much detail, some reference is briefly made to grammatical writing which developed during the Renaissance, that is, somewhat later than the bardic grammars, namely, the humanist grammatical writing comprising grammars, treatises and short manuals.

Disregarding the decreasing prestige of the Welsh language (cf. section 2.2.1.1. and above), some of the humanists sought to safeguard the venerable language by codifying and describing it. One of them was the scholar Gruffydd Robert (cf. section 2.2.1.1.). He published *Dosparth Byrr Ar Y Rhann Gyntaf i Ramadeg Cymraeg* 'A short lesson on the first part of Welsh grammar' in 1567, the final parts of which were probably composed some time after 1584 (cf. G.J. Williams 1939: lv, C. Davies 1995: 70).

The complementary function of the humanists' linguistic works to the bards' grammars is clearly expressed in the following passage from the preface of his book:

> "Yr ydoedd y beirdd rhyd cymru yn ceissio fynghadw rhag colli ne gymyscu a'r saesneg. Ond nid oedd genthynt phordd yn y byd, nag i ddangos yn fyrr, ag yn hyphordd yr odidowgrwydd sydd ynof rhagor nog mewn llawer o ieithoedd, na chwaith i fanegi rhessom am fagod o ddirgelion a gaid i gweled, ond chwilio yn fanwl amdanynt, mal y mae gramadegwyr da yn gwneuthur pawb yn i iaith ihun" (G.H. Hughes 1976: 46).
> 'The bards all over Wales tried to restrain me from getting lost in mixing with English. But they had no way in the world to show briefly and conveniently the magnificence which is it [²¹ the language] beyond other languages, neither did they express a reason for a heap of mysteries, which one would manage to see, were one only to look carefully for them, as good grammarians do each in their own language.'

Since the bards did not teach their craft to ordinary people and Gruffydd Robert, for instance, had no means to study Welsh manuscripts abroad, he complained in his grammar that the traditional poets

> "'kept their art secret, without revealing it unto any, save to some disciple who shall swear that he will not teach it to any other, or to an occasional gentleman who will promise on his honour to keep it secret',[²²] and therefore, he maintained, 'some man else must assume knowledge [of it] and set forth, if it be desired to spread it over the face of the country and to impart it to all who should so desire'" (C.W. Lewis 1997: 39).

It is certainly this context which promotes his readiness to admit Italian metres, as well as the Welsh free or accentual metres, into the compositions of the bards. He, however, also wished to see Welsh poetry in the classcial tradition, which could only have been achieved by using free metres and by giving content precedence over form (cf. Jarvis 1997: 146f.). In the same way, Roberts was concerned to develop Welsh prose writing

> "to enable his native tongue to take its rightful place among those languages capable of dealing with any literary demands made upon them in the new world of Renaissance culture. Such had been Bembo's concern, with regard to the Italian dialects, in his *Prose della volga lingua* (1525) [...]

---

²¹   The author wrote *ynof,* which means 'in me', but it makes little sense in this context.
²²   The major problem was, however, that bardic instruction was traditionally mainly oral rather than secret (cf. G.J. Williams 1930: 30f.). Nevertheless, they guarded their craft and considered it superior (cf. Jarvis 1997: 146 and N. Lloyd 1997: 101).

Of all the Welsh humanist grammarians, [Robert] is the one who is most concerned with prose writing, and within his treatment of the *Questione della lingua* he sees the practice of translation as vital for the process of extending the capabilities of a language to meet all needs" (C. Davies 1995: 71f.).

Robert's grammar is written in Welsh. It contains syntax, morphology and measures of Welsh literature.

"The elevation of a language to the level envisaged by Gruffydd Robert meant patterning its style and rhythms upon the classical masters, but doing so in a manner consistent with that language's own character and native genius" (ibid.: 72).

Although using the terminology of bardic grammars, his work is different from both the early bardic grammars and from those composed in Latin by later humanists (cf. below), in that Robert followed Bembo by couching the discussion of grammar in the form of a dialogue.

"The dialogue form also had a long classical pedigree, used especially for philosophical discussion by both Plato and Cicero. The stylistic advantages of Plato's kind of dialogue, in terms both of clarity and comprehensiveness, are appreciated at the start of the second part of the Grammar" (ibid.: 71).

As a result, Robert's work is not only a grammar as such, but a masterpiece of prose literature, which is by some regarded as the beginning of Modern Welsh prose and

"the work through which - more than any other - the Ciceronianism of Italy came to exert a direct and creative influence on Welsh prose" (ibid.: 74).

Nevertheless, in contrast to other grammars (cf. above and below), Robert's reference book is based on the analysis and observation of the living tongue:

"He aims at the general reader, or rather, the reader with an amateur's interest in reading and writing Welsh, not at the scholar, and he therefore writes in Welsh" (Jarvis 1997 147).

Another grammarian was Siôn Dafydd Rhys (cf. 2.2.1.). He was the most versatile of the Welsh humanists, who travelled to Italy where he became a doctor of medicine.

"He also made a distinctive contribution to classcial teaching. Three books came from his pen during his stay in Italy: a Latin work - now sadly lost - on Greek grammar and syntax, *Della costruttione latina*; and a guide, in Latin, to the pronunciation of Italian; *Perutilis Exteris Nationibus De Italica Pronunciatione et Orthographia Libellus* (1569)" (ibid.: 76).

The guide to the pronunciation of Italian was the only book of its kind in sixteenth century Italy and reflects Rhys' linguistic mastership.

However, the most important of the scholarly works that he produced was *Cambro-brytannicae Cymraecaeve Linguae Institutiones et Rudimenta* 'Rudiments and rules of the Welsh language'. This book, comprising 328 pages and including a grammar of the Welsh language as well as an extensive discussion on poetic art, was written in Latin, thereby introducing Welsh to an international audience (cf. ibid.: 78). With regard to the explanations on *cerdd dafod*, he followed the bardic grammars quite strictly (cf. below), thereby reflecting his respect for bardic learning.

In 1593 Thomas Salesbury, printed the grammar *Grammatica Britannica* 'A British grammar' (Alston 1969a) written by Henry Salesbury (1561-1637?),[23] who was also a lexicographer (cf. below, cf. J.E. Caerwyn Williams 1983: 50f. and section 2.2.2.). His book is the third Welsh grammar in chronological order (cf. above). In contrast to Robert and Rhys's, however,

> "Salesbury appears to have had no direct contact with Italian linguistic theory. All three grammars fall within the 'experimental period' of Welsh grammaticography which can be said to have come to an end with John Davies's *Antiquae linguae Britannicae* [cf. below]. Robert, Rhys, and Salesbury still tried to discover an appropriate descriptive framework for an adequate grammaticographical treatment of the Welsh language" (Poppe 1997: 35).

Poppe (ibid.) shows that H. Salesbury followed the *Grammatica* of the French Petrus Ramus (1515-1572) to a significant extent in approach and many details of classification and definition. Although H. Salesbury includes rules of both Welsh grammar and verse, his explanations of Welsh poetic forms are not extensive (cf. ibid.: 48).

The climax and end of the humanist grammar tradition was marked by the book *Antiquæ Linguæ Britannicæ ... Rudimenta* 'The old British language ... Rudiments' (Alston 1968a), published in 1621 by Dr John Davies, Mallwyd (1567-1644).[24] Written in Latin, it was a work for scholars. Davies

> "wrote it at the end of an era. For eighty years, the Welsh language had been the object of study, analysis and steady enrichment by a body of humanist scholars whose devotion to it was remarkable and whose great efforts, variable in quality though they may have been, had laid some of the groundwork for John Davies" (Jarvis 1997: 148).

Indeed, it remained the most comprehensive work until the early twentieth century (cf. ibid.: 147) providing the Welsh language with a basis for scientific studies. His grammar still includes rules for both grammar and the poetic arts.

Davies' work was to a great extent based on the study of manuscript sources, since, at his time, there were no printed collections of Welsh prose or poetry available. It is significant, however,

> "that it was the manuscripts of poetry which received by far the greater part of his attention. His analysis of the Welsh language is firmly based on the traditional usages of the professional poets, who [...] were considered the guardians of the highest linguistic standards" (ibid.: 149).

His approach is confirmed in the preface to his book, which is written in the form of a dedication to his fellow humanist, churchman, and bard Edmwnd Prys (cf. before). Consequently, Davies' grammar became

---

23 Both belong to the Salesbury family which produced famous scholars and poets (cf. M. Stephens 1997: 657f.). Henry graduated from Oxford in 1584 and afterwards practised medicine in Denbighshire (Poppe 1997: 44, J.E. Caerwyn Williams 1983: 23). Thomas was a London-Welsh stationer who also printed translations of the Pslams of W. Midleton (cf. below, Ch. Parry 1997: 272). There are, however, no details about his date of birth or death.

24 He graduated from Oxford, and was rector, prebendary, scholar, humanist, philosopher, translator, and a collector and copyist of Welsh manuscripts (cf. M. Stephens 1997: 175).

"a very important link in the chain of conservative linguistic usage which stretches from the later Middle Ages to the earlier part of the twentieth century" (ibid.: 149).

Apart from the major grammar books mentioned above, there are a number of further grammars which remain in manuscript form, such as works by Roger Morris (1580-1607)[25] and Tomos Prys (before 1564-1634;[26] cf. G.J. Williams 1930: 31, Jarvis 1997: 40). There are, however, also treatises on grammar and short manuals which, for instance, formed - at least in part - a basis on which John Davies could draw (cf. above). One short manual *Bardhoniaeth, neu brydydhiaeth, y llyfr kyntaf* 'Poetry or poetry, the first book' (cf. G.J. Williams 1930) was written by Wiliam Midleton (1550-1600).[27] Published in 1593, his work was certainly inspired by his friend Siôn Dafydd Rhys whom he helped with his grammar (ibid.: 32, 34). The two books are, however, different in purpose. Whereas Rhys' work contained rules of both grammar and verse explained to the scholar, Midleton's manual aimed at a broad humanist audience, i.e. the cultured gentleman, courtier, or clergyman, rather than at the scholar and poet, imparting a knowledge of the bardic craft to his fellow-countrymen (ibid.: 33f.). Even the method of illustrating *cerdd dafod* differs in the two publications: whereas Rhys strictly follows the bardic grammars, Midleton presents his own explications of Welsh strict metres (cf. pp. 1-21 of Midleton's book in G.J. Williams 1930).

To conclude this section, two other humanists need to be mentioned: Henri Perri (also Parry, 1560/61-1617)[28] wrote *Egluryn Phraethineb sebh Dosparth ar Retoreg* 'An explanation on eloquence, that is, a lesson on rhetoric' in 1595. His book was based on the *Llyfr Rhetoreg* (1552) by William Salesbury (cf. sections 2.2.1.1., 2.2.1.2.2., 2.2.1.2.3., and 2.2.2.) but was more detailed and included more examples from the bard's craft. Both, however, remained in manuscript form.

---

[25]   He was a copyist of Welsh manuscripts (cf. sections 2.2.1.2.1., 2.2.1.2.2., and 2.2.2.).
[26]   He was a bard, soldier and pirate (cf. M. Stephens 1997: 606f.).
[27]   The bards called him Wiliam Miltwn and he referred to himself as Gwilym Canoldref. Midleton was a bard, pirate, and translator, familiar with different languages, and a relative of the prosperous Myddleton family (cf. G.J. Williams 1930).
[28]   He was a cleric and scholar.

2.2.1.2.2. Vocabularies
(A) Bardic vocabularies

As was seen with the bardic grammars, the bards' works were generally important for the evolution of dictionaries. As part of their profession bards also produced early genuine lexicographical material such as vocabularies.

One vocabulary, for instance, has been handed down from Gruffudd Hiraethog (cf. above) with additions from some of his pupils, e.g. Wiliam Cynwal († 1587/88, cf. J.E. Caerwyn Williams 1983: 15),[1] and Wiliam Llŷn (1534/35-80; cf. section 2.2.2. and R. Stephens 1983: 310ff.).[2] Both of them are also known as copyists of bardic grammars (cf. G.J. Williams & E.J. Jones 1934: xxii, xxvi).

Hiraethog's vocabulary dates from about 1560, i.e. it was written after the publication of the first dictionary by William Salesbury (cf. sections 2.2.1.1., 2.2.1.2.1., 2.2.1.2.3., and 2.2.2.). It is part of his considerable lexicographical compilation (MS Peniarth 230), which includes a list of personal names, toponyms of towns, villages, rivers, and other places, a list of verbs, in which explanations of some of their forms are given, some conjunctions and particles, and groups of synonyms. They precede the actual vocabulary, which is sometimes also called an early monolingual dictionary (cf. M. Stephens 1997: 292).

The synonyms are grouped thematically under the following headings:

Henwau arglwydd 'names of the lord', *Henwau brwydr* 'names of battle', *Henwau gwayw* 'names of pain', *Henwau arfau am wr* 'names of weapons of the man', *Henwau baner* 'names of the banner', *Henwau pob/pethau teg* 'names of every/all nice things', *Henwau llaw* 'names of the hand', *Henwau estron Genedl* 'names of foreign races', *Henwau gwledd* 'names of the feast', *Henwau gweiniaid* 'names of sheaths', *Henwau kynhebic* 'names of paromœon', *Henwau kler* 'names of the (wandering) bard'.

Lexical items given for *arglwydd* 'lord' are, for instance, the following: *riawdr, dovydd, peryf, perd, grif, mvner, modur, por, ior, ion, perging, peir, pyr.*

From the actual vocabulary, the following examples are faithfully extrated in order to illustrate its macrostructure. The reading must remain tentative, however, since his handwriting is complicated to read and the manuscript badly damaged and not yet edited:[3]

---

[1] He graduated from the *Eisteddfod* in 1567. Cynwal was a copyist of manuscripts including genealogies, heraldic material, bardic grammar and bruts. He was a wandering bard and is famous for his debate with Edmwnd Prys (for further details, see G.A. Williams 1986 C.W. Lewis 1997: 41ff. and section 2.2.1.2.1.).

[2] Llŷn was qualified in the *Eisteddfod* and, therefore, a bardic teacher, one of the last generation of *Penceirdd* 'chief bards'. In addition, he was a collector of lineages and heraldic material. This bard was not only a bardic pupil of Gruffudd Hiraethog, but also became a copyist of vocabularies and, maybe, of a grammar, too. His and Hiraethog's vocabulary established important material for the first dictionaries (cf. below, J.E. Caerwyn Williams 1983: 18f.). Thomas Wiliems copied the vocabulary of Llŷn - maybe over some years - and separately added words corrected by W. Salesbury (cf. section 2.2.2.).

[3] This seems to be the reason, why some of the words of his vocabulary do not occur in the Welsh historical dictionary *Geiriadur Prifysgol Cymru*, e.g. bwrgin.

Abid		abadwisc	wynebvs yn i abid
			Tvdvr aled
			irr abad sion
Aban	—	Ryvel	aban addaw bevnydd yn
			in bro ni a bair newyn
			Joch medd hen wr imi[4]
abar	—	bvdreð	
aban	—	anvndeb	y yer ... y... ...
abo	—	ysgrwd bvrgvn	abo ...yd bri... bwyd yb...[5]
			ai ddy... ...ewyb man
abwy	—	bwrgin	gwern abwy lle wedi ...gio
abrwysgl	—	amrosgo[6]	
ac ameinau henw gobr			yr gw... ...ameinau aedd ... ...[7]
aytwn,			
ac gwn	—	lluric	
achlan	—	ygyd	g... y... G... ... ...
			...
achre	—	gwisc[8]	bur...d arf... braw dyrfyn[9]
			Deio ... ... du.
adaf	—	llaw	adaf ... ... de... ...
			gan ... ...d

The headwords of the vocabulary are not assembled under a particular heading, but are listed in 'second-letter order'. Hiraethog's alphabetic order, however, differs slightly from the one known today. Whereas his vocabulary follows the order *a b ch d*,[10] the common order today is *a b c ch*. The headwords are all explained by a synonym, and then put in context. The context is formed by poetry and proverbs in order to demonstrate the potential usage of most of the lexical items.

Hiraethog's lexicographical work, taken as a whole, comprises difficult lexical items including those from other periods of time, as for instance, expressions from the *Beirdd y Tywysogion* 'the bards of the princes' and the *Beirdd yr Uchelwyr* 'the bards of the nobles' (cf. J.E. Caerwyn Williams 1983: 16, 41).

---

4   The first part of the couplet was written in black ink and the second in red ink and by another hand. The third line was again written with black ink and in the hand of the first line of the couplet. It is quite likely that the hand in red ink is that of Wiliam Llŷn (cf. R. Stephens 1983: 309f.).

5   This line forms a *cynghanedd*. *Cynghanedd* is a metre which is formed by an intricate system of alliteration, sound chiming and internal rhyme. In this example the sequence of consonants is as follows:
b-d-b -- b-d-b. I could, however, not clearly identify the vowels.

6   'amrosgo' is not a synonym, but the Latin word for *anferth, abrwysgo* 'huge, dreadful'. Either, Hiraethog gave the Latin word, since he could not think of an adequate Welsh synonym or the Latin word itself was accepted as a synonym in the language of the bards.

7   A phrase is interpolated here both on the side of the headword list and that of the context.

8   This word is actually crossed out, but also underlined, and has another word on its top.

9   This line also forms a *cynghanedd*.

10   This order still predominates in modern Breton dictionaries.

With his thematic collection of parts of the Welsh lexicon, his monolingual vocabulary, and his lists of verbs, partly inflected, and toponyms Hiraethog provided a firm basis for further Welsh lexicography. As a representative of the *Bardic Order*, he proved that the scholarship of this institution had reached a high standard (cf. also section 2.2.1.2.1.) and might have taken on dictionary production in a similar way to Ireland (cf. Irish dictionary production in sections 2.2.3. and 3.2.4.), if social changes had not been brought about from the outside (cf. section 2.2.1.1.).

A list of Hiraethog's proverbs was apparently published prior to the appearance of his comprehensive lexicographical compilation. W. Salesbury included them in his book *Oll Synnwyr Pen Kembero Ygyd* 'The Whole Wisdom of a Welshman's Head' (G. Williams 1997a: 211, B.R. Jones 1994: 18f.), published in 1547. The proverbs were again incorporated into the *Dictionarium Duplex* by Dr John Davies, Mallwyd produced in 1632 (cf. section 2.2.1.2.1., 2.2.1.2.3., and 2.2.2.).

Similar lists of synonyms to those preceding Hiraethog's vocabulary can be found in manuscripts written by Sir Huw Pennant (1465-1514),[11] who lived before Hiraethog, and in those copied by Simwnt Fychan (cf. sections 2.2.1.1. and 2.2.1.2.1.).

Vocabularies were also written by Wiliam Llŷn between 1567 and 74 (cf. above and J.E. Caerwyn Williams 1983: 18f.). R. Stephens (1983: 308-319) gave a survey of manuscript parts which might be attributed to Wiliam Llŷn. Unfortunately, certainty of authorship cannot be provided before more research is carried out (cf. ibid.: 313). The fact that becomes evident from the survey, however, is a close co-operation between different individuals.

From the vocabulary in manuscript C 82, which is, for instance, attributed to Wiliam Llŷn, a list of fifty-nine[12] quotations from the bard Dafydd ap Gwilym (1315/20-1350/70)[13] was compiled by R. Stephens (ibid.: 316ff.), some of which are given as an example here:

---

[11] He was a bard and translator of the Latin *Vitae Santes Ursula* into Welsh (cf. M. Stephens 1997: 351).

[12] The quotations are counted according to the number of headwords. Some of them occur more than once, as is seen in the first two examples.

[13] Dafydd ap Gwilym is the most famous bard of mediaeval Wales. He introduced linguistic, metrical and other changes into Welsh literature. For further details with regard to his person and work, see Loomis (1982) and T. Parry (1979).

alaf	golud	alaf ar waessaf wiwsail
		aelaw fv oi hoywlaw hail
aelaw	kyvoeth	alaf ar waessaf wiwsail
		aelaw fv oi hoywlaw hail
amaeth	arddwr	myfi vy hvn ffrwythlvn ffraeth
		o vodd ym a vydd amaeth
amws	ystalwyn	pel oer drom paladr amws
		prennol wrth drossol y drws
anterth	borav	ymddangos Erof kof kerth
		yn nenntyrch wybr yn anterth

Further vocabularies and other lexicographical works were compiled by unknown authors, both bards and humanists (cf. J.E. Caerwyn Williams 1988: 103), thereby forming a firm early basis for Welsh lexicography. Some works of known humanists are discussed in the following section.

(B)   Vocabularies of the Humanists

Before the continuous production of dictionaries from the seventeenth century onwards, more vocabularies and other lexicographical works were produced by some humanists. One of these humanists was William Salesbury (cf. sections 2.2.1.1., 2.2.1.2.1., 2.2.1.2.3., and 2.2.2.) who had his dictionary published in 1547 (cf. section 2.2.2.). Between 1568 and 1574, he worked on a medical herbal compendium *Llysieulyfr* 'Herbal Book'.[1] This work is not listed under dictionaries, since it is rather a scientific compendium (cf. *Allbuchlexikographie* in section 1.3.1.), almost a guide for physicians. Because of its importance to the Welsh lexicon, however, it is briefly mentioned here.

For the compilation of this work, W. Salesbury drew from contemporary scientific material presenting special subjects.[2] Apart from Welsh entries, it comprises mostly Latin, English and Greek equivalents of the names of plants, and occasionally some in French, German or Italian.[3] The descriptions included in his *Llysieulyfr* display the following categories (cf. Edgar 1997):
-   *Y rhywiæ* 'the existing species',
-   *Y phuryf* 'the appearence',
-   *Y lle y tyfant* 'the locations where the herbs grow',
-   *Yr amser* 'the time of growing',
-   *Gradd yr artempr* 'conditions of growing',
-   *Y rhinweddæ* 'qualities of the plants'.

The specialist lexical items W. Salesbury presents in his book are established by loanwords, loan translations, mainly from Latin, Greek, and English, and new inventions, thus enlarging the Welsh lexicon (cf. ibid.: xxix for examples). Assembled systematically and according to his own scientific and linguistic concepts, the lexicon compiled by him influenced other lexicographical works (ibid.: x, xxxii).

A new quality of reference books was achieved by the critical description of some herbs W. Salesbury added to the translation of their denotation (ibid.: xxviif.). His herbal book, therefore, marks an important step in botanical and medical lexicography. It reflects his awareness of developments in Europe where botany was at its height at that time and a subject dealt with in

---

[1]   G. Williams provides the meaning 'Medical Herbal' (1997b: 339).

[2]   For a detailed discussion on the authorship of different parts of the work, see Edgar (1997: xii-xvii). Although W. Salesbury - according to Edgar (ibid.: xxv) - perhaps knew about the *Meddygon Myddfai*, material for the book was drawn from contemporary sources reflecting the most recent knowledge. It is not clear whether the herbal list (cf. sections 2.1.3. and 2.1.4.) was known to him. Some sources of W. Salesbury's book are *De Historia Stirpium* by the German physician Leonhard Fuchs, 1542, *Libellus de Re Herbaria Novvs* by the English physician William Turner, 1538, and *A Nevv Herball or Historie of Plantes* by the Dutch physician Rembert Dodoens (cf. ibid.: xviii).

[3]   The inclusion of lexical items from different languages indicates the degree of his language competence. It is supposed that he had thorough Welsh, English and Latin, a very good knowledge of Hebrew and Greek, and quite a good idea of French and German (cf. also section 2.2.2., B.R. Jones 1994: 7, 62). The unsystematic presentation of equivalents in different languages may, however, be due to a display of learning. Another reason may have been the general popularity multilingual dictionaries enjoyed in the sixteenth century, e.g. the *Calepine* (cf. section 2.2.1.1.), the *Lexicon Tetraglotton* by James Howell (cf. section 2.2.2., cf. also Lehnert 1956: 276).

the main languages of learning on the Continent building on the work of classical writers. W. Salesbury proved that it was possible to keep up with latest trends in research by using the Welsh language.

Another humanist who wrote a vocabulary with similar lists of synonyms as can be found in the works of the bards Gruffudd Hiraethog, Huw Pennant and Simwnt Fychan is Roger Morris (cf. sections 2.2.1.2.1., 2.2.1.2.2., and 2.2.2.). Alike other lexicographers (cf. Dr John Davies, Mallwyd, Wiliam Cynwal, John Jones, or Wiliam Llŷn), he was well acquainted with bardic grammars (cf. G.J. Williams & E.J. Jones 1934: xvi, xxiv). His list (MS Peniarth 169), dated to about 1588, demonstrates that Morris goes back to the 'first-letter order', an algorithm which was characteristic for the first glossaries (cf. section 2.1.3.). What is called a vocabulary actually looks like a combination of a group of synonyms - thematically arranged similarly to that of Hiraethog (cf. section 2.2.1.2.2.) - and a glossary, both unilingual.

J.E. Caerwyn Williams' (1983: 21, 44, Peniarth 169) assumption that Roger Morris' vocabulary might have been inspired by W. Salesbury's dictionary (cf. section 2.2.2.), which exhibits a 'second-letter' order, seems rather unlikely. More probable is an influence by bardic works, such as that of Gruffudd Hiraethog (cf. section 2.2.1.2.2.).

To sum up: it must be said that even with regard to vocabularies, the evidence for Welsh lexicographical production before the first dictionary (cf. section 2.2.2., but also sections 2.1.3. and 2.1.4.) is scanty. This can, however, also be said of English lexicography between 1066 and 1400 which has two vocabularies attested to from that period (cf. Murray 1900: 15).[4]

From Gruffudd Hiraethog's vocabulary onwards, nevertheless, a firm tradition of vocabulary production, now forming a separate branch besides dictionary compilation in Welsh lexicography, becomes apparent (cf. list of vocabularies in the appendix). Some of them seem to be archaic in structure as found in Morris' vocabulary (cf. above).

With regard to bardic works, a close link between vocabulary compilation and bardic grammars is apparent. Some of the early lexicographers were evidently also grammarians, e.g. Gruffudd Hiraethog and Simwnt Fychan (cf. 2.2.1.2.1.), thus being equipped with linguistic knowledge necessary for lexicographical production. Similar skills in the field of linguistics can be attested for humanist lexicographers, e.g. Henry Salesbury (cf. section 2.2.1.2.1.) and Dr John Davies, Mallwyd (cf. section 2.2.1.2.1.) and following scholars (cf. section 2.4.).

Most of the vocabularies of the time of the Renaissance are Welsh-Welsh vocabularies. Some of them contain equivalents in other languages (cf. list of vocabularies in appendix).

Only in the Romantic period (cf. section 2.4.), however, do the vocabularies become regularly bilingual and can be defined as lexicographical reference books apart from dictionaries. Contrary to dictionaries, vocabularies then are mostly confined to specialist subjects and are equally often restricted in linguistic description and consequently in size (cf. definition in section 1.3.2.1.1.).

---

[4]   For reasons concerning the lack of evidence for lexicographical material, see sections 2.1.3. and 2.1.4., but also the state of Welsh society as described in section 2.2.1.1.

2.2.1.2.3. The translation of the Bible

Since the translation of the Bible is important as a source for both literary material and intellectual potential for the development of Welsh lexicography, remarks in its regard are presented in this section. Its catalytic effect becomes apparent if one looks at some of the Bible translators, who also belong to the group of humanists with a key role in the evolvement of Welsh lexicography.[1] The notes on the genesis of the Bible, however, remain brief, since it has already been studied in considerable detail (cf. list of publications on this matter in I. Thomas 1997: 175).

In 1563 in the presence of Bishop Richard Davies (1501?-81),[2] an Act was passed which demanded the translation of the *Scripture* and, thus provided the Welsh language with a semi-official status for preaching following the *Act of Uniformity* from 1549, which had introduced the English language into the divine service. As a result the *Lliver Gweddi Gyffredin* 'The Common Prayer Book' translated by William Salesbury (cf. below and sections 2.2.1.1., 2.2.1.2.1., 2.2.1.2.2., and 2.2.2.) was published in May 1567. It was followed under the same legislation by *Y Testament Newydd* 'The New Testament' published in October 1567. The work was carried out in collaboration with Thomas Huet († 1591),[3] dean of St. David's, Bishop Richard Davies and W. Salesbury. This collaboration, however, came to end before having accomplished the task of translating the whole of the Bible as is illustrated by I. Thomas:

> "[Richard] has none of Salesbury's devices for achieving dignity of diction. On the contrary, his language is marked by non-literary forms and borrowings from English, two things studiously avoided by Salesbury. Whereas Salesbury strives to observe the literary canons of Renaissance letters, Davies is more concerned with the effectiveness of the Protestant mission in Wales and to this end adopts a language much nearer the spoken form. It was this divergence in aims that probably broke up the partnership between Davis and Salesbury and made it impossible for them to go on to produce a version of the Old Testament" (1997: 167).
> "Davies then appeared to have had some intention of proceeding to a joint translation with his nephew, Siôn Dafydd Rhys [cf. section 2.2.1.2.1.], but the plan was never carried out.
> It was left to a young Cambridge graduate, William Morgan, vicar of the remote parish of Llanrhaeadr-ym-Mochnant, to complete the translation" (G. Williams 1997a: 216f.),

which was later perfected by the humanist Dr John Davies, Mallwyd (cf. below and sections 2.2.1.2.1. and 2.2.2.).

William Morgan (1545-1604),[4] could rely on linguistic material which had been produced in the preceding centuries:

> "On the one hand there was the still living bardic tradition with its colourful vocabulary, well suited to capture the poetic quality of so much of the Scriptures. On the other hand

---

[1] Similar trends can also be observed in other countries (cf. Robert Estienne in section 2.2.1.1.).

[2] Richard Davies graduated from Oxford, and was a clergyman, and translator, and later a follower of the Puritans.

[3] No details were available to me with regard to his person.

[4] He was an acquaintance of Richard Davies. Morgan had studied Latin, Greek, and Hebrew at Cambridge and was a doctor of theology. After translating the Bible, he continued his literary work and also supported other men of letters and bards. For details with regard to his person, see G. Williams (1997b: 342f.).

[...] was that remarkable body of medieval prose literature which had encompassed topics as divers as laws, legends, romances, history, geography, medicine and religion, and had done so with considerable elegance and clarity. Of special interest to them were those religious works, mostly translations from Latin, which were the products of the ecclesiastical reforms of the thirteenth and fourteenth centuries. These contained Welsh renderings of the terms and phrases peculiar to Christian theological discourse, and also translations of some significant passages of Scripture" (I. Thomas 1997: 154).

The religious translations listed in section 2.2.1.1. (cf. also ibid.: 154ff.) were now regarded as inadequate, since they were not based on the original Hebrew and Greek texts but on the Latin of the Vulgate. This version was considered an uncertain text and its translations ambiguous. In addition, the adaptations, paraphrases, expansions and abridgements which characterise the Vulgate's pre-Reformation translations (cf. ibid.: 154ff.) were viewed as diminishing the word of God. With the print of the original texts, their subsequent dissemination, and the growth of new intellectual ideas, a new era of Bible translation began. In 1488 the printed Hebrew text of the Old Testament was published for the first time and in 1516 that of the Greek New Testament.[5]

The impact of these publications in Wales became apparent with the book *Yny lhyvyr hwnn* 'In this book' by Sir John Prys (1502-1555)[6] in 1546. This was followed by William Salesbury's dictionary (cf. section 2.2.2.). After receiving a royal license in 1545 to print a dictionary and a variety of translations, his work culminated in the publication of a translation of the epistles and gospels of the 1549 English Prayer Book under the title *Kynniver llith a bann or ysgrythur lan ac a ddarlleir yr eccleis pryd commun, y sulieu a'r gwilieu trwy'r vlwyddyn* 'As many lessons and sections of the Holy Scripture as are read to the church at communion on Sundays and Holy-days throughout the year' published in 1551. As stated above, the New Testament was printed in 1567 and the first complete Welsh Bible was published in 1588 under the title *Y Beibl cyssegr-lan yr Hen Destament a'r Newydd* 'The sacro-sanct Bible, namely the Old Testament and the New'. It contained the translation of the whole of the Hebrew Old Testament (except the Psalms), and of all the Greek and Latin books of the Apocrypha, together with a revision of W. Salesbury's Psalms and the New Testament of 1567.

> "No certainty exists when he began the work, but it can hardly have been later than 1579 for him to have had the work ready for publication by 1587. He completed his task with the enthusiastic encouragement of Archbishop Whitgift and the help of a number of friends from his Cambridge days, and published it in September 1588" (G. Williams 1997a: 216f.).

This greatest achievement of the humanists displayed both the purity of the language of traditional Welsh literature[7] and a greater flexibility of more recent language usage. Capable of using the language in a literary style and producing literature himself, Morgan's work was celebrated

---

[5] For further details on subsequent editions, see I. Thomas (1997: 157f.).
[6] No details were available to me with regard to his person.
[7] In contrast, the English and the German Bibles were based on a language spoken by the ordinary people.

by bards, such as Siôn Tudur, Ieuan Tew Ieuaf (1560-1608), and Thomas Jones (= Twm Siôn Cati, ca. 1530-1609). Some features of Morgan's translation are described as follows:

> "The primary source of Morgan's language was the rich idiomatic Welsh of his mainly monoglot community, but to extend and mould this everyday Welsh into the literary forms required by a version of Holy Scripture, he, like Salesbury, had recourse to the religious prose writings of the medieval period. But unlike Salesbury, his use of this material was not uncritical. He rejected words or phrases whose meaning was unfamiliar, or whose theology was Catholic, or whose inexactness as translations of the biblical texts was clear. This loss Morgan made good by drawing upon the vocabulary of the strict-metre poetry, by borrowing a little from Hebrew and English, but chiefly by the use of new word-formations, many adopted from Salesbury, but most coined by himself. These last are frequently modelled on the compound formations of strict-metre poetry and serve to give his version a poetic tone where required.
> In his sentence structure Morgan[, however,] rarely departs from the 'abnormal' pattern, and it is very rare indeed for him to have the singular verb with a plural subject, the 'normal' but un-Latin Welsh idiom. Indeed, Morgan seems much concerned to bring his Welsh into conformity with the rules of Latin grammar. On the other hand, unlike Salesbury, he makes no attempt to latinize his vocabulary, or his orthography which, with the exception of some oral forms, is that of the strict-metre poetry" (I. Thomas 1997: 169).
> "Throughout, he aimed at fidelity to the original texts, consistency, and regularity. In short, he made a point of eliminating Salesbury's archaisms, Latinizations, and other idiosyncrasies, which had caused the versions of 1567 to be so difficult to understand and so badly read [...] Morgan's handling of the Welsh language bore all the hallmarks of a superb writer as well as an erudite scholar. Not without good cause was he hailed by the poet, Huw Machno, as 'clo'r iaith' ['the lock of the language']" (G. Williams 1997b: 353).

Though not reflecting the spoken language, the Bible soon constituted a standard language of Early Modern Welsh, which was regarded as superior to any particular dialect, and the prose of the Bible became the basis for the Welsh literature produced from the end of the sixteenth century onwards. Thus, in times when the *Bardic Order* was in decline Morgan proved that there could be a continuation of a high quality Welsh language without it. The translation was the answer to the debates of pressure groups that the Welsh would have to learn English:

> "At a fatal juncture for the language, when the bards, hitherto the guardians and exponents of its classic strength and purity, had entered on a period of irreversible and accelerating decline, Morgan embodied in his translation all that was best and finest in their tradition. Yet he did so in a way that was neither obscurantist, nor esoteric, nor inflexible. [His language was] simpler, more natural, and close to the spoken idiom [...], as compared with that of most of the contemporary Welsh humanist writers" (G. Williams 1997b: 353).

The translation of the Scriptures into the vernacular was one of the foremost linguistic and cultural developments of sixteenth-century Europe. Wales was but one of a number of countries where the Bible had been rendered into the mother tongue and set forth in print before 1600.[8] Of

---

[8]   The translation of the Scriptures was completed in France by 1530, in Germany by 1534, in England by 1535, in Sweden by 1541, in Spain and Croatia by 1543, in Finland by 1548, in Denmark by 1550, in Poland by 1553, in Romania by 1563, in Slovenia and Lithuania by 1582, and in Iceland by 1584.

all the Celtic-speaking countries, Wales was the only one which successfully achieved the feat within the sixteenth century. It therefore ensured the future survival of its language and culture for the following five hundred years:

> "Wales had no court, no university, no academy, no salon, as other countries had, to give its language sanction. In the case of Wales, the Bible of 1588 became the canon of bel usage" (B.R. Jones 1994: 65)

Morgan strongly influenced the language of belief, literature and patriotism, thus planting the belief of the Reformation itself among the Welsh people and contributing strongly to the maintenance of and improvement in the language.

The translation of the Bible was supplemented by the production of other religious material. Humanist scholars and clerics of different confessions used translations to conduct religious controversies. Siôn Conwy († 1606),[9] for instance, translated the anti-Puritan work *A Summons for Sleepers* by Leonard Wright (1589) into Welsh under the title of *Deffiniad i Hennadirion* (1593, M. Stephens 1997: 114).

For other humanists, e.g. Siôn Dafydd Rhys (cf. sections 2.2.1.1. and 2.2.1.2.1.), however, the religious motive was, although present, obviously secondary to that of the attention paid to the work of collecting Welsh literature, copying poems, and the researches into pedigrees and antiquities as can be seen from W. Salesbury's statement.

> "E vyddei haws o lawer, ir prechetwr traythy gair Deo yn ddeallus, Ac a vyddei haws i wr dyscedic o Cambro wedy bod yn hir allan oe wlad, ac anghynefino ar iaith, cyfieithy iaith arall, ar iaith einym. Ac am hynny atolwg y chwy nyd er vy mwyn i, anyd er mwyn Deo, nyd er pleser na serch arno vi, anyd er carat ar ddeo, er lles ych eneitieu ych hunein, er tragyvythawl glod ywch (y sawl ae gwnel) a dianck o ywrth poeneu yffernoal, pob un o hanawch ys ydd yn meddy nac y perchenogy llyfreu n y byd o iaith Camberaec, attolwg ew cludo at pwy ryw sawl Gymbry pynac a vo hyspys genwch i bod yn darbod yn naturial tros amgeledd gwladwriaeth yr vnryw iaith."
>
> 'It would be much easier to preach God's word clearly. And it would be easy for a learned Welshman, after having been away from his country for long, and having lost familiarity with the language, to translate from another language into our language. And for this prayer not for my sake, and not for the sake of God, not for my pleasure or passion, and not for the sake of love of God, [but] for the sake of your own souls, for your eternal commendation (whoever does it) and escape from the hellish pains, everyone of you who owns no books in the Welsh language, to carry them to whichever Welsh people known to you that are naturally protecting the state of the same language (W. Salesbury *Oll Synnwyr Pen Kembero Ygyd*, in: G.H. Hugh 1976: 9f.).

Such an attitude was characteristic of the work of both Protestant and Catholic propagandists. The focus on the language may be the reason why differences in religion did not prevent mutual admiration of their work before the seventeenth century when the religious controversy became more acute and the emphasis on learning, in consequence, receded (cf. also G. Williams 1997a: 277-234).

---

[9]   He was a sponsor and translator of bardic literature.

To sum up: during the Renaissance, translation as a means of acquiring and introducing knowledge and arts as well as an educational and creative act expressing modern ideas and applying new linguistic concepts enjoyed a very high prestige. Most translations were made from French, Latin, or English, but also from other languages. They were increasingly produced at the cost of traditional poetry, prose and technical texts. Promoted by the printing press, translating in England, for instance, was at its peak in the sixteenth century which is consequently also called the century of translation; and translation itself was called an Elizabethan Art. In this field, Wales managed to keep up with major international developments even without there being a printing press operating in the country.

2.2.2.   First Welsh dictionaries[1]
(A)   William Salesbury

The first Welsh dictionary *A Dictionary in Englyshe and Welshe* was compiled by William Salesbury (cf. sections 2.2.1.1., 2.2.1.2.1., 2.2.1.2.2., and 2.2.1.2.3.) and printed in 1547. Although titled an English and Welsh dictionary, it was a Welsh-English dictionary (cf. analysis below and J.E. Caerwyn Williams 1983: 20). It has been argued that Salesbury might have intended to write an English-Welsh dictionary but was guided to use bardic Welsh-Welsh vocabularies, which were available in manuscript form, and substituted one Welsh section with English entries (cf. J.E. Caerwyn Williams 1983: 2, section 2.2.1.2.2. and Wiliems' dictionary below). The author himself, however, wrote to the king Henry VIII that he had "[...] writtē a lytle englyshe dictionary with the welsh interpretation" (Salesbury 1547: 3). Such a book tallied with contemporary English governmental policy (cf. section 2.2.1.2.3.) of enabling the Welsh to learn English.

Whatever the truth, Salesbury's dictionary reveals a conflict between obeying royal policy (cf. Salesbury 1547: 1), helping the Welsh to get access to the spheres of belief and learning (cf. ibid.: 4) where English was the only official language between 1549 and 1563 (cf. section 2.2.1.2.3.), and promoting the Welsh language (cf. below).[2] Jarvis (1997: 136) calls Salesbury "the most ambivalent [of all Welsh Renaissance scholars] in his attitude towards his native tongue". Whereas he later clearly attempted to restore the reputation of the venerable Welsh language as a language of learning (cf. his works mentioned in sections 2.2.1.1., 2.2.1.2.2., 2.2.1.2.3. and below), he produced his dictionary predominantly to encourage

> "his fellow Welshmen to learn English, so that they might partake of the learning to be
> found expressed in that language" (ibid.: 136).

Equipped with extensive comments on the pronunciation of English, Salesbury's Welsh-English dictionary is consequently primarily a

> "kyfarwyddyt i ddarllen a deall iaith Saesnec iaith heddyw urddedic o bob rhyw
> oreuddysc iaith gyflawn o ddawn a buddygoliaeth"
> 'guide to reading and understanding the English language, a language today adorned
> with all kinds of highest learning, a language replete with its gifted supremacy'
> (Salesbury 1547: 4).

In this work, therefore, Salesbury does not

> "augment the resources of Welsh by seeking to provide 'new' words where deficiencies
> existed. William Salesbury was later to contribute to the work of enriching and enlarging
> the vocabulary of Welsh, particularly in his *Llysieulyfr* [cf. section 2.2.1.2.2.] and in his
> translation of the New Testament [cf. section 2.2.1.2.3.], which lists alternatives and
> which also offers some very effective, newly minted words. Here, he is endeavouring to
> provide Welsh readers with a means of learning and understanding ordinary English
> words" (Jarvis 1997: 136).

---

[1]   I would like to take this opportunity of thanking William Ll. Griffith, Dinbych/Wales, for helpful discussion and assistance with translation.

[2]   For discussions on this matter, see J.E. Caerwyn Williams (1983: 20f) and B.R. Jones (1994: 15f.).

The introduction to his work reflects that the dictionary was a new learning aid to his intended audience (cf. J.E. Caerwyn Williams 1983: 21, Jarvis 1997: 136). Salesbury, therefore, explains what a dictionary is, how it is arranged and how it is to be used. He also comments on the mutations (Salesbury 1547: 5-7).

The dictionary, however, looks rather like a word list or glossary. Powell (1887: 210, 212) calls it a vocabulary, Stein (1986: 222) a word list. The following sample page, faithfully extracted from Salesbury's dictionary to facilitate its reading and subsequent commenting, demonstrates the structure of his work:

¶ *Kamberaec*	*Saesonaec*	*Walshe*	*Englyshe*
A. o vlaen b.[³]	achwyno		Complaynt
ab ne siak ab	An ape	achwlwm	A roūde knot
ab ne vab	Sonne	achub	
abe ne afon	A ryuer	achub	
aber ne hafyn	Hauen	A. o vlaen d.	
aberth	The sacra-	ad	Re, agayne
	ment	aderyn	A byrde
aberth efferen	Sacryng of	adarwr	A fouler
aberth ne of=	masse	adblygy	To folde a-
frwm	Sacryfyce		gayne
aberthy	Sacryfice	ader	
abledd	Hablenesse	adail	A buyldynge
	habilitie	adeilad	Bylde
Abram	Abraam	adefyn / edau	Threde
absen	Absence	adain	A wynge
absennwr	Bachyter	adain pysco=	
drwc		adnabot (dyn	Knowe
abwy burgyn	Caryen	adliw	A brayde
abwyd	Bayte	adnewyddy	Renewe
abyl	Hable	adwerth	
A. o vlaen c.		adwy bwlch	A gappe
ac	And	adwyth	
acken	Accent	A. o vlaen dd.	
ackw	Yonder	Adda	Adam
acolit		addas	Mete, apte
acolidieth		adaw	Promesse
act	An acte	addwyn	
A. o vlaen ch.		addfed	Rype
ach	Petygrewe	addfedy	Rype
ach diaficach	Hole, founde	addoli	Worshyp
achwyn	Accusation	addunet	A vowe
		A.i.	

The following comments briefly illustrate the main strengths and weaknesses of Salesbury's dictionary in general and can be regarded as applying to the work as a whole:[4]

1. Salesbury's dictionary runs to about 7,000 Welsh headwords, the majority of which have an English equivalent. A number of lexical items, however, remain untranslated, e.g. *achub, ader, adain pyscodyn*. Others seem to be erroneously translated, as can be seen from examples on subsequent pages, e.g. *Alban - Almaygne* (viz. 'Germany' instead of 'Scotland'). The question arises as to why Welsh headwords are left without English renderings (cf. also below). Do they suggest imperfect acquaintance with English on

---

This phrase is an explanation and means 'a before b'. It is repeated for the other letters in turn e.g. 'A. o vlaen c.'.

An analysis of all idiosyncrasies would require a separate study.

Salesbury's part?[5] Or are they due to pressure of time (cf. J.E. Caerwyn Williams 1983: 22)?[6] Or do they reflect lexicographical difficulties, e.g. relating the appropriate equivalents to each other, or a combination of two aspects?

2. A few lexical items are listed twice and in these cases left untranslated twice:

> achub
> achub
>
>
> ymwneuthuriad
> ymwneuthuriad

Others are listed twice in different places:

wi (ne) wy	An egge
wibwrn	
Wiliam	William
wits dewim-wraic	A wytche
witscrefft	Wytche-crafte
...	
ℭ Wy	An egge

3. Salesbury's dictionary reflects features more representative of a vocabulary when he presents the names of the months under the headword *mis* 'month' or the days, the principal sundays, saints' days, and festivals of the year under the headword *dyw* 'day' and not in their proper places in the alphabetical list. In the same way, a number of names of towns is listed under the headword *kaer* 'fort'.

4. His compilation is deficient in covering basic Welsh lexicon. As his translation works (cf. section 2.2.1.2.3. and M. Stephens 1997: 657) prove, he knew, for instance, the pro nouns and numerals, and yet, they are not all included in his dictionary.

5. In order to facilitate the acquisition of English, he introduced a large number of English loanwords in his book. The following examples illustrate this practice:

---

[5] It seems rather unlikely that his knowledge of English was insufficient, since he was, first, adept in nine languages (Green 1997: 108 and section 2.2.1.2.2.) and, second, he admired the English language (cf. also B.R. Jones 1994: 7, 31).

[6] Jarvis (1997: 138) argues similarly:
"There is a sense of urgency about the work of several of the Welsh Renaissance scholars, a sense of huge tasks needing to be done. That it is better that these tasks be done inadequately to begin with than to wait overlong for perfection is a recurrant theme. This sense of urgency is palpable in the early writings of William Salesbury: he insists that unless the work of perfecting and enriching the Welsh language is undertaken in his own generation, it will be too late thereafter - *bydd ry hwyr y gwaith wedyn*. His Welsh-English dictionary, strange as it may seem on the face of things, was part of his urgent scheme." See also, B.R. Jones (1994: 14f.).

warnio rhy-byddio	Warne
wast	Waste
waydys	Wages
waytsio	Watche
[...]	
witscrefft	Wytche-crafte
witsio	Wytche
⟨ Wow ne	
wpian (how	Woope
⟨ Wtla	A outlawe
wtra	
wtrans	Utterance
wtrio	Utter
wtres	Outrage

The high number of English loanwords may also derive from Salesbury's admiration of the English language and its gradually growing status as an intercultural language as expressed in his words: *ac iaith nid chwaith anhawdd i ddyscy vegys y may pop nassiwn yn i hyfedyr ddyscy* 'and a language not difficult to learn so that every nation learns it ably well' (Salesbury 1547: 4). Their number does, however, not say to what extent these loanwords were used in daily speech. Whereas *dragio* 'Drag' is first attested to in the work of the bard Dafydd ap Gwilym (cf. section 2.2.1.2.2.) and *warnio, wast, watsio*, and *witsio* are common in Welsh (cf. above), *walkio* 'Walke' and others did not exist in northern Welsh (cf. also *vario* 'Varye', *ventrio* 'Venture', *waetio* 'Wayte').

For a number of the words Salesbury included in his dictionary, there was certainly no need as can be seen from the example of *warnio* 'Warne' which is immediately followed by its Early Modern Welsh equivalent *rhybyddio*.

Salesbury thus enforced a tradition to give English preference and to facilitate language acquisition, a tradition which - centuries later - affected the language, particulary badly, in the twentieth century (cf. section 4.1.1.). The formation of verbs by adding *-io*, however, remains productive up to the present day (cf. also *tastio* 'tasting', *verneisio* 'Vernysshe').

6. Salesbury's dictionary goes beyond a vocabulary when - although on an irregular basis - presenting Welsh synonyms, definitions, or word families. He thus provides lexical definitions, a feature often missing in twentieth century dictionaries, as for instance, in *Y Geiriadur Cyfoes. The Modern Welsh Dictionary* (sic, cf. sections 3.2.1. and 4.2.).

The following examples illustrate the types of definitions in Salesbury's dictionary:

(a) Types of synonyms: 1. warnyng   Warnyng
                                 rhybydd

                             wits dewim-   A wytche
                                 wraic

	2.	aber ne hafyn	Hauen
		aber ne offrwm	A ryuer
		yspelio ne sillafu	Spell

The first type of synonyms is indicated by the lack of the English renderings of the second lexical item. Such an indication is, however, difficult for dictionary users, since other lexical items remain untranslated without being synonyms (cf. above). In the cases where the second synonym is intended, or begins next to the headword, its identification is easier.

The second type of synonyms is difficult to distinguish from the display of spelling variations according to the context, e.g. *ab ne vab* 'Sonne', or according to the dialect, e.g. *wi (ne) wy* 'An egge' (cf. also B.R. Jones 1994: 16).

(b) Types of definition: 1. wynwyn lly-   An onyon
seun o ddyryr
gwragedd wr-
th eu llygait
er kymel wy-
lo pan vo
meirw eu
gwyr[7]

2. Klwyf   Malady
Klwyfo   Sekyn
Klwyfo march   Cloy
a hoyl yny =
byw[8]

The first definition explains the meaning of *wynwyn* 'An onyon'. The second definition, however, defines an English word for which Salesbury could not find a Welsh equivalent, i.e. *cloy*.

(c)   word family: afiach   Unholesome
afiechyt

anafu   Mayme
anafad

---

[7]   The translation reads as follows: 'A vegetable which women place by their eyes in order to encourage weeping when their husbands die.'

[8]   The translation reads as follows: 'Injurying a horse with a nail to the quick'.

The noun *afiechyt* 'illness' is derived from the adjective *afiach*. The same relation is displayed in the second example. The next example presents the derivation of an adjective from a noun:

> ymryson   Braule
> ymrysongar

In view of the lack of many English renderings (cf. above), it becomes apparent that the dictionary was aimed at Welsh speakers. The question remains, however, how they were expected to form corresponding English word families or find out other English equivalents?

7. The lexical definitions are in no way as regular as the contextual explanation provided in the bardic vocabularies (cf. section 2.2.1.2.2.). Salesbury's headwords, therefore, predominantly remain without context, whereas the bards at that time give poetical quotations and play on the meanings of words in order to illustrate their potential semantic range.

8. Compared with bardic vocabularies, the alphabetical order was improved. Although the metalinguistic Welsh explanations, e.g. *A. o vlaen b*,[9] suggest a 'second-letter order', which is displayed in examples such as *adarwr* following *aderyn* (cf. above), Salesbury follows predominantly a 'third- or fourth-letter order'.

9. New in Salesbury's dictionary is the introduction of the indefinite article in front of a number of nouns, e.g. 'An ape'. Some English infinitives are preceded by 'to', e.g. 'To folde'. Whenever these lexical items precede an English equivalent, its word class is clearly indicated.

8. The hyphenation of Welsh words in Salesbury's dictionary, although not frequent, is at times illogical, e.g. when he splits Welsh letters, such as ⟨ff⟩ in *of-frwm*, or monosyllabic words like *wr-th*, or diphthongs as in *gynyrcha-wl*. Such hyphenation, however, can also be observed in publications of the twentieth century (cf. section 4.3.9.).

9. The spelling of the *Metalanguage* employed in Salesbury's dictionary varies. Whereas he writes *Kamberaec - Saesonaec - Walshe - Englyshe* as the headline of the first page of his dictionary, he later writes *Camraec - Saesnec - Walshe - Englyshe,* and another time *Kymraec - Sasonaec - Walshe - Englyshe.* Perhaps Salesbury thus displayed here what later was described as his

> "delight in variety he extends to his [...] spelling [and which] he achieves by
> alternating words of Celtic Origin with those of Latin Origin, and current forms
> of usage with their medieval equivalents" (I. Thomas 1997: 162).

His later works clearly reflect his favour for Latin elements in Welsh whenever possible (ibid.: 162) and the latinisation of his vocabulary and spelling (ibid.: 169).[10] In addition,

---

[9]   This phrase is an explanation and means 'a before b'.

[10]   "He attempted to convey Latin affinities, some of them spurious, in the way Welsh words were written. One important innovation has survived to this day, although based on a false etymology. The singular and plural forms of the third person possessive pronoun, written as *y* in Middle Welsh, are written as *ei* and *eu* by Salesbury in an attempt to show that they are derived from the

at that time, different theories on orthography influenced the spelling (cf. Ch. Parry 1997: 272) as well as the need to vary the writing of individual words for poetical reason (cf. T. Jones 1688: 7).

Although a revised orthography was also considered a necessary aspect of elevating Welsh to the status of a learned language (cf. Jarvis 1997: 143f.), the drive to standardise orthography is a rather modern phenomenon which does not belong to the Renaissance period.[11]

To sum up: Salesbury's dictionary is a basic learning aid for the acquisition of the English language. It does, however, not yet seem to establish a self-introductory tool, but rather one to be used in class, since whereas he explains English pronunciation in detail and displays his interest in sounds and sound-changes,[12] he leaves a significant number of headwords untranslated. Indeed, his dictionary still displays some features of a vocabulary. However, Salesbury forms word families and exhibits lexicological knowledge, but does not indicate the word classes consistently. In addition, contextual information remains limited thus reducing the applicability of the lexical items as compiled. The complementory function of his dictionary is further implied by Salesbury himself in his introduction as he does in fact advocate his reader to consult native speakers in English:

> "gorau kyngor a vetrwyf vi i'r neb or ni edy anghaffael iddo vyned i loecr lle mae'r iaith yn gynenid ymofyn o honaw ac un a wypo Saesnec (o bleit odit o blwyf ynKymbry et Sasnigyddion yntho) paddelw y gelwir y peth ar peth yn Sasnec [...] a chyd y hyny Kymeryd y llyfer yma yn angwanec o goffaduriaeth yn absen athrawon ac yn diffic dyscyawdywr yr iaith."
>
> '... the best advice I am able [to give] to anyone whom inconvenience prevents from going to England where the language is native to consult one who knows English (for there is hardly a parish in Wales without English speakers in it) how such and such a thing is called in English [...] and along with that take this book as additional record' (Salesbury 1547: last page of his introduction).

However, whatever the deficiencies of his dictionary, Salesbury was the first to commit himself to compiling a bilingual Welsh dictionary. In addition, he reveals himself to be an erudite scholar with considerable linguistic knowledge and sets a new standard in Welsh lexicography.

---

forms of *eius* in Latin" (Jarvis 1997: 144). The reason for Salesbury's attempts to latinise Welsh may perhaps be found in traditional Welsh history (C.W. Lewis 1997: 34).

[11] See also the ideas of the Renaissance as explained in section 2.2.1.1.

[12] For more details, see his later work *A briefe and playne introduction teaching how to pronounce the letters in the British tongue, Londini* (Alston: 1969b). This treatise on the pronunciation of Welsh "was basically a phonetic guide to Welsh intended for those border Welsh people whose work *for their promotions and lyuynges* and trade put them in contact with *them that can not a worde of Englishe,* for those exiled who had lost their Welsh but who wished to renew their roots, and for those scholars who had an interest in language, the *philoglottus* as Salesbury says" (B.R. Jones 1994: 23f.).

(B)   Thomas Wiliems

The second dictionary known to us was produced by Thomas Wiliems (1545/46-1622)[1] some time between 1604 and 1607 (MS Peniarth 228). His Latin-Welsh dictionary *Thesaurus Linguæ Latinæ et Cambrobritannicæ siue Latinæ Linguæ et Britannicæ Veræ, Dictionarum Locupletissimum* was never printed[2] and remains in manuscript form. It consists of three volumes. Volume I comprises the letters A - D, volume II the letters E - P, and volume III the letters Q-Z. At the end of his dictionary, he includes a list of names of British towns in Welsh and English. There is also some material which Wiliems might have intended to use for the compilation of a Welsh or Welsh-Latin dictionary (cf. J.E. Caerwyn Williams 1983: 29), a fact that demonstrates his eagerness to work to promote the Welsh language (ibid.: 28ff.).

Working as a copyist of Welsh manuscripts, he was closely familiar with bardic material,[3] e.g. with the vocabularies of Wiliam Llŷn (cf. section 2.2.1.2.2.) and Roger Morris (cf. sections 2.2.1.2.1. and 2.2.1.2.2.), which he copied and supplemented. Together with other Welsh language material (cf. Jarvis 1997: 139), they provided the lexical basis for his lexicographical work.

His actual way of assembling a dictionary, however, was inspired by the Latin-Latin dictionary of Ambrosius Calepinus (cf. section 2.2.1.1.) and by the Latin-English dictionary, first published in 1587, of Thomas Thomas[4] (1553-88; cf. Green 1997: 100f. and J.E. Caerwyn Williams 1983: 31ff., Jarvis 1997: 139). This becomes apparent when comparing the structure and grammatical description of Wiliems' dictionary with that in the works of Calepinus, Thomas, and Salesbury. Whereas Salesbury's grammatical description is limited to an indirect indication of the word class of some nouns and verbs (cf. above), Wiliems provides systematic and comprehensive information in this respect in Latin (cf. below) - quite similar, although shorter, to the way it is done in Thomas' and Calepinus' dictionaries (cf. J.E. Caerwyn Williams' explanations 1983: 32). In contrast to Salesbury, Wiliems also arranged his headwords in alphabetical order (cf. below).

In view of the structures of Salesbury's and Wiliems' dictionaries, the impression is that the former was more orientated towards Welsh lexicographical material (cf. bardic grammars), whereas the latter had studied English dictionaries, which by the turn of the fifteenth century already displayed alphabetical order, and those of other countries.

---

[1]   Wiliems, also Syr Thomas Wiliems, Trefiw, was a priest and genealogist who spent much of his life as a physician after studying at Oxford University. He was a Catholic and consequently had his problems with some contemporary events and personalities. Wiliems, nevertheless, became famous for copying Welsh manuscripts, e.g. *Y Gododdin* (cf. J.E. Caerwyn Williams 1983: 28). He also sponsored bards (cf. M. Stephens 1997: 52).

[2]   For problems with regard to its printing, see J.E. Caerwyn Williams (1983:36).

[3]   On his difficulties in getting access to appropriate material, see J.E. Caerwyn Williams (1983: 29). In the preface to his dictionary he lists the people who lent him their books (cf. J.G. Evans 1898: 1056).

[4]   He was the first official printer of Cambridge University.

Since Wiliems' dictionary remains in manuscript form in handwriting difficult to read (cf. J.E. Caerwyn Williams 1983: 36), some examples of entries of his work are taken from J.G. Evans (1898: 1055ff.) and presented in the following:

Volume I:

> Thesaurus Linguæ Latinæ et Cambrobritannicæ siue Latinæ linguæ et Britannicæ veræ, dictionarium locupletissimum.
>
> Trysawr yr iaith Latin ar Gymraec, ne'r Geiriadur cywoethocaf, a helaethaf or wir dhiletiaith Vrytanaec, sef heniaith a chyphrediniaith ynys Brydain, ar Latin yn cyfateb pob gair wedy dechrau i scrivenu 4 Maij 1604
>
> [...]
>
> *A* et *Ab* (præpositiones sunt eiusdem significationis, prior longa posterior brevis) O, o'r, er hyny hyt hedhyw, gyferbyn, wedy, ygyd, igan, ywrth, odhywrth, erwyrth, drwy, tûac at, alhan wrth *Abăcēs* rhyw lestri gwaelion y catwer petheû gwerthfawr ynthynt *Abăcion* . N. g. [...] or gair Abax
>
> *Abăctor* . is . M.g. verbal ab Abigo Gyrrwr gwarthec Gwilhiad gwilhiedydh.
>
> *Abactus* . m.g. Gyrriad o nerth braich ac ysgwydh . dygiad yn lhatrat

Volume II:

> *E* præp. serui Ablat. O, or, Alhan or, Ar, odhywrth, drwy, yn ol. *E contrario* yn y gwrthwyneb ..... *E republica* ar y lhes cyphredin, ar les y wald &c [...]

Volume III:

> *Quā.* Adverb. Loci. Pa pfordh, drwy ba ryw phordh, ne pa le, heuyt, bob vn, yn gystal ar, o rann, yn hynny
>
> [...]
>
> *Zythum, thi.* n.g. ... diot a wneler o haidh berwedic, ag a elhir y gymeryt yn lhe Cwrwf ne vir, gwin a wneler or haidh Suid, heiddhgwrw FINIS *Soli deo honor et Gloria . 8 octobris . 1606*
>
> [...]
>
> *Zona, æ,* f.g. Gwregys : rhyw let yn y furuauen ne'r dhaear &c Zinziber vt quidam male colligunt. *finis. 2 Octobris 1607 .*
>
> Deo Gratias .

In general, Wiliems supplies more than one Welsh equivalent for his Latin headwords. In addition, they may also be explained in context as can be seen with *E*. For Latin nouns, however, he tends to provide definitions rather than simple word equivalents in Welsh, such as for *Abăcēs*, *Abactus*. Being aware of the broad lexical basis of his dictionary, he thereby called it a 'thesaurus'.

The fact that Wiliems' dictionary was never printed does not diminish his achievements. As can be seen in the next section, his work proved important for further developments in Welsh lexicography.

(C) Dr John Davies, Mallwyd[1]

The third Welsh dictionary known to us *Antiquae Linguae Britannicae Dictionarium Duplex* (Alston 1968a) was produced by Dr John Davies, Mallwyd (cf. sections 2.2.1.2.1., 2.2.1.2.2., and 2.2.1.2.3.) and printed in 1632. Before compiling his dictionary, Davies had published the leading Welsh grammar book of the Renaissance in 1621 (cf. section 2.2.1.2.1.). His continuous studies of manuscripts of bards' works (cf. section 2.2.1.2.1., 2.2.1.2.2. and G.J. Williams & E.J. Jones 1934: xviiif.), his research in grammar and in lexicographical works of his predecessors are reflected in his dictionary. As a result, the proverbs of Hiraethog (cf. section 2.2.1.2.2.) are also included in his book. Jarvis (1997) comments on Davies' study and usage of bardic material:

> "He was also a highly conservative scholar. His instinct always is to look to the past. His prescription for the perceived paucity of words in seventeenth-century Wales is to search for those words which already exist; new inventions will in most cases be found to be unnecessary. His defence of historical precedent in matters of vocabulary is vigorous. His work, he informs us, is based upon careful study of manuscript sources, and in particular upon the work of the poets: 'for, in order that this laborious work be more complete, I have read almost everything written in British, and especially the work of the poets, who claim for themselves (and that in every language) authority over words ... they were of the greatest help to me concerning writing British words correctly and looking into their true meaning.'" (ibid.: 1997: 140).

The Latin-Welsh section of Davies' dictionary is based on Wiliems' *Thesaurus Linguæ Latinæ et Cambrobritannicæ...* (cf. above and Edgar 1997: xvi, xxxii, J.E. Caerwyn Williams 1983: 36f.).

> "Dr Davies acknowledged his debt to Wiliems and his long labour, but is highly critical of his work and careful to point out that his own dictionary is more of a remaking than a wholesale borrowing: 'As for the Latin-British Dictionary, that of Thomas Wiliems, you will see it here, not directly copied from his manuscript, but having had added to it as many British equivalents of Latin words as possible; cleansed of the almost endless faults of which it was full; so that it might be more concise and perfect ... it could indeed be considered something new and different'.
> John Davies explains in what regard in particular he has pruned and edited Thomas Wiliems' work. He has sought to weed out all words which are derivations of root forms: for example, where an adverb is derived from an adjective, the adjective is only listed. He is similarly stringent in his choice of Welsh words for inclusion in the second half of the dictionary, including only a sufficient number of composite words, which he rightly extols as one of the glories of the Welsh language, to provide exemplary patterns" (Jarvis 1997: 140).

Following the sample page of his dictionary, which is here faithfully extracted in order to illustrate its structure, the presentation of Welsh grammatical phenomena in his book is discussed:

---

[1] I would like to take this opportunity of thanking William Ll. Griffith, Dinbych/Wales, for helpful discussion and assistance with translation.

DICTIONARIVM
BRITANNICO-
LATINVM.

AB	AC	AC

In nomine [...] A [...] Ω.

A,& Ac *Coniunctiones. Et,ac,atque.* A
& Ag *Præpositiones, Cum, Vtrumque*
A *ante initiales consonantes poni solet;*
Ac & Ag *ante vocales.*A *præpositionem*
differentie.e gratiâ cicrcumflectimus, A
coniunctionem non circumflectimus. A
Aduerbium interrogandi significat An,
num, numquid, vt A fu neb,*Numquis*
fuit. vt & *Arabum* A. *Aitem est*
Adverbium seu particula verbis præ-
posita nihil significans, vt Duw a
wnaeth, *Deus fecit;* Duw a ŵyr, *De-*
us *scit;*Bam a fydd, *Indicium est futu-*
rum. A *item est Præpositia in compo-*
sitione vsitata, & vocum significatio-
nem nonnihil augmentat, vt Achadw
ab A & Cadw; Achar *ab* A & Câr ;
Achrwm *ab* A & Crwm;Aphwys *ab*
A & Pwys ; Athrift *ab* A & Trift.
Ab. *Simia.*Ab *in cognominibus pro* Mâb.
Abad. *Abbas. sic Arm. pl.*Ebyd, Abbates.
Abades. *Abbatissa. sic Arm.*
Abadaeth. *Abbatia officium & benefi-*
cium.
Abatty. *Abbatia domus, Monasterium cui*
praest. Abbas sic Arm.
Aball, *Ll. reddit* Anundab, *unde Tw.*
Dissidium reddit ; ego existimo idem
significare quod Pall *Inopia, defectus,*
penuria, indigentia, exiticum ; y mae
trais, a lladrad, ac anudon wedi
gyrru ar aball bob cynneddfau da *R.*
M. in prolog. N.T. & sic Galf.
Aballu,*Perire,deficere.*
*[²]Aban, rhyfel. *Ll. Bellum, prelium.*
Dicitur & Eban. Aban a ddaw beu-
nydd ynn, i'n bro ni a bair newyn.
Iolo.
* *Abar,budreddi.*LL.*videtur esse nomen*
Adiect.& significare corruptus, mar-

---

cidus,*putidus, putris Gr.* ουωρòs. *A.*
lys *est idem quod* Buria, *Cadauer,* vi.
Minsh. *in voce Carcasse.* Abar fe-
ddau, *D.R.* Nid abar y gwnaeth. c.
Cyn bwyf abar a'm bo lludded. *M.*
Br. Lleer gwawr,gwedy bo abar, lle
y mae faint,yn sant diafar. *C.*
Aber,*Casus fluvy, oftium fluvy, portus.*
Venedotis Torrentem significat quòd
in fluvium effundantur.
Aberth,*Sacrificum. Ab Heb.* זבח, *Ze-*
baeb
Aberthu, *Sacrificare.*
Aberthawr & Aberthwr, *Sacrificus.*
Abl, *Habilis, potens,sufficiens.Sic Arm.*
Haber D.G.
Abledd, *Potentia, sufficientia.*
Abo, *idem quod Abwy. Habet P.M.*
Abred. q. Hyd pan ddillyngwys Crist
geithiwed, o ddyfnais aphwys ab-
red. *Tal.vid.* Diabred.
Abrwysgl,*est quod nunc dicimus Am-*
ros, immensus ; ingens. Abrwysgl ei
faran ar gann a glâs. *M..Br.* Gwr
abrwysgl ei faint.
Absen,*Absentia.* Gwydd ac absen, *Præ-*
sentia,& Absentia.Item Calumnia &
obtrectatio in absentes.
Absennwr drwg, *Obtrectator,obloquut*
or, qui absentes rodit.
Absen drwg,& drwg absen, *Oblequutio,*
obtrectatio in absentes. Da ei absen,
dicitur is qui de absentibus benè
loquitur.
Abwy,& Abo, *cadauer, caro morticina,*
moticinum.
Abwyd, *Esca,*δελεάρ.Ab A & Bwyd .A-
licubi Amwyd.
Ac. *vid.* A.
Accen , *Acentus, tenor sermonis , to-*
nus pronunciationis.
Accw,Ibi,illic.Gr. εχοì
A

Ach, *Stemma, prosapia,parentela, gene-*
*alogia. Heb.*וחס, *iachaf, prosapia, ge*
nealogia.Pl. Achau & achoedd.
Achau y tad o chaid dydd,
Achoedd Efa ferch Ddafydd. *L.G.*
Achwr. *Genealogiarum peritus.*
Ach, *particula in compositione vsitata,*
vt in Achludd,achles.
Achadw , *idem quod* Cadw , *ab* A &
Cadw. Corwiliais yn achadw ffin.
Gwal.
Achanog, *idem quod* Anghenog, *Egc-*
nus, indigus.
Achar, *ab* A & Câr, *Amat, amabit, a-*
mans. Neb traha nid achar. *N. Fude*
compositum Diachar , udiosus, áελì-
τος, ἀνέαςος.
* *Achef. q.*
Achen. *vid. an idem quod* Echen.Ce-
nedl *ait Ll. Genus,natio. Sumitur pro*
Ach. Yn achen y ddraig wen wiw
Rownllaes y mae'r arianlliw. Iolo
i arfau mortimer. Mae fyched, masw
ei hachen, meddwodd ith orfod ith
ên. *D.G.* i'r gôg. I brofi vchod ei
brifachen, Ym mysg arafwch y mae
sgrifen. *L.G.*
* *Achenu. vid. an ab* A. &Canu. A-
chenaf vchenaid gyfrin.*M..R.*
* *Achenedd.*
* *Aches,*idem quod* Afon, *Rivus,flumen.*
Achlân. *b.e. i* gyd oll, *Omnes, totus,*
vniversus. in vniversum
Achles. *Confugium, refugium, asylum,*
protectio, locus vbi quid fouetur, de-
fensio. Heb. הלק *Chalak, est lenire,*
blandiri, adulari.
Achlesu. *Indulgere, fouere, confouere,*
refocillare; intutelam, curam, vel
assylum accipere. Y rhai da a achlesir
yn arffed yr eglwys, *Confouebuntur*
boni in gremio ecclesiæ.
Achludd. *Occultare, occultum, occultatio*

This sign indicates old or
obscure words.

The following comments briefly illustrate some achievements of the whole of John Davies' dictionary:[3]

1. On an irregular basis, Davies provides Welsh synonyms before presenting the Latin equivalents, e.g. for *Aban*.

2. In accordance with the Renaissance ideal of versatile educated people (cf. section 2.2.1.1.), Davies displays his knowledge of Greek, Hebrew, and Breton (indicated by *Arm.*)[4] when including equivalents in these languages (cf. also Salesbury in his *Llysieulyfr*, section 2.2.1.2.2.), thereby, however, also defining their meaning as exact as possible.

3. Davies introduces lexical items consisting of more than one consituent as headwords, a practice lacking in some dictionaries of the twentieth century, e.g. in *Y Geiriadur Cyfoes. The Modern Welsh dictionary* (sic, cf. sections 3.2.1. and 4.2.).

4. Also on an irregular basis, his headwords are applied in a Welsh context, which is often taken from bardic compositions, e.g for *Aban* where he presents a *cynghanedd* by Iolo Goch (1325-1398, cf. section 2.2.1.2.2.).

5. Although Davies uses Wiliems' Latin-Welsh part, the headwords in his Welsh-Latin section are assembled according to the 'second-letter order', as indicated by the headline of his dictionary pages (cf. above). The third and fourth letters are frequently in alphabetical order, too.

6. He frequently makes use of cross-references, such as for *Abo, Achanog, Achen, Aches*. Cross-references refer to orthographical variation, e.g. *Abediw, Ebediw, Obediw*, synonyms, e.g. *Aches, Afon*, antonyms, e.g. *Abred - Diabred*, and grammatical phenomena e.g. *Achadw - Cadw* (cf. mutations below).

7. Morphological categories, such as the plural, also form part of the dictionary entries. At times Davies even indicates varying plurals, e.g. for *Ach* when including *Achau & Achoedd*. Feminine forms are also provided, e.g. in *Abbates*.

8. Mutations are contextually explained, i.e. by examples of mutated lexical items and the word causing mutation, as can be seen for *A, Achar* (a + car). Davies also includes mutated words in his headword list, such as *Achadw* (a + cadw), *Achenu* (a + canu). This practice can also be observed in the *Teach Yourself Welsh Dictionary* of 1992 (cf. section 4.2.).

9. Davies provides further systematic knowledge; he, for instance, comments on the pronunciation where it strongly deviates from the written forms, e.g for *Abrwysgl*, and introduces principles of word formation, such as in *Ach*.

10. He also makes an attempt to supply etymological derivations. Before the *Archaeologia Britannica* by Edward Lhuyd (1707), however, etymologies are rather erroneous, for

---

[3] To have all peculiarities of his dictionary exemplified, a separate investigation would be necessary.

[4] Apart from some examples which may be loanwords, Davies does not borrow lexical items from Breton, although he often adapts the Breton lexical items included in his work to Welsh spelling. According to Hincks (1993: 3f., 6f.), there occur only a few Breton loanwords in Welsh before the lexicographer Thomas Jones (cf. below).

146

instance, when Davies assumes that the English word 'denizen' derives from Welsh *dinaswr* 'citizen'.[5]

11. The *Metalanguage* of his dictionary is Latin and graphically indicated by italics.

Nearly ninety years after the publication of the first Welsh dictionary by W. Salesbury in 1547, John Davies' reference book was the second dictionary available in print in Wales. In the meantime, lexicographical activities apart from Thomas Wiliems' dictionary comprised mainly vocabulary production and translating, as is illustrated in sections 2.2.1.1. and 2.2.1.2.2.

Providing synonyms, antonyms, information on word formation and on various grammatical properties of Welsh words, as well as on spelling variation and pronunciation, Davies not only presents himself as a skilled linguist (cf. Jarvis 1997: 140), but more significantly, with this first bi-directional dictionary, he actually produced a linguistic basis for specialisation in Welsh lexicography. Although such specialisation does not occur during the time of the Renaissance, a more continuous production of dictionaries was actually instigated by the publication of the one compiled by Dr John Davies.

---

[5]   There are also some Old Cornish words in Davies' dictionary which he took for Old Welsh, e.g. *Coth* 'old', *Llafrog* 'shoes'. This, however, is a problem which had already occured to Thomas Wiliems (cf. Hincks 1993: 6).

(D)   Henry Salesbury

It seems likely that various scholars acquainted with each other, e.g. Dr John Davies, Mallwyd (cf. above), Henri Perri (cf. section 2.2.1.2.1.), Thomas Wiliems (cf. above), and Henry Salesbury (cf. section 2.2.1.2.1.), prepared or intended to prepare dictionaries over a period of time at the beginning of the seventeenth century (cf. J.E. Caerwyn Williams 1983: 35f., 47, Jarvis 1997: 139). The first to accomplish this task was Wiliems, followed by Davies. H. Salesbury began to compile his Welsh-Latin dictionary *Geiria Tavod Comroig hoc est Vocabvlarivm Lingvæ Gomeritanæ* before the publication of Davies' *Dictionarium Duplex*. He did, however, never finish his compilation. Extending his dictionary continuously, H. Salesbury's work remained incomplete and unpublished at his death around 1637.

Although H. Salesbury's dictionary was never printed, it seems to have been well circulated in manuscript form, as parts of it are incorporated into later works, in particular in a vocabulary compiled by the scholar and poet Ieuan Fardd (also Evan Evans, Ieuan Brydydd, 1731-1788; cf. J.E. Caerwyn Williams, 1983: 23, Jarvis 1997: 137f.).

Henry Salesbury drew from bardic vocabularies and perhaps added to his work after seeing Dr Davies' dictionary (cf. Jarvis ibid.). Like him he had written a grammar, i.e. *Grammatica Britannica* (cf. section 2.2.1.2.1.), before compiling his dictionary, thereby acquiring a linguistic basis for his lexicographical work.

In order to illustrate the structure of Salesbury's compilation, examples are faithfully extracted from the first page of his dictionary entries. The readings are tentative:

Aerwy	"Restis[1]	Alymmic	"Alumine condis
Aeo	"Sonus	Alym	"Alumen
Aille et	"Commodus	Alymedig	"Aluminatus
Aillaw	"Secundarius vol	Alymmog	"Aluminosus
	potius moptas et pleb.	Almys ph Almysen	"s. Amygdala
Airos	"Ostrum	Almwnt	"Adamas
Aib	"Cuneus x Cŷn	Aleanod	"Anchusa
Auad	"Hepatica.	Alcam	"Agalma Stannū
Auon.	"Obolus.Semiscrupulus	Alses	"Fenestra
Aurysu	"Amrosco	Albrast	"Arcubalista
Aurva	"Auraria	Alvarch	"Lancea.
Aurvyd	"Aureum Seculum	Ar gîr y 7euad	"Decreseonto lara
Aurvodrwyog	"Auream gostans	Arabaio	"Puerilitor.
	annglum.	Arymchwel	"Superobruo.
Aurvlodeuog	"Chrysanthemon.	Aryscwydog	"Ephod.
Aurdyvod	"Psegma	Aryfed	"Superbibo
Awenycgar	"Arreptitius	Areiswo	"Accubatio
Awl x	" Gwesi.	[...]	
Awgad 7aw	"		
A7an	Hortus Templum		
	gloris et gloras		
Allawr	"Ara, altare.		
A7[?]wyn	"D: Alltraw. A.		
Al.	"Fatus.		
Alai	"Ambulactirum		
A. ou.	"Arce robuste Full ianū		
Alar	"Fastidium		
Alar	"Tadulus		
Alaneo	"Larlos Hypochantriū		
Alayr	"Politus		
Arawynebydd	Adulator"[2]		

The following comments briefly illustrate some features characteristic of Salesbury's dictionary as a whole:[3]

1. The lexical items in his dictionary are assembled in a rather unusual alphabetical order. At first glance it looks, as if the headwords were listed according to the 'first-letter order' and later in his dictionary in a 'second-' or 'third-letter order'. A closer look, however, reveals that Salesbury probably assembled the lexical items according to sounds being similarly pronounced. His interest in phonetics (cf. Jarvis 1997: 138f.) is confirmed when looking at the symbols he introduces in order to adequately reflect

---

[1]   Whereas "" seems to indicate subsequent Latin equivalents 'x' introduces Welsh synonyms, e.g. *Cŷn* or supplements, e.g. *Arddolw, Arianrif*. In some cases "" is followed by a Welsh lexical item, e.g *Alltraw*.

[2]   This entry looks like a supplement, because it is outside the letter order of the headword list and in smaller and rather squashed writing.

[3]   To have all peculiarities of his dictionary exemplified, however, a separate investigation would be necessary.

grapheme-phoneme-relations. One example is his use of the number 7 for /ɬ/, e.g. in *llaw*. He can thus distinguish between double /l/ at the word boundary in a compound word (Wortfuge), such as *Aillaw* (ail-law), and the phoneme /ɬ/, such as in *A7an* (allan) or *7yma* (llyma),[4] both normally represented by the digraph ⟨ll⟩.

2. In view of some entries, the range of the lexicon included in Salesbury's dictionary is amazing. The headwords, *Alymmic, Alym, Alymedig, Alymmog*, for instance, all refer to sulfates medicinally used as topical astringents and styptics. In such cases the choice of lexical items was probably influenced by Salesbury's work as a physician, thereby introducing specialist lexis (cf. also the considerable number of herbal names he presents). It would be interesting to know as to whether he made use of William Salesbury's *Llysieulyfr* (cf. section 2.2.1.2.2.). This question, however, deserves separate treatment.

3. On an irregular basis, Henry Salesbury introduces synonyms, such as *Tarian.*

4. When he invents new lexical items, he makes frequent use of prefixes, e.g. of *ar-* 'super-', such as in *Aryfed* (cf. Jarvis 1997: 138).[5]

5. Salesbury displays his skills as a grammarian when including collective nouns, that is, nouns whose stem has plural meaning and whose singular inflection is only used when individual items have to be described (cf. sections 1.3.2.3.2. and 4.3.2.2.1.), in the headword list followed by their singulative, as in *Almys ph*[6] *Almysen.* This practise has mostly been ignored by twentieth century lexicographers (cf. section 4.3.2.2.).

Since Salesbury perhaps compiled his dictionary at about the time when Davies was doing the same, but may have based his work on other materials than Davies, the dictionary of the former does not reflect a similarly advanced macrostructure as that of the latter. Salesbury's attempts, however, to indicate Welsh pronunciation and to include relevant grammar as well as his introduction of specialist lexis are of significance in the history of Welsh lexicography.

---

[4] For further explanations, see J.E. Caerwyn Williams (1983: 25).

[5] For further explanations on Salesbury's word formation, see J.E. Caerwyn Williams (1983: 23ff.).

[6] *Ph* stands for 'feminine'.

150

(E) John Jones

Another lexicographer to be mentioned is John Jones, of Gellilyfdy (1585-1657/58).[1] He apparently started to compile a Welsh-Welsh or Welsh-Latin dictionary in 1623 (cf. MS Peniarth 309). Coming from a family who sponsored bards, the compositions of whom he copied, he was naturally well acquainted with their works. He frequently refers to bardic grammars (cf. G.J. Williams & E.J. Jones 1934: xxiii), thereby relying heavily on their works.

Since his work remains unfinished and in manuscript form in a handwriting difficult to read, a few brief remarks will suffice. A few examples from J.G. Evans (1898: 1112) illustrate the kind of dictionary intended by him:

> A
> Abaḷ// Anundeb// Diffic// Dissidum// Exterminatio// Contentio
> Abaḻu// l'erire// Periclitari
> Aban// Bellum// Budreḍ// Ryfel./
> Amkaụḍ// Meḍai// Dywedai ...

Some entries have Latin equivalents, some Welsh, some of them have equivalents in both languages, and some are left untranslated. Jones' headwords are assembled according to the 'second-letter order'. The *Metalanguage* employed in his dictionary is Welsh. Of significance is the morphological variety Jones occasionally presents as can be seen from the following examples:

> Aber: ḷ[²] : Aberau//Aberoedd//Ebyr
> Aberan//

For the first headword, he provides three different plural forms. The second one is actually a diminutive derived by adding the suffix *-an*. He also made an attempt to adequately reflect grapheme-phoneme-relations. Jones, however, used a system employed by Gruffydd Robert in his grammar (cf. section 2.2.1.2.1.) according to which /ɬ/ is represented by ⟨ḷ⟩, /ð/ by ⟨ḍ⟩ and /w/ by ⟨ụ⟩ (cf. also Bowen 1997: 212f.).

Preparations for a trilingual dictionary may perhaps be seen in his word lists kept in MS Peniarth 308 written down in 1639. In 1640 he started to compile the first multilingual dictionary in Wales, that is, a trilingual Welsh-Latin-English dictionary (MS Peniarth 310). It, however, also remains incomplete and unprinted. The type of dictionary intended by Jones is briefly summarised in the manuscript description as follows:

> "The Welsh words are arranged in a column on the pages with the even numbers, while the Latin and English meanings are arranged in double columns on the pages opposite. The meanings however have been given in but very few instances" (J.G. Evans 1898: 1113) .

---

[1]   He was a copyist of Welsh manuscripts (cf. G.C.G. Thomas 1997: 254ff.). Since his father and grandfather sponsored bards, he copied their work for family manuscripts (cf. M. Stephens 1997: 396).

[2]   ḷ stands for *lluosog* 'plural'.

In this compilation, he employed both Welsh and Latin as *Metalanguages* indicating the word class of each headword as is illustrated by the examples below (J.G. Evans 1898: 1112):

A, pan fo Ragdodiad /Præpos : cum
2. pan fo cyssylldiad / Coniunctio Et, ac, atque./ And
A, Ragverf o holiad /Aduerb interrog An, Num, numquid

All considered, his attempt at writing a trilingual dictionary as well as employing Welsh as a *Metalanguage* merits acknowledgement in the development of Welsh lexicography.

152

(F)   Thomas Jones[1]

The last dictionary printed within the period under review is the Welsh-English dictionary *Y Gymraeg yn ei disgleirdeb, neu helaeth eir-lyfr Cymraeg a Saesnaeg Yn Cynwys yr holl eiriau yng Eirlyfr Dr. Davies* by Thomas Jones[2] (1648-1713), published in 1688 (cf. Emanuel 1974: 145). He produced his dictionary[3] for two major reasons - for the maintenance of the Welsh language and for the acquisition of English:

> "We [...] want nothing than the perfection of our Original Tongue [...] We have made too much use of new fashions (in our speaking) to retain our Mother Tongue, which might before now extirpate our Antiquity, had not some faithful lovers of our Language planted small Pillars of this nature to support it in times past [...]
> When I considered how many more of our Country-men are brought up to the learning of English than Latine, and how necessary it is for the Welsh and English to understand one another, I thought that the making of a Welsh and English Dictionary would be the best piece of service that ever could be done for the re-establishing of the Welsh tongue, and for our conduct in learning of English" (T. Jones 1688: A4)[4]

In view of the whole content of the extensive introductory parts of Jones' dictionary, language maintenance seems to be the major purpose of his work; learning, translating[5] (cf. 3. in the following quote), and correctness in spelling being secondary aspects. Under *Am y deunydd a wneir o'r llyfr hwn* 'On the use that should be made of this book'[6] he writes:

> "1. Pan gaffoch y gair Cymraeg a bôch yn ei geisio yn y llyfr hwn, yno gellwch weled, a dysgu y ffordd iw (spelio) ag iw ysgrifennu yn gywir [...]
> 2. Yr ail deunŷdd iw; pan gyfarfyddoch wrth ddarllen Cymraeg a geiriau a fo dieithrol i chwi, neu eiriau na bôch yn eu deall: chwiliwch am y geiriau hynnŷ yn y llyfr hwn; ag wrthŷnt cewch eiriau eraill o gymraeg groŷwach a chynefinach i chwi, yn dangos i chwi feddwl y geiriau dieithrol hynnŷ [...]
> 3. Trydydd deunydd y llyfr hwn iw danghosiad y gair Saesnaeg i bob gair Gymraeg; A hynny sydd gyfleus iawn i bob Cymro a chwenycho ddysgu Saesnaeg, ag angenrheidiol i'r nêb a gyfieutho o'r cymraeg i'r Saesnaeg [...]
> 4. Yn bedwaredd, y llyfr hwn sy ddeunyddiol iawn i'r neb a fynne ddysgu spelio'r Saesnaeg yn gywir [...]

---

[1]   I would like to take this opportunity of thanking William Ll. Griffith, Dinbych/Wales, for helpful discussion and assistance with translation.

[2]   Jones first worked as a tailor, but subsequently took on bookselling and publishing. He was a printer and bookseller in London. Later he established Shrewsbury as the main centre for the printing of Welsh books until the eighteenth century and is also called the father of Welsh publishing (cf. Ch. Parry 1997: 270).

[3]   It has been argued that Jones did not produce the work on his own. For details with regard to this matter, see Hincks (1993: 4f.).

[4]   According to the way of counting pages these days, the quote is on pp. 2f.

[5]   It is interesting to see that translating does not form a separate purpose in his list. It may still have been recognised as a method of learning (cf. section 2.2.1.1.).

[6]   Some parts of his introduction are in Welsh, some are in Welsh and English. The reason for this approach reads as follows:
"I thought it needles to direct the English Reader how to understand, and to make use of this Book, for I suppose there is but few of those that can read English, but are acquainted with the Rules, Method, and Use of a Dictionary" (T. Jones 1688: 14).

5. Yn bumed, ag yn ddiwethâf, y llyfr hwn sydd gyfleus iawn, ag anghenrheidiol (i'r pêth a gwnaed ef yn benna: hynny ydiw) i gadw'r gymraeg rhag ei cholli.

Er amled yr arfero'r Cymru eiriau newyddion o gymhendod; ac er parotted a font i newid eu hên Iaith am ryw gymysgiad a gandrelli'r Saesnaeg; ni newid y llyfr hwn bŷth, pob gair, a sŷlast, a llythyren ag fsŷdd ynddo, a safant yn wastadol fel ag i maent er y dechrau.

'1. When you find the Welsh word you are looking for in this book, there you can see and learn the way to spell and write it correctly [...]

2. The second purpose is: when you come across words which are strange to you whilst reading Welsh, or words you do not understand: search for these words in this book; and near to them you will find other Welsh words plainer and more familiar to you showing you the meaning of those strange words [...]

3. The third purpose of this book is the display of the English for each Welsh word; and this is very convenient for every Welshman wishing to learn English, and necessary for those translating Welsh into English [...]

4. Fourth, this book is very useful for those desiring to learn to spell English correctly [..]

5. Fifth, and lastly, this book is very convenient, and necessary (for the purpose it was mainly made: that is) to safeguard Welsh from extinction.

As frequent as it be that the Welsh employ new words in prudery, and inclined as they may be to change their ancient language for some mixture of fragmentary English; this book will never change, every word, and syllable and letter contained therein, shall remain always as they have been from the beginning' (ibid.: 13f.).'

In reading the last declaration of purpose in combination with other sections of the introduction (cf. also p. 8), it becomes apparent that Jones' prime wish is to purify the Welsh language and that his belief be that language maintenance and purification are closely related to one another. This being probably the reason for placing within brackets such words as:

> "the Britains have (so needlesly) borrowed of the English, (to distinguish them from the True British words) although the Britains had no more need to borrow words of the English, than the English had to become the Frenchmen's Apes, as the Englishman is examoured with the tricks and quillets of the Frenchman's garments, so are the Britains enchanted with the Englishman's dialect, insomuch that the Britains own Language is now become as barbarous as their neighbours" (ibid.: 8).

The following extract from Jones' book is intended to illustrate its structure:

154

AB	AB
A. *And, with, whether.*	Abediw, perthynasan cladde-
Ab, mab. *A Son.*	digaeth, *Funeral Ceremonies*
Ab,(Siancanâp) *an Ape.*	Aber. *a Brook of running Water.*
Abad, pen llywŷdd abatty.	Aberth, (Offrymiad) *an Offer-*
an Abbot.	*ing or Sacrifice.*
Abades, pen llywŷddes, A-	Aberthu, (offrymu.) *to offer*
batty. *an Abbes.*	*or sacrifice.*
Abadaeth, aberthyno i be-	Aberthawr, (offrymwr.) *a*
naeth yr Eglwŷs, megis	*Sacrificer, a Priest.*
Esgobaeth ei Esgob. *an*	Aberthwr, (offrymwr.) *a Sa-*
Abbotship.	*cificer or Priest.*
Abattŷ , math ar Eglwys	Abl) difai galluogrwydd
fawr, mynachlog. *an Abby*	*Sufficient, able.*
or Monastery.	Abledd, galluogrwydd. *Abi-*
Aball, pallder. *Defect or Infir-*	*lity, sufficiency.*
mity.	Abo, bŷrgŷn, corph marw
Aballu, methu, pallu. *To pe-*	*dead carcase*
rish, to fail.	Abrwysgl, braisg, *very large*
Aban, rhyfel. *War, Battle.*	*big, or thick*
Abar, budreddi. *Filthiness.*	Absen) allan o ŵŷdd. *Ab-*
Abdon, henw dyn. *The name*	*sence.*
of a man	Absennwr) drŵg,a ogano un

The following comments briefly illustrate some of the general achievements of Jones' dictionary taken as a whole:[7]

1. Jones generally provides Welsh synonyms or other lexical definitions before presenting the English equivalents. He himself explains that this method is intended (a) to show the semantic range of the headwords included, (b) to explain words which are difficult to understand, (c) to offer synonyms to poets "whereby they may the easier compose their Poems in good Meeters", and (d) to display varying spelling, because "The setting of these various ways of spelling together, is also very necessary for Poets, being a great ease and liberty to them for the Rhiming of their Poems" (Jones 1688: 7).

   In the twentieth century, the practice of including synonyms in Welsh-English diction-aries is only known from *Y Geiriadur Mawr* (cf. section 4.2.).

2. Jones is proud, however, that he managed to reduce the size of Dr John Davies' diction-ary, although he includes more headwords than the latter:

   "And [...] upon many hundreds of other words hath Dr Davies paraphrased, and swelled up his Dictionary: And thereby all persons that would buy it, were tyed to the price of a great Book, for what might (very well) be contained in a little one" (Jones 1688: 11).

This reduction, however, cuts the grammatical information contained in the dictionaries of T. Wiliems, Dr John Davies, Mallwyd, H. Salesbury and J. Jones back to the level of

---

7   To have all peculiarities of his dictionary exemplified, a separate investigation would be neces-sary.

the most rudimentary information provided by W. Salesbury. Similarly to W. Salesbury, T. Jones indicates the word classes of most of the English equivalents only indirectly by placing the indefinite article in front of most of the English nouns and 'to' before most English verbs.

H. Salesbury did not indicate word classes either, but included collective nouns together with their singulative (cf. above). Both form separate entries in T. Jones' dictionary, as can be seen with *adar* 'birds' and its singulative *aderyn* 'bird':[8]

> Adar, *birds.*
> Adar llwch-gwin , *Vultures,*
>   *Griffons.*
> Adar y bwnn. *Birds called*
>   *Bitterns.*
> Adar y drudwy. *Birds called*
>   *Stares or Starlings.*
> Adar y tô. *Sparrows.*
> Adardŷ, cawell adar. *A bird-*
>   *cage.*
> Adblygu, diblygu. *to unfold.*
> Adefŷn, edef. *Thred or yarn.*
> Adeg, treiad y lleuad, neu
>   Rhwng y llawnlloned ar
>   Newid. *The decrease of the*
>   *moon.*
> Adeiniog, adenog, *winged,*
>   *feathered.*
> Adeinŷdd, yr un ag adenŷdd.
>   Adenŷdd. *Wings ; also the*
>   *spokes of a wheel.*
> Aderŷn, *a bird.*

Davies and J. Jones also included the plural forms of the nouns, something that is ignored by T. Jones, too.

3. In addition, like W. Salesbury Jones' dictionary displays a 'second-letter order', whereby *ch* is recognised as a separate letter and follows *c*, although in particular Thomas Wiliems already arranged his headword list in alphabetical order.

4. Jones is the first who makes abundant use of Breton loanwords. He takes many of the Breton lexical items included in Dr John Davies' dictionary (cf. above) for illustrative purposes as Welsh (loan) words, e.g. *caluedd,*[9] <- Bret. caluez 'carpenter', Gwengolo 'September'.[10] It is not clear whether he regarded them as Welsh or chose them deliberately in order to counterbalance English influence. Both aspects seem possible,

---

[8]   This is a method employed for the display of the comparative forms of adjectives in some dictionaries of the twentieth century (cf. section 4.3.3.3.).

[9]   In Modern Breton it is *kalvez.*

[10]   For a complete list, see Hincks (1993: 7-17).

since Jones was not a linguist (cf. also Hincks 1993: 4f.) and, in addition, defined the Bretons as Welsh when writing in his dictionary:

Llydaw, henw man yn ffraingc lle y mae Cymru yn bŷw:[11] Britain in France.

T. Jones apparently only knew of the two dictionaries in print (cf. also his preface, p. 2) and thus could not take notice of major achievements with regard to the grammatical description of individual lexical items. He may, however, not have seen the necessity to include such a description and perhaps ignored, for instance, Davies' grammatical information on purpose as he was keen on producing "inexpensive adequately printed reading matter for the common man" and to supply cheap Welsh-language books of good technical quality (Ch. Parry 1997: 268). In addition, he had no academic background and did perhaps not feel the need to display his knowledge or take notice of works in manuscript form. The emphasis on his printing abilities becomes apparent when looking at the appendices at the end of the dictionary, in which Jones explains symbols, numbers, characters, and provides poetry and a list of corrections. Reading the introductory parts of his work (cf. Jones 1688: 14) leaves us with the impression that the use of dictionaries was at that time still rather uncommon in Wales. A reference book of the type produced by T. Jones may, therefore, have been necessary to popularise such usage.

Although falling behind the achievements of Welsh lexicography particluarly with regard to grammatical description as contained in dictionaries, Jones produced a remarkable dictionary both in quality of print and affordability.

---

[11]   The translation reads as follows: 'Llydaw, place name in France where the Welsh live'.

(G)   Summary

In the period under review, i.e. from 1536/43 to 1689, the Welsh produced two Welsh-English dictionaries, two Welsh-Latin dictionaries,[12] one Latin-Welsh and one Latin-Welsh/Welsh-Latin dictionary. The *Lexicon Tetraglotton* compiled in 1660 by the Welshman James Howell (1593-1666)[13] has not been discussed. Since it is an English-French-Italian-Spanish dictionary which only contains Welsh proverbs but no Welsh headwords, thus allocating Welsh a rather inferior status (cf. Jenkins 1997: 370), it falls outside the scope of this investigation.

There are also various word lists which remain in manuscript form (cf. J.E. Caerwyn Williams 1988: 103) and have not yet been related to individual authors. Their discussion also deserves separate treatment.

Dictionaries in manuscript form were obviously not as well known as those in print (cf. T. Jones). Consequently, they may not have been used as learning and teaching aids for a broader audience, but predominantly served the humanist scholar in order to enlarge his knowledge. The first dictionary was perhaps also limited in its use (cf. W. Salesbury) in that it was maybe difficult to be used as a self-introductory tool and rather constituted one which assisted the instruction of the teacher. Nevertheless, it reflects phenomena of the Welsh language that persist into our days.

Welsh dictionaries produced during the Renaissance as a whole mirror a knowledge of phonetics (cf. W. and H. Salesbury), of grammar, of lexicology, and of lexicographical developments (cf. T. Wiliems) among their compilers. The lexicon included provided material for specialist lexicography, but also rudiments of comparative linguistics and etymological considerations (cf. Dr J. Davies). Whereas specialist lexicography developed in the eighteenth century, some aspects of linguistics where not developed significantly further until the twentieth century, e.g. grammatical description, pronunciation, hyphenation.

Early Welsh dictionaries seem to have emerged from bardic works (cf. W. Salesbury). They at least relied heavily on the materials the bards had produced (cf. T. Wiliems, Dr J. Davies, H. Salesbury, J. Jones). A new quality of compiling dictionaries was introduced after T. Wiliems had studied lexicographical works from a different cultural background, e.g. that of Calepinus and of Thomas Thomas. However, the dictionaries following his successor Dr J. Davies did not keep to the standard previously achieved in the description of the headwords. Nevertheless, dictionary production now became more continuous and the quality of print improved.

---

[12]   In Emanuel (1974: 152), a Welsh-Latin vocabulary in the hand of William Maurice († 1680) is listed, but there are no further details given.

[13]   Howell's biography suggests that he was fluent in several languages. He was a graduate at Oxford, who was fluent in Latin and used his language gift as a representative of traders and politicians. After a carreer in the public sector, which enabled him to travel Europe, and a period in prison he was appointed *Historiographer Royal*. Whilst being imprisoned in the wake of the *Civil War*, he wrote forty books. In addition, Howell became famous as a poet and author who produced more books than any of his contemporaries. His major works were translated into various European languages (cf. M. Stephens 1977: 338).

At the end of the Renaissance, the Welsh humanists could thereby present their language as one equal to others in lexicon available to denote new social contexts. At a time when the traditional learned class, the *Bardic Order*, was already in a state of collapse and could no longer act as the main preserver of the language, the humanists introduced a systematic scholarly linguistic description as a substitution.

2.2.3.   Final remarks

The specific pre-conditions for dictionary production developed in Wales during the Renaissance, when education was no longer restricted to elitist groups, but was accepted as part of profound and comprehensive education for larger groups of people, particularly for those working as specialists in new professions (cf. section 2.2.1.1.). In this context, new conditions for learning developed, such as learning in an educational system with schools and universities,[1] as well as new learning methods and aims. Further social conditions were established by new scientific, economic and technical achievements, which laid the foundations for extensive book production, and by a new stage of intellectual and cultural exchange.

Within these social contexts, dictionaries developed from the habit of glossing and explaining difficult passages from the Bible and other religious and non-religious texts, while at the same time teaching languages and related subjects (cf. sections 2.1.-2.1.4.). The new quality of dictionaries, in contrast to glossaries and vocabularies, can be characterised by the following features:

- they developed from being mainly supplementary tools into basic teaching aids (cf. in particular T. Jones), into tools for translation (cf. T. Jones) and, in addition, into compendia of the language to describe and to handle knowledge (cf. T. Wiliems, Dr J. Davies, H. Salesbury);
- dictionaries contained as many lexical items as were considered necessary to meet the needs of contemporary communication (cf. T. Wiliems, J. Davies, H. Salesbury, T. Jones);
- they regularly included additional linguistic information, particularly on grammar, semantics, phonetics, stylistics, and/or etymology in order to (a) display knowledge (cf. J. Davies), (b) enrich the language of the dictionary users (cf. T. Jones), (c) make the meaning of lexical items explicit, or (d) guide correctness in spelling (T. Jones) and pronunciation (cf. W. Salesbury);
- they were aimed at a particular audience (cf. W. Salesbury, T. Jones) and produced on the basis of concepts which were acquired by studying preceding dictionaries or other lexicographical material (cf. W. Salesbury, T. Wiliems, Dr J. Davies, T. Jones);
- they were intended to increase the prestige of the vernacular language and to develop it;
- in the case of languages of limited social influence, such as Welsh, they were produced to maintain and purify, and thereby stabilising them (cf. T. Jones).

When Welsh dictionary production began, the compilation of English dictionaries had already been flourishing for more than a century[2] (cf. section 2.2.1.1.). Shortly after the publication of the first Welsh dictionary, the English started with specialist lexicography and produced dictionaries for beginners, of synonyms, a picture and a monolingual dictionary (cf. section

---

[1]   The Welsh attended English universities, since there were none in Wales at that time.
[2]   Some scholars regard the English glossaries from the seventh and eighth centuries still in use in the fifteenth century as the first dictionaries (cf. section 2.1.3. and Lehnert 1956: 271).

2.2.1.1.).

The first Breton dictionary the *Catholicon*, a Breton-French-Latin reference book, was compiled by Jehan Lagadeuc in 1464 and printed by Jehan Calvez in 1499 (cf. section 3.2.2.). It placed Breton ahead of its sister languages as far as the first dictionary was concerned (J.E. Caerwyn Williams 1983: 10).[3]

The Gaels were somewhat late in contributing a dictionary.[4] The first Irish dictionary was Ó Cléirigh's monolingual *Foclóir no Sanasan Nua* published in 1643 (cf. Welch 1996: 148 and below).[5] The first Scottish Gaelic dictionary was the *Focloir Gaoidheilge-Shagsonach no Bearladoir Scot-Sagsamhuil: An Irish-English Dictionary*, compiled by F.O. Molloy (cf. sections 2.3. and 3.2.6.) and published by Edward Lhuyd in his *Archaeologia Britannica* in 1707.[6] The first dictionary for Manx was the *Triglot Dictionary of the Celtic Languages*, a Manx-Irish-English dictionary compiled by Dr John Kelly in 1808.[7] For Cornish, there do not seem to have been any lexicographical works, except the *Vocabularium Cornicum* (cf. section 2.1.4.) before the disappearance of this language.[8]

With regard to the quantity of dictionaries produced during the Renaissance, Wales can in no way compete with England, although it comes first within the Celtic regions (cf. chapter III). The level of linguistic description in them also remained behind that of English dictionaries. The latter, for instance, displayed the lexicon in alphabetical order, which was internationally not yet contemporary common practice (cf. Lehnert 1956: 277, Stein 1986: 219). In Welsh dictionaries, however, the second-letter order was dominant.

Early English dictionaries seen as a whole would include indication of pronunciation by diacritical signs, exemplifying contexts, idiomatic expressions, definitions of words, basic etymological explanations, grammatical classification, and elementary usage notes covering style and register.

Early Welsh dictionaries seen as a whole would claim to provide synonyms (cf. W. Salesbury, T. Wiliems, Dr J. Davies, J. Jones, T. Jones), to exemplify lexical items in context, to present definitions of words and some lexical variation, to introduce to different degrees basic

---

3   For further dictionaries, see chapter III.

4   The question as to whether the late appearance of Irish dictionaries was due to the still flourishing bardic and clerical system which covered any scholarly need and/or due to its territorial isolation falls outside the scope of this investigation and is not discussed here. For further dictionaries, see chapter III.

5   In other publications it counts as a vocabulary, e.g. in Best (1913: 7). In de Bhaldraithe (vol. 6, no. 1: 7) the *Foclóir Laidin-Gaeilge*, compiled by Risteárd Pluincéad in 1662, is introduced as the first Irish dictionary. This, however, was never published.

6   This dictionary was intended for both the Irish and the Scottish, a fact confirmed in the appendix of the dictionary, which reads:

> "Having since the Printing this *Irish Dictionary*, sent Copies to *Ireland* and *Scotland*, in order to have it improv'd ; the following Supplement consists chiefly of some Notes return'd thence by two Gentlemen [...]" (Lhuyd 1707: 426).

7   This dictionary, however, was not printed before 1866. The first Manx dictionary in print was that by A. Cregeen published in 1835 (cf. also section 3.2.5.).

8   For more details, see Ternes (1991: 2348) and section 3.2.3.

morphological categories (cf. Dr J. Davies, H. Salesbury, J. Jones) and to a limited extent pseudo-etymological explanations (cf. Dr J. Davies). There are no indications of pronunciation, although some Welsh scholars, including W. Salesbury, were familiar with phonetic descriptions (cf. Siôn Dafydd Rhys in section 2.2.1.2.1. and W. Salesbury in section 2.2.2.). Some of the contexts included in Welsh dictionaries can be specified as poetry and some as proverbs.

These contexts, therefore, rather reflected idiomatic usage found in literature, which was not necessarily easily or broadly applicable in everyday communication and scientific language. Appendices explaining rhetoric or artistic composition can also be found.

The earliest lexicographical works in Western Europe were predominantly compilations which presented the vernacular language together with the important or dominant language that was to be understood, that is, the first dictionaries were mainly bilingual and displayed the vernacular language first and then Latin.[9] As is illustrated in the following, this was different in Wales (and also in Ireland):

1.	Monolingual lexicographical works dominated here first. Apart from a Latin-Welsh herbal list from the fourteenth century, they are attested for Wales at least from the fifteenth century (cf. sections 2.1.4. and 2.2.1.2.2.), that is, earlier than in England.[10]

2.	Monolingual compilations demonstrate an interest in mastering and developing the vernacular language at an early date in history. They were mainly compiled by bards, that is, by the feudal elite oriented towards literary scholarship, a phenomenon that can also be observed in Ireland. The first dictionary to be produced in this country was monolingual (i.e. Irish-Irish, cf. development before Pluincéad's dictionary, above).[11]

3.	The decline of the *Bardic Order* during the Renaissance and the rise of the humanists marked, as far as can be assumed from the material handed down to us, a change of emphasis in lexicographical work away from monolingual vocabularies to bilingual dictionaries starting

4.	with a Welsh-English one, thereby reflecting new political constellations in society.

---

[9]	This is also true for early English dictionaries. The first English dictionaries were two English-Latin ones. After 1460, they were followed by two Latin-English dictionaries (cf. Stein 1996).

[10]	English-English dictionaries were not published before the seventeenth century (cf. Osselton 1986 and section 2.2.1.1.).

[11]	In contrast to Wales Ireland had a strong tradition of glossary production (cf. section 2.1.3.). Nevertheless, with regard to the first Irish dictionary, Harrison (1986: 51f.) describes the situation in comparison to English lexicographical works as follows:
"Is é an chéad fhoclóir Gaeilge a cuireadh i gcló an *Sanasán Nua* le Mícheál Ó Clérigh a cuireadh i gcló i Lobhían i 1643. Féachaimis ar theideal an leabhair sin: Focloir no Sanasan Nua ina mínighthear cáil eigin de fhoclaibh cruaidhe na gaoidheilge, [...]
Is spéisiúil an rud é freisin a chosúla a bhí aidhm fhoclóir Uí Chléirigh agus aidhm an chéad fhoclóra Béarla : Béarla a d'fhoilsigh Robert Cawdrey sa bhliain 1604."
'The first printed Gaelic dictionary was the *New Vocabulary* by Mícheál Ó Cléirigh, printed in 1643 in Louvain. We see in the title of that book:
The dictionary or new vocabulary in which some meanings of difficult words in Gaelic are explained [...]
It is interesting to compare the scope of Ó Clérigh's dictionary with that of the first English-English dictionary published by Robert Cawdrey in 1604.'

5. Although the dictionaries were mainly produced outside the bards' spheres, they were not compiled independently from these as was previously illustrated (cf. above). Indeed a kind of labour division emerged, whereby the scholars predominantly dealt with bilingual and the bards with monolingual material[12] - useful for literary training and composition - as well as with some grammatical tracts.

Keeping close to the fading feudal elite (cf. sections 2.2.1.2.2. and 2.2.2.) as well as practising translating, copying and enlarging copies themselves, Welsh humanists codified a language in their grammars, vocabularies and dictionaries, which were mainly based on the literary language. They thus followed similar trends in European lexicography in which a preference for written to spoken sources was evident (cf. Kibbee 1986: 146) and emphasised the importance of the bards' linguistic inheritance.

In keeping with the Renaissance ideal of versatile and educated people, the early lexicographers were erudite and possessors of comprehensive knowledge and skills, rather than specialists in lexicography. But only by being so versatile could they succeed in developing any aspect of linguistics, laying the foundation for later specialisation in the field of linguistic research and thus the basis for modern lexicography. Special professions, such as language teachers, translators, and other specialists in related fields developed as a social phenomenon mainly in the wake of the processes described (cf. section 2.2.1.1.), i.e. after the period under review.

At the very moment, therefore, when dictionaries became popular Europe-wide and the first methods of compiling were established, the Welsh joined in with their own fund of knowledge. Although subject to delay, they succeeded in keeping up with basic trends in European linguistics.

At the same time, however, they fell behind in the field of specialist lexicography. In addition, deficiencies in the description of the Welsh language, such as the grammatic and phonetic description of the lexicon, became apparent as early as at that time. Because of harmful and adverse developments imposed on Welsh society from the outside (cf. section 2.2.1.1.), the Welsh ended up in a situation in which they failed to keep up with the latest European ideas in science. Welsh scholars did not reproduce European linguistic trends in the same complexity, quantity or of a comparatively high standard for their own language, thus leaving a gap in the quantity and quality of dictionary production in comparison with England, a situation from which Wales has never fully recovered.

> "The valuable linguistic groundwork laid by the humanist scholars [did not] herald a new crop of writing in diverse branches of learning in succeeding generations. Welsh humanist learning remained confined by the problem of limited human and material resources: Given the constraints imposed by the social conditions of the Welsh language in the sixteenth and seventeenth centuries, it can be seen that the humanists embarked upon a programme which was nigh on impossible to realize" (Jarvis 1997: 152).

---

[12]   One of the last bards known to have produced a vocabulary was Ieuan Fardd (cf. section 2.2.2.).

Events in the wake of the incorporation of Wales into England, therefore, caused more retardation for the development of Welsh society than inspiration for it.

> "In their own terms [the humanists] did not succeed. From a wider historical perspective, however, two great areas of achievement stand out: the first is that they ensured that the Welsh language [...] was refined and enhanced as a dignified and flexible instrument of learning and creative expression. They were the fathers of the modern tradition of Welsh prose. The second great achievement is less tangible. It is the bequeathing of a spirit of almost fierce love and the conviction that, for the Welsh language, given the right conditions, all things are possible. Such was the inheritance that they passed on to their heirs, the scholars of the eighteenth-century revival of learning" (ibid.).

2.3.   The Classical Period

The Classical period and its philosophical and social movement of the Enlightenment derived from the conditions in society at the end of the Renaissance period. Rational thoughts and the belief of human tolerance dominated the ideas of this period.

The Classical period can roughly be dated to a time from the end of the seventeenth century to the second half of the eighteenth century (cf. M. Stephens 1997: 107). Problems of strict distinction between the Classical and the following Romantic period become apparent when realising that Ieuan Fardd, for instance, is attributed to both of them (ibid.: 107, 640 and section 2.2.2.).[1] Although basically different, the periods under review actually developed from each other and overlapped one another.

The Classical period witnessed a step forward in Welsh lexicography, although in the context of Celtic linguistics. The enlightened scientist Edward Lhuyd (1660?-1709)[2] compared the three most thriving Celtic languages he identified at his time, i.e. Breton, Irish,[3] and Welsh, thereby inaugurating comparative studies of Celtic languages and establishing etymological relations between them. As a result, firm etymological considerations became part of Welsh lexicography as soon as his *Archaeologia Britannica* was published in 1707.

This work, the biggest part of which remained unpublished,[4] was the result of a four-year voyage of discovery through all Celtic regions of Britain, as well as through Ireland and Brittany (cf. G.H. Jenkins 1997: 376). Important parts of Lhuyd's compendium with regard to lexicography are: *Comparative etymology, A comparative vocabulary of the original languages of Britain and Ireland*, an *Armoric-English vocabulary*[5], a Welsh vocabulary under the title *Some Welch Words Omitted in Dr Davies's Dictionary, A British etymologicon; or, The Welsh collated with the Greek and Latin and some other European languges*, and a *Focloir Gaoidheilge-Shagsonach: an Irish-English Dictionary* compiled by F. O. Molloy (cf. sections 3.2.6.). Added to these works is an appendix which displays Irish and Scottish words sent to him after he had distributed his dictionary for corrections in both countries.

---

[1]   The same is true for the German composer Ludwig van Beethoven (1770-1827).

[2]   Lhuyd was born in South Wales as an illegitimate child. Because of monetary considerations, he never completed his degree as a lawyer at Oxford university, but studied natural history with the first keeper of the Ashmolean Museum Dr Plot. In 1684 Lhuyd was appointed under-keeper of the Museum. He became the head keeper of the Museum in 1690. "He moved in erudite circles and was at the hub of a constant and invigorating traffic and exchange of ideas" (G.H. Jenkins 1997: 376). Lhuyd was well known for his expertise in botany and geology. Sir Isaac Newton paid for the publication of one of his books. In 1701 he was granted an honorary M.A. in Oxford, in 1708 he was elected a fellow of the Royal Society, and in 1709 he was elected to be an esquire beadle of divinity.

[3]   He did not consider Irish and Scottish Gaelic as separate languages, although he realised differences between them (cf. Lhuyd 1707: 426).

[4]   The Ashmolean Museum refused to publish any of his writings that were left and sold them at an auction. In subsequent years most were lost, since the private library which kept many of his unpublished works was destroyed by a fire. The Museum fell into disrepair and many manuscripts were damaged beyond repair.

[5]   This vocabulary is based on the work of Julien Maunoir (1659, see section 3.2.2.) which was translated into English by M. Williams.

Among the unpublished material of Lhuyd's *Archaeologia Britannica* is a Manx vocabulary (cf. D. Ifans & R.L. Thomson 1979/80: 129-165).[6]

Lhuyd was well aware of the distinction between the term 'vocabulary' and 'dictionary'. Apart from some definitions illustrating the precise meaning of a few headwords, the Welsh vocabulary, therefore, is rather a word list which indicates the verbs by preceding 'to' and the nouns by the article. Lexical definitions would be in Welsh, such as for *Bettus* 'Abbatis'[7] or English, such as for *Pil* 'Dim'. Equivalents in Latin, Greek or German may in rare cases also be included:

> Lòlio, *To babble.* Πξ[8]
> λαλιᾶς, *Babblers, news-*
> *mongers.* D.[9]
> Lhever, *Light. Lux.* V.[10]
> *& alii.*
> Rheidyr, *A Knight.* V.
> *It's the same with the*
> *German* Ritter.q.d.[11] An-
> glicè *A Rider.*

The Irish dictionary is more comprehensive and contains definitions on a more regular basis, now in Irish or English, often plurals or finite verb forms as is illustrated by the following examples:

> Ainm, *A name. A noun,* pl. An-
> manna.
> Ainmnughadh, *To name* : D'ain-
> mnigh se, *He named*; go ain-
> mnighe, *namely.*

It is interesting to realise that Lhuyd based his Welsh vocabulary on the dictionary of Dr John Davies, Mallwyd, and not on that of Thomas Jones (cf. section 2.2.2.). Since Lhuyd himself refers for comparative reasons to foreign languages in his compilations, he might have had more interest in Davies' work or might have esteemed it higher. In this context, however, it is perhaps not surprising that his Welsh vocabulary is still not in strict alphabetical order as is displayed in the following examples:

> Adhien, *Fair*
> Adhia, *A stranger.* V.
>
> Beirniad, *A Judge.* S.[12]
> Beirion, *Kites* V.

---

6   I am indebted to Dr Habil G. Broderick for bringing this vocabulary to my attention.
7   He does not give an English equivalent for *Bettus*, but only a similar Latin expression.
8   This word is not readable.
9   'D' stands for 'Davies's Welsh Dictionary and MS. Notes'.
10   'V' indicates references to 'An old Welsh vocabulary out of Mr. Vaughan of Hengwrt's Study'.
11   'q.d.' is Latin 'quasi dicas'.
12   'S' indicates a reference to the dictionary of Henry Salesbury.

Lhuyd, nevertheless, also consulted lexicographical works in manuscript form, e.g. the diction-ary of Henry Salesbury and others (cf. section 2.2.2. and Lhuyd 1707: The Abbreviations). In contrast to the preceeding lexicographers, however, he did not seem to be familiar with Welsh poetry and prose (cf. Carr 1983: 72 and his definition of *englyn* as an epigram in Lhuyd 1907: The Abbreviations).

To conclude, it has to be emphasised that within his *Archaeologia Britannica* Lhuyd detected the common origin of the Celtic languages and formulated

> "the Celtic p and q languages theory. He had also broken new ground by discovering the significance of Old Welsh and recognizing the continuation of the orthography from the earliest days of the inscriptions" (ibid.: 376).

It was the greatest achievement of the enlightenment and its concept of rational thought to put Celtic studies on a firm scientific basis. Not surprisingly, the task was accomplished by a versatile and talented scientist.

Apart from Thomas Richards' (1710-1790)[13] *Antiquæ linguæ Britannicæ thesaurus* (cf. chap-ter III) published in 1753, English-Welsh dictionaries dominated in this period. The basis of his work was the translation of the dictionary of Dr John Davies, Mallwyd.[14] Richards extended the dictionary by lexical items he took from Edward Lhuyd including scientific lexis and quotations from ancient authors as well as by synonyms and equivalents from other languages (cf. dictionaries of Dr John Davies and T. Jones in section 2.2.2., Hincks 1993: 18). Adding a Welsh grammar to his dictionary, he offered a broad lexical basis and a compendium of the language to the bards (Carr 1983: 70).

The four English dictionaries (cf. chapter III) produced in this period, however, were intended for the Welsh who wanted or needed to read English, but did not know the language. The status of Welsh is clearly expressed when William Evans (fl. 1768-1776)[15] says in his *English-Welsh Dictionary: containing All Words necessary for Reading an English Author; wherein not only the Corresponding British is given to the English, and the various Significa-tions properly arranged; but also Every English Word is accented to prevent a bad Pronunciation, The Part of Speech added to which each Word respectively belongs, And proper Authorities subjoined where necessary*:

> "The mutual intercourse between the natives of this Principality and their neighbours the English, has rendered the study of the English Tongue necessary to every one in this Country, whose views are raised above the plowman and the labourer; and the great number of English publications continually circulated among us, make an Undertaking of this kind, not only useful, but necessary [...] It may also be of great service to young Divines, who [...] have had their education at the Universities, or other Seminars of learning, where only the English and learned languages are studied. --- The tradesman likewise must find a work of this kind extremely serviceable, as all commerce is carried

---

13   No details were available to me with regard to his life.
14   His dictionary, therefore, contains Breton lexical items which can als be found in the dictionary of Dr John Davies, Mallwyd (cf. section 2.2.2.). They are, in contrast to the dictionary of Thomas Jones, clearly indicated again.
15   No details were available to me with regard to his life.

on in English, which must at first be difficult to a Cambro-Briton, without the assistance of an English-Welsh Dictionary" (Evans 1771: Preface).

In Evans' dictionary, an attempt was made to indicate English pronunciation by diacritical signs and occasionally also by the spelling, e.g. when *ache* is spelled *ake*. His work was based on Robert Ainsworth's (1660-1743) *Thesaurus Linguae Latinae compendarium*, an English-Latin Dictionary, published in 1736 (cf. Green 1997: 182f.) and other English authors (cf. Evans 1771: Preface). His dictionary consequently follows strict alphebtical order (cf. section 2.2.1.1.).

In order to have the emphasis on displaying first of all the Welsh language in lexicographical works again, social developments carried by new social movements were necessary. Such developments are briefly introduced in the next section.

2.4. The Romantic period

The Romantic period evolved at the end of the eighteenth century. Whereas it had reached its climax in England, France and Germany by the middle of the nineteenth century it lasted in Wales into the twentieth century (cf. M. Stephens 1997: 640). In this period major inventions in the sciences and industries (Industrial Revolution) laid the economic foundation for industrial capitalism.[1] A positive effect for Wales was the establishment of four university institutions in the nineteenth century, that is, St. David's College Llanbedr Pont Steffan in 1827, the Aberystwyth College in 1872, the Cardiff University in 1883, and the Bangor University in 1884. This allowed the development of a new Welsh elite.

Reflecting gradually evolving contradictions in society, dominating philosophical ideas now emphasised on the independent thought of the free individual. A mixture of mystical, idealist and humanist values demanded through education the formation of the character of modern people as independently thinking individuals allowing also emotions.

The influence of such romantic ideas effected Welsh lexicography. Without going into too much detail, some remarks will suffice in order to briefly illustrate major developments in this field. Although essentially new kinds of lexicographical works were not developed during this period, achievements in the description of the lexicon, however, generated various types of dictionaries.

One of the key figures of Romantic philologists was William Owen Pughe (1759-1835).[2] He belonged to the *Gwyneddigion Society*[3] whose members, similar to Johann Gottfried Herder (1744-1803) in *Über den Ursprung der Sprache* (1772), thought that language could arouse a sense of identity within a nation and thereby shape the character of its people. Members of the *Gwyneddigion Society* believed, therefore, that there was an obligation to nurture and strengthen the association between language and identity. These ideas are reflected in Pughe's dictionary *Geiriadur Cynmraeg a Saesoneg: A Welsh and English Dictionary ... to which is prefixed a Welsh Grammar* published between 1793 and 1803 (cf. chapter III). Since his work has already been studied in considerable detail,[4] some brief remarks will suffice. Related to ideas expressed,

---

[1]   For further information with regard to the industrial revolution, the transition of society into industrial capitalism and related philosophical ideas, see Bartel, H. & D. Fricke et al. (1984) and Klaus, G. & M. Buhr (1975).

[2]   He spent most of his life in London. Although married to an English woman, he eagerly worked for the sake of the Welsh language (cf. Carr 1983: 71). Pughe was familiar with, and published on, early Welsh literature (cf. list of publications in Carr 1983: 295).

[3]   The society *Y Gwyneddigion* 'The people of Gwynedd' was founded in London in 1770. The majority of its members came from the north of Wales. However, one of its most influential figures, Edward Williams (1747-1826), the bardic names of whom were Iolo Morganwg and Y Bardd Glas, was a stonemason from Glamorgan.

    To become a member of the society, one had to master Welsh and love singing to the harp. The society succeeded in publishing Welsh manuscripts, magazines and re-introducing the bardic competition, the *Eisteddfod* (cf. section 2.2.2.). After 1837 nothing more was heard of *Y Gwyneddigion* (cf. M. Stephens 1997: 312).

[4]   For comprehensive information with regard to his person and works, see Carr (1983). Further information can also be obtained in G.H. Jenkins (1997) and Hincks (1993).

for instance, in the book on *The Origins of Language and Nations* by Rowland Jones (1722-74),[5] many peculiarities can be found in Pughe's dictionary. They are described by Jenkins (1997: 397) as follows:

"Pughe was so enchanted by the notion that languages could be broken down into particles or atoms that he adopted it as the fundamental principle of his study of Welsh orthography. Spurred on by a burning desire to breathe new life into 'a nearly expiring language', Pughe began work on a new dictionary of the Welsh language in 1785. The first part was published in June 1793 and the complete edition, containing over 100,000 words, in 1803. Unlike John Walters, who remained firmly attached to well-established lexicographical and orthographical principles, Pughe believed that self-expression, creativity and even fabrication were required in order to prove to the Welsh themselves and the world at large that the Welsh language was virile, flexible and strong. His dictionary, therefore, was riddled with the most grotesque orthography which kept printers and proof-readers on their toes and almost totally baffled the common reader. In place of the letters ch, dd, f, ff, and ph, Pughe had substituted ç, z, v, f and f. Such orthographical horrors were compounded by the inclusion of strange-sounding words like 'cynnorthwyolion', 'gwrthymchwelogion', 'llewyrchiannawl', and 'ymddygymmysgiad'. Not all words, of course, were uncongenial, and it should not be forgotten that it was Pughe who coined words like 'alaw' (tune), 'awyren' (aeroplane), 'dathlu' (celebrate), and 'diddorol' (interesting), which are widely used in our own times. Pughe and his ally, Iolo Morganwg, genuinely believed that his orthography was erudite and impressive. In reality, however, it was dangerous bunkum which was greeted at the time with a torrent of vituperation.The dictionary [...] mystified and infuriated the ordinary reader. More critically, the bizarre orthography, bogus archaisms and turgid sentences which informed all his works made them a minefield for the unsuspecting scholar and especially for those who sought to emulate him. Even with the best will in the world, it is hard not to conclude that Pughe's lexicographical and orthographical enterprise was a colossal waste of time, effort and money" (G.H. Jenkins 1997: 397, cf. also Carr 1983: 73).

Nevertheless, Pughe apparently met the expectations of the audience which most enthusiastically furthered the Welsh language and literature. As a result, his work dominated the first half of the nineteenth century and remained important in its second half (cf. chapter III, but also Hincks 1993: 7). This fact is confirmed by the number of publications of Pughe's dictionaries (cf. chapter III) and illustrated in the preface of the dictionary of Gweirydd ap Rhys (cf. Pryse 1807-1889)[6] *Geiriadur Cymraeg a Saesneg*:

---

[5]   The ideas of Rowland Jones are described by G.H. Jenkins (1997: 397) as follows:
      "For the modern critic, his work is as useless as a ceiling fan in an airless room, but even in his own day reputable Welsh scholars were justly sceptical of his theories and ready to cast doubt on his sanity".
      Rowland Jones also claimed that Celtic was a primitive tongue that passed through 'Babel' (cf. Evangelische Haupt-Bibelgesellschaft: Moses, first book, section 11, 1-9) unharmed (Wight 1896: 192).

[6]   His English name was Robert John Pryse. He was an author and historian, born in Anglesey. Pryse was an orphan and had only four days of education in school. He began to read and write Welsh when working on a farm. Whilst running a shop he learned Latin, Greek and English. He contributed to the Welsh encyclopedia *Y Gwyddoniadur Cymreig* published between 1854 and 1879 and was also a distinguished writer (cf. M. Stephens 1997: 606).

"Y mae ein Geiriaduron Cymraeg a Saesneg talfyredig diweddar oll wedi cymmeryd o Eiriadur y Dr Pughe, ac anfynych y mae neb o'r Casglyddion wedi anturio rhoddi unrhyw eiriau i mewn sydd heb fod yn y Geiriadur ardderchog hwnw" (ap Rhys 1866: Rhagymadrodd).
'All the latest abridged Welsh and English dictionaries were taken from Dr Pughe's dictionary and rarely did one of the compilers venture to introduce any word which is not in this excellent Dictionary' (ibid.: Preface).

In 1806, Pughe published an abridgement of his dictionary titled *Geiriadur Cymraeg a Saesoneg: An Abridgement of the Welsh and English Dictionary.* In 1832 the second edition of Pughe's original dictionary was produced and in 1866 a third one under the title *Geiriadur Cenhedlaethol Cymraeg a Saesneg: A National Dictionary of the Welsh Language with English and Welsh Equivalents* was enlarged by Gweirydd ap Rhys.

Pughe's orthography, however, was not as influential as his lexical work as is illustrated by ap Rhys (1866: 5) and by the fact that it was not employed in the abridgement of Pughes' dictionary in 1806 (cf. section 3.2.).

Pughe's lexicographical work was based on the study of the dictionaries previously published, but also on vocabularies which remained in manuscript form, e.g. those of Wiliam Llŷn (cf. section 2.2.1.2.2.), Ieuan Fardd (cf. section 2.2.2.), or unpublished complete or incomplete dictionaries, such as those by John Jones (cf. section 2.2.2.), William Gambold (1672-1728, cf. Carr 1983: 70), and Lewis Morris (1701-65).[7] Not surprisingly, therefore, he included some of the Breton words found in the dictionaries by Dr John Davies, Mallwyd and Thomas Jones (cf. section 2.2.2.), e.g. *ceginwr* 'cook', *golfan* 'sparrow'.[8]

Pughe also produced a Welsh grammar keeping close to the tradition of earlier lexicographers, e.g. the bards Gruffudd Hiraethog and Simwnt Fychan (cf. sections 2.2.1.2.1. and 2.2.1.2.2.), the humanists Dr John Davies and Henry Salesbury (cf. section 2.2.2.), as well as Siôn Rhydderch (1673-1735, cf. list of Welsh dictionaries in section 3.2.1.), E. Lhuyd (cf. section 2.3.),[9] John Walters (1721-1797),[10] and William Gambold (cf. Carr 1983: 70, cf. also lexicographers of Scottish Gaelic in section 3.2.6.).

The nineteenth century also brought specialisation into Welsh lexicography which was first observed in England in the sixteenth century (cf. section 2.2.1.1.). After the bards' Welsh-Welsh vocabularies (cf. section 2.2.1.2.2.), the first Welsh-Welsh dictionary, i.e. the *Cyneirlyfr: neu*

---

[7]   Lewis, whose bardic name was Llewelyn Du o Fôn, belongs to the Morris family of Anglesey which became famous for its learning. Lewis, the oldest, is well known as a bard, scholar, and teacher of later bards and writers. He worked as a land-surveyor at the customs office and in the mining business. Intending to provide a corpus of literature for the Welsh, he published prose and poetry in his own publishing house. His intention to revise Dr John Davies' dictionary gave way to comprehensive lexicographical works, which however, remained unpublished.

[8]   For a complete list, see Hincks (1993: 7-17).

[9]   He did not publish a Welsh grammar, but a Breton grammar preceding his *Armoric-English vocabulary.*

[10]   The Rector of Landough included his *Dissertation on the Welsh language* (1771) also in his dictionary (cf. section 3.2.1.).

eiriadur Cymraeg, was compiled by Edward Williams and published in 1826. Two leading Welsh lexicographers, i.e. Thomas Richards (cf. section 2.3.) and John Walters (cf. chapter III), both natives of Glamorgan, had influenced Williams. He played a central role in the campaign to redefine, enrich and enhance the native language.

> "He was a prodigiously learned authority on the language and literature of Wales, a historian of great subtlety and imagination, and a highly skilful romantic poet. To these gifts and attributes might be added encyclopaedic knowledge, elephantine memory, egoism, volatility, demonic energy and caustic wit. Nothing was of greater importance to him than 'yr hen ddywenydd' (the old happiness) i.e. the study of Welsh language, literature and history. He dedicated around sixty years of his life to recovering - and embelleshing - the literary history of his native land and his name is greatly honoured to this day as one of the most successful literary forgers in the history of Europe" (G.H. Jenkins 1997: 398).

In particular because of the influence of Richards, Williams also made use of the Breton and Cornish languages in order to enrich Welsh. Although also borrowing lexical items from Latin, French and Irish, he found loanwords or loan translations from the p-Celtic languages much more natural (cf. Hincks 1993: 18ff.). He drew most of the Breton words from Lhuyd's *Archaeologia Britannica*[11] (cf. the work of Julien Maunoir, 1659 in section 3.2.2.).

Two years later, another Rowland Jones (fl. 1828)[12] published thirty-two pages on difficult Welsh lexical items in 1828 under the title *Geiriadur poblogaidd : yn cynnwys mwy nag wyth gant o eiriau a'nghyfiaith a arferir yn gyffredin yn lle geiriau Cymraeg, wedi eu hegluro a geiriau dealladwy dilediaith* (cf. appendix). Another Welsh-Welsh dictionary was compiled in this period, i.e. *Geiriadur Cymreig Cymraeg : sef, geiriau Cymraeg yn cael eu hegluro yn Gymraeg* by Robert Ellis (Cynddelw, 1812-1875)[13] in 1868 as well as *A dictionary of the Welsh language ... Geiriadur Cymraeg* compiled by Daniel Silvan Evans (1818-1903)[14] from 1887 to 1906.

Another type of dictionary was introduced by Robert Ellis and Iolo Morganwg in 1874, only a decade later than the first English dictionary of its kind. It was a rhyming dictionary,[15] which helped the bards compose poetry in the traditional metres, i.e. *Geiriadur y bardd : neu yr odlydd cyffredinol, at wasanaeth y beirdd, yn yr hwn y trenir y geiriau yn ol eu hodlau.*

---

[11] For further details with regard to the formation of the loanwords and loan translations and their interpretation by Williams, see Hincks (1993: 20f-88).

[12] No details were available to me with regard to his life.

[13] He was a bard, editor of poetry and two journals, and a minister (cf. M. Stephens 1997: 251).

[14] He was a lexicographer and bard. Evans studied in Llanbedr Pont Steffan and was appointed rector in Llanwrin before lecturing Welsh in the college of Aberystwyth from 1875 to 1883. He contributed to the Welsh encyclopedia (cf. above), translated Welsh manuscripts, edited Welsh literature, and was the editor of two journals (cf. M. Stephens 1997: 240).

[15] The first English rhyming dictionary was compiled by John Walker in 1865 under the title *A rhyming dictionary : answering at the same time the purposes of spelling, pronouncing, and explaining the English language, on a plan not hitherto attempted.*

172

Relatively late, a dictionary of synonyms titled *Cyfystyron y Gymraeg* followed, compiled by Griffith Jones (1836-1906)[16] and published in 1892.

Whereas the indication of pronunciation in English language dictionaries was indicated systematically from the seventeenth century,[17] the first pronouncing dictionary in Wales *An English-Welsh pronouncing dictionary: Geiriadur cynaniaethol Seisoneg a Chymraeg* (sic)[18] was published by William Spurrell (1813-1889)[19] in 1850. Two others appeared, that is, *An English-Welsh pronouncing dictionary: also an analysis of the orthography of the Welsh language*, by Thomas Edwards (Caerfallwch, 1779-1858)[20] in 1850 and *An English and Welsh pronouncing dictionary, in which the pronounciation is given in Welsh letters* by Gweirydd ap Rhys in 1857 (cf. above and section 4.4.). However, they all provided the pronunciation of the English lexical items, thereby first of all promoting the acquisition of English (cf. section 2.3.). Up to the present day, no general-purpose dictionary[21] has been compiled which indicates the pronunciation of Welsh lexical items. The facilitating of the learning of Welsh in this respect, therefore, remains a desideratum.

16	No details were available to me with regard to his life.
17	For further details on the development of the indication of pronunciation in English lexicography, see Bronstein (1986).
18	For the changing spelling in the title in the next edition of the dictionary, see chapter III.
19	He was a printer and publisher who set up a printing company in Carmarthen, which became more influential after his son took over the business and published books for libraries and universities as well as dictionaries, e.g. compiled by his father and others (cf. M. Stephens 1997: 678).
20	He was a self-educated saddler. While a pupil of Pughe (cf. above) he compiled specialist vocabularies for trade and science. He also worked on Welsh orthography illustrated in the book *Analysis of Welsh Orthography* (1845).
21	The only dictionary which includes the indication of pronunciation is H. Gruffudd's *The Welsh Learner's Dictionary* (1998). It is based, however, on the method of 'imitated pronunciation' (for further details with regard to the dictionary and the disadvantages of the method of 'imitated pronunciation', see section 4.4.).

2.5. Summary

Searching for a way to maintain their language and to turn it into an effective means of communication under new social conditions (cf. section 2.2.2.), Welsh bards continued to produce predominantly monolingual vocabularies during the Renaissance, whereas Welsh humanists stepped into the production of new types of lexicographical works, i.e. mainly (bilingual) dictionaries (cf. sections 2.2.3. and 2.2.1.2.2.). Those compilations the macrostructure of which was modelled on European dictionary structures, came very close to the standards of European lexicography at that time (cf. T. Wiliems). Specialisation in lexicography, however, was leaping behind. Nevertheless, Welsh dictionary production developed continuously after the Renaissance and the number of works produced increased considerably (cf. list of dictionaries in chapter III).

The dictionary which influenced Welsh lexicography the most thereafter was that of Dr John Davies, Mallwyd (cf. Carr 1983: 70). At the end of the Renaissance, it formed the major basis for the work of T. Jones (cf. section 2.2.2.). In the Classical period, it was the reference book for Edward Lhuyd, the founder of comparative Celtic linguistics, who based his Welsh lexicographical work on it, as well as for T. Richards (cf. section 2.3.).

The dictionary of Dr John Davies also remained important in the Romantic period when the maintenance and development of the language again became the major concern of Welsh intellectuals. Lewis Morris and Pughe, for instance, studied Davies' work intensively (cf. section 2.4.)

Nevertheless, vocabularies and unpublished dictionaries were also examined. Although they did not attract the same attention as printed lexicographical works (cf. T. Jones in section 2.2.2. and E. Lhuyd in section 2.3.), they provided important material for all those who wished to study Welsh language and literature thoroughly. As such the works remaining in manuscript form not only provided valuable material for lexicographers up to the Romantic period, in particular for Pughe (cf. Carr 1983: 72), but they continued to do so for contemporary lexicography, e.g. for the compilation of the historical dictionary *Geiriadur Prifysgol Cymru* (cf. chapter IV). They may also hold material for future projects, such as the compilation of a Welsh-Welsh dictionary, or an etymological dictionary.

Strict alphabetical word order first appeared in Welsh dictionaries when they were modelled on Latin or English dictionaries (cf. T. Wiliems in section 2.2.2. and W. Evans in section 2.4.). Only in the Romantic period, however, this became the common principle of arranging headwords in Welsh lexicography.

Although the comprehensive work of the lexicographers of the Renaissance had laid the foundation for specialisation, specialist dictionaries only developed as late as in the ninteenth century, i.e. in the Romantic period (cf. section 2.4.). In this context, vocabularies, well attested to since Gruffudd Hiraethog (cf. section 2.2.1.2.2.), were attributed a new function. After the first Welsh-Welsh dictionary had been published in 1826, the function of the vocabularies to provide monolingual material had ceased. They became now predominantly bilingual lexicographical works mainly restricted to special subjects and reduced in the grammatical description of their lexical items. This is quite similar to the function they serve today (cf. section 1.3.2.1.1. for a definition of vocabulary).

In the Romantic period, language decline had reached a new stage. Nevertheless, the question of the language was related to that of the nation, thereby turning the language into a politicial issue again (cf. W. Salesbury 1547: 4 and section 2.4.).

This, however, was a general phenomenon evolving from the interplay of humanist, enlightened and romantic ideas in a time of emerging industrial capitalism. Resulting developments brought forth the modern university - this time also in Wales and elsewhere.

The universities evolved from a relatively autonomous community directed to collecting and passing on knowledge to an institution preserving existing and producing new knowledge while gradually getting tied to social ambitions of governments and industries. These developments, however, early contradicted the Romantic ideal that the independent thought of the free individual was to develop at universities. For a while this thought served, on the one hand, the spirits for enforced capitalist development. On the other hand, it furthered inventions made during the industrial revolution, thereby forming the ideological and economic basis for industrial capitalism and its restrictions on the individual (cf. section 1.1. and 4.1.1.).

In order to fully meet the spiritual needs of the bourgeoisie, a lot of place was devoted to the arts. Philology as the science of text and culture was for decades a most prominent modern science. Through Renaissance source-studies it traced a line to the great examples of antiquity and systemised knowledge so far acquired as a firm basis for new discoveries. Part of these discoveries were, for instance, the re-orientation of history from initially Greek culture to 'Indo-Germanic' culture and related to it the evolvement of comparative linguistics (cf. Thorne 1991),[22] as well as in the Welsh microcosmos, the specialisation in lexicography.

In view of the social developments briefly summarised above, it is logical that bardic literature no longer constituted the main lexical basis for the compilation of lexicographical works in the Romantic period. Instead, other dictionaries and field work supplied lexical material, a tendency that had already begun in the Classical period (cf. section 2.3. and 2.4.). Bards had long before ceased to be an influential social group and the intended dictionary users now belonged to various social groups (cf. W. Evans 1771: The Preface). Evolving specialisation in lexicography, however, offered specialist reference books, such as dictionaries of synonyms and rhymes, which served the needs of particular users, in this case, writers and bards (cf. also T. Edwards and the pronouncing dictionaries in section 2.4. and the appendix).

As the Welsh language became the subject of major study in the Romantic period, orthography was also re-discovered as a field of experiment and research. As did W. Salesbury during the Renaissance, Pughe introduced new and individual ways of spelling in the Romantic period, though on a different basis (cf. sections 2.2.2. and 2.4.). Other scholars published treasises on this matter as well, e.g. Thomas Edwards (cf. section 2.4.) and Thomas Stephens (1821-1875; cf. preface of Gweirydd ap Rhys 1866: 5).

To conclude, the works of the lexicographers of the eighteenth and nineteenth centuries filled gaps in Welsh lexicography, an achievement also important for the further development of

---

[22]   The terminology has meanwhile changed. Whereas 'Indo-Germanic' paid tribute to the provenance of famous scholars in related fields, e.g. Franz Bopp (1791-1867, cf. Thorne 1991 for further details), the term 'Indo-European' is given preference in English-speaking areas today.

Welsh linguistics and research methods. Nevertheless, gaps regarding the description of the Welsh lexicon, e.g. its phonetic and etymological description, remained. The range of specialisation reached is also restricted. Welsh-Welsh dictionaries were thereafter not much further developed, although the effect of later social developments would have needed revised or new compilations of that kind.

A detailed analysis of dictionaries produced in the course of the twentieth century, and compiled on the basis of lexicographical achievements up to 1900, is pursued in chapter IV. The next section, however, first provides an overview of the number and types of dictionaries generated in Wales and in the other Celtic regions.

III.   Welsh lexicography and its context
3.1.   Preliminary remarks

Before analysing Welsh dictionaries, a brief survey of Welsh works is given by presenting the corpus of dictionaries from the first one published up to the present day. This gives the reader some idea of the continuity, extent and variety of the production of lexicographical reference books from the Renaissance period until today. This survey also enables the reader to place the dictionaries surveyed in their historical context. A list of Welsh vocabularies provided in the appendix of this investigation indicates a long and firm tradition of lexicographical production in Wales.

In order to accurately assess developments in Welsh lexicography, a comparison with the production of dictionaries in the other Celtic countries, i.e. Brittany, Cornwall, Ireland, the Isle of Man, and Scotland, is included. Such an approach is given preference over a comparison of lexicographical productions in England and France, since:

(a)   Cultures of languages of limited diffusion like Wales can hardly generate a similar number or range of dictionaries to that of cultures with dominating languages.

(b)   Whenever direct influence of particular English, French or other lexicographical work in a Welsh dictionary is attested this influence is discussed in related sections (cf. the influence of English dictionaries during the Renaissance and Romantic periods illustrated in sections 2.2.2. and 2.4.).

(c)   The Celtic languages exhibit a similar structure to each other.

(d)   They all suffer the minority status in their countries.[1]

As the attempt has been made to grasp all Welsh dictionaries printed up to 2001, I have also tried to obtain dictionaries of the other languages in their entirety. However, the completeness of the dictionary corpora cannot be guaranteed. Particularly for the Breton, Cornish, Irish, and Scottish dictionaries, I had to depend to a large extent on catalogues and bibliographies and had to try to match their different systems of presenting the data stored either electronically or on

---

[1]   Although the Irish language is the first official language in Ireland and promoted by the Irish government, it is in severe decline and, therefore, treated as a minority language here. This approach is justified by the *European Charter for Regional Languages* which defines 'less widely used official languages'. In Article 3, paragraph 50 is written that

"The wording of Article 3 takes account of the position in certain member states whereby a national language which has the status of an official language of the state, either on the whole or on part of its territory, may in other respects be in a comparable situation to regional or minority languages as defined in Article 1 (a), because it is used by a group numerically smaller than the population using the other official language(s). If a state wishes such a less widely used official language to benefit from the measures of protection and promotion provided for by the Charter, it is therefore enabled to determine that the Charter shall apply to it."

For further information concerning reasons of Irish language death, see Hindley 1991.

paper. Some major problems of tracing dictionaries which affect the completeness and correctness of the lists of dictionaries are mentioned in the following:[2]

First of all, even at a time of electronic exchange of data, the accessibility of information is often unsystematic. This is partly due to the method of transferring data stored on catalogue slips to electronic data carriers or storage devices. The following examples illustrate the situation:

(a)   Harold E. Palmer's grammar (1924) is not to be found under the categories 'author' or 'title' in the *Staatsbibliothek* Berlin, but under the category 'grammar'.

(b)   The situation noted in (a) is similar in the *National Library of Wales* and the *National Library of Scotland* when searching for the authors Cassie (1930), Hogan (1900, cf. list of Scottish Gaelic dictionaries in section 3.2.6.).

(c)   Examples from the *Bibliothèque nationale de France* (BnF) include the catalogue entries for Jaffrennou and Taldir (1914, the latter being Jaffrennou's pseudonym, cf. list of Breton dictionaries in section 3.2.2.). Neither contains his dictionary *Giriadur gallek ha brezonek. Dictionnaire français-breton de poche* (cf. list of Breton dictionaries in section 3.2.2.), which can only be found by searching under the keyword 'dictionnaire français-breton'.

Second, libraries cannot stock all lexicographical works produced and have to prioritise.

Third, not all dictionaries or vocabularies are necessarily kept in their respective national libraries (cf. dictionary by Peter M'Farlane 1815, in section 3.2.6.). An explanation for this situation can be found in the history of lexicographical production; a look at the list of dictionaries reveals that the first Welsh dictionaries, for instance, were produced outside Wales (cf. section 3.2.1.).

Fourth, in many libraries it takes quite some time for newly published dictionaries to appear in the library catalogues.

Fifth, another problem is the degree of variation in title, date, location, author and publisher. Sources such as catalogues, bibliographies, and even books themselves are not altogether reliable in the information they provide. Some of the problems the researcher is faced with are illustrated in the following:

(a)   Frequent spelling mistakes, as for instance in Ernault's *Gériadurig brézonekgallek* 'Little Breton-French dictionary' (1927, cf. list of Breton dictionaries in section 3.2.2.).

(b)   Wrong data input, e.g. when the publications of four volumes of Hemon's *Geriadur istorel* are dated to the years 1401, 1501, 1701 and 1801 (1958-1979, cf. list of Breton dictionaries in section 3.2.2.).

(c)   At times, different versions of the author's name are provided, thus suggesting two authors, as in the case of Émile Ernault, who is once listed in the catalogue of the *BnF* under this name with seventy-seven publications and once with the first name Émile-

---

[2]   Some general problems with regard to Breton language material are illustrated on the following website: http://webbo.enst-bretagne.fr/Brezhonet/LevraBzh/savia-fr.htm (20.10.2001).

Jean-Marie with eight publications.

(d)   The online catalogues of the universities of Galway and Cork do not make use of any diacritics.

(e)   Some publications do not reveal the full name of the author (cf. *Geiriadur Cymraeg/Saesneg* in section 3.2.1.).

(f)   Scottish Gaelic personal names are particularly tricky as they frequently reflect different stages of anglicisation or varying standards of orthography. In such cases there is no 'correct spelling' for a personal name or a title, even more since spelling is also linked to varying attitudes towards the language or other implications, such as political or personal views. D. Thomson (1993: 99-101) describes the situation for Scotland as follows:

> "The historical development of Scottish Gaelic orthography has not been researched as yet [...] There is a strong thread of continuity in the history of Gaelic orthography. It is primarily an etymologically based system, and in its essentials is the same for the old and modern stages of the language, deriving from the system most familiar in Middle and Old Irish. Our earliest Scottish sources are in the literary language we describe as Classical Common Gaelic, but at all times this language is open to modification in the direction of spoken Scottish Gaelic [...] This often results in 'pronunciation spellings' [...] and can explain some of the variation in orthographical forms even within the one text [...]; often, however, such variation is arbitrary [...] The present century has seen a gradual tidying up of minor features of the spelling system [...] Some of these reforms had been introduced, or reintroduced into Gaelic writing, especially by the periodical *Gairm* over the period from 1952 onwards, and [...] by a special Committee on Gaelic Orthography set up by the Scottish Certificate of Education Examination Board (1978; with minor modifications 1980)."

A rather distant attitude is taken by W. Gillies (1993: 147):

> "Modern Scottish Gaelic is founded on that of Classical Irish as practised by the literati in the Early Modern period. Some Scottish Gaelic features were incorporated as the modern standard evolved, but others went unrecognized. As a consequence Scottish Gaelic orthography bears a complex, though basically regular relationship to the language (an orthographical revision took place in the 1980s, but although this is now taught in schools and used by many writers, it is less serviceable for present purposes, and is ignored here)."

Both scholars provide explanations for the vagaries of Scottish Gaelic spellings, which occasionally occur even within one printout of the same catalogue of the *National Library of Scotland*, for instance, in that of Robert Macfarlan (1815, cf. list of Scottish Gaelic dictionaries in section 3.2.6.).

In order to circumvent the problems mentioned above, I decided to use the spelling presented in the first edition of the particular work accessible to me. In the case of re-editions for which the originals were not available, this means that the title and the author of the respective dictionary may be presented in modern spelling.

Problems also occur with regard to Breton orthography. The application of a particular type of Breton orthography today always reflects a certain political attitude or points to the institution in which the language was learned.[3]

(g)   The reason for variation of personal names for one and the same author in Breton and also in Welsh is often the use of pseudonyms, e.g. Iolo Morganwg for Edward Williams (cf. section 2.4.). Whereas in Wales these are mainly bardic names,[4] pseudonyms were often used for protection of Breton intellectuals (cf. Malo 1994). Some authors became even better known under their pseudonyms, for instance, the Breton *Louis-Paul Némo* = Roparz Hemon. As a result, Christian names and pseudonyms are often listed separately in the catalogues of the libraries mentioned above. The most important pseudonyms are, therefore, included in the lists of dictionaries in sections 3.2.1.-3.2.6.

The variety of the majority of personal names in the lists of dictionaries, however, is mainly due to the switch between Breton and French or other Celtic and English versions of names (cf. above).

(h)   Another question to answer is which words really belong to the title, since in former times the title often consisted of the first sentence(s) of a book (cf. titles of early dictionaries in the lists of the following sections or in sections 2.3. and 2.4.). The situation is aggravated by re-editions, for they may have titles different from their original, mostly as a result of shortening the former title of the book. This is predominantly a characteristic of Welsh or Scottish Gaelic dictionaries, such as Dwelly's work (1901-1911, cf. list of Scottish Gaelic dictionaries in section 3.2.6.). In general, therefore, an attempt was made to follow the spelling and wording of the title provided by the first edition available to me.

(i)   Some data is not even obtainable in the reference books themselves. Breton works, for instance, frequently do not provide the location of publication. Reprints, e.g. of Scottish Gaelic dictionaries, seldom include the front page of the original, thus obscuring the location where it was first published. This phenomenon can, at least partly, be explained by the background knowledge of close-knit communities of the speakers of lesser used languages for which the dictionaries were intended. These people would have been familiar with the location of their publishing houses. In present-day society, however, with a high mobility also among speakers of these languages as well as international contacts, this practice is counter-productive.

Sixth, even if data relating to the lexicographical works were completely listed, an exact number of all published dictionaries is somewhat difficult to obtain, since some reference books occurred first on their own and were later re-published and at the same time bound together with

---

[3]   For details about the controversies with regard to Breton orthography, see section 4.4.

[4]   The use of pseudonyms by intellectuals is a historic phenomenon (cf. Laugaa 1986). Particularly during the Romantic period, it was very popular in Europe to use pseudonyms (cf. Délecourt 1863, Sintenis 1899, Barbier, A. & M. Barbier et al. 1822-27), and to discuss them (cf. Franklin 1875). This certainly was also a reflex of the love for mysticism at that time (cf. section 2.4.).

another dictionary (cf. the dictionaries of Gweirydd ap Rhys (1866) in section 3.2.1.). Sometimes the two parts of a bi-directional dictionary were first published separately and later in one volume or vice versa. The former is the case with the *Learner's English-Irish dictionary* by Pádraig Ó Siochfhradha (1957-1966) and his *Irish-English pronouncing dictionary* (1959 and 1967), which were after his death published together under the title *Easy reference Irish/English-English/Irish dictionary. Foclóir Gaeilge/Béarle-Béarle/Gaeilge* (1996 and 1998, cf. list of Irish dictionaries in section 3.2.4.).

In addition, at times it is impossible to distinguish between extended editions and new dictionaries (cf. list of dictionaries produced by Roparz Hemon or Raymond Delaporte in section 3.2.2.).

The language of one and the same institution can even switch from one edition to the next, although Irish is the first official language in Ireland. It may, however, also be used exclusively (cf. Bunreacht na hÉireann. Constitution of Ireland http://www.irlgov.ie/taoiseach/publication/constitution/english, 1.1.2002). Welsh is to be granted 'equal status in the conduct of public affairs' (cf. section 4.1.1).

In view of the legal premisses and the fact that a scientific investigation like this is written to become a 'public affair', I have decided to use the vernacular languages in order to name the location and institution of publication of the respective lexicographical works after 1937 in Ireland and 1993 in Wales. This is even more justified, since not all Irish or Welsh locations have an English equivalent. Before 1937 and 1993, however, the names of locations and publishers are given in the form presented in the first edition of the particular work available to me.

Re-editions are in so far of interest as they indicate the importance and impact of a particular dictionary. The information on re-editions of lexicographical works is, therefore, given in a way that the significance of the dictionaries becomes clear rather than the actual number of editions.[5] Some dictionaries have seen so many re-editions over the years that it seemed more reasonable to mark the period of their date of publication (cf. *Collins Spurrell Welsh dictionary, Y Geiriadur Bach,* and *Y Geiriadur Mawr* in section 3.2.1.). Only with regard to Scottish Gaelic dictionaries, a comprehensive account of the editions of individual dictionaries was aimed at. The reason for this approach is the apparent deviant kind of lexicographical production in Scotland in comparison with the other Celtic countries (cf. sections 3.3.).

Apart from minor comments, it is not within the scope of the present survey to consider whether the dictionaries were produced in the same country as the language described, since the emphasis is placed on the availability of lexicographical material. In view of the fact that Irish lexicographical works were, far more than others, produced by non-Irish scholars, e.g. Marstrander (1913, cf. list of Irish dictionaries in section 3.2.4.), it becomes apparent that the question as to who produced what for whom and why, deserves an investigation of its own. It is also of minor significance to this investigation whether a lexicographical work remained un-

---

[5]   This approach is even more justified, since the staff from the *Welsh Book Council* told me that they have no statistical data of printed dictionaries (cf. personal correspondence).

finished such as Hessen's Irish Lexicon (1933, cf. list of Irish dictionaries in section 3.2.4.) or that of Daniel Silvan Evans (1887-1906, cf. list of Welsh dictionaries in section 3.2.1.), as long as it was published.

Since reference books on the Bible, bibliographers, saints, bards, place and personal names, or those on dialects do not form part of this study (cf. section 1.3.1.), they have not been included in the survey. Indeed, they merit separate research.

It is also possible that some works unavailable to me or which are listed as 'vocabularies' may in fact have to be classified as dictionaries. Others, which are called 'dictionaries', may only contain a vocabulary. The classification of lexicographical works is a particular problem for Irish, e.g. with *Foclóir ceoil* 'Dictionary of Music' (1985, cf. list of Irish dictionaries in section 3.2.4.), since *foclóir* 'dictionary' is used for both dictionaries and vocabularies, although the word *foclóirín* 'little dictionary' (Wörterbüchlein) could also be employed (cf. *geriadur - geriadurig* 'little dictionary' in Breton and section 4.3.2.2.2. for the functions of diminutives). Occasionally, the term *focal*, which clearly denotes a vocabulary, is employed.

The subsequent sections present the lists of dictionaries produced in the individual Celtic countries. Thereafter follows a comparison of the different lexicographical traditions in these countries.

3.2. The Corpora
3.2.1. The Corpus of Welsh dictionaries

	Date	Author	Title - published dictionaries only	Location	Publisher
1	1547	Salesbury, William	A dictionary in Englyshe and Welshe moche necessary to all suche Welshemen as wil spedily learne the englyshe tõgue thought unto the kynges majestie very mete to be sette for the to the use of his graces subjectes in Wales:whereunto is p̃fixed a litle treatyse of the englyshe pronuciacion of the letters,by Wyllyam Salesbury (sic)	London	John Waley
2	1632	Davies, John	ANTIQUÆ LINGUÆ BRITANNICÆ, Nunc vulgo dictæ Cambro Britannica A suis Cymraecae, vel cambricae, Ab aliis wallicæ; ET LINGUÆ LATINÆ, DICTIONARIUM DUPLEX, Prius BRITANICO LATINUM Plurimus venerandæ antiquitatis Brittannicæ monumentis pespersum POSTERIUS LATINO BRITANNICUM. Accesserunt ADAGIA BRITANNICA, plura & emendatiora quam antebac edita (sic).	London	R. Young[1]
3	1688 (1707; 1977)[2]	Jones, Thomas	Y Gymraeg yn ei disgleirdeb, neu helaeth eir-lyfr Cymraeg a Saesnaeg Yn Cynwys yr holl eiriau yng Eirlyfr Dr. Davies (sic)	Caerlydd (Y Mwythig)	Lawrence Baskerville (Stafford Prys)
4	1725	Rhydderch, Sion[3]	The English and Welch dictionary - y geirlyfr Saesneg a Chymraeg	Y Mwythig	no data[4]
5	1737	Rhydderch, Sion	Y geirlyfr Saesneg a Chymraeg: neu'r Saesneg o flaen y Gymraeg	Y Mwythig	Thomas Durston
6	1753 (1759; 1815; 1839)	Richards, Thomas	Antiquæ linguæ britannicæ thesaurus. A Welsh and English dictionary: wherein the Welsh words are often exemplified by select quotations from celebrated ancient authors; and many of them etymologized, and compared with the Oriental and other languages ... It is also adorned with many valuable British antiquities, to elucidate the meaning of obscure words. To which are annexed, a Welsh and English Botanology; and a large collection of Welsh proverbs; and to the whole is prefixed, a compendious Welsh grammar, with the rules in English.	Bristol (Trefiw)	Felix Farley (I. Davies, Thomas Price)

---

[1] If the first name is not listed here, it was unavailable.

[2] Data in brackets indicate re-editions, also for purposes of research rather than every-day use.

[3] The English version of his name is John Roderick.

[4] The information 'no data' means that no information was given in the book or catalogue from which the title was taken.

7	1770-1794 (1815; 1828)	Walters, John	An English and Welsh dictionary: wherein, not only the words, but also, the idioms and phraseology of the English language, are carefully translated into Welsh, by proper and equivalent words and phrases: with a regular interspersion of the English proverbs, and proverbial expressions, ranged in their alphabetical order, and rendered by corresponding ones in the Welsh tongue. To which is subjoined a dissertation on the Welsh language, pointing out it's antiquity, copiousness, grammatical perfection, with remarks on it's poetry (sic).	London (Dolgelley; Dinbych)	Rhys Thomas (R. Jones - Gomerian Press; Thomas Gee)
8	1771 (1812)	Evans, William	An English-Welsh Dictionary: containing All Words necessary for Reading an English Author; wherein Not only the Corresponding British is given to the English, and the various Significations properly arranged; but also Every English Word is accented to prevent a bad Pronunciation, The Part of Speech added to which each Word respectively belongs, And proper Authorities subjoined where necessary (sic).	Carmarthen	John Evans
9	1793	Pughe, William Owen	Geiriadur Cynmraeg a Saesoneg. A Welsh and English dictionary … to which is prefixed a Welsh grammar[5]	London	Evan Williams
10	1798 (1839; 1846)	Richards, William	Geiriadur Saesoneg a Chymraeg. An English and Welsh dictionary: in which the English words and sometimes idioms and phrases are accompanied by those which correspond with them in the Welsh language.	Carmarthen (Utica)	J. Daniel (M. Jones; E.E. Roberts)
11	1800	Jones, Thomas	Geiriadur Saesoneg a Chymraeg: an English and Welsh dictionary	Chester	W.C. Jones
12	1805 (1815)	Lewis, Titus	A Welsh-English dictionary: Geirlyfr Cymraeg a Saesneg: yr hwn sydd yn cynnwys ynghylch deugain mil o eiriau Cymraeg, a Rhan-ymadrodd i bob un honynt, ac amrywiol o Eiriau Saesneg pridol gyferbyn a hwynt; hefyd, arwyddoccad Geiriau anghyfiaith yn yr ysgrythur lan; a pha ran ohoni y maent hwy, ac amrywiol o rai eraill, i'w cael; y mae hefyd yn rhoddi, Hanes gryno am rai o Deyrnasoedd, Gwledydd, Dinasoedd, Trefydd, &c., mwyaf enwog yn amrywiol Barthau y Byd (sic).	Carmarthen	John Evans

[5] This is the title of part I. Later parts were published under the title: *A dictionary of the Welsh language : explained in English : with numerous illustrations : from the literary remains and from the living speech of the Cymry*. The title page of 1793 is included as an additional title page in the complete work. The *Grammar of the Welsh language* has a separate title page and pagination.

13	1806 (1836[6])	Pughe, William Owen	Geiriadur Cymraeg a Saesoneg: An Abridgement of the Welsh and English Dictionary	London	Evan Williams
14	1826	Williams, Edward	Cyneirlyfr: neu eiriadur Cymraeg;yn cynnwys tadogiad geiriau, rheolau barddoniaeth,hanes enwogion Cymru,darluniad byr o wledydd,at yr hyn y chwanegwyd llysieudraith,ynghyd a'r diarebion Cymreig wedi eu hesbonio (sic).	Aberhonddu	William Williams
15	1832	Pughe, William Owen	A Dictionary of the Welsh Language: explained in English: with numerous illustrations: from the literary remains and from the living speech of the Cymry: to which is prefixed, a Welsh grammar	Denbigh	Thomas Gee
16	1833 (1834)	Thomas, John Williams (Arfonwyson)	Geiriadur Cymreig a Seisonig: a chydymaith i'r ysgol Sabbathol; yn dri dosbarth. Yn y sawl yr amlygir ansawdd a gwraidd y Gymraeg, tarddiad geiriau dyrys, cynnulliad o eiriau o gyfelyb sain, a chrynoad helaeth o eiriau tywyll yr ysgrythyr, efo eu cyfystyron (sic).	Caernarfon	H. Humphreys (William Potter)
17	1835	Williams, Owen & Isaac Jones[7]	Welsh encyclopedia: Y Geirlyfr Cymraeg, yr hwn sydd yn cynnwys geiriadur ysgrythyrol, hanesol, ac ieithyddol, lle y danghosir arwyddocad geiriau annghyfiaith.... hefyd, hanes y diwygwyr a'r merthyron yn y byd crefyddol ... Hefyd hanes y Cymry (sic)	Llanfair-Caereinion	H. Humphreys
18	1840	Jones, Ellis	A new pocket dictionary of the Welsh and English languages: Geiriadur llogell Cymreig a Seisonig, yn nghyda Geiriadur llysieuol; wedi ei gasglu gan Ellis Jones o'r geiriaduron a'r awduron cywiraf (sic).	Caernarfon	W. Potter & co (sic)
19	1847	Evans, John	Geirlyfr Seisonig a Chymreig: a new English and Welsh dictionary, with a botanical dictionary subjoined (sic)	Llannwst	John Jones
20	1847	Griffiths, Evan (Ieuan Ebblig)	Welsh and English dictionary, in which Welsh words are explained by corresponding English words: designed to assist enquiring youths, and others, to acquire a knowledge of the English language. Geiriadur Cymraeg a Saesonaeg, yn yr hwn yr eglurir geiriau Cymreig trwy amrywiol o eiriau Seisnig cyfatebol: er cynnorthwy ieuenctyd, ac eraill, a awyddant am wybodaeth o'r iaith Saesoneg (sic).	Abertawe	E. Griffiths

---

[6] Carr (1983: 76) gives the date 1836, whereas the printout of the *National Library of Wales* contains an entry for 1826.

[7] This work falls at least in two categories of lexicographical reference books (cf. section 1.3.1). It does, however, contain a dictionary.

#	Date	Author	Title	Place	Publisher
21	1848 (-72; 1903; -13; -15; -16; -22; -25; -26; -34; -37)	Spurrell, William (from 1916 onwards together with Anwyl, John Bodfan)	Geiriadur Cymraeg a Saesonaeg, ynghyd a grammadeg o iaith y Cymry. A dictionary of the Welsh language: with synonyms and explanations: to which is prefixed a grammar of the Welsh language. (later: Spurrell's Welsh-English dictionary)	London (Carmarthen)	Spurrell (H. Hughes)
22	1850 (-61; -86; 1916; -22, -26, -37)	Spurrell, William (from 1916 onwards together with Anwyl, John Bodfan)	An English-Welsh pronouncing dictionary with preliminary observations on the elementary sounds of the English language, a copious vocabulary of the roots of English words, and a list of scripture proper names. Geiriadur cynaniaethol Saesonaeg a Chymraeg. (later Spurrell's English-Welsh dictionary)	London (Carmarthen)	Spurrell (H. Hughes)
23	1850 (1861-64)	Edwards, Thomas (Caerfallwch)	An English-Welsh pronouncing dictionary: also an analysis of the orthography of the Welsh language. Geirlyfr seiniadol (neu gynaniaethol) Saesoneg a Chymraeg: ynghyd ag agoriad ar lythyriaeth yr Iaith Gymraeg (sic). [8]	Holywell/London (Treffynnon)	P.M. Evans/H. Hughes (P.M. Evans)
24	1852-1858[9]	Evans, Daniel Silvan	An English and Welsh dictionary adapted to the present state of science and literature; in which the English words are reduced from their originals, and explained by their synonyms in the Welsh language.	Dinbych	Thomas Gee
25	1857 (1880; 1888; 1899)	Gweirydd ap Rhys	An English and Welsh pronouncing dictionary: in which the pronunciation is given in Welsh letters. Geiriadur cynaniadol Saesneg a Chymraeg: yn yr hwn y silliadir y geiriau Saesneg a llythyrennau Cymraeg (sic).	Dinbych	Thomas Gee
26	1861	Richards, William	A pocket dictionary, Welsh-English: geiriadur llogell Cymraeg a Saesoneg	London/Wrexham	R. Hughes
27	1866	Gweirydd ap Rhys (ed.) for Pughe, William Owen	Geiriadur Cenedlaethol Cymraeg a Saesneg: A National Dictionary of the Welsh Language with English and Welsh Equivalents	Denbigh	Thomas Gee
28	1866	Gweirydd ap Rhys	GEIRIADUR CYMRAEG A SAESNEG: AT YR HWN YR YCHWANEGWYD ENWADUR DAEARYDDOL, HEFYD, GEIRIAU O GYFFELYB SAIN, OND YN GWAHANIAETHAU MEWN YSTYR, &c/WELSH-ENGLISH DICTIONARY TO WHICH IS ADDED, A GEOGRAPHICAL NOMENCLATURE, ALSO, WORDS SIMILAR IN SOUND, BUT DIFFERING IN SIGIFICATION (sic).	Caernarfon	H. Humphreys

[8] The titles vary in bibliographies.
[9] The library of the University College Galway also keeps editions dated from 1848 and 1854.

29	1866[10]	Johnson, Webster & Hughes	AN-ENGLISH-WELSH DICTIONARY TO WHICH IS ADDED, A LIST OF PROPER NAMES OF PLACES, &c. WITH THEIR SYNONYMS/GEIRIADUR SAESONEG A CHYMRAEG; AT YR HWN YR YCHWANEGWYD RHESTR O ENWAU PRIODOL LLEOEDD, &c, GYDA'U CYFYSTERON CYMRAEG.	Caernarfon	H. Humphreys
30	1868	Ellis, Robert (Cynddelw)	Geiriadur Cymreig Cymraeg: sef, geiriau Cymraeg yn cael eu hegluro yn Gymraeg (sic)	Caernarfon	H. Humphreys
31	1874	Morganwg, Iolo & Ellis Robert (Cynddelw)	Geiriadur y bardd: neu yr odlydd cyffredinol, at wasanaeth y beirdd, yn yr hwn y trefnir y geiriau yn ol eu hodlau, ac nid yn ôl y llythyren gyntaf, fel y trefnir geiriaduron yn gyffredin (sic)	Caernarfon	H. Humphreys
32	1887-1906	Evans, Daniel Silvan	Geiriadur Cymraeg. A dictionary of the Welsh language	Carmarthen	W. Spurrell & Son
33	1892	Jones, Griffith	Cyfystyron y Gymraeg	Wrexham	Hughes and Son
34	1905	Edwards, Owen Morgan	Geiriadur Cymraeg a Saesneg byr: yn bennaf ar sail 'Dictionarium Britannico-Latinum' Dr. John Davies o Fallwyd: ac ar 'Y Gymraeg yn ei disgleirdeb' Thomas Jones o'r Amwythig (sic)	Llanuwchllyn	Ab Owen
35	1911	Williams, Peter	A key and guide to the Welsh language. A Welsh-English dictionary and grammar combined	Liverpool	Hugh Evans
36	1915	James, David	Geiriadur y Plentyn	Caerdydd	Educational Publishing company
37	1919 (1930)	Anwyl, John Bodfan	Spurrell's pocket dictionary, Welsh-English and English-Welsh	Carmarthen	W. Spurrell & Son
38	1931-38 (1963; 1988)	Lloyd-Jones, John	Geirfa Barddoniaeth Gynnar Gymraeg	Caerdydd	Gwasg Prifysgol Cymru
39	1932	Rees, David	Llawlyfr technoleg : geiriadur darluniadol ac esboniadol	Caerdydd	Gwasg Prifysgol Cymru
40	1932	Rees, E. Cook	Cymraeg i'r Werin. Welsh Simplified. A Practical Modern Dictionary of Words and Phrases for Teachers and Students.	London	Foyle's Welsh Press
41	1937	Anwyl, John Bodfan	Spurrell's schools' dictionary	Carmarthen	W. Spurrell & Son
42	1950-2002	Bwrdd Gwybodau Celtaidd	Geiriadur Prifysgol Cymru	Caerdydd	Gwasg Prifysgol Cymru
43	1950	Jones, Thomas Gwynn & Gwynn ap Arthur	Geiriadur Cymraeg-Saesneg a Saesneg-Cymraeg	Caerdydd	Hughes a'i Fab
44	1953 ... 1998	Evans, Harold Meurig & William Owen Thomas	Y Geiriadur Newydd	Llandybie	Llyfrau'r Dryw

---

[10] This and the *Geiriadur Cymraeg a Saesneg…* by Gweirydd ap Rhys (1866) were published together in one volume.

#	Date	Author	Title	Place	Publisher
45	1955	James, David, Defynnog	Geiriadur ysgol. Cymraeg-Saesneg/Saesneg-Cymraeg	Caerdydd	Hughes a'i Fab
46	1958 ... 2001[11]	Evans, Harold Meurig & William Owen Thomas	Y Geiriadur Mawr	Llandybie	Llyfrau'r Dryw a Gwasg Aberystwyth (Christopher Davies, Gwasg Gomer)
47	1959... 1996	Evans, Harold Meurig & William Owen Thomas	Y Geiriadur Bach	Llandybie (Abertawe)	Llyfrau'r Dryw (Christopher Davies)
48	1960 ... 1999	Lewis, Henry; later Convey, Anne & David Thorne	Collins-Spurrell Welsh dictionary	London, Glasgow	HaperCollins
49	1968	Williams, Ina Tudno	Geiriadur Dysgwr	Llandybie	Llyfrau'r Dryw
50	1969	Jones, Bobi	Geiriadur Lluniau	Llandybie	Llyfrau'r Dryw
51	1973	Williams, Jac L.	Y Geiriadur Termau	Caerdydd	Gwasg Prifysgol Cymru
52	1978 (-86; -91; -95)	Stephens, Roy	Yr Odliadur	Llandysul	Gwasg Gomer
53	1979	Thomas, Huw	Geiriadur Lladin-Cymraeg	Caerdydd	Gwasg Prifysgol Cymru
54	1979	Hincks, Rhisiart	Geiriadurig kembraeg-brezhoneg	Plufur	Ober
55	1979 (1997)	Armery, Heather	Y Geiriadur Lliwgar (for Welsh speakers and learners: the most popular Welsh children's picture dictionary ever! (sic)	Caerdydd	Gwasg y Dref Wen
56	1982 ... 2001	Evans, Harold Meurig	Y Geiriadur Cyfoes. The Modern Welsh Dictionary (sic)	Abertawe	Christopher Davies
57	1984	Hill, Leslie Alexander	Geiriadur lluniau y plant (sic)	Abertawe	Gwasg Mynydd Mawr
58	1985	Wells, John Christopher	Geiriadur Esperanto. Kimra vortaro (sic)	Teddington	Group Five
59	1985	Williams, Rita	Geiriadur Bach Llydaweg-Cymraeg	Aberystwyth	Canolfan Uwchefrydiau Cymreig a Cheltaidd
60	1987	Zimmer, Stefan	Geiriadur Gwrthdroadol Cymraeg Diweddar	Hamburg	Helmut Buske Verlag
61	1988	Lovell, P.A.	Geiriadur Cymraeg/Saesneg	Yr Wyddgrug	P. A. Lovell
62	1988	Hill, Eric, translated by Dilwen M. Evans	Llyf Mawr Geiriau Smot	Llandysul	Gwasg Gomer
63	1990	CBAC[12]	Geiriadur 50 Awr	Caerdydd	CBAC

11 In 1989 the 15th edition was launched.
12 CBAC stands for *Cyd-bwyllgor Addysg Cymru* 'Welsh Joint Education Committee'.

No.	Year	Author	Title	Place	Publisher
64	1990	Williams, Rita	Geiriadur Cymraeg-Llydaweg: Geriadur Kembraeg-Brezhoneg	Aberystwyth	Canolfan Astudiaethau Cymreig a Cheltaidd
65	1991	Hincks, Rhisiart	Geiriadur Cymraeg-Llydaweg	Lesneven	Hor Yezh
66	1992 (-93; -96; -99)	Convery, Anne & David Thorne	Collins Gem Welsh Dictionary	Glasgow	HarperCollins
67	1992 (2000)	Lewis, Edwin C.	Teach Yourself Welsh Dictionary	London	Hodder & Stoughton
68	1992	CBAC	Geiriadur Termau Cyfrifiadureg	Caerdydd	MEU[13]
69	1992 (-96)	Lewis, Robyn	Geiriadur y Gyfraith	Llandysul	Gwasg Gomer
70	1993 (-99; 2000)	no data	Y Thesawrws Cymraeg/ Y drysorfa eiriau	Abertawe	Gwasg Pobl Cymru
71	1993	Evans, Bethan W. et al.	Gair i Gall. A word to the Wise: A Basic Dictionary for the Learner	Caerdydd	Acen
72	1993 (-95)	Greenwood, Mike	The Welsh Dictionary Phrasebook	no data	Bagnol Greenwood Partners
73	1994	Gunn, Marion	Da mihi manum (terms and phrases in six languages)	Dublin	Everson Gunn Teo.
74	1994	Wilkes, Angela	Geiriadur Cymraeg Cyntaf. My first Welsh picture dictionary (sic)	Caerdydd	Dref Wen
75	1994	Morgan-Jones, Lis	Geiriadur 1	Caerdydd	CBAC
76	1994	Lewis, Geraint David	Geiriadur Gomer i'r Ifanc	Llandysul	Gwasg Gomer
77	1995 (-97; 2001)	Griffiths, Bruce & Dafydd Glyn Jones	The Welsh Academy English-Welsh Dictionary/Geiriadur yr Academi Gymreig	Caerdydd	Gwasg Prifysgol Cymru
78	1996	Davies, Elizabeth	Geiriadur 2	Caerdydd	CBAC
79	1996	Greller, Wolfgang et al.	Geiriadur Almaeneg	Aberystwyth	Canolfan Astudiaethau Addysg
80	1996	Russon, Linda et al.	Y Geiriadur bach: Ffrangeg-Cymraeg/Cymraeg-Ffrangeg	Aberystwyth	Canolfan Astudiaethau Addysg
81	1996	no data	A first bilingual dictionary/English-Welsh	Huddersfield	Schofield & Sims
82	1996	Jones, Medwyn	Y Cleciadur	Llanrwst	Gwasg Carreg Gwalch
83	1997 (2000)	Lewis, David Geraint	Welsh-English/English-Welsh Dictionary	New Lanark	The Works
84	1998	Canolfan Safoni Termau	Y Termiadur Ysgol	Caerdydd	ACCAC[14]
85	1998	Knox, William	The Pan-Celtic Phrasebook	Talybont	Lolfa

13   MEU stands for *Microelectronics in Education Unit Wales*.
14   ACCAC stands for *Awdurdod Cymwysterau, Cwricwlwm ac Asesu Cymru* 'Qualifications, Curriculum & Assessment Authority for Wales'.

86	1998	Jones, Dafydd G.	Sight + Hearing/Golwg a Chlyw	no data	Sense Cymru
87	1998	Gruffudd, Heini	The Welsh Learner's Dictionary	Talybont	Lolfa
88	1999	Gruffudd, Heini	The Pocket Welsh Learner's Dictionary	Talybont	Lolfa
89	1999	Boore, Roger	Geiriau bob dydd - Children's picture dictionary	Caerdydd	Dref Wen
90	1999	McNeir, Clive Leo	Geiriadur Terminoleg Trefniadaeth	Caerdydd	Bwrdd Yr Iaith Gymraeg
91	1999	Lewis, D. Geraint	Geiriadur Cynradd Gomer	Llandysul	Gomer
92	1999	Williams, John Ll. & Bruce Griffiths et al.	Geiriadur termau archaeoleg/A dictionary of archaeological terms in English and Welsh	Caerdydd	Gwas Prifysgol Cymru
93	1999	Greller, Wolfgang et al.	Geiriadur Almaeneg	Aberystwyth	Y Ganolfan Astudiaeth-au Addysg
94	2000	Davies, Meirion & Menna Wyn et al.	Geiriadur Ffrangeg	Aberystwyth	Y Ganolfan Astudiaeth-au Addysg
95	2000	King, Gareth	Pocket Modern Welsh Dictionary	Oxford	University Press
96	2001	Cownie, Alun Rhys	Geiriadur Idiomau/A Dictionary of Welsh and English Idiomatic Phrases	Caerdydd	Gwasg Prifysgol Cymru
97	2001	Lewis, Edwin C.	Y Geiriadur Cryno/The Concise Welsh Dictionary	Llandybie	Gwas Dinefwr Press

Five other major dictionaries were compiled, but remain in manuscript form to the present day:

1608	Willems, Thomas	Thesaurus Linguæ Latinæ et Cambrobritannicæ siue Latinæ Linguæ et Britannicæ Veræ. Dictionarum Locupletissimum	Pen. 228
1625-37	Salesbury, Henry	Geira Tavod Comroig hoc est Vocabvlarivm Lingvae Gomeritanae	
no data	Willems, Thomas	Dictionarium Latino-Cambricum	Pen. 228
1725	Lewis, Erasmus	An English-Welsh Dictionary	NLW 321
1968[15]	Lis, Frantiszek	Geiriadur Cymraeg-Pwyleg	National Library of Wales

More lexicographical material in dictionary or vocabulary form is available in manuscripts (cf. John Jones in section 2.2.2., Lewis Morris, William Gambold in Carr 1983: 72 and appendix). However, this is often incomplete or otherwise complex to deal with and merits an investigation of its own.

Two dictionaries were deliberately designed for the use on the computer, i.e. *CySill*, a spell checker on floppy disk/CD-ROM produced by Canolfan Bedwyr (Bangor, 1995) and *CysGair*, a dictionary on CD-ROM, compiled by Cathair Ó Dochartaigh (1996). Another dictionary on floppy disc is *The Welsh Dictionary Phrasebook*.

Another dictionary is called *Y Geiriadur Gweol* and presents equivalents in Welsh, Catalan, and English (http://www.estelnet.com./catala-/gbssampl.htm, 20.10.2001). On this website, there are also links to various other lists of vocabularies, e.g. Basque-Welsh, Norwegian-Welsh, Occitan-Welsh, Russian-Welsh and so on (cf. http://pssst-heyu.com/dictionarydownloads/wlanguages.html, 20.10.2001[16]). More word lists, often as part of Welsh courses, are temporarily accessible (cf. information provided by the news group TESTUNAU@JISCMAIL.AC.UK (20.10.2001). Terms on education and finance can be found online on the website of *Bwrdd yr Iaith* 'The Welsh Language Board' (cf. section 4.1.).

Many of the online dictionaries or vocabularies which are not produced by larger institutions, however, are of varying standard and, at times, difficult to use. Online dictionaries are currently a field of extensive experiment. Their analysis, therefore, merits a separate investigation.

---

15   Date of arrival in the *National Library of Wales* (cf. personal correspondence with R. Lacey, Assistant Librarian in the *National Library of Wales*, 13.9.2000).

16   Information on other online Welsh dictionaries can also be obtained here.

A download Welsh-English dictionary designed by Paul and David Houghton is available under http://www.linguru.com (20.10.2001).

Geiriadur yr Academi is in the process of going online. As a result, it is only temporarily accessible at the moment (cf. http://www.melin.bangor.ac.uk/ga/ga.asp or the homepage of the university of Swansea). Knowledge on the progress of the production of Welsh online dictionaries can be obtained from the news group TESTUNAU@JISCMAIL.AC.UK (20.20.2001). *CySill* is also partly online (ibid.).

Originally printed dictionaries on CD-ROM are *Y Termiadur Ysgol* and *Geiriadur Gomer i'r Ifanc* (cf. list of dictionaries above). The former is also in the process of going online (cf. http://www.melin.bangor.ac.uk/, temporarily available). Courses for Welsh on CD-ROM can also include word lists, which are entitled dictionaries, e.g. *Teach Me! Welsh*, produced by the Welsh Language Board (2001). It contains interactive Welsh learning courses in French, German, English and Spanish.

The preceding list of dictionaries reveals a constant production of dictionaries from the seventeenth century onwards, thereby reflecting a firm tradition of Welsh lexicography. A comparison of dictionary production in the Celtic regions, however, is presented following the individual lists of dictionaries in section 3.3.

3.2.2. The Corpus of Breton dictionaries[1]

	Date	Author	Title - published dictionaries only	Location	Publisher
1	1499 (1521; 1975; -77)	Lagadec, Jehan; de Quoatqueveran, Auffret & Yves Roperz	Le Catholicon amoricain (français, breton, latin)	Tréguier (Paris; Rennes; Mayenne)	Jehan Calvez (Yvon Quillivere; Ogam-tradition celtique; J. Floc'h)
2	1626-1759	Quiquer de Roscoff, Guillaume[2]	DICTIONNAIRE ET COLLOQVES FRANCOIS ET BRETON. (sic)[3]	Morlaix (St. Briec, Quimper)	George Allienne (Guillaume Doublet, Vve J. Périer & S.M. Périer)
3	1659	Maunoir, Julien	Dictionnaire français-breton et breton-français[4]	Quimper	Jean Hardouin
4	(1699) 1979[5]	Harinquin, Robert	(Le dictionnaire breton de Harinquin 1699)	(Rennes)	(Hor Yezh)
5	1717 ... 1893	unknown author	Nouveau Dictionnaire[6]	Morlaix	de Ploesquellec
6	1732 (1834)	de Rostrenenn, Père F. Grégoire	Dictionnaire françois-celtique ou françois-breton	Rennes (Guingamp)	Julien Vatar (Benjamin Jollivet)
7	1751 (1975)[7]	Le Pelletier, Dom Louis	DICTIONNAIRE DE LA LANGUE BRETONNE, OU L'ON VOIT SON ANTIQUITÉ, SON AFFINITÉ AVEC LES ANCIENNES LANGUES, L'EXPLICATION DE PLUSIEURS PASSAGES DE L'ECRITURE SAINTE; ET DES AUTEURS PROFANE, AVEC L'ETYMOLOGIE DE PLUSIEURS MOTS DES AUTRES LANGUES (sic)	Paris	François Delaguette
8	1752 (1975)	Le Pelletier, Dom Louis	Dictionnaire étymologique de la langue bretonne	Paris	François Delaguette

[1]   I would like to take this opportunity of thanking Dr Iwan Wmffre for helpful discussion on this matter. For an extensive description of Breton lexicography, see Le Menn (1981, cahiers 1-13).

[2]   It is not indicated when Quiquer's dictionary was edited by another lexicographer.

[3]   The edition of 1632 also contains Latin equivalents. For a complete list of the twenty-one dictionaries initiated by his work including their places of publishing, see Le Menn (1981, cahier 1: 60, cahier 2: 4).

[4]   Translated by Moses Williams into English, it became part of Lhuyd's *Archaeologia Britannica* (cf. section 2.3.) as the *Armoric-English vocabulary*.

[5]   The manuscript by Harinquin was only partly kept by Le Pelletier. Various notes and references attributed to Harinquin, however, were collected and published in 1979 (Le Menn 1981, cahier 1: 61, cahier 6: 21-30).

[6]   Thirty-five editions were produced of this dictionary (cf. Le Menn 1981, cahier 1 and cahier 2: 5).

[7]   Although the re-editions of historical dictionaries serve mainly research purposes, they are listed here, since they are thus easily accessible for various users.

9	1821	Le Gonidec, Jean-François-Marie-Maurice-Agathe	Dictionnaire celto-breton ou breton français	Angoulême	F. Trémeau
10	1842	Troude, Amable-Emmanuel	Dictionnaire français et celto-breton	Brest	J. B. Lefournier
11	1847	Le Gonidec, Jean-François-Marie-Maurice-Agathe	Dictionnaire français-breton de Le Gonidec, enrichi d additions et d'un Essai sur l'histoire de la langue bretonne, par Th. Hersart de La Villemarqué	St.-Brieuc	L. Prud'homme
12	1850	La Villemarqué, Théodore-Claude-Henri Hersart	Dictionnaire breton-français de Le Gonidec, précédé de sa Grammaire bretonne, et enrichi d'un avant-propos, d additions et des mots gallois et gaëls correspondants au breton, par Th. Hersart de La Villemarqué - Dictionnaire français-breton de Le Gonidec, enrichi d'additions et d'un Essai sur l'histoire de la langue bretonne, par Th. Hersart de La Villemarqué (sic)	St.-Brieuc	L. Prud'homme
13	1883-1886 (-95)	Du Rusquec, Henri	DICTIONNAIRE FRANÇAIS-BRETON	Morlaix	A. Chevalier
14	1885 (-87)	Ernault, Émile	Dictionnaire étymologique du breton moyen	Nantes (Paris)	Société de les bibliophiles bretons (E. Thorin)
15	1901	Vallée, François	Dictionnaire anglais, irlandais, gaëlique, manois, breton (sic)	no data	Celtia
16	1902 (1997)	Normand, J.-M.	Lexique breton-français nouvelle methode pour faciliter aux commencants l'etude de la language bretonne (sic)	Quimper (Nimes)	de Kerangal (Lacour)
17	1914	Jaffrennou, François[8]	GIRIADUR GALLEK HA BREZONEK/DICTIONNAIRE FRANÇAIS-BRETON DE POCHE COMPRENANT 25.000 Mots (sic)	Keraez	Moullerez ar Bobl
18	1927 (1984)	Ernault, Émile	Geriadurig brezoneg-galleg	St.-Brieuc (Brest)	L. Prud'homme (Brud Nevez)
19	1927	Hemon, Roparz[9]	Geiriadur Brezoneg-Galleg a gorfadurez (sic)	Brest	Gwalarn
20	1928	Hemon, Roparz	Petit dictionnaire pratique breton-français/Geriadurig-Dourn Brezonek-Gallek	Brest	Gwalarn

---

8   He is also known under his pseudonym *Taldir*.
9   His real name is *Louis-Paul Némo*.

No. (date)	Author	Title	Place	Publisher
21	1931 (1934; 1980)	Vallée, François[10]	Grand dictionnaire français-breton, par François Vallée, avec le corcours de É. Ernault et R. Le Roux	Rennes (Glomel)	Édition de l'Imprimerie commerciale de Bretagne (Association bretonne de culture)
22	1933-39	Berthou, Yves	Dictionnaire des rimes[11]	Carhaix	An Oaled
23	1935-36 (-62; -90)	Hemon, Roparz	Petit dictionnaire français-breton des expressions populaire/ Geriadurig an troiou lavar galleg-brezhoneg	Brest (Lesnesven)	Gwalarn (Hor Yezh)
24	1938-39 (-50; -65; 74; -78; -84; -85; -95)	Hemon, Roparz	Dictionnaire français-breton	Brest	Gwalarn (Al Liamm)
25	1941	Abeozen[12]	Geriadurig brezonek krenn	Lambézellec	Sterenn
26	1941	Hemon, Roparz	Dictionnaire de poche français-breton	Brest	Gwalarn
27	1943 (-48; -64; -70; -73; -78; -85; -93)	Hemon, Roparz (Ronan Huon)	Dictionnaire breton-français	Brest	Skridoù Breizh
28	1948	Vallée, François	F. Vallée. Supplement au Grand dictionnaire français-breton	La Baule	Skridoù Breizh
29	1956 (-79; -80; -93; -98)	Séité, Visant & Naïg Rozmor et al.[13]	Lexique breton-français et français-breton/Geriadurig brezoneg-galleg ha galleg-brezoneg	Brest	Pressess libérales du Finistère (Emgleo Breizh)
30	1958-1979 (1979-98)	Hemon, Roparz	Geriadur istorel ar brezhoneg	Brest (Plomelin)	Al Liamm (Preder)
31	ca. 1960	Even, Arzel	Geriadur bach llydaweg-cymraeg	Aberystwyth	no data
32	1960	Abanna	Abanna. Geriadur a gorfadurezh. Gallek-latin-brezhonek (sic)	no data	H. Le Mée
33	1963-1971	Hemon, Roparz	Geriadur broadel	no data	Ar Bed Keltiek
34	1964	Fleuriot, Léon	Dictionnaire des Gloses en Vieux Breton	Paris	Librairie C. Klincksieck

---

10   He is also known under his pseudonym *Abherve*.

11   Only seventy-six pages of this dictionary were printed. Its publication stopped when the journal *An Oaled* ceased to exist. For details on the book and author, the pseudonym of whom is *Erwan Vertoù-Kaledvoul'ch*, see Châtel (1997: 117ff.).

12   Pseudonym for *Jean-François-Marie Éliès*. Another variation of his name is *Fañch Eliès*, by which he was known in his later years.

13   Authors apart from Séité vary for this lexicographical work, which saw its twentieth edition in 1979.

#	Year	Author	Title	City	Publisher
35	1970 (-78; -85; -93; -98)	Hemon, Roparz	Nouveau dictionnaire breton-français; suivi du dictionnaire français-breton (1985)	Brest	Al Liamm
36	1970-1984 (-89; -93)	Gros, Jules	Dictionnaire breton-français des expressions figurées Le Trésor du breton parlé	St.-Brieuc (Lannion, Brest, Rennes)	Presses bretonnes (Éditions "Barr-Heol", Emgleo Breiz, Brud Nevez)
37	1973-1977	Guyonvarc'h, Christian-J.	Dictionnaire étymologique du breton ancien, moyen et moderne	Rennes	Ogam-Celticum
38	1974	no data	Geriadur bras ar brezhoneg	Rennes	Hor Yezh
39	1976-1986	Le Dû, Jean & Yves Le Berre	Dictionnaire pratique français-breton	Brest	Université de Bretagne occidentale
40	1977	Hemon, Roparz	Ur geriadur unyezhek	Brest	Al Liamm
41	1978 (-80)	Menga, Erwan	Deskomp esperanteg/Geriadur esperantek-brezhonek	Lesneven	Hor Yezh
42	1979;[14] (1990; -95)	Delaporte, Raymond[15] (Kervella, Divi & Christian Brisson)	Elementary breton-english & english-breton dictionary/ Geriadur bihan brezhoneg-saozneg ha saozneg-brezhoneg (sic)	Cork (Lesneven)	University Press (Hor Yezh)
43	1979	Hincks, Rhisiart	Geriadurig kembraeg-brezhoneg	Plufur	Ober
44	1980	Olier, Youenn	Geriadur ar Brezhoneg Arnevez	Questembert	Imbouc'h
45	1982	Bouessel du Bourg, Yann	Geriadur Yezh ar barzhig	Lesneven	Hor Yezh
46	1983	Andouard, Loeiz	Brezhoneg ar mor/Le breton de la mer	Lesneven	Al Liamm
47	1983-1994	Le Gléau, René	Dictionnaire classique Français-Breton	Brest	Al Liamm
48	1983	Étienne, Guy	Geriadur bredel fennerezh/Dictionnaire de psychanalyse en quatre langues: français, allmand, anglais, breton	Quimper	Preder
49	1984	Rous, Anna-Vari; Gwilhamot, Yann & Yann-Bêr Trousset	Kentañ geriadur Eflamm ha Rivanon	Ar Gelveneg	Moulerezh ar Martolod
50	1984 (-93; -94)	Kadored, Iwan	Geriadur bihan brezhoneg-galleg, galleg-brezhoneg	Lesneven	Hor Yezh
51	1984 (-94)	Kervella, Divi; Kadored, Iwan & Yann Desbordes	Geriadur bihan brezhoneg-galleg, galleg-brezhoneg	Lesneven	Hor Yezh

---

[14] This edition is not listed in the catalogue of the *BnF*.

[15] He is also known under the pseudonym *Remon Ar Porzh*.

#	Year	Author	Title	Place	Publisher
52	1985	Herbert, Perig & Jil Ewan	Geriadur bihan ar sonerezh: vocabulaire musical breton-français, français-breton	Lesneven	Hor Yezh
53	1985	Williams, Rita	Geriadur Bach Llydaweg-Cymraeg	Aberystwyth	Canolfan Uwch-efrydiau Cymreig a Cheltaidd
54	1986 … 1995	Delaporte, Raymond	Geriadur brezhoneg-saozneg gant skouerioù: elementary breton-english dictionary with examples (sic)	Cork (Lesneven)	University Press (Hor Yezh)
55	1986	Hélias, Pierre Jakez	Dictionnaire breton: breton-français; français-breton	Paris	Garnier
56	1986	Evans, Claude & Léon Fleuriot	A Dictionary of Old Breton. Historical and Comparative. In two Parts.	Toronto	no data
57	1987	Andouard, Loeiz & Éamon Ó Ciosáin	Geriadur Iwerzhoneg-Brezhoneg gant Iavarennoù/Foclóir Gaeilge-Briotáinis Ia samplaí	Lesneven	Hor Yezh
58	1988	Hill, Eric	Spot e bro ar gerioù	Kemper	An Here
59	1990	Berr, Alan-Gwennog	Geriadur an anoiou Ioened mor	Brest	Brud Nevez
60	1990	Williams, Rita	Geiriadur Cymraeg-Llydaweg: Geriadur Kembraeg-Brezhoneg	Aberystwyth	Canolfan Astud-iaethau Cymreig a Cheltaidd
61	1991	Hincks, Rhisiart	Geriadur kembraeg-brezhoneg	Lesneven	Hor Yezh
62	1992 (-93; -97; -98)	Favereau, Francis	Geriadur ar brezhoneg a-vremañ. Dictionnaire du breton contemporain	Morlaix	Skol Vreizh
63	1993	Cornillet, Gérard	Geriadur Brezhoneg-Alamaneg	Lesneven	Hor Yezh
64	1993	no data	Les 1000 premiers mots en breton	Rennes	Skol an Emsav
65	1994	Gunn, Marion	Da mihi manum (terms and phrases in six languages)	Dublin	Everson Gunn Teo.
66	1995 (2001)	Ménard, Martial	Ar geriadur brezhoneg (gant skouerioù ha troiennoù - dictionnaire monolingue breton)	Ar Releg Kerhuon	An Here
67	1995	Ménard, Martial	Alc'hwez braz ar baradoz bihan pe Geriahudur ar brezhoneg (dictionnaire du breton érotique)	Ar Releg Kerhuon	An Here
68	1995	Delanoy, Arnaud	Geriadurig etimologel ar brezoneg	Brest	Mesidou
69	1995	An Noalleg, Yann-Baol	Geriadur an armerzh ar c'henwerzh hag an arc'hant: e div yezh, gilleg, brezhoneg Dictionnaire de l'économie politique du commerce et des finances en deux langues: français, breton	Plomelin	Preder
70	1995	Cadieu, Marie-Paule & Christophe Lazé	Mon premier dictionnaire français-breton en images	Paris	Éditions Jean-Paul Gisserot

	Year	Author	Title	Place	Publisher
71	1995	Étienne, Guy	Geriadur ar stlenneg e teir yezh: galleg, saozneg, brezhoneg Dictionnaire de l'informatique en trois langues: français, anglais, breton	Plomelin	Preder
72	1996	Fulup, Jakez	Diccionario básico español-breton: geriadur diazez brezhoneg-spagnoleg	Rennes	Skol-Uhel ar Vro
73	1997 (-98)	Hemon, Roparz & Ronan Huon	Dictionnaire breton-français/français-breton	Brest	Al Liamm
74	1997	Delanoy, Arnaud	Geriadurig etimologel ar brezoneg	Brest	Ar Skol vrezoneg, Emgleo Breiz
75	1997	Conroy, Jospeh F.	Breton-English, English-Breton Dictionary and Phrase Book	New York	Hippocrene
76	1998	Knox, William	The Pan-Celtic Phrasebook	Talybont	Lolfa
77	1999	Étienne, Guy	Geriadur ar gorfadurezh hervez an destladur etrevroadel P.N.A. e teir yezh: galleg, latin, brezhoneg Dictionnaire de l'anatomie conforme à la nomenclature internationale P.N.A. en trois langues: français, latin, breton	Plomelin	Preder
78	1999	Favereau, Francis	Geriadur krenn ar brezhoneg a-vremañ Dictionnaire usuel du breton contemporain. Brezhoneg-galleg/galleg-brezhoneg	Morlaix	Skol Vreizh
79	2000	Le Moal, Pascal & Etienne Guy	Geriadur ar mediaoù, firveier, video e teir yezh: galleg, saozneg, brezhoneg Dictionnaire des Médias, Cinema, vidéo en trois langues: français, anglais, breton	Plomelin	Preder
80	2000	Cornillet, Gérard	Geriadur brezhoneg-alamaneg/deutsch-bretonisch	Lesneven	Hor Yezh

In contrast to other Celtic regions, there is a relatively large number of dialectal dictionaries available in Britain, particularly of the Vannetais dialect, which is very different from the *KLT*-dialects. The importance which is attributed to particular dialects can be seen in the following table:

1723	Châlons, Pierre de	Dictionnaire breton-français du diocèse de Vannes	Vannes	Jacques de Heuqueville
1744-56	Cillart de Kérampoul, Claude-Vincent[16]	Dictionnaire françois-celtique du dialecte de Vannes	Leyden (Holland)	la Compagnie
1869 (-76; -86; 1979)	Troude, Amable-Emmanuel	Nouveau dictionnaire pratique breton-français du dialecte de Léon, avec les acceptions diverses dans les dialectes de Vannes, de Tréguier et de Cornouailles, et la prononciation quand elle peut paraître douteuse. Suivi d'un Receuil de proverbed bretons et d'un Dictionnaire de rimes bretonnes, dans lequel sont indiqués quelque règles de la prosodie bretonne, ainsi que les particularités des consonnances finales de cette langue (sic)	Brest (Mayenne)	J.B. & A. Lefournier (J. Floc'h)
1890	Moal, Jean	SUPPLÉMENT LEXICO-GRAMMATICAL AU DICTIONNAIRE PRATIQUE FRANÇAIS-BRETON du Colonel A. Troude. EN DIALECTE DE LÉON (sic)	Landerneau	J. Desmoulins
1895	Du Rusquec, Henri	NOUVEAU DICTIONNAIRE PRATIQUE ET ETYMOLOGIQUE DU DIALECTE DE LÉON AVEC LES VARIANTES DIVERSES, DANS LES DIALECTS DE VANNES, TRÉGUIER ET CORNOUAILLES (sic)	Paris	Ernest Leroux
1895	Châlons, Pierre de	Dictionnaire breton-français du dialecte de Vannes	Rennes	J. Plihon et L. Herve
1904 (-19; -83; -91)	Ernault, Émile	Dictionnaire breton-français du dialecte de Vannes	Gwened (Brest)	Ti Lafoyle Frères (Brud Nevez)
1980-1988	Denez, Per	Geriadur brezhoneg Douarnenez	Lesneven	Hor Yezh
1981 (1999)	Herrieu, Meriadeg[17]	Dictionnaire français-breton vannetais	Hennebont (Brest)	Bleun-Brug Bro-Gwened (Emgleo Breiz)

---

[16] The same dictionary is also attributed to *Abbé Armeyrie* in a separate entry. *L'Abbé Armeyrie*, however, is the pseudonym of Cillart de Kérampoul.

[17] The French form is *Mériadec Henrio*.

| 1984-1993 | Guilloux, Gabriel Louis | Grand dictionnaire français-breton du dialecte de Vannes: recueil de mots bretons empruntés aux dictionnaires breton-français et francais-breton de Guillevic et Le Goff, au dict-ionnaire breton-français d'Émile Ernault, au grand dictionnaire français-breton de François Vallée, à la collection complète de "Dihunamb" ainsi que de mots recueillis par l'auteur | Lesneven | Hor Yezh |
| 1995 | Le Gal, D. | Geriadur Groe (diwar yezhadur Ternes) | Rennes | no data |

At the moment, there are five lexicographical works online for Breton. One is the dictionary by Favereau (cf. 1992-98 in the list above[18]), which was put on the internet as a Breton-French-Breton data base by Phillippe Argouarch (http://www.bretons.org/dico.gci, 20.10.2001). Another is the *Breton-German-Breton Dictionary* by Johannes Heinecke (http://www.compling.hu-berlin.de/~johannes/dict/brezhoneg/, 20.10.2001). The other three cannot be regarded as dictionaries: the *Alternative Breton Dictionary* by Hans-Christian Holm lists only twenty-seven headwords in Breton and their English equivalents (http://www.notam.uio.no/~hcholm/altlang/ht/Breton.html, 20.10.2001); *Breizh.Net* produced by the TermBret Computer Commission provides one hundred computer terms in English, Breton and French (http://www.breizh.net/saosg/mahtmals.htm, 20.10.2001). The *Dictionnaire Breton-Français-Anglais* produced by Gildas Perrot gives five hundred entries and presents at least a vocabulary (http://www.-francenet.fr/~perrot/breizh/dico.html, 20.10.2001).

---

[18] As *Dictionnaire vocal du breton contemporain* it is also available on CD-ROM.

3.2.3. The corpus of Cornish dictionaries

	Date	Author	Title - published dictionaries only	Location	Publisher
1	1665 (1972)	Williams, Robert	Lexicon Cornu-Britannicum : a dictionary of the ancient Celtic language of Cornwall, in which the words are elucidated by copious examples from the Cornish works now remaining ; with translations in English, the synonyms are also given in the cognate dialects of Welsh, Armoric, Irish, Gaelic, and Manx, shewing at one view the connexion between them (sic)	London (Menston)	Trübner (Scholar Press)
2	1887 (1980)	Jago, Frederick William Pearce	An English-Cornish dictionary	London (redruth)	Simpkin, Marshall & co. (sic) (Dyllansow Truran)
3	1934 (1990; -94)	Nance, Robert Morton	A New Cornish-English Dictionary	St. Ives	Federation of Old Cornish Societies
4	1981 (1997)	Snell, J. Anthony N.	Cornish dictionary. Python an gegyn. War an fordhow-Kitchen things. On the roads/Supplement no. 1.	no data (Portreath)	Cornish Language Board (Agan Tavas)
5	1984	Snell, J. Anthony N.	Cornish dictionary/Supplement no. 2	no data	Cornish Language Board
6	1986 (-98; 2000)	Truran, Christine	A short Cornish dictionary/Gerlyver ber	Redruth	Dyllansow Truran (Tor Mark)
7	1990	Gendall, Richard	A students dictionary of modern Cornish (sic)	Liskeard	Cornish Language Council
8	1991	Kennedy, Niel P.	Gerlever bear Geiriadur byr Saesneg-Cernyweg-Cymraeg	no data	Neil P. Kennedy
9	1993	George, Ken	Gerlyver Kernewek kemmyn An Gerlyver meur Kernewek-Sowsnek/Cornish-English dictionary	Cornwall (sic)	Cornish Language Board
10	1994	Sanderock, Graham	The first thousand words in Cornish. With pronunciation guide.	Liskeard	Kesva an Tavas Kernewek
11	1995	George, Ken	Gerlyver Kernewek kemmyn Sowsnek-Kernewek/English-Cornish dictionary	no data	Cornish Language Board
12	1995	Morris, William	Cornish dictionary. Geryow divers-general words/ Supplement no. 3.	Portreath	Agan Tavas
13	1997	Gendall, Richard	A practical dictionary of modern Cornish	Liskeard	Teere ha Tavaz

14	1998	Gendall, Richard	A new practical dictionary of modern Cornish, English-Cornish	Cornwall (sic)	Teere ha Tavas
15	1998 (2000)	George, Ken	GERLYVER KERNEWEK KEMMYN An Gerlyver Kres KERNEWEK - SOWSNEK/SOWSNEK - KERNEWEK CORNISH-ENGLISH/ENGLISH-CORNISH DICTIONARY (sic)	Bosprenn	Kesva an Tave Kernewek
16	2000	Williams, Nicholas	English-Cornish dictionary Gerlyver Sawsnek-Kernowek	Dublin & Redruth	Everson Gunn & Agan Tavas

There is one Cornish course on the internet which contains an English-Cornish word list (cf. http://www.clas.demon.co.uk/html/body_lexicon.htm, 20.10.2001).

There are two other dictionaries listed on the *Cornish Language Page* (http://www.summerlands.com/marketplace...ore2/amazon_store/language/cornish.htm, 20.10.2001), i.e. a *Cornish English dictionary* (1974) and a *Cornish-English Dictionary* (1989). Neither could be found in the library catalogues.

A comparison of dictionary production in the Celtic regions is presented following the individual lists of dictionaries in section 3.3.

3.2.4. The Corpus of Irish dictionaries

	Date	Author	Title - published dictionaries only[1]	Location	Publisher
1	1643	Ó Cléirigh, Micheál	Foclóir no Sanasan Nua ina minighthear cáil éigin de fhoclaibh cruaidhe na gaoidheilge	Louvain	no data
2	1707	Molloy, F.O.	FOCLOIR GAOIDHEILGE-SHAGSONACH: AN IRISH-ENGLISH DICTIONARY (sic)[2]	Oxford	Edward Lhuyd
3	1732	Ó Beaglaoich, Conchobhar[3] & Aodh Buidhe Mac Cuirtín	The English Irish Dictionary. An focloir bearla gaoidheilge ar na chur a neagar le Conchobhar O Beaglaoich mar son aon le congnamh aodh bhuide mac cuirtin agus fós. a bpairis. (sic)	Paris	Seamus Guerin (sic)
4	1740 (1825; 1969)	no data	The Irish spelling book	R.C. Alston	The Scholar Press Ltd. Menston
5	1768 (-86; 1832)	O'Brien, John Dr.	Focalóir Gaoidhilge-Sax-Bhéarla, or An Irish-English Diction-ary. Whereof the Irish part hath been compiled not only from various Irish vocabularies, particularly that of Mr. Edward Lhuyd, but also from a great variety of the best Irish manu-scripts now extent; especially those that have been composed from the 9th & 10th centuries, down to the 16th: besides those of the lives of St. Patrick & St. Brigit, written in the 6th and 7th centuries. (sic)	Paris (Dublin)	N.F. Valleyre; Printed for Hodges and Smith
6	1780	Shaw, William[4]	A Galic and English Dictionary, containing all the Words in the Scotch and Irish Dialects of the Celtic, that could be col-lected from the Voice, and Old Books and MSS. Vol. i An English and Galic dictionary, containing the most useful and necessary Words in the English Language, explained by the correspondent Words in the Galic. Vol. ii (sic)	London, Edinburgh, Oxford, Paris	W. & A. Strachan; D., C. Elliot, J. Balfour and R. Jamieson; Prince; Pissot

---

[1] I would like to take this opportunity of thanking Prof. Séamus Mac Mathúna for providing me with material with regard to Irish dictionaries and advising me on that matter. In the same way I would also like to thank Theresa Illés, Vienna/Austria.

[2] This dictionary became part of Lhuyd's *Archaeologia Britannica* as an Irish and Scottish Gaelic dictionary (cf. sections 2.2.3., 2.3., and 3.2.6.).

[3] The English version of his name is *Conor Begley*.

[4] See also section 3.2.6.

7	1814 (-63)	Connellan, Thaddæus	An English Irish dictionary, intended for the use of schools: containing upwards of eight thousand English words, with their corresponding explanations in Irish.[5]	Dublin (London, Edinburgh, Melbourne)	Graisberry & Campbell (Simpkin, Marshall & Co; Oliver & Boyd; George Robertson)
8	1817 (-21; -64)	O'Reilly, Edward	Sanas Gaoidhilge-Sagsbhearla. An Irish-English dictionary, containing upwards of twenty thousand words that never appeared in any former Irish lexicon: with copious quotations to elucidate the meaning of obscure words, and numerous comparisons of the Irish words, with those of similar orthography, sense, or sound, in the Welsh and Hebrew languages. In their proper places in the dictionary, are inserted, the Irish names of our indigenous plants, with the names by which they are commonly known in English and Latin. The Irish words are first given in the original letter, and again in Italic, for the accomodation of those who do not read the Language in its ancient character. To which is annexed a compendious Irish grammar (sic)	Dublin	John Barlow (O'Neil, J. Duffy and Co ltd.)
9	1849	de Vere Coneys, Thomas	Foclcir guoidilge-sucs-beurlu, or an Irish-English dictionary (sic)[6]	Dublin	Hodges & Smith
10	1855	Foley, Daniel	An English-Irish dictionary: intended for the use of students of the Irish language	Dublin	William Curry
11	1900	Hogan, Edmund F.	Luibhleabhrán: Irish and Scottish Gaelic names of herbs, plants, trees etc.	Dublin	M.H. Gill
12	1900 (-03; -05; -07; -10)	Fournier d'Albe, Edmund Edward	An English-Irish dictionary and phrase book with synonyms, idioms, and the genders and declensions of nouns	Dublin	The Celtic Association (M.H. Gill)
13	1901	Vallée, François	Dicticnnaire anglais, irlandais, gaēlique, manois, breton (sic)	no data	Celtia
14	1904 (-21)	O'Neill Lane, Timothy	Lane's English-Irish Dictionary (Foclóir Béarla-Gaedhilge) compiled from the most authentic sources	Dublin - London	Sealy, Bryers and Walker - David Nutt (Talbot Press)

[5] The title found in the catalogue of the *National Library of Ireland* deviates from that written in the bibliography by Best (1913), which reads as follows: *An English-Irish Dictionary intended for the use of Schools; containing upwards of eight thousand words, with their corresponding explanations in Irish.*

[6] The spelling in the catalogue of the *National Library of Ireland* deviates from that in the bibliography by Best (1913), which reads as follows: *Focloir Gaoidhilge-Sacs-bearla.*

15	1904 (-27; -29; -34; -65; -79; -96)	Ó Duinnín, Pádraig[7]	Foclóir Gaedhilge agus Béarla/An Irish-English Dictionary, Being A Thesaurus Of The Words, Phrases And Idioms Of The Modern Irish Language. (sic)	Dublin (London)	M.H. Gill (David Nutt; Educational Company of Ireland)
16	1910 (-19; -20; -22; -23; -29; -34; -38; -41; -45; -51; -53; -65; -75; -79)	Ó Duinnín, Pádraig	A Smaller Irish-English dictionary for the Use of Schools (sic)	Dublin - London	M.H. Gill - Simpkin, Marshall & Co
17	1911 (-22)	MacKenna, Lambert Andrew Joseph[8]	English-Irish phrase dictionary, compiled from the works of the best writers of the living speech	Dublin	M.H. Gill
18	1912 (-22; -59)	Ó Duinnín, Pádraig	A Concise English-Irish Dictionary for the Use of Schools	Dublin	M.H. Gill
19	1913-1976	Marstrander, Carl Johan Sverdrup & Joynt, Maud et al.[9]	Dictionary Of The Irish Language Based Mainly On Old And Middle Irish Materials (sic)	Dublin	Royal Irish Academy
20	1915 (-16; -21; -22)	O'Neill Lane, Timothy	Larger English-Irish Dictionary/Foclóir Bearla-Gaedhilge.	Dublin	Phoenix Publication (The Talbot Printer)
21	1922	Ó Duirinne, Séamus & Pádraig Ó Dálaigh	The educational pronouncing dictionary of the Irish language	Dublin	Educational Company of Ireland
22	1927	Dinneen, Patrick Steven.	Foclóir Gaedhilge agus Béarla/An Irish-English dictionary, being a thesaurus of the words, phrases and idioms of the modern Irish language	Dublin	Educational Company of Ireland

---

7 The English version of his name is *Patrick Steven Dinneen*.
8 *MacKenna*'s name - also *McKenna* - is occasionally listed in its Irish spelling *MacCionnaith* or *McCionnaith*.
9 Other editors were Eleanor Knott, David Green, Ernest Gordon Quin, Myles Dillon, Maura Carney, Máirín O Daly, and Anne O'Sullivan. For more details with regard to the compilation of this lexicographical work, see E.G. Quin (1976: III-VI).

No.	Year	Author	Title	Place	Publisher
23	1933	Hessen, Hans & Séamus Caomhánach et al.	Hessen's Irisches Lexikon Kurzgefaßtes Wörterbuch Der Alt- Und Mittelirischen Sprache Mit Deutscher Und Englischer Übersetzung Hessen's Concise Dictionary Of Early Irish With Definitions In German And English (sic)	Halle	Niemeyer
24	1935 (-43)	MacKenna, Lambert Andrew Joseph	Foclóir Béarla agus Gaedhlige/An English-Irish Dictionary	Baile Átha Cliath	Oifig Díolta Foill-seatcháin Rialtais 4
25	1949	Ní Ghráda, Máiréad	Foclóir Gaeilge-Béarla: an litrú caighdeánach	Baile Átha Cliath	Brún agus Ó Nualláin
26	1952	de Hae, Risteárd	Foclóir Gaedhlige agus Frainncise	Baile Átha Cliath	Oifig an tSoláthair
27	1953 (-69)	Department of Defence, Training Section	Foclóir Béarla-Gaeilge de théarmaí mileata agus de théarmaí gaolmhara. (English-Irish dictionary of military and related terms)	Baile Átha Cliath	Oifig an tSoláthair
28	1957 (-58; -60; -63; -66)	Ó Síochfhradha, Pádraig (An Seabhac)	Learner's English-Irish Dictionary	Baile Átha Cliath Corcaigh	Cló Thalbot
29	1958 (-93)	Ó hUallacháin, Colmán	Foclóir Fealsaimh/Dictionary of Philosophical Terms (German, English, French, Latin and Irish)	Baile Átha Cliath	An Clóchomhar (An Gúm)
30	1958 (-71; -73)	Ó Síochfhradha, Micheál	Irish-English Dictionary and English-Irish Dictionary	Baile Átha Cliath, Corcaigh	Cló Thalbot
31	1959 (-67)	Ó Síochfhradha, Pádraig (An Seabhac)	Foclóir Gaeilge-Béarla. Learner's Irish-English pronouncing dictionary in new standard spelling	Baile Átha Cliath, Corcaigh	Cló Thalbot
32	1959 (-87; -92)	de Bhaldraithe, Tomás	English-Irish Dictionary (later: with terminological additions and corrections)	Baile Átha Cliath	Oifig an tSoláthair (An Gúm)
33	1959-1996	Vendryes, Joseph (Pierre-Yves Lambert)	Lexique étymologique de l'irlandais ancien	Baile Átha Cliath, Paris	Dublin Institute for Advanced Studies & Centre National de la Recherche Scientifique
34	1965 (-77)	Oireachtaigh, Bríd Bean & Piaras Ó Muirgheasa	An Mionfhoclóir Irish-English Dictionary	Baile Átha Cliath	Ó Fallúin
35	1966 (-77; -78)	Oireachtaigh, Bríd Bean	Nuafhoclóir English-Irish dictionary	Baile Átha Cliath	Ó Fallúin
36	1966 (-94)	An Roinn Oideachais	Foclóir Eolaíochta/Dictionary of Science	Baile Átha Cliath	An Gúm

37	1968 (-78; -93)	An Roinn Oideachais	Foclóir Bitheolaíochta/Dictionary of Biology	Baile Átha Cliath	An Gúm
38	1968 (-71)	Ó Siochfhradha, Mícheál	Nuafhoclóir Gaeilge-Béarla Learner's Irish-English Dictionary Nuafhoclóir Béarla-Gaeilge Learner's English-Irish Dictionary	Baile Átha Cliath	Comhlacht Oideachais na hÉireann
39	1972 (-82)	An Roinn Oideachais	Tíreolaíocht agus Pleanáil/Geography and Planning (Foclóir Tíreolaíochta agus Pleanála mar aon le Téarmaeí Sean-dálaíochta/Dictionary of Geography and Planning in-corporating Archaeological Terms)	Baile Átha Cliath	Oifig an tSoláthair
40	1972	no data	Foclóir Ceirdeanna agus Teicneolaíochta	Baile Átha Cliath	An Gúm
41	1973 (-91)	Ó Droighneáin, Muiris	Nua gach bia: a dictionary of culinary terms Béarla-Gaeilge/Gaeilge-Béarla	Baile Átha Cliath	Sairséal agus Dill
42	1977	Mac Cionnaith, Séamus	Foclóir don aos óg 1. Séamus Mac Cionnaith a rinne na pictúir.	Baile Átha Cliath	Oifig an tSoláthair
43	1977 (-92)	Ó Dómhnaill, Niall[10]	Foclóir Gaeilge-Béarla	Baile Átha Cliath	An Gúm
44	1978	Oifig an tSolathair	Foclóir Modúlach/Modular Terminology	Baile Átha Cliath	Oifig an tSolathair
45	1979	Leonard, Pamela	Foclóir don aos óg 2. Leonard, Pamela a rinne na pictúir.	Baile Átha Cliath	Oifig an tSolathair
46	1981	Oifig an tSolathair	Fiseolaíocht agus Sláinteachas/Physiology and Hygiene	Baile Átha Cliath	Oifig an tSolathair
47	1981	Ó Dómhnaill, Niall & Tomás de Bhaldraithe	An Gearrfhoclóir Gaeilge-Béarla	Baile Átha Cliath	An Roinn Oideachais
48	1981	de Bhaldraithe, Tomás	Innéacs Nua-Ghaeilge don - Dictionary of the Irish Language	Baile Átha Cliath	Acadamh Ríoga na hÉireann
49	1982	Leonard, Pamela	Foclóir don aos óg 3. Leonard, Pamela a rinne na pictúir.	Baile Átha Cliath	Oifig an tSolathair
50	1982	Oifig an tSolathair	Eacnamaíocht Bhaile/Home Economics	Baile Átha Cliath	Oifig an tSolathair
51	1983	Oifig an tSolathair	Foclóir Déiríochta/Dictionary of Dairying	Baile Átha Cliath	Oifig an tSolathair
52	1983 (-90)	Quin, Ernest Gordon	DICTIOANARY OF THE IRISH LANGUAGE BASED MAINLY ON OLD AND MIDDLE IRISH MATERIALS COMPACT EDITION (sic)	Baile Átha Cliath	Acadamh Ríoga na hÉireann
53	1983	Dorris, Paul	Pocket Irish Phrase Book	Belfast	Appletree Press

---

10   His name is mostly written in its modernised form as *Ó Dónaill*.

	Year	Author	Title	City	Publisher
54	1983	no data	Hippocrene Practical Dictionary Irish-English/English-Irish Dictionary and Phrase Book[11]	New York	Hippocrene books
55	1984	Ó Baoill, Dónall	English-Irish/Irish-English Dictionary	Baile Átha Cliath	Cló Thalbot
56	1985	An Roinn Oideachais	Foclóir Ceoil/ Dictionary of Music	Baile Átha Cliath	An Gúm
57	1985	Watson, Seosamh	Pocket Irish dictionary	Belfast	Appletree Press
58	1986 (-90; -93; -94; -98; -94)	An Roinn Oideachais	Foclóir Póca	Baile Átha Cliath	An Roinn Oideachais
59	1987	An Roinn Oideachtais	Foclóir Talmhaíochta/Dictionary of Agriculture	Baile Átha Cliath	An Gúm
60	1987	Andouard, Loeiz & Éamonn Ó Ciosáin	Geriadur Iwerzhoneg-Brezhoneg gan Iavarennoù/Foclóir Gaeilge-Briotáinis le samplaí	Lesneven	Hor Yezh
61	1988 (-90)	Davies, Helen & Yvonne Carroll	Beginner's Irish Dictionary	Baile Átha Cliath	Gill and Macmillan
62	1989	An Roinn Oideachais	Foclóir Staidéir Ghnó/A Dictionary of Business Studies	Baile Átha Cliath	An Gúm
63	1991 (-99)	Rialtas na hÉireann	An Foclóir Beag: Gaeilge - Gaeilge	Baile Átha Cliath	An Gúm
64	1992	Oireachtaigh, Bríd Bean	Foclóir: English-Irish-English Dictionary[12]	Baile Átha Cliath	Ó Fallúin
65	1992	An Gúm	FOCLÓIR CEIRDEANNA agus TEICNEOLAÍOCHTA ceirdeanna agus teicneolaíochta (Innealtoireacht, foirgníocht, líníocht, etc.)/A Dictionary of Trades & Technology (Engineering, Construction, Drawing, etc.) (sic)	Baile Átha Cliath	An Gúm
66	1994	Gunn, Marion	Da mihi manum (terms and phrases in six languages)	Baile Átha Cliath	Everson Gunn Teo.
67	1994	An Roinn Oideachais	Foclóir Scoile	Baile Átha Cliath	An Gúm
68	1995 (-96)	Mac Mathúna, Séamus & Ailbhe Ó Corráin	Collins Gem Irish Dictionary English-Irish/Irish-English	Glasgow	HarperCollins
69	1996	An Roinn Oideachais	Foclóir Réalteolaíochta/Dictionary of Astronomy	Baile Átha Cliath	An Gúm
70	1996	Doyle, Aidan & Edmund Gussmann	A Reverse Dictionary of Modern Irish	Lublin	Wydawnictwo Folium

11 This book could not be found in Irish libraries, but under http://www.cs.vu.nl/~dick/Summaries/Misc/NatLang.html (20.10.2001).
12 This dictionary could not be found in any catalogues of Irish libraries, but under http://www.cs.vu.nl/~dick/Summaries/Misc/NatLang.html (20.10.2001).

71	1996 (-98; -99)	(Ó Síochfhradha, Pádraig)[13]	Easy reference Irish/English - English/Irish Dictionary: Gailge/Béarla - Béarla/Gaeilge	Baile Átha Cliath	Comhlacht Oideachais na hÉireann
72	1997	Mac Mathúna, Séamus & Ailbhe Ó Corráin	Collins Pocket Irish Dictionary	London	HarperCollins
73	1998	Knox, William	The Pan-Celtic Phrasebook	Talybont	Lolfa
74	1999	Caldas, Thomas Feito & Clemens Schleicher	Wörterbuch Irisch-Deutsch Mit einem deutsch-irischen Wortindex	Hamburg	Helmut Buske Verlag
75	1999	Ó Cróinín, Brendán & Grundy, Valerie	The Oxford Irish minidictionary: Béarla-Gaeilge, Gaeilge-Béarla	Oxford	Oxford University Press
76	1999	Ó Luineacháin, Dáithí	An foclóir pictiúrtha The picture dictionary	Baile Átha Cliath	Comhlacht Oideachais na hÉireann
77	1999	no data	Children's illustrated Irish Dictionary Irish-English/English-Irish	New York	Hippocrene Books[14]
78	2000	Ó Cróinín, Brendán & Grundy, Valerie	The Oxford pocket Irish dictionary Béarla-Gaeilge/Gaeilge-Béarla	Oxford	Oxford University Press
79	no data	Johnson, Walter	The Leinster English-Irish & Irish-English dictionary containing most of the principal words commonly used in both languages	Baile Átha Cliath	Leinster Printing

Another Irish dictionary was compiled by Teig O'Nachter (Ua Neachtain, Tadhg Ó Neachtain) in 1739, but never published (Reid 1832: 52).

Organised by Caoimhín Ó Donnaíle, a number of q-Celtic dictionaries has been put on the internet (cf. also list of dictionaries of Manx and Scottish Gaelic and http://www.ceantar.org/Dicts/index.html, 20.10.2001), including the Irish online dictionary An Foclóir Beag (cf. list above, 1991, http://www.csis.ul.ie/focloir/ 20.10.2001).

He also produced an Irish-English word list for computer terminology (http://www.smo.uhi.ac.uk/gaeilge/foclora/riomhaire.html#comheadan, 20.10.2001) and a kind of vocabulary of terms (http://www.smo.uhi.ac.uk/~smacsuib/bng/tobar/, 20.10.2001).

An online dictionary Irish-[any of the eleven official languages of the EU including Latin] can be found under http://www.foreignword.com/-Tools/dictsrch.asp?p=files/f_40_87.htm (20.10.2001). A short online dictionary English-Irish is available under http://www.geocities.com/kswicca/-

---

13   This dictionary consists of the two individual dictionaries of Ó Síochfhradha (cf. above 1957 and 1959).
14   This book was listed under http://www.his.com/~rory/idicts.html (20.10.2001) and in the National Library of Scotland.

gaelic.html (20.10.2001) and a word list for travellers under http://www.travlang.-
com/languages/cgi-bin/langchoice.cgi?page=main&lang1=english&lang2=irish (20.10.2001).
Quite substantial are the English-Irish dictionary of bird names (http://gofree.indigo.ie/-
~cocaomh/English-Irish%20Dictionary.htm, 20.10.2001), the English-Latin-Irish word list on
the same subject (http://gofree.indigo.ie/~cocaomh/EnglishLatinIrish.htm, 20.10.2001), and a
German-Irish/Irish-German dictionary as part of an Irish language course (http://ireland-
man.de/curgail/kurs-dic.pdf, 20.10.2001), which all need to be downloaded.

More smaller word lists and phrases can be found under http://www.mavicanet.com/direc-
tory/eng/13428.html (20.10.2001).

A dictionary created for the use on hard disk *GaelDict98* was produced by Ciarán Ó Duibhín
in 1998 and can be obtained from the internet. Cathair Ó Dochartaigh is currently developing a
computer version of Ó Dónaill's dictionary which will be available on CD-ROM soon.

3.2.5. The corpus of Manx dictionaries

	Date	Author	Title - published dictionaries only	Location	Publisher
1	1838 (1910)	Cregeen, Archibald (Yn Cheshaught Ghailckagh)	A DICTIONARY OF THE MANKS LANGUAGE, WITH THE CORRESPONDING WORDS OR EXPLANATIONS IN ENGLISH; INTERSPERSED WITH MANY GAELIC PROVERBS: THE PARTS OF SPEECH, THE GENDERS, AND THE ACCENTS OF THE MANKS WORDS ARE MARKED: WITH SOME ETYMOLOGICAL OBSERVA-TIONS, NEVER BEFORE PUBLISHED. A dictionary of the Manks language, with corresponding words or explanations in English, interspersed with Gaelic proverbs (sic) (Fockleyr ny gaelgey)	Douglas	J. Quiggin
2	1866[1] (1977)[2]	Y Kelly, Yuan	FOCKLEYR MANNINAGH AS BAARLAGH	Douglas	(Scholar Press)
3	1901	Vallée, François	Dictionnaire anglais, irlandais, gaëlique, manois, breton (sic)	no data	Celtia
4	1938	Knee, J.J.	Fockleyr Kneen English-Manx Pronouncing Dictionary	Douglas	Isle of Man Examiner
5	1938	Kneen, J.J.	Manx Idioms and Phrases	Douglas	Isle of Man Examiner
6	1979	Fargher, Douglas C.	Fargher's English-Manx dictionary	Onchan	Shearwater Press
7	1984	Broderick, George	A handbook of late spoken Manx, Part 4	Tübingen	Niemeyer
8	1991	Kelly, Phil	Fockleyr Gaelg-Baarle[3]	Kirkmichael	Phil Kelly
9	no data	Robert L. Thomson et al.	The First Thousand words in Manx (sic)	no data	no data

---

[1] The English version of his name is *John Kelly*. He produced his dictionary in 1808. "It was in fact a triglot dictionary of Manx, Irish, and Scottish Gaelic equivalents of an amplified version of Shaw's English-Gaelic half of his dictionary of 1780 [cf. list of Irish and Gaelic dictionaries]. However, due to a catalogue of disasters the book never appeared and partially exists in manuscript form [... H]is dictionary of Manx (1805-08), like his grammar, was prepared for Bishop Hildesley and the Bible translators (Thomson 1977), and was to follow his grammar to the press, but never appeared until printed by the Manx Society (Vol. VIII) in 1866, along with an English-Manx version edited by the Rev. J.T. Clarke and John Ivon Mosley." (Broderick 1999: 48).

[2] The reprint only contained the Manx-English part (Broderick 1999: 48).

[3] This book is the Manx-English version of Fargher's dictionary. It was privately published and cannot be found in the *British Library*.

The staff of Sabhal Mòr Ostaig (cf. also sections 3.2.3. and 3.2.6.) has also produced two download Manx dictionaries: An English-Manx/Manx-English dictionary (http://smo.uhi.ac.uk/~kelly/LIST/DICTIONARY/dict/index.html, 20.10.2001) and Phil Kelly's dictionary *Fockleyr Gaelg-Baarle* (http://www.ceantar.org/Dicts/search.html and http://www.smo.uhi.ac.uk/~stephen/Fockleyr.pdf, 20.10.2001). A comprehensive word list of bird names is available under http://www.smo.uhi.ac.uk/~kelly/LIST/BIRDS/bird.html (20.10.2001).

Another Manx dictionary produced by Phil Kelly, Brian Stowell and Peter Hayhurst is available as part of Manx lessons (http://homepages.enterprise.net/kelly/LIST/LESSONS/LESSONS.html, 20.10.2001).

The only online dictionary *Interactive Manx Dictionary* created by J.F. Craine can be used under http://www.embedded-systems.ltd.uk/ManxStart.html (20.10.2001).

3.2.6. The Corpus of Scottish Gaelic dictionaries

	Date	Author	Title - published dictionaries only	Location	Publisher
1	1707	Molloy, F.O.	FOCLOIR GAOIDHEILGE-SHAGSONACH: AN IRISH-ENGLISH DICTIONARY (sic)[1]	Oxford	Edward Lhuyd
2	1741	M'Donald, Alexander[2]	A Galick and English Vocabulary, with an Appendix of the terms of Divinity in the said Language. Written for the use of the Charity-schools, founded and endued in the Highlands of Scotland. Leabhar a Theagasc Ainminnin: no, a Nuadhfhocloir Gaoidheilg & Beurla. (sic)	Edinburgh	Robert Fleming
3	1780	Shaw, William[3]	A Galic and English Dictionary, containing all the words in the Scotch and Irish dialects of the Celtic, that could be collected from the voice, and old books and MSS. Vol. i
An English and Galic dictionary, containing the most useful and necessary Words in the English Language, explained by the correspondent Words in the Galic. Vol. ii	London, Edinburgh, Oxford, Paris	W. & A. Strachan; D., C. Elliot, J. Balfour and R. Jamieson; Prince; Pissot
4	1795	M'Pharlain's, Robert[4]	Nuadh Fhocloir Gaidhlig agus Beurla. A new alphabetical vocabulary, Gaiilc and English: with some directions for reading and writing the Gaiilc	Edinburgh	John Moir
5	1803	Dewar, Daniel	Gaelic dictionary	Edinburgh	no data
6	1815	M'Farlane, Peter[5]	A New and Copious Vocabulary, in two Parts: the first part consisting of English and Gaelic; the second, of Gaelic and English ; with a few Directions for Reading the Gaelic. Focalair ur Gaelig agus Beurla. (sic)	no data	no data

---

[1]   This dictionary became part of Lhuyd's *Archaeologia Britannica* as an Irish and Scottish Gaelic dictionary (cf. sections 2.2.3., 2.3., and 3.2.4.).

[2]   In some editions, the spelling *M'* for *Mac* is preferred. The Gaelic spelling is *Alistair Macdomhnuill* (Reid 1832: 54). He was known as a bard of high reputation under the name of *Mac Mhaighistir Alasdair*.

[3]   See also section 3.2.4.

[4]   *Pharlain* is the Scottish Gaelic version for *M'Pharlain*, *Macpharlain*, *Macfarlan(e)*, *MacFarlan(e)*, *M'Farlan(e)*, and *Farlan(e)*. Other personal names containing *Mac* can exhibit similar variations.

[5]   This dictionary which is described in Reid (1832: 57), Thomson (1993: 61) and listed under http://www.electronicscotland.com/history/literat/dictiona.htm (10.10.2000) could not be found in the catalogue of the *National Library of Scotland*.

7	1825	Armstrong, Robert Archibald	A Gaelic Dictionary in Two Parts. I. Gaelic and English. II. English and Gaelic. In which the words, in their different acceptations, are illustrated by quotations from the best Gaelic writers ; and their Affinities traced in most of the languages of ancient and modern times with a short historical appendix of ancient names, deduced from the authority of Ossian and other poets: to which is prefixed, a new Gaelic grammar (sic)	London, Edinburgh, Glasgow, Dublin	J. Duncan, Howell and Stewart; Bell and Bradfute; W. Laing; W. Blackwood; M. Ogle, R.M. Tims
8	1828	Maclachlan, Ewen & M'Leod of Dundonald et al. (Irvine of Little Dunkeld; Mackay)	Dictionarium Scoto-Celticum, a dictionary of the Gaelic language, comprising an ample vocabulary of Gaelic words, as preserved in vernacular speech, manuscripts, or printed works, with their signification and various meanings in English and Latin, illustrated by suitable examples and phrases, and with etymological remarks, and vocabularies of Latin and English words, with their translations into Gaelic: to which are prefixed an introduction explaining the nature, objects and sources of the work, and a compendium of Gaelic grammar compiled under the direction of the Highland Society of Scotland. (sic)	Edinburgh, London	W. Blackwood, T. Cadell
9	1831 (-33; -39; -47; -53; -76; 1901; -09)	M'Leod, Norman & Daniel Dewar[6]	A Dictionary of the Gaelic language, in Two Parts. I. Gaelic and English. II. English and Gaelic. First Part comprising a comprehensive Vocabulary of Gaelic words, with their different significations in English ; and the Second Part comprising a Vocabulary of English words, with their various meanings in Gaelic.	Glasgow, London Edinburgh	Hutchison & Brookman; W.R. M'Phun, Trongate; and Simpkin and Marshall W.R. M'Phun, J. Grant

---

6   The name of *Daniel Dewar* is not always mentioned.

10	1831; (-32; -33; -66; -72; -90; -98; 1929; -34; -55; -71; -73)	M'Alpine, Neil[7]	A Pocket Pronouncing Gaelic Dictionary, for Schools in the Highlands and Islands ; containing a far greater number of pure Gaelic words than any other Dictionary, and three times, in some instances ten times, the number of Illustrations and Examples in the large Gaelic Dictionaries, from the Bible, and other sources : also, all words that are exclusively Irish pointed out, and reasons given for rejecting them. By N. M'Alpine, Student in Divinity, and Parochial Schoolmaster, Islay. Sold, in Parts, by all the Teachers in the Highlands, price Sixpence on Coarse Paper, - Ninepence on Royal. To be finished in from Ten to Twelve Numbers, including an abridgement of Gaelic Grammar (sic).	Edinburgh (Glasgow)	Maclachlan & Stewart (Gairm)[8]
11	1842 (-47; 1902; -06; -22; -36; -70)	Maceachen, Evan[9] (Alexander Macbain, John Whyte)	Faclair Gaidhlig is Beurla. Maceachen's Gaelic-English dictionary (based on Macleod & Dewar)[10]	Inverness, Edinburgh	Highland News Office; Maclachlan, Northern Counties Newspaper and Printing and Publishing Co.
12	1845 (-47; -66; -72; -90; -98; -29; -30; 1971)	Mackenzie, John	An English-Gaelic Dictionary being part second of the pronouncing Gaelic dictionary[11]	Glasgow (Edinburgh)	MacLaren (Maclachlan; Gairm)
13	1896 (1911; -82)	Macbain, Alexander	An Etymological Dictionary of the Gaelic Language	Inverness (Stirling, Glasgow)	The Northern Counties Printing and Publishing Company Ltd (Mackay, Gairm)
14	1900	Hogan, Edmund F.	Luibhleabhrán: Irish and Scottish Gaelic names of herbs, plants, trees etc.	Dublin	M.H. Gill

---

7 The dictionary is based on a work on the Argylleshire dialect and is normally titled *A pronouncing Gaelic dictionary*.

8 When the number of re-editions is very high, it is impossible to list all publishers and their locations. In this case a selection is presented.

9 Another version of his name is *Eoghaim Mac Eachain*. Both versions are listed separately in the catalogue of the *National Library of Scotland*. Another variation of his first name is *Ewen*.

10 This dictionary became the standard school dictionary in the twentieth century (cf. Thomson 1993: 62).

11 This work formed part II of MacAlpine's *Pronouncing Gaelic Dictionary* and was originally published separately.

	Date	Author	Title	Place	Publisher
15	1900 (1912)	MacFarlane, Malcolm	The School Gaelic Dictionary. Am briathrachan beag i air a dheasachadh a chum feum luchd-ionn sachadh na Gàidhlig le Calum Mac Phàrlain.	Stirling	Eneas Mackay
16	1901	Vallée, François	Dictionnaire anglais, irlandais, gaëlique, manois, breton (sic)	no data	Celtia
17	1901-1911 (-20; -30; -41; -49; -67; -71; -73; -77; -88; -93; -94; -98)	Dwelly, Edward	Faclair gadhlig, air son nan Sgoiltean, le Dealbhan. The Illustrated Gaelic-English Dictionary: specially designed for beginners and for the use in schools, including every Gaelic word in all other Gaelic dictionaries and printed books, as well as an immense number never in print before.[12]	Herne Bay (Glasgow)	E. Macdonald & Co (Gairm)
18	1902-1911	Macdonald, E.[13]	A Gaelic dictionary: specially designed for beginners and for the use in schools: profusely illustrated, and contains every Gaelic word in all the dictionaries hitherto published, besides many hundred collected from Gaelic-speakers and scholars all over the world, now printed for the first time. (sic)	Herne Bay	E. Macdonald
19	1925 (1979; -82; -84; -85; -86; -88; -92; -95)	MacLennan, Malcolm	A pronouncing and etymological dictionary of the Gaelic language: Gaelic-English, English-Gaelic[14]	Edinburgh	John Grant (Acair and Mercat)
20	1930	Cassie, R.C.	A comparative Gaelic-Scots vocabulary	Stirling	Eneas Mackay
21	1932 (1992)	Dieckhoff, Henry Cyril	A Pronouncing Dictionary of Scottish Gaelic (based on the Glendary dialect)	Edinburgh et al. (Glasgow)	Johnston (Gairm)
22	1975	McKay, Girvan	English-Gaelic key to Dwelly's illustrated Gaelic-English dictionary	Glasgow	Gairm
23	1979 (-86; -88; -90; -93; -94; -96)	Renton, Robert Wemyss & J.A. MacDonald	Abair! Faclair Gaidhlig-Beurla, Beurla-Gaidhlig[15]	Glasgow	Gairm
24	1979	I.A.R.R.	Abair faclan! Gaighlig-beurla, beurla-Gaidhlig[16]	Glasgow	Mingulay Publications

12 The title of this dictionary varies considerably in the individual editions. This is confirmed by a note in the catalogue of the *National Library of Scotland.*

13 According to Derick Thomson this is 'virtually' the same dictionary as Dwelly's (cf. personal correspondence, 25.7.2000).

14 This dictionary is based on that of MacAlpine (cf. above).

15 This quaint spelling is indeed used on the cover of the dictionary.

16 According to Derick Thomson, the two 'Abair'-dictionaries are identical (cf. personal correspondence, 25.7.2000).

				New York	Hippocrene Books
25	1979 (1994)	Renton, Robert Wemyss & J.A. MacDonald	Scottish Gaelic-English/English-Scottish Gaelic[17]	New York	Hippocrene Books
26	1981 (-86; -94; -96)	Thomson, Derick S.	The New English-Gaelic Dictionary	Glasgow	Gairm
27	1985	Clyne, Douglas	An English-Gaelic dictionary of expressions, idioms and phrases	Glasgow	Gairm
28	1986 (-91; -92; -98)	Macleod, Iseabail	Pocket guide to Scottish words	Glasgow (Edinburgh)	Glasgow Drew (Chambers)
29	1987	Amery, Heather & Iain MacDhòmhnaill	The first thousand words. Gaelic. Dealbh is Facal	Steòrnabhagh	Acair agus Comhairle nan Sgoiltean
30	1991	Cox, Richard A.V.	Brìgh nam facal: faclair ur don bhun-sgoil (the first ever Gaelic-Gaelic dictionary)	Glasgow	Roinn nan Cànan Ceilteach
31	1991	Clyne, Douglas	Appendix to Dwelly's Gaelic-English Dictionary	Glasgow	Gairm
32	1993	Owen, Robert C.[18]	The modern Gaelic-English dictionary: specially recommended for learners, containing pronunciation, irregular verb tables, grammatical information, examples of idiomatic usage Faclair ur Gaidhlig-Beurla	Glasgow	Gairm Publications
33	1993	no data	An Stor-data briathrachais Gaidhlig. The Gaelic terminology database. Leabhar 1[19]	An Teanga	Clò Ostaig
34	1994	Gunn, Marion	Da mihi manum (terms and phrases in six languages)	Dublin	Everson Gunn Teo.
35	1994	Climo, Eadaidh	Feuch Facal: faclair le dealbhan	Glasgow	Gairm
36	1996	PRG & Acair[20]	Mo Chiad Fhaclair (Children's Gaelic dictionary)	Steòrnabhagh	PRG & Acair
37	1998	Buchanan, Dougal	Gaelic-Engl.sh/English-Gaelic Dictionary	Edinburgh	Lomond Books
38	1998	Knox, William	The Pan-Celtic Phrasebook	Talybont	Lolfa
39	1999 (2001)	Watson, Angus	Gaelic-English Dictionary	Edinburgh	Birlinn

17   This dictionary could only be found under http://www.cs.vu.nl/dick/Summaries/Misc/NatLang.html (20.10.2001).

18   The Scottish Gaelic version of his name is *Raibeart C. MacEòghainn.*

19   A deviant spelling could be found on the internet and can be seen in the text (cf. infra).

20   PRG stands for *The Primary Review Group.*

| 40 | 1999 | Hippocrene books | Hippocrene children's illustrated Scottish Gaelic dictionary: English-Scottish Gaelic, Scottish Gaelic-English | New York | Hippocrene Books |
| 41 | 2000 | Boyd, Robertson & Iain McDonald | Teach Yourself Scots-Gaelic Dictionary | London | Hoddon & Stoughton |

There are also seven major unpublished dictionaries:[21]

1732	McColm, David	Focloir Gaoidheilge-Shagsonach[22]	no data
1776	(clergymen)	Highland Gentlemen's Dictionary	NLS MSS. Adv. 73.3, 7-12, 22-3
no data	James Foulis	The dictionary of James Foulis of Colinton	NLS MS. Ad. 72.2.16
late eighteenth-century	Archibald Fletcher	no data	NLS MS. Adv. 72.217; Ingliston MS. A. vi.17)
1800	Alexander Robertson	no data	NLS MS. Adv. 72.2.18; NLS MSS. Adv. 72.2.19-21)
no data	Alexander MacLaurin	An English-Gaelic dictionary	NLS MSS. Adv. 72.2.22-5
no data	no data	Supplement to Dwelly's dictionary	NLS MSS. 14957-8

The major Scottish Gaelic dictionaries on the internet were prepared by the staff of the only college in which a Celtic language, i.e. Scottish Gaelic, is the medium of communication Sabhal Mòr Ostaig (cf. sections 3.2.3. and 3.2.5.) on the Isle of Skye/Scotland (cf. http://www.ceantar.org/Dicts-/search.html, 20.10.2001). These are the following download dictionaries: *An Etymological Dictionary of the Gaelic Language* compiled by MacBain,[23] (cf. above, 1896, and http://www.ceantar.org/Dicts/MB2/index.html, 20.10.2001), the *Dictionary of the Gaelic language* produced by MacLeod (cf. above, 1831, and http://psst-heyn.com/dictionarydownloads/slanguages.html, 20.10.2001), *The School Gaelic Dictionary* by MacFarlane (cf. above, 1815, and http://www.ceantar.org/Dicts/MF2/index.html, 20.10.2001), and *An Stòrdàta Briathrachais Gàidhlig*

---

21   The data presented in the table were mainly taken from Thomson (1993: 62).
22   According to Reid (1832: 54).
23   Note the different spelling to the originals.

218

(http://www.smo.uhi.ac.uk/cgi-bin/sbg, 20.10.2001).[24] These lexicographical works, however, are merely electronic versions of previously published dictionaries and are thus not specifically geared towards electronic use.

Nevertheless, there is more lexicographical material on the webpages from Sabhal Mòr Ostaig. Ciaran Ó Duibhín, for instance, produced *Gluais Albanach-Éireannach* 'A glossary of the Gael and Irishman' to be downloaded (http://www.smo.uhi.ac.uk/gaidhlig/ga-ge/gluais.html, 20.10.2001). It mainly comprises lexical items from prose and songs and is quite substantial. In addition, there are some comparisons between the Irish and the Gaelic language under http://www.smo.uhi.ac.uk/gaidhlig/ga-ge/faclair.html and .../ga-ge/coimeashtml (20.10.2001) and the *Gaelic-L Dictionary* (sic, cf. http://www.smo.uhi.ac.uk/~smacsuib/focloir/gaelic-l/, 20.10.2001):

Faclair Gàdhlig-Beurla/Gaelic-English (http://www.sst.ph.ic.ac.uk/angus/Faclair, 20.10.2001) is quite a comprehensive download dictionary. Another minor word list is available under http://www.estelnet.com/catalunyacymru/catala/dicgae_a.htm (20.10.2001).

Based on the previous list of dictionaries, the next section presents a comparison of the dictionary production in the Celtic regions.

---

[24] It can be assumed that Caoimhín Ó Donnaíle is responsible for this work (cf. http://www.-ceantar.org/Dicts/search.html, 20.10.2001). The spelling of the version on the internet deviates from that of the printed version (cf. above).

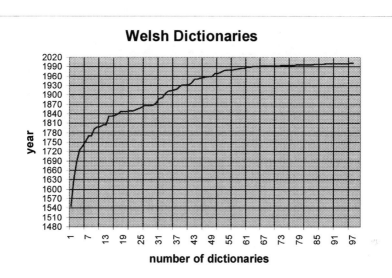

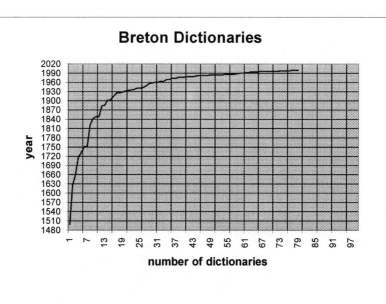

220

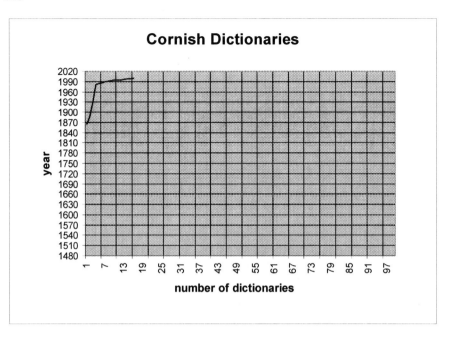

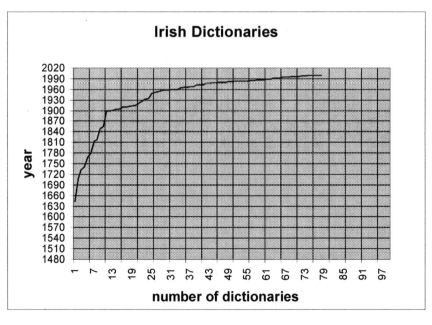

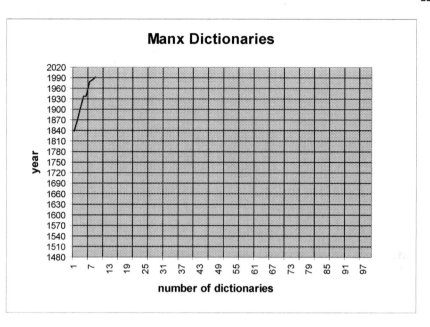

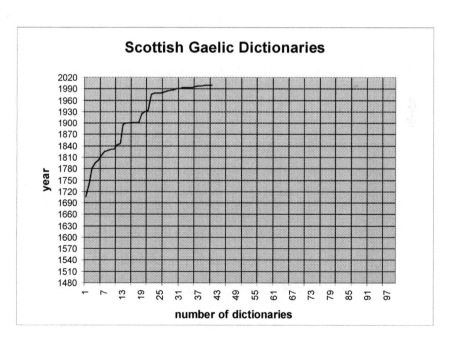

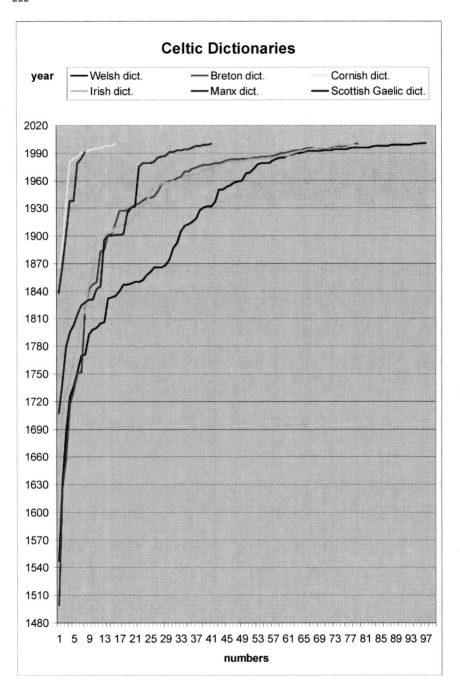

Celtic Dictionaries

year	—— Welsh dict.	﹌﹌ Breton dict.	﹌﹌ Cornish dict.
	﹌﹌ Irish dict.	—— Manx dict.	—— Scottish Gaelic dict.

numbers

3.3. Comparison of the corpora

Some basic conclusions can be drawn from the comparison of the corpora of dictionaries compiled in the preceding lists and displayed in the diagrams. Questions as to why the developments stated below took shape, however, should be more thoroughly discussed in a separate investigation, which examines issues in detail, such as the correlation of dictionary production with language policy in all Celtic countries. Some first ideas in this regard, however, are expressed in the context of the major conclusions introduced in the following, in particular, when concerning the Welsh language:

It is interesting to realise that the first dictionary of a Celtic language, a trilingual one, was produced in Brittany (Lagadec 1499). The next Breton dictionary, however, occurred later than the first Welsh dictionary (cf. sections 3.2.1. Salesbury 1547, and 3.2.2. Quiquer de Roscoff 1626-1759, cf. also below).

The number of dictionaries produced in the individual Celtic regions seems to correspond with the number of the speakers there (cf. Heinz 2000). This is on the one hand somewhat surprising, since the range of lexicon needed in order to communicate in modern life is not dependent on the number of speakers. Living in culturally very similar and closely related areas, the speakers of Celtic languages have to denote about the same kind and range of objects, relations, phenomena and realities in society.

On the other hand, the correspondence of the number of dictionaries with the numbers of speakers gives apparently an idea of the actual status of the Celtic communities in their countries. Part of the correlation of dictionary production with the number of speakers are also economic aspects. The fewer the number of speakers the less is the acceptance of financial support for them and questions as to the purpose and efficiency of the production of abundant lexicographical or other material for such minorities occur. Economy, however, is not the only factor which influences societies - one reason why more money has been spend on matters of minority in the last forty years (cf. sections 4.1.1. and 4.1.2.).

Looking at the lists and diagrams above, it becomes apparent that the first substantial increase in the number of dictionaries produced in the Celtic countries occurred in the period of the Romantic (cf. also section 2.4.). This is also the period of beginning specialisation in Celtic lexicography (ibid.) and continous dictionary production.

The second increase in the number of dictionaries produced for Irish was at the turn of the ninteenth and twentieth centuries and for Breton between the end of the twenties and the end of the fourties. Lexicography here mirrored the 'dawn and decline' of the Breton language in the twentieth century which was strongly related to the influence of Roparz Hemon (cf. sections 3.2.2. and 4.4.).

In all Celtic countries a more intensive lexicographical production was noticable after the Second World War. Part of this development was the compilation of dictionaries and vocabularies which contained specialist lexis, thereby reflecting new specialisation in society (cf. section 1.1.).

In particular in Ireland, this trend in lexicography was supported by its status as the first official language of Ireland (cf. section 3.1.) and the subsequent demand of inventing new lexical items in order to cover communicational needs according to social developments.

In Wales the struggle for the language gradually improved its status and helped to establish a network of institutions working in its support (cf. Phillips 2000 and section 4.1.1.). Consequently, a third major increase of lexicographical activities was apparent in the nineties.

Quite apparent are differences in the development of lexicographical material in the individual Celtic countries. Scotland, for instance, seems more different from the others in that it depends more on re-editions of particular works than Wales, Ireland, or Brittany. Although there are Breton, Irish and Welsh dictionaries which have seen very many re-editions (cf. in the preceding lists: *Nouveau Dictionnaire*, 1717-1893; H.M. Evans *Y Geiriadur Mawr*, 1958-2001; P. Ó Dinneen *A smaller Irish-English dictionary*, 1910-1979), the emphasis on re-printing seems to dominate Scottish Gaelic lexicography. As a result, general-purpose dictionaries from the first half of the nineteenth century were still being used at the end of the twentieth (cf. M'Alpine 1831, Maceachen 1842, and Mackenzie 1845), which is not the case with early dictionaries in Brittany, Ireland, or Wales. In these countries, new dictionaries have consistently been produced. The currently most popular reference book is still Dwelly's dictionary, which was first produced between the years 1901 and 1911. M' Farlane (1815), M'Leod (1831), and Macbain (1896) even benefited from computer age.

More basic developments in Celtic lexicography can be recognised by looking at various types of dictionaries[1] as presented in the following tables:

---

[1]   For a definition of individual types of dictionaries, see section 1.3.2.1.3.

Specialist dictionaries in the Celtic countries

	Brittany	Cornwall	Ireland	Manx	Scotland	Wales
first dict.	1499	1865	1643	1838	1707	1547
number of dict.[2]	80	16	79	9	41	97
monolingual general-purpose dictionaries	1941 Geriadurig krenn brezhonek 1963-1971 Geriadur broadel 1974 Geriadur bras ar brezhoneg 1977 Ur geriadur unyezhek 1995 Geriadur brezhoneg	--	1991 Foclóir beag: Gaeilge-Gaeilge	--	1991 Brigh nam facal	1868 Geiriadur Cymreig Cymra-eg ...[3]

[2] First, the number of dictionaries given here refers to printed books only. Second, the dictionaries mentioned here are listed with the date of their first publication only. For re-editions, see previous lists. Third, space-consuming titles are abbreviated. The complete titles can also be obtained from the previous lists. Fourth, the spelling of the dictionary titles in the tables has been unified by the author.

[3] The Welsh also produced a thesaurus (1993, cf. below). This, however, is a dictionary of synonyms and antonyms.

	Breton		Irish		Gaelic	Welsh
historical dictionaries[4]	1958-1979 Geriadur istorel ar brezhoneg 1964 Dictionnaire des Gloses en Vieux Breton 1986 A dictionary of Old Breton	--	1913-1976 Dictionary of the Irish language based mainly on Old and Middle Irish materials 1933 Hessens's Irisches Lexikon 1983 Dictionary of the Irish language	--	--	1950- Geriadur Prifysgol Cymru
etymological dictionaries[5]	1752 Dictionnaire étymologique de la langue bretonne 1885 Dictionnaire étymologique du breton moyen 1973-1977 Dictionnaire étymologique du breton ancien, moyen et moderne 1995 Geriadurig etimologel ar brezoneg	--	1954-1996 Lexique étymologique de l'irlandais ancien	--	1896 An etymological dict. of the Gaelic language ... 1925 A pronouncing and etymological dictionary of the Gaelic language ...	--

---

4   Historical dictionaries are those reference works which were primarily compiled in order to display as many historical lexical items as possible.
    Dictionaries which contain historical lexical items on an irregular basis or for elucidating headwords do not form part of this type of dictionaries.
5   Historical or general-purpose dictionaries which contain etymologies of their headwords on an irregular basis do not belong to this category.

pronoun-cing dic-tionaries[6]	--	1922 The educational pronouncing dictionary of the Irish language 1959 Learner's Irish-English pronouncing dictionary ...	1938 Fockleyr Kneen English-Manx pronouncing dictionary	1831 A pocket pronouncing Gaelic Dict. ... 1925 A pronouncing and etymological dict. of the Gaelic language... 1932 A pronouncing dict. of Scottish...--	
spelling dict.	--	1740 The Irish spelling book	--	--	
reverse dict.	--	1996 A reverse dict. of modern Irish	--	--	1987 Geiriadur gwrthdroadol
bardic diction-aries[7]	1933-1936 Dictionnaire des rimes	--	--	--	1874 Geiriadur y bardd: neu yr odlydd cyffredinol ... 1978 Yr Odliadur 1996 Y Cleciadur

[6] First, here are only those pronouncing dictionaries listed which reflect the pronunciation of the Celtic languages. Second, the display of pronunciation should be the major purpose of these dictionaries. General-purpose dictionaries which contain the pronunciation of the headwords, therefore, do not belong to this category of specialist dictionaries.

[7] Bardic dictionaries are those which help to find rhymes, consonantal clusters or other metrical features of the Celtic languages.

term- inology[8]	1960 body 1982 bardic words 1983 the sea 1983 psycho- analysis 1985 music 1990 animals of the sea 1995 economy 1995 computer science 1995 eroticism	1981 kitchen	1953 military terms 1958 philosophy 1966 science 1968 biology 1972 geography 1972 psychotherapy 1973 culinary terms 1978 modular term 1981 physiology and hygiene 1982 home econom- ics 1983 dairying 1985 music 1987 agriculture 1989 business 1992 trades and technology 1996 astronomy	–	1993 general	1931 bardic words 1932 technology 1973 general 1992 computer 1992 law 1998 school terminology 1998 sight + hearing 1999 organisation 1999 archaeology
multilin- gual dict.[9]	1499 Le Catholicon (French, Bret- on, Latin) 1901 English, Irish, Gaelic, Manx, Breton 1983 French, Ger- man, English, Breton 1995 French, Eng- lish, Breton	1865 Lexicon Cornu- Britannicum (Welsh, Breton, Irish, Gael- ic, Manx)	1901 English, Irish, Gaelic, Manx, Breton 1958 German, Eng- lish, French, Latin	1901 English, Irish, Gael- ic, Manx, Breton	1828 Dictionarium Scoto- Celticum (English, Latin, Gael- ic) 1901 English, I- rish, Gaelic, Manx, Bret- on	

8 In order to facilitate comparisons, only the subject of the dictionaries are displayed here.

9 Multilingual dictionaries are those who contain the same headword list in different languages. Occasional references to other languages, as found for instance, in Dr John Davies' dictionary (1632, cf. section 3.2.1.) are not considered multilingual dictionaries. Some of the multilingual dictionaries are specialist reference books. In order to facilitate the comparison, only the languages displayed in the dictionaries are mentioned here.

1994 Da mihi manum (terms and phrases in six languages)
1998 The Pan-Celtic Phrasebook

other lan- guages[10]					
1960 Welsh	‡	1952 French	‡	1985 Esperanto	‡
1978 Esperanto		1987 Breton		1979 Breton	
1979 English		1999 German		1985 Breton	
1979 Welsh				1990 Breton	
1985 Welsh				1991 Breton	
1986 English				1996 French	
1987 Irish				1996 German	
1990 Welsh				1999 German	
1991 Welsh				2000 French	
1993 German					
1996 Spanish					
1997 English					
2000 German					

10   Here are those bilingual dictionaries listed which have another language than that of the 'mother country' as their target language.

learners' dictionaries[11]	--	1990 A students dictionary of modern Cornish[12]	1855 An English-Irish dict. … 1957 Learner's English-Irish dict. 1959 Learner's Irish-English pronouncing dict. … 1968 Learner's English-Irish dict. 1968 Learner's Irish-English dict. … 1988 Beginner's Irish dict. …	--	1983 The modern Gaelic-English dict. … 2000 Teach yourself Scots-Gaelic dict. …	1932 Cymraeg i'r Werin … 1968 Geiriadur Dysgwr 1990 Geiriadur 50 awr 1992 Teach yourself Welsh dict. 1993 Gair i Gall 1998 The Welsh learner's dict. 1999 The Pocket Welsh learner's dict. 2000 Pocket Modern Welsh dict.
school dict.	--	--	1814 An English I-rish dict. … 1910 A smaller Irish-English dict. … 1912 A Consice English-Irish dict. 1994 Foclóir scoile	--	1831 A Pocket pronouncing Gaelic dict. 1900 The School Gaelic dict. 1901-1911 Faclair gadhlig… 1902 A Gaelic dict. -1911 …	1937 Spurrell's schools' dict. 1955 Geiriadur ysgol 1999 Geiriadur Cynradd Gomer

11   The distinction between learners' and school dictionaries is that learners' dictionaries are intended for self-tuition and further education whereas school dictionaries are primarily for the use in schools. Learners' dictionaries often present a simplified language (cf. remarks below).

12   Students' dictionaries could actually be separated from learners' dictionaries. Since specialisation in languages of limited diffusion is not as far advanced as in dominant languages (for reasons in this respect, see section 1.2.), however, this distinction is not made here.

	Breton	Cornish	Irish	Manx	Scottish Gaelic	Welsh
children's dictionaries[13]	1984 Kentañ geriadur Eflamm ha Rivanon	1994 The first thousand words in Cornish	1977 Foclóir don aos óg 1	no date The first thousand words in Manx	1987 The first thousand words in Gaelic	1915 Geiriadur y plentyn
	1988 Spot e bro ar gerioù		1979 Foclóir don aos óg 2		1991 Brigh nam facal ...	1979 Y Geiriadur lliwgar
	1993 Les 1000 premiers mots en breton		1982 Foclóir don aos óg 3		1996 Mo Chiad Fhaclair	1984 Geiriadur lluniau plant
	1995 Mon premier dictionnaire français-breton en images		1999 An foclóir pictiúrtha		1999 Hippocrene children's illustrated Scottish Gaelic dict.	1988 Llyfr Mawr Geiriau Smot
			1999 Children's illustrated Irish dict. and phrase book			1994 Geiriadur
						1994 Cymraeg cyntaf
						1994 Geiriadur Gomer i'r Ifanc
						1994 Geiriadur 1
						1996 Geiriadur 2
						1996 A first bilingual dict.
						1999 Geiriadur bob dydd
						1999 Geiriadur Cynradd Gomer
synonym /antonym dict.[14]	--	--	--	--	--	1892 Cyfystyron y Gymraeg
						1993 Thesawrws Cymraeg (2000)

---

13   Children's dictionaries are to be separated from school dictionaries. The former are intended for younger children or those who do not learn the respective language in school. As with any categorisation, however, it is apparent that the individual dictionaries cannot always be clearly assigned to one single category only, but fall in two or even more categories, if the authors intended to appeal to a broader audience.

14   Dictionaries of synonyms and antonyms are those whose first purpose it is to present synonyms and antonyms and not equivalents of other languages. Bilingual general-purpose dictionaries often also contain synonyms of the source language, i.e. Y Geiriadur Mawr (1958, cf. section 3.2.2.). An English-Irish dictionary (1900, cf. section 3.2.4.), but do not belong to the category of dictionaries of synonyms.

	Breton		Irish	Manx	Gaelic	Welsh
online dictionaries[15]	- Breton-French-Breton dict. - Breton-German-Breton dict.	--	- An Foclóir Beag Irish-[official languages of the EU and Latin]	- Interactive Manx Dictionary	- An etymological dict. of the Gaelic language - Dict. of the Gaelic language - The school Gaelic dict. - An Stòrdata Briathrachais Gàidhlig	- English-Welsh-English (Nodine) - Welsh-German-Welsh - English-Welsh-English (Walters) - Cymraeg.lamp.ac.uk - Y Geiriadur Gweol[16]
download dict.	--	--	- English-Irish dict. of bird names - German-Irish/Irish-German dict. - GaelDict98	- English-Manx/Manx-English dict. - Fockleyr Gaelg-Baarle	- Faclair Gàidhlig-Beurla/Gaelic-English	- Welsh-English dict.

---

15 The online dictionaries do not include so called 'download dictionaries'. Online dictionaries as defined here cannot be downloaded from the internet, but have to be used whilst being online.

16 CySill, Geiriadur yr Academi and Y Termiadur Ysgol are currently being prepared to be presented on the internet. It is not known to me, however, whether they will be available online or as download dictionaries.

Some further conclusions can now be drawn from the comparison of the availability of different types of dictionaries as presented in the previous table:

With regard to **monolingual general-purpose dictionaries** it is somewhat surprising that these are available in Brittany, Ireland and Scotland, but not in Wales, although they form essential reference books for native speakers, learners, translators, researchers, writers and many other people (cf. H.Ll. Humphreys 2000: 27). Cornwall and the Isel of Man do not have this type of dictionary either.

A kind of restricted but unfinished monolingual dictionary is *Geirfa Barddoniaeth Gynnar Gymraeg* (Lloyd-Jones 1988). It is, however, very specific, since it explains words used by the early bards and includes grammatical forms that they employed.

Wales is with regard to current monolingual general-purpose dictionaries in the same situation as are Cornwall and the Isle of Man.

Historical dictionaries were produced for the Irish, Breton and Welsh languages. The Irish historical dictionary is somewhat specific, since it concentrates on Old and Middle Irish material. The Welsh historical dictionary has been finished in 2002.

For Scottish Gaelic, a historical dictionary was intended to be produced (Thomson 1993: 62). Answering my question as to what has happened to it, I received the following reply from the *National Library of Scotland*:

> "The Historical Dictionary of Scottish Gaelic Project was based at the Department of Celtic, University of Glasgow [...] We are not sure whether the Project has finished or has run out of funding" (personal correspondence with H. Robertson, Assistant at the *National Library of Scotland*, 16.8.2000).

Etymological dictionaries were produced for Breton, Irish and Scottish Gaelic, but not for Welsh, Cornish and Manx.

In view of the historical and etymological dictionaries produced for Breton, one gets the impression that the former periods of the language seem to be of particular importance to Breton lexicographers.

Pronouncing dictionaries have only been compiled for the q-Celtic languages, thereby suggesting that the pronunciation of the p-Celtic languages is strongly phonetic.[17] Nevertheless, Breton lexicographers have produced general-purpose dictionaries, which include phonetic transcription, e.g. the *Elementary breton-english/english-breton dictionary* (Delaporte 1986), *Geriadur ar vrezhoneg a vremañ* (Favereau 1977), and *Geriadur brezhoneg-alamaneg hag alamaneg-brezhoneg* (Cornillet 2000) which prove an easy phonetic pronunciation wrong.

There are, however, no recent pronouncing dictionaries for the q-Celtic languages either. Nonetheless, looking at Irish lexicographical works it is apparent that phonetic descriptions are included in several modern dictionaries, thereby meeting the task of phonetic guidance. There are at least five dictionaries which include phonetic transcription, either based on a system of 're-spelling' as the *Learner's Irish-English Pronouncing Dictionary* (Pádraig Ó Siochfhrada

---

[17] For a discussion on this subject, see section 4.4.

1959), or on IPA, e.g. *Foclóir Póca* (An Roinn Oideachais 1986), *Foclóir Scoile*, (An Roinn Oideachais 1994), the *Children's Illustrated Irish Dictionary and Phrase Book* (http://www.his.-com/~rory/idicts.html, 20.10.2001), and the *Wörterbuch Irisch-Deutsch* (Caldas & Schleicher 1999).

Phonetic description is also included in the Manx dictionary contained in *A Handbook of late spoken Manx*, Part 4 by Broderick (1984).

Spelling dictionaries do not seem to be considered important in Celtic lexicography, except from Ireland. The Welsh book *Orgraff yr Iaith Gymraeg* (Lewis 1987), is very limited in the lexicon presented and is rather a report on Welsh Orthography (ibid.: I/viiiff.). There is, however, the spellchecker *CySill* (1995) on floppy disk/CD-ROM available in Wales. Nevertheless, the need for a spelling dictionary as well as for a thesaurus for Welsh is also felt by the staff of *Geiriadur Prifysgol Cymru* (cf. section 4.2.).

Reverse dictionaries exist only for Welsh (Zimmer 1987) and Irish (Doyle & Gussmann 1996), both produced outside their respective country.

Dictionaries of syllables and of clusters of consonants for poetic purposes have been generated in Wales. Such dictionaries do not exist for the other Celtic languages except from an older and incomplete *Dictionnaire des rimes* (Berthou 1933-39) for Breton. The existence of such dictionaries reflects a peculiarity of Welsh literary production, that is, the production of strict metre poetry, such as the *cynghanedd* (cf. section 2.2.1.2.2.). These complex metres based on consonance and assonance patterns deriving from the Middle Ages are still in popular use and productive in Wales today.

Terminology has been broadly developed for the Welsh, Breton and Irish languages. Apart from various terminological lexis contained in dictionaries and presented in the tables above, more specialist lexis has been compiled in vocabularies which were produced by these countries. These works, however, do not form part of this investigation.

Cornish and Scottish Gaelic lexicographical production is less advanced in the field of specialist lexicography, although some terminology is available in vocabularies, e.g. *Faclair Eòrpach* (Commission of the European Community: 1983). Particular terminology does not seem to have been developed for Manx.

The provision of lexicographical material for the translation into **languages other than the dominant language** of the respective Celtic country is most advanced in Breton. It seems that the location of Brittany on the continent and outside English spheres encourages the production of dictionaries reflecting intensive cultural contacts with various countries. This trend is confirmed by the number of multilingual reference books produced here.

Scottish Gaelic lexicography generated only vocabularies in order to have the language translated into other languages, i.e. German, Spanish, French and Italian, such as in the *Facal*-series (Fàilte: 1995/6).

The table of specialist dictionaries also reveals that the closely related sister languages, i.e. the q-Celtic languages on the one hand and the p-Celtic languages on the other, form the preferred content of bilingual dictionaries rather than the more further related Celtic languages.

A relatively large number of **learners' dictionaries** has been produced in Wales, particularly in recent times. The respective Irish works are on average a few decades older.

In both countries, the production of learners' dictionaries reflects the status of the languages (cf. sections 3.1. and 4.1.1.), which is much greater here than in the other Celtic countries. The higher number of learner's dictionaries in Wales certainly mirrors one of the cornerstones of Welsh language education, i.e Welsh for adults (cf. section 4.1.1.).

For Breton and Manx there do not seem to exist particular learners' dictionaries.

Children's dictionaries have been produced for all Celtic languages, but particularly for Welsh, thereby reflecting another cornerstone of Welsh language education, i.e. Welsh-medium education for the young children (section 4.1.1.).

School dictionaries are best represented in Irish, thereby reflecting the official status of the Irish language as the first language of the country and Irish as a compulsory subject in Irish schools. The Scottish Gaelic reference books of this kind are out of date and Breton school dictionaries are not available.

Although the teaching of Welsh is the third cornerstone of the revival of the language, little attention has been paid to the production of school dictionaries. This fact indicates that language policy is not always properly implemented. Dictionary production, therefore, does not necessarily reflect actual policy, but rather the status of the language or the status of the fulfilment of the policy (cf. also section 4.1.1.).

This phenomenon is underlined, on the one hand, by the fact that Irish has not really recovered, although the language policy in Ireland has been very supportive (cf. Hindley 1991). On the other hand, we have Cornish and Manx which no longer exist as community languages (cf. section 1.3.2.1.3.). Nevertheless, dictionary production in these countries continues. In the case of Cornish the generation of lexicographical works only began when the language was in fatal decline (cf. W. Robert 1865, and P.F.W. Jago 1887, and also section 2.2.3.).

Online dictionaries are available for all languages except for Cornish. Their production reveals that those countries who have well established research centres, benefit from latest technology and use it in support of their languages. This trend is confirmed by the production of download dictionaries.

Online dictionaries are, however, still limited in scope (cf. section 3.2.1.).

To sum up: in view of the survey of the dictionary corpora, three major characteristics could be found which are shared by the lexicographical productions in Celtic countries: all of them make use of modern computer technology, generate children's books, and have generally produced only a limited range of specialist dictionaries featuring linguistic properties of the respective languages. Apart from these three common features, the language specific situations differ strongly. In Wales, the highest number of dictionaries has been produced (97), thereby reflecting the prestige of the language. Unlike in most of the other Celtic countries, however, no current monolingual general-purpose dictionary is available here, nor an etymological reference book and only one current school dictionary. The pronunciation of the Welsh language is not adequately included in any of the existing dictionaries.

Breton lexicography has also concentrated on the provision of lexis and consequently produced a considerable number of dictionaries. It has comprehensively recorded lexical items of former periods of its language. There is, however, a lack of learners' dictionaries.

Irish lexicographical works also form a considerable corpus and cover a comparatively broad range of specialist dictionaries with regard to the lexicon included in them.

Scottish Gaelic lexicography apparently pursues a different way of presenting the Scottish Gaelic lexicon altogether in that it concentrates on re-editing older popular dictionaries. The number of dictionaries produced, therefore, is relatively small, and current works including terminology are underrepresented. As with Breton dictionaries, there seems to be a lack of learners' tools. A historical dictionary or one exhibiting synonyms and antonyms is not available either.

With regard to monolingual lexicography Brittany is most advanced (cf. the number of historical, etymological and monolingual general-purpose dictionaries). Current work on terminology is predominantly done for the living Celtic languages. However, the need to produce dictionaries for young learners has been recognised for all languages.

The survey of the dictionary also reveals that the production of dictionaries rather reflects the actual status and prestige of the respective languages than official language policy.

After Welsh lexicography has been placed in its historical perspective and Celtic context, an indepth analysis of the most important current general-purpose dictionaries based on the theoretical approaches as outlined in chapter I is pursued in the following section. One of the questions to be answered is whether the lack of presentation of linguistic features is also reflected within individual works. In addition, it is interesting to examine as to how the status quo of Welsh lexicography effects language maintenance and the construction of Welsh identity.

IV.   Welsh Dictionaries in the twentieth century
4.1.   Two major functions of Welsh dictionaries in the twentieth century

The compiling of dictionaries has always been part of social processes and has been carried out in the interest of particular cultural or political groups. Some driving interests are listed in Wiegand (1998: 59):

- the spread of religious beliefs,
- the promotion of commerce,
- the promotion of international tourism,
- the strengthening of national consciousness,
- the strengthening of group consciousness,
- language maintenance and the prevention of language decline,
- the purification of a language,
- the establishment of a unified written language,
- the development of a variety into a standard variety
- the establishment of linguistic norms and conventions,
- the establishment of conventions with regard to language, culture and pedagogy,
- the support of language politics,
- language planning with regard to the political lexicon,
- the promotion of science,
- the social integration of people by reducing linguistic barriers,

The development of English lexicography seems to confirm the intricate relationship between lexicography and social developments. Murray (1900: 50) described this relationship briefly in his summary of the historical stages of English lexicography (cf. also Ross 1996: 64ff., Stein 1995: 127-142):

"These are: the glossing of difficult words in Latin manuscripts by easier Latin, and at length by English words; the collection of the English glosses into Glossaries, and the elaboration of Latin-English Vocabularies; the later formation of English-Latin Vocabularies; the production of Dictionaries of English and other modern languages; the compilation of Glossaries and Dictionaries of 'hard' English words; the extension of these by Bailey, for etymological purposes, to include words in general; the idea of a Standard Dictionary, and its realization by Dr. Johnson with illustrative quotations; the notion that a Dictionary should also show the pronunciation of the living word; the extension of the function of quotations by Richardson; the idea that the Dictionary should be a biography of every word, and should set forth every fact connected with its origin, history, and use, on a strictly historical method. These stages coincide necessarily with stages of our national and literary history; the first two were already reached before the Norman Conquest; the third followed upon the recognition of English as the official language of the nation, and its employment by illustrious Middle English writers. The Dictionaries of the modern languages were necessitated first by the fact that French had at length ceased to be the living tongue of any class of Englishmen, and secondly by the other fact that the rise of the modern languages and increasing intercourse with the Continent made Latin no longer sufficient as a common medium of international communication. The consequences of the Renascence and of the New Learning of the sixteenth century appear in the need for the Dictionaries of Hard Words at the beginning of the seventeenth;[1] the literary polish of the age of Anne begat the yearning for a standard dictionary, and inspired the work of Johnson; the scientific and historical spirit of the nineteenth century has at once called for and rendered possible the Oxford English Dictionary."

Despite the scarce evidence for Welsh lexicographical material before the Renaissance, a close relationship between social phenomena and lexicographical production can also be confirmed for Wales.

Welsh lexicography, as far as can be established, focused at an early stage on the vernacular language (cf. sections 2.1.2., 2.1.3., 2.1.4., and 2.2.1.2.), beginning with Welsh glosses, and some Welsh words in a Latin-Cornish vocabulary (cf. *Vocabularium Cornicum* in section 2.1.4.). Although there is a Latin-Welsh list of herbs from the second half of the fourteenth century, the first vocabularies, written by bards, were Welsh-Welsh ones. The first dictionary was Welsh-English, reflecting a shift of political power in Wales. By then it was the English who ruled the country and who strongly influenced its culture (cf. section 2.2.). The second dictionary was Latin-Welsh, indicating the still lasting importance of Latin in the world of learning. Thomas Wiliems emphasised this fact in the foreword to his dictionary with the words:

> "... Llatin sydd gyphredinaf iaith yn holl Europa." 'Latin which is the most common language in the whole of Europe' (G.H. Hughes 1976: 112).

When the Welsh language faced severe decline in the nineteenth century, lexicographical activities increased remarkably, giving birth to new types of dictionaries (cf. sections 2.4., 3.2.1. and 3.3.). A similar outbreak of lexicographical activity can be observed in the second half of the twentieth century when the language was in serious peril (cf. section 3.2.1. and 3.3.):

> "By the middle of the century, the position of Welsh seemed to be extremely precarious, with virtually no public status whatsoever. The language was not recognized in the law courts and was seldom seen on official forms or administrative documents" (M.C. Jones 1998: 15).

Despite social necessities, there are some major types of dictionaries which have not been fully developed in Welsh lexicography up to the present day (cf. section 3.3.). Those are an etymological dictionary (cf. section 4.3.9.),[2] a Standard Welsh-Welsh dictionary,[3] a pronouncing dictionary and a spelling dictionary. The current potential of information technology for linguistic purposes with regard to the Welsh language is not fully developed either (cf. sections 3.2.1. and 4.2.):

---

[1]   For more details with regard to the first English-English dictionary, see also Osselton (1986).

[2]   However, the etymology of a large number of lexical items is provided in the historical Welsh dictionary *Geiriadur Prifysgol Cymru*. More can be found in the *Etymological glossary of Old Welsh* by Falileyev (2000).

[3]   Good examples for such dictionaries in English are, for instance, the *Shorter Oxford Dictionary* or the *American Heritage Dictionary*. The latter contains definitions, some etymological explanations, English variants, pronunciation, hyphenation, word class labels, inflected forms of verbs, nouns and adjectives, notes on the registers of the language, and special usage of lexical items. Syntactic information is provided by contextual examples. The method of presenting English variants could serve as a model for a possible treatment of Welsh dialect words in dictionaries. Highly recommended is also the *Cambridge International Dictionary of English* (2000).

"It might consist of constructing databases of standard and specialist terms so that one Welsh term would correspond to one English term and vice versa; the upgrading of *CySill* and *CysGair*; the licensing of Welsh versions of standard computer packages and office systems; the development of speech to text procedures [...]" (C.H. Williams 1998: 112).

Looking at Welsh lexicography as a whole, there are three major forces which hastened its development: (a) the spread of religious beliefs, mainly during the Renaissance (cf. section 2.2.),[4] (b) the strengthening of national consciousness (cf. section 2.4.), and (c) language maintenance and prevention of language decline (cf. section 2.4.).[5]

Language maintenance is a major interest for current lexicographical production. It is, however, generally important as is explained by Crystal:

"We should care about dying languages for the same reason that we care when a species of animal or plant dies. In the case of language, we are talking about intellectual and cultural diversity [and potential, i.e. about an intellectual circuit], not biological diversity, but the issues are the same.
Diversity occupies a central place in evolutionary theory because it enables a species to survive in different environements. Inreasing uniformity holds dangers for the longterm survival of a species. The strongest ecosystems are those which are most diverse. The need to maintain linguistic diversity stands on the shoulders of such arguments. If the development of multiple cultures is a prerequisite for successful human development, then the preservation of linguistic diversity is essential, because cultures are chiefly transmitted through spoken and written languages. Encapsulated within a language is most of a community's history and a large part of its cultural identity [...] Sometimes what we might learn from a language is eminently practical, as when we discover new medical treatments from the folk medicine of an indigenous people. Sometimes it is intellectual, as when the links between languages tell us something about the movements of early civilisations. Sometimes it is literary: every language has its equivalent - even if only in oral form - of Chaucer, Wordsworth and Dickens. And of course, very often it is linguistic: we learn something new about language itself - the behaviour that makes us truly human, and without which there would be no talk at all. Ezra Pound summed up the core intellectual argument: "The sum of human wisdom is not contained in any one language, and no single language is capable of expressing all forms and degrees of human comprehension" (Crystal *The Guardian*, 25.10.99).

Questions of identity are particularly closely related to a language when the actual language suffers from a minority status or struggles to survive (cf. section 4.1.2.3.). As a result, aspects of the strengthening of national consciousness or identity feeling have formed an important part of the driving forces of Welsh lexicographical activities since the incorporation of Wales into England (cf. section 2.2.).

The two major driving interests for Welsh lexicography, i.e. language maintenance and prevention of language decline, on the one hand, and dictionaries and identity, on the other, are therefore briefly discussed in the following section, touching at the same time on other driving forces for lexicography, such as the establishment of linguistic norms.

---

[4]   These main driving forces can also be observed for Ireland (cf. Harrison 1986: 56).
[5]   The close relationship between lexicography and language maintenance is underlined by the fact that some languages are only described in the form of dictionaries (cf. Ickler 1985: 360 and section 1.1.).

4.1.1. Dictionaries and language maintenance[6]

From the nineteenth century onwards, new conditions in society and subsequent new requirements for the language developed with emerging industrial capitalism, and this prompted a
severe crisis within the Welsh language and culture down into the twentieth century. Faced with
the rapid decline of the Welsh language particularly after the Second World War and new accelerated developments in social structure, work, religion and the media, a modern revival movement evolved in the fifties accompanied by growing lexicographical work. After massive pro-
tests by language campaigners in the sixties (cf. Phillips 1998, 2000), planning and development
control of the Welsh language were gradually undertaken (cf. Aitchison & Carter 2000: 148-154)
and formed little by little also a basis for comprehensive lexicographical work.

First successes in favour of the language were the establishment of (a) the *Cyngor Llyfrau
Cymraeg* 'The Welsh Book Council' in 1961, of (b) the *Cyngor Celfyddydau Cymru* 'The Welsh
Arts Council' in 1967, (c) the passing of the *Welsh Language Act* 1967 which, among other
things, removed the restrictions on the speaking of Welsh in the law courts, (d) the introduction
of *Radio Cymru*, the Welsh-language BBC station in 1977,[7] and (e) the use of the fourth
television channel under the name *Sianel Pedwar Cymru* (S4C) 'Channel Four Wales' for
Welsh-language broadcasting in Wales since November 1982.[8] Since 1998, S4C also broadcasts
digitally.[9]

That a continuous campaigning for Welsh even in these media is necessary, however, has
been shown by the deteriorating standard and decreasing quantity of the language presented in
them in recent years. This trend is illustrated by figures 1 and 2 (cf. also *Cylch yr Iaith* below).

---

[6]   I would like to take this opportunity of thanking William Ll. Griffith, Dinbych/Wales, for
       helpful discussion on this subject as well as Siôn Williams, University of Cardiff, who, in
       addition, provided me with valuable material.
[7]   The range of programmes is quite wide with substantial amounts of news and current affairs,
       phone-ins, quizzes and music.
[8]   The channel currently transmits around thirty-three hours a week of Welsh language broad-
       casting, i.e. more than four hours a day. Ten hours a week are provided by BBC Wales. Some
       are produced by independent producers, including HTV. The general range of programmes,
       therefore, is rather broad, comprising news, current events, classical and popular music, sport,
       film, soap opera, satire, documentaries, chat and quiz shows. There are programmes for young
       children at lunch time and for older children at tea time, both traditional slots in Britain.
       Including programmes for learners, up to eight hours transmission per day may be reached at
       peak seasons (cf. *Sbec* 18.1.-24.1.1997, Mungham & K. Williams 1998: 121). When there is a
       major event, such as a rugby international or the *Eisteddfod*, the expected saturation coverage
       can be provided.
       Those who want to listen to and watch Welsh continuously can keep going for most of the day
       between radio and television.
[9]   Potential consumers, however, have to have a special decoder.

Daily Post, Tuesday, March 21, 2000

Bid to force S4C to axe 'English' news

By Emyr Williams
Daily Post Correspondent

CAMPAIGNERS against the use of English on S4C are calling for the scrapping of the channel's news magazine programme Heno.

A deputation of representatives from Cylch yr Iaith, Merched y Wawr and the Welsh teaching union UCAC will tomorrow present a petition to S4C chiefs in Cardiff.

Signed by thousands of viewers, it expresses dissatisfaction with the use of English on the channel's Welsh language programmes.

During their meeting with S4C's chief executive Huw Jones, they will be pressing strongly for a written language policy stating that Welsh language programmes will in future be through the medium of standard spoken Welsh.

They will also be calling for a programme to replace Heno, which they say is the chief cause of most of the complaints and argue that Heno has failed to justify itself in terms of viewing figures.

The deputation is also expected to press S4C to reveal the cost of funding the Heno programme. To date, despite repeated requests, S4C has refused to reveal such figures.

Already several well-known figures in Welsh language circles have been fined for not renewing their television licences as part of the Cylch yr Iaith campaign.

One of them, retired headmaster Geraint Jones, from Trefor, near Caenarfon, is waiting to be imprisoned for refusing to pay the fine imposed by magistrates in Caernarfon last September [...]

Figure 1

10,000 sign petition supporting pair fined for TV licence protest

Still smiling, the pillars of society who took

Figure 2a

Daily Post, Wednesday, August 18, 1999

ALMOST 10,000 people have signed a petition calling on BBC Cymru and S4C to reduce the amount of English used on Welsh language programmes.

The growing groundswell of opinion on a subject that has split the Welsh establishment emerged during a rally attended by around 150 language campaigners outside Aberystwyth Magistrates Court yesterday.

Earlier, local magistrates had imposed fines of £75 and costs of £45 each on both Dr Mererydd Evans, 79, who was in charge of BBC Cymru's light entertainment department for 10 years until 1973, and science writer, Dr Eirwen Gwynn, 82, of Talybont, who had pleaded guilty to charges using television sets without a licence last April.

They both told the two magistrates that they had not renewed their licences in protest against the vast amount of English on Radio Cymru and S4C Welsh language programmes.

Statements

Both read out lengthy statements in Welsh explaining why they had not renewed their licences and were prepared to face fines for such offence.

On view of the limited size of the court-room, only 25 members of the public were allowed inside, with the remainder of the 150 campaigners standing in the corridors within the court building.

Many of the campaigners had travelled long distances to be present to support both Dr Evans and Dr Gwynn.

Among them was retired Presbyterian minister, Rev Meirion Lloyd Davies, who is due to appear at Pwllheli Magistrates Court on a similar charge next month.

Dr Evans, of Cwm Ystwyth, was given 28 days to pay the fine and costs, while science writer Dr Gwynn paid on the spot, after telling the magistrates: "I am paying today as I am too old to go to prison."

Both made it clear to the court that they had not renewed their TV licences as a protest against the Anglicisation of

By Emyr Williams
Daily Post Correspondent

programmes on Radio Cymru and S4C.

They are part of a campaign launched several month ago in the name of Cylch yr Iaith (Language Circle), and are believed to be the first protesters to appear in court for failing to renew TV licences.

Cylch yr Iaith campaigners want both the BBC and S4C to be more answerable to Welsh people.

The campaign is backed by Cymdeithas yr Iaith Gymraeg, Merched y Wawr, the Welsh teaching union UCAC, Mudiad Ysgolion and Gorsedd y Beirdd, and many of their members were present in the court building yesterday.

Making it clear that he was guilty of breaking the law, Dr Evans added: "I wish the court to realise that I am withholding payment of the licence fee in protest until such time as the situation improves."

"As soon as I am satisfied that there are clear indications that the broadcasting authorities haved turned their backs on the use of English on Welsh language programmes, then I will renew my licence."

Opinion - Page 6

Figure 2b

244

There are also accusations of insufficient variety in the Welsh media, particularly concerning the younger generation (cf. M.C. Jones 1998: 233f.). Figure 3 (*Golwg* 12 (2000) 18) reflects on the discontent of younger Welsh speakers with the range of programmes offered by *Radio Cymru*. Since they are unhappy with the provision of transmissions for young people made by *Radio Cymru*, the record company R-Bennig set up a radio station on the internet:

Radio Newydd Cymru

Oherwydd eu bod nhw'n anfodlon â darpariaeth Radio Cymru i bobol ifanc, mae cwmni recordiau R-Bennig wedi sefydlu gorsaf radio eu hunain ar y we.

STORI: IWAN ENGLAND

YN Y DADLAU parhaol dros ddarpariaeth Radio Cymru, mae llawer wedi dechrau crybwyll yr angen am ail donfedd ac ail orsaf radio yn Gymraeg. Fe fyddai hynny, medden nhw, yn helpu i blesio cynulleidfaoedd o bob oed a bob chwaeth gerddorol.

Yn hytrach na siarad, mae Johnny R, a label recordiau R-Bennig ym Môn, wedi mynd tuag at sefydlu'r fath wasanaeth, gan ddefnyddio'r we fydeang fel modd o ddarlledu. Fe fydd Radio-D, gorsaf radio mwya' newydd Cymru yn darlledu unwaith yr wythnos am y flwyddyn nesa' o leiaf.

Yn ogystal â rhoi dewis arall i bobl, mae'r datblygiad yn rhoi cip ar y math o ddrysau a fydd yn agor gyda datblygiad y cyfryngau newydd electronig.

"Mae o wedi cychwyn fel rhyw fath o sbŵff," meddai Johnny R. "Ond mae'r peth wedi tyfu fel gorsaf go iawn. Ydan ni'n trio rhedeg awr o adloniant pob wythnos, efo lot o stwff arbrofol a stwff dawns.

"Mae pobol wedi dechrau danfon stwff i fewn yn barod. Do'n i ddim yn disgwyl cymaint o ymateb. Nawr mae'n rhaid chwilio am DJs, gwneud cyfweliadau a chael cwpl o DJs gwadd i fewn."

Dros y blynyddoedd diwethaf mae rhaglenni radio fel **Heno Bydd yr Adar yn Canu** oedd yn arbenigo ar gerddoriaeth newydd ac arbrofol wedi diflannu oddi ar y gwasanaeth cenedlaethol. Gobaith Johnny R yw llenwi'r bwlch sydd wedi datblygu.

"Ar Radio Cymru mae *all over the shops*. Mae hyd yn oed gan Radio Wales *dance* DJs. Dydi bobol sy'n gwneud y rhaglenni ar Radio Cymru ddim yn gwybod bod y stwff yna. Ers talwm oedd lot o adnoddau da yn Radio Cymru, nawr mae popeth yng Nghaerdydd." [...]

Figure 3

A break-through in Welsh language promotion was attained when the first institutions for language planning were established, e.g. *Bwrdd yr Iaith Gymraeg* 'The Welsh Language Board' in 1988. This advisory body was set up in order to formulate language policies (cf. G. Jenkins & M.A. Williams 2000: 22). It was followed by the establishment of government quangos (quasi autonomous non-governmental organisations), which act on behalf of the government (cf. Phillips 2000: 486), in the nineties.

An enforcement of systematic language planning was achieved with the second *Welsh Language Act* in 1993.

The Act stated for the first time that Welsh and English were to be given equal status in the conduct of public business[10] and administration of justice in Wales. The Act's central function was to re-establish *Bwrdd yr Iaith Gymraeg* as the first official statutory body to promote the Welsh language (cf. also C.H. Williams 2000: 675ff.). It was now responsible for developing and overseeing the implementation of Welsh language schemes by organisations in the public sector as well as in schools, for distributing grants to promote and facilitate the use of Welsh and for developing goods and services such as a Directory of Translators, a Welsh spell-checking and grammar-checking software package.[11] Despite their limitations, the Acts and developments initiated by them have served to enhance the validity of the language by giving it greater status, encouraging its use in many sectors of society and furthering its public image, a process found decisive in the vote for the Assembly in September 1997.

---

[10]   In light of the overwhelming dominance of the private sector and the accelerated tendency towards total privatisation in the current type of society, crucial limitations of the law become immediately obvious, even if some businesses try to use the Welsh language for competitive reasons, i.e. the banks (cf. C.H. Williams 1998: 111). Second, in areas in which Welsh dominates, the *Act* allows a weakening of its position. Third, although section 46 of the *Government of Wales Act* (1988) sets a more far reaching norm than that previously envisaged under the *Welsh Language Act* by saying:

> "1 The Assembly shall in the conduct of its business give effect, so far as is both appropriate in the circumstances and reasonably practicable, to the principle that English and Welsh should be treated on a basis of equality",

economic restrictions are put on the language with the phrase 'so far as is both appropriate in the circumstances and reasonably practicable' (cf. also H. Gruffudd 1999b: 10, C.H. Williams 1998: 107, cf. below Dafydd Elis-Thomas). E. Jones (1992) observed that economical factors are often underestimated in their importance, especially for linguistic minorities (cf. also figure 6 below, *Cash Threat To Language* in *Daily Post*, 29.12.2001). In view of the serious weaknesses of the 1993 *Act*, it is hardly surprising that there have been calls for a new Language Act (cf. flyer *Y Tafod dyddiol* by *Cymdeithas yr Iaith* from the 11 August 2000, http://www.cymdeithas.com/gwybodaeth/deddfiaith/canrifnewydd/, 20.10.2001).

[11]   For more details with regard to the implementation of the *Welsh Language Act 1993*, see Williams, G. & D. Morris (2000).

Even within the Assembly, however, voted for by the majority of Welsh speakers (cf. figures 4 and 5, *Wales on Sunday*, 21.9.1997, Osmond 1998: 312), campaigning for the Welsh language remains necessary, since its language policy does not go far enough.[12]

---

[12] The National Assembly's language policy, outlined in *The National Assembly. A Handbook for the First Four Years* (Osmond 1998), reads as follows (C.H. Williams 1998: 105f.):

"· The Assembly should adopt and extend the Welsh Office's existing Welsh language scheme;

· Members should be able to use English and Welsh in Assembly debates and Committee Meetings;

· Members of the public should be able to use English and Welsh when communicating with the Assembly.

On the basis of submitted evidence [it is anticipated] that there will be practical barriers to full implementation of these principles and [it is suggested] that a target date be set by which comprehensive bilingual provision will be in place [...]. Until then [...] the following key priorities [are suggested]:

· Simultaneous translation (Welsh into English) for Assembly debates and committee meetings:

· Simultaneous translation (Welsh into English) available for meetings with the public;

· Publications, and documents available to the public being in both English and Welsh;

· Papers submitted for consideration by Assembly Members in plenary sessions and committee meetings to be available in both English and Welsh [...];"

First of all, as M. James (1998: 32) explains, the Welsh Office did not operate bilingually and the adoption of its language scheme is, therefore, insufficient for the Assembly. Second, whereas there is simultanuous Welsh -> English translation, this is not the case the other way round. On page 111 (C.H. Williams 1998), 'the right of every member (and of course the public, which is not a matter for Standing Orders) to have simultaneous translations into English' is stated, but not the right to have translations into Welsh. All new vocabulary with regard to matters related to the Assembly, therefore, will hardly be memorised, not to speak of being used productively by Welsh speakers. Taken as a whole, there are crucial problems in maintaining the language policy outlined above (cf. figure 6, *Golwg* 12 (2000) 48, figure 7, *Golwg* 13 (2000) 7 below).

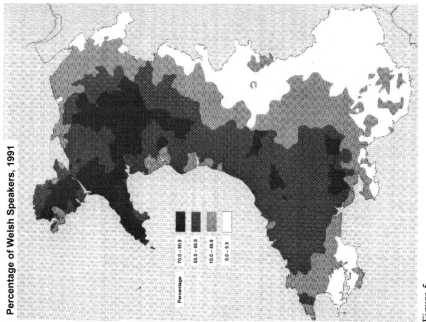

Percentage of Welsh Speakers, 1991

Figure 5

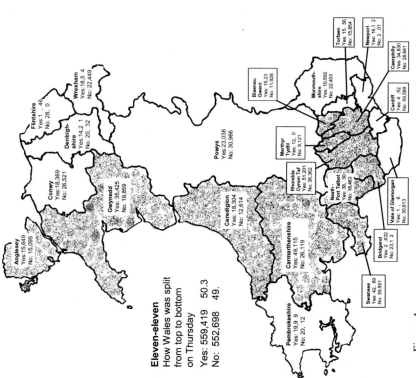

Figure 4

248

This and the following figure illustrate problems within the *National Assembly* to maintain its language policy. The first reflects the wish of the president of the Assembly to stop the habit of translating reports of the Assembly into Welsh, since he regards this as too expensive.

Dim Cymraeg i'r Llywydd

Mae Llywydd y Cynulliad am ddod â'r arfer o gyfieithu cofnodion y Cynulliad i ben. Mae'r Gymraeg yn rhy ddrud, meddai, yn ôl negeseuon cyfrinachol ...

Mae Llywydd y Cynulliad Cenedlaethol wedi awgrymu y dylen nhw ddod â'r arfer o gyhoeddi fersiwn Cymraeg llawn o Gofnod y Cynulliad i ben.

Mae gohebyddiaeth e-bost gyfrinachol rhwng staff Swyddfa'r Llywydd a chlerc i'r Cynulliad yng Nghaerdydd yn ystod y mis diwetha', yn dangos fod Dafydd Elis-Thomas yn gweld talu cwmni o gyfieithwyr i wneud y gwaith fel "gwastraff adnoddau".

Mae un o'i weithwyr agosa' hefyd yn dweud fod gan y Llywydd gefnogaeth Prif Weithredwr Bwrdd yr Iaith Gymraeg yn hyn o beth, a bod John Walter Jones yn gweld y cyfieithu fel "sumboleiddiaeth (*tokenism*) di-fudd."

Fe gyrhaeddodd copi o'r negeseuon - i gyd yn Saesneg - swyddfa Golwg yn ddi-enw ddiwedd yr wythnos diwetha'.

Yn y cyfamser, mae un o brif swyddogion y wasg y Cynulliad wedi cadarnhau eu bod nhw'n rhai dilys, ond mae Bwrdd yr Iaith Gymraeg wedi methu ag ymateb.

Mae'r negeseuon e-bost yn honni nad yw Dafydd Elis-Thomas yn credu bod angen cyfieithu cofnodion o'r cyfraniadau yn y siambr o'r Saesneg i'r Gymraeg, a bod y broses yn wastraff adnoddau gwerthfawr wrth iddynt nhw dalu contractwyr allanol i wneud y gwaith. [...]

Figure 6

The next figure mirrors the criticism of *Cymdeithas yr Iaith* and *Plaid Cymru* that there is no longer a definite reference to the Welsh language in the wake of re-organisations in the Cabinet of the Assembly.

After the basis for language planning had developed as illustrated above, the first major success towards the future of the language was the growing absolute number of Welsh speakers shown in the census of 1991 (cf. Aitchison & Carter 1993: 6). A second success was the boost of lexicographical works which were produced in the nineties (cf. section 3.3.) as a result of the developments mentioned above.

The relative number of Welsh speakers, nevertheless, is still declining, thus diminishing efforts to stabilise and normalise the use of the Welsh language (cf. figures 8-11 from Aitchison & Carter in G.H. Jenkins 2000: 53, 54, 66, 89).

Y Gymraeg - un ymhlith llawer

Mae Cymdeithas yr Iaith wedi disgrifio'r ad-drefnu yng Nghabinet y Cynulliad fel "cam yn ôl" yn y ffordd y mae'r iaith yn cael ei hystyried.

Roedd gan y cyn Ysgrifennydd Addysg ôl-16, Tom Middlehurst gyfrifoldeb arbennig am y Gymraeg, ond o dan y trefniant newydd fe fydd y Gweinidog Addysg a Dysgu Gydol Oes, Jenny Randerson yn gyfrifol am "ieithoedd Cymru" yn gyffredinol.

Fe fydd ei chyfrifoldeb hi hefyd yn cynnwys y celfyddydau, chwaraeon, llyfrgelloedd ac amgueddfeydd.

"Yr ydym yn derbyn fod Cymru yn wlad aml-ieithog, ond mai'r Gymraeg yw priod iaith Cymru," meddai Dafydd Morgan Lewis o Gymdeithas yr Iaith. "Fe ddylai fod cyfeiriad at hyn yn y disgrifiad o gyfrifoldebau Ms Randerson."

Mae'r Gymdeithas hefyd wedi mynegi pryder ynglyn â'r ffaith nad yw Ms Randerson yn siarad Cymraeg, ond mae nhw wedi cael eu calonogi gan y ffaith ei bod hi wedi pleidleisio o blaid yr egwyddor o Ddeddf Iaith Newydd yn y Cynulliad yn gynharach yn y flwyddyn.

Er bod Plaid Cymru wedi mynegi consyrn ynglŷn â diddymu'r cyfeiriad penodol at yr iaith Gymraeg yn rhestr dyletswyddau'r Cabinet, mewn cynhadledd i'r wasg ddechrau'r wythnos fe ddywedodd yr Aelod Cynulliad Jacelyn Davies nad oedden nhw yn pryderu llawer ynglŷn â'r ffaith fod Jenny Randerson yn methu siarad Cymraeg.

Figure 7

250

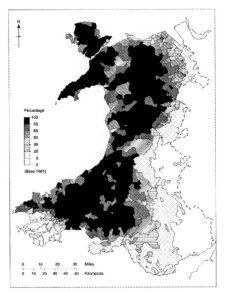

Figure 8: The percentage of the population able to speak Welsh in 1961

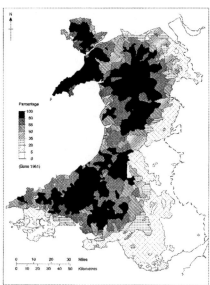

Figure 9: The percentage of the population able to speak Welsh in 1971

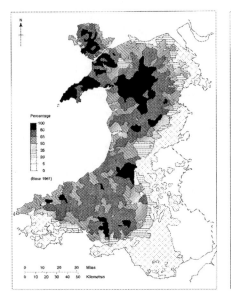

Figure 10: The percentage of the population able to speak Welsh in 1981

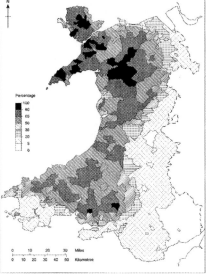

Figure 11: The percentage of the population able to speak Welsh in 1991

The trend illustrated by the figures above emphasises that the Welsh language at the end of the twentieth century was in a fragile situation (cf. M.C. Jones 1998: 37, 236, 238) which was itself more complex and difficult than ever before (cf. also flyer by *Cymuned*,[1] 2001). *Bwrdd yr Iaith Gymraeg* described the threat to the language resulting from four major phenomena (1999: 9):[2]

- migration patterns from rural to urban areas
- inward migration of English speakers to rural areas
- increased availability of English-language news and entertainment media
- a general secularisation of society, leading to a decline in chapel attendance, on which traditional Welsh-medium activities were centred.

With regard to the migration patterns from rural to urban areas, *Plaid Cymru* 'The Party of Wales' referred to the BSE crisis as the most serious in agriculture since the 1930s (cf. *Plaid Cymru* Newsletter Spring 1996). The whole agricultural economy in Britain is involved, but as Wales has worse natural conditions, it might suffer more heavily from the outcomes of the crisis, which was reinforced by the foot-and-mouth disease in 2000/2001.[3] In addition, there is a coincidence of disadvantageous demographical and economical factors in Welsh rural areas,[4] such as:

---

[1]   *Cymuned* 'Community' is a pressure group which warns that the Welsh language might die within the next ten years as a community language (*Golwg* 13 (2001) 40, BBC News, 27.02.2002). *Cymuned* comprises well-known language activists, bards, students, and former representatives of official bodies who intend to provide evidence to the Assembly and other official bodies that the language is in severe decline (cf. www.cymuned.org, 20.10.2001). See also the article by Angharad Tomos 'Nid marw ond newid siwr iawn' (*Yr Herald*, 4.8.2001).

[2]   At http://www.netwales.co.uk/byig/strats.htm (1.11.2000), a detailed report to *The present state of the language* is given.

[3]   One of the short-term changes caused by the BSE is the ban on exporting beef and a number of bovine products into several countries which had been good customers before. There has also been a severe drop in consumer confidence in quality, so that major chains such as McDonald's now process imported beef almost exclusively. The price policy of supermarkets is often disadvantageous, particularly to small producers. These changes caused major reductions in income to producers and even to dependent industries (cf. *Cambrian News* 17.10.1996). A study of the impact of the BSE crisis estimated that the labour market will be loosing between 4,000 and 7,000 jobs out of a total of 56,800 in Welsh agriculture, i.e. about 8 to 12%. Not only producers are among the victims, however, but also all dependent and supply industries, such as carriers, abattoir workers, meat processors, livestock traders, auctioneers, victuallers, and maybe even machine builders (cf. *Cambrian News*, 3./17.10.1996). In Welsh dairying, 100 jobs support 40 jobs in dependent industries. In sheep and beef farming the ratio is 100:53 (cf. *Y Tir & Welsh Farmer*, March 1989: 10).

On 3 April 1996, the British government implemented a culling scheme according to which all cattle over 30 months old and in the UK for at least six months were to be slaughtered (cf. House of Commons). This was the most serious of all short term consequences. Within three years from May 1996 onwards, about 2.5 million cattle had to be slaughtered. Only two Welsh abattoirs, however, had been given a culling licence within the limits of this programme by September 1996. As a result, a considerable back-log developed, which caused further difficulties to the farmers as they had to feed and care for their animals for a further three years without ever gaining profit from them. In addition, special breeds of dairy cows and premium bulls were lost.

[4]   This becomes evident in the following figures: Areas with little prosperity are particularly obvious in the 'border areas' of former Gwynedd, Clwyd and Powys. The poorer regions of Dyfed also have a

- little prosperity
- disproportionately unfertile farm land
- few *assisted areas*[5]
- high number of second homes
- high average age of population.

With regard to English-language media and social changes (cf. above), one has to bear in mind that the world is facing rapid technical developments which impinge heavily on human society which the Welsh have to cope with if they want their language and culture to survive. One of the bodies responsible for standardising the Welsh language, *The Panel for Official Welsh* stated, therefore:

> "In many ways, the task which the Welsh language is faced with today in the secular world, is similar to that which it faced successfully in the ecclesiastical field at the end of the sixteenth century" (Elis-Thomas 1995: 12).

At the end of the Renaissance, religious controversies formed a major driving force for the employment of Welsh and its linguistic description, e.g. in the form of dictionaries. In this context, Wales also made successful use of the latest technology of that period, i.e. the printing press (cf. section 2.2.1.). Looking at Welsh society at the end of the twentieth century, Wales managed in a similar way to employ computer technology to its own advantage (cf. chapter III and above).[6]

Nevertheless, the range of media available in Welsh is still reduced (cf. above and the research of the Mercator Centre/Aberystwyth into the possibilities of running a daily newspaper illustrated under http://www.aber.ac.uk/~merwww/papurdyddiol/PapCefn.htm, 20.10.2001). The very availability of the language in different media, however, provides the language with the prestige that it is worthy of being promoted, learned and used:

> "The forms of media accessed or stored by libraries are a powerful force in promoting and consolidating language use. They are probably the first entry point, even before education, to a minority language for most people" Axford (2000: 16).

The more the language is presented in any kind of media the more it will be accepted in the age of information overflow or even taken up. In addition, media has wide influence and can shape the opinions of its viewers, listeners and readers (cf. Axford 2000: 16f.).

High prestige for the language is, moreover, of particular importance for attracting non-Welsh speaking Welsh people and incoming Englishmen/women to encourage them to accept and learn Welsh.

---

larger Welsh-speaking population (Lowson 1991). 78.5% of the poorest areas in Gwynedd were predominantly Welsh-speaking in 1981, but only 49.5% of the least impoverished areas (Morris 1992: 142). Welsh-speaking areas belong almost exclusively to those with poorer natural conditions.

[5] *Assisted areas* are those which receive more financial help from the government.

[6] Nevertheless, there are many difficulties in trying to have Welsh equally used in computer technology. One of them is the trial to launch a Welsh spell and grammar check version with the software company Microsoft.

The mass influx of the latter[7] is the most crucial problem for Wales in its attempt to stabilise its language[8] (cf. figures 8-11 above, Aitchison & Carter 1985: 14, idem 2000: 110). This major problem is briefly reflected, for instance, in a report on a Local Plan of Dwyfor:[9]

> "there is firm evidence from the Census of 1981 and 1991 that the cultural fabric is being undermined, and that the position of the Welsh language is becoming increasingly fragile. The percentage of Welsh speakers in Criccieth fell from 72.1 % in 1981 to 69.4% in 1991. 30% of the resident population was born outside Wales, and are mainly in the older age groups, suggesting that the area continues to be popular for retirement. There is also a high percentage of housing which is not used permanently (20%)" (quoted from Aitchison & Carter 2000: 153).

Particularly over the last few years there has been an increase in English speakers moving into Welsh-speaking areas, to such an extent that schools and whole communities are being anglicised.[10] English immigrants look first of all for a quiet life and do not really wish to learn another language.[11] The problems arising from this rather common phenomenon of relatively remote and touristically attractive areas (cf. other minority languages, Heinz 1999) can in the first instance best be met, if at all, by comprehensive education society-wide provided for the socialisation also of the migrants (cf. Basque and Catalan country). Other elements in the process of supporting the language are the promotion of Welsh media, a consequent usage of the language at the political and administrative level and an active marketing and promotional campaign (cf. C.H. Williams 2000: 677f.).[12]

These four factors in the process of normalising the language need to be backed by linguistic training and this in turn by linguistic material. As a result, continuous lexicographical materials need to be developed in order to provide enough lexis for communication in all fields of society and illustrate its usage. This view is supported by Crystal when saying:

> "To save a language you must get linguistics into the field, support the community with language teachers, publish grammars and dictionaries, write materials for the use in schools [...]" (*The Guardian*, 25.10.1999).

One area which contributes most to the rise in number of speakers is education as is illustrated in the following quote:

---

[7] Seimon Glyn (2001: 19ff.) illustrates how migration into Wales was artificially enforced.

[8] From a certain point onwards, high mobility and intense migration not only destroy families as the smallest social units in society, but also the dialect and even the language, both a means of communication of larger social units, themselves social phenomena which change according to social dispositions. For the purpose of this investigation, however, further facets and factors contributing to the situation of the language can only be briefly mentioned. The focus in this investigation is on learning aids, translating tools and resources of research and communication accompanying and supporting basic steps in encouraging the maintenance and use of the language society-wide under the currently given societal circumstances.

[9] See also M.C. Jones on the decline of Welsh in Glamorganshire (1998: 45-154), but also on the effect of English immigration on areas with a high percentage of Welsh speakers (ibid.: 155-238).

[10] This is the reason why the pressure group *Cymuned* has been set up (cf. above).

[11] "If a group of people is linguistically mixed, then English is the language likely to be spoken, a phenomenon which often restricts the use of Welsh within the community" (M.C. Jones 1998: 152). For problems resulting from an environment deprived of Welsh speakers, see below.

[12] For detailed steps with regard to Reversing Language Shift, see Fishman (1991: 111-141, 395) and D. Jones (1997: 139-154).

"The role of the classroom in language revitalisation is highly notable in the former counties of Glamorganshire and Gwent where numbers of pupils coming from non-Welsh-speaking backgrounds often amount to about 95 per cent of a school's total intake. In such cases, therefore, the school has replaced the family to a large extent as the vehicle for language transmission" (M.C. Jones 1998: 24).

E.P. Jones & D. Reynolds simply say: "The learner is the key" (1998: 232).

Education in Wales is based on three cornerstones.[13] The first is Welsh for Adults, which can be characterised as follows:

"At present, a whole gamut of both day and evening classes are available and include taster courses, progressively structured classes at beginner, intermediate, and advanced levels, intensive courses, both residential and non-residential, day schools, Saturday schools, specialized courses such as Welsh for business purposes, Welsh for catering, and Welsh for the workplace, as well as courses at the National Language Centre at Nant Gwrtheyrn in Gwynedd. Through its Learners' Officer, the National Eisteddfod of Wales has also been responsible for creating a series of Welsh for Adults initiatives in different areas of the country. Welsh for Adults courses are organized on three levels [...]. In year 1-3, learners study by means of weekly sessions. During this time, they are assessed at entry level and level 1/(2) (beginners). The assessment covers four types of skill [...] By and large, after approximately 150 hours of teaching, students at level 2 (intermediate) can start to study *Defnyddio'r Gymraeg* ('Use of Welsh'), a national qualification awarded by the national examining board of Wales, the Welsh Joint Education

---

[13] Although education is of foremost importance, it must not be idealised and has to be put in conducive contexts if the language is to survive. First, it is also necessary to reflect upon the extent to which pupils of immersion programmes are likely to transmit that language to their offspring. If this were to prove negative the whole point of immersion schooling must be questioned. Second, the vital role of family and community must not be ignored:

"Without considerable and repeated societal reinforcement schools cannot successfully teach either first or second languages [...] the fact remains that just as the basics of a subject such as geography are forgotten by most individuals in their post-school years unless there is any specific reason to retain them, so a language learned in this way will be lost in early adulthood due to the lack of societal reinforcement" Fishman (1991: 371).

Third, with little or no extra-curricular back-up in highly anglicised areas, children tend to associate a language with school and the dominating language, i.e. English, with leisure. As for those who do favour Welsh, they

"find themselves in a [...] situation when, having learned Welsh, they have little opportunity to practise it due to its near total absence beyond the school's perimeter [...] A similar situation is faced by the [...] growing number of adult learners who, having made the effort to learn Welsh, may find that once they graduate from the advanced class it is difficult to find an opportunity to speak the language in the community. It cannot be denied that, since 1982, S4C has provided Welsh with an inroad into every home, but a language cannot be improved by passive use alone" (M.C. Jones 1998: 152).

The statements above taken together with a look at the developments in the Republic of Ireland since the twenties, show that a language cannot be saved solely by a comprehensive educational system. This truth remains even in light of the fact that there were no Irish-medium schools outside the *Gaeltachtaí* up to the 1970s in Ireland, which are much more effective with regard to language learning (cf. also the article 'Classroom holds the key to survival of the language', *Western Mail*, 2.1.2001).

Committee. This may be followed by entry to level 3 (Advanced) by the end of which adult learners will have completed 3000 hours of instruction and are eligible to sit *Defnyddio'r Gymraeg Uwch* ('Advanced Use of Welsh') [...] the Consultative Paper published by the Welsh Language Board's Welsh for Adults Strategic Planning Group stated that the field has grown by 60 per cent during the last decade and that it is foreseen that this growth will continue [...] If coupled with the likelihood that adult converts to Welsh will send their offspring to Welsh-medium schools, this indicates a steady gain for the language" (M.C. Jones 1998: 17-19).

According to *Bwrdd yr Iaith Gymraeg* (1999: 29), there were 20,000 adults learning Welsh in such schemes in 1998.[14]

The second cornerstone is Welsh-medium education which itself is seen as one of the cornerstones of the whole movement towards the revitalisation of Welsh. Its development can be briefly described as follows:

"Despite [Welsh] being used in the circulating schools [...] it was English that became the medium of all formal education, with Welsh only being allowed back into the classroom in the 1890s, following the Royal Commission on elementary education, and then only as a subject rather than a medium of instruction. At secondary level, however, provision remained scanty. The Welsh Intermediate Education Act of 1889 led to the establishment of 95 secondary schools by 1900 but fewer than half had Welsh as part of the curriculum, despite the fact that following the creation of the Welsh Central Board in 1895, examinations were prepared in the language at both senior and higher levels [...] However, even in Welsh-speaking areas, Welsh was not used anywhere as a medium of instruction at this level. In 1927 came the publication of a report entitled *Y Gymraeg mewn Addysg a Bywyd* ('Welsh in Education and Life'). As a direct consequence of the report, several primary schools in Welsh-speaking areas began using the language as a teaching-medium for subjects other than Welsh itself. [...] One of the most significant events in Welsh education this century was undoubtedly the establishment, in 1939, of an officially Welsh-medium primary school at Aberystwyth [...] this first *Ysgol Cymraeg* (Welsh-medium school) proved highly successful and in due course led to the establishment of large numbers of such schools [...] all over the country including Anglicized areas" (M.C. Jones 1998: 22f.).

With Welsh-medium schools 'Ysgolion Cymraeg' in anglicised areas, immersion-type programmes[15] evolved in Wales. Immersion-type schools are, as mentioned above, not the result of deliberate language planning, but are rather, in origin, Welsh-medium schools now attended by an increasing number of second-language learners. These often outnumber their native-speaker counterparts, particularly in more anglicised parts of the country. This fact is confirmed by data provided by *Bwrdd yr Iaith Gymraeg* (1999: 29):

"In 1997-98, over 30% of children in Wales were attending Welsh-medium schools. The majority of these pupils came from non-Welsh speaking homes."

The *Ysgolion Cymraeg* are well supported by a second element of Welsh-medium education, that is, by pre-school education in the form of *Mudiad Ysgolion Meithrin* 'The (Welsh) Nursery School Movement' by means of which many non-Welsh children aged between two and four are first introduced to the language.[16]

---

[14]   In 2001 the number was 24,000 (cf. http://www.bwrdd-yr-iaith.org.uk/, 20.10.2001).
[15]   For definitions and further explanations, see D. Jones (1997) and M.C. Jones (1998).
[16]   For further elements of pre-school education, see E.P. Jones (no date: 15).

The success of Welsh-medium primary education meant that people were soon calling for an analogous secondary school, i.e. the third element of Welsh-medium education. Here progress was relatively slow. In 1956 *Ysgol Glan Clwyd* was established as a secondary school teaching all subjects other than science through the medium of Welsh.[17] Figure 12 (*Golwg* 13 (2000) 12) reflects groundless fears of parents wishing to sent their children to Welsh-medium schools that their offsprings might not succeed in science.

Chwerwder tros addysg Gymraeg

Un o'r pethau mwya' trist am y dadl tros addysg Gymraeg yng Nghaerfyrddin ydi'r teimladau chwerw sy'n cael eu corddi ar y ddwy ochr.

Y peryg ydi y bydd rhai rhieni sy'n simsanu ag anfon eu plant i ysgolion cyfrwng Cymraeg yn penderfynu peidio, a hynny am y rhesymau anghywir.

Mae'r dadl ynglŷn â dysgu gwyddoniaeth a mathemateg trwy gyfrwng yr iaith yn corddi ers sefydlu'r ysgol uwchradd Gymraeg gynta' ond, erbyn hyn, mae yna filoedd o blant wedi astudio'r pynciau hyn yn Gymraeg ac wedi llwyddo.

Mae taflen newydd gan Fwrdd yr Iaith yn pwysleisio fod canlyniadau TASau Gwyddoniaeth a Mathemateg mewn ysgolion Cymraeg eu cyfrwng yn "cymharu'n arbennig o dda" gyda rhai mewn ysgolion Saesneg eu cyfrwng [...]

Figure 12

The fourth element of Welsh-medium education is higher education. Wales has been served by her own university since 1827, with the establishment of St. David's College Llanbedr Pont Steffan. In 1875 a chair of Welsh was created at the University College at Aberystwyth. Until the 1920s, however, most lectures in Welsh university departments were given in English. Further developments in this area of education are described as follows:

"The provision of undergraduate degree courses through the medium of Welsh has taken considerably longer to achieve and was initiated by education departments in the different University Colleges, each of which determined to appoint one lecturer who would be responsible for training teachers to teach various subjects through the medium of Welsh [...] but it was not until 1970 that a decision was taken to develop Welsh-medium courses in two of the Colleges, namely Bangor and Aberystwyth. Numbers of students availing themselves of such courses are small yet not insignificant and it is also possible to take any degree examination and to submit any form of postgraduate dissertation, including a Ph.D. thesis, through the medium of Welsh" (M.C. Jones 1998: 23).

The employment of Welsh in higher education, however, remains difficult. This is dicussed in figure 13 (*Golwg* 12 (2000) 48) in which the job of the then newly appointed *Officer for Developing Education through the Medium of Welsh in the University of Wales* is described:

---

[17] The teaching of science remains a point hotly discussed in Welsh-medium education (cf. figure 8, flyer of *Bwrdd yr Iaith Gymraeg*, 2001), although it is well accepted in Breton-medium schools.

Y Kevin Keegan Cymraeg

Ef sydd â'r swydd newydd o Gymreigio Prifysgol Cymru. Ef yw'r Prifardd Cen Williams ...

"Rhyw swydd fel Mark Hughes neu Kevin Keegan ydi hi. Gorfod defnyddio pobol o dimau pobol eraill fydda' i, ac yn cydweithio gyda nhw am gyfnodau byr."

Mae'r gymhariaeth yn un ysgafn, ond mae'r pwynt yn un difrifol. Wrth i Dr Cen Williams ddisgrifio yr her sy'n ei wynebu ar ôl cael ei benodi yn Swyddog Datblygu Addysg Cyfrwng Cymraeg i Brifysgol Cymru, mae'n pwysleisio y bydd angen cydweithrediad colegau trwy Gymru arno.

Mae'n pwysleisio na all un ffigwr yn gweithio ar ei ben ei hun wneud gwahaniaeth gwirioneddol. Mae'n gobeithio y bydd y gystadleuaeth sydd bellach yn bodoli rhwng colegau i ddenu myfyrwyr yn cael ei roi i'r naill ochr er mwyn sicrhau dyfodol dysgu drwy gyfrwng y Gymraeg.

"Arwain tîm fydda' i," meddai. "Nid un dyn yn gweithio yn yr anialwch ac yn cynnig rhyw syniadau rhyfedd ei hun ydw i."

"Mi fydd gen i gyswllt ar lefel uchel ym mhob sefydliad fydd yn cydweithio efo ni. Mi fydd gen i hefyd gyswllt, maes o law, efo'r rhai sy'n dysgu trwy gyfrwng y Gymraeg, trwy'r un person cyswllt yma."

Gan ei fod wedi treulio ei fywyd yn gweithio ym maes addysg - mewn ysgolion, colegau ac yn fwy diweddar fel Cyfarwyddwr Canolfan Bedwyr yng ngholeg Prifysgol Cymru, Bangor - dyw hi'n fawr o syndod fod gan Cen Williams res o ffeithiau moel i ddisgrifio'r her fydd yn ei wynebu yn ei waith.

Mae'n dadlau fod:
- 12% o ddisgyblion Cymru yn sefyll arholiadau Cymraeg iaith gyntaf yn 16 oed.
- 5-6% yn gwneud eu pynciau Lefel A drwy gyfrwng y Gymraeg.
- mae'r ffigwr yn syrthio mor isel ag 1.5% mewn sefydliadau addysg uwch [...]

Figure 13

A third cornerstone of education contributing to the rise in the number of Welsh speakers within the process of language maintenance is Welsh teaching in English-medium schools. Major changes in the recognition of Welsh as a subject are reflected in the following paragraph:

"The 1988 Education Act which, as part of the National Curriculum, gave Welsh the status of a core subject (and therefore made it compulsory) in the officially designated Welsh-medium schools also made it a foundation subject in all other schools in Wales [...] Until then no school in Wales was statutorily required to teach Welsh. In most [parts of Wales], the language was introduced gradually, starting with the pupils in the first year of primary and secondary education in September 1994. However, in highly Anglicized areas such as the former county of Gwent, the introduction of Welsh was postponed by several years in order to enable teachers to be properly trained, but from September 1996 Welsh has been compulsory for all pupils in every primary school in Wales (Key Stages 1 and 2 as defined by the National Curriculum) and those pupils in Key Stage 3 (11-14 year olds) attending secondary education" (M.C. Jones 1998: 24).

In this kind of education, Welsh is often taught via a number of timetabled classes per week,

"where the grammar and form of the language are focused upon and various excercises are performed, including 'drilling' on patterns and irregularities in the language and elementary translation tasks. This style of learning is the means by which most British students acquire modern languages such as French and Spanish and, as mentioned above, is also used quite widely in the teaching of Welsh" (M.C. Jones 1998: 25).

In addition, since 1999 there is a statutory requirement for all children in Key Stage 4 (14-16 year olds) to study Welsh. From 2000 onwards, therefore, all sixteen year old pupils had to sit a compulsory public examination in the language.

The brief description of Welsh education given above illustrates this institution as a well established element in the process of normalising the language (cf. above). It can, however, only fulfill its function as intended, if the language taught corresponds with that of the mother tongue speakers.

In the middle of the eighties the 'functional-notional approach' was generally introduced into schools, concentrating on teaching the language according to the communicative situation. As a result, grammar was almost totally excluded, a demand I found imposed on myself, when I was teaching German in a Welsh-medium school in 1994. With the *National Curriculum* following the *Education Reform Act* of 1988, different achievement skills were set leading to SATs (Standard Attainment Tasks) at four different key stages (Bwrdd yr Iaith Gymraeg 1989). Since then no manuals have been available for teaching Welsh as a second language. Grammar is largely neglected, so that a whole generation of pupils went through the educational system without an idea of how languages work. Teachers now tend to extract material from various Welsh books according to their own choice and provide the children with loose working sheets. Such a lack of descriptive and prescriptive material causes confusion and frustration among learners and diminishes efforts of language acquisition and application. It does not come as a surprise - that people between 25 and 44 years of age, i.e. the age group with the highest social impact, write and read less frequently and fluently than any other age group as is illustrated by the following article (*Golwg* 12 (2000) 46):

Cymry ifanc a'r iaith

Mae pobol ifanc yn yr oedran 25-44 yn sgrifennu a darllen Cymraeg yn llai aml ac yn llai rhugl na grŵpiau oedran eraill yng Nghymru.

Yn ôl Adroddiad Arolwg Cyflwr yr iaith Gymraeg a gafodd ei gomisiynu gan Fwrdd yr Iaith Gymraeg a'i gyhoeddi mewn cyfarfod o'r Bwrdd yn Aberystwyth yr wythnos ddiwetha', pobol ifanc sy'n gadael yr iaith i lawr.

Yn ôl yr ystadegau ar gyfer darllenwyr Cymraeg, mae'r gallu i ddarllen yn dda iawn yn gostwng ar gyfer y grŵp 25-55, cyn codi'n sylweddol wedyn.

Mae 57% o bobl ifanc rhwng 16 a 24 oed yn gallu darllen yn dda iawn, 54% o bobol rhwng 25 a 44, 63% o bobol rhwng 45 a 64, a 72% dros 65 oed.

Mae'r un duedd yn wir gyda'r gallu i sgrifennu'r Gymraeg. Mae 55% o bobol ifanc rhwng 16-24 oed yn ystyried eu hunain yn sgrifennwyr rhugl, o gymharu â grŵp 25-64 oed, 56% o bobl rhwng 45 a 64 oed, a'r un canran o bobl dros 65 oed.

Er hynny, mae'r gallu i siarad yr iaith yn rhugl yn cynuddu'n weddol gyson gydag oedran - o 52% rhwng 16-24 oed; 71% rhwng 25-44 oed; 76% yn y grŵp oedran 45-64 oed, a 75% o'r bobl dros 65 oed.

Figure 14

In addition, a number of the teaching materials for Welsh still suffers from the invention of *Cymraeg Byw* 'Living Welsh'. This was introduced in 1964 with the booklet *Cymraeg Byw: Rhifyn 1* (Cyfadran Addysg Coleg y Brifysgol 1964) in order to simplify Welsh for second-language learners. The intention was to regulate the language and avoid any difficulties, an attitude which immediately lowered the prestige of standard Welsh.

Cymraeg Byw was described in books such as *Cymraeg i Oedolion* 'Welsh for Adults' (B. Jones 1965-68), *Siarad Cymraeg* 'Speak Welsh' (Jones, A. & A. Jones 1967) for use in schools, *Gweld, Dweud a Gwneud* 'See, Say and Do' (C. Davies 1975), and the grammar book *Gramadeg Cymraeg Cyfoes* 'A Contemporary Welsh Grammar' (Uned Iaith Genedlaethol Cymru 1976). For teaching *Cymraeg Byw* successfully, comprehensive didactic methods were developed, described by Roberts, M.E. & R.M. Jones (1974) and D.L. Jones (1974) and others.[18] Although *Cymraeg Byw* was intended as an oral standard for the whole of Wales, it was gradually also adopted as a medium for writing by Welsh native speakers (prescriptive power of language material). One reason for this develoment is given by Knowles (1995):

> "Dictionaries and grammars and popular literature about language questions become the instrument of national culture in [circumstances when a nascent state is geopolitically threatened by a powerful neighbour] and are imbued with an authority which it is difficult for anyone to contest. The "mode of exposition" of dictionaries and grammars easily adopts a prescriptive and proscriptive tone" (ibid.: 321).

The power of written material increases if, at the same time, important types of dictionaries or other reference books are unavailable (cf. above and section 3.3.) and, moreover, the representation of the language in the media is insufficient (cf. above and section 4.3.9.).

Some of the results of the introduction of *Cymraeg Byw* were the enforced use of periphrastic and a simplification of inflected verb forms (M.C. Jones speaks of 'over-simplification' in many areas of grammar 1998: 356, cf. also *Cwrs Wlpan* 1991), as a result of which the morphology of the Welsh verb was reduced (cf. above). In *Cwrs Wlpan*, for instance, the plural forms of the past

---

[18] I would like to take this opportunity of thanking W. Ll. Griffith, Dinbych/Wales, for advising me on this matter.

tense have been replaced by those of the subjunctive (cf. S.J. Williams 1980: 104f.). As a result, the latter is now largely neglected or expressed by imperfect (predominantly in the south) or pluperfect forms. However, the neglect of the subjunctive in such a manner is an element of language death, in particular if the language is in a weak position. Altogether it can be stated that:

> "[M]ae genhedlaeth gyfan o blant wedi mynd trwy'n hysgolion bellach heb rithyn o glem am ramadeg, gan fod y drefn addysgu yn gwgu ar gyflwyno'r fath beth. Mae'r Gymraeg heddiw yn dioddef yn enbyd o'r herwydd ac yn sicr ni all lleiafrif ieithyddol, megis ag ŷm ni, fforddio dibrisio'r iaith safonol. Yr eironi trist yw fod statws ffurfiol yr iaith ar gynnydd ond y feistriolaeth ffurfiol arni yn prinhau. Ac mae'r peth yn newid llawer mwy enbyd nag y gellir ei anwybyddu fel y gwneir drwy ddadlau'n arwynebol fod pob iaith yn newid" (personal correspondance with a former teacher of Welsh, 11.10.2000).[19]
> 'A whole generation of children went through our schools without the slightest clue of grammar, since the educational system frowns on introducing such things. Thus Welsh today suffers heavily and certainly a linguistic minority, such as ours, cannot afford to disregard the standard language. The sad irony is that the formal status of the language is on the rise but its formal mastery becomes rare. And this change is much more severe, that it cannot be ignored, as it is the case by superficially arguing that every language changes.'

In addition, since the introduction of *Cymraeg Byw* it has often been argued that there is no standard for the Welsh language, and complicated explanations have been introduced in order to explain current registers of Welsh (cf. *Canllawiau Ysgrifenedig Cymraeg Llafar* 'Guidelines for Written Oral Welsh', Welsh Joint Education Committee 1991). As a result, the confusion on the part of Welsh speakers with regard to the choice of forms of the language increased, a phenomenon called 'linguistic insecurity' (M.C. Jones 1998: 330). At this point, learners often give up using the language (cf. J.E. Caerwyn Williams 1995: vii).

Moreover, *Cymraeg Byw* was felt by many Welsh speakers to be highly artificial (cf. M.C. Jones 1998: 356). The kind of Welsh now produced also discourages native Welsh and, at times, tends to make them give up using their language. In the case of *Cymraeg Byw* the status of a construct with reduced morphology, idiom, and stylistic range was promoted instead of that of a living register of Welsh with full morphology, idiom, and stylistic range.

A consequence of the linguistic insecurity mentioned above was the introduction of linguistic descriptions of the spoken language, thereby creating a kind of *Standard Oral Welsh*. This was mistaken as the 'speech of the people' (cf. King 1993: 3), which would rather be their dialect (cf. M.C. Jones 1998: 152).

As seen with *Cymraeg Byw*, this new construct in turn is now often taken as the sole guide for learners, thus further reducing Welsh morphology (cf. the series of language material written by *Gareth King*).[20] Printed by powerful and influential publishers, such as Routledge or Collins in the case of general-purpose dictionaries (cf. section 3.2.1. and 4.2.), there is a real danger to the language (prescriptive power of language material, cf. above), because of potential pidginisation (cf. below).

---

[19] The name is known to the author.
[20] With regard to a critical discussion of his grammar and language course, see Heinz 1995, 1998a. For information on his dictionary, see the following sections.

However, if the language is likely to be given up by its learners and native speakers, that is, all its potential users, it is in severe decline (cf. also section 4.1.2.3.). Indeed, the predominant use of a reduced or anglicised morphology (cf. for example nouns, section 4.3.2.; verb, section 4.3.1.; adjectives, section 4.3.3.), the presentation of a reduced syntax (cf. for instance the government of words; particles, section 4.3.8.), and the preference of an anglicised idiom (cf. verbs, section 4.3.1.; one-word headwords, sections 4.3.5. and 4.3.6.; word formation, sections 4.3.2.2. and 4.3.2.) are elements of language death rather than language change (cf. section 4.1.1.). Investigating the decline of other languages, research has shown that, first,

> "[i]f a rule is optional with the older generation which has a full and varied command of a still vigorous language system, it is lost in the disintegrating language of a younger generation" (Dressler 1972: 425)

and, second, "[w]hen a language surrenders itself to foreign idiom [...] the penalty is death" (T.F. O'Rahilly 1988: 121). The reasons for such developments are clear; morphology and syntax form the structure of the language, that is, its skeleton. Collocations and idioms add linguistically to the unique component parts which make up the conception of the language, thereby arousing particular feelings and associations among its speakers. They are part of what furnishes the language with a soul which makes it cherished by native speakers and learners and distinct to foreigners.

The situation of the language looks more disadvantageous considering that the higher the percentage of Welsh learners the deeper is the impact of education on the language taught. The language can change significantly when it is inadequately described and insufficiently and/or erroneously taught. M.C. Jones (1998: 45-154), for instance, argues that even in Welsh schools, a dominating number of second-language learners in immersion schools alongside their native-speaker counterparts may influence the speech of the latter. Historically inappropiate forms become increasingly prevalent in situations when second-language learners dominate and societal monitoring is absent (cf. ibid.: 358, cf. C.H. Wiliams concering the need to establish an office of a Language Ombudsman 2000: 679 and the first steps of monitoring done by *Cylch yr Iaith*,[21] below). M.C. Jones (ibid.: 236) also attests to the fact that development of a simplificatory or reductive nature with regard to Welsh morphology and vocabulary can to a lesser degree be found in the speech of native speakers receiving English-medium education.

The impact of education on the language becomes more apparent when considering the high percentage of Welsh learners. Indeed, it is difficult to give an exact percentage of Welsh learners, i.e. people actually learning the language or having acquired Welsh as a second language, among the 508,098 speakers of Welsh,[22] who were identified in the census of 1991 (*Bwrdd yr Iaith*

---

[21]   *Cylch yr Iaith* 'The Language Circle' is a pressure group, which is strongly campaigning against tendencies of anglicisation in Welsh media. Members of the group are monitoring the quality of Welsh presented in the media and the quantity of English. That their campaigning is highly reasonable will be understood by reading the ideas of the media for Wales as outlined in the *National Assembly Agenda. A handbook for the first five years* by Mugham and K. Williams (1998: 116-132). For current developments in relation to their protest, see consecutive numbers of *Golwg, Western Mail, Daily Post* and the website of *Cylch yr Iaith* http://cylch.members.beeb.net/, 10.1.2001)

[22]   J. Davies (1993: 67) gives the number 510,920.

Gymraeg 1999: 59).[23] There were about 20,000 adult learners in 1998 (cf. above), a majority of pupils from non-Welsh speaking homes in Welsh-medium education and an even higher percentage of such pupils in English-medium schools who take Welsh as a second language. According to *Data Regarding Welsh-medium Education* (*Bwrdd yr Iaith Gymraeg* 1998), (a) 47,619 children received bilingual education in pre-schools compared with 15,119 children who had Welsh only, (b) 209,103 children were taught Welsh as a second language in primary schools compared with 50,327 who had Welsh as the first language, and (c) 112,680 pupils took Welsh as a second language in secondary education compared with 32,973 who were taught Welsh as a first language. Adding the 20,000 adults learning Welsh in 1998, there was a total of 389,402 Welsh learners, i.e. a percentage of 76.6% of the total of Welsh speakers in 1997/1998.

In a publication from 1992 the *Welsh Office* identifies about 55% mother tongue speakers among those who speak Welsh (1995: 4). The basis for these figures, however, remains unclear, even more, since the percentage of Welsh speakers of the total resident population in Wales is relatively high in this publication, too, i.e. 21,5% whereas the census of 1991 indicated 18,6% (Jenkins & M.A. Williams 2000: 85). In addition, the figures above display a number of learners which is always at least two or three times higher than that of the first-language speakers (15,119 : 47,619; 50,327 : 209,103; 32,973 : 112,680).

However, the figures above do not exactly reflect the number of Welsh learners. First, there are pupils in Welsh-medium schools who come from a non-Welsh speaking background and who would, therefore, have to be added to the number of learners (cf. above). Second, there are Welsh-speaking children who attend English-medium schools and take Welsh as a second language, although they are not second-language learners. The first percentage, however, seems to be higher (cf. below). Third, it has to be borne in mind that there are learners who acquired the language to different degrees in the past or who never went through state supported education but who use the language for large parts of their daily communication. Fourth, in view of the ongoing immigration, a percentage of 76% learners of the total of Welsh speakers, based on figures from 1991/1997-98, is the minimum percentage we can assume, even if the total number of speakers has increased since 1991. This fact is confirmed if we consider the figures for Welsh-medium education for previous years. In 1996-7, the number of learners was 384,176, i.e. a percentage of 75.4%. The number of adult learners increased up to 24,000 in 2001 (cf. above). In addition, when talking about the percentage of learners of Welsh speakers, who can - because of their age - not fill in censuses have also to be counted, since they are natural and vital members of any Welsh speech community. This is a fact which may not have been considered when identifying 55% mother tongue speakers (cf. above).

These figures and the situation of teaching Welsh as described above not only underline the fragile state of the language[24] and the danger for its future (cf. Fishman 1991: 371-5), but also reinforce the demand of excellent teaching materials, learning aids, such as manuals and refer-

---

[23]   First results of the census 2001 will be published in August 2002 (http://www.statistics.gov.uk/census2001/censuslatest.asp, 24.10.2001).

[24]   For details, see above and M.C. Jones (1998: 236. 238). On page 37, she describes the degree of advances made in Reversing Language Shift in Wales.

ence books including dictionaries (cf. Crystal above), available on paper and/or new media, if the language is to survive as Welsh and not as a kind of pidgin[25] (cf. J.E. Caerwyn Williams 1995: vii).

Carchar i aelod o'r cylch

Mae'r mudiad protest Cylch yr Iaith yn bygwth gweithredu uniongyrchol yn erbyn Radio Cymru ac S4C, yn dilyn carchariad un o'u haelodau am beidio â thalu am drwydded deledu.

Fe gafodd Emyr Llywelyn ei ddedfrydu i saith niwrnod o garchar yng Ngharchar Abertawe, wedi iddo wrthod talu dirwy o £175. Mae e a Chylch yr iaith yn protestio yn erbyn Seisnigeiddio honedig y gwasanaeth teledu a radio Cymraeg.

"Rwy'n cyhuddo Radio Cymru ac S4C o danseilio gwaith yr holl bobol hynny sy'n llafurio i ddysgu Cymraeg mewn ysgolion a dosbarthiadau nos ledled Cymru," meddai Emyr Llywelyn yn ei ddatganiad yn y llys.

"Mae i gyfrwng mor gryf â theledu a radio hyrwyddo'r defnydd o fratiaith a Saesneg yn fwriadol ar raglenni Cymraeg, yn gyfystyr â chondemnio'r Gymraeg i farwolaeth."

Figure 15

A trend towards pidginisation becomes apparent when looking at other areas using Welsh. A corrupted language is currently presented, for instance, in a number of official translations (cf. *Golwg* 11 (1999) 24) and in the media (cf. above). The low standard of the presentation of Welsh in the media is mirrored in figure 15 (*Golwg* 13 (2000) 14). In this article the arrest of a language campaigner is taken as an opportunity to announce that the work of those who further the Welsh language is undermined when influential media like television and radio promote inadequate language usage of Welsh.

In a survey of *Cylch yr Iaith*, launched in the Eisteddfod in 2001, an analysis of the percentage of

---

[25] Pidgin here is understood as a simplified language that is usually a mixture of two languages, has a rudimentary grammar, vocabulary, and stylistic range. The term is mainly applied when such a language emerges in multicultural settings and is not employed as a first or native tongue (otherwise it would turn into a creole). The development of linguistic phenomena of Welsh in highly anglicised areas bears resemblances to those seen in pidginisation, e.g. reduced vocabulary, reduction of morphological complexity, reduced use in register, syntactically calqued language use (cf. *Cymraeg Byw* and *Standard Oral Welsh* infra and M.C. Jones 1998: 235). M.C. Jones (ibid.: 41ff.) argues that sociological and linguistic similarities between pidginisation and language obsolescence may emerge from immersion education. The consequences for the language, however, may remain the same. If immersion education is carried out in highly anglicised areas, the best results which can be expected may be that, apart from enthusiasts or those who manage to find a job in which Welsh is essential, most pupils retain a pidgin (cf. Fishman 1991: 371, cf. J.E.C. Caerwyn Williams 1995: vii). This, however, may have the potential to develop into a new dialect or variety of Welsh (M.C. Jones 1998: 236, 358), but it can equally become totally lost when its practical use is not required.

For a relation between pidgin and language death, see Dressler and Wodak-Leodolter (1977: 37). However, there seems as yet insufficient evidence about terminal language stages

"due to the fact that, until very recently, linguists tended to neglect what they deemed to be 'imperfect' or 'aberrant' speakers" (M.C. Jones 1998: 43f.).

A detailed discussion as to how and why features of pidgin and creoles parallel developments in language obsolescence and those of a variety acquired via immersion education merit further attention, but are beyound the scope of this investigation.

English in individual radio programmes was carried out and examples were given of inadequate Welsh language usage, such as '*full-length mirrored wall* efo *voluptuous television star*', '*y carriage* yn *non-smoking*', or '*merit* mewn *music technology*' (Cylch yr Iaith 2001).

It is the situation illustrated in the preceding paragraphs which urges the production of linguistic material (cf. Crystal above), that describes an unsimplified or otherwise modified language, and its application in school. If Welsh is really to be taught as is French or Spanish (cf. M.C. Jones above), the need for adequate teaching material becomes even more apparent. These languages are normally not taught in a simplified version and without manuals or appropriate dictionaries.

In fact, the *National Curriculum* suggests that pupils learning Welsh should be encouraged and enabled to use reference books, such as dictionaries early. At level 3 (out of ten), second-language learners should begin to develop into independent readers, that is, texts are to be understood with the help of dictionaries (decoding function). Apart from learning how to use reference books, therefore, dictionaries are essential to acquire a good standard of skills like reading and understanding. In addition, good writing skills at a higher level can only be achieved when using dictionaries, e.g. in order to find correct word meanings and to produce comprehensive texts (encoding function). There is, however, no current school dictionary for learners in secondary schools (cf. section 3.3.).

Since dictionaries are also self-introductory tools, their use in school is to generally enable pupils learn independently whilst in school, but in particular after leaving school.

To sum up: in the context of language maintenance, dictionaries are essential for the following reasons: first, dictionaries are popular tools of learning, research and communication, but also subject of personal advancement (cf. also chapter I).

Second, the availability of dictionaries provides the language with the prestige that it is worthy of being used and learned, a message important also for immigrants and non-Welsh speaking Welsh people.

Third, dictionaries as fundamental teaching and learning aids are either introduced as complementory aids to the teacher's instruction or they are used as self-introductory language tools.

Fourth, the school has to a large extent to compensate for the lack of home-based transmission. In areas, such as the South-East of Wales, but increasingly also in areas with a higher percentage of Welsh speakers (cf. M.C. Jones 1998: 155-238), school-based language acquisition has become the principle means of transmission of Welsh to the younger generation. The fact that an increasing number of people learning Welsh comes from relatively anglicised backgrounds means that the language must be learned formally and in a somewhat clinical environment. The learners, therefore, have to be guided by as much and as good additional and supplementary teaching materials and self-introductory tools as possible, an important part of which are dictionaries. It is to a considerable extent due to deficiencies in the area of describing and presenting the language, i.e. in manuals and reference books such as dictionaries (but also in the media), that the language spoken by children from immersion-schools in highly anglicised areas is often rather poor.[26]

Fifth, the language in English-medium education has second-language status. As a consequence, Welsh has to be acquired here like a foreign language in other countries, i.e. ideally with the help of manuals and dictionaries as the main instructional tools. In Wales, however, where manuals for second-language Welsh learners have not been in existence for the last few years[27] (cf. above), the reference books teachers and pupils have to rely on are older or self-introductory manuals, grammars and dictionaries available on the market and chosen rather individually.

Sixth, the spread of Welsh in higher education and most other spheres of life also demands new teaching materials. Vast numbers of terms have been created and many teaching materials have had to be written in order to make possible the teaching of all subjects through the medium of Welsh. Again, dictionaries form part of these materials as repositories of lexical items and guides for the application of the created lexicon.

Seventh, dictionaries are also needed for the training of translators and for the training of members of the public who act on behalf of the Assembly.[28] This institution has become important within the process of aiming at a bilingual policy (cf. C.H. Williams 1998: 110, 112, 2000: 680).

---

[26]   In an evaluation of immersion schooling by Cummins and Genese (1985: 43), it was revealed that although the method was found to be effective at the infant stage (4-7 years), it was less successful in teaching Welsh at the junior level (7-11 years) owing to a less favourable attitude among teachers, the unavailability of adequate teaching materials, and other factors. For the quality of Welsh used in daily communication in general, see above.

[27]   It is hoped that the lack of manuals in second-language teaching is not due to an attitude towards education as expressed by E.P. Jones & D. Reynolds (1998: 233) when saying that:

"As knowledge in many areas is obsolete in maybe five to ten years, the conventional role of the educational system as one of knowledge transmission is increasingly irrelevant. Skills to access information, together with broader conceptual understanding, are required priorities."

This position is not only an exaggeration of knowledge obsolescence, it is, above all, not valid for language acquistion. Language needs predominantly to be practised and not read about.

[28]   C.H. Williams (1998: 114) demands a stronger appreciation of linguistic qualification acquired and a higher recognition of language tuition when he says:

"Currently there is an acknowledged shortage of competent accredited translators, experienced language tutors, and skilled bilingual administrators and technical specialists. The training infrastructure for a bilingual workforce is woefully inadequate. Consequently, special attention should be paid to how the Government's training agencies [...] are resourcing or failing to resource the required training programmes for an increasingly sophisticated, bilingual economy [...] Government agencies should recognise Welsh language courses as a necessary skills-based training qualification for those searching for employment. In recognising the necessity for such skills, agencies should pay both course and examination fees and lobby to receive government assistance for upgrading the skills level of its employment force [...]."

Eighth, through dictionaries the Welsh lexicon continuously developed and created can be made broadly applicable to its potential speakers thereby furthering the adoption of language schemes and the promotion of a permanent use of the language throughout society.

A successful production of dictionaries can best be guaranteed by a *National Language Planning Centre* (C.H. Williams 200: 679) responsible for language planning,[29] standardising, maintenance, and monitoring.[30] The need for a standardising body was already formulated by *Bwrdd yr Iaith Gymraeg* in 1995[31] after having compiled a list of lexicographical works and other reference books of the Welsh language so far published. Since this need has not yet been met adequately,[32] it is now the task of the Assembly to think about introducing one or more effective authorities.

Altogether, in view of the decoding and encoding function of dictionaries, their prescriptive and proscriptive power (cf. above), their role for the improvement of language proficiency, their broad acceptance by large parts of the population (cf. chapter I, in particular 1.3.2.2.4.), and their part in the development and spread of the Welsh language their resulting importance for language maintenance becomes immediately clear and has been recognised as such by the Welsh authorities (cf. Elis-Thomas 1995). In light of the importance of linguistic descriptions and introductory tools, such as dictionaries these must be of an excellent quality in order to meet their descriptive and creative tasks as well as their codifying, compensatory and supplementary functions as described above. Such a quality, however, can only be maintained if dictionaries are being continously kept up-to-date.

The next section sheds light on another function of dictionaries, that is, their function to contribute to the construction of cultural identity.

---

[29]   According to H. Gruffudd (1999b: 9) language planning in Wales is still of a somewhat *accidential nature* 'natur ddamweiniol'.

[30]   Detailed monitoring is currently only being pursued by the pressure group *Cylch yr Iaith* (cf. above).

[31]   For reasons as to why it was not fully established, see
http://www.netwales.co.uk/byig/estyns.htm. (1.11.2000).

[32]   A first step in this direction is the *Centre for Standardization of Welsh Terminology* 'Canolfan Safoni Termau' in Bangor (http://bangor.ac.uk/addysg/cyrsiau/cstc.html, 20.10.2001).

4.1.2.   Dictionaries and cultural identity
4.1.2.1.   Defining cultural identity

In this section the correlation between cultural identity and dictionaries is discussed. A generally accepted definition has not yet been developed and may never be (cf. M. Heinz 1993: 358f.), despite a huge corpus of literature on the subject.[1] As in other fields of research, various phenomena tend to be denoted by the same term. Nevertheless, a few recurrent factors are often mentioned which seem to establish the broadly acceptable essentials for a definition of ethnic or cultural identity,[2] and which will serve the purpose of this investigation. Following Tovey, H. & D. Hannan et al. (1989) and M. Heinz (1993), cultural identity here is understood as:

- First, a socio-physical phenomenon of a group of people which is established cumulatively and consists of various elements
- encapsulating all other identities and roles (gender, class, occupational, local, regional, religious)
- defining and delimiting the acceptable range of relationships one may claim with both insiders and outsiders to the group, i.e. cultural identity is always the result of social processes and never purely individual
- emerging out of a reciprocal process of identification (by the insiders) and of ascriptions (by outsiders) of cultural characteristics which are thought to typify the distinctive 'being in the world' of a given group.
- Second, the cultural characteristics and symbols or sets of symbols[3] identified and ascribed in defining identity are matters of social definition and selection out of a broader range of cultural features
- which encompass roughly three main domains: (a) communication in a language, (b) values, norms and behaviour, (c) political organisation.
- Third, identity is independent of power
- and results from a particular way of defining, ordering and perceiving reality, including the symbolic representation of the past.
- Fourth, cultural identity persists over time dependent upon the continued production and confirmation in interaction of the meaning attached to identity, i.e. it is historically restricted.

A similar approach is expressed by Tovey, H. & D. Hannan et al. (1989):

"What is selected by a group as its chief 'marker' or badge of identity [...] is a negotiated outcome of historical relations with the principal other groups with which it has, willingly or unwillingly, had to contrast itself [...] Whatever cultural elements emerge to symbolise identity, over time these develop an accretion of additional meanings which amplify the group's representation of itself to itself and to others. They become bearers of an interpretation of historical continuity [...]; they come to stand for a much broader, explicit or implicit ethos and set of aspirations for the future of the people; they represent in shorthand how the people are or have been part of

---

[1]   M. Heinz (1993) gives a survey on the most important concepts of identity.
[2]   Following M. Heinz (1993: 15), no distinction is made between 'ethnic identity' and 'cultural identity' in this investigation. The term 'national identity', which could be used in the same way (cf. Tovey, H. & D. Hannan et al. 1989: 8), is avoided in order not to come close to nationalism (cf. M. Heinz 1993: 15) and not to relate cultural identity necessarily to the form of a state.
[3]   Symbols can be names of people and places, food, ceremonies, rituals, stereotypes etc.

broader systems of social, political or economic relationships. Thus, they both define the epitome of peoplehood and express in a multidimensional way a common consciousness of kind" (Tovey, H. & D. Hannan et al. 1989: 6).

Identity is thus established by a great number of factors,

"of which language may form only a small part, and the group thus identified may be a social class, a profession, a religious community, a tribe, etc. - the nation being, again, only one of the many possible units" (Görlach 1997: 1).

4.1.2.2. Welsh and the cultural identity of Wales

In the following, the restricted topic of language and identity is pursued as only one of a number of possible approaches to the concept of identity. It is, however, an essential one, since any phenomenon in a given society is mediated by its language:

> "When the members of a society share their experiences in order to improve their lives, they use their resources of repeating the experiences that are important, of analyzing the elements that form them, of distinguishing their tones in their variety, of maximizing them metaphorically, and, later, of incorporating them in the memory and education of the rest of its members. This cultivation in the agricultural, handcraft, industrial, scientific, sentimental, social, political, judicial, artistic, religious, etc. is what constitutes culture [and as such cultural identity]. And the language is the best vehicle to fix it, to remember it, to teach it and to improve it. That is why a language turns out to be so crucial in every thought about culture" (Lara 1995: 44)

- and why language problems are always liable to cause turbulence in society (cf. also infra)[4] or, at least, to engender passionate discussion of the concept of identity. It is no surprise, therefore, that the discussion of the correlation between cultural identity and language has always been a driving force behind the production of Welsh lexicographical material. Welsh lexicography developed a new quality when the Welsh language came for the first time in history under severe threat, i.e. during the Renaissance (cf. section 2.2.). Thomas Wiliems (cf. section 2.2.2.) illustrates the correlation between language and cultural identity as he saw it:

> "Ond y daluyrru, ag ar hyder y mawrha'n Cymru ni eu priawt ymadrodd a u cyseuniaith loewdec eglurloew 'n wello hynn allan, rhag dannot gwarth a chywilydd, wely'r modd a r llyuer helaethlawn, a r Gymraec yn cyfateb pob gair llatin, er eu mwyn, ag er cadw heuyt y Gymraec loewlan byth bythoedd, ag hyt ddiwedd y byt val y mae n gobeith ar dduw, a i cadwodd mor rhyuedd yn disothach ddigymmysc ac yn ddilwgr er ys mwy na dwyuil a seithgant o vlynyddoedd, ymysc cymeint a chyniuer o ieithoedd estron wledydd val datganodd Taliesin Benbeirdd: [...] Ag velly' erfyniaf, ag yr attolygaf ar dduw Celi 'ch noddi ach cadw (v arglwyddi gwiwryw a bonheddicon vrddasol) a phawb oll o m anwylgu wladwyr, eich hyrwyddo a ch cynysgaeddu, val y parhao cymrodedd, vndeb, twymder a thirion gariat rhyngoch oll yn y byt haearnawl hwn [...]" (G.H. Hughes 1976: 115, 117).
> 'But to resume, and with the confidence that our Welsh people will henceforth better increase their proper speech and their fair and shiningly clear tongue to avoid the reproach of shame and disgrace, here is the cure with the complete book, and the Welsh having a word corresponding to each Latin word, and also to maintain the shining pure Welsh language for ever and ever, and to the end of the world as is our hope with God, who kept it so strangely unspoiled, unmixed and uncorrupted for over two thousand and seven hundred years, in the midst of so many languages of foreign countries as was declared by Talisien the Chief Bard: [...] And therefore, I pray and beseech God the Lord to protect you and preserve you (my esteemed lords and dignified noblemen) and every one of my dear countrymen, to promote you and endow you, so that Welshdom can continue, the unity, the warmth and dear love between you all in this iron world [...]'.

---

[4]   With regard to Irish, for instance, Tovey, H. & D. Hannan et al. (1989: 33) state: "The humanistic and democratic perspectives available within Irish have tended to become sub-merged the more the use of the language and control over its use was confined to a narrow section within the Irish population as a whole".

Despite being under threat, the Welsh language continued to be the essential criterion for Welsh identity till the 1950s, as is illustrated by Welsh terminology. Until then, the Welsh terms *Cymro* 'Welshman' and *Cymraes* 'Welsh woman' were used to refer to those who spoke the Welsh language.[5] Research has shown that the language continued to remain a major criterion for Welsh identity until the end of the seventies (cf. M. Heinz 1993: 106-109).

Today, however, a difference is made between persons being born in the political unit of Wales (cf. figure 17) and those who speak Welsh. The latter are called *Cymro Cymraeg* 'Welsh-(speaking) Welsh(man)'. As a result, C.H. Williams (1998: 101) proposes that Welsh no longer acts as a badge of distinct Welsh identity and that the Welsh language per se is of less importance to its people. In contrast to Tovey, H. & D. Hannan et al. (1989) and Kabel (1995, cf. above), he formulates that:

> "The Scottish and Irish experience is cited, where the Celtic languages are not greatly relevant to the maintenance of national identity for the vast majority of Citizens" (C.H. Williams 1998: 101).

He goes even further and claims that "countries like the USA and Australia have no distinct linguistic basis" (ibid.: 102).[6] C.H. Williams apparently follows a different concept of cultural identity (cf. above) and also ignores recent developments in Wales, Europe and other parts of the world[7] (cf. above) when stating that:

---

[5] Such linguistic criteria have been important throughout Europe in history (cf. Görlach 1997: 3f.), particularly at the time when the concept of the nation was introduced (cf. Hobsbawm 1993). However, they tend currently to be increasingly re-applied in European countries, as for instance, in Germany. Here the ability to speak German has gradually come to be an essential condition for immigrants to apply for German citizenship or to claim income support (cf. developments in Bavaria and Northrhein-Westphalia). In the USA, immigrants have had to be able to speak English since 1906 if they want to become US citizens (cf. Görlach 1997: 15). Also in England, the ability to speak English may become increasingly important and is seen in correlation with identity (cf. *The Independent*, 3.1.2002).

[6] In contrast to his opinion, a strong English-only movement has developed in the USA (cf. http://www.aclu.org/library/pbp6.html, 20.10.2001 and http://ourworld.compuserve.com/home-pages/JWCRAWFORD, 20.10.2001). I would like to take the opportunity of thanking Dr Orin Gensler for bringing this matter to my attention.

[7] In view of the different varieties of English (cf. various publications of Görlach; Tristram 1997, 2000, 2002), however, as well as in light of the functions of dialects and varieties in general, these statements have to be doubted. It is rather obvious that any larger group of people who share major cultural phenomena will develop their specific speech and thus express their cultural distinctiveness. As the USA forms a political unit, English has become essential there too.

> "The pressure to conform has made all groups English-speaking, and this shift has speeded up in the twentieth century. This includes even speakers of Spanish, which many Americans have seen as a local or even national threat to an anglophone country. It is remarkable that this shift to English has been brought about without legislation: there has never been a national language mentioned in the constitution (which is of course written in English)" (Görlach 1997: 15f.).

In a similar way, English became important for Australia (cf. ibid.: 27f. and Tovey, H. & D. Hannan et al. 1989: 29).

"Social scientists have argued that the Welsh language is no longer the central symbol defining our separate identity within the UK. Major institutions established in the post-war era have taken its place as the key marker of national separateness [...] Identity does not depend on specific cultural markers but can be established, or even manufactured, around institutions" (C.H. Williams 1998: 101f.).[8]

The first devolution referendum in 1979, however, in fact reinforced linguistic and cultural divisions in Wales. In the referendum for a Welsh Assembly in September 1997, the language factor (and also that of identity) was consequently still significant[9] (cf. figure 17 *Golwg* 43 (1997) 9) in gaining the very narrow majority (cf. figure 16 *Wales on Sunday*, 21.9.1997).[10]

---

[8]   May be based on a similar view, the *National Assembly* currently promotes Welsh culture and identity at home and abroad (cf. publications in newspapers, e.g. *South Wales Echo*, 28.11.2000-).

[9]   The importance of the language factor also holds for Northern Ireland, when assessing the vote for the Assembly in this region:

> "The resulting data suggest a broad level of support for increased use of the Irish language in various fields within the public domain" (MacGiolla Chríost 2000: 52).

[10]   The majority, however, was gained by only half of the voters, who in turn represented half of the population. Altogether, only 25% of the population of Wales actually voted for the Assembly. This percentage is ca. 6% higher than that of the official census figure of Welsh speakers (cf. section 4.1.1.).

272

Now Assembly may get law-making powers

TONY: 'So half the people didn't vote; half who voted said 'No' but Wales said 'Yes'-right?' RON: 'simple, innit?'....

NATIONAL RESULT (Cumulative)
CANLYNIAD CENEDLAETHOL (Cronnol)

Agree Cytuno	559,419	50,3%
Disagree Cytuno	552,698	49,7%

Still to declare / Heb gyhoeddi eto: 0

Turnout / Maint y bleidlais: 51,3%

Figure 16

In figure 17 (*Golwg* 34 (1997) 9,[11] and section 4.1.1.) some reasons are given which explain the vote, e.g. the fact that 61% of the fluent Welsh speakers voted for the devolution, and the fact that fluent Welsh speakers were more likely to vote in the first place (79% vs. 57% of the non-Welsh speaking population). Place of birth, however, was also important for the feeling of being Welsh and for voting in favour of devolution.[12]

---

[11] Linguistic problems in this article are due to its author.

[12] Other important factors were social problems in the valley areas in South Wales where both former coal mining and the closure of the mines have left disastrous effects on the environment, social health, unemployment etc. (cf. figures 4 and 5 in section 4.1.1.).

Y REFFERENDWM - MWY YN ERBYN!

Roedd nifer o wrthwynebwyr datganoli wedi peidio â phleidleisio yn refferendwm 1997.
Pe baen nhw wedi gwneud, fe fyddai'r canlyniad yn hollol wahanol.

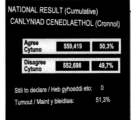

NATIONAL RESULT (Cumulative)
CANLYNIAD CENEDLAETHOL (Cronnol)

Agree Cytuno	559,419	50,3%
Disagree Cytuno	552,698	49,7%

Still to declare / Heb gyhoeddi eto: 0
Turnout / Maint y bleidlais: 51,3%

Dylanwad plaid [...]

Dylanwad cenedl
Un esboniad posibl o'r gwahaniaeth rhwng barn swyddogol plaid y Democratiaid Rhyddfrydol a barn ei chefnogwyr yw'r teimlad o genedl.
Yn ôl yr arolwg, mae yna lai o'r Democratiaid erbyn hyn yn eu gweld eu hunain fel Cymry yn hytrach na Phrydeinwyr ac yn hynny y mae un o'r cliwiau eraill i ganlyniad pleidlais Medi 1997.
Mae ffigyrau'n dangos:
• Fod pobol sy'n teimlo'n fwy Cymreig na Phrydeinig wedi pleidleisio'n gry' o blaid, fod pobol sy'n teimlo yr un mor Gymreig â Phrydeinig yn erbyn o ychydig, a'r 'Prydeinwyr' yn wrthwynebwyr cry' iawn.
• Fod lle geni - Cymru neu Loegr - yn gwneud gwahaniaeth i'r balans Cymreictod-Prydeindod a bod y rhai a anwyd yng Nghymru yn fwy tebyg o gefnogi datganoli.
• Mae pobol o dan 45 oed yn fwy tebyg o feddwl amdanyn nhw'u hunain fel Cymry yn hytrach na Phrydeinwyr ac roedd y rheiny hefyd yn gryfach o blaid datganoli. Roedd mwyafrif y bobol tros 45 oed yn erbyn.

Dylanwad iaith
Mae'r ffigyrau'n awgrymu fod yna wahaniaeth o ran iaith hefyd.
• Mae 73% o siaradwyr Cymraeg rhugl yn eu hysytried eu hunain yn fwy o Gymry nag o Brydeinwyr a dim ond 2% sy'n dweud fel arall. Ymhlith pobol ddi-Gymraeg 34-27 yw'r rhaniad.
• Roedd 61% o siaradwyr Cymraeg rhugl wedi pleidleisio o blaid datganoli a dim ond 18% yn erbyn. Ymhlith siaradwyr llai rhugl, roedd y rhaniad yn 31-34 ac ymhlith pobol ddi-Gymraeg yn 24-33.
• Roedd siaradwyr Cymraeg rhugl yn fwy tebyg o bleidleisio yn y lle cynta' - 79% o'i gymharu â 57% ymhlith pobol ddi-Gymraeg.

Figure 17

Although the language factor proved important in the vote for the Assembly in 1997, C.H. Williams expressed the view in 1998 that the Assembly itself might now become the most important marker of Welsh identity.[13]

> "None is more significant than the proposed National Assembly, which together with similar developments in Scotland and Northern Ireland will recognise in formal terms the internal cultural political distinctiveness of the United Kingdom [...] The operation of the Assembly might itself become the defining characteristic of national identity" (C.H. Williams 1998: 102).

However, looking at the aforementioned factors establishing identity and at developments in Ireland (cf. above), it seems, first of all, rather unlikely that the Assembly will become the most important marker of identity ever (cf. also Tovey, H. & D. Hannan et al. 1989: 4-72).

Second, doubts remain as to how quickly and how far governmental institutions are accepted as an identity marker for large parts of the population. This question becomes particularly acute when social inequalities remain, i.e. those phenomena which partly led to the establishment of the Assembly (cf. different groups of voters as exemplified above).

Third, it must be borne in mind that the Assembly is overwhelmingly English-speaking and as such may not meet the expectations of the decisive Welsh-language voters (cf. above, figure 17). This situation is clearly illustrated in an article from *Y Cymro* (30.12.2000, cf. figure 18).

---

[13] Such an attitude is occasionally also expressed with regard to Ireland, with some authors arguing that Irish identity is primarily focused on and articulated through the medium of the state itself (cf. Tovey, H. & D. Hannan et al. 1989: 25). To the degree that the state, however, fails to solve social problems, e.g. poverty, unemployment, environmental devastation (BSE, nuclear pollution, see *Der Standard*, 19.11.2001), and emigration, its function as an important marker of identity decreases.

> "Moreover, a sense of national identity which was defined purely through subjection to the institutional arrangements of the state seems more likely to be a temporary condition signalling a crisis of identity [and being dangerous ...]. The role of the state in maintaining Irish ethnic identity [...] has become more and more symbolic and ritualistic than dynamic [...A]lthough the state has generally achieved a remarkable appearance of consensus in presenting its own vision or 'project' for the future of Irish society as a project shared by the whole nation, it has been able to do this by, broadly, leaving to other groups (the church, educationalists, sporting and cultural associations and the Irish language movement) the task of continuing to define and articulate the social and cultural distinctiveness of that nation. Yet its own activities, in many respects, work to deny the validity of the definitions that these groups offer [...I]n the specific Irish case [...] language is a particularly salient and consistent element in what constitutes our identity" (ibid.: 26, ii).

C.H. Williams may perhaps have been thinking of Scotland after the devolution of Parliament from Westminster Parliament in London and the establishment of a Scottish Parliament in Edinburgh in May 1999 (cf. Axford 2000) when formulating his statements above. The linguistic situation there, however, is different from that in Wales. In the latter the Assembly will certainly give a new expression to Welsh identity (cf. MacGiolla Chríost 2000b: 4). Nevertheless, in an international context in which political arrangements have an insecure future an 'identity' which depends mainly on official administration cannot provide the resources needed to comprehensively construct identity (cf. above). The language, therefore, as a traditional marker of group identity remains essential.

Here a sixth-form student expresses her disappointment following an invitation to the Assembly session *Hawl i Holi* 'The right to question'. She describes her experiences there as *sarhad cenedlaethol* 'a national insult'. Not only were the pupils welcomed by *Seisnigrwydd graenus* 'professional Englishness' and faced with three English-speaking panellists out of four, including the representative of *Plaid Cymru* 'The Party of Wales', but their right to ask for better Welsh-medium education was also denied. The educational system was characterised as satisfactory and the question why new subjects, such as Information Technology, had to be done in English was not answered. As a consequence, the author asks in conclusion whether the vote for the Assembly was the last nail in the coffin for the Welsh nation.

A FU GWAWR NEWYDD I GYMRU WEDI'R CYFAN?

[...] Medi 18, 1997 - 18 mlynedd yn ddiweddarach daeth machlud y dydd a hunanlywodraeth i Gymru (o drwch blewyn). Bu i Gymru blannau ei gwreiddiau gwleidyddol ei hun a rhyddhawyd ychydig ar y cadwyni dros Glawdd Offa.

Fel un o'r genhedlaeth ifanc yn Nyffryn Nantlle yr oeddwn yn eithriadol o obeithiol fy enaid a'm ffydd pan ddaeth y grym o hunanlywodraeth i Gymru, oblegid yr oedd yn eithaf amlwg hyd yn oed i ferch ifanc fel myfi mai cornel anghysbell ddiystyr yng Ngogledd Cymru oedd Dyffryn Nantlle i San Steffan. Credwn bryd hynny fod goleuni ynghlwm wrth wraidd dyfodiad Cynulliad Cenedlaethol. Ond ar Ragfyr 6, chwalwyd fy ngobeithion yn llwyr, a theimlais gysgod hynod drom ym meddiannu'r genedl wrth i 30 o genhedlaeth ifanc werinol Dyffryn Nantlle eistedd yn siambr y Cynulliad yn wynebu sarhad cenedlaethol. Sarhad a greithiodd agweddau'r

genhedlaeth ifanc yn Nyffryn Nantlle tuag at Cynulliad Cenedlaethol a thuag at wleidyddiaeth.

Yn dilyn 18 mis o weithredu'r Cynulliad, aeth gwahoddiadau lu i ysgolion y wlad yn eu gwahodd i sesiwn 'Hawl i Holi'. Bu i Ysgol Nantlle dderbyn gwahoddiad. Ac felly ar Ragfyr 6, ffarweliodd 30 o ddisgyblion gyda Dyffryn Nantlle, ac yn dilyn pedair awr mewn bws cawsom ein croesawu mewn Seisnigrwydd graenus yn y Cynulliad. Dau air perthnasol sydd gennyf yn fy ngenau i ddatgan fy marn pendant ynglyn â'r Cynulliad - brad cenedlaethol.

Os mai ymgais y Cynulliad fu'r sesiwn hwnnw i geisio magu agweddau gwleidyddol ymysg y genhedlaeth ifanc, ofer fu eu hymgeision. Fy mwriad yw cyflwyno i chwi annwyl ddarllenwyr ymgeision bondigrybwyll y Cynulliad yn y sesiwn 'Hawl i Holi'. Yn eistedd yn urddasol bwysig o'n blaenau yn y siambr roedd pedwar panelwr, sef cynrychiolydd o bob plaid, ac un cadeiryddes. Siom mwyaf oedd canfod fod tri o'r panelwyr yn ddi-Gymraeg. Gwarth pur oedd i Blaid Cymru anfon aelod Seisnig i wynebu ieuenctid y wlad.

Wedi'r cyfan os na wnaiff hi o bob plaid ddangos y ffordd o ran yr iaith Gymraeg, gan bwy y gellid disgwyl arweiniad? Clywais sôn yn y wasg yn ddiweddar fod y blaid Lafur yn honni mai hwy yw'r blaid i Gymru, dirmygu'r ffaith hwn a wnes - ond gyda Delyth Evans ym AS Lafur yn glynu wrth ei mamiaith yn ystod y sesiwn, credaf bellach fod elfen o wirionedd yn yr honiad. Yr iaith fain oedd iaith y gadeiryddes yn ogystal, a gellir dadlau fod hynny'n siarad cyfrolau o ran parch y Cynulliad tuag at yr iaith Gymraeg.

Pan ddaeth yr iaith Gymraeg i gynnu grym bob hyn a hyn, fe'i boddwyd yn syth gan atsain y Saesneg o'r clustffonau, a daeth y llif Seisnig fel bradwriaeth i sarhau'r Gymraeg. Trowyd y llif yn dôn bwerus pan y bu i

un o'r panelwyr ddatgan yn gadarn ac yn hynod rymus fod addysg Gymraeg yn well na dim, ni ddylem gwyno, yn hytrach dylem fod yn fodlon gyda'r hyn sydd gennym. Pa obaith sydd i addysg Gymraeg gyda gwleidyddion yn datgan yr uchod? Roedd ei geiriau yn un mor arwyddocaol a rhoi cortyn am wddf pob disgybl sydd yn benderfynol a gadw'r Gymraeg yn yr ysgolion.

Neges un o'r pleidiau i Gymry'n gyffredinol oedd - nodwch y ffaith eich bod yn Gymro wrth ochr y blwch 'arall' ar y ffurflen cyfrifiad. Ac nid oedd cynrychiolydd y blaid yn deall pam fod y genedl am fynnu cael blwch yn y flwyddyn 2000. Wedi'r cyfan meddai'r cynrychiolydd, yr un oedd y drefn ddeng mlynedd yn ôl ac ni fu awgrym o wrthwynebiad ym 1990. Pa obaith sydd yna i ddyfodol Cymru os yw'r genhedlaeth ifanc yn gorfod eistedd yn gwrando ar ddatganiadau fel yr uchod?

Bu i'r Cynulliad Cenedlaethol anwybyddu cwestiwn Ysgol Dyffryn Nantlle, a chredwn fel ysgol mai'r rheswm pennaf am hyn yw na wyddent yr ateb i'r cwestiwn. Gyda'r Lefel A newydd daeth y Sgiliau Allweddol, sef Cymhwyso Rhif, Cyfathrebu a Thechnoleg Gwybodaeth. Ac mae'n ofynnol i ddisgyblion y chweched newydd eistedd arholiad Sgiliau Allweddol ym mis Ionawr, ond trwy cyfrwng y Saesneg yn unig. A'r cwestiwn syml a dealladwy oedd, pam? Ble roedd cynt frwdfrydedd a gobaith yn fy nghalon, mae bellach anobaith ac anfodlonrwydd, gadewais y Cynulliad gan nodi fy anfodlonrwydd yn y 'Visitors Book'.

Ai rhyddhau'r genedl a wanethom yn '97, yntau rhoi'r allwedd i gadwyno'r Gymraeg a tharo hoelen olaf yn arch y genedl a'r iaith? [...]

Figure 18

Fourth, most of those who voted for the Assembly apparently favour the concept of a nation state and, partly defined in terms of this concept, that of the correlated national language. This concept has been of the greatest importance in the recent history of Europe (cf. Görlach 1997: 2f., MacGiolla Chríost 2000b: 6), of which Wales forms a part, since a language has two major functions: it is (a) a means of communication and (b) a system of symbols (cf. Hartung 1998: 41):

> "Als Symbolsystem ermöglicht es Sprache, dank ihres Verflochtenseins mit der Geschichte einer Sprechergruppe/Sprachgemeinschaft und den historisch-konkreten Biographien ihrer einzelnen Mitglieder, Zusammengehörigkeiten wahrzunehmen und Identität zu definieren.
> Indem also eine bestimmte Sprache gebraucht wird, wird Zusammengehörigkeit angezeigt und empfunden. Sprache wird so zu einem wichtigen und für die Beteiligten leicht wahrnehmbaren Hinweis auf Identität, allerdings nicht zum einzigen [...]
> Ginge es nur um Sprache als Kommunikationsmittel, könnten Konflikte in gewissem Umfang vermieden werden. Verschiedensprachigkeit kann die Verständigung einschränken, aber nicht verhindern. Weil Sprache aber mehr als ein Kommunikationsmittel ist, greifen die für die Konfliktüberwindung empfohlenen sprachpolitischen Maßnahmen, die mehr oder weniger auf die Verpflichtung oder die Befähigung zum Gebrauch der dominierenden Sprache hinauslaufen, in den meisten Fällen zu kurz" (Hartung 1998: 41f.).[14]

> 'As a system, language - being interwined with the history of a group of speakers/speech community and with the concrete historical biographies of its individual members - is able to realise a sense of group membership and to define identity. Through the use of a given language, group membership is indicated and experienced. Language thus becomes an important (albeit not the only) indicator of identity, and one which is easily perceptible to those involved [...]
> If it were only a matter of language as a means of communication, conflicts could be avoided to a certain extent; language differences can restrict understanding, but not prevent it. Because language is more than a means of communication, however, the language-political measures recommended for conflict resolution in most cases fall short, involving as they do the empowerment or obligatory imposition of the dominant language'.[15]

In light of the facts mentioned above, it is apparent that the language factor becomes increasingly important the more a culture is politically underrepresented (cf. the situation in Ireland, Scotland and Wales). Language, but also personal thinking, are those possessions which are most difficult to politically eradicate.

---

[14] In the way the speakers of a given language discuss identity-constructing features of the language, they reflect a certain ideology of the language, i.e. a system of assumptions and beliefs with regard to the value of the language. However, ideology and consciousness of a language should not be understood as a cognitive coining, which is difficult to overcome, but rather as strategic resources with the help of which symbolic power can be created and be presented as something naturally given.
  Generally, such ideologies may be supported by linguistics. An extreme kind of support is language purism which emphasises one's own language, rejects foreign elements (cf. infra and Zorc's considerations on *Philippine Regionalism versus Nationalism and the lexicographer*) and can, under certain circumstances, even provoke xenophobia (cf. Hartung 1998: 42).

[15] Translation by courtesy of Dr Orin Gensler.

Fifth, taking language in its function as a symbol, even larger groups of people who do not speak it, may regard the language as a badge of identity. This becomes clear when looking at Ireland, where Irish is in a much weaker situation:

> "Even in its present attenuated form and threatened condition the Irish language still offers both an authentic, dynamic link with our past and the potential for a more self-liberating participation in the contemporary world. As it is, the Irish people, though not using the language widely in everyday affairs, value it highly as a symbolic expression of their cultural distinctiveness and are reluctant to see it disappear from the experience of future generations [...] The majority of Irish people still appear to believe that the Irish language is a central, even irreplacable, constituent in our distinctive national identity" (Tovey, H. & D. Hannan et al. 1989: iv, 3).[16]

The identity-constructing feature of the language is due to symbols, such as personal and local names,[17] and to stereotypes spread throughout a given society by social interaction, by the media, by various kinds of literature[18] and other cultural outlets, and by education. Anglo-Welsh people, for instance, are effected by the language through the *Welsh Curriculum*, introduced as a result of the 1988 *Education Reform Act*, since:

> "The *Curriculum Cymreig* is made up of:
> a sense of place and heritage
> a sense of belonging
> awareness of the part that a language and literature play
> a better understanding of the creative and expressive arts
> awareness of factors which have shaped religious beliefs and practises" (Axford 2000: 8).

All these issues can only be discussed by referring to the language, thereby furthering its importance for cultural identity.

In addition, it should be borne in mind that, as in the case of Wales and Ireland, the name of the region/country is closely related to the denotation of the language and recognisable as such. This relationship is explained in dictionary entries as follows:

> **Irish** *adj., n.* About 1205 *Īrisce* of or native to Ireland, an Irishman, in Laymon's *Chronicle of Britain*; developed from *Īr-*, stem of Old English *Īras* inhabitants of Ireland + *-isc* -ish. The Old English form was borrowed from a

---

[16] Although only a very small percentage of the Irish population uses Irish as a daily means of communication, its function as identity constructing is also confirmed by M. Heinz (1993: 111) and Kabel (1995).
Language as a constituent of identity is particularly in evidence when well-known Irish authors refuse to have their works translated into English. Some of these are Biddy Jenkinson, Liam Prút, Gearailt Mac Eoin or Aodh Ó Canainn, whose statements on this matter can be read in *Eolaire Chló Iar-Chonnachta de Scríbhneoirí Gaeilge* (Uí Nia 1998).

[17] Welsh names are particularly obvious when they contain letters not available in the English alphabet, such as <ll> and <ff>, e.g. in Llanelli, Llanfair. Welsh people, even if they do not speak the language, can mostly pronounce Welsh place names well, whereas English people fail in doing so (cf. section 4.4., see also below).

[18] Literature, in particular, furthers the growth of a sense of the collective self viewed through the prism of the symbols and mythologies of the community's heritage (cf. Axford 2000: 5).

Scandinavian source (compare Old Icelandic *Īrar*, from Old Irish *Ēriu* Erin). There is also evidence of some influence of Old French *irais, irois* angry and *Irais, Irois* Irish (Barnhart 1988: 544).

Irish /'ʌɪrɪʃ/ *a. & n.* ME [f. OE *Īr*(as inhabitants of *Īrland* Ireland (obscurely based on Oir. *Ériu*: see HIBERNIAN) + -ish¹. Cf. ON *Írskr*. See also ERSE.] A *adj.* 1 Of, pertaining to, or native to Ireland, an island lying west of Great Britain, now divided into the Republic of Ireland and Northern Ireland. ME. † b Of or belonging to (the Gaelic inhabitans of) the Scottish Highlands. M16-M18. 2 In, of, or pertainig to the language Irish. M16. 3 Having a nature or quality (regarded as) characteristic of Ireland or its people; (of an expression or statement) paradoxical, (apparently illogical), self-contradictory. L16 (L. Brown 1993: 1416).

Welsh welʃ pert. to the native British population as opp. to the Anglo-Saxons, (hence) pert. to Wales OE. (Anglian, Kentish) *Wēlisc, Wælisc* (WS.) *Willisc, Wȳlisc* corresp. To OHG *wal(a)hisc, walesc* (G. *wälsch, welsch*), Roman, Italian, French, Du. *waalsch* WALLOON; ON. *valskr* Gaulish, French ; f. OE. *Walh, Wealh*, corr. to OHG *Wal(a)h*, ON. **Valr*, pl. *Valir* :- Germ. **walχaz* foreign (Celtic or Roman), pl. *-ōs* - L. *Volcæ* name of a Celtic people, of unkn. origin. Cf. WALACH, VLACH. The two Anglian and Kentish OE. forms co-existed till xvi, after which *Welsh* became the only form in gen. use, *Walsh* sur-viving as a surname ; the pl. of *wealh, Wēalas*, is repr. by *Wales* and *Cornwall* ; the var. *Welch* is retained in the titles of regiments. ¶ AN. var. *waleis* remains as the personal name *Wallace* (Barnhart 1988: 999).

Welsh /wɛlʃ/ *a. & n.* Also † **Welch**. [OE (Anglian, Kentish) *Wēlisc, Wælisc,* (WS) *Willisc, Wȳlisc* corresp. to OHG *wal(a)hisc, walesc* (G *welsch*) Roman, Italian, French, Du. *waalsch* WALLOON; ON *Valskr* Gaulish, French; f. OE *(W(e)alh* corresp. OHG *Wal(a)h*, ON *Valir* pl., f. Gmc wd meaning 'foreign (Celtic or Roman)' f. L *Volcae* a Celtic people, of unkn. origin. Cf. VLACH, WALACH.] A *adj.* Orig. (*Hist.*), of or pertaining to the native Celtic population of England as distinguished from the Anglo-Saxons. Now, designating a native or inhabitant of Wales, a western part of Great Britain and before union with England an independent country; of, pertaining to, or characteristic of Wales, its inhabitants, or its language. OE (L. Brown 1993: 3556).

In view of the above facts, the conclusion can be drawn that even for non-speakers the choice to regard a particular language as emblematic of their country's culture (e.g. Gaelic for the whole of Scotland, cf. Axford 2000: 11, 15) is important to them to ensure that they belong to a distinct group of people.[19] Thus, research in Wales suggests that:

---

[19] This is also true for Northern Ireland where the percentage of Irish speakers is only about 8.8.% (for a discussion of this figure, see MacGiolla Chríost 2000: 46-48):
  "The primary importance of the Irish language lies in its significance as an indicator of cultural identity, a fact recognised as one of the key issues in the discussions leading up to the political settlement of 1998 [...] the Irish language functions as a cultural signifier for many groups in Northern Ireland, and in this

"even Welsh people who do not speak Welsh find Welsh-speaking Welshmen more desirable and evaluate them more favourably on a number of affective dimensions than Welshmen who speak only English" (Tovey, H. & D. Hannan et al. 1989: 22).

Sixth, identity construction is also a process of social emancipation and, therefore, of vital importance to any speaker of a language in a fragile situation, as illustrated by the authors cited above:

"Human beings construct and reproduce themselves and their cultural meanings. But in the modern world not only do our cultural building blocks come in pre-assembled forms but even the assemblage of the buildings and streetscapes often appears pre-determined. In such a world, the use of the Irish language and the cultural and ideological possibilities contained within it may be the only means whereby we can ourselves become the architects" (ibid.: 34).[20]

Seventh, were Welsh ignored as a constituent in the identity system of the majority of Welsh people, they would not only be deprived of a most valuable resource in the task of ethnocultural construction and social emancipation; they would also find it difficult to replace it with an effective alternative.[21]

Altogether, in view of the facts mentioned above, another statement of C.H. Williams - contrasting sharply with that cited on page 275 - seems much closer to the reality of Welsh society: that the Welsh language is and will remain a significant component of 'national identity' in the foreseeable future (ibid.: 1998: 102). In fact, an all-Wales study conducted on behalf of *Bwrdd yr Iaith Gymraeg* showed that 88% of the population regarded the Welsh language as something

---

sense transcends political ideology" (ibid.: 45-54; for further comments on the complexity of the Irish language and socio-cultural identity, see ibid.: 49).
This statement is confirmed by Kabel (1995: 5) when illustrating how the language has recently been presented as a cultural possession of both traditions in Northern Ireland, thus creating the image of Irish being a bridge between Nationalists and Unionists. With regard to the status and function of the language he confirms:
"The interest in Irish seems to have been growing since the eighties [...] Irish creates symbolic boundaries towards the outside world, i.e. first of all towards the security forces who usually see Irish language street signs on patrols in Nationalist areas, and secondly towards those who don't identify with Irish culture" (ibid.: 4, 16).

[20] With regard to the Irish, the aspect of emancipation of a people is characterised as follows:
"While English is the major medium through which we interact with other peoples, and for that very reason gives us access to an arena within which we can enrich our knowledge of our difference from others, our use of it also continually reinforces our understanding of our position within the wider English-speaking world as a marginal, provincial variant, derivative of the cultural attitudes and standards generated within the core. Exclusive use of English has the effect of displacing awareness of our peoplehood, away from the centre of our attention and interest. Only the Irish language appears able to offer us a medium through which we can place ourselves at the centre of our own world" (Tovey, H. & D. Hannan 1989: 4).

[21] For a discussion of an English variety in its place, see Tovey, H. & D. Hannan et al. (1989: 29f.). The maintenance of Welsh as a living language should, if anything, also contribute to the survival and development of such a variety.

to be proud of (Bwrdd yr Iaith Gymraeg 1999). It is not surprising, therefore, that the correlation between Welsh identity and the Welsh language has become a hotly disputed issue in the year 2001 (cf. comments by Harold Carter, *Western Mail*, 25.10.2001,[22] *Cylch yr Iaith* in section 4.1.1. and other pressure groups), with many Welsh speakers feeling that their language is severely threatened.

By this point, the close correlation between language maintenance and cultural identity has become immediately apparent. This correlation in turn is a driving force for dictionary production, as was illustrated at the begining of this section. Further aspects of the correlation between cultural identity and dictionary production are explained in the next section.

---

[22]   Carter, an emeritus professor, emphasised that only people who speak Welsh can call themselves Welsh. Carter has written extensively on language issues and is regarded as one of Wales's leading cultural commentators.

4.1.2.3.   Welsh dictionaries and cultural identity in Wales

In light of the facts presented in the preceding sections, it is of crucial importance that a variety of books using and describing the language should be sufficiently available, thereby providing material for the purpose of the continued construction of identity.

The very availability of books, including reference books, such as grammars, manuals and dictionaries, provides a language with prestige in that it is thereby shown to be worthy of being printed, promoted and used. The same applies, of course, to the presentation of the language in other media, i.e. on television, radio, theatre, and internet (cf. section 4.1.1. and Axford 2000: 16f.).

Offering a broad variety of linguistic descriptions also provides the language with the status of normalcy, showing that it is normal for everybody to learn and use it (cf. section 4.1.1.). A look at the types of dictionaries currently available in Wales, however, immediately reveals that their range is limited. Although the Welsh compiled monolingual vocabularies at a comparatively early date in their history (cf. sections 2.2.1.2.2., 2.2.3., 2.5.), they have not yet produced a modern Standard Welsh-Welsh dictionary.

Such a dictionary is, first of all, intended for native speakers. It is the vehicle of their culture, since both its content and its organisation are strongly indicative of the values, judgements, and priorities of the society in which the dictionary is compiled (cf. Cowie 1995: 283). As a consequence, dictionaries of this kind contribute considerably to the construction of identity. In addition, the description of lexical items in the vernacular enhances the overall feeling of linguistic confidence.

In this regard, English lexicography has been successful in reflecting and furthering the growth of feelings about English identity since the beginning of the seventeenth century (cf. section 2.2.1.1.). At that time, an attempt was made to produce a standardised English orthography presented in monolingual dictionaries (cf. Ross 1996: 64). In addition, difficult words were explained and the lexicon was enriched. Related to these attempts was also the interest in older stages of the English language (cf. ibid.: 64f.).

Welsh dictionary production, however, is clearly deficient in the field of monolingual lexicography, which has thus failed to add its contribution to the construction of Welsh identity. This failure is reinforced by the lack of other types of dictionaries, e.g. an etymological dictionary (cf. section 4.3.9.), a pronouncing dictionary, a spelling dictionary, and a school dictionary for learners in secondary schools (cf. section 4.1.1.).

In particular in circumstances where a social group is geopolitically threatened by a powerful neighbour, dictionaries and grammars as well as popular literature about language questions become the instrument of national culture (Knowles 1995: 321), partly in order to emphasise cultural particularities, but also to strengthen the political aspect of language by

1.   fighting widespread linguistic insecurity (cf. the effects of *Cymraeg Byw* in section 4.1.1.);

2.   opposing the linguistic inferiority complex of many Welsh speakers (cf. the effects of *Cymraeg Byw* in section 4.1.1. and quote by J.E. Caerwyn Williams below);

3.   preventing a situation where the communicating partners do not feel comfortable using the language and communication remains limited. As a consequence, the integration of English-speaking Welshmen/women or willing English people, i.e. learners, fails. Their integration, however, is essential to the language's viability, since it is known that a language under threat tends increasingly to be a means of communication used only among family and friends, thus further reducing its chances of survival (cf. the situation in Brittany). Learners are often disappointed and give up, as is indeed all to frequently the case in Wales.[23] Limited integration and language acquisition, however, can show fierce backlash effects as soon as learners and non-Welsh speakers form a majority, since the 'inferior' kind of Welsh then produced discourages native Welsh speakers and tends to make them give up their mother tongue (cf. 4.1.1. and below). In addition, a lack of integration makes it difficult to share common cultural traditions, such as the *Eisteddfod* (cf. section 2.2.1.2.), which, as a promoter of literature, is also part of the Anglo-Welsh literaturary milieu. Indeed,

> "research in Wales has suggested that world-views assumed by many Welsh cultural nationalists to be characteristic of English speakers and antipathetic to Welsh culture are in fact quite often reproduced in the Welsh language, particularly by those who are not native speakers or who have learned their Welsh within institutions (such as schools)" (Tovey, H. & D. Hannan et al. 1989: 31).

4.   Another argument for first-rate linguistic description is provided in the following:

> "The human race shares a number of mental and physiological functions. However, the way we think and talk about them differs from one culture to another. Language provides a form to our conceptualizations and each language uses a unique combination of morphological and syntactic tools to perform this task. Some of these can be shared by a number of different languages but a particular combination is singular and unique to a given code. It would be untenable to claim that language predetermines our thinking, however the presence of labels for specific concepts as well as the expression of messages by synthetic or analytic means do bring about different cognitive implications (cf. Bloom 1984). Morphological, syntactic and discourse structures are the devices that bound the reality we perceive and express the focussing of our attention on some of its aspects" (Lewandowska-Tomaszczyk 1995: 234f.)

In this context, collocations and idioms, for instance, are part of to what furnishes the language with a soul which makes it cherished by native speakers and learners and distinct to foreigners. As a consequence, if linguistic devices, such as morphological, syntactic, semantic and discourse

---

[23]   This trend is confirmed by the asymmetry between the large number of learners doing beginners' courses and the few who do advanced levels. In 2001 only 94 adult individuals succeded in passing the exam *Cymraeg Safon Uwch* (http://www.penllyn.com/cymuned/papurau/cym1.html, paragraph 9.4., 7.11.2001). Giving up language learning is, however, not only a question of the quality of the language materials provided but has much to do with the social situation in which the learner finds himself, with the community he is living in, his abilities, the necessity of learning, etc.

structures become too strongly adapted to the structure of another language, they lose the force of their culture-specific way of perceiving reality, a process which is part of the construction of identity (cf. description of factors which establish identity above).

In view of the facts mentioned above, an attempt should be made to contribute to the maintenance of the morphology, syntax and semantics of the Welsh language whenever possible. Dictionaries, as repositories of the lexicon of a language and guides to its potential usage, are particularly suited and qualified to creating a sense of identity and fostering a healthy confidence in linguistic identity (cf. also section 1.3.2.2.4. on the recourse to dictionaries). If they do not describe the language adequately, which is mostly the case with Welsh dictionaries,[24] the language is reduced in function

(a)   as an effective means of communication of a specific speech community (language maintenance) and
(b)   as a system of symbols and values which contributes to the construction of cultural identity.

In addition, dictionaries always contain information that is culturally specific to speakers of the language, whether such information is purposefully introduced or not. The incontrovertible truth, that dictionaries tell us more than they are consciously intended to tell, is

> "due to the fact that they are based on philological data widely collected over the centuries from multiple sources [...] and also because they expose specific cultural facts about the linguistic communitiy under consideration (Lara 1995: 41)."
> "Dictionaries always tell us something about the characteristics of their compilers, about the characteristics of their intended users and about the characteristics of the society and culture in which their compilers intend to be used. Indeed, as with all cultural artefacts, dictionaries *must* tell us these things, whether or not they wish to do so [...]
> Thus, we must interpret dictionaries in context and see them as both resultant of and constructive of their contexts. Indeed, this is what we do with other cultural artefacts. We recognize them as reflections of their contexts but as more than reflections we recognize them as constitutents of those contexts" (Fishman 1995: 29, 34).

Yiddish and Breton dictionaries, for instance, quite consciously include additional ideological attitudes by using specific orthographies (cf. section 4.4. and Fishman 1995: 33), and native lexicographers of non-Tagalog Philippine languages do so by refusing to include Tagalog words (cf. Zorc 1995). Instances of ideologically based and culture-constructing political language planning are widespread. One such case is reflected in the monolingual German dictionary produced by the former German Democratic Republic:

> "In den sprachlichen Unterschieden zwischen der DDR und der BRD manifestiert sich die ökonomische, politische, insbesondere aber die ideologische Konfrontation zweier Weltsysteme. Das Wörterbuch der deutschen Gegenwartssprache wird das erste

---

[24]   For details with regard to the reflection of idioms and collocations in Welsh dictionaries, see section 4.3.1.2. Even the comprehensive *Geiriadur yr Academi* does not systematically provide the valency of verbs, collocations and idioms. This, however, is not surprising, since it is a unidirectional English-Welsh dictionary. From an English-language perspective it is, of course, difficult at times to include Welsh phenomena which are structurally and semantically very distinct from English.

semantische Wörterbuch sein, das dieser Konfrontation auf linguistischem Gebiet Rechnung trägt. Es wird vom 4. Band an den gesamten Wortschatz konsequent auf der Grundlage der marxistisch-leninistischen Weltanschauung darstellen. Das gilt für die Auswahl der Stichwörter, für die Bedeutungsangaben, die kommentierenden Bemerkungen und auch für die Auswahl der Beispiele. Das Wörterbuch läßt dadurch vor allem diejenigen gesellschaftspolitisch relevanten Sprachwandlungen, die sich in der DDR vollzogen haben, deutlich hervortreten." (Klappenbach & Steinitz 1981: Preface) 'In the linguistic differences between East and West Germany is mannifest the economic, political, and above all ideological confrontation of two world orders. The Dictionary of contemporary German will be the first semantic dictionary which takes this confrontation into consideration linguistically. From Volume 4 on, the entire vocabulary will be presented consistently against the background of the Marxist-Leninist worldview. This holds for the selection of headwords, the definitions, the commentary, and also the selection of examples. The dictionary thereby allows the sociopolitical relevant language changes that have occurred in East Germany to emerge clearly.'[25]

The attitude expressed in the quote reflects an explicit desire for language divergence enforced for political reasons - more divergence, at least, than is warranted by differing social realities and by the mere passage of time.[26] Similar phenomena can also be observed in other cultures which were split as a result of political decisions, e.g. Korea (cf. Kim 1995: 231-223). They may also occur in societies which have experienced drastic social changes (cf. Farina 1995 and her considerations on *Marrism and Soviet Lexicography*).

A subtle way of introducing identity-related politics is found in *Geiriadur yr Academi* when explaining the lexical item 'prince':

> **prince** *n.* **1.** tywysog(-ion) *m; S.a.* **crown**[1] **1; the P~ of Wales,**
> Tywysog Cymru; **P~ Charles,** y Tywysog Siarl; **The P~ of**
> **Peace** Tywysog Tangnefedd; **Llywelyn, the last P~ of Wales,**
> Llywelyn ein Llyw Olaf; [...]

This entry indicates that *Llywelyn* († 1282) was the last Welsh Prince of Wales,[27] but also implies that the title was then (in 1301) taken over by the English for the successor to the English throne, currently Prince Charles.

The vocabulary used to describe the *Eisteddfod*, a cultural event quite unique to this country (cf. section 2.2.1.2.), is another example. Here and in other cultural domains, it is noteworthy that *Geiriadur yr Academi* may itself become to a certain extent a symbol of Welsh identity (cf. below) by virtue of selecting, introducing and defining headwords denoting specific cultural

---

[25]   Translated by courtesy of Dr Orin Gensler.

[26]   For further details with regard to linguistic controversies in East and West Germany up to the present day, see Hartung (1998: 46f.).

[27]   At the outset of his revolt in 1400, Owain Glyndŵr crowned himself 'Prince of Wales' again. By 1403 he effectively controlled the countryside from Anglesey to Glamorgan. Even the Edwardian fortresses of Harlech and Aberystwyth surrendered to him in 1404, and at this zenith of his success, he held a Welsh parliament at Machynlleth. Thereafter, however, the English gradually gained ground again and in 1409, his last stronghold fell to English heavy cannon. For further details with regard to Owain Glyndŵr, see Skidmore 1996.

aspects of Welsh society. An example is 'chair', for which the dictionary entry singles out and highlights its relationship to the *Eisteddfod* and Welsh literature:

chair[1] *n.* **1.** *(a)* cadair (cadeiriau) *f, S: occ:* stôl (stol[i]au, stolion) *f*; **eisteddfodic~,** cadair eisteddfodol, cadair eisteddfod; **bardic** ~, cadair bardd (cadeiriau bardd/beirdd), cadair farddol (cadeiriau barddol); [...]

Other identity-constructing vocabulary covers subjects like rugby, special breeds of animals, e.g. the *corgi*, particular food, such as *bara brith, laverbread* etc. (cf. Greenslade 2000). In addition, with the inclusion of North-East, North-West, South-East, South-West and Midland dialects the dictionary furthers linguistic confidence and identity by appealing to all sectors of the country. Generally, however, an enforced convergence of Welsh and English linguistic properties can be observed when looking at descriptions of the Welsh language as presented in dictionaries (cf. analysis of Welsh dictionaries in the following sections and section 4.1.1.).

This situation is in contrast to the stated aim of *Geiriadur yr Academi*. In its preface the idea is clearly expressed that the dictionary is to provide Welsh speakers and learners with a basis for linguistic confidence:

> "Unless Welsh can offer a means of communcation adequate to compete with English in every sphere of life, its speakers will be under pressure to borrow more and more words from English and will end up speaking a patois with the feeling of linguistic inferiority which has given some Welsh men the excuse to abandon their native tongue" (J.E. Caerwyn Williams 1995: vii).

Nevertheless, since this dictionary in fact looks at the Welsh lexicon from the viewpoint of an English database, there will necessarily be limitations to the construction of cultural identity. In addition, the linguistic description in this dictionary is at times minimal or inadequate, e.g. the grammar of the verb, and may thus fail to engender linguistic confidence and foster a sense of identity (cf. following sections). Indeed, a Welsh-English side would contribute enormously to the construction of linguistic and cultural identity. Such a supplement to the *Welsh Academy English-Welsh dictionary* would not only present the world from a Welsh point of view, but would also confirm the prestige of the language as one worthy of a complete linguistic description and a comparison with other languages.

To sum up: first, language has two major functions: it is (a) a means of communication and (b) a system of symbols, historically and culture-specifically shaped.

Second, as a consequence, the Welsh, like any people, need a specific language for the construction of their cultural identity (cf. chapter 4.1.2.2.). As such, language - reflected in part in dictionaries as popular tools of reference - may be enlisted in aid of enforced construction of identity (cf. above). If, on the other hand, a social group is politically oppressed or underrepresented and the language is under threat, the language question per se and the correlation between language and identity become central issues in political controversies.

Third, such controversies themselves can act as a driving force for lexicographical production (cf. section 4.1.).

Fourth, because a language and its linguistic particularities (system of symbols and values) express a specific way of perceiving reality of a social group in all spheres of life, they must be adequately and comprehensively described in all linguistic domains. In the area of lexicology, for instance, the Welsh language has not yet been sufficiently described, a fact also disadvantageous for lexicography.

Fifth, the very availability of a wide range of popular tools of reference, e.g. dictionaries, provides the language with a prestige value, an acknowledgement that it is worthy of being used, and that it is normal to learn it, and that it is an essential component in becoming part of a specific cultural group (cf. above). Welsh lexicography, therefore, needs to offer a wider range of dictionaries: first of all, a Standard Welsh-Welsh dictionary, but also a pronouncing, a spelling and an etymological dictionary (cf. section 4.3.9.), a school dictionary and a comprehensive modern bi-directional general-purpose dictionary modelled on *Geiriadur yr Academi*.

Sixth, by virtue of the lexical items selected for the compilation of dictionaries, an indication is given of the values, judgements, and priorities of the society in which the reference book was generated.

Seventh, adequacy of linguistic description is also fundamental in order to prevent linguistic insecurity and linguistic inferiority complexes, which limit the identity-constructive function of the language (cf. above and section 4.1.1.).

All in all, therefore, without being purist, a high goal for linguistic description should be envisaged. This is a real desideratum for Welsh dictionaries, as is illustrated in the following sections. However, before turning to an analysis of the description of linguistic properties seen in modern Welsh dictionaries, those dictionaries to be investigated are first introduced to the reader in the next section.

4.2.   Choice of corpus

The following investigation focuses on the description of bilingual general-purpose dictionaries which reflect synchronic language use and range between 20,000 and 46,000 headwords. It has to be stressed, however, that it is generally very difficult to provide a reliable number of head-words contained in Welsh dictionaries, since figures are very rarely given by their lexicographers. Where numbers are provided, the base of counting often remains unclear.

Bilingual general-purpose dictionaries of the size indicated above are those most likely to be bought by the non-linguistically trained native speaker and learner. Consequently, they are of predominant interest in this investigation. In addition, the works under review are those diction-aries which are most frequently edited and, therefore, most widespread. They are predominantly descriptive and produced on paper. Moreover, they are based on a semasiological approach, compiled of words arranged in alphabetical order, set out in common reading direction and presented graphically.

For reasons of comparison, further lexicographical works are also included or briefly referred to, e.g. some produced on electronic data carriers as well as uni-directional and most popular learners' dictionaries.

4.2.1.   Y Geiriadur Cyfoes. The Modern Welsh Dictionary

The first bilingual general purpose dictionary under review is *Y Geiriadur Cyfoes. The Modern Welsh dictionary* (H.M. Evans 1992, henceforth *Y Geiriadur Cyfoes*). It claims that it is:

> "[a] revised edition of an essential reference book first published in 1982, containing over 100,000 words and definitions used in the Welsh language today. Revised edition first published in 1992" (www.gwales.com, 20.10.2001).

Despite this statement, however, there are hardly any definitions in this dictionary (cf. the sections of the analysis). In addition, the figure presented reflects rather the words contained in the whole of the volume. Another figure can be produced by using the American system which counts 'references', that is all source language items. An estimation according to this system - 50,000 references - was made by Campbell, a lexicographer interested in Welsh dictionaries (http://members.tripod.com/gwybodiadur/dicts2.htm, 20.10.2001).

Unfortunately, the author does not keep to this system for all dictionaries presented on his website. I therefore decided to use my own system of counting in order to have a basis of com-parison. I took the headwords counted on each page as the basic unit. The results of several - sample pages were then multiplied by the number of pages containing the lexicon, but reduced by those pages which are not completely filled. Thereby I counted ca. 37,000 headwords for *Y Geiriadur Cyfoes*. Apart from a Preface, the dictionary has an introduction dealing with the history of the Welsh language (pp. 11-12), "Hints on Pronunciation of Welsh" (pp. 12-16), ex-planations on mutations (pp. 17-21), and a list of abbreviations. Between the Welsh-to-English and the English-to-Welsh section, there are explanations on Welsh lexicology and a list of pro-verbs. Added are also appendices on proper names, creatures and plants. The word class label-ling is in English introduced by a bilingual key. *Y Geiriadur Cyfoes* looks rather like a word list, often with 1:1 translations (cf. following individual sections), that is, one lexical item in Welsh has only one corresponding lexical item in English. Since there is hardly any sub-entered material,[1] no marking of regional variants or registers of the language can be expected.

4.2.2. Y Geiriadur Mawr

The next dictionary under review is *Y Geiriadur Mawr* (Evans, H.M. & W.O. Thomas 1987). It is advertised as "The complete Welsh-English, English-Welsh dictionary" (www.gwales.com, 20.10.2001). The only figure available is 60,000 references provided by Campbell (http://members.tripod.com/gwybodiadur/dicts2.htm, 20.10.2001). I estimated ca. 46,000 headwords.

Y Geiriadur Mawr only contains a foreword and a preface, a bilingual key for the Welsh word class labels and field markers in the Welsh-to-English section. In the English-to-Welsh section, they are in English with a monolingual key.

As in *Y Geiriadur Cyfoes*, there are explanations on Welsh lexicology between the two sections of the dictionary. Some technical terms are put into miscellaneous lists which have been used as addenda in the various revisions of this work. Since the Welsh-English half provides sub-entered material, such as definitions, but also presents different registers of the language, it is quite a comprehensive reference book, which serves the purposes of advanced learners and native speakers (cf. individual sections of analysis). This section also contains numerous synonyms and a special category of further words, i.e. archaisms and obsolete words, signalled by an asterisk. Their inclusion enlarges the size of the book significantly.

The English-to-Welsh section is described by W.S. Dodd as follows:

> "[It] mostly gives no more than a list of potential translation equivalents, with no indication other than putting them in numbered groups that they have major sense differences. Even senses associated with differing wordclasses are gathered under the same headword, in a manner familiar to the users of the COBUILD dictionary series in English. It likewise has relatively few phrases or compounds under headwords, and gives only very terse indications of wordclasses, effectively not much more than noun, verb, and similar broad classes" (1998: 56).

That is, the microstructure in the Welsh-English section differs from that in the English-to-Welsh part.

In 2001 its fifteenth edition was launched, which qualifies *Y Geiriadur Mawr* as one of the most popular dictionaries in Wales.

---

[1]   Sub-entered material is needed in case of multiple meanings of the headword. In such instances "the entry is sub-divided into (usually numbered or otherwise marked) sections called 'sub-entries' or 'sub-senses', each of which provides the same basic information categories" (Hartmann & James 1998: 50, cf. section 1.3.2.1.2.).

4.2.3. Y Geiriadur Bach

A third dictionary analysed here is *Y Geiriadur Bach* (Evans, H.M. & W.O. Thomas 1986). It is described for commercial purposes as:

> "A pocket-sized Welsh-English, English-Welsh dictionary, based on *Y Geiriadur Mawr*, but smaller both in size and in content" (www.gwales.com, 20.10.2001).

It looks, however, like a miniature version of *Y Geiriadur Newydd* (cf. below, Campbell http://members.tripod.com/gwybodiadur/dicts2.htm, 20.10.2001, W.S. Dodd 1998: 56), but without its forewords, its introduction to Welsh and an appendix dealing with the conjugation of verbs. Whereas Campbell estimates 30-35,000 references on his website, I suggest more than 25,000 headwords. The front matter is as short as in *Y Geiriadur Mawr*. Miscellaneous lists are included accordingly. The dictionary saw its latest edition in 1996 thus being similarly popular to *Y Geiriadur Mawr*. Both, however, are at times badly printed or bound.

4.2.4. Collins Spurrell Welsh English/English-Welsh Dictionary

The fourth dictionary investigated is the *Collins Spurrell Welsh-English/English-Welsh Dictionary* (Thorne, D. & A. Convery 1991), which is referred to here as the *Spurrell* dictionary. Its description for commercial purposes reads as follows:

> "A fully revised and updated edition of this popular dictionary which was first published in 1960. Welsh-English and English-Welsh sections" (www.gwales.com, 20.10.2001).

Claiming 35,000 references on its cover, I estimated more than 26,000 headwords, slightly more than in *Y Geiriadur Bach*.

Apart from an introduction, there is a section on the history of the Welsh language (pp. viii-ix), on pronunciation (pp. x-xi), on mutations, and a bilingual key for the English word class labels. The miniature version of *Collins Spurrell* is the *Collins Gem Welsh-English/English-Welsh Dictionary*, in the following called the *Gem Dictionary*.

4.2.5. Welsh-English/English-Welsh Dictionary

The last general-purpose dictionary under review is the *Welsh-English/English-Welsh Dictionary* (D.G. Lewis 1997), which provides the number of headwords itself; 'over 20,000' is written on its back cover. It is advertised as:

> "An up-to-date, comprehensive and clearly presented compact dictionary, suitable for learners and speakers of Welsh, with over 20,000 headwords including irregular forms. First published in 1997" (www.gwales.com, 20.10.2001).

Its introduction (pp. 7-8) contains a few remarks on the alphabet and on mutations. In addition, a monolingual key to the English word class labels is provided and an appendix presenting the inflection of some irregular verbs. Just as the *Spurrell* and *Gem* dictionaries, however, it neither provides any sub-entered material nor additional specialist lexical items. The dictionary contains less vocabulary than the other dictionaries of small size and focuses on 1:1 translations. As a result, it cannot be called comprehensive at all. It is, however, together with *Geiriadur yr Adcademi* (cf. below), and *CysGair* (cf. below) the only Welsh one which includes the gender of the equivalent noun of the target language. In no other dictionaries under review, are there word class labels provided for lexical items in the target language.

Based on what is written on its front cover, Lewis' reference book is referred to as the *Works-Dictionary* from now on.

4.2.6.   Y Geiriadur Newydd

Y Geiriadur Newydd (H. Meurig Evans & W.O. Thomas 1953) is another general-purpose dictionary. It is currently available in its twenty-first edition (1995) after being first published in 1953, and supplanted by *Y Geiriadur Mawr* back in 1958. It contains a useful introduction and an appendix (cf. *Y Geiriadur Bach*). Since preference was given to its reduced-size edition *Y Geiriadur Bach* in this investigation, it will not be separately analysed.

4.2.7.   Geiriadur Prifysgol Cymru

As said at the beginning, for reasons of comparison, other Welsh dictionaries are also referred to in this investigation. The first one to serve comparative studies is the historical dictionary *Geiriadur Prifysgol Cymru*. It is advertised as:

> "an authoritative dictionary of the Welsh language prepared under the auspices of the University of Wales" (www.gwales.com, 20.10.2001).

The dictionary is methodologically orientated on the *Oxford English Dictionary*. Its completion was envisaged by the end of the year 2001 by which time it was to comprise some 60 parts (for further plans, see http://www.aber.ac.uk/~gpcwww/, 20.10.2001). It will eventually consist of ca. 85,000 headwords illustrated by nearly half a million citations, with 340,000 Welsh definitions and 300,000 English equivalents (cf. sample page). It is a reference book for the academic or serious enthusiast, not one that learners would normally consider buying (cf. Campbell http://members.tripod.com/gwybodiadur/dicts2.htm, 20.10.2001):

Figure 19:

bŷn: resisting. **1722** *Llst* 189, *Rhagter.* m. Resistance, reluctance. **1803** *P* d.g. *Rhagder.*

rhacto [*rhag-*+*to¹*] *eg.* ll. *-ion.* Pentis; bwth, oriel, arcêd: *penthouse*; *booth*, *gallery*, *arcade.*

1632 *D*, *rhagto* d.g. *Præstega*, *Protectum.* **1722** *Llst* 189, *Rhagto.* m: A pent-house. **1725** *SR*, *rhagto* d.g. *Booths*, *Cabbins*, *or Standings.* **1772** *W*, *rhagto* colofnog d.g. *Cloister.*

rhactref, rhactrws, gw. **rhagdref, rhagddrws.**

rhacty [*rhag-*+*tŷ*] *eg.* ll. *-au.* Portsh, cyntedd, porth, mynedfa; tŷ allan: *porch*, *vestibule*, *portal*, *entry*; *outhouse.*

1632 *D*, *rhagty* d.g. *vestibulum.* **1722** *Llst* 189, *Rhagty.* m. A porch, portal. **1725** *SR*, *Rhactŷ* d.g. *A Porch.* **1773** *W* d.g. *Entry*, *Porch or vestibule.* **1803** *P*, *Rhagdy*, s. m.—pl. t. *au* . . . An outhouse.

rhactyb, rhactyddyn, gw. **rhagdyb, rhagdyddyn.**

rhacw, racw [ff. adfl. ar yr ardd. *rhag*, gw. *GMW* 60] *adf.* a hefyd gyda grym enwol ac ansoddeiriol.

(*a*) Acw, y[illegible] *there*, *yonder*; *see* (*o*[illegible]

13g. *LlI* 63, [illegible] ymbreynt am tyr, a'r neyll [illegible] hyt ema. [illegible] ddamor pôr eurddor pert, / Hwyl [illegible] Ricert [i Owain Glyndŵr]. **15g.** [illegible] ac ofn briw / yt Edwart ydiw / o [illegible] gwiriant. **1469** (**15–16g.**) *RWM* i. 415, Ni bo i berchen bwa / *Rakw* n swydd iork vnnos dda [marwnad Wiliam Iarll Penfro gan Hywel Swrdwal]. **15–16g.** *GLM* 195, Mae *racw* lys am war [illegible]

(*b*) [illegible] fan.) (Y . . .) hwnnw (honno, hynny, yna): *that*, *those*, *yonder* (*adj.*).

13g. *LlI* 38–9, bu well ganthau ef menet en uab e'r gur *racu* er e da no bot en argluyd. *id.* 75, Sef yu gyrr keureythyaul, llv e perchennauc ar uot en wyr ar e den *racu* e lledrat a yrr ef. **13g.** *BD* 17, Guisgvch avch arueu, wyr, a bydinvch, a chyrchvch yr hanner [illegible] *racv* megys deueit. **14g.** *RC* xxxiii. 187, da oed [illegible]nyf beth or aualeu *rackw* pei gellit yw caffel. *Dchr.* [illegible] *B* ii. 191, gwraic wenn i throet . . . kyt boet g[illegible]iw troet y gair *rackw* gwenn a dygir ar y wraic ac nyt ar y troet. **15g.** *BB* 123, dan y broynsswrn *rackw* yssyt ymherued y plas. ymae yr llyn teckaf. *id.* 139, ymledwch yn duhun diueiriawc ar castell *rackw.* *Diw.* **16g.** *LBS* iv. 421, Os daw neb yma . . . a fynno dyrchafel y corph kyssegredic *rhackw* mogel rhac y wrafyn. **1716** T. EVANS: *DPO* 81, A'r amser hwnnw y beichogais i ac y ganwyd y mab *rhaccw.* *c.* **1730** *Thos. Lloyd D* (LlGC) 197b.

Gw. hefyd **acw, rhaco.**

rhacymeriad, rhacytundeb, gw. **rhaggymeriad, rhag-gytundeb.**

rhad [Crn. C. *ras*, yr e. prs. H. Lyd. *Rad*(*uueten*), yr e. prs. Gal. (*Su*)*ratus*, H. Wydd. *rath* 'gras', be.'r f. *ern*(*a*)*id* 'cyflwyna, rhydd', cf. Gr. πορεῖν 'darparu'] *eg.* ll. *-au*, (prin) *-oedd*, a hefyd fel *a.*

(*a*) Gras, bendith, ffafr; haelioni, daioni, graslonrwydd; dawn, rhodd: *grace*, *blessing*, *favour*; *generosity*, *bounty*, *goodness*, *graciousness*; *talent*, *gift.*

9g. (*Ox* 1) *VVB* 208, *rat.* *Dchr.* **12g.** *GMB* 7, O Morccanhvc, o Ricinvc, *radew* rwytheint. *ib.* Vrten arnav, *rad* ac anaw a ffav a phlant! **12g.** *id.* 142, Boed kyuoed dy *rad* a'th wlad a'th wawd. *id.* 152, Medressid mawr ri mawr rann gan deithi, / Arwystli arwystyl *rad.* **12–13g.** *GLlLl* 4, Prif deyrn kedyrn, kydwet *rad*, / Preityei bawb, y bob digarad. *id.* 25, Gwallouyad eur *rad*, Rodri—essillyt. *id.* 218, Minheu o'm *radeu*, rym anant, / Yn ruteur, yn rwyt ardunyant. **13g.** *C* 68. 20–69. 1, Piev ybet ar lan ryddnant. Run .y. env *radew* keucant. **14g.** *T* 20. 10–11, Gogwn dedyf *radeu* awen pan deffreu. **14–15g.** *IGE²* 120, Mawr yw *rhadau* llyfrau llên, / Rho Duw, nid llai *rhad* awen (Gruffudd Llwyd). **1632** *D*, *Rhâd*, Gratia, benedictio. *id.* *Rhâd* . . . quod gratis venit. **1639** *NBSB* 62, Mae'n d'wyneb, man a 'dwaenynt, / Mawr *radoedd* gwaed M'redudd gynt. **17g.** HUW MORUS: *EC* ii. [370], Mae *rhad* fy nghariad, fy nghwyn—a'm hannerch, / A'm heneid i'th gynllwyn. **1803** *P*

(*b*) (mewn cyd-destun crefyddol: *in a religious context*).

12g. *GCBM* ii. 331, Neud oedd fwy no rhaid *rhad* mwyaf / Rhwyf cedyrn yn cadw ar eithaf [marwysgafn Cynddelw]. **13g.** *Brut B* 137, Arthvr . . . ydav e rodassey Dyw e veynt *rat* hon o daeony. **14g.** *T* 46. 21–3, Meint dy godet boet im dy *rat.* Gwyeiliesse a*rat* iessu llathyr yblodeu. **1346** *LlA* 159, henpych gwell gyfulawnn o*rat.* **14g.** *GDG³* 368, Rhoed Duw hoedl a *rhad* didlawd, / Rhinllaes frân, i'r rhawnllaes frawd. / . . . / Rhwyd yw'r bais yn rhodio'r byd, / Rhyw drawsbren, *rhad* yr ysbryd. *c.* **1400** *YCM²* 4, A'r Galiscyeit a bregethassei Iago a'e disgyblon udunt, ac aymchoelassei ar anffydlawn genedyl paganyeit. adatennynhwys o *rat* y bedyd trwy law turpin archescob. **1551** W. SALESBURY: *KLl* liiib, Deo a wrthlad y beilchion, ac ir gestyngedigion e dyry *rat* [:– ras]. *id.* lxiib, *Rat* ewn [*sic*] Arglwydd Iesu Christ a vo y gyd ach yspryt chwi. **1567** *TN* 176b, rhoes yr Apostolon testiolaeth cyfodiat yr Arglwydd Jesu, a' *rrat* mawr ytoedd arnwynt oll. **1606** E. JAMES: *Hom* ii. 263, gweled pa fendithion y mae Duw yn eu rhoddi, a pha *radau* nefol sydd yn dyfod i'r fath bobl, ac a arferant o ddyfod i'w eglwysydd yn ewyllysgar. **1672** R. PRICHARD: *Gw* 160, Cais gan Dduw dy brûdd fendithio, / A rhoi *rhâd* [:– Bendith] ar waith dy ddwylo. **1718** E. SAMUEL: *HDdD* 31, rhydd Duw ychwaneg o *râd* ir sawl a wnaeth y goreu or hyn sydd ganddo eusys. **1793** DAFYDD IONAWR: *CD* 14, E luniwyd holl olwynion / Y Gre'digaeth helaeth 'hon [*sic*], / O *râd* y mawr Greawdydd.

(*c*) Defnydd (diwastraff); yr ansawdd neu'r cyflwr o fod yn rhadus: (*economical*) *use*; *the quality or state of being economical or good value.*

1722 *Llst* 189, *Rhad* . . . Cheapness. *c.* **1730** *Thos. Lloyd D* (LlGC) 197b. **18–19g.** *Llr* C 41, 463, *Rhâd* œconomy, Glam, prudence. Gwneuthur *rhad* ar beth: nid oes dim *rhad* ar hyn a hyn.—Nid yw nhwy'n ceisio gwneuthur y gronyn lleiaf o *rad* ar ddim yn y byd. Ar lafar ym Morg., "Wi wedi nuthur *ræd* o'r ffowlyn 'na, cofia, ma fa wedi nuthur dou bryd i bump o' ni!', *GTN* 680.

Fel *a.* Heb fod yn ddrud, tsiêp, a geir am dâl bach; a roddir am ddim, di-dâl, di-gost, digyflog; diwerth, gwael, isradd; rhadlon, graslon, llawn gras; rhoddgar, hael, rhydd; hefyd yn *ffig.*: *cheap*, *costing little*; *free* (*of charge*), *without cost*, *gratis*, *unpaid*; *valueless*, *poor*, *inferior*; *gracious*, *full of grace*; *giving*, *generous*, *free*; *also fig.*

12g. *GMB* 274, Hi yn wam wy Thad, hi yn wyry heb wad, / Hi yn hollawl *rad*, yn recouyt. **12–13g.** *GLlLl* 88, Mab cor dor dewred, ef dwyre—prifgat / Megys y hendat o'y *rat* rodre. **13g.** *LlI* 12–13, Ef a dele medegynyaeth *rat* e'r a uo en e llys ac e'r teylu. **15g.** *GO* 177, O rroed ym aur *rrad* a medd. **15g.** *ID* 100, ni bu *rad* iawn i bridwerth / y gorffai roi i gorff ar werth. **1547** *WS*, Newid da ne *rad* Good chepe. *id.* *Rad* eb werth ne diddrud For nought. *a.* **1587** *Y* 225, Dy ddawn ym nid oedd iawn iach, / Dy ddireidi oedd *radach.* **1588** *2 Sam* xxiv. 24, nid offrymmaf i'r Arglwydd fy Nuw boeth offrymmau *rhad.* **16–17g.** EDWARD URIEN, &c.: *Gw* 263, Ni ddôi'r un awenydd *rhad* / O ddwyfil i'w ddyfaliad. / Siôn oedd, heb gwrs anweddol, / Saer yr heirdd fesurai rôl. **1606** E. JAMES: *Hom* i. 25, er bod y cyfiawnhâd hyn yn *rhâd* ini, etto nid ydyw yn dyfod mor *rhâd*, megis pe byddid heb dalu vn rhyw daledigaeth drosto. **1632** *D*, *Rhâd*, Gratis . . . minimè carus. *id.* *rhad* iawn d.g. *Pervilis.* **1675** R. JONES: *HCh* 134–5, ystyried, fod Duw yn edrych ar ei ddaioni ei hun . . . a bod ei râs ef bob ffordd o'r fath *rattaf.* **1677** R. JONES: *BB* 180, y drugaredd o lechydwriaeth a brynwyd cyn ddrutted, ac a gynygiwyd cyn *rhated* iddynt. **1771** *PDPh* 88, eli'r Banadl . . . y mae yn atteb diben y tar, ac yn llawer *rhattach* nâ thar. **1803** *P.* Ar lafar yn gyff. yn y Gogledd ac mewn rhai ardaloedd yn y De, *LGW* 229.

Cfn.: **rhad ac am ddim:** *free* (*of charge*), *without cost*, *gratis*, *unpaid.* **1910.** Ar lafar, *WVBD* 457. **rhad a phenllad:** *grace and blessing.* **1722** S. RHYDDERCH: *Alm* [6], Gwir *Râd a Phenllâd* fo'n lledu 'amgylch / Yn ymgais a'th Lettu. **1801** *MMf* 298. Gw. hefyd *rhad penllad.* **rhad ar (arno, arnynt, &c.):** *bless* (*him*, *them*, *&c.*), *a blessing on* (*him*, *them*, *&c.*), *also used ironically.* **15g.** *GGl²* 9, *Rhad ar* eu dewrder a'u hynt, / Rhyw flodau rhyfel ydynt. **1755** *ML* i. 383, Dyna fal y gwelais i fy meistred i erioed; Duw ro *rad arnynt*, yn gadel pob peth dan y dydd diwaethaf. Ar lafar yn Arfon, *WVBD* 456–7. Cf. D. OWEN: *RL* 81, Am Mr. Brown, *rhad arno* fo!; *Traeth* cxii. (1957) 40, Pan fo dyn wedi gwneud tro sâl â rhywun, clywir yn aml . . . 'Fydd 'na byth *rad* na bendith *arno* fo am wneud y fath beth'. Gw. hefyd *rhad Duw ar.* **rhad gariad:** *unmerited favour*, *gracious love.* **1793** B. JONES: *AD* 89–90, am *rad-gariad* Duw tu âg attom yn ei Fab. **1803** *P.* **rhad Duw:** (i) *the grace of God*, *God's blessing.* **14g.** *LlB* 1, Hywel Da o *rat Duw*, mab Kadell, tywyssawc Kymry oll. **14g.** *GDG³* 309, *Rhad Duw* wyd ar hyd daear, / Rhuad blin doriad blaen dâr [i'r gwynt]. **1567** *TN* [xxi], Richard can '*rat Dyw* Episcop Menew. **1803** *P* d.g. *Rhâd.* (ii) (*dict.*) *surplus*, *excess.* **1604–7** *TW* (*Pen* 228), y *rhat duw* d.g. *Corollarium* (hefyd *D*). **1722** *Llst* 189. *c.* **1730** *Thos. Lloyd D* (LlGC) 202a. (iii) *grace of God*, *gratia Dei* (*kind of ointment or plaster for cleaning and healing wounds*). *c.* **1400** *Études* vii. 312, Llyma vedeginyaeth diballedic a elwir *Rat Duw* . . . kanys y lle y dotter wrth vratheu . . . mae gwyrtheu Duw neu wyrtheu nefawl a wna yn vynychach no gweithredoed bydawl. **rhad Duw ar (arnat, arnynt, &c.):** *God's blessing upon* (*you*, *them*, *&c.*), *God bless* (*you*, *them*, *&c.*), *also used ironically.* **13g.** *C* 44. 14–15, y randir a *rad duw erni.* **1604–7** *TW* (*Pen* 228), *rhat duw arnoch* d.g. *Aue.* **1757** *ML* ii. 14. **1786** TWM O'R NANT: *PCG* 17, Mae nhw fel cenau y Llwynog . . . / Yn ymroi i gyd ysbailio'n gas, / Ein teyrnas, '*rhad Huw arnyn*'. **1803** *P* d.g. *Rhâd.* **rhad Duw ar y gwaith (eich gwaith, eu gwaith,** &c.**):** *God's blessing on the work* (*your work*, *their work*, *&c.*). **1567** *TN* [xxxix], *Rhad tuw ar y gwaith.* *a.* **1587** *Y* 167, [illegible] *ar ych gwaith.* **1604–7** *TW* (*Pen* 228) d.g. *A*[illegible] R. VAUGHAN: *YPS* 17, am yr hon [athrawi[illegible] ddylent gael *rad Duw ar eu gwaith.* **1803** *P*, *R*[illegible] *Rhâd Duw ar y gwaith!* God prosper the work! **rhad fel baw:** *dirt cheap.* Ar lafar. **rhad mochyn:** *dirt cheap.* Ar lafar yn Arfon, *WVBD* 457. **rhad ras:** *free grace.* **1676** W. JONES: *GB* 58. **1679** C. EDWARDS: *GGG* 135, Mabwysiad yw Gwaith *Rhâd Râs* Duw yn ein cymmeryd ni i rifedi ei blant. **1798** T. ROBERTS: *CG* 14. Cf. J. THOMAS: *Rhad Ras* (1810), d.d. **rhad penllad (benllad):** *the greatest gift or grace*, *the chief or supreme good*, *the summum bonum*, *special favour*, *abundance*, *surplus.* **1588** *2 Br* iv. cs., A honno yn cael *rhâd penllâd*, ai mab o farw i fyw. *Dchr.* **17g.** *J* 10, 13a, *Rhad penllad* . . . Auctarium. **1632** *D*, Llâd . . . *Rhad penllâd*, Summa gratia, summum beneficium. **1722** *Llst* 189, *Rhâd penllad.* An exuberant bounty, cornucopia. **18–19g.** *IMCY* 233, A rhannu gwenau'r hinon / Yn *rad benllad* i'r wlad lòn. **1803** *P* d.g. *Rhâd.* Gw. hefyd *rhad a phenllad* uchod. **rhad rodd,** gw. *rhadrodd.* **gan rad:** *fortunately.* **13g.** *GDB* 521. **yn rhad:** *as a gift*, *free* (*of charge*), *without cost*, *gratis*, *unpaid*; *gratuitously*, *for no* (*good*) *reason*; *cheaply*; *freely*, *unchecked*, *unrestrained.* **12g.** *GLlF* 441, Mab Sant syw gormant, gormes heint—ny ad / Na lledrad *yn rad*, rwyd ysgereint. **13g.** *GDB* 303, Yn llutwaw Llidwm *yn rat.* **13g.** *LlI* 8, Ef [ynad llys] a dele barnu ar e llys . . . *en rat.* **14g.** *WM* 153. 19–20, ny chaffei y eneit genhyf nac *yn rat* nac ar werth. **15g.** *GLGC* 461, Gwin *yn rhad* ac enrhydedd / a gâi'r beirdd ar gwr ei bedd. **1551** W. SALESBURY: *KLl* lxxxiva, Wy am casasant i *yn rhat* (**1588** *Io* xv. 25, yn ddi-achos). **1604–7** *TW* (*Pen* 228), *yn rhat* d.g. *Gratuito.* **1620** *Hos* xiv. 4, caraf hwynt *yn rhâd* (**1588** *ib.* yn ewyllyscar). **1672** R. PRICHARD: *Gw* 497, os tyngaist, yr hwn sydd yn bechod y mae dynion yn ei wneuthur *yn rhâd* ac yn fynychaf. **1728** T. BADDY: *DDG* 89–90, Ynysoedd Solomon a Chaersalem . . . gwyr y Wlad . . . megis y rhei'ny o'r Ynys gynta, aca [*sic*] ddaethont a Defaid a ffrwythydd ac Ymborth iddynt, y rhai a roddasant iddynt *yn rhad* ac yn rhwydd. Ar lafar ym Morg. clywir y ddihar. 'A geir yn *rad* a gerdd yn rwydd'.

rhadaf: rhadu [bf. o'r e. *rhad*; ansicr yw'r ail engh.] *ba.*

(*a*) Rhoddi gras ar, bendithio; rhoddi'n hael: *to bestow grace upon*, *bless*; *give generously.*

c. **1400** *R* 1027. 9, Vyn dillat mi ae *radaf.* *id.* 1209. 20–2, Gwnaeth tudur aervur aruot lymder. kynn rudg[illegible] best[illegible]

(*b*[illegible] bet[illegible] *som*[illegible]

18[illegible]

rhadaidd [*rhad*+*-aidd*] *a.* Rhad, rhydd: *free.*

1803. Cf. **16–17g.** *PhA* 345, Yr Iessu mynn o'i ras maith / anrhydeddu yn rhadeiddwaith / porth ras power a thryssawr / priodas mewn urddas mawr (Siôn Phylip).

rhadbost, gw. **rhatbost.**

rhadedd [*rhad*+*-edd¹*] *eg.* Rhadr[illegible] graslonrwydd: *cheapness*; *graciousness.*

1803 *P.*

rhadeiddwaith, gw. **rhadaidd**+**gwaith².**

rhadell¹ [bnth. dysg. o'r Llad. *rādula* dan ddyl. yr e. *gradell*] *eb.* Gratiwr, rhatheil: *grater.*

1707 *AB* 219d, *Rhadelh*, A grater, &c, D. *c.* **1730** *Thos. Lloyd D* (LlGC) 202a, *Rhadell.* Radula. D. **1774** *W* d.g. *Grater* [*an instrument for grating*].

rhadell², gw. **gradell** (At.).

Cipair / Catchword

Diffiniadau Cymraeg a Saesneg
Definitions in Welsh and English

Croesgyfeiriad
Cross-reference

Dyddio manwl gywir
Accurate dating

Enghreifftiau llafar a thafodieithol
Colloquial and dialect examples

Dangosair
Headword

Cyfuniad
Combination

Rhan ymadrodd (gan gynnwys ffurfiau lluosog, &c.)
Part of speech (including plural forms, &c.)

Tarddiad
Etymology

Paragraff ystyr / Sense paragraph

Enghreifftiau â dyddiadau mewn trefn gronolegol
Dated examples in chronological order

The front matter consists of a bilingual introduction explaining the "General Order And Arrangement Of The Dictionary" and of abbreviations. It also presents a bibliography (no pages are given). In a leaflet produced by the staff of *Geiriadur Prifysgol Cymru*, the following description is given:

> "*Geiriadur Prifysgol Cymru* is the first standard historical dictionary of the Welsh language, broadly comparable in method and scope with *The Oxford English Dictionary*, but midway in format between that dictionary and the *Shorter Oxford English Dictionary*. It presents in alphabetical order the vocabulary of the Welsh language from the remnants of Old Welsh, through the abundant literature of the Medieval and Modern periods, to the explosion of vocabulary arising from the ever-increasing use of the language in all fields of contemporary life. This vocabulary is defined in Welsh, but English equivalents are also given. Detailed attention is given to variant forms, common collocations, and etymology. The work is based upon a collection of well over two million citation slips, amassed by voluntary readers as well as members of the Dictionary staff and is still being augmented. [...] Once the present work is completed, it is intended to revise the earliest parts of the Dictionary (A-B), with an online version provided on the Web. It is also hoped to produce a concise version of the Dictionary for the Web (and, eventually, a full version on CD-ROM), a spelling dictionary, and an index to the definitions that will form the basis of a Welsh thesaurus. We shall continue to augment our collections by gathering examples of new words and usages and by acquiring further electronic texts. Much fuller details about the Dictionary and its history are available on the Dictionary's website: www.aber.ac.uk/~gpcwww" (cf. figure 19).

Another description is provided by W.S. Dodd (1998: 55):

> "This dictionary is to Welsh what Murray's New English Dictionary was for English, and has a certain similarity in approach and appearance to the Oxford dictionaries [...] In effect, because of the inclusion of translation into English at the end of the definitions provided for most major entries, it can also be seen as a mono-bilingual Welsh-Welsh-English dictionary. Nevertheless, the strong emphasis on etymologies, and the extensive coverage of historical development, prevent it from being seen as just the Welsh-English part of a large bilingual dictionary. There is, for instance, a much greater range of archaisms than would be normal in a purely synchronic contemporary bilingual volume [... B]ecause of the catholic descriptive approach adopted, there are many words which are taken from other languages, and especially from English, which indubitably have been and are used in Welsh, but which would equally not be the phrasing of first preferences for more than a few speakers."

The dictionary was chosen because, first, it is of major importance for Welsh lexicography. Second, according to its description, it is expected to include more linguistic features of individual lexical items than any other dictionary thus reflecting potential range and type of information in relation to lexical items which may be provided in Welsh lexicographical works. A thorough analysis of the dictionary, however, reveals some deficiencies, e.g. it lacks etymology for many lexical items and semantic precision (cf. Humphreys 2000: 27). More details are illustrated in the following individual sections.

4.2.8.   Geiriadur yr Academi. The Welsh Academy English-Welsh Dictionary

The second important dictionary analysed for comparative purposes is *Geiriadur yr Academi.*
The Welsh Academy English-Welsh Dictionary by Griffiths, B. & D.G. Jones (1995, henceforth,
Geiriadur yr Academi) which reflects current language use. It is advertised as:

> "The most comprehensive English-Welsh dictionary ever compiled including synonyms,
> illustrative quotations, idioms, specialist and technical terms etc. together with a concise
> morphology of the Welsh language. First published in 1995" (www.gwales.com,
> 20.10.2001).

Unfortunately, there is no number of headwords or references anywhere suggested. Campbell
(http://members.tripod.com/gwybodiadur/dicts2.htm) provides the following figures on his
website:

> "The total number of words in the entire text (i.e. not just headwords) is around two
> million; the monumental *Geiriadur Prifysgol Cymru* itself has only four times that
> number."

I myself counted more than 100,000 headwords[2] in the first edition. It is, therefore, an enormous
and important work in Welsh lexicography. Campbell (ibid.) assesses the dictionary as follows:

> "Enormous, ambitious, arcane, unwieldy, largely archaic in both form and content, al-
> most excessively comprehensive in some areas and definitely inadequate in others [...]
> the breadth impresses more than the depth [...] The typography too is years behind the
> times, and high-quality printing and paper are marred by a cheap, flashy binding un-
> likely to withstand serious use for long."

Looking at the dictionary in detail, W.S. Dodd provides the following statement:

> "The general framework employed is aligned on the English portion of the Harrap bi-
> lingual French and English dictionaries. Although it is the *Shorter English and French*
> *Dictionary* of 1975 and subsequent editions that is specifically acknowledged in this
> context, there is also some family resemblance to Harrap's larger *Standard French and*
> *English Dictionary*" (1998: 57).

The physical format, and also some sections are very similar, such as those presenting abbreviations and field markers (pp. xv-xxviii), those on orthography and pronunciation (pp. xx-lxxix),
and also the select bibliography (pp. lxxx-lxxxi).

All of the word class and field label abbreviations are in English, with a monolingual English
key. Clarificatory comments given in italics in brackets are also entirely in English (cf. following sections) with the exception of some French (cf. section 4.5.) and Latin synonyms, the latter
for plants only. The syntax of the *Metalanguage* is only partly standardised.

For many lexical items, there are alternative variants according to the region. Sometimes the
lexicographers go as far as distinguishing North-East, North-West, South-East, South-West, and
Midland dialects. Although the more global North and South division is the most striking, this
approach furthers linguistic confidence and identity for native speakers. Colloquial, literary and
poetic versions, i.e. variation of register, are also conspicuous. The headword inventory is rich

---

[2]   Sorlin (1999: 334) mentions "some 200,000" entries but does not reveal the source of the figure.

in technical terms drawn from specialist fields, such as law, medicine, architecture, and sciences. They are always indicated by a field label. For this area of lexicography, the editors of *Geiriadur yr Academi* could certainly rely on the extensive terminological work that has gone on in Wales in recent years (cf. chapter III and the list of vocabularies in the appendix), as one of the various aspects of language planning. Dictionary users can also find a large number of proper nouns, i.e. place names and personal names, as for instance *London, Londonderry*, but also titles of literary works (cf. below). Examples of literary works as is illustrated by the following example:

> **lady** *n.f. S.a.* **woman. 1.** *(a)* boneddiges(-au); **~-in-waiting,**
> boneddiges breswyl [...]; *W.Lit:* **The L~ of the Fountain,**
> Iarlles y Ffynnon; *Eng.Lit:* **The L~ of Shalott,** Y Feinir o
> Sialót; *W.Myth:* **The L~ of the Lake,** Morwyn y Llyn, Rhiain
> y llyn [...] **L~ Mayoress,** Arglwydd Faeres(-au); **~ friend,**
> cyfeilles(-au); **(Miss X) first ~ of song,** (Miss X) y brif gantores,
> [...] *Ecc:* **Our L~,** y Forwyn Fair; Mair Wyry, *occ:* Ein
> Harglwyddes; *(in name of plants &c):* Mair. **3.** *(as title):*
> bonesig *f*, boneddiges(-au) *f*; **L~ Jones,** y Fonesig Jones; *(peer
> or wife of peer):* arglwyddes(-au) *f*; **L~ Huws,** yr Arglwyddes
> Huws; *(in comb. with place name):* **L~ Llanover,** Arglwyddes
> Llanofer; **my L~,** f'Arglwyddes, Madam; [...]

Campbell (http://members.tripod.com/gwybodiadur/dicts2.htm, 20.10.2001) assesses the entries in *Geiriadur yr Academi* with the following words:

> "[they] adhere to an arcane, counter-intuitive set of conventions not fully explained in the front matter; and the haphazard presentation of the material makes it painfully hard to negotiate. -- just try finding your way around the solid columns of dense text at the larger units. As for the target language how are we supposed to choose between 16 translations of *puffball*?"

In short, the access structure of *Geiriadur yr Academi* is not clear.

The inventory of this dictionary includes a number of phrases which are not yet naturalised, being therefore italicised, especially many French loans, as for instance *amour* and *faux-*:

> ***amour*** *n.* carwriaeth(-au) *f*; helynt(-ion) *(f)* caru. **~ *propre*** *n.*
> hunan-barch *m.* **~ *courtois*** *n.* Lit: serch cwrtais *m.*

> ***faux-*** *Fr.a.* ffug- + *soft mut.*, gau- + *soft mut.* **~ *bonhomme*** *n.*
> Ffug-fonheddwr (~-fonheddwyr) *m*, dyn(-ion) *(m)* gwên-blês,
> dyn gwên-deg. **~-*bourdon*** *n.* *Mus:* **faux-bourdon(-s)** *m.* **~ *naif***
> *n.* cam gwag (camau gweigion) *m*, camgymeriad(-au) *m.*

In some cases, the question arises as to why the French lexical items were included in this English-Welsh dictionary. The French word *cantatrice* is certainly gender specific, i.e. more precise, than the English word *singer* when the female artist is meant. What, however, is the need to include *fauteuil* 'armchair', or *escargot* 'snail' when there is no explanation that the latter stands for snails as priced food items in English? It is certainly desirable to include lexical items of a very precise semantic meaning. However, the lexicographer can hardly expect dictionary users to know all the borrowed and foreign words in order to make the target language more precise.[3]

As a comprehensive dictionary including some detailed grammar, *Geiriadur yr Academi* has a major impact (cf. also section 4.1.2.3.). It was the Book of the Year 1995; nearly 10,000 copies were sold after a few months following its publication (cf. G. Wiliams 1996: 3f.). As a result, a wave of new dictionaries based on the lexicon presented in this work was initiated, e.g. *Geiriadur termau archaeoleg. A dictionary of archaeological terms in English and Welsh* (J.LL Williams, John Ll. & Bruce Griffiths et al.: 1999).

Where the uni-directional English-Welsh dictionaries of the 18th and 19th centuries intended to encourage the Welsh to learn English (cf. in section 2.4.), the contrary is true for *Geiriadur yr Academi*. In light of this fact, however, the question may be posed as to why the target language, i.e. Welsh, is not consistently provided with word class labels. Such labels are only given to nouns and adjectives when the gender is indicated. Nevertheless, the dictionary presents quite comprehensive information in relation to adjectives and mutations thus including basic information for the application of this part of the lexicon.

Geiriadur yr Academi is largely descriptive, but also prescriptive when introducing new words, or when referring to incorrect language use (more examples can be found in the following sections):

> **ask** *v.t. &i.* **1.** *(=inquire) :* **to ~ s.o. sth,** [...]; **to ~ s.o. a
> question**; gofyn cwestiwn i rn (*not* holi cwestiwn); **I ll' ~ whether
> she's there**, mi holaf i a yw hi yna (*not* os yw hi yma); **I've often
> asked myself whether she was right**, yn aml mi feddyliais tybed
> a oedd hi'n gywir; (*not* os oedd hi'n gywir); [...]

> **provisional** *a. & n.* **1.** *a* dros dro, am y tro, tymhorol, *occ:*
> darpariaethol; **the P~ I.R.A.**, *usu., but incorrectly:* yr I.R.A.
> Ddarpariaethol; *preferably:* yr I.R.A. Dros Dro, yr I.R.A.
> Answyddogol; *Golf:* [...]

To sum up: *Geiriadur yr Academi* illustrates productive word formation (cf. Sorlin 1999: 335) and demonstrates

> "that Welsh has all the resources of any modern language, that it has a technical
> vocabulary adequate for the needs of all the multivarious areas of academic endeavour,
> trades, crafts and skills of the present day. [...] All in all, *Geiriadur yr Academi* is a
> valuable record of the wealth of vocabulary in existence in Welsh" (W.S. Dodd 1998:
> 59).

As indicated by Campbell (cf. http://members.tripod.com/gwybodiadur/dicts2.htm, 20.10.2001), it has its inadequacies mainly in the field of grammar, a few of which are described in the following sections.

---

[3]   Cf. also statements by Gareth King in an interview between himself and Dewi Rhys-Jones for
Cambria on the occasion of the publication of his *Pocket Modern Welsh Dictionary*.

4.2.9.   The Welsh Learner's Dictionary

As the need arises to illustrate trends in Welsh lexicography or in order to exemplify specific problems in this field, other Welsh language dictionaries are also included into this investigation, such as learners' dictionaries. They generally focus on the use of their lexicon and provide more explanations for given lexical items than other dictionaries. The provision of extensive explanations is, of course, at the cost of the number of headwords.

One of the recent learners' dictionaries referred to is *The Welsh Learner's Dictionary* by H. Gruffudd (1998). It is advertised as:

> "A Welsh-English, English-Welsh dictionary for Welsh learners, ideal for evening classes, schools and tourists, comprising over 20,000 words and phrases, pronunciations, mutations and grammatical explanations, words in context and place-names" (www.gwales.com, 20.10.2001).

The dictionary has about 10,000 headwords, two pages on pronunciation (pp. 6-7), two on mutations (pp. 8-9), seven pages on the verb inflection (pp. 10-16), three on syntax (pp. 17-19), and two more on adjectives, the article and pronouns. In addition, it contains a list of personal and place names. The word class labels are in English with a key in English only. The dictionary comprises lexical items and units actually used and provides idioms that have not appeared anywhere else. Above all, it indicates which mutation, if any, is triggered at the relevant entry.

Apart from Gruffudd *The Welsh Learner's Dictionary*, none of the bilingual dictionaries includes phonetic transcription. The section on phonetic transcription in this investigation (section 4.4.), however, proves that the improvised phonetic transcription is not a good guide for learners of Welsh.

4.2.10.   Pocket Modern Welsh Dictionary

The *Pocket Modern Welsh Dictionary* (King 2000) is described for commercial purposes as follows:

> "A new Welsh-English/English-Welsh dictionary comprising examples of speech and written phrases, detailed information on mutations, grammar characteristics and pronunciation, and a list of place names" (www.gwales.com, 20.10.2001).

On the internet Welsh language discussion list *the Welsh-L@listserv.heanet.ie*, the dictionary was praised by L.K. Sherman as:

> "[...] the Pocket Modern Welsh Dictionary [...] will be a milestone in Welsh lexicography, representing a modern and user-friendly approach to the Welsh language as a vibrant and dynamic medium of communication in the new millennium.
> This two-way dictionary, designed and compiled primarily with the needs of learners of the language in mind, comes with a range of revolutionary innovations:
> – illustrative sentences and examples from everyday Welsh as spoken and in the media for many headwords on the Welsh-English side
> – translation guidelines giving help in problem areas where Welsh and English usage differ
> – full grammatical information for all word categories: genders and plurals of all nouns, unpredictable verb stems, comparative forms of adjectives, special personal forms of prepositions

- detailed coverage of the system of initial mutations - what they are, where they are used, and how to spot them. In addition, all incidences of mutation in the illustrative sentences and examples are marked by special typographical devices
- special usage boxes dealing in detail with major points of difficulty, e.g. numbers, verb 'to be', particles *yn* and *yn°*, particle *mo*, focused sentences [...]
- a completely up-to-date wordbase, including terms for a wide variety of modern concepts [...]

The *Pocket Modern Welsh Dictionary* is to be Waterstones bookstore chain's Book of the Month in April 2000 - recognition of an important publishing event for the Welsh language and all its friends.

This modern, new-look and user-friendly dictionary, backed by the considerable lexicographical expertise and reputation of the Oxford imprimatur, truly brings the Welsh language into the 21st century" (L.K. Sherman 10.2.2000).

A close look at the dictionary and the analysis in the following sections, however, reveal that the quality of this work does not correspond with that which is overwhelmingly praised in the above and other descriptions.[4] Indeed, the second-year students of Welsh in Vienna were rather unhappy with this reference book. Because of the reduced number of lexical items, they could not understand any given text completely without using a more comprehensive dictionaries, such as *Y Geiriadur Bach* or *Y Geiriadur Mawr*.

The dictionary may reach the number of 10,000 headwords. The actual number of headwords is particularly hard to estimate, since huge boxes explaining the usage of some individual lexical items take unpredictable amounts of space. The front matter contains five pages on "How to Use the Dictionary" (pp. ix-xiii), two on pronunciation (pp. xiv-xv), two on mutations (pp. xvi-xvii), seven pages "Grammar Reference" (pp. xviii-xxiv) and four explaining grammatical terms (pp. xxv-xxviii). At the end of the book personal and place names are added. The *Metalanguage* is in English only and without using abbreviations.

As King says himself (2000: preface), the *Pocket Modern Welsh Dictionary*

"represents a departure from traditional dictionaries which, particularly for Welsh, have confined themselves to more or less word-for-word entries without explanations."

Since comprehensive boxes strategically placed with lengthy explanations follow quite a lot of entries, the book may even be called a combined dictionary and grammar. However, the explanations and examples in the boxes are, at times, unsystematically presented (cf. ibid.: 25, for further details, see the following sections).

The dictionary is problematic in the way that it provides "numerous illustrative examples taken from actual speech and writing" (King 2000: Preface), since the focus is almost exclusively on 'actual speech'. This approach, based on J. Fife (1990) is confirmed when looking at King's grammar book (cf. King 1993), which largely forms the linguistic basis of his dictionary[5] and in which it is clearly stressed that the emphasis is on the spoken language. As a con-

---

[4] In the interview with Dewi Rhys-Jones for *Cambria* (cf. above) Gareth King states: "Any point that might present translation problems between Welsh and English has been explained with examples." This statement appears to present the dictionary as a perfect all-purpose reference book.

[5] For details, see section 4.5.

sequence, there are forms of words in the dictionary which would rarely be used in writing, but which are not clearly indicated as such (cf. King 2000: 26, 111).[6]

Nevertheless, a real innovation is described by the author himself as follows:

> "all instances of mutation (except fossilized/fixed mutation) are explicitly indicated by special typographical signs throughout the dictionary on both sides" (ibid.: preface).

The dictionary is clearly aimed at the beginner and intermediate learner by providing essential core-language items. It does, however, include a relatively high number of anglicisms. Nevertheless, the learner can find information on regional variation and different registers in the language.

4.2.11. CysGair

The last dictionary to be introduced here is *CysGair*, a dictionary on CD-Rom produced by C. Ó Dochartaigh (1977). It is advertised as follows:

> "CysGair is invaluable to both native speakers and learners of Welsh as it is an English-Welsh and Welsh-English dictionary. Both the Tool Bar and the language of the CysGair screen can either be in English or Welsh, and the pull-down menus are bilingual.
> − CysGair has about 45,000 headwords, including technical terms and phrases.
> − The program can recognise mutations and verb conjugations. For example, CysGair can identify *gath* as a mutated form of *cath* and *ysgrifennodd* as a form of *ysgrifennu*.
>
> − CysGair can carry out wildcard searches, finding words containing combinations of particular letters, vowels or consonants.
> − A comprehensive Help file is included to assist you when learning to use the program effectively.
> − CysGair can cut and paste Welsh and English words from the dictionary to your document.
> − The program can be used as a standalone program or can be integrated with the most popular Windows word processors including Microsoft Word, WordPerfect, AmiPro and WordPro. Used this way, you can click on any word in your document to see its translation, and copy any word or phrase from CysGair into your document.
> − CysGair can be called upon from within CySill" (http://hydraulix.bangor.ac.uk/-ar/cb/english/cysgair.htm).

The word class labelling is in English. The user quickly realises that the lexicon presented in the dictionary is limited. Core-language items are missing. Some of them are *dwyael* 'eyebrows', *plant* 'children', *t@r* 'tower', *tâl* 'payment', *gr@p* 'group', *blwydd* 'year old', *blynedd* 'years',[7] *Cymru* 'Wales', and *G@yl* 'holiday, festival', the latter two identity-constructing.

Another problem is the alphabetical order, which is English, thus ignoring the existence of the Welsh digraphs *ch, dd, ff, ng, ll, ph, rh, th*. Further problems with regard to the description of lexical items are illustrated in the following sections.

---

[6] For problems concerning the approach of King, see section 4.1.1.
[7] However, *blwydd* and *blynedd* occur in phrases.

A few other lexicographical works are mentioned briefly in individual sections and characterised there as far as necessary. Dictionaries of related languages, such as Irish, Breton, Scottish Gaelic and Manx are also included as the need arises. They predominantly exemplify in which way particular features of the Celtic languages may generally be presented.

4.3.   Analysis of dictionary entries
4.3.1.   The Welsh verb
4.3.1.1. Inflection

Although the importance and complexity of Welsh verb inflection is acknowledged (cf. section 1.3.2.3.1.) and shown in individual works (cf. D.G. Lewis 1995), it does not form a regular part of dictionary entries in Welsh bilingual bi-directional general-purpose dictionaries. The examples below suffice for the purpose of illustration:

Y Geiriadur Cyfoes:	**cadeirio,** *v.* CHAIR
	cadw, *v.* KEEP, SAVE, PRESERVE [...]
	cael, *v.* HAVE, GET, FIND

Y Geiriadur Mawr and *Bach:*	**bod,** *be.* bodoli, byw. TO BE.
	bodio, *be.* teimlo â'r bodiau neu'r bysedd, trafod, trin. TO THUMB, TO FINGER.
	bodoli, *be.* bod. TO BE, TO EXIST.

Spurrell:	**gwneud, gwneuthur** *vb* do, make
	gwnïo *vb* sew, stitch
	gwobrwyo *vb* reward

Works-Dictionary:	**dod, dyfod** *v* to come (*see* Appendix).
	dodi *v* to put.
	mynd, myned *v* to go (*see* Appendix).

A study of dictionaries of Celtic sister languages reveals ways of a more comprehensive display of the verb inflection. In medium-size Irish dictionaries, for instance, the verb stem is regularly given. Entries of irregular verbs may also include a second present form, the verbal noun and the past participle (cf. Rialtas na hÉireann 1981, Caldas/Schleicher 1999):

> **aifir,** *v.t.* (*pres.* -fríonn, *vn.* ~t, *pp.* -feartha), Rebuke [...]
> **aor,** *v.t.* (*vn.* ~adh *m, gs.& pp.* -tha). Satirize [...]
> **leasaigh,** *v.t. & i.* **1.** Amend, reform [...]

> **aifir** [afər] *v₁* (*präs.*: -**fríonn,** *pp.*:
> -**feartha,** *vn.*: ~t) tadeln, vorwerfen [...]
> **aitheasc²** [ahək] *v₁* (*pp.*: ~**tha,** *vn.*: ~)
> ansprechen, anreden
> **diasraigh** [d'iəsri] *v* (*vn.*: -**rú**] <Agr.>
> nachlesen

Whereas the verb stem is indicated in even the smallest Breton/English - English/Breton dictionary (Delaporte 1995, cf. also the French/Breton - Breton/French dictionary, Desbordes & Kervella 1994), this is not the case in any modern Welsh dictionary (cf. above), apart from the historical dictionary *Geiriadur Prifysgol Cymru* (henceforth *GPC*, cf. also S. Heinz 1994 and cf. section 4.3.1.2.):

faltaziañ [ˌfaltaˈ ziã] *v.* to imagine, to fancy, to picture.

falvez*out* [falˈveːzut] *v.* *(used only in the 3rd sg. followed by indir. object introduced by **da** or **gant**) to want, to wish.*

ober [ˈoːbɛr] *irr.v.* *[see Table] (radic.* **gra-**) to do, to make; **en em o.**, to adapt oneself, to get used (**diouzh**, to); **o. da u.b.** (**mont**), to make (s.o.) (go); **o. erc'h, glav, h.a.**, to snow [...]

rise (rose, risen) *v.* sevel (*radic.* sav-); en em sevel (*radic.* en em sav-); (of dough) go*iñ*; **risen** (of dough) go.

rouse *v.* *(awake)* dihun*iñ*; *(fire)* tabarc'h*at*

rout *v.* trec'h*iñ*, faezha*ñ*

The indication of the verb stem is also regularly included in the dictionary of Favereau (1992):

BERADiñ [beˈraːdi], [beradɛŋ] vb. *goutter.*
BERañ,-iñ,-o⁺ [ˈbeːrə], [berɛŋ] vb. *(s')égoutter, & couler* (C. -aff, kmg beru) : [...]
BERiañ, BERIAOiñ⁺ [ˈberjə], [berjɛɲ], a-w. [beˈrjowi] vb. *embocher:* beriaouiñ un to(u)sseg (gw. brochañ).

Welsh/Breton - Breton/Welsh dictionaries, produced by Welsh authors (Hincks 1991, Rita Williams 1990), also lack information on verb inflection.

The only general-purpose dictionary which allows the indication of verb inflection to a limited degree is *Geiriadur yr Academi*. It lists the inflected present tense forms of the verb *bod* 'to be'.[1] In addition, phrases which illustrate the usage of a particular verb may contain an inflected verb form. Moreover, inflection paradigms, and longs lists of verbal nouns classified by their ending as well as exceptions are presented in the introductory section of *Geiriadur yr Academi* (Griffiths, B. & D.G. Jones 1995: lvii-lxxix). Such lists, however, are of little help for immediate guidance on the usage of lexical items, since the dictionary user must carry out a complete new search procedure in order to find the relevant rules or exceptions, in particular when the access structure is not clear (cf. ibid.: lxxv).

The *Works-Dictionary* refers at least to an appendix, in which the irregular forms are listed separately. However, identifying the stems of other verbs remains impossible for dictionary users.

Only in *GPC*, the first person singular present - according to P.W. Thomas the future tense (cf. section 1.3.2.3.1.) - is chosen as the headword, thus presenting the verb stem. In addition, the irregular form of the third person singular present - again future tense according to P.W. Thomas (cf. section 1.3.2.3.1.) - is occasionally listed under 'Etymology' (cf. *arhosaf* 'I (will) wait' and *GPC* 1950 *General order and arrangement of the dictionary*). However, since it is a historical dictionary, its users cannot be sure that the presented verb form is still in use.

---

[1]   Another exception can be found in S. Heinz (1994) where the first person singular present and the third person singular past tense are given in the verb entry. As this work, however, does not count as a dictionary it is not subject to analysis here.

The learners' dictionaries are better in this respect. *The Welsh Learner's Dictionary* (Gruffudd 1998) includes inflected verb forms of the irregular verbs in the headword list. In the *Pocket Modern Welsh Dictionary* (King 2000), inflected irregular verb forms are contained in the dictionary entry. In addition, the stem of difficult verbs is indicated as exemplified in the following entry:

mwynhau (*stem* **mwynheu-**)
verbnoun
= enjoy

In the case of the inflected forms of *gwneud* 'do', however, King presents so much reduced forms that these can only be used in informal communicative situations (cf. King 1993, 1995, S. Heinz 1995, 1998, and section 4.1.1.).

In short, owing to the peculiarities of the usage of the Welsh verb, it remains a requirement for Welsh bi-directional general-purpose dictionaries to provide the speaker with some guidance on the usage of the verb inflection.

The best way to give safe instructions on verb inflection is to include the first and third person singular present in the dictionary entry. Particularly the third person is often unpredictable (cf. section 1.3.2.3.1.) for non-native speakers, but in the current communcative situation increasingly also for young native speakers (cf. section 4.1.1. under linguistic insecurity and increasing use of the periphrastic). However, this form is the basis for further verb inflection, such as the imperative.

The third person singular present is difficult when vowel affection occurs, as in *egyr* 'he opens' (< *agor*), *pair* 'he causes' (< *peri*), *bwyty* 'he eats' (< *bwyta*), *hyllt* 'he splits' (< *hollti*). In addition, *n* can geminate in the first person singular, i.e. the stem, but not necessarily in the third person singular, e.g. in *gofyn* -> *gofynnaf* -> *gofyn* 'to ask', *gorffen* -> *gorffennaf* -> *gorffen* 'to finish'. In other verbs this can be different (cf. section 1.3.2.3.1.), e.g. in *darllen* -> *darllenaf* -> *darllen*. Despite these unpredictabilities, a comprehensible or easily accessible list of all verbs cannot be found in any reference book, although relatively long lists are available in *Geiriadur yr Academi* and P.W. Thomas (1996). However, in the former, the access structure is not clear (cf. Griffiths, B. & D.G. Jones 1995: lxxv and section 4.2.) and basic verbs appear to be missing in both books, e.g. *gobeithio* 'to hope'. Since it is nearly impossible to compile a complete list of verbs, unless in a separate book (cf. D.G. Lewis 1995) or in a dictionary of verbs, it is advocated to regularly include the first and third person singular present in the dictionary entries. A similar approach was taken by S. Heinz (1994), although in an inefficient manner.

4.3.1.2. Valency, government of the verb, collocation and idioms

The presentation of the verb in dictionaries is of major interest, since it forms the structural centre of the sentence (cf. Buchholz/Beyrer et al. 1977: 1; Helbig/Schenkel 1973: 24ff.), a basic unit of any speech act.

Whereas the dependent subject is relatively easy to link to the verb in order to form simple sentences, this is not the case with the other dependents or complements. The relations between the verb and its other complements, e.g. objects, including oblique objects, *yn*-complements and adverbials are more complicated. All these syntactically based relations between the verb and its dependent elements are subsumed under the term syntactic valency (cf. section 1.3.2.2.1.). This term is also referred to as government of the verb.

In this section the syntactic and the semantic valency as well as idiom (cf. section 1.3.2.2.1.) form the subject of the analysis. Another term for semantic valency is collocation[2] (cf. sections 1.3.2.2.1. and 1.3.2.3.1.). Since both aspects of valency, and ideally also idiom, should be reflected in dictionary entries, as is explained in sections 1.3.2.2.1. and 1.3.2.3.1., they are analysed together in this section.

As is illustrated in section 1.3.2.3.1., the categorisation of verbs according to their syntactic behaviour by P.W. Thomas (1996) is limited. Aspects of the semantic behaviour of the Welsh verb are not mentioned, thus reflecting the state of linguistic description in this field. As far as I am aware, no Welsh term has been applied to the description of these phenomena either.

As a result, syntactic and semantic valency as well as idiom have largely been ignored in Welsh general-purpose dictionaries, that is to say, they do not belong systematically to their dictionary entries. This situation is illustrated by the following examples from *Y Geiriadur Cyfoes:*[3]

    cael, *v.* HAVE, GET, FIND
    cynnig, *v.* ATTEMPT. TRY. OFFER. PROPOSE.
      APPLY. BID.
    dyfod, dod, *v.* BECOME. COME.

The indication of minimal syntactic valency would include the word class label and the basic government, e.g. *cynnig rhywbeth i rywun* 'to offer something to someone' or *cynnig am* 'to apply'.

---

[2]   *Cyfosodiad* 'collocation' (cf. Griffiths, B. & D.G. Jones 1995) could be an appropriate Welsh term.

[3]   No comment will be made here as to the fact that the most uncommon and rather archaic form of *dod* 'to come' has been chosen as the headword.

In some cases, syntactic and semantic valency are arranged rather stochastically, e.g. in *Y Geiriadur Mawr*, 1987:

> **cael,** *be.* dyfod o hyd i, derbyn, meddu, ennill, cyrraedd, canfod. TO HAVE, TO GET, TO OBTAIN, TO GAIN, TO WIN, TO FIND.
>> Cael a chael. TOUCH AND GO.
>> Ar gael. TO BE HAD.

> **cynnig[1],** *be.* 1. ceisio, ymgeisio. TO ATTEMPT, TO TRY.
>> 2. estyn er mwyn rhoi, cyflwyno. TO OFFER.
>> 3. awgrymu rhywbeth (mewn cyfarfod). TO PROPOSE.

> **dyfod : dod : dŵad,** *be.* agosáu, dynesu, cyrraedd, digwydd. TO COME, TO BECOME, TO COME TO PASS.

In the entry of *cael*, there is no indication of syntactic valency. There is, however, an idiom cited, i.e. *cael a chael*, and an adverb formed by preposition + verbal noun, i.e. *ar gael*.

For *cynnig* syntactic valency is indirectly provided under 3. in the entry.

The headword *dyfod* is again left without even minimal syntactic valency, e.g. *dod at rywun* 'to come to someone', *dod i rywle* 'to come somewhere', *dod ar* 'come upon' (cf. below). Collocations would be *dod i gasgliad* 'to come to a conclusion', *dod i benderfyniad* 'to come to a decision'.

Occasionally, however, dictionary users have the benefit of some collocations in *Y Geiriadur Mawr*, such as in the following entry:

> **torri,** *be.* mynd yn ddarnau, darnio, rhannu, briwio, archolli; methu (mewn busnes). TO BREAK, TO CUT; TO GO BANKRUPT.
>> Torri enw. TO SIGN.
>> Torri ar. TO INTERRUPT.[4]
>> Torri dadl. TO SETTLE A DISPUTE.
>> Torri geiriau. TO UTTER WORDS.
>> Torri bedd. TO DIG A GRAVE.
>> Torri cytundeb. TO BRAKE AN AGREEMENT.

---

4   Whereas 'to interrupt' would rather be the equivalent to *torri ar draws*, *torri ar* has further meanings, e.g. 'to run somebody down'.

tynnu, *be.* achosi i ddod at, llusgo at, denu. TO PULL.
Yn tynnu ato. SHORTENING.
Tynnu llun. TO PHOTOGRAPH, TO SKETCH.

Although basic syntactic valency is excluded from the entries of *torri* and *tynnu*, some collocations made their way into them.

Confusion concerning valency and idiom is apparent in the dictionary entries of *Geiriadur yr Academi*:

> **offer**[2] *v.t.&i.* l. *v. t. (a)* cynnig; **to ~ sth to s.o., to ~ s.o. sth,** cynnig rhth i rn; **I was offered some wine,** cefais gynnig gwin; cynigiwyd gwin imi; **to ~ [up] some prayers to God,** offrymu gweddïau i Dduw; **to ~ oneself (for a post),** ymgynnig, eich cynnig eich hun (am swydd); **to ~ goods for sale,** cynnig nwyddau ar werth; **a house offered for sale,** tŷ ar werth; **to ~ to do sth,** cynnig gwneud rhth; *(b) (= try):* **to ~ resistance,** ceisio gwrthsefyll; *0:* **he offered to strike me,** cynigiodd fy nharo i; *N: occ:* mi cynigiodd fi; *Th:* **"offers to go",** "yn cynnig mynd". 2. *v. i.* ymgynnig; **if a good occasion offers,** os daw cyfle da.
>
> **come** *v.i.* **1.** *dod, F:* dŵad, *Lit:* dyfod; *(a)* **to ~ to a place,** dod i le, cyrraedd lle; *F:* **let 'em all ~; ~ one, ~ all,** croeso i bawb ddod; **he comes this way every week,** mae'n dod heibio bob wythnos; **he never comes to chapel,** nid yw byth yn dod i'r capel; *F: m* fydd byth yn t'wyllu'r capel; **coming!** dyma fi! 'rwy'n dod 'nawr! dŵad! **~ to/and see me tomorrow,** tyrd (dewch) i'm gweld i yfory; **to ~ for sth.** *N:* dod i nôl rhth, *S:* dod i mo'yn rhth, dod i ôl rhth, *M. W:* dod i mofyn rhth; **to ~ to s.o.,** dod at rn; *B:* **~ unto me,** deuwch ataf fi; **[...]**[5]

Whereas syntactic valency comes first in the entry for the headword *offer*, it is more difficult to discover for the headword *come*. Here the basic syntax for Welsh verbs of movement, i.e. *i* 'to' for moving to a place and *at* 'to' for moving to a person, is split. Whereas *i* comes first in the entry, *at* comes somewhere further down. Checking with other lexical items, e.g. *go*, basic syntactic valency may not occur at all in verb entries of *Geriadur yr Academi* (cf. Griffith 1995: 612-615). For the headword, i.e. the English verbs, however, minimal syntactic valency is regularly provided by the word class labels, such as *v.t.*

---

[5]   Selective representation from pp. 267-270.

308

The historical dictionary *GPC*[6] is the only Welsh lexicographical work which provides most cases of syntactic and semantic valency in its entries. As well as some idiom, the government of the verb and collocations are listed in alphabetical order under *Cfn.* 'combinations' (cf. below) without indicating any distinction between them. Nevertheless, for a historical dictionary which has other uses than general-purpose dictionaries, this is a justifiable approach. The following examples illustrate the way of displaying valency and some idioms in its entries:

caf, †cahaf, caffaf: cael, †cahel, caff-(a)el, caffu [Crn. *caf(f)os, cafes,* Llyd. C. *caf(f)out:* y bôn *caff-, cah-* < amr. Brth. **kab-* ar y gwr. **ghabh-* 'gafael'] *ba.;* fe'i defnyddir yn aml yn ei gwahanol ffurfiau o flaen *rh.bl.* a *be.* i gyfleu ystad oddefol, a'r *be.* hefyd fel *eg.*

   I. Derbyn, meddiannu, dod i feddiant, perchenogi, mwynhau; ennill, cipio, dal, adennill; dod o hyd i, darganfod, dod ar draws; cyrraedd, cyfarfod â: *to have, get, obtain, receive, &-c.; win, seize, regain; find, discover, come by, come across; reach, arrive at.*

   10g. *(Cpt)* B iii. 256, ismod. *cephitor.* did. hanaud ... ha *chepi.* hinn inguir. c. **1200** *LIDW* 5. 2, ef adele *kafael* y guasanaet en rat. **12-13**g. C 53. 13, Oes imi gan iessv *gaffv* guaessaf. *id.* 89. i, anhaut *caffael* clid. […][7]

2. Cenhedlu, beichiogi, peri geni, cynhyrchu, epilio; tarddu, deillio, hanfod: *to procreate, beget, conceive, produce, bring forth; derive, issue.*

   14g. *R* 1292. 20-1, Y nos vat y *kaat* or kyt orwed balch oronwy aerwalch oreu rinwed. *id.* 1299. 43-4. **1346** *LIA* 16, Y pedrieirch. Ar prophwydi. *agaffat* ac aanet ympechodev. c. **1400** *GP* 12, A'r mod hwnnw a *gaffat* wrth vod Lladin. **1547** *WS,* dyddgwyl vair Pan *gad,* conception of our lady. **1567** *TN* 18oa, Isaac a *gavas* laco. **1618** J. SALISBURY: *EH* 23, y *caed,* neu ycenhedled Mâb Duw. **1672 R.** Rho dy gorph ir ddaer lle *cafad.*

   Amr.: **celat*** : **cael** [lluniwyd bôn yr amr. hwn, a ddigwydd yn yr amserau amhff., grff. a grb., ar ddelw y be. *cael;* fe'i ceir yn gyff. yn y Deau, yn enw. ym Mynwy a Morg.]. **1651** SIÔN TREREDYN : *MDD* 59, efe a *celsei [sie]* fywyd tragwyddol.[…]

   Cfn.: fel *bf. gynorthwyol* + *be.* i gyfleu caniatad, bwriad, gweithred neu gyflwr yn y dyf., e.e. *caf fynd, caf weld,* &c. **cael a chael** : *to just manage it, to have a narrow shave, touch-&-go.* Ar lafar yn gyff. **c. ail** : *to be foiled of one's expectations, be disappointed.* Ar lafar yng Ngwynedd. **c. allan** : *to discover, find out, trace.* **1588** *Barn* xiv. 18. **1775** *W* d.g. *to know by inquiry.* **1784** M. WILLIAMS: S i. 199. **c. (ei) anadl (gwynt) (ato)** : *to get one's breath (back), breathe.* **1632** *D* d.g. *orthopnœa.* **c. (yr) annwyd** : *to catch cold.* **1759** J. EVANS: PF 19, 69. Ar lafar yn gyff. **c. ar lab** : *to obtain on credit.* Ar lafar yng Ngwynedd. **c. benthyg** : *to have the loan {of}, borrow.* **1632** *D* d.g. *commodatorius.* Ar lafar. **c. blaen ; c. y blaen (ar)** : *to have (be given) advantage; to have precedence or preference, excel, outdo, outrun.* **1632** *D* d.g. *præcurro, prægredior, prœuerto.* **1676** *W.* JONES: *GB* 23. **1699** T. JONES: *T P* 77. **1703** E. WYNNE: BC 30. **1778** *W* d.g. *to out-go.* **1782** D. WILLIAM : GMS 14. **c. blas ar:** *to enjoy.* **1703** E. WYNNE: *BC* 151. Ar lafar yn gyff. **c. bodd** : *to please, to win the approval of.* **14**g. *GDG* 211. **14**g. DGG² 64. **15**g. *H* 88a. 27. **1567** TN 214b. **c. cam** : *to be wronged, be dealt unfairly with.* **15**g. *Pen* 109, 54 (Lewis Glyn Cothi). **16**g.WLl 45. **1632** *D* d.g. *patrocinor.* Ar lafar yn gyff. **c. cas ar** : *to grow to hate.* Ar lafar yng Nghered. **c. cawell** : *to be jilted (of lover).* Ar lafar yn y Gogledd a Chered. **c. cefn** : *to see one's back, find someone's back turned, have opportunity when someone is absent.* **15**g. *Pen* 109, 58 (Lewis Glyn Cothi). Ar lafar. **c. ei gefn (ato)** : *to recover oneself, get over it; get started properly in business &c.,be set on one's feet.* Ar lafar yn gyff. **c. cennad** : *to have permission.* **1455-85** LGC 28. **1588** *Job* ii. es. **c. cip :** *to catch a glimpse.* Ar lafar. **c. codwm** : *to fall.* **1632** *D* d.g. *recido.* Ar lafar. **c. coel** : *to gain credence; obtain credit,* **1703** E. WYNNE : BC 134. **c. crap ar** : *to get a smattering of, get hold of.* Ar lafar yn gyff. **c. dolur (niwed)** : *to sustain an injury.* Ar lafar yn y Deau. **c. dychryn** = **c. ofn. c. gafael (ar)** : *to catch hold of, seize, grip, apprehend, discover, find.* **14**g. *R* 1272. 12. **1588** *Phil* iii. 13. **1632** *D* d.g. *apprehendo, comprehendo, deprehendo, inuado, occupo.* **c. y gair** o+be.: *to have the reputation of, be reputed to be.* **1685** *Art-lo.* **c. gan**+be.: *to induce to.* **15**g. *FfBO* 32. **c. gan Duw :** *God grant!* **14**g. *RC* xxxiii. 221. **1740** T. EVANS : D PO 98. **1793** *P* d.g. *cael.* **c. y gorau ar (o)** : *to get the better of, overcome, overpower.* **1536** LBS iv.376. **16**g. *Pen* 86, 199. **1778** *W* d.g. *to out-breathe one.* **Caffael y Groes,** gw. **caffael².** **c. gwared,** — **o** (ar, rhag): *to find deliverance; get rid of.* […] Ar lafar yn gyff. **c. yn ei feddwl :** *to conceive in one's mind, decide.* **13**g. *WM* 34. 7-8. **c. yn ei (i'w) gyngor :** *to determine, decide, resolve.* **13**g. *WM* 40. 17, 53. 28-9. **14**g. *GDG* 175. **1590** *RC* xlvi. 55. **ar gael :** *in existence, existing, extant, available.* **1776** D. ELLIS: *HI* 152. Ar lafar yn gyff. **ar g. a chadw :** *extant, preserved.*

---

  6   *GPC* is listed for comparison and exemplification in order to display the range of valency of Welsh verbs. The format of *GPC* was adapted to the width of the page in order not to waste too much space.

  7   Since it is very space-consuming to present the entire dictionary entry, a representative part of it has been selected.

cynigiaf, cynigaf: cynnig, cynigio [bnth. Llad. *condico*, Llyd. Diw. *kinnig*] *ba.* Estyn neu gyfleu *(peth)* i'w dderbyn neu i'w wrthod gan arall, cynwyno; gosod gerbron, gosod neu gyflwyno (penderfyniad) i'w gymeradwyo neu i'w anghymeradwyo (gan bwyllgor, *&c.*); cystadlu, ceisio; ymgeisio *(am); gwneud osgo* (i daro), bygwth (ergyd); taro, ymosod: *to offer, bid, tender, present; propose, move* (a *resolution, &c.*); *compete, attempt; apply (for); threaten (a blow); strike, set upon.*

c. **1200** *LIDW* 54. 4-5, A guedi er eisteter ena emae jaunt yr haulur *kenic* ydevnidieu jam etestion ay keidveit. *id. 121. 25,* 134. *26.* **13g.** *WM 30.* 26-8, *Kynnic* ywestei a phellynic y dwyn ar y cheuyn yr *Ilys. id.* 158. 29-31, A *chynnic* awnaethant wynteu idaw yr un a dewissei oe teir chwiored. *id.* 168. 5, Llawer o arueu a *gynigwyt* idaw. **13g.** *W ML* 83. *c.* **1300** *BD* 123, *kynnyc (cepit)* Heingyst a wnaeth trwy varyfle y benffestin. **14g.** *YCM 25,* ydoeth allan o'r gaer y *gynnic* ymlad un ac un. **14g.** *RB* ii. 315, 398. **1567** TW 183a, e *gynygawdd* yddwynt ariant. **1588** *Deut* **xx.** es., Bod yn rhaid *cynnig* heddwch yn gyntaf i bawb ond i bobl Canaan. **1595** *Egl Ph 100, rhac* iddo ei fwrw ei hun allan ... wrth *gynnic* gormod. **1632** *D d.g. do, ministro, offero, propono, tendo.* **1675** .R. JONES: *HCh* 25, cyn gynted ac y *cynnhygio ef* ddyfod i mewn, cau drws dy galon yn ei erbyn. **1703** *E.* WYNNE: *BC* 42, ni wiw i chwi *gynnyg* mynd trwodd â'ch teganeu gyda chwi. *id. 60, ac a* aeth i'm *cynnyg* i drachefn. **1759** T. THOMAS: *WWDd 10-11, mi* a *gynnigaf* . . . osod allan ychydig am druenus gyflwr Dyn trwy bechod. *id.* 98, *[c]ynnigodd* Satan... beri i Grist fwrw ei hun oddi ar Binacl y Deml. **1771** *PDPh* 57, *cynnigwch* ddwfr twymn iddo i'w yfed. **1776** *W* d.g. *to move, to offer or attempt.*

Cfn.: **cynnig cam :** *to offer abuse, wrong.* **15g.** H 109b. 5. **1774** H. JONES: *CH* 53. **1778** *W* d.g. *to offer abuse to one.* **c. o (ar) hyd braich :** *to offer something in the hope that it will not be accepted.* Ar lafar yn gyff. **c. tros (dros) ysgwydd :** *to offer half-heartedly (lit. to offer over the shoulder).* Ar lafar yn gyff.

deuaf, dof, doaf: dyfod, dod [y be. *dyfod* (< *dy-*+*bod³*), Crn. *devos (dos),* devones (*dones*), Llyd. C. *donet,* Llyd. Diw. *dont* (ar ddelw *monet, mont*) [...] un yn eu lle priodol] *bg.* a'i dilyn yn fynych gan yr ardd. *i* ac *at* ac *ar* yn dra chyff. gynt (*i* le ac *at* berson).

 I. (*a*) Symud, ymdaith, treiddio, &c., i ryw le neu gyrchfa neu at ryw berson neu bobl [...] *to come, arrive, sometimes fig.; come to a subject or section in a speech, &c.; occur, come to pass, happen, befall, betide; appear as a public figure or fulfiller of prophecy; issue, be descended (from)* [...]

10g. *(Cpt) B iii.* 256, Irni*didibid* ir\ oyr di. a, **10g.** *(Juv) B* vi. 206, di*cones* ihesu dielimlu pbetid / a guirdou pan *dibu.* [...]

(b) (Yn y modd grch. weithiau defnyddir y ferf yn rhetoregol i galonogi, croesawu ac annog (*Beibl.* fynychaf); hefyd i [...]

1567 *TN* 67a, *debre [:- dyred],* dilyn vi. **1588** *Gen* **xi.** 3, *deuwch* gwnawn briddfeini. [...]

 2. (o flaen yr ardd. *yn, o*) Newid ystad neu gynwr, datblygu (i ryw ffurf neu gyflwr arall): *to become, develop (into).*

1585 G. ROBERT: *DC [v],* pan *ddoeth* Cystennin Gymro yn Emherodr, [...]

Amr.: **dawaf: dawod** *[y ff. dawaf, dawant* wedi eu ffurfio o'r 3 un. *daw],* **13g.** *WM* 425. 16. **14g.** *Haf I, 10b.* [...]

Cfn.: **doed a ddêl (ddelo), del a ddêl, deled a ddelo, deued a ddêl :** *come what may, whatever comes or happens.* **1455-85** *LGC* 82. **1592** S. D. RHYS: *Inst [xvii].* **1630** *R.* LLWYD: *LIH* 67, 438. **1759** T. THOMAS: *WWDd* 194. **dyfod (dod) â :** *to bring, convey, come or carry with; bring forth (young); bring or induce (to believe, &c.). c.* **1200** *LIDW* 19. 31, 36. 14. **13g.** *WM* 17. 1-2. **14g.** *R* 1235.30-1. **l5g.** H 38b.5. **1588** *2 Sam* xviii. 27. **1632** -D d.g. *pario. c.* **1658** R. VAUGHAN: *E [vi].* **1681** S. HUGHES: *AC* 42. **1728** T. BADDY: *DDG* 2. **d. â chathod (-an) bach :** *to kitten, bring forth kittens.* **1722** *List* 189 d.g. *dyfod.* **1775** *W* d.g. *to kitten or kittle.* **d. â chenawon :** *to cub, wheip, litter.* **1632** *D* d.g. *pario.* **1772** *W* d.g. *to cub, to litter,* **d. â chwn :** *to wheip, litter.* **1722** *List* 189 d.g. *dyfod.* **1775** *W* d.g. *to litter,* **d. â chywion :** *to hatch chickens.* **1632** *D* d.g. *pario.* **1722** *List* 189 d.g. *dyfod.* **1774** *W* d.g. *to hatch chickens.* **d. âg ebol :** *to foal.* **1722** *List* 189 d.g. *dyfod.* **1773** *W* d.g. *to foal.* **d. â llo :** *to calve.* **1771** *W* d.g. *to calve.* **d. ag oen :** *to yean.* **1722** *List* 189 d.g. *dyfod.* **1794** *W* d.g. *to yean.* **d. â pher-chyll :** *to pig, litter.* **1632** *D* d.g. *pario.* **1722** *List* 189 d.g. *dyfod.* **1775** *W* d.g. *to litter,* **d. â rhai bychain :** *to bring forth young, kindle.* **1775** *W* d.g. *to kindle.* **d. am ben :** *to come upon (with hostile intent), fall upon, attach.* [...]⁸

Some dictionary entries in *GPC* contain information about syntactic valency immediately after the word class label as is illustrated by the examples below. This, however, does not form a regular part of entries in *GPC* (cf. GPC 1950 *General order and arrangement of the dictionary*):

---

8 This is a brief but representative selection of the dictionary entry for *dod* 'to come'.

arswydaf: arswydo [bf. yr e. *arswyd*] *bg.a.* a'i dilyn yn fynych gan yr ardd. *rhag* ac *at*.
Ofni'n fawr, brawychu, dychrynu; ofni â pharchedig ofn, parchu:
to fear greatly, dread [...]

deuaf, dof, doaf: dyfod, dod [y be. dyfod (< *dy-+bod³*), Crn. *devos* (*dos*), *devones*
(*dones*), Llyd. C. *donet*, Llyd. Diw. *dont* (ar ddelw *monet, mont*); [...] un yn eu lle
priodol] *bg.* a'i dilyn yn fynych gan yr ardd. *i* ac *at* ac *ar* yn dra chyff. gynt (*i* le ac *at*
berson).
　　1. (*a*) Symud, ymdaith, treiddio [...]
　　to come, arrive, sometimes fig.; come to a subject or section in a speech, [...]

Bg.a. means 'verb transitive/intransitive' and is followed by the explanation *a'i dilyn yn fynych
gan yr ardd. rhag ac at* 'and is often followed by the prepositions *rhag* and *at*'. Only for *dod ar*,
however, the semantic range is explained, namely further down under *Cfn.* 'combinations'. The
semantic difference concerning the relation between *dod* ac *i* and *dod* ac *ar* remains unexplained.

As a result, information about syntactic valency given before the equivalent of the target language is (a) not sufficiently elucidated and (b) rather casually provided. The question arises,
therefore, as to why this minimal syntactic information is not provided regularly and when given,
why not clearly explained?

It is interesting to discover that the insufficient presentation of the valency of the verb in Welsh
general-purpose dictionaries is somehow counter-balanced by other reference books, such as
Torri'r Garw. Idioms for Welsh Learners based on verbs (sic., C. Davies, 1995: selection from
pp. 49-61, 107, 137-143). In this book, syntactic and semantic valency are subsumed under
idioms. All together they are listed in alphabetical order, again without being distinguished from
each other:

CAEL
ar gael—available
　　Oes llysiau ffres ar gael heddiw?
　　Are there fresh vegetables available today?

ar gael a chadw—to have been preserved; to exist
　　Rydyn ni'n ffodus bod llawer o hen lawysgrifau ar gael a chadw o hyd.
　　We are fortunate that many old manuscripts have been preserved.

cael a chael—touch and go; a narrow shave
　　Enillodd Cymru'r gêm 13-12, ond cael a chael oedd hi, fel yr awgryma'r sgôr.
　　Wales won the game 13-12 but, as the score suggests, it was touch and go.

cael blaen tafod llym—to be reprimanded; to receive a talking to
　　Cafodd y bechgyn flaen tafod llym eu mam am ddod adre'n
　　hwyr y noson cynt.
　　*The boys were severely reprimanded by their mother for coming home late the previous
　　evening.*

cael blas ar—to acquire a taste for; to enjoy
　　Erbyn hyn rydyn ni'n cael blas ar arddio er nad oedd
　　gennym ddiddordeb i ddechrau.
　　By now we enjoy gardening although we didn't have any interest initially.

cael bys ym mhob brywes—to have a finger in every pie
Hoffai'r teulu gael bys ym mhob brywes yn y pentref.
The family liked to have a finger in every pie in the village.

cael bywyd ci—to have a dog's life; to be badly treated
Cafodd e fywyd ci gan ei wraig ac yn y diwedd fe wahanon nhw.
He had an awful life with his wife and in the end they separated.

cael caff gwag—to fail in one's efforts
Er iddo geisio ei orau i berswadio Mari i ddod allan, cael caff gwag wnaeth o yn y diwedd.
Although he tried to persuade Mari to come out, he failed in the end.

Mostly idioms and collocations, such as *cael blas ar*, are found under the verb *cael*. For *cynnig*, there are two idiomatic verbs listed first, followed by an idiom and then by the verb and its government:

CYNNIG
cynnig am swydd—to apply for a job
Penderfynodd Branwen gynnig am swydd newydd.
Branwen decided to apply for a new job.

cynnig ar—to attempt to
Doedd hi ddim yn ddoeth cynnig ar ddringo'r mynydd.
It wasn't wise to attempt to climb the mountain.

cynnig o hyd braich—to offer grudgingly or halfheartedly
Er i Geraint ddweud y gallwn i aros yn ei dŷ, teimlwn mai cynnig o hyd braich ydoedd.
Although Geraint said that I could stay in his house, I felt that it was a halfhearted offer.

cynnig rhywbeth i—to offer something to
Cynigiais lifft adref iddi.
I offered her a lift home.

DOD
ar ddod—about to come
Roedd y trên ar ddod.
The train was about to come.

daw tro ar fyd—things will change
Mae e'n ifanc ac yn llwyddiannus nawr, ond daw tro ar fyd, coeliwch chi fi.
He is young and successful now, but things will change, believe me.

dod â—to bring
Dewch â'r plant i'r parti.
Bring the children to the party.

dod â chŵn bach/chathod bach/chywion—to whelp/to kitten/ to hatch chickens etc.
Mae'n ymddangos y bydd yr âst yn dod â chwn bach cyn diwedd yr wythnos.
It seems that the bitch will have pups before the end of the week.

dod â dau ben llinyn ynghyd—to make ends meet
Er ei bod yn dlawd, llwyddai'r farn i ddod â dau ben llinyn
ynghyd rywsut.
Although she was poor, the mother somehow managed to make ends meet.

dod allan o gragen—to come out of one's shell
Ar ôl mynd i'r coleg, daeth y ferch allan o'i chragen.
After she went to College, the girl came out of her shell.

dod ar draws—to come across
Daeth y ferch ar draws y fodrwy wrth lanhau'r tŷ.
The girl came across the ring whilst cleaning the house.

Judging by what has been deemed necessary for the description of verbs relating to their syntactic and semantic valency in sections 1.3.2.2.1. and 1.3.2.3.1., dictionary users will be disappointed when looking into Welsh lexicographical works: *Y Geiriadur Cyfoes, Spurrell,* and the *Works-Dictionary* offer nothing but the verb itself.

Although *Y Geiriadur Mawr* and the two learners' dictionaries (H. Gruffudd 1998, King 2000) do not indicate any syntactic sub-groups of Welsh verbs, the government of the verb and collocations, however, may be included on an irregular basis. Nevertheless, shift of government linked to different semantic meanings, such as in *cynnig rhywbeth i* 'to offer something to' or *cynnig am* 'to apply', is not sufficiently presented.

As a result, the actual range of syntactic and semantic valency of a given verb can only be deduced from the entries of the historical dictionary *GPC*, the reference book of C. Davies (1995), and to some extent from *Geiriadur yr Academi.*

GPC regularly supplies, at least, the syntactic sub-groups transitive and intransitive verbs with the word class labels *ba* 'verb transitive', *bg* 'verb intransitive' or *ba.g/bg.a* 'verb transitive.intransitive/intransitive.transitive'. The dictionary may, however, also specify the government of the verb immediately after the word class label. In addition, the range of syntactic and semantic valency and some idioms can be obtained from the ample examples of usage of a given verb provided in alphabetical order under 'combination' in the entries of *GPC*. Their alphabetical arrangement attests for the lack of a comprehensive concept of the categorisation of Welsh verbs based on their syntactic complementation (cf. section 1.3.2.3.1.) on the one hand and its distinction from semantic complementation on the other.

In the publication of C. Davies, the government of the verb - in case it takes a preposition as connector to complements - together with collocations and idioms is subsumed under idioms.

Geiriadur yr Academi does not reflect a systematic approach of valency either. Syntactic valency is not necessarily part of its dictionary entries. Instead, lexical units which exemplify syntactic or semantic usage of a given verb or its idioms are sometimes abundantly included in the dictionary entries, but without a clear access structure.

Altogether, in none of the Welsh bilingual general-purpose dictionaries the syntactic sub-groups of verbs are indicated. The maximum information on valency is provided by the historical dictionary *GPC*. One may also find the government of a given verb in *Geiriadur yr Academi*. The search procedure for this discovery, however, is somewhat laborious. Generally, a clear differentiation between government, collocations and idiom does not appear to have been made in those works which include guidance in the use of Welsh verbs.

Since most dictionary users do not have the historical dictionary at home, and may not have the restricted, since uni-directional *Geiriadur yr Academi* either, they will mainly depend on the smaller bi-directional general-purpose or learners' dictionaries. These, however, cannot be considered remotely adequate for the needs of any dictionary user.

In the following table, an attempt has been made to suggest a categorisation of verbs according to their syntactic and semantic behaviour which may be used for lexicographical purposes:

Syntactic and semantic valency of the Welsh verb in selection - Falensi'r ferf Gymraeg

	intransitive - cyf-lawn (PWT, 401)	transitive - anghyflawn (PWT, 401)	verbs governing prepositions - berfau arddodiadol (PWT, 560)	verbs to be complemented - berfau dibeniadol (PWT, 401)	verbs governing other verbs	verbs governing adverbs - berfau gan adferfol (PWT, 402)	collocation - cyfosodiad (semantic valency)	idioms - priod-ddull
adnabod 'to know'	x	x (GPC)	wrth (CD)					adnabod rhywun ym mhig y frân, adnabod y bluen (CD)
aflonyddu 'to disturb'	x (GPC)*	x (GPC)	ar (O, CD, PTW)					
agor 'to open'	x (GPC)	x (GPC)						
anghofio 'to forget'		x (BG, GPC)	am (CD)		x			
arbenigo 'to specialise'	x (GPC)	x (GPC)	yn/mewn, yn/ar (BG)					
aros 'to wait'	x	x (GPC)	am, ar (GPC), wrth (GPC), i m[9] wneud rb (PWT)	yn; yn ... am				
aros 'to dwell upon'	x							aros ar draed, aros yn y gwt (CD)
arswydo 'to fear'		x (GPC)	rhag (CD), at (GPC)		x			
barnu 'to judge'	x (GPC)	x (BG)	wrth					
bod 'to be'	x		o blaid, yn erbyn	yn				
bod â 'to have'		x					bod ag angen, ~ eisiau	
bod am 'to want'		x						
bod ar 'to owe'		x					bod ar fai,* ~ goll, ~ gael, ~ frys, ~ dân	
bod gan/gyda 'to have'		x						

---

9   *rn* stands for *rhywun* 'someone' and *rb* for *rhywbeth* 'something'.

Entry					
bod yn gefn 'to support'		i			
brifo 'to hurt'	x (GPC)				
bwyta 'to eat'	x				bwyta mêl o'r cwd (CD)
cael 'to have, get, to be allowed to'	x	oddi wrth, trwy, at, i, gan (BG)	x	cael cinio, ~ blas ar, ~ hwyl am, ~ mynediad i, ~ cas ar, ~ gair â, ~ goleuni ar, ~ golwg ar, ~ gwybod gan, ~ yn euog, ~ yn ei feddwl, ~ plant (CD)	cael llond bol ar/o, ~ a chael, ~ achlust, ~ ail, ~ bachiad, ~ blaen tafod llym, ~ bys ym mhob brywes, ~ caff gwag, ~ ei thraed dani, ~ ei wynt ato, ~ ffit binc, ~ hyd fy nhafod, llaw drom, ~ pen llinyn ar, ~ rhwydd hynt, ~ y blaen ar ~ traed, ~ y ddau ben llinyn ynghyd, ~ y llaw uchaf ar, ~ yn brin, ~ y maes ar, ~ y maen i'r wal, ~ y gorau ar/o, ~ gwynt ar, ~ rhagor ar, ~ tafod gan (CD)
cael gwared 'to rid of, to get rid of'		â 'to rid of'; i; o (Ô), ar (Ô)		cael hwyl	
cael gafael 'to get hold of'		ar			
canu 'to sing'	x			canu cloch, ~ offeryn, ~ clodydd (CD)	canu ar ei fwyd ei hun, ~ cnul ar, ~ corn, ~ crwth i fyddar, ~ cywydd y gwcw, ~'n iach i (CD)
ciniawa 'to dine'	x (PWT)				
cludo 'to transport'	x (PWT)	at, i (and other prep. of direction)			
codi 'to rise, lift, raise'	x	i		codi arian ar/at, ~ calon, ~ braw/chwant/blas/awydd ar, ~ clustiau, ~ siawns (CD)	codi a gostwng, ~ aeliau, ~ bwganod, ~ bys i/at, ~ bys bach, ~ canu, ~ cefn, ~ cloch, ~ cnoi ar (CD)
codi ar 'to charge'	x		x		
cofio 'to recall'	x (GPC)	am, at			cofio afflhw o ddim (CD)
credu 'to believe'	x (GPC)	yn/mewn; o (GPC), ar (GPC)			

Verb							
creu 'to create'	x	x					
crynu 'to quiver, shake'	x (PWT)	x (GPC)					
cydnabod 'to acknowledge, recognise'	x						
cyfansoddi 'to compose'	x						
cyfeirio 'to address, refer'	x (GPC)	x (GPC)	at				
cyflwyno 'to introduce'	x		i		cyflwyno hawl, ~ dogfen, ~ hysbysiaeth		
cyfrif 'to count'	x		â, am, i (GPC)				
cymryd 'to take'	x				cymryd lle		
cymryd ar 'to pretend'	x						
cymryd at 'to enamour'	x						
cynllunio 'to design, plan'	x						
cynnig 'to offer'	x		rb i m (BG)				~ o hyd braich (CD)
cynnig am 'to apply'	x						
chwarae 'to play'	x (PWT)	x	ar (BG), â/am/dros (O)		chwarae cast ar, ~ blerwm-blerwm, ~ teg, ~ siawns (CD)	x	chwarae chwiw â, ~ bodiau, ~ chwic chwiw, ~ i ddwylo'i gilydd, ~ mig, ~ plant, ~ troi chwerw, ~'r diawl, ~'r ffôn ddwybig
chwynnu 'to weed'	x						

Verb								
chwythu 'to blow'	x	x (BG)					chwythu bygyth-ion, ~ trwyn	~ yng nghlust rhywun
dal 'to hold, to keep'	x (GPC)	x	at, i, ar (PWT)			x	dal anadl, ~ anmwyd, ~ bws/trên, â perthynas â (CD)	dal pen rheswm gyda, ~ ar y camfa, ~ cannwyll i, ~ craff ar, ~ dan, ~ dwylo, ~ ei drwyn ar y maen (CD)
dal allan 'to maintain'	x							
darllen 'to read'	x	x						darllen ffawd (CD)
datblygu 'to develop'	x (GPC)	x (GPC)		yn (PWT)				
dawnsio 'to dance'	x	x (GPC)						
dechrau 'to begin, to start'	x	x (CD)	ar	yn	x			
derbyn 'to receive, accept'	x	x	gan/oddi wrth (CD)					
dewis 'to choose'	x	x			x			dewis rhwng y diawl a'i gwt (CD)
dianc 'to escape'	x	x (GPC)	rhag; o (GPC), ar (GPC)					
diflannu 'to disappear'	x (PWT)	x (GPC)						diflannu fel iâr i ddodwy
disgleirio 'to shine'	x (PWT)							
dod 'to come'	x (PWT)		at, i (and other prep. of direction); ar (PWT)	yn			~ i gasgliad, ~ dod i benderfyn-iad	dod ar ofn, ~ ar warthaf, ~ at ei goed, ~ at ei stumoch, ~ drwy deg (CD)
dod â 'to bring'	x						dod â chwn bach/cathod ... (CD)	dod â dau ben llinyn ynghyd (CD)
dod ar draws 'to find'	x							

Verb							
dod dros ben 'to overcome'	x (CD)						
dod i 'to reach, to get'	x	â				dod i arfer â, ~ ben â, ~ oed, ~ nabod, ~ feddiant	dod i ben ei denmyn, ~ y dalar
dod o hyd 'to find'		i					
dodi 'to inflict'	x (GPC)				yma 'to place'		
dotio 'to dot'	x	at; am (GPC), ar (CPG)					
dweud 'to say'		wrth, am (Ó); i (GPC)					dweud y drefn
dychmygu 'to imagine'	x (GPC)						
dygymod 'to put up (with)'	x (GPC)	â					
dyrchafu 'to elevate, promote'	x						
dysgu 'to learn, teach'	x	gan (GPC), rb i m	yn	x			dysgu ar gof, ~ pader i berson
edrych ar 'to look'	x (GPC)						
edrych ar 'to watch'	x (GPC)						
edrych am 'to search'	x (GPC)						
edrych at 'to attend'	x (GPC)						
edrych ymlaen 'look forward'	x	at					
effeithio 'to effect'	x (GPC)	ar	yn (PWT)				

eistedd 'to sit'	x	x (GPC)	i, ar		wrth (PWT)			
ennill 'to win'	x	x (GPC)					ennill arian, ~pwysau, ~iawndal, ~bywolaeth	
enwebu 'to nominate'	x				yn (PWT)			
enwi 'to name'	x				yn (PWT)		enwi darnau	
ethol 'to elect'	x				yn (PWT)			
ffurfio 'to form'	x				yn (PWT)			
gadael 'to leave'	x		i		yn (PWT)			~ ar ynys anial
gadael mewn ewyllys 'to bequeath'	x		i					
gafael 'to grasp'	x	x (GPC)	yn/mewn		yn (PWT)			
galw 'to call'	x		ar rn am rb		yn (PWT)			
geni 'to be born'	x				yn (PWT)			
gorwedd 'to lie'	x				yn (PWT)			
graddio 'to graduate'	x	x (GPC)			yn (PWT)			
gwaedu 'to bleed'	x (PWT)	x (GPC)						
gwasanaethu 'to serve'	x (PWT)	x (BG)	ar, i, o (GPC)					
gwasgu 'to pressurise'	x	x (PWT)	ar, at (GPC), wrth (GPC), yn (GPC)					
gwasgu at 'to snuggle'		x						

Verb							
gwegian 'to dodder'	x (PWT)						
gweiddi 'to shout'	x	x (PWT)	ar rm am rb (GPC)				
gweld 'to see'	x			yn (PWT)			
gweld eisiau 'to want, to miss'	x						
gwneud 'to do'	x (GPC)	x		yn (PWT)			gwneud ei orau glas, ~ cawl o bethau
gwneud cam 'to wrong'	x	â (O)					
gwneud iawn 'to atone'			am (BG)				
gwywo 'to wit'	x (PWT)	x (GPC)					
gyrru 'to drive, send'	x	x (PWT)	at, i (and other prep. of direction)				gyrru i'w aped
gyrru ar 'to prosecute'	x	x				gyrru ar ffo	
hoffi 'to like'	x (GPC)	x		yn (PWT)			
hollti 'to split'	x (GPC)	x				hollti geiriau	hollti blew am
hyfforddi 'to coach, to train'	x (PWT)	x			x		
lladd 'to kill'	x (PWT)					lladd gwair	
lladd ar 'to denounce'	x	x					
llenwi 'to fill'	x	x					
llewygu 'to faint'	x (PWT)	x (GPC)					

lliwio 'to colour'	x		yn (PWT)				
llosgi 'to burn'	x (PWT)						
llunio 'to construct, draw'	x		yn (PWT)				
llygru 'to corrupt; to pollute'	x (PWT)	ar (GPC)					
magu 'to nurture'	x		yn (PWT)		magu plu		
marw 'to die'	x (PWT)						
methu 'to fail'	x (GPC)	(â)		(x)			
mwynhau 'to enjoy'	x		yn (PWT)				
mynd 'to go'	x (PWT)	at, i (and other prep. of direction)	yn; yn … am/i/at				
mynd â 'to take'							
mynd am dro 'to stroll'	x	at/i					
mynd ar 'to get'	x				mynd ar y sbri, ~ drywydd, ~ frys, ~ pererin-dod, ~ ffo, ~ goll, ~ led, ~ nerfau, ~ dân	mynd ar droed cadno	mynd ar ôl ysgyfarnog, ~ dros ben llestri, ~ i ganlyn y llif
mynd rhagddo 'to progress'							
mynd ymlaen 'to proceed'							
newid 'to change'	x		yn (PWT)	x	newid lle â		newid er gwaeth

Verb								
ordeinio 'to ordain'	x	x (GPC)		yn (PWT)				
paentio 'to paint'	x	x		yn (PWT)				
palu 'to dig'	x (PWT)	x (PWT)						
para 'to last'	x			yn	x			
pendwmpian 'to drowse'	x (PWT)							
penodi 'to appoint'	x (GPC)	x		yn (PWT)				
perthyn 'to belong'	x (GPC)	x (GPC)	i					
petruso 'to hesitate'	x (PWT)				x			
pwyso 'to weigh'	x (GPC)	x (PWT)	ar					
rhoi 'to give'	x	x	i/ar	yn (PWT)		yma 'to put'	rhoi cyfraith (ar)	rhoi gorau i, ~ cildwrn, ~'r ffidl yn y tô, ~ bys yn llygad (CD)
rhoi ar herw 'to outlaw'		x	am?					
siarad 'to talk'	x	â ... am					siarad aflan	siarad trwy ei het, siarad o'r frest, ~ yn ei gefn, ~ yn ei gyfer, ~ wrth y pwys a byw, ~ trwy'r trwch, ~ siprys, ~ dan ddannedd, ~ dan ddwylo, ~ mewn damhegion (CD)
siglo 'to shake'	x	x (PWT)						
swnio 'to sound'	x		yn (PWT)					
symud ymlaen 'to move on'			yn (PWT)					
synhwyro 'to sense'	x	x		yn (PWT)				synhwyro cyfeiriad y gwynt
syrthio 'to fall'	x	x	i	yn (PWT)			syrthio i'sgu, ~ mewn cariad	syrthio ar dir garegog (CD)

syrthio ar 'to devolve, to fall out'	x					
taro 'to hit'	x	yn erbyn	yn (PWT)			taro'r hoelen ar ei phen, ~ gair ar bapur (CD)
torri 'to break'	x (PWT)	oddi ar (BG)	yn (CD)		torri syched, ~ ffos, ~ calon, ~ gofyn-ion, ~ cig, ~ dannedd (CD), ~ dadl, ~ geiriau (GM), ~ enw (ar, BG)	torri ar yr edau, ~ asgwrn cefn gwaith, ~ crib, ~ cyt, ~ dadl, ~ iaith, geiriau â, ~ gwynt, ~ garw, ~ tir newydd (CD)
torri ar 'to interrupt'	x					
torri allan 'to erupt'	x					
trefnu 'to arrange, organise'	x		yn (PWT)	x		
troi 'to turn'	x	at/i	yn (PWT)			troi o'r neilltu, ~ cleddyfau'n sachau, ~ clust fyddar i, ~ cof, ~ ei fol at yr haul, ~ fel cwpan mewn dŵr, ~'r drol trwy, ~'r ffantol, ~'r stori, ~'r tu min at, ~ trwyn ar (CD)
troi llygaid 'to goggle'	x					
troi heibio 'to cease to use'	x (CD)					
trwyddedu 'to license'	x		yn (PWT)	x		
tyfu 'to grow'	x (PWT)		yn			
tyngu 'to swear'	X	i/wrth (CD)			tyngu llw	
tyngu anudon 'to commit perjury'	x					
yfed 'to drink'	x (PWT)					yfed ar ei dalcen (CD)

ymarfer 'to practise'	x	x	â (PWT)		x
ymddangos 'to appear'			i m (PWT)	yn (PWT), gerbron	
ysgrifennu 'to write'	x	x	ar/i		
ystyried 'to consider'	x			yn (PWT)	y

°   A number of verbs are differently classified in *GPC* and PWT. This may perhaps be due to different definitions of the category of intransitive verbs.

*   Units formed with *ar* 'on' and *dan* 'under', e.g. *ar dro* 'from time to time', are difficult to assign to the different word classes. 120 of such units were not classified in *GysGair*, about 30 were assigned to adjectives, about 35 to adverbs. Some were classified as prepositions and some were assigned to more than one word class. Therefore, the classification of the complement of the verb remains somewhat problematic when introduced by *ar, dan*.

BG = Griffiths, B. & D.G. Jones, 1995, *Geiriadur yr Academi*, Caerdydd.

CD = Davies, C, 1996, *Torrir 'r Garw. Idioms for Welsh Learners based on the verb-noun*, Llandysul.

GPC = *Geiriadur Prifysgol Cymru*

Ó = Ó Dohartaigh, Cathair, 1997, *CysGair*, Bangor.

PWT = Thomas, P.W., 1995, *Gramadeg y Gymraeg*, Caerdydd.

Since the indication of the sub-categories of the verbs is limited in the dictionaries and grammar books used here (cf. above), it is likely that the valency of individual verbs is not completely registered in this table.

Looking once more at the dictionary entries presented above and linking them to the problem of reflecting the basic syntactic and semantic use of verbs within them, it becomes clear that the provision of valency would not take up unnecessary space. More importantly, it would provide basic information in order to ensure the encoding function of the dictionaries. This would thus make a whole range of vocabulary easily applicable as illustrated by the examples proposed in the following:[10]

> **cynnig** (cynigi-; cynnig), *v.tr.*[11] to propose; *pr.*[12] ~ **rhywbeth i rywun** to offer; ~ **am** to apply.

> **dod** (do-, deu-, daw-; daw), *v.itr.*[13] to come; *pr.* ~ **at rywun** to come to someone; ~ **i rywle** to come to somewhere, *other dir. acc. to prep.*;[14] ~ **ar** come upon; *adv.*[15] ~ **yn nes** to come closer; *c.*[16] ~ **yn rhywbeth/un** 'to become some-one/thing'; ~ adj.; *coll*[17] ~ **i gasgliad** to come to a conclusion *i.*[18] ~ **dod at ei goed** to come to one's right senses...

> **dod â**, *v.tr.* to bring; *coll.* ~ **â chŵn** to whelp, *acc. other animals*;[19] *i.* ~ **dau ben llinyn ynghyd** to make ends meet.

> **dod i ben**, *v.itr.* to end; *v.tr.* to finish; *pr.* ~ â; *i.* ~ **ei dennyn** to reach the end of his tether.

Minimum information is also provided by the smallest Breton/English - English/Breton dictionary (Delaporte 1995). When no additional information is given, then the direct object follows the verb or a look under the reverse section reveals necessary facts:

> **chalañ** ['ʃa:lã] *v.* **1.** to worry; **en em ch. (gant)**, to get uneasy, to worry (about); **2.** to be anxious to (used in neg: **ne oa ket chalet da chom,** he was not anxious to stay).

> **worry** *v. (cause w.)* nech*iñ*, chal*añ*, tregas*iñ*.
> **run** (ran, run) *v.* redek, (of liquid) ber*añ*, diver*añ*; (of machine) mont (*radic.* a-) en-dro; **r. away**, skar*añ*, tec'h*el*.

---

[10] The examples also enlcose the indication of the respective verb inflection.
[11] Verb transitive.
[12] Verb governing a preposition.
[13] Verb intransitive.
[14] Other directions according to the meaning of further prepositions.
[15] Adverb.
[16] Verb to be complemented.
[17] Collocation.
[18] Idiom.
[19] Accordingly other animals.

The provision of verb inflection as well as syntactic and semantic valency ensures the decoding and encoding function of the dictionary. In addition, it improves the potential contribution of a dictionary to the development of linguistic confidence as well as to the construction of linguistic and cultural identity (cf. section 4.1.2.3.). Linguistic devices, such as morphological, syntactic, semantic, and discourse structures form a culture-specific way of perceiving reality, a process which is part of the construction of identity. With such devices, members of a specific society maximise the expression of their common experiences. As a result, particularly syntactic and semantic valency as well as idioms belong to what furnishes the language with a soul which makes it lovable to the native speakers and learners and distinct to foreigners.

Dictionaries as popular repositories of the lexicon of a language and guide to its potential usage are markedly suited and qualified to give way to linguistic confidence and cultural identity. Consequently, if they fail to reflect the inflection, syntactic and semantic valency of the Welsh verb these are reduced in their sentence and identity-constructing functions. In addition, in view of Wales' English neighbourhood, its high percentage of learners of Welsh who can rarely communicate with native speakers (cf. section 4.1.1.), the valency system of the Welsh verb and its idioms are liable to converge easily with the English system. Moreover, the English system is not only adequately described in numerous reference books, but also omnipresent everywhere.

To sum up: according to their specific syntactic behaviour, seven types of verbs may be distinguished in Welsh dictionary entries (cf. a-g in section 1.3.2.3.1.B). For semantic reasons idiomatic verbs and collocations should be included in the dictionaries (linguistic confidence, cf. section 4.1.2.3.). Phrasal verbs and idioms may be considered according to the intended size of the dictionary. Where there is limited space, the priority has to be given to idiomatic verbs, since they are frequently used and cover basic semantic meanings in the Welsh language. They have to be treated as individual lexical items which feature a particular government.

Next in the hierarchy of importance come collocations, since the combination of their constituents are semantically unpredictable, although they syntactically follow the governmental rules of their base verb. Another reason to include them is that they themselves can impose a government on following lexical items. In addition, collocations, as do idiomatic verbs and idioms, express particular concepts of the Welsh language which make it distinct to others and constitutes strongly to the construction of linguistic and cultural identity (cf. above and section 4.1.2.3.).

That is why idioms should be included in dictionaries as soon as the size of the dictionary may allow. They are representatives of the wealth of the language conceptually, semantically and syntactically.

May be all that is needed for Welsh general-purpose dictionaries with regard to valency is the inclusion of large parts of works, such as *Torri'r Garw. Idioms for Welsh Learners based on verbs* (sic., C. Davies, 1995). Although distinctions between the individual verb categories remain fuzzy, a classification which provides a good guide to the uses and applications of verbs through dictionary references is also entirely feasible.

4.3.2.   The Welsh noun[1]
4.3.2.1. Gender inflection

Since it is known that the *gender* of Welsh nouns can vary, it would be useful to provide dictionary users with the most significant reasons for changes in order to enable them to use this part of the lexicon correctly and prevent misunderstanding.

Close scrutiny of the dictionaries in use reveals, however, that this matter has not been treated with sufficient care so far. Whereas the fact of varying gender is often indicated as 'egb',[2] the context which causes this variation is mostly lacking.

This is always true for dialectally based changes. As gender variations present in the use of dialect do not pose a major obstacle to general comprehensibility, however, no particular emphasis will be placed upon this phenomenon.

Problems arise when shifts of gender are linked to different semantic meanings; a phenomenon which is often not satisfactory indicated. Although some dictionary entries in *Y Geiriadur Cyfoes* provide full information, e.g. for *gwaith* 'work, occurrence', this is not the case in the following examples:

> **ewyllys,** (-iau, -lon), *n.f.* WILL. DESIRE.
> TESTAMENT.

> **golwg,** (-ygon), *n.f.m.* SIGHT. VIEW.
> ELEVATION. APPEARANCE
> *pl.* EYES
> *golwg doriadol,* SECTIONAL VIEW
> *golwg ochrol,* SIDE VIEW

The situation is better in *Y Geiriadur Mawr*. Nevertheless, the lexical item *golwg* (cf. below) and others remain undifferentiated:

> **ewyllys,** l. *eb.*[3] *ll.*-iau. datganiad mewn
> ysgrifen o'r hyn y dymuna person
> ei wneud â'i eiddo ar ôl ei farw,
> cymynrodd, llythyr cymyn, testa-
> ment. WILL.
> > 2. *eg.*[4] y gallu i ddewis a phender-
> > fynu, dymuniad, pwrpas. ewyll-
> > ys rydd. DESIRE, WILL.
> > Rhyddid ewyllys. FREE WILL.

---

[1]   I would like to take this opportunity of thanking William Ll. Griffith, Dinbych/Wales, for his helpful comments on this section.
[2]   The abbreviation 'egb' means *enw gwrywaidd/benywaidd* and indicates that the noun can act in both genders.
[3]   *Eb* stands for *enw benywaidd* 'feminine'.
[4]   *Eg* stand for *enw gwrywaidd* 'masculine'.

golwg, *egb. ll.* golygon. l. y gallu i
weld, trem. SIGHT.
   2. drych. APPEARANCE.
   3. golygfa. VIEW.
   O'r golwg. OUT OF SIGHT.
   Golygon. EYES.

ton[1], *eb. ll.*-nau. ymchwydd dŵr,
gwaneg. WAVE.

ton[2], l. *eg.* tir porfa sydd heb ei droi yn
ddiweddar, gwndwn, gwyn-dwn.
LAY-LAND.
   2. *eb.* croen, arwyneb. SKIN, SURFACE.

That the manner in which semantic variation is treated is not necessarily linked to the size of any particular dictionary becomes apparent when looking at *GPC*[5] and *Y Geiriadur Bach* (1986). As usual, the first supplies abundant information, but does not make a gender-coupled distinction in cases like *ewyllys*:

ewyllys [y bôn *ewyll-+trf.* amrywiol *-ys, -is, -us, -wys;* am. y bôn *ewyll-,* cf. Crn. *awel, awell* 'blys', H. Lyd. *aiul,* gl. *ultro,* Llyd. C. *eoull, youll* 'awydd, dymuniad' o'r gwr. **au-, *auē̆-, *auēi-* 'dymuno, chwennych'] *eb.g.* 11. *-iau, -ion.*
   l. *(a)* y gynneddf mewn dyn sy'n mynnu (penderfynu, cymell, ymroi, cydsynio, &c.) fel y bo'r weithred neu'r ymddygiad o fodd ac nid o anfodd, bwriad pwyllog a sefydlog, sef gwir fwriad calon, bryd neu feddwl bwriadus, yr hyn a fynnir (a geisir, a ddymunir, &c.); awdurdod (hawl, gallu) i ddewis a phenderfynu; gallu'r meddwl i reoli'r nwydau a'r cyffroadau elfennol, &c. ; awydd, chwant, dymuniad, tueddfryd; hyfrydwch: *will, what is willed,* &c; *volition; will-power; desire, inclination, urge; pleasure, delight.*
   c. **1200** *LIDW* 47. 9-10, nidoes keureith erug egil a gilid namin *evvlis* diu. *id.* 134. 29-135. l, ar ynuyt ny ellyr kymell dym namyn y *ewyllys.* **13g.** *WM* 53. 20-I, doro dy urenhinaeth yny *ewyllus.* [...]
   (b) Chwant (bwyd, &c.), blys (cnawdol) neu gyflawniad blys, nwyd: *appetite, lust or fulfilment of lust, passion.*
   c. **1200** *LIDW* 40. 10, apan del *yeuellys.* yellug ar ellenlyeyn. **13g.** *YBH* la, y serchawl damunedic *ywyllus* ymdanaw. **14g.** [...]
   (c) Tynged, ffortun: *fate, fortune.*
   14g. *BT* 215, yr ymchwelawd yr *ewyllys* dracheuyn
   2. Llythyr cymyn, ewyllys ddiwethaf, dogfen gyfreithiol a lofnodir gan berson wrth gymynnu neu rannu ei eiddo erbyn ei farw: *(legal) will, last will and testament.*
   1632 J. DAVIES: *LIR* 120, gosod dy dŷ mewn trefn, a gwna dy *ewyllys* a'th lythyr cymmyn. **1672** J. LANGFORD: *HDdD* 490, Trefna hefyd dy achoision [sie] bydol . . . trwy wneuthur dy *Ewyllys.* **1710** *LIGG (Gos)* 13, Na ddyfynner neb i amryw Lysoedd i [...]
   Amr.: **gwyllys** [drwy golli'r llaf. ar ddechrau ewyllys a bod yr *w* > *gw*]. **l6g.** *HG* 36. **1588** *CLIC* ii. 10. **1672** R. PRICHARD: *Gw* 89. **1688** S. HUGHES: *TSP 100,* 219. **1750** J. THOMAS: *AIG* 11. **1752** J. THOMAS: *FG* 60, 111. **1764** DEWI NANTBRÂN: *CB vi. 12,* 7i. [...]
   Cfn.: **ewyllys y cnawd :** *the will or desire of the flesh.* **1567** *TN* 121a. **1588** *lo* i. 13. **1620** *Eff* ii. 3. yr e. **gyffredin :** *the general will.* **20g.** e. da : *good will or pleasure, affection, benevolence, kindness, favour; offertory.* **13g.** *YBH* 45a. **14g.** *R* 1152. 35. **14g.** *HMSS* i. 46, 146, 190. **1567** *TN* 83b, 291a, 293a. **1567** G. ROBERT: *GC* 7. **1588** *Salm* lxxxix. 17, cxiv. 16, *Diar* xiv. 9, *Eccius* xlv. 29, 2 *Mac* xiv. 37, *i Cor* vii. 3. [...]

Y Geiriadur Bach, on the other hand, provides the gender-coupled differentiation in the meaning of *ewyllys* in the same way as does *Y Geiriadur Mawr* (cf. above).

The entries are very similar in both dictionaries. Differences between them are apparent, however, in entries, such as *ton* (cf. below). Whereas *Y Geiriadur Mawr* presents the semantic variation in two separate entries *Y Geiriadur Bach* gives only one:

> **ton,** 1. *eb. ll.*-nau. ymchwydd dŵr,
> gwaneg. WAVE.
>> 2. *eg.* Tir porfa sydd heb ei droi
>> yn ddiweddar, gwndwn, gwyn-
>> dwn. LAY-LAND.
> Troi ton. TO PLOUGH LAY-LAND.

Only the briefest of information is presented by *Spurrell*, thus restricting the semantic meaning of lexical items severely at times: **ewyllys** (-iau) *nf* will.

What may be referred to as a subtype of gender-coupled semantic variation, occurs where the grammatical gender of a lexical item is at variance with natùral gender. This is the case with some nouns referring to people, e.g. *cariad* 'love, lover (feminine, masculine)', *nyrs* 'nurse', *priod* 'spouse' or *perthynas* 'relation' and others. There are, however, striking differences in the way dictionaries deal with this phenomenon as is illustrated in the following:

	Geir. Cyfoes	Geir. Mawr	Geir. Bach	G. yr Acad.	Spurrell	Works Dict.	GPC	Learners' Dict.
cariad	n.m.f.	n.m.f.[6]	n.m.	n.m.f.	n.m.f.	n.m.f.	n.f.m.	n.m.//n.m.
nyrs	n.m.f.	n.f.	n.f.	n.f.	n.m.f.	n.m.f.	n.f.m.	n.f.//n.m.f.
perthynas	n.f.	n.f.m.	n.f.	n.f.	n.f.	n.m.f.	n.f.m.	n.f.//n.f.
priod	n.m.f.	n.m.f.	n.m.f.	n.m.f.	n.coll.	n.m.f.	n.m.f.	--//--

The examples show that only *GPC* provides sufficient information about the gender of the given nouns. It apparently deals adequately with gender variation in lexical items within a corresponding biological context.

The extent to which the other dictionaries focus the ramifications of gender change, varies considerably. The word priod, however, is well described in the general-purpose dictionaries analysed here by giving the English equivalent 'husband, wife'. In the learners' dictionaries, on the other hand, is does not occur.

To sum up: the amount of attention paid to the gender-coupled semantic variation of lexical items differs widely. Whereas the subtype 'natural gender linked to grammatical gender differ-

---

[6] For ease of comparison, English abbreviations are used, although some of the dictionaries use Welsh as the *Metalanguage*.

entiation' is well reflected in the historical dictionary *GPC*, this is not consistently the case in the general-purpose dictionaries.

In addition, when the variation in gender is due to dialectal or semantic variation dictionary users have often to decide for themselves how to interpret the dictionary entries. In no general-purpose dictionary are these cases of semantic variation of lexical items consistently dealt with (cf. also the analysis in the following section). Dictionary users may, therefore, miss the appropriate meaning for their utterance.

4.3.2.2. Number inflection
4.3.2.2.1. Simple number inflection

The presentation of the number category by P.W. Thomas (1996: 150ff.) is primarily semantically based. Altogether, he defines four sub-groups within the number category (cf. section 1.3.2.3.2). Apart from the group which exhibits the 'normal' singular-plural opposition, these are illustrated in the following tables. Each table commences with a rough definition of the respective sub-category of nouns as given by P.W. Thomas (ibid.).

The nouns actually displayed are also taken from this author (ibid.). However, their description is supplemented by information obtained from *GPC*.

'Non-countables'[7] *enwau cynnull* (PWT: 150f.): nouns which have no definite plural; the partitive is necessary for their use; they behave in some instances like nouns in the singular and plural.					
Lexical item	**Grammatical description**	**Plural inflection**	**Singular inflection**	**Diminutive[8]**	**Commentaries**
arian 'money'	nm, ncoll				*cf. singularia tantum*
bara 'bread'	nm				*cf. singularia tantum*
caws 'cheese'	nm				*cf. singularia tantum*
cwrw 'beer'	nm	cyrfau			number-coupled semantic variation remains unexplained°
diddordeb 'inter-est'	nm	-au			number-coupled semantic variation remains unexplained°
dŵr 'water'	nm	dyfroedd			number-coupled semantic variation remains unexplained°
eira 'snow'	nm	-oedd			number-coupled semantic variation remains unexplained°
garlleg 'garlic'	npl		-en, -yn		
glaw 'rain'	nm	-ogydd			number-coupled semantic variation remains unexplained°
glo 'coal'	nm, ncoll	-eau			number-coupled semantic variation remains unexplained
gwallt 'hair'	nm	-iau, -ach		-yn,	number-coupled semantic variation remains unexplained°
gwlan 'wool'	nm	-au		gwlenyn	
haearn 'iron'	nm, ncoll	heyrn 'iron armour'		-ach	number-coupled semantic variation is clear
hiraeth 'longing'	nm	-iau			number-coupled semantic variation remains unexplained°
llafar 'speech'	nmf	(lleferoedd)			no indication whether the shift in gender is semantically related
newyddion 'news'	pl. of newydd				*cf. pluralia tantum*
sebon 'soap'	nm	-au, -s			

°Although P.W. Thomas lists the nouns given above as those which do not have a definite plural, most of them are not marked in *GPC* as words which should not be used in the plural. As a result, semantic variation between their singular and plural forms is not indicated and mostly not deducable from entries in general-purpose dictionaries either (cf. also explanations for sub-groups (b), (c), below).

---

[7]   In Bussmann (1996: 296) such nouns are defined as mass nouns and described as nouns which have no number distinction and cannot be immediately combined with a numeral. Among mass nouns, a distinction can be made between nouns which refer to elements, e.g. *wood*, and those which refer to collectives, e.g. *cattle*.

[8]   For the diminutive, see section 4.3.2.2.2.

'Collective nouns'[9] *enwau torfol* (PWT: 154): sub-group of nouns which refer to gatherings of people, creatures or things.					
Lexical item	Grammatical description	Plural inflection	Singular inflection	Diminutive	Commentaries
bonedd 'lineage'	nm	-ion			
branes 'flight of crows'	nf	-ion			
byddin 'army'	nf	-oedd, -au...			no indication whether the shift in plural is semantically related
cenfaint 'herd'	nf.	-iau			
côr 'choir'	nmf	-au			no indication whether the shift in gender is semantically related
cyfryngau 'media'	pl. of cyfrwng				cf. *pluralia tantum*
cyngor 'counsel, council'	nm	-ion, -au			no indication whether the shift in plural is semantically related
cyhoedd 'public'	nm				cf. *singularia tantum*
cynulleidfa 'audience'	nf	-oedd			
diadell 'flock'	nf	-au, -oedd			no indication whether the shift in plural is semantically related
gwasg 'pressure, press'	nfm	-au, -oedd			number-coupled semantic variation remains unexplained
gorsedd 'mound of earth, throne, court...)'	nfm	-au, -i, -ion			no indication whether the shift in gender and plural are semantically related
gre 'stud of horses'	nf	-oedd, -on			no indication whether the shift in plural is semantically related
gwerin 'people, folk'	nfm, ncoll	-oedd		-yn, -ach	no indication whether the shift in gender and diminutive are semantically related
gyr 'drive'	nm	-oedd			
haid 'swarm'	nf	heidiau			
haig 'shoal of fish'	nm	heigiau			
llywodraeth 'government'	nfm	-au			no indication whether the shift in gender is semantically related
praidd 'flock'	nfm				no indication whether the shift in gender is semantically related

---

[9]   According to Bussmann (1996: 81, 369), *collective nouns* are semantically defined as a class of nouns that express a group or set of several members in terms of a single unit, e.g. *cattle*. With certain collective nouns the plural can have individualising function, e.g. *people - peoples*. Whether the latter is the case, however, is mostly not indicated in the dictionary entries.

'Plural Nouns' *enwau lluosog* (PWT: 166): nouns which refer to things the distinctions between them are not easy to detect; mostly feminine.					
Lexical item	**Grammatical description**	**Singular inflection**	**Plural inflection**	**Diminutive**	**Commentaries**
abwyd 'bait'	nm		-au, -iaid...		no indication whether the shift in plural is semantically related
adar 'birds'	nm.pl	-yn (-nod)[10]			
bresych 'cabbage'	npl	-yn, -en			
cacwn 'hornet'	npl	-yn, -en	cacyniaid		
ceirios 'cherries'	npl	-en			
cynrhon 'maggots'	npl	-yn			
chwain 'fleas'	npl	-en (-au)			
ffawydd 'beech trees'	npl.f				cf. *pluralia tantum*
gellyg 'pears'	npl	-en, -yn			
gewyn 'sinew'	sg. of giau (npl.)		gewynnau, -ion		no indication whether the shift in plural is semantically related
gwybed 'gnats'	npl	-yn			
llau 'lice'	npl	-en			
llygod 'mice'	npl	-en, -yn (-au)		-ach	
meillion 'clover'	npl	-en	meillionau		
morgrug 'ants'	npl	-yn	-ion, -iaid		no indication whether the shift in plural is semantically related
moron 'carrots'	npl	-yn, -en			
nedd 'nits'	npl	-en			
poplys 'poplar trees'	npl	-en			
pysgod 'fish'	npl	-yn (-au)	pysgotau		
rhedyn 'ferns'	npl	-en			
For reasons of space not all possible plural inflections are displayed here; neither vowel affection is indicated nor the doubling of the final consonant when a suffix is added; rare plural forms are in brackets.					

---

[10] Some of the nouns which occur mostly in the plural may exhibit singular inflection (cf. under sub-group (b), below) in order to designate single entities, thus forming singulatives. These singulatives (for further explanations of this term, see below) in turn can occasionally also inflect their number, that is, they can take plural endings.

A study of the tables presented above reveals that the description of the number inflection for nouns may vary considerably, even in entries of the historical dictionary *GPC*; that is, number-coupled semantic variation is as heterogeneously treated as gender-coupled semantic variation (cf. section 4.3.1.2.).

In addition, looking at the nouns of the three semantic groups displayed in the tables, it becomes apparent that their morphology differs within these groups. *Non-countable nouns* may, for instance, be morphologically characterised as those with a 'normal' singular- (nm, nf) plural opposition, e.g. *sebon*. They can, however, also be defined as collective (ncoll), e.g. *arian, glo*, or plural nouns (npl), *garlleg*. Indeed, although P.W. Thomas claims that *non-countables* have no definite plural (cf. above), most of the examples provided by him exhibit plural inflection. However, whether the plural in these cases indicates individualisation or specification, as in *rock - rocks*, i.e. number-coupled semantic variation, remains mainly open.

The situation is similar in the sub-group defined by P.W. Thomas as *collective nouns*. Only one of the lexical items assigned by him to this group is actually described as such in *GPC*, i.e. *gwerin* 'people, folk'. Otherwise the nouns are characterised as *nm* or *nf* and exhibit plural inflection. In addition, existing number-coupled variation is rarely indicated.

The sub-group *plural nouns* is less heterogeneous. Nevertheless, in view of the facts above it becomes apparent that relating the brief semantic grouping[11] given by P.W. Thomas to morphological forms for the number category is somewhat difficult. For dictionary users, however, this is the major question. First of all, they need to know, which ending out of the variety of Welsh plural endings and/or vowel changes is the right one to chose for a given lexical item. In cases where more than one ending is possible, explanations which indicate selection priorities are necessary.

Ideally, the grammatical description of the noun in the dictionary entry should provide the necessary information. This descriptive need may be served quite effectively by a categorisation of nouns which places emphasis on the morphology of the number category. Such a categorisation is suggested in the following and distinguishes also between four sub-groups:

(a) Nouns which exhibit plural inflection following the basic <u>singular-plural opposition</u>. They form the major part of the nouns, e.g. *drws - drysau* 'door', *byddin - byddinoedd* 'army'.

(b) Nouns the stem of which has plural meaning. They are called <u>collective nouns</u>. Such nouns predominantly denote a group or a complex of realities and use singular inflection only when single individuals or realities have to be described, e.g. *mefus - mefusen* 'strawberry', *moch - mochyn* 'pig'; that is, they form singulatives. They tend to occur in special semantic fields, such as denotations for living things, creatures and weather phenomena.
Some of them can exhibit additional plural inflection, e.g. *coed* (ncoll) - *coeden* (nf) - *coedydd* (npl), thereby indicating different species or kinds of the denoted living things, creatures, or phenomena.

(c) A limited number of nouns has no plural form, thus being called <u>singularia tantum</u>. They mostly denote abstracta, but also plants and other

---

[11] A much more detailed analysis is offered by Burgschmidt (1984, 1990).

realities. They cannot be immediately combined with numerals and need a partitive, as in *llawer o fara* 'much bread'.

(d) A limited number of nouns has no singular form, thus being called pluralia tantum. Only if they do not refer to a particular group they can be counted, otherwise they need a partitive, e.g. *llawer o newyddion* 'a lot of cattle'.

There is no doubt that the motivation for the number category is semantically based. The category of the number expresses, basically, attitudes towards countability of entities and items. The singular, therefore, refers to entities and items which are seen as a unit. The plural emphasises countability but can also have individualising function with certain nouns, e.g. *sheep - sheeps*. Most nouns are able to occur in both numbers, that is, they are formed by a stem denoting a countable individual which takes plural inflections referring to the largest possible number of entities. There are, however, restrictions or particular conceptions of the reality which lead to the focus on either the unit of objects and subjects or their countability, mostly concentrated on special semantic fields. This is the case in the groups (b) - (d). The most important group is (b). For a number of conceptual fields, e.g. fruits, vegetables, trees, corn, animals, weather phenomena, Welsh prefers the emphasis on an unmarked collective view rather than on individualisation (cf. Burgschmidt 1984, 1990), thus indicating that the entities are often primarily associated with existing in a group or being fragments, e.g. *briwsion* 'crumbs'. As a result, there is a long list of nouns which comprises those whose stem expresses plural meaning. For singularisation they can take a singulative, i.e. the marked singular form of collective nouns (Bussmann 1996: 436). This singular is formed by the suffix *-yn* (masculine) or the suffix *-en* (feminine). Both are etymologically diminutive suffixes, which still functioning as such (cf. Burgschmidt 1984: 218, S. Heinz forthcoming).

Although being called plural nouns by P.W. Thomas, they are named *collective nouns* in this investigation (cf. also Bussmann 1996: 436) in order not to confuse them with the *pluralia-tantum* group and suggest that they do not take a singular. This approach is also reflected in King (1993: 48, 67ff.) and, furthermore, justified by the definition of such nouns as *ncoll* in many dictionary entries. In addition, in languages which also emphasis collective views, e.g. Arabic in *dabbān* 'fly, flies' (unspecified) vs *dabbāne* 'a fly', the same collective-singulative opposition can be found.

The sub-groups established primarily on a morphological categorisation of Welsh nouns are displayed in the following tables. The selected lexical items are described by information obtained from *GPC*. Again, the nouns which exhibit the basic singular-plural opposition are not included.

Collective nouns	Grammat. descript.	Singu-lative	Plural	Diminu-tive	Commentaries
Creatures, birds					
adar 'birds'	nm.pl	-yn (-nod)			
ednog 'gnats'	ncoll.	-yn	-ion, -od, -iaid...		no explicit explanation for varying plural'
gwenyn 'bees'	npl, ncoll	-en			no explicit explanation for varying number category
llygod 'mice'	npl	-en, -yn (-au)		-ach	
moch 'pigs'	npl, ncoll	-yn	-od		no indication whether the shift in plural is semantically related
morgrug 'ants'	npl	-yn	-ion, -iaid		no indication whether the shift in plural is semantically related
plant 'children'	npl	-yn	-au	-ach	no indication whether the shift in plural is semantically related
Plants					
blodau 'flowers'	npl	blodeuyn	-oedd		no indication whether the shift in plural is semantically related
bresych 'cabbage'	npl	-yn, -en			
bricyll 'apricots'	npl	-en			
callod 'moss'	npl	-yn, -en			
cawn 'reeds'	npl	conyn, (-au) cawnen	conion		no indication whether the shift in plural is semantically related
castenwydd 'chestnut-trees'	npl	-en			
ceirch 'oats'	npl	-en, -yn	ceirchau		
ceirios 'cherries'	npl	-en			
cnau 'nuts'	npl	-en			
coed 'trees'	npl, ncoll	-en	-ydd, -au		no indication whether the shift in plural is semantically related
collwydd 'hazel trees'	npl	-en			
dail 'leaves; herbs'	ncoll	deilen (-au)	deiliau		no indication whether the shift in plural is semantically related
danadl 'nettles'	npl	danhadlen, danhaden...			
erfin 'turnips'	ncoll, npl	-en			
ffa 'beans'	npl	ffäen, ffeuen			
garlleg 'garlic'	npl	-en, -yn			
gellyg 'pears'	npl	-en, -yn			
gwellt 'grass'	npl, ncoll	-en, -yn (pl. -i)	-ydd, -au		no indication whether the shift in plural is semantically related
gwiwydd 'poplars'	npl	-en			
gwinwydd 'vines'	npl	-en			
larswydd 'larch trees'	npl	-en			
llus 'bilberries'	npl	-en	-au, -i		no indication whether the shift in plural is semantically related

lluswydd 'bilberry bushes'	npl	-en			
llysiau 'vegetable'	npl, ncoll	llys, llysyn, llys(i)euyn...	llys(i)euau, -oedd, -wedd		no indication whether the shift in plural is semantically related
madarch 'fungus, mushrooms'	npl, ncoll	-en	medyrch, madeirch		no indication whether the shift in plural is semantically related
maip 'turnips'	npl	-en		meipennig	
moron 'carrots'	npl	-yn, -en			
pupur 'pepper'	npl	-en, -yn (-au, -od)			
Denotations for groups of things, including fragments					
blew 'hair'	npl, ncoll	-yn			
cenllysg 'hail'	npl, ncoll	-en, -yn			
dillad 'clothes'	npl, ncoll	-yn	-au		no indication whether the shift in plural is semantically related
gro 'pebbles'	npl, ncoll		groydd, groeon	gröyn	
had 'seed'	npl, ncoll	-en, -yn			
mellt 'lightening'	npl	-en, -yn (-au, -oedd)			
briwsion 'crumbs'	npl	-yn			
cnewyll 'kernels; tonsils'	npl	-yn	-(i)on, -od		no indication whether the shift in plural is semantically related
dellt 'laths'	npl	-en (-au, -i)			
plu 'feathers'	npl.	plu(f)yn, plu(f)en	pluawr		no indication whether the shift in plural is semantically related
The semantic grouping follows roughly the suggestions of Burgschmidt (1994: 220ff.).					
* Some of the varying plural forms are indirectly explained by examples provided in the entries of *GPC*. => Collective nouns are also those which are derivations from adjectives, e.g. *newyddion* 'news'. Some of them have developed singulatives, e.g. *israddolion* 'inferiors' -> *israddolyn*.					

In group (c), there are nouns which normally have no plural forms, i.e. *singularia tanta*. In case they do exhibit plural inflection, however, this is to indicate different species or kinds of denoted people, creatures, things, or phenomena.

Singularia tantum	Grammat. description	Commentaries
adareg 'ornithology'	nf	
arian 'money'	nm (-nau)	
bara 'bread'	nm	
barlys 'barley'	nmf, ncoll	no indication whether the shift in gender and number is semantically related
brasgig 'fat meat'	nf	
bretyn 'rag'	nm	
breuder 'brittleness'	nm	
callrwydd 'prudence'	nm	
deublygrwydd 'duality'	nm	
deubwys 'two pounds'	nm	
deucannwr 'two hundred men'	nm	compound nouns with a prefix expressing a number occur very often in the singular only
cawl 'soup'	nm	(diminutive: cawlen)
caws 'cheese'	nm	(diminutive: cosyn, Pl.: -nau, -nod)
copr 'copper'	nm	
cyhoedd 'public'	nm, ncoll	no indication whether the shift in number is semantically related
cyngordioledd 'accordance'	nm	
cyngryn 'contention'	nm	
cyngwedd 'conformity'	nf	
cyngweddoldeb 'compatibility'	nm	
chwerthin 'laughter'	nm	
dywrthred 'trouble'	nf	
eiddo 'property'	nm	
engirioldedd 'cruelty'	nm	
garllegog 'hedge-garlic'	nf	
garment 'cloak'	nm	
garmlais 'scream'	nmf	no indication whether the shift in gender is semantically related
garnais 'garnish'	nm	
gellygwin 'perry'	nm	
gerwinwuch 'roughnes'	nm	
geuedd 'falsehood'	nm	
gewynnwst 'rheumatism'	nfm	no indication whether the shift in gender is semantically related
girad 'bitterness'	nm	
gitêt 'playtime'	nm	
gitwn 'banner'	nm	
githran '(kind of wild) parsli'	nf	
giwana 'guano'	nm	
gwidan 'minnow'	nm	
glais 'stream'	nm	
gwenydd 'muse'	nf	
hâl 'moor'	nf	

hiraethdod '(object of one's) longing'	nf	
hirbwyll 'caution'	nm	other compound words which take *hir* or other adjectives as a prefix often belong to the same number category
iâ 'ice'	nm (-au, -on)	
llaeth 'milk'	nm (-au)	
mêl 'honey'	nm	
miled 'millet'	nm	
milfodaeth 'zoology'	nf	
milfodeg 'fauna'	nfm	no indication whether the shift in gender is semantically related
Whereas the diminutive suffixes *-ach* and *-os* may form *pluralia tanta*, the suffix *-aeth* may derive feminine *singularia tanta* from the same noun, e.g. *dilladaeth* (cf. under *pluralia tanta*).		

Group (d) subsumes nouns which exhibit no regular singular inflection, i.e. *pluralia tanta*:

Pluralia tantum	Grammatical description	Diminutive	Commentaries
adarach 'game-birds'[12]	npl		
ceirs 'turns'	npl		
crasgalaf 'parched reeds'	npl, ncoll		no explicit explanation for varying number category
crasgeirch 'oats dried in kiln'	npl		
chwalcs 'whelks'	npl		
cyngogion 'a series of englynion'	npl		
dwylo 'two hands'	npl, ndual*		
gwefusflew 'moustache'	npl		
lloffion 'gleanings'	npl		
lloffonad 'crutches'	npl		
llusw 'oven ashes'	npl		
môr-fresych 'sea-kale'	npl		
môr-lysiau 'seaweed'	npl		
nawyr 'nine men'	npl		
* It is debatable whether *dwylo* is a real 'dual'. The dual category occurs only in fossilised forms (cf. section 1.3.2.3.2). Instead, what may be expressed in the word *dwylo* is a semantic field in which the occurrence of the object in pairs is emphasised. This is quite a common phenomenon in the Welsh language which works also with other numbers, for instance, three, five, nine, one hundred and others, e.g. *deuddarn* 'two parts', *cantroed* 'a hundred feet' (cf. section 1.3.2.3.7.). The phenomenon of the occurrence of objects in pairs is known to other languages, too, e.g. to Russian, where such nouns belong to the *pluralia tanta*.			

The kind of number inflection exhibited by collective nouns (cf. sub-group (b) above) does not exist in English or German. What is referred to as collective noun in German, for instance, has

---

[12]   Nouns ending in *-ach* are very often formed by the plural form of a noun + the diminutive suffix *-ach*. Quite a few of them form separate dictionary entries, e.g. *dilladach, cwnach* and others. The same is true for nouns ending in *-os*, another diminutive suffix, e.g. *dillados, gwerinos* (cf. the discussion of the Welsh diminutive in section 4.3.2.2.2.).

mostly no plural inflection, thus forming a group within the *singularia tanta* (cf. Buscha 1981: 246ff.). Semantically they would belong to P.W. Thomas' group of *non-countables* (cf. above). Whenever German or English emphasis needs to be placed on group formation, which is characteristic for sub-group (b) in Welsh (cf. above), use has here to be made of either plural forms, syntactic groups or compound words (cf. Burgschmidt 1990: 207). Neither language has the means of inflection to produce singular forms by morphological addition.

In light of the facts presented above, Welsh lexicographers are asked to pay particular attention to *collective nouns* as defined in sub-group (b) (cf. above) and to make their system of number inflection clear to the dictionary users. A look at the entries of general-purpose dictionaries reveals, however, that this is not the case. On the contrary, in most instances the English system is, at least partly, imposed on that of the Welsh language. This becomes apparent when looking at Welsh equivalents given for English headwords. Whereas the English equivalents of the Welsh headwords are mostly adequately translated and furnished with grammatical description, this is often not the case the other way round. In the English-to-Welsh section, the secondary singular form is given without referring to its stem, i.e. the basic and plural form of the respective lexical item. The following examples from *Y Geiriadur Cyfoes*, *Y Geiriadur Mawr* and *Geiriadur yr Academi* illustrate this problem:

moch, *(-yn, n.m.)*, *n.pl.* PIGS, SWINE   **pig**, *n.* MOCHYN

moch, *ell. (un. g.-yn)*. anifeiliaid ffarm   **pig**, *n.* mochyn.
a leddir er mwyn eu cig, hobau.
PIGS.
Mochyn bychan : broch : pryf
llwyd: mochyn daear. BADGER.
Chwarae mochyn coed. PLAYING
LEAP-FROG.
Moch y coed. WOODLICE.

pig[1] *n.* **1.** *(a)* mochyn (moch) *m;* *S.a.* **boar, sow; sow in ~,** hwch
dorrog (hychod torrog) *f;* **a drove** [...]

ceirios, *(-en, n.f.)*, *n.pl.* CHERRIES   **cherry**, *n.* CEIRIOSEN

ceirios, *ell. (un. b.* -en). ffrwythau bach   **cherry**, *n.* ceiriosen.
coch, sirian. CHERRIES.

cherry *n.* **1.** *Bot: (Prunus):* *Lit:* ceiriosen (ceirios) *f, occ :*
sirianen (sirian) *f, F:* tsieren (tsieris) *f;* **American ~,**
black ~, *(P. serotina):* ceiriosen ddu (ceirios duon);
bird~, [...]

coed, (-ydd), *c.n.m.* TREES, TIMBER. WOOD

coed bach, BRUSHWOOD

tree, *n.* COEDEN, PREN

tree line, COEDLIN

wood, *n.* COED, PREN, GWŶDD, COEDWIG

ply wood, PREN HAENOG

synthetic wood, PREN GWNEUDCOED

timber, *n.* COED, COEDWYDD

coed, *ell.* (*un. b.* coeden). prennau, gwŷdd; coedwig. TREES, TIMBER; WOOD

tree, *n.* pren, coeden, colfen *(coll.)*

wood, *n.* **1.** coed, gwŷdd, coedwig

2. pren

timber, *n.* coed, pren.

tree[1] *n.* **1.** *(a)* coeden (coed) *f, occ:* pren(-nau) *m, S: occ:* colfen(-ni, -nau) f, Lit: occ: (in pl.): gwŷdd: fruit~[...]
wood *n.* **1.** *(=forest):* coed *pl* (*with double pl.* coedydd), coedwig(- oedd) *f; Lit: Poet:* gwig(-oedd) *f;* [...]
timber[1] *n.* **1.** *(a) Carp:* coed *m,* pren *m;* *(b) (=trees):* standing~, coed tal *pl,* [...]

gwenith, (-en, *n.f.*), *n.pl.* WHEAT

wheat, *n.* GWENITH

wheaten bread, BARA GWENITH/CAN

gwenith, *ell.* (*un. b.*-en). yr ŷd y gwneir blawd (can) ohono. WHEAT.

wheat, *n.* gwenith.

WHEATEN BREAD, bara gwenith, bara can.

wheat *n.* gwenith(-oedd), -au) *m; S.a.* **buckwheat;** **grain of** ~, gwenithen (gwenith) *f,* tywysen(-nau, tywys) *f;* ~ **in the ear,** [...]

The treatment of denotations for 'trees' is even more heteregeneous. To begin with, the authors of *Y Geiriadur Cyfoes* assign most of the lexical items for trees in the Welsh language to a more specialised section of the lexicon dealing specifically with 'Planhigion - Plants', in which the linguistic description is even more limited:

pisgwydden, LINDEN. LIME TREE (in the 'Planhigion'-Section)

linden, *n.* PISGWYDDEN (in the English-Welsh section)

The English language entries, however, are assigned to the general lexicon. This leads to the question of whether the English speaker is better acquainted with trees than the Welsh language speaker, a rather discriminating question. The authors of *Y Geiriadur Mawr* see denotations for trees generally as part of the common lexicon.

pisgwydd, *ell.* palawyf. LINDEN-
TREES

linden, *n.* palawyfen, pisgwydden.

Geiriadur yr Academi: **linden [tree]** *n.* = **lime⁴.**
lime⁴ *n. Bot: (ornamental tree = linden):* ~ **[tree],**
palalwyfen (palalwyf) *f*, pisgwydden (pisgwydd) *f*,
pisgen(-ni, pisg) *f*, gwaglwyfen (gwaglwyf) *f*,
eurwernen (eurwern) *f*. [...]

It is apparent from the examples, that the number inflection is reflected in a rather haphazard manner in Welsh general-purpose dictionaries and that there does not seem to be a clear theoretical concept behind their terminology (cf. also Burgschmidt 1994: 218, 228). As a result, *coed* 'trees', for instance, is described as a masculine collective noun (c.n.m.) in *Y Geiriadur Cyfoes*, as a plural noun (ell.) in *Y Geiriadur Mawr*, and as a plural and collective noun in *GPC* (not exemplified here).

A problem occurs when dictionary users look up the equivalent for an English lexical item, e.g. *pig*, and can only find the Welsh equivalent presented in the singulative, i.e. *mochyn* 'one pig', in the English-to-Welsh section. The commonly used and etymological basic plural form *moch* 'pigs' remains unrecorded in *Y Geiriadur Cyfoes*, *Y Geiriadur Mawr* and *Spurrell* (not exemplified here). In addition, since *mochyn* as a secondary singular form is correctly not selected as a headword in the Welsh-to-English section of the three dictionaries, the lexical item remains untraceable when cross-checking or looking for its plural form. Such a way of dealing with lexical items presents a mixture of two systems of plural inflection.

In the *Works-Dictionary*, the Welsh system is simply adapted to that of the English language, that is, the secondary singular form comes first.

coeden *f* (coed) tree.
ceiriosen *f* (ceirios) cherry; cherry tree.
gwenithen *f* (gwenith) wheat.
mochyn *m* (moch) pig.

In the case of *gwenith* this approach goes totally wrong, since *gwenithen* is a 'grain' or 'stalk of wheat' rather than 'wheat'.

A mixed approach is taken by *The Welsh Learner's Dictionary*. Here some nouns are contained in the headword list with their singulative, e.g. *ceirios* and *moch* and some are represented by their etymological basic form, e.g. *gwenith* - in this case the English equivalent is also a collective noun - and *llus*. Others are included twice in the macrostructure as is illustrated by the following examples:

ceiriosen/ceirios (f) *[ke-eeryosen]* cherry
coed (pl) *[koeed]* forest, trees, wood,
timber
see coeden
coed tân firewood
coedydd (double plural) forests,
woods, timbers

coeden/coed (f) *[koeeden]* tree
   coeden afalau (or **afallen**) apple tree
   coeden ceirios cherry tree
[...]
gwenith (pl) *[gooenith]* wheat
[...]
llus (pl) *[llees]* winberries
[...]
mochyn/moch (m) *[mochin]* pig
[...]
plant (pl) *[plant]* children
   see **plentyn**

Such an approach is also reflected in the *Pocket Modern Welsh Dictionary*. This is rather disappointing, since King was the first to explain the phenomenon of etymological basic plural forms in a grammar book (1993).

The best solution currently on offer among the Welsh-to-x/x-to-Welsh dictionaries can be found in *Geiriadur Almaeneg-Cymraeg/Cymraeg-Almaeneg* (Greller et al. 1999). It includes the plural forms in a way that they can all be traced. As a result, mistranslations may be avoided. The system of collective nouns as defined under sub-group (b) (cf. above), however, is not explained and will remain hidden to German dictionary users, since some of the nouns are contained twice in the headword list, e.g. *coed/coeden* and *plant* 'children' and *plentyn* 'child'. Others are introduced with their singulative. Nevertheless, at least all forms are presented in a way that they can be found in the reverse section.

In *Geiriadur yr Academi*, only the English system is reflected. As a result, the secondary singular form is chosen as the appropriate equivalent for the English headword, although it is the lesser used form. The basic plural form is only provided first when the English lexical item is itself a collective noun as shown in 'wood' and 'wheat'. In this case the singular may also form part of the entry (cf. *wheat*).

Looking at the entry for the headword 'wood', *Geiriadur yr Academi* reveals the information *pl* for its Welsh equivalent *coed*. As an equivalent to 'timber', however, the grammatical description of the number category of *coed* is quite misleading when this lexical item is characterised as a masculine noun (*m*).

Whereas, apart from obvious mistakes, such a description may be justifiable from an English language viewpoint it has to be argued that, first, the dictionary has also a prescriptive function with regard to its target language Welsh. In addition, the presentation of the number inflection is equally unsatisfactory in the bi-directional bilingual dictionaries.

Apart from the facts presented above, this is confirmed by referring to *CysGair*. Whereas the lexical item *plant* 'children' is adequately detailed in *Y Geiriadur Cyfoes* it occurs like 'plant, *ell.* gweler *plentyn*' in *Y Geiriadur Mawr*, thereby providing the meaning of the noun in the entry in its secondary word form. In *CysGair*, however, *plant* in the meaning of 'child' is not traceable at all. The definitions found under the headword *plant* are:

clinig cyfarwyddo plant nm, child guidance clinic
clinig lles plant nm, child welfare clinic
lles mamau a phlant nm, maternity and child welfare
lles plant nm, infant welfare
theatr nf, children's theatre
therapydd nm, child therapist

Only if one knows the singulative of *plant* does the entry become accessible (cf. also *mefus* 'strawberries', *deilen* 'leaf'). Usually, the programme itself jumps to the secondary singular form when typing the plural form, e.g. with *madarch* 'mushrooms', *moch* 'pigs', *ceirios* 'cherries'. In other cases, the plural form is given as it should generally be the case, e.g. with *coed* 'trees, wood', *dillad* 'clothes', *garlleg* 'garlic'. In these instances, however, the singulative is lacking. Altogether, this approach obscures Welsh morphology.

The only dictionary which presents the basic word forms in the headword list is the historical dictionary *GPC*. Occasionally can a singulative be found as a headword, but only in order to refer to its basic (plural) word form, an approach that makes lexical items easier traceable.

The inconsistencies in the presentation of the number inflection of the Welsh noun in general-purpose dictionaries may be the result of morphological obscuring of this phenomenon in Welsh linguistics up to 1977 (Jones, M. & A.R. Thomas 1977: 157-163). For dictionary users such inconsistencies are irritating, since they cause frustration or at least confusion as the impression is created that there are two systems of number inflection for certain Welsh nouns.

Altogether a presentation of this phenomenon as illustrated above, first, harms the morphology of the language. Second, it leads to linguistic insecurity on the part of the learner of Welsh who may recognise the system as non-understandable, or incomplete, or illogical. Third, a system which presses Welsh lexical items into English categories affects the linguistic identity of native speakers. Again, cultural identity may be spoiled considering that the Welsh number system belongs to those morphological devices which contribute to the construction of the culture-specific way of perceiving reality in Welsh culture. Fourth, dictionary users will, in the end, not be provided with guidance in the application of lexical items or will not be able to trust the dictionary for encoding purposes.

All considered, the dictionaries under review do not adequately meet their purposes. It is surprising that the phenomenon collective noun as defined in sub-group (b) (cf. above) has not been described in a Welsh grammar before 1993 (King 1993: 48, cf. other grammars, e.g. S.J. Williams 1981: 9-22, Morris-Jones 1970: 213, Watkins 1961: 146, 1992: 51f., Thorne 1993: 100, 106ff.) and has consequently been neglected by Welsh lexicographers. Nevertheless, the latter could have consulted dictionaries of the sister language Breton. The English-Breton and French-Breton dictionaries, for instance, found a solution for exhibiting different systems of number inflection in one entry:

 tree *n.* gwez *coll.* -enn. (Delaporte 1995)
 arbre(s) *m.* gwez *coll.* (Desbordes & Kervella 1994)

Welsh lexicography should follow these examples as well as latest descriptions of the Welsh language as soon as possible.

4.3.2.2.2.   Relation between multiple number inflection and the diminutive[1]

Upon a close examination of Welsh grammar books it can be established that the diminutive does not seem to be recognised as a very important phenomenon in the Welsh language (cf. King 1993). S.J. Williams refers to the diminutive as a kind of plural inflection (1980: 17f.). J.J. Evans (1960), Thorne (1993), and P.W. Thomas (1996) include the diminutive under the heading 'noun endings'/morphology. In S. Heinz (forthcoming), a variety of diminutive suffixes and their usage is discussed, demonstrating that the actual choice of such suffixes depends on criteria relating to additional connotations or grammatical aspects of this particular noun. These criteria include gender and number as well as formal aspects of the lexical items, such as whether they end in a vowel or not.

As in grammar books, the diminutive is not regularly included in entries of general-purpose dictionaries. On an irregular base, the suffixes *-ach* (or *-an*[2]) and *-os* form part of the entries of the historical dictionary *GPC* as can be seen in the first four tables of section 4.3.2.2.1. The reason for a more regular inclusion of the suffixes *-yn/-en*[3] is that they may form singulatives. This, however, is only one of their features. Etymologically these are diminutive suffixes (cf. Burgschmidt 1984: 218) which have become polyfunctional.[4] According to Burgschmidt (ibid.), the diminutive meaning strongly supports the concept of particulation with collective nouns and consequently that of singularity.

The diminutive suffix *-ach* is considered by S.J. Williams (1980: 17f.) as a suffix to be added to the plural form of a noun and by P.W. Thomas (ibid.: 668) characterised as one to be added to the plural or singular form of nouns. In *GPC*, however, nouns ending in *-ach* are assigned to various categories. They are defined (a) as *ll. (lluosog)* 'plural' category, e.g. *gwalltach* 'hairs', *cryddionach* 'shoemakers'[5] or (b) as *ll.bach.* 'diminutive plural', e.g. *haearnach* 'old iron, scrap iron', or (c) as *ll.dwbl* 'double plural' (when the noun exhibits singular-plural opposition), e.g. *dyneddach*. Some nouns ending in *-ach* form (d) separate dictionary entries, e.g. *dynionach* 'contemptible men', *dilladach* 'old clothes', *cwnach* 'curs', *peth(eu)ach* 'things of little value', or (e) they are listed, as done here, under 'diminutive', e.g. *deiliach* 'little leaves'.

---

[1]   I would like to take this opportunity of thanking William Ll. Griffith, Dinbych/Wales, for his helpful comments on this section.

[2]   For instance in the entries of *ebill* 'auger', *gafr* 'goat', and *llyweth* 'tress'.

[3]   *-en* is the feminine form of *-yn*.

[4]   For other functions, see S. Heinz (forthcoming).

[5]   Both forms are indicated as derogative.

The diminutive suffix *-os* which can only be added to the plural form of a noun and, in contrast to *-ach* expresses endearment, is similarly treated. A representative example to illustrate the situation is the entry of *plant* 'children' in *GPC*:

> **plant** [...] *ell.* (un. g. *plentyn*) bach. *-ach*, ll. dwbl *-au*.[6]

Plantos 'little children, infants, tots (usually expressing affection but sometimes derog.)', which means nothing but the opposition of *plantach* 'dammed children' (cf. entry above), however, forms a separate dictionary entry. In other instances, the same diminutive opposition may also be displayed in one dictionary entry, such as in that for *draen* 'thorn':

> **draen** [...] *eg.b.* (un b. *draenen* ll. *-nau*; ll. bach. *dreiniach, dreinos, -ios*) ll. *drain*

Another type of inconsistency is seen in the entry of *dyn* 'man'. One plural diminutive is listed as the plural form of the singular diminutives. This approach is irritating, since the plural diminutive is derived from the unmarked plural form. The others are listed under the double plural forms:

> **dyn** [...] *eg.b.* (bach. *dynyn, dynionyn*, ll. *dynionos* [...]) ll, *-(i)on*, ll. dwbl †
> *dynionau, dyn(i)addon, dyneddon, dyneddach.*

Similar inconsistencies are noticeable with singular diminutive suffixes. For some of them separate dictionary entries are provided, e.g. for *coesan, coesig* 'little leg', *croesig* 'little cross'. Other diminutive forms of the same base word *coes* 'leg', however, are correctly to be found within its dictionary entry, e.g. *coesyn* and *coesen*.

Were diminutives regularly included in the headword list would the dictionary swallow a lot, since there are ten suffixes for nouns to denote Welsh diminutive derivations as well as the prefix *lled-* 'half, part(ly)' for the diminishing of verbs, e.g. in *lledferwi* 'simmer'. However, a separation of the diminutive forms from their base word obscures Welsh word formation.

Nevertheless, since diminutive derivations are not unmarked plural forms but express connotations as exemplified for *-ach* and *-os*, they should not be assigned to the plural inflection either. In the same way, the description 'double plural' is misleading, since it is a second[7] unmarked plural ending that is normally called a 'double plural' form of a noun, as for instance in *engylion* 'angels', *seintiau* 'saints', *pelydrau* 'beams', *negeseuon* 'messages', *caneuon* 'songs'.[8]

In some cases the diminutive form has developed a secondary meaning or is recognised as a separate lexical item. In such instances its description in a separate dictionary entry is justified. Moreover, such nouns may take an additional diminutive suffix:

---

[6] *Ell. - enw lluosog* 'plural noun', *un. g. - unigol gwrywaidd* 'singular masculine', *bach. - bachigol* 'diminutive', *ll. dwbl - lluosog dwbl* 'double plural'.

[7] With the word *gwraig* 'women' even a triple plural is possible (GPC 1968).

[8] Double plurals may develop when vowel affection or plural endings are not considered sufficient to indicate the plural.

cor [...] *eg.* (bach. g. *corryn,* ll. *corynnod,* b. *corren, corres,* ll. *coresau*) ll. *coriaid* [...][9]
  1. *dwarf, pigmy, little urchin* [...]
  2. *spider* [...]

corrach [cor+ -ach²][10] *eg.* (un. bach. *corechyn*)[11] ll. *corachod, -iaid.* [...] *dwarf, pygmy.*

To sum up: lacking systematic research in Welsh lexicology may be the reason for the inconsistent handling of diminutive derivations. Diminutive forms should, however, neither make up an own dictionary entry as long as the semantic meaning and the formal presentation has not changed noticeably nor should they be treated as a sub-category of the plural. Diminutives, either in the plural or singular, are first of all derivations which specify the semantic meaning of the base word. The different diminutive suffixes for singular and plural are used to derive diminutive forms from nouns in the singular, in the plural and from collective, singular and plural nouns (cf. section 4.3.2.2.1. for these sub-groups) according to grammatical and formal aspects of them. Lexical items which have both a diminutive for their singular and their plural forms, such as *draen* 'thorn' (cf. above), however, are rare. The same is true for those nouns from which diminutive paradigms exhibiting gender and number inflection can be derived, e.g. *ffril* 'a little':

ffril [...] *eg.* (un. bach. *ffrilyn,* b. *ffrilen,* ll. *ffrilach*) ll. -iau, -od [...]

Although some examples in *GPC* may be considered somewhat archaic, diminutive derivations are still being used in Modern Welsh. They should consequently be contained in general-purpose dictionaries and in a manner easily understood. Since the different diminutive derivations are grammatically and formally restricted semantic specifications of a base word, they should be detailed in its dictionary entry, unless the semantic meaning of a diminutive form differs drastically from that of the base word.

Although the diminutive is far more regular in Breton (cf. T.A. Watkins 1961: 88f., Hemon 1976) and diminutive forms here are easier to derive it is part of the entries in the dictionary by Favereau (1993):

---

[9] *Eg.* - *enw gwrywaidd* 'noun masculine', *bach. g.* - *bachigol gwrywaidd* 'diminutive masculine', *ll.* - *lluosog* 'plural', *b.* - *benywaidd* 'feminine'.

[10] The '2' means that the suffix -*ach* in this case is the diminutive suffix.

[11] *Un. bach.* stands for *unigol bachigol* 'singular diminutive'.

BERAD[+] ['beːrəd-t], berad-t] g. -où *gouette (de...)*, bih.
-IG *-ette*: ur berad dour [...]
BERADENN[+] [beˈraːdən], [beradɛn] b. -où *coulée, gouttelette* (bih. -IG): an ddra-se en doa gwraet evel ur veradenn [...]
BERR[+] [bɛr], a-w. [bɛːr] & [ber] Ph, [-eː-] bih. -IG ad. *court,-e, & à court, de court, bref,-ève* (C., kmg byr g. ber b.): berr an dewezhioù bremañ [...]

By using this reference book models can be found for the indication of diminutive forms of Welsh lexical items in dictionaries.

4.3.3. The Welsh adjective
4.3.3.1. Gender inflection

The *gender inflection* of the Welsh adjective is relatively well covered by the dictionary entries[1] as can be seen in the following table. The lexical items are taken from the section on adjectives in P.W. Thomas (1996: 192ff.).

Adjectives	Geiriadur Cyfoes	Geiriadur Mawr	Geiriadur Bach	GPC	Geiriadur yr Academi	Works Dict.	Spur-rell
brith 'speckled'	√	√	√	√	√	√	√
brwnt 'dirty'	--	√	√	√	--	√	√
brych 'freckled'	√	√	√	√	√	--	√
bychan 'small'	√	--	no entry	√	√	--	√
byr 'short'	--	√	√	√	√	--	√
crwm 'bent'	√	√	√	√	√	--	√
crwn 'round'	--	√	√	√	√	--	√
cryf 'strong'	√	√	√	√	√	--	√
cwta 'short'	--	√	√	√	√	--	no entry
dwfn 'deep'	--	√	√	√	√	--	√
gwlyb 'wet'	--	√	√	√	√	--	--
gwyn 'white'	√	√	√	√	√	--	√
gwyrdd 'green'	--	√	√	√	√	--	--
hysb 'dry'	√	√	√	√	√	--	√
llwm 'bare'	√	√	√	√	√	--	√
llyfn 'smooth'	√	√	√	√	√	--	√
llym 'sharp'	√	√	√	√	√	--	√
melyn 'yellow'	√	√	√	√	√	--	√

Some entries from general-purpose dictionaries and *GPC* are given in the following in order to show how the gender distinction is illustrated in them:

---

[1]   Some variation in the handling of the gender inflection of Welsh adjectives in dictionaries may be due to the approach of the respective author to the contemporary use of existing feminine forms of adjectives (cf. P.W. Thomas 1996: 191).

Y Geiriadur Cyfoes: **brith,** (*braith, f.*) *a.m.* SPECKLED.
MOTLEY. VAGUE. INDISTINCT. PARTLY
GREY. SHADY
brith gof, FAINT RECOLLECTION.

Y Geiriadur Mawr: **brith,** *a.* (*b.* braith). brych, amryliw;
aneglur, llwyd. SPECKLED, MOTLEY;
INDISTINCT, VAGUE; GREY.
Ceffyl brith. PIEBALD HORSE.
Brith gof. FAINT RECOLLECTION.
Yn frith gan (o). STUDDED WITH

Y Geiriadur Bach: **brith,** *a.* (*b.* braith). brych, amryliw;
aneglur, llwyd. SPECKLED,
Ceffyl brith. PIEBALD HORSE.
Brith gof. FAINT RECOLLECTION.

Geiriadur yr Academi:

speckled *a.* brych (*f.* brech, *pl.* brychion), brith (*f.* braith, *pl.*
brithion), *Lit: occ:* bannog, mannog; **bird ~ with white,** aderyn
gwyn brith. [...]

Spurrell: **brith** *adj* mottled, speckled; *f*
braith

GPC: **brith**[1] [H. Gym. *brith, -breithet,* Llyd. [...]]
a. (b. *braith*) [...]
1. (*a*) Cymysgliw, brych [...]: marked with different colours [...]
9g. (*Juv*) *VVB* 59, *brith,* gl. *pictam.* 12g. *LL* 191 [...]

A look at the above table and the examples reveals that the space devoted to the gender
inflection is again not necessarily linked to the size of the dictionaries. Indeed, it is *Y Geiriadur
Cyfoes* which is worse than the small dictionaries, i.e. *Spurrell* and *Y Geiriadur Bach*.

Very peculiar is the *Works-Dictionary*. Only two feminine forms occur in the respective entry
of their masculine base words. All the other feminine forms are contained as separate headwords
in the dictionary, thus making morphological features of lexical items difficult to ascertain. Such
an approach severely reduces the flexible usage of lexical items. In contrast to nouns (cf. section
4.3.2.), the compiler seems to take morphological features of adjectives as criteria for separate
dictionary entries as is illustrated by the following examples:

bechan *adj (f)* small.
[...]
ber *adj (f)* short.
[...]
brech *f* **(-au)** pox. • *adj (f)* speckled.
[...]
brith *adj* speckled; faint (*f* **braith**).
[...]
brwnt *adj* dirty; nasty (*f* **bront**).
[...]
brych *m* **(-au)** speck. • *adj* speckled.
[...]
bychan *adj* little.
[...]
byr *adj* short
[...]
crom *adj (f)* round.
[...]
crwm *adj* curved.

With some adjectives D.G. Lewis even attributes different meanings to the feminine and masculine forms, thereby aggravating morphological obscuring.

Only in *Geiriadur yr Academi* and in the historical dictionary *GPC* is gender inflection nearly comprehensively covered in the dictionary entries. Disappointing, on the contrary, are *The Welsh Learner's Dictionary* and the *Pocket Modern Welsh Dictionary*; the former hardly recognises feminine forms and the latter exhibits a very limited lexicon.

4.3.3.2.   Number inflection

The *number inflection* is not as well represented in Welsh dictionary entries as is the gender inflection. The selection of lexical items in the following table, which illustrates the situation, is based on P.W. Thomas (1996: 193):

Adjective	Geiriadur Cyfoes	Geiriadur Mawr	Geiriadur Bach	GPC	Geiriadur yr Academi	Works Dict.	Spurrell
amddifad 'destitute'	--	--	--	√	√	--	--
arall 'other'	√	√	√	√	√	√	√
balch 'proud'	--	--	√	√	√	--	--
buan 'swift'	--	√	√	√	√[1]	--	--
cadarn 'firm'	--	--	--	√	√	--	√
caled 'hard'	--	--	--	√	√	--	--
cyfan 'whole'	--	--	--	√	√	--	--
garw 'harsh'	√	√	√	√	√	--	√
hardd 'beautiful'	√	√	√	√	√	--	--
ifanc 'young'	√	--	--	√	√	--	√
llydan 'wide'	--	--	--	√	√	--	--
marw 'dead'	√	√	√	√	√	--	√

Some variation in the presentation of the number inflection may again be due to assumed language usage. The plural form of *buan* 'swift', for instance, is listed in *Y Geiriadur Bach* and *Y Geiriadur Mawr*, both elder dictionaries, but not consistently in *Geiriadur yr Academi*, the most recent of importance. However, this dictionary has additionally in its explanatory section an extensive list of adjectives which take plural forms (1996: xliif.).

The *Works-Dictionary* nearly totally excludes the number inflection from its dictionary entries. A few plural forms of adjectives form separate entries. As with the gender inflection, the *Works-Dictionary* obscures the morphology of Welsh adjectives.

Looking at the table it becomes apparent that the number inflection of Welsh adjectives is only well presented in *Geiriadur yr Academi* and in the historical dictionary *GPC*.

---

[1]   Under the headword 'swift' *buan* is given without its plural form and under the headword 'quick' with its plural form.

354

The following table lists those adjectives which exhibit both gender and number inflection, thereby confirming the tendencies established in sections 4.3.3.1. and 4.3.3.2. above:

Adjective	Geiriadur Cyfoes	Geiriadur Mawr	Geir. Bach	GPC	Geiriadur yr Academi	Works Dict.	Spur-rell
brith 'speckled'	(√-g)	(√-g)	(√-g)	√	√	(√-g)	(√-g)
brwnt 'dirty'	(√-n)	√	√	(√-g)	(√-n)	(√-g)	(√-g)
bychan 'small'	(√-g)	--	no entry	√	√	--	(√-g)
byr 'short'	(√-n)	√	√	√	√	--	(√-g)
crwm 'bent'	(√-g)	(√-g)	(√-g)	(√-g)	√	--	(√-g)
crwn 'round'	--	√	√	√	√	--	(√-g)
cryf 'strong'	(√-g)	√	√	√	√	--	(√-g)
cwta 'short'	--	(√-g)	(√-g)	√	√	--	no entry
dwfn 'deep'	--	√	√	√	√	--	(√-g)
gwlyb 'wet'	--	√	√	√	√	--	--
gwyn 'white'	√	√	√	√	√	--	(√-g)
gwyrdd 'green'	--	√	√	√	√	--	--
llwm 'bare'	(√-g)	√	√	√	√	--	(√-g)
llyfn 'smooth'	(√-g)	(√-g)	(√-g)	√	√	--	(√-g)
llym 'sharp'	(√-g)	√	√	√	√	--	(√-g)
melyn 'yellow'	(√-g)	√	√	√	√	--	(√-g)

As in the preceding tables, it becomes clear that more notice is taken of the gender (√-g) than of the number inflection (√-n). If only one inflection is stated, it is nearly always the gender inflection.

This is somewhat surprising and not user-friendly, since the plural forms of adjectives can often be used as nouns, either as plural nouns (for a definition, see section 4.3.2.2.1.), such as in *beilchion* 'the proud (people)' or as nouns in the plural form, e.g. *cleifion* (< *claf*) 'patients (< patient, cf. next section)'. In view of the facts presented above it can be said that word formation patterns are not sufficiently supported by most Welsh general-purpose dictionaries.

4.3.3.2.1. The formation of de-adjectival nouns by grammatical suffixes

Listing those adjectives in a table the plural forms of which are regularly employed as nouns illustrates the lack of exhibiting their number inflection in Welsh dictionary entries clearly. This insufficiency causes the obscuring of the close relation between nouns and adjectives and consequently limits the range of their applicability. The lexical basis is again drawn from P.W. Thomas (1996: 194f.).

Adjective	Geir. Cyfoes	Geir. Mawr	Geir. Bach	GPC	Geir. yr Acad.	Works Dict.	Spur-rell
bonheddig 'noble'	--	--	--	√ (eg, ll)	--	--	√
caredig 'kind'	--	--	--	√ (eg, ll)	--	--	--
claf 'ill'	√	√	√ (eg)	√ (eg, ll)	√	√ (eg)	√
clwyfedig 'wounded'	no entry	√	--	√ (eg, ll)	--	no entry	no entry
colledig 'damned'	--	--	--	√ (eg, ll)	--	--	--
cyfoethog 'rich'	--	√	--	√ (eg, ll)	√ (ell)	--	--
dall 'blind'	√	√ (eg, ll)	√	√ (eg, ll)	√ (ell)	--	√
dewr 'brave'	√ (eg, ll)	√ (eg, ll)	√	√ (eg, ll)	--/√	--	√
dirgel 'occult'	√	√	--	√ (eg, ll)	--	--	√ (eg)
doeth 'wise'	--	√ (eg)	√	√ (eg, ll)	--[1]	--	√
dychweledig 'returned'	ell	√ (ell)	√	√ (eg, ll)	--	no entry	--
dysgedig 'learned'	--	--	--	√ (eg, ll)	√	--	√
graddedig 'graduated'	√	--	--	√ (eg, ll)	eg, ll[2]	--	ell[3]

---

[1] *Doethion*, the plural of *doeth*, is included as the plural of *doethyn*, which, however, is its singulative (cf. sections 4.3.2.2.1. and 4.3.2.2.2. and *Y Geiriadur Mawr* 1987: 193). In addition, the plural of *doethyn* would rather be *doethynion* (cf. section 4.2.2.2.1.).

[2] *Graddedig(-ion)* as an equivalent to 'graduate' is only characterised as a noun. The equivalent to 'graduated' *graddedig* is only included in its singular form.

[3] *Graddedigion* is only characterised as a noun, the adjective *graddedig* is not contained in the dictionary.

hoyw 'gay'	--	√	√	√	egb, ll[4]	--	--
hynod 'extraordinary'	ell	ell	√ (ell)	--	--	--	ell
mawr 'big'	√	√	√	√ (eg, ll)	√	--	√
meddw 'drunk'	√	√	√	√ (egb, ll)[5]	--	--[6]	√
mud 'dumb'	--	--	--	√ (eg, ll)	--	--	--
newydd 'new'	√ (eg)	√ (eg, ll)	√	√ (eg, ll)	√ (eg, ll)	√ (eg, ll)[7]	√ (eg)

Looking at the above table, it becomes immediately apparent that the dividing line between adjectives and nouns is recognised somewhat idiosyncratically.[8] √ (eg, ll) stands for *enw gwrywaidd, lluosog* 'masculine noun, plural' and indicates that the plural (and singular) form of an adjective may be used as a noun, which itself occurs in the same entry as the adjective, such as in an example from *Y Geiriadur Mawr*:

> **dall**, 1. *a. ll.* deillion. yn methu gweld, tywyll. BLIND.
> 2. *eg. ll.* deillion. dyn tywyll. BLIND PERSON.

√ is used when the plural form of an adjective is only defined as a noun or only assigned to the adjective but is part of the dictionary entry. Such entries can, for instance, be found in *Y Geiriadur Mawr* and *Y Geiriadur Cyfoes*:

> **claf**, 1. *a.* sâl, tost, afiach, anhwylus.
> ILL.
> 2. *eg. ll.* cleifion. un sâl, person tost, dioddefydd. SICK PERSON.

> **claf**, (cleifion), *a.* ILL. SICK.
> *n.m.* SICK PERSON. PATIENT.

√ (eg) stands for *enw gwrywaidd* 'noun masculine' and is employed when the plural form of the adjective is in the same entry also characterised as a masculine noun in the singular (cf. below *claf*). √ (ell), i.e. *enw lluosog* 'plural noun', is written when the plural form of the adjective is in the same entry also assigned to a noun in the plural as in the following example from *Y Geiriadur Mawr*:

---

4   *Hoyw(on)* is only included as a noun and is characterised as feminine and masculine.
5   The noun derived from the adjective *meddw* is characterised as feminine and masculine.
6   *Meddwon*, the plural of *meddw*, is included but as the plural of *methwyn* which, however, is its singulative (cf. sections 4.3.2.2.1. and 4.3.2.2.2. and *Y Geiriadur Mawr* 1987: 328).
7   In this entry the adjective is primarily defined as a noun.
8   Some variation in the reflection of the relation between nouns and adjectives in Welsh dictionaries may be due to the approach of the respective author to the contemporary use of existing forms of adjectives.

dychweledig, *a. ll.-ion.* wedi dychwel-
yd, wedi dod yn ôl. RETURNED.
Dychweledigion. CONVERTS, REVENANTS.

Ell is used when the plural form of the adjective constitutes a separate 'plural' headword, e.g. (cf. *hynodion, dewrion* (below) and collective nouns in section 4.3.2.2.1.).

A study of the above table reveals that morphological relations between Welsh adjectives and nouns are neither consistently nor sufficiently included in entries of general-purpose dictionaries. If the plural forms are contained as separate entries in the headword list the relation between the adjective and the noun is not visible to the dictionary user.

Similar insufficiencies can be observed in *The Welsh Learner's Dictionary* and in the *Pocket Modern Welsh Dictionary*, which thereby fail to support easy language aquisition because of obscuring regularities of Welsh word formation.

Very peculiar is again the *Works-Dictionary*. With regard to adjectives the limited lexicon of this dictionary is introduced as a compilation of isolated lexical items. This tendency is supported by the exemplification of the relation between Welsh nouns and adjectives in its dictionary entries: whereas the plural form of *claf* is introduced as a noun in the singular, the plural forms of other adjectives constitute separate headwords, e.g. *caredigion, dewrion, doethion*. The plural form of *bonheddig*, i.e. *boneddigion*, is assigned to the noun *bonheddwr*, the plural form of which, however, is *bonheddwyr*:

> **bonheddig** *adj* courteous.
> **bonheddwr** *m* **(boneddigion)** gentleman.
> [...]
> **claf** *adj* sick. • **(cleifion)** patient.
> **dewr** *adj* brave.
> [...]
> **dewrion** *pl* braves.
> [...]
> **newydd** *m* **(·ion)** news. • *adj* new.

In view of the facts presented above, it would appear that a vital link between an adjective, a possible plural and its potential usage as a noun has not been acknowledged by the compiler of the *Works-Dictionary*. This phenomenon, however, is usually well applied in the speech of native Welsh speakers.

The reflection of the morphological relation between nouns and adjectives in an English-Welsh dictionary, e.g. in *Geiriadur yr Academi*, is somewhat difficult. Some inconsistencies in dealing with different morphological forms of lexical items are apparent. A number of Welsh adjectives is listed with and without their plural forms in individual dictionary entries, such as *dewr* 'brave', which is included with its plural form on pages 315 and 1609 and without its plural form on page 163.

In addition, some plural forms of adjectives are introduced as the plural inflection of the secondary singular form of the noun derived from this adjective, e.g. *doethyn -> doethion*, instead *doeth -> doethion -> doethyn*. This approach follows the problematic reflection of the number inflection of collective nouns in *Geiriadur yr Academi* as exemplified in section 4.3.2.2.1. With regard to adjectives it is ignored here that some of their plurals form collective nouns as defined in section 4.3.2.2.1., which have later developed singulatives, e.g. *israddol -> israddolion -> israddolyn, meddw -> meddwon -> meddwyn* (cf. sections 4.3.2.2.1. and 4.3.2.2.2.).

Inconsistencies as illustrated above occur in all general-purpose and learners' dictionaries. This is rather unfortunate, since the chance is missed to present patterns of productive Welsh word formation systematically to the dictionary user. An even greater ignorance of morphological links between nouns and adjectives would become apparent, when investigating the presentation of the formation of de-adjectival nouns by the diminutive suffixes, e.g. *pwysig* 'important' -> *pwysigyn* 'V.I.P.' (cf. section 4.3.2.2.2.). Welsh dictionaries thus fail to maximise efficient language acquisition or translation or to provide accurate language material for researchers.

4.3.3.3. The category of degree

In this section, the presentation of the *category of degree* in entries of Welsh general-purpose dictionaries is analysed. Lexical items for this analysis have been taken from the preceding tables:

Adjective	Geir. Cyfoes	Geiriadur Mawr	Geiriadur Bach	GPC	Geiriadur yr Academi	Spur-rell
balch 'proud'	--	--	--	--	mor falch, cyn falched	--
brith 'speckled'	--	--	--	--	--	--
brwnt 'dirty'	--	--	--	--	--	--
brych 'freckled'	--	--	--	--	--	--
buan 'swift'	--	--	--	cynted, cynt, cyntaf	cynted, cynt, cyntaf; buaned, buanach, buanaf[1]	--
bychan 'small'	--	--	no entry	bychaned, lleied, llai, llaiaf (bychanaf)	cyn lleied, llai, lleiaf	--
byr 'short'	--	--	--	--	byrred, byrrach, byrraf	--
cadarn 'firm'	--	--	--	--	--	--
caled 'hard'	--	--	--	--	caleted, caletach, caletaf	--
crwm 'bent'	--	--	--	--	--[2]	--
crwn 'round'	--	--	--	--	--[2]	--
cryf 'strong'	--	--	--	--	--[2]	--
cwta 'short'	--	--	--	--	--[2]	no entry
cyflym 'swift'	--	--	--	--	cyflymed, cyflymach, cyflymaf[3]	--
cynnar 'early'	--	--	--	--	cynhared, cynted; cynharach, cynt; cynharaf, cyntaf	--

---

[1]   Under the headword 'swift' *buan* exhibits only the comparison with *cynted* ..., under 'quick' both comparisons and under the headword 'speedy' there is a reference to 'quick'.

[2]   The comparison of this adjective is presented in the explanatory section of *Geiriadur yr Academi* (Griffith, B. & D.G. Jones 1996: xlivf.).

[3]   This comparison is only given under the headword 'fast', not under 'swift', 'quick' or 'speedy'.

da 'good'	--	--	--	cystal, cynna, daed; gwell; gorau, goraf	cystal, gwell, gorau	--
dwfn 'deep'	--	--	--	--	dyfned, dyfnach, dyfnaf	--
garw 'harsh'	--	--	--	--	--	--
gwlyb 'wet'	--	--	--	--	--[2]	--
gwyn 'white'	--	--	--	--	--[2]	--
gwyrdd 'green'	--	--	--	--	--	--
hardd 'beautiful'	--	--	--	--	--	--
hysb 'dry'	--	--	--	--	--	--
ifanc 'young'	--	--	--	ianged, ienged, iangach, iengach, iau, iangaf, iengaf, ieuaf	ieuenged, ienged, ifenged, 'fenged, ifanced; iau, ieuangach, ifengach, 'fengach, iengach, ifancach; ieuaf, ieuangaf, ifengaf, 'fengaf, ifancaf	--
llwm 'bare'	--	--	--	--	--	--
llydan 'wide'	--	--	--	cyfled, lled, lletaf; lleted, lletach, llydanach, llydanaf	lleted/cyfled, lletach, lletaf	--
llyfn 'smooth'	--	--	--	--	--	--
llym 'sharp'	--	--	--	--	--	--
mawr 'great'	--	cymaint, mwy, mwyaf	cymaint, mwy, mwyaf	--	cymaint, mwy, mwyaf	--
melyn 'yellow'	--	--	--	--	--	--
uchel 'high'	--	uched, cyf- uwch, uwch, uchaf	uched: cyf- uwch, uwch, uchaf	letter 'u' not yet reached	cyfuwch, cuwch, cyn uched; uwch; uchaf	--

The above table shows that with the exception of *Geiriadur yr Academi* the comparison of the adjectives does not form a regular part of entries of Welsh general-purpose dictionaries. The entries of *uchel* and *mawr* in *Y Geiriadur Mawr* and *Y Geiriadur Bach* look rather like a mistake or accident.

In *Geiriadur yr Academi*, most of those adjectives are listed which show peculiarities in their comparison. However, some of them are not exemplified, e.g. *gwlyb - gwlyped, gwlypach, gwlypaf* 'wet, so wet, more wet, most wet', *gwyn - gwynned, gwynnach, gwynnaf* 'so white, more white, most white', *cwta - cwteued - cwteuach - cwteuaf* 'so short, shorter, shortest'. This inconsistency is misleading, since dictionary users may (mis)assume that those adjectives whose comparison is not included in the dictionary entries compare regularly and without additional changes; i.e. when monosyllabic synthetically and when polysyllabic analytically (cf. Griffith 1995: xlv, 909;[4] P.W. Thomas 1996: 225). In addition, as observed with the presentation of the number category of adjectives in entries of *Geiriadur yr Academi*, its users do not necessarily find the entire information concerning a Welsh equivalent each time it is included in an entry. Only some entries provide comprehensive information (cf. sections 4.2.3.2.). On the other hand, the comparison of some adjectives not exemplified in dictionary entries is illustrated in the explanatory section of *Geiriadur yr Academi* (1996: xlivf.).

The complete absence of the comparison of adjectives in the entries of the bi-directional general-purpose dictionaries, such as in *Y Geiriadur Cyfoes*, the *Works-Dictionary*, and *Spurrell*, is somewhat surprising, since this category is linguistically demanding and causes a number of problems (cf. sections 1.3.2.2.7. and 1.3.2.3.3.). In particular the equative is not known to English, but the Welsh learner does not learn anything about this category if relying on the aforementioned dictionaries.

Even the most comprehensive dictionary, the historical *GPC* does not contain the comparison of adjectives on a regular basis in their entries. The learners' *Pocket Modern Welsh Dictionary* includes irregular comparisons of adjectives in its entries as well as some of those which induce changes in the lexical items. This approach is very user-friendly, but diminished in its effect by the limited number of lexical items compiled in this reference book.

As illustrated in the preceding sections, Welsh general-purpose dictionaries, except from *Geiriadur yr Academi*, tend to separate morphological categories of adjectives. This is also the case with the category of degree when equative, comparative, or superlative forms make up separate dictionary entries, as seen in the following examples:

Y Geiriadur Cyfoes: **cystal,** *a.* AS/SO GOOD, EQUAL
                ad. AS/SO WELL.
                [...]
                da, *a.* GOOD, WELL
                (-oedd), *n.m.* good, goods, stock,
                cattle.
                [...]
                gorau, *a.* BEST
                [...]
                gwell, *a.* BETTER, SUPERIOR
                o'r gorau, VERY WELL

Y Geiriadur Mawr and Bach: **cystal,** *a.* mor dda, cyfartal. AS GOOD,
                EQUAL
                [...]

---

[4]   The comparison of adjectives is explained twice in Griffith, B. & D.G. Jones (1995), once under 'The Morphology of the Welsh language' and once in the entry of the headword 'most'.

da, *a.* mad, buddiol, llesol, addas,
cyfiawn, dianaf. GOOD, WELL.
  Os gwelwch yn dda. IF IT PLEASE
  YOU.
  Da gennyf. I AM GLAD.
  Da chwi. I PRAY YOU.
  [...]
gorau, *a.* gradd eithaf *da.* BEST.
  O'r gorau. VERY WELL; OF THE
  BEST.
  Rhoi'r gorau i. TO GIVE UP.
  [...]
gwell, *a.* gradd gymharol *da.* BETTER.
  GWELL. BETTER AND BETTER.

Both dictionaries indicate at least for the comparative form of *da*, i.e. *gwell*, and for its superlative, i.e. *gorau*, the adjective the two forms of degree derive from. This, however, is not the
case with the following dictionaries:

Spurrell: **cystal** *adj* as good, so good ♦ *adv*
       as well, so well
       [...]
       da *adj* good, well ♦ (-oedd) *nm*
       Good; goods; stock, cattle
       [...]
       gorau (-euon) adj best. **o'r g.** very
       well
       [...]
       gwell *adj* better, superior

Works-Dictionary: **cystal** *adj* as good as.
           [...]
           da *adj* good. • *m* cattle
           [...]
           gorau *adj* **(goreuon)** best.
           [...]
           gwell *adj* better.

The Welsh Learner's Dictionary: **cystal** (adj.) *[kuhstal]* as good, so good
                  cystal â +A.M. as good as
                  rydw i cystal â fe I am so good as he
                  [...]
                  da^2 (adj) *[da]* good
                  merch dda a good girl
                  mae'n dda 'da fi 'ch gweld chi I'm
                    glad to see you
                  os gwelwch chi'n dda please
                  dda gen i mo'r dyn I don't like the
                    man

[...]
gorau (adj) *[goraee]* best
o'r gorau all right
[...]
gwell (adj) *[gooell]* better
gwell na better than

There is no doubt, that irregular forms of comparison may be listed separately. The least that should be done, however, is to include a reference in the separate entry linking the individual irregular forms of the adjective to each other (cf. *Y Geiriadur Mawr* and *Y Geiriadur Bach* above). A constant separation of different morphological forms of lexical items undermines the morphology of the language thus reducing its communicative potential and learner-friendly acquisition, in particular when the separated entry does not provide the different meaning as in the entry '**cynted** *from cynnar.*' in the *Works-Dictionary*.

The best way of presenting different forms of adjective comparison, therefore, is to arrange them together in the entry of the adjective they are derived from, as is the case with dictionaries of other Celtic languages. Although the comparison of adjectives is far more regular in the Breton language, it is even included in the small *Elementary breton-english & english-breton dictionary* (Delaporte 1995, cf. section 3.2.2.) whenever the comparison induces the slightest change in the given lexical items:

kozh *a. [comp.* **koshoc'h**, *sup*
koshañ] 1. ['koːs] *(after noun)* old,
aged; former; **ar maer k.,** the
former mayor; **2.** ['kɔs] *(bef noun)*
(mut.1b) bad; **ur c'hozh ti,** a
miserable house

Irregular comparisons are also inluded in the dictionary entries of the *Dictionnaire Du Breton Contemporain* (Favereau 1993):

MAD⁺ /&-T^X [maːd-t] *(var.* MAT [mad-t] ad., d-ll Argoad
KTW) bih. -IG ad. *bien, bon (& appr. moral),*
g. -où *bien (immobilier, surt. pl.) & (l') intérêt (fin.), (un)*
bon produit, & appr. morale, & b. bien(fait), dim (-ig-où)
bonbon (C. mat, h-br. id., kmg mad good(ly), iwg. maith
id. & gln mat-) : an dra-se n'eo ket mat? [...]
a-w matoc'h & matañ
(gwaliessoc'h GWELL(OC'H), GWELLAÑ): krampouezh
gwinizh ha laezh tro / matañ traou zo er vro [...]

The same is true for Irish dictionaries which include the class of declension of the adjectives, thus indicating the different kinds of comparison. Or they provide full paradigms of irregular forms on a far more regular basis than Welsh dictionaries present morphological features of adjectives to dictionary users (cf. also Irisch-Deutsches WB) as is illustrated by the following examples:

Foclóir Póca, Gearrfhoclóir Gaeilge-Bèarla
> **maith¹** mah *f2, gs & pl* ~ **e** good, [...]
> > *a*1, *comp* **fearr** good, [...]
> **maith²**, *a1. (comp.* **fearr**). Good **1.** Morally [...]

> **gearr²** g´a:r *a*1. *gsm* ~ *gsf & comp* **giorra**
> > short; near [...]
> **gearr²**, *a. (gsm.* ~, *gsf. comp.* **giorra**, *npl.* ~ **a**)
> > & *s.* **1.** Short. [...]

The Scottish Gaelic *The illustrated Gaelic-English Dictionary* (Dwelly 1994, cf. section 3.2.6.) also offers more information and includes irregular comparisons in its entries:

> math, *pl.* -a, a. *1st. comp.* fèarr *or* feabha, *2nd.*
> *comp.* fèairrd or feabhaid, *3rd. comp.* feabhas.
> [‡ says fearr is a comp. from the prep. ver =
> Gaelic far, for, *super.* Now *comp.* for math,
> but evidently once for fern. *good* [...].

As is shown by Celtic sister languages of Welsh, the learner needs information on the degree of adjective comparisons. Most Welsh dictionaries seem to take the command of them for granted and thus do not cater for learners. That a good command of the category of degree, however, cannot be taken for granted is illustrated in section 4.1.1. More likely is a loss of morphological features in this part of the Welsh lexicon as well, especially when considering the high percentage of learners and their potential impact on the situation of the Welsh language (cf. ibid.).

Specific to the Welsh language is the use of affixes of adjective comparison by nouns, thus turning them into adjectives. The representation of this particularity in dictionary entries is displayed in the following table. The lexical basis is, once more, taken from P. W. Thomas (1996: 228f.).

Adjectives in Welsh-to-English sections	Geiriadur Cyfoes	Geiriadur Mawr	Geiriadur Bach	GPC	Geiriadur yr Academi	Spurrell	Works-Dictionary
blaen 'point front' - **blaenaf** 'foremost'	--	--	--	--	(blaenaf)[5]	--	--
dewis 'choice' - **dewisach** 'rather'	--	--	--	dewis(ach)	--	--	--
diwedd 'end' - **diweddaf** 'last'	--	--	--	diwethaf - separately under c	(diweddaf, olaf)	--	--
elw 'benefit' - **elwach** 'better off'	--	--	--	--	(rhagorach, cyfoethocach)[6]	--	elwach - separately under c
gradd 'rank' - **cyfradd** 'of equal rank'	cyfradd - separately under c	--	--	cyfradd - separately under c	(cydradd)	cyfradd - separately under c	cyfradd 'rate' - separately under c

[5] The Welsh lexical items found in *Geiriadur yr Academi* are in brackets because they can only be found under English headwords in a uni-directional English-Welsh dictionary.

[6] *Cyfoethocach* is also a de-adjectival noun.

gwedd 'appearance' - **cyfwedd** 'similar in appearance'	--	--	--	cyfwedd - separately under c	--	--	--
gwerth 'value' - **cyfwerth** 'of equal value'	--	--	cyfwerth - separately under c	cyfwerth	(cyfwerth)	cyfwerth 'equivalent' - separately under c	cyfwerth 'equivalent' - separately under c
lled 'breadth' - **cyfled** 'of the same breadth'	cyfled 'how wide' - separately under c	cyfled 'as broad as' - separately under c	cyfled 'of equal breadth or wide' - separately under c	cyfled 'equal in breadth' - separately under c	(cyfled)	cyfled 'as broad as' - separately under c	'cyfled *from* llydan.' [no meaning given]
lles 'benefit' - **llesach** 'more advantageous'	--	--	--	--	--	--	--
lliw 'colour' - **cyfliw** 'of the same colour'	cyfliw - separately under c	cyfliw - separately under c	cyfliw - separately under c	cyfliw - separately under c	--	cyfliw - separately under c	--
nifer 'number' - **cynifer** 'of the same number'	cynifer 'so many' - separately under c	cynifer 'as many' - separately under c	cynifer 'as many' - separately under c	cynifer 'so great a number' - separately under c	(cynifer)	cynifer 'as many' - separately under c	cynifer 'as many' - separately under c
oed 'age' - **cyf-oed** 'of the same age'	cyfoed - separately under c	cyfoed - separately under c	--	cyfoed - separately under c	(cyfoed)	cyfoed - separately under c	--
ôl 'rear' - **olaf** 'last'	olaf - separately under o	olaf - separately under o	olaf - separately under o	olaf - separately under o	(olaf)	--	olaf - separately under o

pen 'head' - pen**naf** 'chief'	pennaf - separately under p	pennaf - separately under p	pennaf - separately under p	pennaf - separately under p	(pennaf)	pennaf - separately under p
rhagor 'difference' - rhagor**ach** 'superior'	--	--	--	--	(rhagorach)	--
rhaid 'need' - rheitied, rheit**iach**, rheit**iaf** 'fitting'	--	--	--	(rheitiaf)	(rheitiach)	'rheitied' *from* rhaid (no meaning)
rhyw 'kind' - **cyf**ryw 'of the same kind'	cyfryw 'such' - separately under c	cyfryw 'such' - separately under c	--	cyfryw	(cyfryw)	cyfryw 'such' - separately under c

Morphological relations between Welsh nouns and adjectives are generally not well clarified in bi-directional general-purpose dictionaries as is illustrated in the preceding sections. This applies also to dictionaries which include synonyms, context or even idioms in their entries, such as *Y Geiriadur Mawr* and *Bach*. Some items which are exemplified by context are *ar led* 'abroad', *lledled* 'throughout' for *lled* 'breadth'; *yn ôl* 'ago...', *ar ôl* 'after', *y tu ôl i* 'behind' for *ôl* 'track...'; or *ar ben* 'on top of', *ymhen y mis* 'in a month's time', *da dros ben* 'exceedingly good' for *pen* 'head, end, chief'. Adjectives derived from nouns, such as *cyfled, olaf, pennaf*, however, are not regularly contained in these entries. Only in four cases of the entire examples above do we find the 'noun in comparison' being turned into an adjective in the dictionary entry.

Much better are the historical dictionary *GPC* and the uni-directional *Geiriadur yr Academi*, which present most derivations. The latter additionally provides some comments on this phenomenon in its explanatory section (Griffiths, B. & D.G. Jones 1995: xlvi).

De-nominal derivations of adjectives are particularly inadequately reflected in the learners' dictionaries by Gruffudd and King (cf. section 4.2.).

In order to counter any possible claim that the derived adjectives are not been used, the following table is given.[7] Cross checking the English equivalents of the above table in the English-to-Welsh section, it becomes apparent that most of the adjectives derived from nouns by affixes of comparison are listed there as Welsh equivalents:

Adjectives in the English-to-Welsh section	Geiriadur Cyfoes	Geiriadur Mawr	Geiriadur Bach	Geiriadur yr Academi	Spurrell
(blaen) foremost	blaenaf	blaenaf	blaenaf	blaenaf, pennaf...	blaenaf
(dewis) rather	--	--	--	--	--
(diwedd) last	olaf, diwethaf	olaf, diwethaf	olaf, diwethaf	olaf, diwethaf, diweddaf	olaf, diwethaf
(elw) better (off)	rhagorach	--	(rhagorach)	rhagorach, cyfoethocach	rhagorach
(gradd) of equal rank	--	--	--	cydradd	--
(gwedd) similar in appearance	--	--	--	--	--
(gwerth) equivalent	cywerth	cywerth	cywerth	cyfwerth	cywerth
(lled) of the same breadth	--	--	--	cyfled	--
(lles) more advantegeous	--	--	--	--	--
(lliw) of the same colour	--	--	--	--	--
(nifer) as many	cynifer	cynifer	cynifer	cynifer	cynifer
(oed) contemporary	--	cyfoed	--	cyfoed...	--
(ôl) last	olaf, diwethaf	olaf, diwethaf	olaf, diwethaf	olaf, diwethaf	olaf, diwethaf
(pen) chief	pennaf	pennaf	pennaf	pennaf...	pennaf

7   Only those adjectives which have been dervied from nouns by the suffix -ach seem to be less popular.

(rhagor) superior	--	--	--	rhagorach...	rhagorach
(rhyw) such	cyfryw	cyfryw	cyfryw	cyfryw...	cyfryw

It is apparent from the preceding tables that the derivation pattern of de-nominal adjectives is as inadequately reflected in Welsh general-purpose dictionaries as is that of de-adjectival nouns (cf. preceding section). This inadequacy is aggravated when the English language has no single lexical item for existing words in Welsh, such as for *cyfradd* 'of equal rank'. Consequently, if multi-word lexical items formed regular parts of the dictionary entries, or peculiarities of the Welsh language were given preference more Welsh equivalents could be expected in the second table, e.g. *cyfled* 'of the same breadth' or *cyfliw* 'of the same colour'.

When, however, English has a single lexical item for which there exists a de-nominal adjective in Welsh this normally forms its equivalent in the English-to-Welsh section, even if this adjective is not contained in the headword list of the Welsh-to-English section.

In view of the facts presented above, it has to be concluded that Welsh general-purpose dictionaries do not sufficiently support patterns of Welsh word formation for de-nominal adjectives. In addition, the bi-directional dictionaries are not user-friendly in that there is no proper correspondence between their Welsh-to-English and English-to-Welsh sections.

4.3.3.4. Semantico-grammatical information

Some adjectives in the Welsh language vary in meaning according to their position, that is, whether they come before or after their referent. In the following table, the meaning of the adjective when pre-positioned is given first and then the meaning of the adjective when post-positioned. The lexical items are taken from P.W. Thomas (1996: 209f.).

Adjectives	Geiriadur Cyfoes	Geir. Mawr	Geir. Bach	GPC	Geir. yr Acad.	Spurrell
aml 'regular; many'	FREQUENT. ABUNDANT	--; FREQUENT.	--; FREQUENT.	(a) many, numerous. (b) large, abundant ... (c) often	under meaning before the referent	frequent, abundant
cam 'wrong; crooked'	CROOKED. BENT. FALSE. BANDY	1. CROOKED, BENT. 2. WRONG, FALSE.	1. CROOKED. 2. WRONG, FALSE.	1. (a) crooked, bent ... (b) one-eyed ... 2. wrong, wrongful ...	meaning after the referent	crooked, wry; wrong
cwta 'not full; short'	SHORT. ABRUPT	1. SHORT. 2. ABRUPT. 3. NIGGARDLY.	1. SHORT. 2. ABRUPT.	short, cut short, clipped; succinct; meagre, mean, stingy; curt, abrupt ...	under both meanings	short, curt
diweddar 'dead; modern, late'	--; LATE. MODERN	--; LATE, MODERN.	(--); LATE, MODERN.	(a) late. (b) recent; modern; late (of person), deceased. (c) backward, tardy	under both meanings	--; late, modern
eithaf 'quite; extreme; outermost'	EXTREMITY. END. TERMINAL. EXTREME. SUPERLATIVE; -	VERY, QUITE, UTMOST.	VERY, QUITE, UTMOST.	extreme, farthest, uttermost, most distant or remote, outer; highest (of degree or quality) ...	(under both meanings)	extreme; superlative; --
gau 'false; wrong'	FALSE; --	FALSE; --	FALSE; --	false, counterfeit, lying, deceitful, erroneous.	u. meaning before the referent	false; hollow
gwahanol 'dissimilar; various'	DIFFERENT. VARIOUS	DIFFERENT. VARIOUS	DIFFERENT. VARIOUS.	different, other than, unlike, various, diverse; set apart ...	under both meanings	different; --
gwir 'genuine; true'	TRUE. REAL. NET	--; TRUE	--; TRUE.	true, certain, undoubted, genuine, real, very ...	under both meanings	--; true
hen 'old; ancient'	OLD. AGED. ANCIENT	OLD, ANCIENT.	OLD, ANCIENT.	(a) old, aged; ancient ... (b) stale, mouldy ...	under both meanings	old, aged, ancient, of old

hoff 'favourite; dear'	DEAR. FOND. FAVOURITE.	--; FOND.	--; FOND.	beloved, dear, favourite, pet; lovely, chouce, desirable, pleasant ...	under both meanings	dear, fond, favourite
iawn 'right; sufficient'	RIGHT; --	RIGHT; --	RIGHT; --	right, correct, true, real, genuine, exact; ?straight, direct; ... --	u. meaning before the referent	right; --
mân 'trivial; small'	TINY. SMALL. MINUTE. FINE. PETTY	TINY, SMALL, MINUTE. FINE; PETTY.	--; TINY, SMALL.	(a) small, little (in seize). (b) fine, thin ... (c) unimportant, trifling, insignificant ...	under both meanings	small, fine, petty
perffaith 'absolute; faultless'	--; PERFECT. IDEAL	--; PERFECT.	--; PERFECT.	perfect, faultless, blameless, pure, correct; complete ...	under meaning after the referent	--; perfect
prin 'meagre; limited'	--; RARE. SCARCE	--; RARE, SCARCE.	--; RARE, SCARCE.	1. (a) rare, uncommon; scarce ... (b) niggardly, mean; needy ...	under both meanings	--; scarce, rare
priod 'proper; married'	OWN. PROPER. MARRIED	1. OWN, PROPER. 2. MARRIED.	1. OWN, PROPER. 2. MARRIED.	(a) proper, right, appropriate ... (b) specific, particular, peculiar ... (c) rightful, true ...	under both meanings	own; proper; married

A look at the table shows that changing meaning according to the position of adjectives, i.e. positionally dependent semantic variation, is often neglected in Welsh general-purpose dictionaries. This variation is most inadequately reflected in the *Works-Dictionary*. Here the basic semantic range of a given adjective is often not covered:

> **cam** *m* (·**au**) step. • *adj* crooked.
> **eithaf** *adj* quite.
> **hen** *adj* old.

Spurrell, provides more equivalents and tends to mark basic differences in meaning by a semicolon.

The analysis confirms again that the size of the dictionary is not a decisive criterion for its quality. *Spurrell*, for instance, includes nearly as many positionally dependent semantic meanings as the more comprehensive dictionaries *Y Geiriadur Mawr* and *Y Geiriadur Cyfoes*.

Apart from the learners' *Pocket Modern Welsh Dictionary*, however, not a single bi-directional dictionary links differing meanings of given lexical items to their actual position in relation to their referent. Since *Y Geiriadur Mawr* provides regularly contextual information, such as for *mân - oriau mân y bore* 'the small hours of the morning'; *priod - enwau priod* 'proper nouns', it offers limited indirect information. In this dictionary, definitions and explanations of headwords by Welsh synonyms contained in their entries may present a broader semantic range than the English equivalent(s) given for them. This phenomenon is illustrated by the following examples:

> **gau,** *a.* ffug, coeg, ffals, anwir, ang-
> hywir, cyfeiliornus, twyllodrus, cel-
> wyddog. FALSE.
> **diweddar,** *a.* hwyr, ar ôl amser, yn y
> dyddiau hyn, wedi marw. LATE,
> MODERN.

The situation is similar in the historical dictionary *GPC*. Although a broad semantic range is presented and sorted according to major differences in meaning, an indication of the positionally dependent semantic variation is often lacking and not regularly deducible from the examples and context provided, as is possible in the case of *hen* 'old'. Comparing *GPC* with the general-purpose dictionaries, it becomes apparent that the semantic fields of individual lexical items are slightly differently defined in the historical dictionary. This, however, is not a problem to be discussed here.

In *Geiriadur yr Academi*, most of the adjectives are in dictionary entries which cover broad semantic fields. The dependence of the meaning from the position of the adjective, however, is often not made clear. Where the relation is exemplified it looks rather unsystematic. The following approaches of presenting positionally dependent semantic variation were found:

(a)　the variation is not explained, e.g. for *cwta, eithaf, prin,*

(b) the positionally dependent meaning becomes clear, since only one meaning is given, e.g. for *aml, cam, gau, iawn, perffaith* (cf. table above),

(c)　explicit indications for the usage of given adjectives are included, e.g. for *hen* and *gwahanol*;

> **old** *a.* [...] hen (*usu. precedes n. + soft mutation*);
> **small** *a.* [...] mân (*usu. only with pl. nouns; can follow, or precede + soft mut.*)
> **petty** *a.* [...] mân + *soft mut.* (*precedes usu. n.pl.*),
> **various** *a.* **1.** *(=varied):* amrywiol, gwahanol *(precedes n. in this sense)*, [...]
> 　**2.** *(a) (=differing, unlike):* gwahanol *(follows n. in this sense)* [...]
> **different** *a.* **1.** gwahanol (**from sth,** i rth) *(can precede noun + soft mut.)* [...]
> 　**2.** *(= diverse, various):* amryw gwahanol; ~ **people saw him,** fe'i gwelwyd ef gan amryw/wahanol bobl [...]
> **sundry** *a. & n.* **1.** amryw [...]; gwahanol, amrywiol, *both + soft mut. Can precede or follow n.;* [...]

As can be seen from the examples, the explanations of positionally dependent semantic variation are of differing quality. The best exemplified lexical item is that of *various*. The meanings of the others are somewhat incomplete.

(d)　the variation is well exemplified by phrases, e.g. for *hoff* - dear ... fy mrawd hoff; (fy hoff frawd = **my favourite brother**);

(e)　the variation is deducible from the given context when looking up both English equivalents, e.g. for *gwir, diweddar, priod.*

Some examples of the presentation of positionally dependent meanings in *Geiriadur yr Academi* demonstrate that there is a way of providing the dictionary user with minimal guidance on this matter. In addition, there are more illustrations on this phenomenon in the explanatory section of this dictionary (Griffiths, B. & D.G. Jones 1995: xlviif.).

Such guidance is also necessary in bi-directional dictionaries, since some adjectives always precede their referents. A number of these is taken from P.W. Thomas (1996: 203) and listed in the following table in order to analyse the syntactic information given for these adjectives in dictionary entries, that is, the government they impose on a subsequent lexical item, such as mutation.

Adjectives	Geir. Cyfoes	Geir. Mawr	Geir. Bach	GPC	Geiriadur yr Academi	Works-Dict.	Spurrell
ambell 'occasional'	AMBELL WAITH	AMBELL WAITH	AMBELL WAITH	a. waith ...	ambell + *soft mut.* [...; example]	--	a. waith
amryw 'diverse'	--	--	--	Ei ddilyn gan y tr. ml.+e.[1]	amryw + *soft mut. (precedes n.)*	--	--
cryn 'considerable'	--	CRYN DIPYN	CRYN AWR ... ~ DIPYN	(yn wreiddiol yn elf. flaenaf gair cfns.)[2]	cryn *(before n. + soft mut.);* [... example]	--	--
holl 'all'	--	--	--	(rh. enghrau o flaen enw neu rhagenw)[3]	holl + *soft mut. preceding n.*	--	--
prif 'prime'	--	--	--	prif achos, prif afon ...	prif + *soft mut. preceding noun*	--	--
rhyw 'some'	--	--	RHYW DDYN	Bron yn ddieithriad pair dr. ml. i air y mae'n ei oleddfu[4]	rhyw *(precedes noun and in sing. is followed by soft mut.)*	--	--
unrhyw 'any'	---	--	--	letter not yet reached	unrhyw + *soft mut. preceding n;*	--	--

A look at the table reveals that the indication of the government of Welsh adjectives which precede their referent is insufficiently indicated in bi-directional general-purpose dictionaries. In most of them both government and position of adjectives must predominantly be guessed from

---

[1]   'Followed by soft mutation + noun.'
[2]   'Originally the first element of compound words.'
[3]   *Holl* is only defined as a pronoun (*rh.*) in *GPC*.
[4]   'Almost without exception does it cause soft mutation in the word it modifies.' This statement implies that *rhyw* precedes its referent, but only for those dictionary users who are familiar with Welsh grammar. Other users, however, may in this case be guided by examples following the explanation.

the given examples. Such indirect information, however, is not sufficiently explicit, since users may take the given examples as exceptions.

The *Works-Dictionary* does not contain any syntactic information for adjectives. Only the unidirectional *Geiriadur yr Academi* provides nearly consistent explicit information on the syntax of Welsh adjectives. The information included here, however, is not standardised or formulaic but varies considerably as can be seen from the table.

Similarly inconsistent in the description of the syntax are the entries in the learners' dictionaries:

The Welsh Learner's Dictionary: **ambell** (adj) *[ambell]* some
  ambell un a few
  ambell ferch a few girls
  ambell waith sometimes, occasionally

  cryn (adj) *[krin]* quite a, a fair
  + S.M
  cryn dipyn quite a lot
  cryn nifer a fair number

Only in the second type of entry, dictionary users get to know directly that the mutation is regularly imposed on the following lexical item. The information about the position of the adjective, however, is always indirect:

Pocket Modern Welsh Dictionary: **ambell**[5] *adjective (precedes the noun)*
  = occasional
  mae'n ˈ fater o ˈbobl eisiau ennill
  ambell ˈbunt yn ychwanegol = it's a
  question of people wanting to win an
  occasional extra pound

  crynˈ
  cryn ˈdipyn = quite a bit
  cryn nifer = quite a few, quite a
  number: [...]

In the second type of entry the information of the regular position of the adjective is only indirectly provided.

The situation becomes worse when looking at idioms formed by adjectives which precede their referent. From twenty-eight idioms listed in P.W. Thomas (1996: 211) and some more in Thorne (1993: 135) only one could be found in *Y Geiriadur Cyfoes* and *Y Geiriadur Mawr*, i.e. *brith gof* 'faint recollection'. This is not surprising for *Y Geiriadur Cyfoes*, which often presents 1:1 equivalents only. *Y Geiriadur Mawr*, however, is known for providing context and idioms, but apparently none based on the position of adjectives.

---

[5]   'ˈ' indicates soft mutation in all reference books written by King (cf. section 6.2.2.).

4.3.3.5.   Summary

I hope to have demonstrated in the preceding sections that the *gender inflection* is relatively adequately exhibited in the entries of Welsh bi-directional general-purpose dictionaries (cf. section 4.3.3.1.). An exception is *Y Geiriadur Cyfoes* and in particular the *Works-Dictionary*.

The number category of Welsh adjectives is less well reflected (cf. section 4.3.3.2.). This weakness becomes more apparent where their plural forms derive de-adjectival nouns, i.e. where the word class of a given lexical item may change (cf. section 4.3.3.2.1.).

Although grammar books try to provide some guidelines about when to use synthetic or analytic *comparison* (cf. Thorne 1993: 193), the regularities are somewhat vague and difficult to remember when to be applied on spot. This is confirmed by P.W. Thomas (1996: 225) who states, that there are no definite rules but rather tendencies. Considering possible interior changes of the adjective in the process of comparing, raises the demand to reflect the *category of degree* adequately in dictionaries. However, this category does not form a regular part of Welsh bi-directional general-purpose dictionaries (cf. section 4.3.3.3.). Not even in the historical dictionary *GPC* is the comparison regularly included, but only for those adjectives which compare irregularly. Only in *Geiriadur yr Academi* more attention is paid to the comparison. The adjectives which compare irregularly are included as well as some which exhibit regular degree. The presentation of the category of degree is similar in the *Pocket Modern Welsh Dictionary* but diminished in its effect because of the limited number of lexical items included in this book.

The relation between adjectives and nouns in the case of the derivation of adjectives from nouns by means of adding affixes of comparison is also poorly represented (cf. section 4.3.3.3.1.). If such adjectives are included in dictionaries they are predominantly separated from their related nouns, apart from some examples in *GPC*. However, the English-to-Welsh sections in bi-directional dictionaries provide these adjectives as equivalents, as long as they correspond to English headwords consisting of single lexical items.

Position-bound semantic variety of adjectives is frequently neglected in bi-directional general-purpose dictionaries (cf. section 4.3.3.4.). Different semantic meanings of individual lexical items are generally not linked to their position. There are only some indications in the historical dictionary *GPC* and in the learners' *Pocket Modern Welsh Dictionary*.

The best treatment can be found in *Geiriadur yr Academi* where a number of explicit explanations on how to use Welsh adjectives is provided. The explanations, however, are not formulaic or standardised, but use a differing *Metalanguage*, i.e. abbrevations, syntax and extralingual signs.

Since some adjectives generally precede their referent, their position should be clearly indicated in dictionary entries in order to support their comprehensive applicability. If an adjective is characterised as one which precedes its referent, its government is often not sufficiently indicated in Welsh bi-directional general-purpose dictionaries (cf. section 4.3.3.4.). Idioms based on adjectives are mainly excluded from them.

In light of weaknesses in the exemplification of linguistic features of Welsh adjectives in bi-directional general-purpose dictionaries (cf. preceding sections), it is no wonder, that learners of

Welsh often complain how difficult this language is. However, it is not the difficulty of the language which distresses the learner, but the deficient description of Welsh in some popular reference books in a socio-linguistic context as illustrated in section 4.1.1.

The presentation of linguistic features of Welsh adjectives in bi-directional general-purpose dictionaries is generally weak and not user-friendly. This also holds to a considerable degree for learners' dictionaries. This standard of the description of peculiarities of adjectives consequently undermines their morphology and does not support Welsh word formation patterns. The situation is better in the historical and uni-directional dictionary but it is completely insufficient in the *Works-Dictionary*.

4.3.4. The Welsh pronoun

As mentioned in section 1.3.2.3.4., the government of different Welsh pronouns, defined as such by P.W. Thomas (1996: 241ff.), is now looked at in detail. The analysis predominantly focuses on the provision of direct information:

Pronouns	Geir. Cyfoes	Geiriadur Mawr	Geiriadur Bach	GPC	Geir. yr Acad.	Works-Dict.	Spur-rell
a^L 'which, who(m)'	--	provided by context	provided by context	✓	✓	--	--
beth $^{(L)}$ 'what'	--[1]	--	--	provided by context	✓	--	no entry
$dacw^L$ 'there'	--[1]	--[1]	--[1]	--[1]	✓[1]	--[1]	--[1]
dy^L 'you(r)'	--	--	--	✓	✓[1]	--	--
$dyma^L$ 'here is/are'	--[1]	--[1]	provided by context[1]	--[1]	--[1]	--[1]	--[1]
$dyna^L$ 'there is'	--[1]	--[1]	provided by context[1]	provided by context[1]	✓[1]	--[1]	--[1]
ei^L 'him, his'	--[2]	--	--	--	✓[1]	--[2]	--[2]
$ei^{S/H}$ 'her, it, its'	--[2]	--	--	--	✓[1]	--[2]	--[2]
ein^H 'us, our'	--[2]	--	✓	✓	✓[1]	--[2]	--[2]
eu^H 'them, their'	--[2]	--	--	✓	✓[1]	--	--[2]
fy^N 'me, my'	--[2]	--	--	✓	✓[1]	--	--[2]
pa^L 'which, what'	--[1]	--[1]	--[1]	✓	✓[1]	--[1]	--[1]
$pwy^{(L)}$ 'who(m)'	--	x[3]	provided by context	provided by context	✓[1]	--	--
$un^{L,4}$ 'one'	--[1]	--[1]	--[1]	letter not yet reached	✓[1,5]	--[1]	--[1]

---

[1]   This lexical item is not defined as a pronoun in the dictionary.

[2]   Meaning when lexical item is used as an object is not provided.

[3]   Page is not existing in the dictionary used for the analysis.

[4]   The mutation is gender-distinguishing and only occurs when the following referent is feminine.

[5]   The word class label of Welsh lexical items does not form a regular part of *Geiriadur yr Academi*. Their classification had, therefore, to be guessed from their description in the dictionary entries or taken from the introductory section (Griffiths, B. & D.G. Jones 1995: xxxiii-xli).

Looking at the table, it becomes, first, apparent that the lexical items defined as pronouns by P.W. Thomas (1996: 241ff.) are assigned to different word classes in the bi-directional dictionaries under review. However, this problem may partly be due to different concepts of defining individual word classes, as for instance in *Geiriadur yr Academi*. That the dividing line between them is not easy to draw is shown by P.W. Thomas whenever he defines a word class and its sub-groups in his grammar (1996). *Dyma, dyna,* and *dacw,* for instance, are also defined as *berfau dangosol* 'demonstrative verbs' by him (ibid.: 271). However, they do not inflect and have a different complementation from verbs (cf. section 4.3.1.), that is, they are morphologically and syntactically very different from verbs. In addition, they may replace a phrase and do not meet the logical category of 'process' (cf. section 1.3.2.2.7.). As a consequence, *dyma, dyna,* and *dacw* are, according to their major function, assigned to the word class of pronouns.

Second, the table reveals that the dictionaries under review do not supply sufficient information concerning the government of the pronouns. *Y Geiriadur Cyfoes* and the *Works-Dictionary* do not provide a single item of information on the mutation the pronouns cause in their referents. Since both dictionaries generally include very limited context their users cannot even guess any influence the lexical items may have on others.

Comparing *Y Geiriadur Cyfoes,* the *Works-Dictionary, Y Geiriadur Mawr* and *Y Geiriadur Bach* it becomes apparent that the indication of mutations imposed on the referents of the pronouns is not necessarily linked to the size of the dictionary.

The comment 'provided by context' implies that the government is indicated by examples in which the lexical item performs in its different functions, or is assigned to a different word class, or is only applied in historic examples. Historic usage, however, cannot be considered reliable information, since it is not necessarily the case that this is also kept in modern language use. In addition, the other examples can be similarly unreliable, since the government may change according to the function or the word class of the respective lexical item. This becomes clear when looking at *ei,* which causes spirant or soft mutation according to the gender it represents (cf. section 1.3.2.3.4.). Is the government not explicitly indicated, therefore, the dictionary user may use this lexical item incorrectly.

Third, the semantic range of the pronouns governed by their functions is not always completely reflected, for example, when the use of *ei, ein, eu* and *fy* as object pronouns is not covered by English equivalents. The following translations can be found in *Y Geiriadur Cyfoes:*

ei, *pn.* HIS, HER, ITS	('him' and 'it' are lacking)
ein, *pn.* OUR	('us' is lacking)
eu, *pn.* THEIR	('them' is lacking)
fy, *pn.* MY	('me' is lacking)

The applicability of pronouns is generally limited when a lexical item defined as a pronoun is not characterised as such, but only as, for instance, an adjective, such as *unrhyw* in the *Works-Dictionary. Y Geiriadur Bach* provides, at least, examples in which it is used as a pronoun, that is, in which it is indirectly defined, such as in sentences like *Gwna unrhyw un y tro.* 'Anyone will do'.

As can be expected from a historical dictionary, the situation in *GPC* is much better, although not satisfactory. Aspects of the valency of pronouns do not form a systematic part of its dictionary entries. Direct information is predominantly given for the prefixed personal pronouns (cf. section 1.3.2.3.4.). Otherwise, explanations relating to the government have to be drawn from the context illustrating the usage of the pronouns or from grammar and other reference books, as for instance, from *Y Treigladur* by D. Geraint Lewis (1993).

An acceptable way of treating the government of pronouns is presented in *Geiriadur yr Academi*. Apart from three exceptions, that is, *aml, dyma* and *dyna*, information on the mutation which pronouns may cause in their referent forms a regular part of the dictionary entries. Occasionally, the whole sentence structure is explained thus providing further aspects of the valency of the respective lexical item:

> **who** *pers.pron.nom.* **1.** *(a) (interr.):* pwy a + *soft mut.* + *conjugated verb form, or* pwy + sydd + yn + *vn; (b) (before forms of* bod = *to be): before present tense forms:* pwy; *before other tense forms*: pwy a + *soft mut. (the* a *is often omitted in speech); (c) negative:* pwy na + *soft mut. of* b, d, g, m, ll, rh. *spirant mut. of* p, t, c; [...].

The learners' dictionaries also include information on the government of pronouns in their entries. They do, however, not recognise all of the pronouns displayed in the above table as such.

The absence of the government of pronouns in Welsh dictionaries is somewhat surprising. Even in the small *Elementary breton-english & english-breton dictionary* (Delaporte 1995, cf. section 3.2.2.), the government on pronouns is indicated. In addition, the government of any word class is well covered in this dictionary (cf. also *Geriadur brezhoneg-alamaneg hag alamaneg-brezhoneg*, Cornillet 2000, section 3.2.2.).

In short, only in *Geiriadur yr Academi*, the information on the government a pronoun can impose on its referent is nearly adequately provided. *Y Geiriadur Mawr* and *Bach* supply some examples of how the necessary minimum information can be indirectly included. Otherwise, dictionary users are badly guided by Welsh general-purpose dictionaries as to the usage of pronouns and may fail to express themselves clearly when using them.

A few remarks on the reflection of the only possessive pronoun in the Welsh language *eiddo* in dictionary entries are given in the following:

Y Geiriadur Cyfoes:	**eiddo,** *n.m.* PROPERTY.
	pn. HIS, etc.
	rhestr eiddo, INVENTORY [...]

Y Geiriadur Mawr,	**eiddof,** (-ot, -o, -i, -om, -och, -ynt),
Y Geiriadur Bach:	ansoddeiriau meddiannol. MINE,
	THINE, etc.

Spurrell:	**eiddo** *nm* property, possessions ♦
	pron his, *etc.*

As in *Y Geiriadur Mawr* and *Bach*, the inflected forms of *eiddo* are part of its dictionary entry in *GPC*, too. In *Geiriadur yr Academi*, the appropriate inflected form of the pronoun is listed each time under the equivalent English headword. For the compilers of the learners' dictionaries the pronoun does not seem to exist. In *Y Geiriadur Cyfoes* and *Spurrell*, dictionary users may be puzzled to be informed that *eiddo* as a pronoun corresponds to 'his, *etc*' (cf. above). No explanation is given as to which other English equivalents are to be assigned to 'etc'. In the *Works-Dictionary eiddi*, the feminine form (third person singular) of *eiddo*, is characterised as a form of the noun *eiddo* 'property'.

4.3.5. The Welsh Preposition
4.3.5.1. Compound prepositions

The analysis of Welsh prepositions first examines compound prepositions and their presentation in the macrostructure of general-purpose dictionaries. The following twenty seven lexical items are drawn from the list of compound prepositions given by P.W. Thomas (1996: 355).

Preposi-tions	Geiriadur Cyfoes	Geiriadur Mawr	Geiriadur Bach	GPC	Works-Dict.	Spurrell
am ben 'on, upon'	no entry	no entry	no entry	under *am* - **prep.**	no entry	no entry
ar ben 'on top of'	no entry	under *pen* 'head' - **noun**	under *pen* 'head' - **noun**	under *pen* 'head' - **noun**	no entry	no entry
ar bwys 'near'	no entry	under *pwys* 'pound' - **noun**	under *pwys* 'pound' - **noun**	under *pwys* 'pound' - **noun**	no entry	no entry
ar draws 'across'	no entry	under *ar* - **prep.**	under *ar* - **prep.**	under *traws* 'cross' - **adj.**	no entry	no entry
ar fedr 'for the purpose of'	no entry	no entry	no entry	under *medr* 'skill' - **noun**	no entry	no entry
ar fin 'on the point of'	no entry	under *ar* - **prep.**	under *ar* - **prep.**	under *min* 'margin' - **noun**	no entry	no entry
ar gefn 'on top'	no entry	no entry	no entry	under *cefn* 'back' - **noun**	no entry	no entry
ar gorn 'at one's ex-pense'	no entry	no entry	no entry	under *corn* 'horn, might' - **noun**	no entry	no entry
ar gyfer 'for'	under *cyfer* 'di-rection' - **noun**	no entry	under *cyfer* : *cyfair* 'oppo-site' - **prep.**	under *cyfer* : *cyfair* 'oppo-site' - **prep.**	under *cyfer*, *cyfair* 'acre' - **noun**	under *cyfer* 'direc-tion' - **noun**
ar gyfyl 'near'	no entry	under *cyfyl* 'vicinity' - **noun**	under *cyfyl* 'vicinity' - **noun**	under *cyfyl* 'vicinity' - **noun**	no entry	under *cyfyl* 'vicinity' - **noun**
ar hyd 'along'	no entry	under *hyd* 'length' - **noun**	under *hyd* 'length' - **noun**	under *hyd* 'length' - **noun**	no entry	no entry

ar ôl 'after'	no entry	under *ôl* 'track' - **noun**	under *ôl* 'track' - **noun**	under *ôl* 'track' - **noun**	no entry	no entry
ar warthaf 'upon'	under *gwarthaf* 'summit' - **noun**	under *gwarthaf* 'summit' - **noun**	under *gwarthaf* 'summit' - **noun**	under *gwarthaf* 'summit' - **noun**	under *gwarthaf*[1]	under *gwarthaf* 'summit' - **noun**
ar ymyl 'on the edge'	no entry	no entry	no entry	letter not yet reached	no entry	no entry
er gwaethaf 'in spite of'	no entry	under *gwaethaf* 'worst' - **ansoddair**	under *gwaethaf* 'worst' - **ansoddair**	under *er* - **prep.**	no entry	no entry
er mwyn 'for the sake of'	under *er* - **prep.**	under *er* - **prep.**	under *er* - **prep.**	under *mwyn* 'benefit' - **noun**	no entry	no entry
i blith 'into the midst of'	no entry	under *plith* 'midst' - **noun**	under *plith* 'midst' - **noun**	under *plith* 'midst' - **noun**	no entry	no entry
o achos 'because of'	no entry	under *achos* 'reason, cause' - **noun**	no entry	under *achos* 'because of...' - **prep.**	no entry	no entry
o amgylch 'round about'	under *amgylch* 'circuit' - **noun**	no entry	no entry	under *amgylch* 'circuit' - **noun**	under *amgylch*[1]	under *amgylch* 'circuit' - **noun**
o blaid 'in favour'	no entry	under *plaid* 'party' - **noun**	under *plaid* 'party' - **noun**	under *plaid* 'party' - **noun**	no entry	no entry
o blith 'from among'	no entry	under *plith* 'midst' - **noun**	under *plith* 'midst' - **noun**	under *plith*	no entry	no entry
o flaen 'in front of'	no entry	no entry	no entry	under *o* - **prep.**	no entry	no entry
o fewn 'within'	no entry	under *mewn* 'in' - **prep.**	under *mewn* 'in' - **prep.**	under *mewn* 'in' - **prep.**	no entry	no entry
o fysg 'amongst'	no entry	no entry	no entry	under *mysg* 'mixture' - **noun**	no entry	no entry

---

[1] No meaning is given for this lexical item, which is defined as a noun in this dictionary.

o gwmpas 'about'	no entry	no entry	under *cwmpas* 'round' - **noun**	under *cwmpas* 'round' - **noun**	under *cwmpas*[1]	under *cwmpas* 'round' - **noun**
o gylch 'around'	no entry	under *cylch* 'circle' - **noun**	under *cylch* 'circle' - **noun**	under *cylch* 'circle' - **noun**	under o *ogylch* 'about'	no entry
o ran 'in part'	no entry	under *rhan* 'part'- **noun**	under *rhan* 'part'- **noun**	under *rhan* 'part'- **noun**	no entry	no entry

Concentrating on one-word equivalents and providing a limited context, *Y Geiriadur Cyfoes* includes only three of twenty-seven compound prepositions chosen here. *Spurrell*, the *Works-Dictionary*, and *The Welsh Learner's dictionary* are slightly better. However, all three dictionaries largely ignore the existence of compound prepositions. The awareness of and sensitivity towards a system of compound prepositions, therefore, is undermined. Their usage is indirectly suppressed and cannot even be considered by dictionary users. These may thus also fail to use this highly metaphorical part of the Welsh lexicon.

The situation is better in *Y Geiriadur Mawr*. This reflects at least fifteen out of the twenty-seven prepositions. *Y Geiriadur Bach* steps further ahead and includes eighteen compound prepositions. Similarly good is the *Pocket Modern Welsh Dictionary*. The best treatment, however, is to be found in the historical dictionary *GPC*.

The question remains, as to what the principle of including compound prepositions in Welsh general-purpose dictionaries is. In the dictionaries under review, they are mostly compiled under their second constituent part. This is often a noun, e.g. in *ar gefn*, but can also be an adjective, such as in *er gwaethaf*, or another preposition, as in *o fewn*. When listed under a noun, compound prepositions are predominantly given as a phrase or an idiom. In *GPC*, compound prepositions are generally listed under 'combinations' together with collocations and other phrases.

Only some of the compound prepositions are given under their initial preposition, e.g. *ar draws* in *Y Geiriadur Mawr* and *Bach*. Very rarely, however, are they defined as prepositions, such as *ogylch* as contained in the *Works-Dictionary* (cf. above).

The situation illustrated above is exemplified by the following two dictionary entries of the compound preposition *ar ôl* 'after' and *yn ôl* 'behind':

Y Geiriadur Bach:

> **ôl,** 1. *eg. ll.* olion. nod, marc. MARK,
> TRACK.
> Yn ôl ei draed. IN HIS STEPS.
> Olion. REMAINS.
> 2. *a.* dilynol. BEHIND.
> Yn ôl ac ymlaen. BACKWARDS AND
> FOREWARDS.
> Yn ôl. AGO, BACK; ACCORDING TO.
> Ar ôl. AFTER.

Y tu ôl i : y tu cefn i. BEHIND.

Blwyddyn yn ôl. A YEAR AGO.

Apart from the difficulty of identifying the compound preposition as such, the approach practised above makes it difficult to find the appropriate semantic meaning of the lexical item, when the word class label is not provided but its meaning changes with this label. Consequently, the morphological and syntactic behaviour of the compound preposition cannot be deduced. The inflection of *ar ôl*, as for instance in *ar fy ôl* may perhaps be collected from entries like the following from *GPC*:[2]

ôl [Crn. C. *olow* (ll.), Crn. Diw. *ooll;* ?cf. H. Wydd. Ôl 'canys'] *eg.* ll. *olion, -au,* a hefyd fel *a.* [...]
(yn y ff. l. *olion)* manyd, gwehilion, tinion: *footprint, hoofprint, pawmark, track, trail, path, mark, stamp, remains, trace, residue, hint, also fig., rear,* [...]

12g. *LL 42,* dio/igabr. 13g. C 70. 14 [...], Ny charaw alaw ôl difod bressuil. 14g. *WM* 118. 17-22, tri [...]

Cfn.: 20g. ô. llaw: *mark or trace of human activity.* 1896. ô. troed: *footprint, footstep, also fig.* 15-16g. LLAWDDEN, &c.: *Gw* III, *Olau 'y nhraed* ar lan rhiw. 1547 *WS, ol troed,* steppe of a fote. 1588 *Esth* (Apocr.) xiii. 10, buaswn fodlon i gussanu *ôl* ei *draed* ef er iechydwriaeth i Israel. 1684 H. Owen: DC48, Mae eu *hôl-traed* hwynt [y Tadau Sanctaidd], sydd etto'n parháu, yn testiolaethu mai gwŷr berffaith a sanctaidd ddynion oeddent. ar ô.: (i) *after* (of place), behind, also fig. 14g. *YBH* 54b. 1588 *Gen* xxxi. es. 1803 *P* d.g. *ôl.* Ar lafar, 'Dwn i ddim be' ddaw o'i flaen ne' *ar* 'i *ôl* o', *WVBD* 405. (ii) *after (of time).* 14g. *YBH* 65a, ac *ar y ol* ynteu coronhau iosian. *c.* 1730 *Thos. l.loyd D* (LlGC) 183a, *ar ôl* iddo syrthio, postquam. 1770 *W, ar ôl* y dyddiau hynny d.g. *after. . . After those days.* Ar lafar; hefyd ynglŷn ag etifeddu, 'Gei di weld be' gei di *ar ôl* d'ewyrth', *WVBD* 405. (iii) *for, after (used with words expressing longing, desire, wish, &c.).* 1708 *EGE* 133. 1709 H. POWEL: G 6. 1790 T. JONES: *TOS* 289. Ar lafar, 'Bydda i'n chwith *ar*'ch ôl chi', 'Bydd yn chwith iddo *ar ôl* Bangor', 'Mae gynno fo hirath *ar* eu *hola* nw', *WVBD* 405. (iv) *after, about (used with words expressing care, concern, &c.).* 1672 J. LANGFORD: *HDdD* 50. 1762 G. JONES: *CFfOG* 24. Ar lafar, 'edrach *ar ôl* y tân', *WVBD* 405; 'wêdd da fi ratach gwaith na poeni mhen *ar* 'u *giole* nhw', *Wês wês* 18. (v) *according to, in accordance with, by.* 1551 W. SALESBURY viiib, y rhai'n a gerddynt *ar ol* y fydd. 1567 *TN* I a, Cysecrlan Euangel lesu Christ, *ar ôl* [:- [Ys] ef yr hon y escrivenwyt ac addyscwyt y gan Vatthew] Mathew. 1588 *Deut* i. 41. 1603 E. KYFFIN: *PS d.d.,* Rhann o Psalmae Dafydd Brophwyd Iw Canu *ar ôl* y dôn arferedig yn Eglwys Loegr. 1615 R. SMYTH: *GB* 8, i galw hwy *ar ôl* i henwau priodawl. 1777 W. WILLIAMS: DN 39. (vi) *(left) behind; left, remaining; after, following, afterwards; backward(s); late.* 1567 *l.IGG (Sall)* xxxvib, Y cantorion aent or blaen, a'r cerddorion *ar ôl.* 1632 *D,* a ddêl *ar ôl* d.g. *posterus. id.* y dydd *ar ôl* d.g. *posterus . . . postera dies.* 1676 W. JONES: *GB* 6, yr hwn sydd yn myned *ar ôl.* 1707 *AB* 27la, backward, *ar ôl.* 1803 *P,* ôl ... myned *ar ôl.* Ar lafar, 'Mae 'na un *ar ôl'*, *WVBD* 405; 'Pwy sy'n dod *ar ôl?*', ''W' i *ar ôl* gyda'r gwaith tŷ 'eddi''. (vii) *(left) out, wanting, lacking, deficient, out of place, wrong, defective.* Ar lafar yn Arfon, 'gadal rhyw air *ar ôl'*, 'rwbath *ar ôl'*, 'Rodd 'i olwg *ar ôl'*, *WVBD* 405. ar ô. delw: *in the image of, in the form of.* [...]

Even in this kind of entry, however, it remains doubtful, whether dictionary users discover that the first four meanings of *ar ôl* are bound to a compound preposition and whether they may deduce its inflection (cf. i., ii, iii. and iv., cf. also *ar ben* - *GPC*: 2729).

Assigning a lexical item to a particular word class may be difficult, since prepositions and conjunctions, for instance, are not easy to keep apart. As is discussed in the following sections, *am* 'at; because', *gan* 'by; because', *cyn* 'before; as', *ar ôl* 'after' and other lexical units can belong to both word classes and may be distinguished by different morphological and syntactic behaviour.

In addition, the question arises whether the examples provided in *GPC* can really function as a guideline for current language usage and whether they are representative. Some direct information would solve all problems and make things clear for current and historic language use. The situation becomes worse, when no context is provided as is the case with the compound preposition *ar gefn* (ii, iii):

---

2 The format of *GPC* was adapted to the width of the page in order not to waste too much space.

cefn [cf. H. Grn. *chein*, gl. *dorsum* [...]
   (a) Y rhan honno o gorff dyn neu anifail sydd nesaf at yr asgwrn cefn cyferbyn â'r bol ac yn ymestyn [...]: *back, fig. support, second* [...]
   c. **1200** *LlDW* 24.14-15, buyta ... ay *keuen* ar etan. **1346** *LlA* 136, ef aduc ygroes ary*gefuyn* hyt ymynyd caluaria. **14g** [...]
   Cfn.: **cefn gefn, cefngefn:** *(i) back to back* [...] **ar gefn:** *(i) in addition to, as a consequence of, with regard to.* **1455-85** *LGC* 122. **1703** E. WYNNE: *BC* 55. **1762** D. ROWLAND: *PA* 79-80. **18g.** *W.Ballads* [5]. *(ii) at the expense of.* Ar lafar yn gyff. *(iii) on top, upon; up to.* **1807.** Ar lafar yn y Gogledd, *WVBD* 255. **ar g. ei geffyl:** [...]

Without context and word class label, dictionary users may, first, interprete the actual lexical unit as a collocation or idiom, since these are normally listed under the section *Cfn* 'combinations' (cf. section 4.3.1.2.). Second, with lacking direct information, they can hardly be expected to recognise that *ar gefn* can be a compound preposition which, third, exhibits inflection. Fourth, users may not be able to ascertain that only the third meaning listed in the dictionary entry (iii) can be expressed where the lexical unit is used as a preposition.

To sum up: the presentation of the system of compound preposition in Welsh general-purpose dictionaries is inadequate. Many lexical units are not contained in their macrostructure. In addition, the compilation of compound prepositions under other consituent parts than the prepositions themselves undermines their recognition as a prepositions and consequently the acknowledgement of their respective morphological features, syntactic behaviour and semantics.

Another important aspect is that linguistic confidence and identity are undermined when common lexical items are not presented in dictionaries as such. Moreover, if these form part of linguistic devices with a high metaphorical value for the language, they loose their force when not supported by popular reference books (cf. section 4.1.1.). As a result, the identity-constructing function of the language is gradually reduced.

Consulting the *Pocket Modern Welsh Dictionary* or the small *Gaelic-English/English-Gaelic Dictionary* (Buchanan 1998), the ignorance of lexical units in Welsh general-purpose dictionaries which consist of more than one part becomes more incomprehensible. In both reference books these form seperate dictionary entries. A list of some compound prepositions illustrates the approach taken by Buchanan (1998):

   a chionn *prep* because of.
   a dh' ionnsiagh *prep* to, towards; against.
   air beulaibh *prep* in front of.
   air cùl *prep* behind.
   air cùlaibh *prep* behind.
   air feadh *prep* throughout, all over.
   air sgàth *prep* on account of.
   am broinn *prep* inside, within.
   an aghaidh *prep* against.
   an àite *prep* instead of.
   an ceann *prep (of time)* in after.
   an coinneimh *prep* towards.
   an comhair *prep* in the direction of.

an crochadh air *prep*[3] depending
on.
an dèich *prep* after.
ann an *prep* in.
an tairc ri *prep* leaning on/against;
in comparison with.
an tòir air *prep* in pursuit of;
looking for.
an urra ri *prep* responsible for; in
charge of.
às aonais *prep* without.
as bith cò *prep* whoever.
as bith dè *prep* whatever.
às eugmhais *prep* without.
às leth *prep* on behalf of.
a-steach do *prep* into.

The entries of the *Pocket Modern Welsh Dictionary* look as follows:

arbennig *adjective*
• = special
mae hi heddiw yn ˈddiwrnod arbennig [...]

ar ˈbwys *preposition (South)*
= near
personal forms: **ar ⁿmhwys (i), ar dy
ˈbwys (di), ar ei ˈbwys (e), ar ei
ʰphwys (hi), ar ein pwys (ni)** [...]

archeb (*plural* -**ion**) *noun, feminine*
= order
diolch am eich archeb = thank you for
your order

Although compound prepositions forming a dictionary entry on their own (cf. Buchanan) are separated from their base prepositions, they are, at least, accessible to dictionary users. In entries as illustrated by the examples from the *Pocket Modern Welsh Dictionary*, they are adequately described.

---

[3]   Compound prepositions for Scottish Gaelic are not discussed here. The relevant aspect for this analysis is the treatment of lexical units which consist of more than one constituent part.

4.3.5.2.   Government

In this section, the reflection of the government of Welsh prepositions is examined. As was exemplified in section 1.3.2.3.5., there are three possible kinds of government; soft (L), spirant (S) and nasal mutations (N). Some prepositions, however, do not impose any changes with subsequent lexical items, e.g. *cyn* 'before', *er* 'for', *erbyn* 'by', *ers* 'since'. The prepositions in the following table are again drawn from P.W. Thomas (1996: 340f.):

Preposi-tions	*Geiriadur Cyfoes*	*Geiriadur Mawr*	*Geiriadur Bach*	GPC	*Geiriadur yr Academi*	*Spurrell*
â[S] 'with'	--	provided by context	provided by context	may be guessed from context[1]	+ asp. mut.	--
am[L] 'about, at'	--	--	--	ei ddilyn gan y tr. meddal[2]	+ soft mut. (+ soft mut.)[3]	--
ar[L4] 'on, upon'	--	may be guessed from context	may be guessed from context	ei ddilyn gan y tr. meddal ...[5]	+ soft mut.	--
at[L] 'to, at'	--	--	--	ei ddilyn gan y tr. meddal	+ soft mut.	--
dan[L6] 'under'	--	--	--	may be guessed from context[1]	+ soft mut.	--
dros[L] 'over'	--	may be guessed from context[4]	may be guessed from context[4]	letter not yet reached	+ soft mut.	--
drwy[L] 'through'	--	--	--	letter not yet reached	+ soft mut.	--
gan[L] 'with, by'	--	--	--	may be guessed from context[3]	+ soft mut.	--

---

[1]   The context here is not totally clear for dictionary users, since the examples provided are compound prepositions or idioms which may follow different rules among their constituent parts, such as in *gan mwyaf* 'mostly', *i mewn* 'into'.

[2]   'Followed by soft mutation.'

[3]   Changingly indicated.

[4]   Before the word 'twenty', the preposition *ar* demands a 'h'.

[5]   There are also exceptional mutations listed.

[6]   <t> is the original initial letter of *drwy, dan, dros*. Since they are mainly used as adverbials - in which cases they suffer mutation - their mutated forms are often taken as the radical forms. The same applies for *gan* 'with, by', *ger* 'at, near', *gerbron* 'before', *gerfydd* 'by', *gerllaw* 'near', *gyda* 'with', *gyferbyn* 'against' (cf. Thomas ibid.: 343f.).

gyda[S] 'with'	--	--	--	may be guessed from context[3]	+ asp. mut.	--
heb[L] 'without'	--	--	--	ei ddilyn gan y tr. meddal	+ soft mut.	--
hyd[L] 'till'	--	--	--	tr. meddal yn dilyn bellach	+ soft mut.	--
i[L] 'to, into'	--	may be guessed from context[3]	may be guessed from context[3]	ei ddilyn gan y tr. ml.[2]	+ soft mut.	--
o[L] 'from'	--	may be guessed from context[3]	may be guessed from context[3]	ei ddilyn gan y tr. meddal...[2]	(+ soft mut.) + soft mut.	--
yn[N] 'in'	--	may be guessed from context[3]	may be guessed from context[3]	letter not yet reached	+ nasal mut.	--

It can again be stated that *Y Geiriadur Cyfoes* does not adequately reflect basic grammatical particuliarities of its lexical items. Not a single government of the prepositions is indicated. The same applies for *Spurrell* and the *Works-Dictionary* which are also bare of any indication of the prepositions' government. The situation is slightly better in *Y Geiriadur Mawr* and *Y Geiriadur Bach* in which the government may, at times, be assumed from provided examples. Such an approach, however, is misleading, since the included examples often have idiomatic character and constituents of idioms do not necessarily follow general grammatical rules (cf. section 1.3.2.2.2.).

In the historical dictionary *GPC*, the lenition is mostly indicated and occasionally some exceptional mutations. In view of this, the question remains why the spirant mutations of *â* 'with' and *gyda* 'with' and the soft mutation of *gan* 'by' are not included. Since *GPC* had not been completely compiled when this investigation was undertaken, the conclusions have to be left incomplete. It seems, nevertheless, that the treatment of the government of prepositions is slightly inconsistent.

Geiriadur yr Academi, provides regularly comments on mutations in dictionary entries, although, as stated in the preceding sections, not necessarily formulaic (cf. *am* 'about, at' *o* 'from'). The inclusion of these comments, however, underlines the need of basic information on mutations, that is, which lexical items cause which kind of morpho-syntactically motivated sound changes at the beginning of a word.

Prepositions are important connectors, e.g. between the verb and a following complement (cf. sections 1.3.2.2.2., 1.3.2.3.5. and 4.3.1.2.) or as parts of compound prepositions (cf. 4.3.5.1.). Their usage may generally cause difficulties, also for native speakers at times. Even if that was not the case it has to be taken into consideration that a very high percentage of Welsh speakers consists of learners (cf. section 4.1.1.), without whom the Welsh language has no chance of survival. Their needs must be considered when compiling dictionaries, that is, a more adequate reflection of the syntactic behaviour of prepositions is demanded in dictionary entries.

4.3.5.3. Inflection

In this section it is examined whether the inflection of simple and compound prepositions is regularly included in entries of Welsh bi-directional general-purpose dictionaries. As with government, not all the prepositions exhibit inflection. In addition, with some prepositions the inflection is restricted to certain meanings, e.g. *ar ôl* 'after (temporal)', so that its occurrence should be indicated.

The lexical base of the analysis is formed by the prepositions looked at in the preceding sections, that is, simple prepositions consisting of one item and compound prepositions consisting of more than one item. Examples containing '&' are taken from the dictionary entries exactly as they occur in them.

Preposi-tions	*Geiriadur Cyfoes*	*Geiriadur Mawr*	*Geiriadur Bach*	*Geiriadur Prif-ysgol Cymru*	*Geiriadur yr Academi*	*Spurrell*
am 'about, at'	--	amdanaf, amdanat...	amdanaf, amdanat...	amdanaf, -at...	amdanaf, amdanat...	--
am ben 'on, upon'	no entry	no entry	no entry	--	(am ei phen)[1]	no entry
ar 'on, up-on'	--	arnaf, ar-nat...	arnaf, ar-nat...	arnaf, -at...	arnaf, arnat...	--
ar ben 'on top of'	no entry	--	--	(ar ei ben, ar dy ben)	(ar eu pennau nhw)	no entry
ar bwys 'near, next to'	no entry	--	--	(ar ei bwys)	[ar fy mhwys (i)...][2]	no entry
ar fedr 'for the purpose of'	no entry	no entry	no entry	ar ei fedr, &c.	--	no entry
ar draws 'across'	no entry	--	--	letter not yet reached	ar ei draws	no entry
ar gefn 'on top'	no entry	no entry	no entry	--	[ar fy nghefn (i)...]	--
ar gorn 'at one's ex-pense'	no entry	no entry	no entry	--	--	no entry
ar gyfer 'for'	--	no entry	--	(ar ei gyfer)	(ar eich cyfer)	--

---

[1]   Brackets indicate indirect information.
[2]   Square brackets indicate that the information was obtained from the introductory section of the dictionary.

ar gyfyl 'near'	no entry	--	(ar ei gyfyl)	(yn ei gyfyl)	[ar fy nghyfyl (i)...]	(ar ei g.)
ar hyd 'along'	no entry	--	--	ar ei (fy, eu &c.) h., ar hyd-ddo, &c.	ar hyd-ddo, ar hyd-ddi ...	no entry
ar ôl 'after'	no entry	--	--	(ar 'i *ol* o, ar 'ch ôl chi, ar eu hola nhw...)	(ar ei ôl)	no entry
ar warthaf 'upon'	--	(ar ei warthaf)	(ar ei warthaf)	ar fy ngwarthaf, ar ei warthaf, &c.	[ar fy ngwarthaf (i)...]	--
at 'to, at'	--	ataf, atat...	ataf, atat...	ataf, -at....	ataf, atat...	--
dros 'over'	--	--	trosof, trosot...	letter not yet reached	trosof, trosot, drosof...	--
drwy 'through'	--	--	trwof, trwot...	letter not yet reached	trwof, trwot...	--
er mwyn 'for the sake of'	--	--	--	er ei f., &c.	er ei mwyn hi, er fy mwyn i	no entry
gan 'with, by'	--	gennyf, gennyt...	gennyf, gennyt...	gennyf, gennyt...	gennyf, gennyt...	--
heb 'without'	--	hebof, hebot...	hebof, hebot...	hebof, hebot...	[hebof...]	--
i 'to, into'	--	imi, iti...	imi, iti...	im, imi, it...	i mi, i ti...	--
i blith 'into the midst of'	no entry	--	--	i'n p., &c.	[i'n plith (ni)...]	no entry
o 'from, of'	--	ohonof, ohonot...	ohonof, ohonot...	ohonof, ohonot...	[ohonof...]	--
o achos 'because'	no entry	--	no entry	(om hachaws i)	o'm hachos i, o'th achos di...	no entry
o amgylch 'round about'	--	no entry	no entry	--	o'm hamgylch, o'th amgylch...	--
o blaid 'in favour'	no entry	--	--	o'm p. (o'th b., &c.)	[o'm plaid (i)...]	no entry
o blith 'from among'	no entry	--	--	o'n p., &c.	o'ch plith chwi, o'u plith nhw	no entry

o flaen 'in front of'	no entry	no entry	no entry	o'i flaen, o'n blaen(au), &c.	o'm blaen, o'th flaen ti...	no entry
o fewn 'within'	no entry	--	--	o'i fewn, &c.	[o'm mewn (i)...]	no entry
o fysg 'amongst'	no entry	no entry	no entry	--	[o'n mysg (ni)...]	no entry
o gwmpas 'about, round'	no entry	no entry	--	(o' ch. hi)	o'm cwmpas, o'th gwmpas	--
o gylch 'around'	no entry	--	--	o'm gylch, o'th g., &c.	--	no entry
o ran 'in part'	no entry	--	o'm rhan i	o'm rhan (o'th ran, &c.)	(o'i ran)	no entry
yn 'in'	--	ynof, yn-ot...	ynof, ynot	letter not yet reached	--	--

The above table shows that *Y Geiriadur Cyfoes* continues to neglect most of the basic grammatical information for its lexical units which make them applicable in speech or writing. As the government of the prepositions is totally ignored so is the inflection excluded from its dictionary entries. *Spurrell* is not much better. Only one indirect item of information could be found in this dictionary. The *Works-Dictionary* includes the first person singular of *am, ar, drwy, gan, o* and *yn* in its headword list as well as the third person singular and plural of *i*. Its author thus retains his general approach of separating morphological categories of lexical items (cf. section 4.3.3.) as can be seen from the following examples:

> **am** *prep* at; for; on.
> [...]
> **amdan(af)** *from* am.
> [...]
> **gan** *prep* with, by.
> [...]
> **genn(yf)** *from* gan.
> [...]
> **gyda, gydag** *prefix* with.[3]
> [...]
> **i** *prep* to. • *pron* me; my.
> [...]
> **iddi, iddo, iddynt** *from* i.

In the entries of *Y Geiriadur Mawr* and *Y Geiriadur Bach*, the forms of simple inflecting prepositions are regularly contained. The inflection of compound prepositions, however, does not form systematic part of their entries. Only some inflected forms may be obtained, e.g. for *o*

---

[3]   This item is included in order to show incorrect word class labelling.

ran and indirectly, when the use of a preposition is exemplified by the third person singular, as in *ar ei gyfyl*.

A similar approach can be observed in *The Welsh Learner's Dictionary* and in the *Pocket Modern Welsh Dictionary*, although the latter does not provide the inflection of *heb* 'without'. In particular the *Pocket Modern Welsh Dictionary* includes complete inflection paradigms of major compound prepositions as is illustrated by the example below (cf. also section 4.3.5.1.):

> **o 'blaid** *adverb*[4]
> = in favour (of)
> *personal forms:* **o ⁿmhlaid (i), o dy 'blaid (di), o'i 'blaid (e), o'i ʰphlaid (hi), o'n plaid (ni), o'ch plaid (chi), o'u plaid (nhw)** [...]

The few compound prepositions included in *The Welsh Learner's Dictionary* look as follows:

> **achos**[2] **(prep)** *[achos]* because of
> **rydw i'n hwyr (o) achos y glaw** I'm late because of the rain
> **mae e'n hwyr o'm hachos i** he's late because of me
> **o'm hachos i, o'th achos di, o'i achos e, o'i achos hi, o'n hachos ni, o'ch achos chi, o'u hachos nhw** because of me etc.

The historical dictionary *GPC* and *Geiriadur yr Academi* comment on most of the prepositions grammatically. Both dictionaries, nevertheless, have not standardised their patterns of description. Whereas the simple inflecting prepositions are accompanied by all their different forms - apart from *heb* in *Geiriadur yr Academi* - the compound prepositions are only represented with some selected forms, e.g. *o'ch plith chwi* 'from among you', *ar ei draws* 'across him' in *Geiriadur yr Academi* and *o'n p.* 'from among us', *er ei f.* 'for his sake', *ar fy ngwarthaf* 'upon me' in *GPC*. With the examples of the inflection of selected compound prepositions in its introductory section, however, *Geiriadur yr Academi* nearly supplements the missing forms of these prepositions in the dictionary entries (cf. Griffiths, B. & D.G. Jones 1995: li-lvii). Nevertheless, the principle of including particular forms or comments thus remains unclarified. The example of *am* 'about, at' illustrates varying structures entries may take in *Geiriadur yr Academi*:

I. At pages 4 and 5 one can find *am* + inflected forms + indication of mutation (rth vs rhth):[5]

---

[4]   The word class is labelled differently from that in the other dictionaries.
[5]   *rth* stands for *rywbeth*, the mutated form of *rhywbeth* 'something'.

about *adv & prep.* 1. *(= around):* o amgylch (rhth), o bobtu (i rth), o gylch (rhth), o gwmpas (rhth) [...]
      7. *(usu. with parts of the body):* am (rth), o gylch (rhth), o amgylch (rhth), *F:* am dan (rth); *N.B.* am *has pronominal forms: sing.* **1.** amdanaf, **2.** amdanat, **3.** amdano, amdani; *pl.* **1.** amdanom, **2.** amdanoch, **3.** amdanyt; [...]

A variant of this version can be found at page 1189:

round[2] *adv. & prep.* I. *adv.* **1.** *(a)* [...] II. *prep.* **1.** *(a)* o amgylch, o gwmpas, oddeutu (rhth); o bob tu (i rth) [...]
      3. o'u hamgylch/cwmpas hwy; in [...]; *(b) Measurement:* am (rth), o gwmpas (rhth); am *is conjugated thus: sing.* **1.** amdanaf i; **2.** amdanat ti; **3.** *m.* amdano fo/fe, *f.:* amdani hi; *pl.* **1.** amdanom ni; **2.** amdanoch chi; **3.** amdanynt hwy [..]

II.   Page 556 displays *am* + inflected forms + direct indication of mutation:

for[1] *prep.* I. **1.** am *(+ soft mut.) with forms:* (amdanaf, amadanat amdano, amdani; amdanom, amdanoch, amdanynt) [...]

III.   Page 81 exhibits *am* + direct indication of mutation:

at *prep.* **1.** *(position): usu:* yn + *nasal mut.;* ~ **the centre** [...]
      2. *(time) usu.* am + *soft mut.;* ar + *soft mut.;* [...]

The *Metalanguage* employed to describe the lexical units grammatically in the dictionary entries of *Geiriadur yr Academi* varies widely. In the example of page 1189, the most detailed grammatical information is provided, although the preposition is listed here under a rather marginal meaning of *am*. Some users may even regard this description as hypercorrect, since literary forms, such as *amdanaf* 'about me', are normally not followed by a separate personal pronoun. Under a more central meaning of *am* (cf. page 81), however, only the indication of the mutation is included.

To sum up: Welsh prepositions are troublesome for dictionary users, since they behave morphologically and syntactically in a different way from those in Standard Average European languages. If they are used incorrectly communication remains inefficient, since relations among sentence constituents may not become clear or parts of speeches are ill-formed.

The grammatical information included in the historical dictionary *GPC* and in the unidirectional *Geiriadur yr Academi* forms the basic grammatical information necessary for the use of prepositions in speech. Although this information could be improved by a more formulaic coding, both dictionaries provide examples which could serve as a model for entries of bilingual and bi-directional Welsh general-purpose dictionaries.

4.3.6 The Welsh conjunctions

As discussed in section 1.3.2.3.6., Welsh general-purpose dictionaries need to give information on the word class and the complementation of Welsh conjunctions. Based on conjunctions defined as such by P.W. Thomas (1996: 461-479), this section investigates whether this information is adequately provided in entries of the aforementioned dictionaries. The study focuses on a representative selection of subordinating conjunctions, which can be assigned to different word classes and which, therefore, cause major difficulties in usage (cf. section 1.3.2.3.6.).

Con-junctions	Geir. Cyfoes	Geir. Mawr	Geir. Bach	GPC	Geiriadur yr Academi[1]	Spur-rell
am[(L)2] 'be-cause' (causal)	prp., c.[3]	prp.	prp.	c.	conj.,[(L)4] [prp.]	prp., c.
ar ôl 'after' (temporal)	no entry	(phrase)[5]	(phrase)	(phrase)	conj. [...] ar ôl i + soft mut. + n. or pron. + soft mut. + vn.	no entry
cyhyd â/g 'as long as, if only' (cond.)	(a.)[6]	(a.)	(a.)	c.	conj.	(a.)

396

cyn[7] 'before' (temporal)	c., prp., px.	c.[8]	c.[7]	prp., c. Fel cys. (a'i ddi-lyn gan *no*, *na* neu'n un-iongyrchiol gan ffurf-iau'r ferf)[9]	*conj.* cyn + y[r] + *verb*, cyn + i + *subject* + *soft mut.* + *vn.*, cyn + *verb noun*, cyn + *vn.* + *o* + *soft. mut.* + *subject*; *occ:* cyn + *subjunctive* [ad., prp.]	ad.
er 'though' (con-cessive)	prp., c.	prp.	prp.	prp., c. Fel cys.[10] [...] (y, na)	*conj.* er y + *indicative (negative:* er na + *soft mutation)* (er nad *before vowel)* [...], *in the present & future tense the usual construction in af-firmative clauses is a noun clause containing* bod, *mutated according to person* [...], *in em-phatic clauses:* er mai [...], *in past time the usual construction is* er i + *soft mut.* + *vn., Lit:* er + *vn.* + *o* + *n. pron* [...], *with adjectives:* er + *poss.pron* + *equative degree*[11] [prep]	prp., c.
erbyn 'by the time that' (tem-poral)	prp.	prp.	prp.	prp., c., n.m. Fel cys. (erbyn + pan, y)	*conj.* [...] erbyn i + *soft mut.* + *subject* + *soft mut.* + *vn.* [prp]	prp.
er mwyn '(in order) that' (final)	(phrase)	(phrase)	(phrase)	(phrase)	*conj.* [...] er mwyn i + *subject* + *vn.* [prp]	no entry
fel 'as, so' (consec.) (modal) (temporal)	c.	c.	c.	prp., c., ad.	*conj.* [context] [context] [ad.] fel y/yr	ad., c., prp.

---

7   *Cyn* can cause mutation when used as a particle of comparison. In *Geiriadur yr Academi* (Griffiths 1995: 73) it is defined as an 'adverb' in this function. It can also be a preposition meaning 'before'.

8   The context for the conjunction *cyn* in *Y Geiriadur Mawr* and *Y Geiriadur Bach*, i.e. *cyn ddued â* 'as black as' exemplifies its usage as a particle of comparison (cf. above), not as a subordinate conjunction with temporal meaning. The concept of conjunction in *Y Geiriadur Mawr* and *Bach* and P.W. Thomas seems to differ from each other.

9   'As a conjunction (followed by *no*, *na* or directly by verbforms).'

10   *Fel cys.* stands for 'as conjunction'.

11   Similar information is provided for the headword *although*. It is, however, differently formulated.

gan^(L) 'as, because'	prp.	prp.	prp.	prp., c.^(L)	*conj.* gan; + *soft mut.*+ *vn*; [...] gan ... na + *soft mut.* gan fod/mai^12 [prp]	prp.
hyd^13 'as, as far as' (temporal)	n.m., prp.	prp.	prp.	n.m., prp., c. (fel cys. a'i ddilyn gan y gn. pth. traws y(r)^14	*adv.* (context) [prep.]	prp.
lle 'where' (local)	n.m., ad.	n.m., ad.	n.m.	n.m., c., ad.	*rel.conj.*	n.m.
nes 'until' (temporal)	a.	a., ad.	a., ad.	a., prp., c.	*conj. + inflected form of verb*; nes y/yr nes i + *subject* + *vn. (mutated)*	ad.
o^1 'if' (cond.)	c.	prp., c., pr.	prp., c., pr.	c. [...] i ddilyn yn aml gan y tr. llaes^15 in-terr.-p	no entry [c.]	prp.
o achos 'because'	(n.m., c.)	prp.	c.	(prp., n.m.)	*conj.* o achos bod/mai^16	(c.)
oddi ar 'from' (temporal)	no entry	phrase	phrase	(phrase)	*prep.* oddi ar *(+ soft mut.)*^17	no entry
oherwydd 'because'	c. & prp.	c.	c.	prp., c.	*conj.*, oherwydd bod/mai; oherwydd *&c are followed by* bod/mai + *clause; when introducing a negative clause* oherwydd *&c are followed by* na + *soft mut. of* b, d, g, *spirant mut. of* p, t, c, nad *before vowels + conjugated verb form*	c. & prp.
onid^(L/S) 'unless' (concess.)	c., adv, prp.	c.	c.	c.^(L/S)	*conj.*^(L/S)	ad., c., prep.

12	Further explanations are given in context of the equivalent *oherwydd* (cf. below).
13	*Hyd* causes soft mutation when used as a preposition.
14	'As conjunction followed by the relative particle y(r).'
15	'Often followed by spirant mutation.'
16	Further explanations are given in context of the equivalent *oherwydd* (cf. below).
17	*Geiriadur yr Academi* and the *Pocket Modern Welsh Dictionaries* are the only sources which indicate mutation after *oddi ar* P.W. Thomas does not indicate mutation either.

o ran 'as regards' (causal)	no entry	(phrase)	(phrase)	(phrase)	(phrase: o ran rhth)	no entry
pan^L 'as, when' (temporal)	c., a.	c., ad.$^{(L)}$	c.$^{(L)}$	c.^{L}, prp.^{L}	*conj.* pan + *soft mut.* + *indicative; or, where* **when=whenever** + *subjunctive*	c.
tan[18] 'until' (temporal)	prp.	prp.	prp.	prp., ad., c.[19]	*conj.* + *inflected form of verbs* tan y/yr [prp.]	prp.
tra[20] 'while' (temporal) (concess.)	ad., c.	ad., c.	ad., c.	c.[21]	*conj. (usu. followed by indicative mood, but in the literay style by the subjunctive when referring to an indefinite time,* tra na + *spirant mut. of* p, t, c, *soft mutation of* b, d, g, tra nad *before vowel;* tra *is occ. followed by soft mut. of the forms of* bod *in the Biblical style* tra [context]	ad., c.
trwy^L 'by reason of'	prp.	prp.	prp.	not yet reached	*prep.* trwy + *soft mutation*	prp.
wrth^L 'while'	prp.	prp.	prp.	not yet reached	*conj.* [...] wrth + *soft mut.* [prp.]	prp.

The above table corroborates what has already been said about pronouns (cf. section 4.3.4.) and prepositions (cf. section 4.3.5.), namely that the word class definition of individual lexical items may vary considerably. One reason for this variety may be different concepts of defining individual word classes (cf. above and below). Another, however, may also be the ignorance of the comprehensive use of a number of lexical items. Whatever the reason, the varying or indirect labelling of word classes can cause problems for dictionary users (cf. below). It would be useful, therefore, if lexicographers detailed their grammatical approach in such a manner that dictionary users can find corresponding explanations in the grammatical books (cf. section 1.3.2.2.6.). Another option were the comprehensive provision of context which enables dictionary users to deduce the correct usage of individual lexical items from indirect information.

---

[18]   *Tan* causes soft mutation when used as a preposition.
[19]   There is an example in the entry which illustrates how to form negative sentences with *tan*.
[20]   *Tra* causes spirant mutation when used as an adverb.
[21]   The usage of *tra* with forms of *bod* 'to be' is indicated.

However, the impression is, that grammatical concepts of the lexicographers are not always that clear. Whereas some conjunctions are recognised as syntactic connectors, e.g. *fel* 'as, so', *oherwydd* 'because', *ond* 'but', *pan* 'as, while', *tra* 'while' and defined, or at least, decribed as such (cf. below) in all dictionaries, this is not the case with others. *Tan* 'until', *trwy* 'by reason of' and *wrth* 'while', for instance, are predominantly characterised as prepositions, others are defined as adjectives *cyhyd â/g* 'as long as, if', or nouns and adverbs, e.g. *lle*, or adjectives and adverbs, e.g. *nes*. Some are mostly reflected as a phrase only, such as *oddi ar* 'from', *o ran* 'as regards'.

Irrespective of the word class label provided in their entries, *Y Geiriadur Mawr* and *Y Geiriadur Bach* cover the main meanings of their lexical items, such as for *am, er, o ran* (predominantly characterised as prepositions, cf. above), *lle* (noun, adverb), or *nes* (adjective, adverb) by context, i.e. by indirect information. The meanings for these items, however, are bound to different word classes, which in turn demand different kinds of complementation, features which are not reflected in the respective dictionary entries (cf. also W.S. Dodd 1998: 56). The following examples illustrate this point:

> **am,** *ardd.* (amdanaf, amdanat, amdano,
> amdanom, amdanoch, amdanynt.
> ABOUT ME, ETC.).
> > 1. oherwydd, oblegid, o achos, os.
> > BECAUSE.
> > 2. ar, o gwmpas, o boptu, oddeutu,
> > ynghylch, ynglŷn â. ABOUT, AT,
> > ABOUND, ETC.

The preposition *am* 'about' inflects and induces lenition in the subsequent lexical item. The conjunction *am* is non-inflectable and can only cause soft mutation in *bod* 'to be'.

> **rhan,** *eb. ll.*-nau. cyfran, dogn, darn,
> dryll, peth, siâr; adran; tynged.
> PART, SHARE; SECTION, FATE.
> Rhannau ymadrodd. PARTS
> OF SPEECH.
> O ran. IN PART, AS REGARDS.
> O'm rhan i. FOR MY PART.
> Rhannau cyplysol. MATING PARTS.

As a preposition *o ran* inflects as is shown in the phrase *O'm rhan i*. As a conjunction *o ran* 'as regards' introduces subordinated causal clauses and is non-inflectable.

In the case of *cyn* conceptual aspects of the word class conjunctions may have been responsible for the following entry:

> **cyn**[1], *ardd.* o flaen (amser), yn gynt.
> BEFORE (TIME).
> **cyn**[2], *cys.* mor. as
> Cyn ddued â : mor ddu â.

Here, however, the phrase- or sentence-connecting function of conjunctions while characterising semantic relations between these elements is not clearly illustrated (cf. Bussmann 1996: 94). Indeed, there are definitions which specify conjunctions only as words which connect words (P.W. Thomas 1996: 461; he, however, goes far beyond this definition himself, cf. 462-480). For dictionaries such a theoretical approach is too restricted, since conjunctions and particles (cf. section 4.3.8.) are the only word classes which provide the lexicographer with the opportunity to illustrate the construction of complex sentences, a necessary device for comprehensive communication.

In addition, if a lexical item is defined as a preposition only, its potential use as a connector of sentences, i.e. its syntactic function, remains hidden. However, even if dictionary users know about its usage as a conjunction, they may want to know how to use it in speech or writing. In this case they must, first, have the information that conjunctions - in contrast to prepositions such as *trwy* and *wrth* (cf. section 1.3.2.3.5.) - do not inflect. Second, they should be informed that the complementation of prepositions differs from that of conjunctions. Consequently, *tan* and *tra* do not cause mutation when used as a conjunction because they are followed by the particle *y/yr* (cf. section 1.3.2.3.6.). *Wrth* may precede the preposition *i* + lenition (cf. also *ar ôl*, *cyn*, *er*, *erbyn*, *er mwyn*, *nes* and section 1.3.2.3.6.).

The situation is similar with the nouns *hyd*, *lle* and the adjective/adverb *nes*. When used as conjunctions they may be followed by the particle *y/yr*. *Hyd*, therefore, only causes mutation in the subsequent lexical item when used as a preposition. *Nes*, however, may also precede the preposition *i* + mutation or an inflected verb.

Those conjunctions which are recognised as such by the two learners' dictionaries are predominantly well explained in them, particularly in the *Pocket Modern Welsh Dictionary*.

In dictionaries which generally do not provide contextual information and which include a restricted number of equivalents, such as in *Y Geiriadur Cyfoes*, *Spurrell* and the *Works-Dictionary*, the word class label 'preposition' even limits the semantic range of the lexical items as is illustrated by examples form the *Works-Dictionary*:

>**am** *prep* at; for; on.
>**gan** *prep* with, by.

How is the dictionary user to understand the following sentences when using the *Works-Dictionary*?

>*Penderfynnodd weithio am fod angen arian arno.* 'He decided to go to work because he needed money.'
>*Gan mai chwaraewr oedd ef cafodd ef wahoddiad i'r parti.* 'Because he was a player he got an invitation to the party.'

Some of the lexical items which are characterised by their complementation as conjunctions in entries of *Geiriadur yr Academi* are defined differently in its explanatory section (Griffiths, B. & D.G. Jones). Nevertheless, the maximum information which can be provided for conjunctions is offered by many dictionary entries in *Geiriadur yr Academi*. Here, however, the *Metalan-*

guage varies widely, a problem which has already been observed in preceding sections (cf. sections 4.3.3. and 4.3.5.). The following examples illustrate the varying *Metalanguage* in this dictionary:

> **and** *conj.* [...] na + *spirant mut. of* p, t, c; [...]
> **or**[1] *conj.* **1.** [...] na + *spirant mut.* [...]

The information 'of p, t, c' is not necessary, since other consonants are not aspirated. Consequently, this information is not always provided when spirant mutation is mentioned (cf. *or*). Another inconsistency is illustrated by the next examples which demonstrate the varying codification of the sentence structure following the conjunctions:

> **altho', although** *conj.* **1.** [...] er i + *soft mut.* + *n* [...]
> **though** *conj. & adv.* **I.** *conj.* [...] er i + *soft mut.* + *vn.* [...]

> **that**[3] *conj.* [...] nes i + *subject* + *vn. (mutated)* [...]
> **till**[3] *prep. & conj* [...] nes i + *pron.* + *vn.* [...]

> **from** *prep.* **1.** [...] oddi ar *(+ soft mut.)* [...] oddi ar + *soft mut.* [...]

> **whereas** *conj.* [...] **2.** tra *(correctly not followed by any mut.)* [...]
> **while**[3] *conj.* **1.** [...] tra *is occ. followed by soft mut. of the forms of* bod [...]

The following examples show how the syntax of the type *Ar ôl i fam gyrraedd bwytaon ni* 'After mum had arrived we ate' is exhibited differently in the various dictionary entries of *Geiriadur yr Academi*:

> **after** *adv., prep., conj. & a.* [...] **III.** *conj. (a)*
> ar ôl i + *soft mut.* + *n. or pron.* + *soft mut.* + *vn.* [...]
> **altho', although** *conj.* **1.** [...]
> er i + *soft mut.* + *n* [...]
> **before** *adv., prep., conj.* **3.** *conj. (a)* [...]
> cyn + *i* + *subject* + *soft mut.* + *vn.* [...]
> **that**[3] *conj.* [...]
> nes i + *subject* + *vn.* [...]
> **time**[1] *n.* [...]; **by the ~ that...,**
> erbyn i + *soft mut.* + *subject* + *soft mut.* + *vn.* [...]

The first example correctly reflects government and word classes which may follow the conjunction (*ar ôl*). The second entry does not provide the full sentence structure. The third example omits the mutation of the subject (characterised as noun in the first example). The fourth example omits the indication of mutation twice, i.e. for the subject and the verbal noun. In the last example, all information is contained again.

The historical dictionary *GPC* tends to separate different word classes of lexical items by providing different dictionary entries, that is, the same lexical item may form more than one headword, such as with the word *o*:

402

o¹ [...] *ardd.rhed* (weithiau yn y ff. og o fl. llaf., yn enw. o fl. y rh. prs. dib. bl. ll.) gyda'r ff. prs. cfns. *ohonof* (Cym. C. *ohonof, ohonaf*), *ohonot* [...] Ei ddilyn gan y tr. meddal, ac yn eithriadol dan y tr. llaes [...]

o², O [...] *ebd.* a hefyd gyda grym enwol [...]

o³, od² [...] *cys.* yn cyflwyno cym. amod, a'i ddilyn yn aml gan y tr. llaes [...]; a hefyd fel *gn.gof.*

For some lexical items this approach can also be found in *Y Geiriadur Mawr* (cf. *cyn* above) and in the *Works-Dictionary* as is illustrated by the following examples:

nes *adj* nearer.
nes *adv* until
[...]
tra *adj* very.
tra *conj* while.

Some of the conjunctions not recognised as such or only as phrases in the Welsh-to-English sections may occur in the English-to-Welsh sections of the dictionaries, e.g. *ar ôl* 'after' in *Y Geiriadur Mawr* and *Bach* and *Spurrell*. Again, the description of lexical items is often more precise in the English section (cf. section 4.3.2.1.). This is certainly helpful for learners. The native speaker, the advanced learner or translator, however, also needs the Welsh section to be as precise as possible. In addition, for the prestige of a language such unequal treatment is not helpful.

A number of conjunctions hardly appears anywhere, e.g. *oddi ar, o ran*, or *ar ôl*. As observed in the preceding section (cf. 4.3.5.), it is apparent that lexical units consisting of more than one item may cause problems for Welsh lexicographers.

To sum up: Welsh conjunctions are troublesome, since they may perform syntactically in a different way from those in Standard Average European languages. In addition, some of them resemble lexical items of other word classes. This multifunctionality and polysemy of lexical items is, however, inadequately presented in entries of Welsh bi-directional general-purpose dictionaries. As a result, conjunctions which by form can fall into different word classes are restricted in their semantic and syntactic potential when they are not recognised as conjunctions or when their complementation is not indicated.

The historical dictionary *GPC* and the uni-directional *Geiriadur yr Academi* are much better in the definition of conjunctions as well as in the presentation of their government. They - embody necessary mutations and provide comprehensive contexts. Some lexical items in *GPC*, however, are left without an indication of their government, e.g. *am, cyhyd â/g.* Given a more formulaic *Metalanguage* which, moreover, is restricted to the most necessary information, *Geiriadur yr Academi* provides entries which could serve as a model for entries of bi-directional Welsh general-purpose dictionaries (cf. section 4.3.5.).

4.3.7. The Welsh numeral

In English, numerals form a word class on the basis of mainly lexical features. Syntactically, the individual members of this word class act as nouns, adjectives, pronouns, or adverbs and would consequently be delt with under the respective word classes (cf. section 1.3.2.2.7.). In Welsh, however, numerals can be defined on the basis of semantic, morphological, and syntactic properties.

In certain environments, Welsh numerals may exhibit features similar to nouns, such as *mil* (cf. section 1.3.2.3.7.) or to pronouns, e.g. *un* 'one' (cf. P.W. Thomas (1996: 276, 287f.). *Cyntaf* 'first' is orginally an adjective (cf. word class label in the *Works-Dictionary*) and consequently predominantly takes its normal position (cf. section 1.3.2.3.3.), i.e. after its referent.[1] In addition, as do nouns, many numerals exhibit number inflection and some cardinals and ordinals show gender inflection (cf. section 1.3.2.3.7. and the following table).

However, Welsh numerals regularly require complementation which is different from that of nouns, pronouns, and adjectives. The lexical items defined as numerals in this analysis form a larger group of words, which can all be followed by the partitive *o*, or by their referent in the singular, although they denote quantities. In addition, apart from *cyntaf* they normally precede their referent (cf. section 1.3.2.3.7.)

A number of numerals, e.g. *un* and ordinals except *ail* 'second', may cause lenition in the subsequent lexical item as do adjectives when preceding their referent (cf. also various pronouns and prepositions in sections 1.3.2.3.4. and 1.3.2.3.5.). In contrast to adjectives, however, these numerals induce mutation in order to indicate the gender of their feminine referents and not to take different semantic meanings (cf. positionally dependent semantic meaning of adjectives in section 4.3.3.4.). Other numerals, such as *ail*, *dau/dwy* 'two', *tri* 'three', and *chwe* 'six' induce lenition or spirantisation in their referents. *Pum* 'five', *saith* 'seven', *naw* 'nine', *deng* 'ten', however, cause soft or nasal mutation in a restricted group of nouns.

In view of a semantic-structural approach chosen here to define the word class numeral, the words *digon* 'enough', *gormod* 'too much/many', *tipyn* 'sufficient(ly)', and *llawer* 'many/much' are also assigned to this category (cf. section 1.3.2.3.7.), since they (a) denote quantities as do cardinals, ordinals and fractions, (b) they take the same position as do genuine numerals, and (c) they demand the same complementation. This complementation cannot be taken by other quantifiers, such as *amryw* 'divers', *sawl* 'many', *unrhyw* 'any', *rhyw* 'some', *holl* 'all', *ambell* 'occasionally', *cryn* 'considerable', *nemor* 'hardly any'. These are adjectives (cf. P.W. Thomas 1996: 203)[2] which cause positionally dependent mutation in their referent (cf. section 4.3.3.4. and above).

---

[1]   It may, however, also precede its referent (cf. P.W. Thomas 1996: 234).
[2]   There are also nouns which may denote vague quantities, e.g. *peth* 'thing', *lliaws* 'multitude', *llu* 'host', pronouns such as *rhai* 'some' and adverbs, e.g. *rhagor* 'more' (cf. P.W. Thomas 1996: 285).

Although some members of the group of numerals listed above can also behave like adverbs, e.g. *Bwytais ormod* '1 got enough', the decisive criterion for defining them as numerals is their government linked to their position in relation to their referents and their semantics.[3]

In this section, the presentation of the gender and plural inflection of Welsh numerals in general-purpose dictionaries is investigated as well as the inclusion of their government.

Numerals	Geiriadur Cyfoes	Geiriadur Mawr	Geiriadur Bach	Geiriadur Prifysgol Cymru	Geiriadur yr Academi[4]	Spurrell
un[L of fem.] referents: -au 'one'	**un,** (-au) *a. & n.m.*	**un,** [...] 3. *a.* (y rhifol cyntaf).[5]	**un,** [...] 3. *a.* (y rhifol cyntaf).	letter not yet reached	**one** [...] 1. *num.a.* **1.** (*a*) un (+ *soft mut. of f. nouns*)[6] [num.adj.]	**un** *adj*
dau[L: deuoedd] (masc.) 'two'	**dau,** *(dwy, f.) a. & n.m.*	**dau,** *a.* ac *eg. ll.* deuoedd. (*b.* dwy). y rhifol ar ôl un.[7]	**dau,** *a.* ac *eg. ll.* deuoedd. (*b.* dwy). y rhifol ar ôl un.	**dau** [...] y ddwy ff. fel rheol yn treiglo ar ôl y fannod [...] - *rhif.* ac *a.* (un. b. *dwy*; ll. -oedd) ll. *deuoedd, deuwedd* [...][8]	**two** *num.a.* [...] dau (deuoedd) *m,* dwy(oedd) *f; both dau and dwy mutate after the def. article* [...]*; dau and dwy are followed by the soft mut.*	**dau** *adj,* nm two; *f* **dwy**
dwy[L: -oedd] (fem.) 'two'	**dwy,** see dau	**dwy,** *a. rhifol b. (g.* dau)[9]	**dwy,** *a. rhifol b. (g.* dau)	**dwy** gw. dau	*(although occ.* [...]) [num.]	**dwy** *see* **dau**

---

[3] With some lexical items it is generally difficult to assign them to a particular word class (cf. preceding sections). This fact is also reflected in dictionary entries when phrases such as the following are given: *a hefyd gyda grym adferfol* 'and also with adverbial potency' (GPC, entry of *tri*, cf. below).

[4] The word class label of Welsh lexical items does not form a regular part of *Geiriadur yr Academi*. Their classification had, therefore, to be guessed from their description in the dictionary entries (cf. below) or taken from the introductory section (Griffiths, B. & D.G. Jones 1995: xxxiii–xli) and was then put in square brackets.

[5] 'The numeral first.'

[6] 'The numeral after one.'

[7] *Num.a.* is the abbreviation for 'numeral adjective' in *Geiriadur yr Academi*.

[8] 'Both forms usually mutate after the article' [...]. Lenition is only indicated by the context provided in this dictionary entry.

[9] 'Feminine numeral.'

tri⁻ᵒᵉᵈᵈ, ⁻ᵃᵘ (masc.) 'three'	**tri,** *(tair, f.) a. & n.m.*	**tri,** *a. (b.* tair*). y rhifol ar ôl* dau.¹⁰	**tri** [...]; pair *tri* dr. llaes i c-, p-, t- [...] *rhif.* (b. *tair*, ll. *teir-(i)au, teiroedd*) ll. *-oedd, -au*	**three** *num.a. & n.* **1.** *a. m.* tri, *f.* tri, *f.* tair (f), *foll. by sing. noun or by* o + *n.pl.* [...] tri *is foll. by the spirant mut. of* p-, t-, c- [...] **2.** *n.* tri(-oedd) *m* [num.adj.]	**tri** *adj, nm* three; *f* **tair**
tair⁻ᵒᵉᵈᵈ, ⁻ᵃᵘ (fem.) 'three'	**tair,** *a. & n.f.* of *tri*	**tair,** *a. (g.* tri*). dwy ac un.*¹¹	**tair** gw. **tri**	**tair** *adj f.* of **tri**	
pedwar⁻ᵒᵉᵈᵈ, ⁻ᵃᵘ (masc.) 'four'	**pedwar,** *a.*	**pedwar,** *a. (b.* pedair*). y rhifol ar ôl* tri.¹²	**pedwar** [...] *rhif.* (b. *pedair*) ll. *-oedd, -on, -iaid, -au, pedweiriau*	**four** *num.a. & n.* **1.** *a. m.* pedwar, *f.* pedair; *(a) foll. by sing. noun or* o + *n.pl.* [...]; *(b) neither* pedwar *nor* pedair *mutate the noun following, nor do they mutate after the article* [...] **2.** *n.* pedwar(-au) *m.* [num.conj./num.]	**pedwar** *adj* four; *f* **pedair**
pedair⁻ᵃᵘ (fem.) 'four'	**pedair,** *a.* f. of *pedwar*	**pedair,** *a. tair ac un. (g.* pedwar*)*	**pedair** [...] gw. **pedwar**		**pedair** *adj f.* of **pedwar**
pum(p)⁽ᴺ⁾; ⁻ᵒᵉᵈᵈ (masc.) 'five'	**pum(p),** *a.*	**pump : pum,** *a. y rhifol ar ôl* pedwar.¹³ Pump + o + *lluosog enw (fel yn* pump o bunnoedd*)* Pump + *unigol enw (fel yn* pum punt*).*¹⁴	**pump, pum, pym(p)** [...] *weithiau pair dr. trwynol i* b-, d- [...]; *am y tr. ml. i eiriau sy'n dechrau â* gw-, *ac ychwanegu* h- *o flaen llaf.,* gw. [...] *rhif. a hefyd fel eg.* ll. *pumoedd, -au* [...]¹⁵	**five** *num.a. & n.* **1.** *a.* pum, *foll. by a sing. noun, or* pump + o + *n.pl.* [...]: *it is foll. by the nasal mut. of* blynedd, blwydd *and occ. of* diwrnod [...] **2.** *n.* pump (pumau, pumoedd) *m* [num.]	**pum, pump** *adj*

---

10   'The numeral after two.'
11   'Two and one.'
12   'The numeral after three.'
13   'The numeral after four.'
14   'Pump + o + noun in the plural (as in *pump o bunnoedd*). Pump + o + noun in the singular (as in *pump punt*).'
15   'Causes sometimes nasal mutation with *b-, d-*; for the soft mutation with words which commence with *gw-*, and for placing *h-* before vowels, see [...].'

chwe(ch) (L, N); -au, -oedd (masc.) 'six'	chwe, a. six (with singular noun)[16] chwech, a. six	chwe, a. y rhifol ar ôl pump (definyddir hwn o flaen enwau unigol, e.e. chwe thŷ [...]) chwech, a. [...] (definyddir hwn heb enw neu gydag o ac enw lluosog [...])[17]		chwech[1], chwe [... definyddir chwech a chwe o flaen e.un. (ac weithiau e.ll.) a threiglir p-, t-, c-, yn llaes ar ôl chwe] rhif. ac a. a hefyd eg. ll. -au, -oedd[18]	six num.a. & n. 1. a. chwe foll. by spirant mut. of p-, t-, c- and by a sing. noun; chwech + o + n.pl. [...] 2. n. chwech(-au) m [num.]	chwe adj six (before a noun) chwech adj six ◆(-au) nm
saith (L, N); -oedd, au (masc.) 'seven'	saith, a. & n.m.	saith, a. y rhifol ar ôl chwech[19]	saith, a. y rhifol ar ôl chwech	saith[1] [[...]; weithiau pair dr. meddal [...], a thr. trwynol i b-, d- [...]] rhif. a hefyd fel eg. ll. seith(i)au[20]	seven num. & n. saith (seith-oedd) m (foll. by singular noun, occ: foll. by soft mut.)	saith adj, nm
wyth (L, N) 'eight'	wyth, (-au), a. & n.m.	wyth, a. y rhifol 8[21]	wyth (ŵy), a. y rhifol ar ôl saith[22]	letter not yet reached	eight num.a. &n. 1. a. wyth; (a) wyth is foll. by a sing. noun, or by o + n.pl. [...]; wyth is foll. by the unmutated form of the noun [...], (b) or by the soft mutation (except of m, d) [...]; (c) wyth is foll. by the nasal mut. of blwydd, blynedd, and occ. of diwrnod [...] 2. n. Sp: &c: wyth(-au) m [num.adj.]	wyth (-au) adj, nm

16   In a dictionary which normally provides no explanation, this entry seems to explain something very particular. The given explanation, however, is somewhat misleading. Welsh numerals are regularly followed by a noun in the singular, unless the partitive particle o is placed between the numeral and the noun (cf. section 1.3.2.3.7.). Chwe is a form which is used in a particular formal environment. Such forms also exist for pump 'five' -> pum, cant 'hundred' -> can, deg 'ten' -> deng, deudeg 'twelve' -> deuddeng, and pymtheg 'fifteen' -> pymtheng (cf. P.W. Thomas 1996: 302f.).

17   'the numeral after five (this is used before nouns in the singular, e.g. chwe thŷ [...]) chwech, adjective [...] (this is used without a noun or with o and a noun in the plural [...].'

18   'Chwech and chwe are used before a noun in the singular (and sometimes in plural) and p-, t-, c- suffer spirant mutation after chwe.'

19   'The numeral after six.'

20   'Causes sometimes soft mutation with b-, d- and spirant mutation with p-, t-, c-.'

21   'The numeral 8'.

22   'The numeral after seven'.

naw (N, L); -au 'nine'	naw, *a. & n. m.*	naw, *a.* rhifol, wyth ac un[23]	naw, *a.* rhifol. un yn llai na deg, wyth ac un[24]	**naw**[1] [...] weithiau pair dr. trwynol i *b-, d-* (*naw mlynedd, naw niau*), a thr. ml. i *g-* (*naw radd*) *rhif.* a hefyd fel *eg.* ll. *-(i)au, -oedd,* ac fel *adf.*[25]	**nine** *num. a. & n.* **1.** *a.* now *foll. by sing. noun or by o + n.pl; it is foll. by the unmutated form of the noun, except that it is foll. by the nasal mut. of* blynedd, blwydd, diwrnod [...] **2.** *n.* naw-[i]au) *m* [*num.*]	**naw** *adj, nm* nine
deg/deng(N); -au 'ten'	**deg,** (-au), *a.* deng, *a..*	**deg : deng,** *a. ll.* degau. y rhifol sy'n dilyn naw[26]		**deg, deng** [...] o flaen e.un (ac eithrio rhai e. yn dechrau â *b, d, g, m, n*), neu gydag *o* ac *e.ll.*; defnyddir *deng* o flaen rhai e.un. yn dechrau â *b, d, g, m, n* a threiglir *b, d* yn drwynol [...] ag *g* yn feddal [...] *rhif.* ac *a.* a hefyd *eg. ll. -au*[27]	**ten** *num.a. & n.* **1.** *a.* deg, *foll. by sing. noun or by o + n.pl.* [...]; *before m-, and occ. before a vowel, deg is replaced by deng; deng is also foll. by nasal mutation of* blynedd, blwydd, diwrnod [...] **2.** *n.* deg(-au) *m* [*num.*]	**deg** *adj* ten ◆ (-au) *nm*
ugain(N); -au 'twenty'	**ugain,** *a.*	ugain *a. ll.* ugeiniau. dau ddeg	ugain *a. ll.* ugeiniau. dau ddeg	letter not yet reached	**twenty** *num.a. & n.* **1.** *a.* ugain [...]; *foll. by sing. noun or by o + n.pl.* [...]; *ugain is foll. by the nasal mutation of* blynedd, diwrnod [...] **2.** *n.* ugain (ugeiniau) *m* [*num.adj.*]	**ugain** (ugeiniau) *adj, nm*

---

23 'Numeral, eight and one.'

24 'Numeral, one less than ten, eight and one.'

25 'Causes sometimes nasal mutation in *b-, d-* (*naw mlynedd, naw niau*), and soft mutation in *g-* (*naw radd*), and as adverb.'

26 'The numeral which follows nine.'

27 'Before noun in the singular (except from those which begin with *b, d, g, m, n*), or with *o* and nouns in plural; *deng* is used before nouns in the singular which begin with *b, d, g, m, n* and *b, d* suffer nasal mutation and *g* soft mutation.'

can(t)(N);-oedd 'hundred'	cant, (can-noedd), n.m.	cant², eg. ll. -nnoedd. pum ugain[28]	cant : can, eg. ll. cannoedd. pum ugain.	cant¹, can [[...]; can yw'r ff. reolaidd o flaen e., ac weith-iau fe'i dilynir gan y treiglad trwynol] rhif. ac eg. a hefyd fel a.[29] cannoedd [...]	hundred¹ num.a. & n. 1. a. can + sing. noun, or cant + o + n.pl. [...] (b) can is foll. by the nasal mut. of blynedd, blwydd, diwrnod [...] 2. n. cant (cannoedd) [num.]	cant (can-noedd) nm
mil⁻oedd (fem.) 'thousand'	mil, (-od), n.m. ani-mal (-oedd), n.f. thou-sand	mil², eb. ll. -oedd. deg cant.[30]	mil², eb. ll. -oedd. deg cant.	mil¹ [...] rhif. ac eb.g. ll. -(i)oedd	thousand num.a. & n. mil (-oedd) f. occ: m, now usu. foll. by o + soft mut. [num.]	mil (-oedd) nf
miliwn⁻au (fem.) 'million'	miliwn, (-iynau), n.f.	miliwn, eb. ll. miliynau. mil o filoedd	miliwn, eb. ll. miliynau. mil o filoedd	miliwn, million² [...] rhif. a hefyd fel eb. ll. miliynau [...]	million n. miliwn (miliynau) f	miliwn (-iynau) nf
ail^L 'second'	ail. a.	ail. a. yn dilyn y cyntaf[31]	ail. a. yn dilyn y cyntaf	ail¹ [...] yn wr. yn peri tr. meddal cts.[32]	second² a. & n. 1. a. 1. ail, occ: eilfed (preceding noun, and foll. by soft mut.) [ord.adj.]	ail adj
trydydd (masc.) 'third'	trydydd, (trydedd f.), a.	trydydd, a. (b. trydedd). yr olaf o dri[33]	trydydd, a. (b. trydedd). yr olaf o dri	letter not yet reached	third num.a. & n. 1. a. m. trydydd, f. trydedd [...]; trydedd is foll. by a soft mut. of a fem. noun, and itself mutates after the article [ord.adj.]	trydydd adj third; f trydedd
trydedd^L (fem.)	--	--	--	letter not yet reached		--

---

28   'Five twenty.'
29   '[[...] can is the regular form before a noun, and sometimes it is followed by nasal mutation] numeral and masculine noun and also adjective.'
30   'Ten hundred.'
31   'Following the first.'
32   'Causes originally soft mutation in consonants.'
33   'The last of three'.

pedwerydd (masc.) 'fourth'	--	**pedwerydd**, *a.* (*b.* pedwar-edd). yr olaf o bedwar[34]	**pedwerydd**, *a.* (*b.* pedwar-edd). yr olaf o bedwar	**pedwerydd** [...] *rhif.* (*b.* pedwaredd) [...] *eg. ll.*-au	**fourth** *num.a. & n.* **1.** *a. m.* pedwerydd. *f.* pedwaredd; pedwaredd *mutates after the article and mutates the noun following* [ord.adj.]	--
pedweredd[L] (fem.) 'fourth'	--	--	--	**pedwaredydd, pedwaredd** [...] *gw.* **pedwarydydd pedwerydd**		**pedwaredd** *adj* f. of **pedwerydd**
chwarter[-i, -au] (masc.) 'quarter'	**chwarter,** (-i, -au), *n.m.*	**chwarter,** *eg. ll.* -i, -au. un rhan o bedair[35]	**chwarter,** *eg. ll.* -i, -au. un rhan o bedair	**chwarter** [...] *eg. ll.* -(i)au, ion, -i	**quarter**[1] *n.* **1.** (*a*) chwarter(-i) *m*, pedwaredd ran *f. Lit: occ:* pederian(-nau) [noun, adv.]	**chwarter** (-i, -au) *nm*
deuparth (masc.) 'two thirds'	**deuparth** *d.n.*[36]	**deuparth,** *a.*	**deuparth,** *a.*	**deuparth, deubarth** [..] *eg.*	**two thirds,** y deuparth *m*	**deuparth** *nd*[67]
hanner[hanerau, haneri] (masc.) 'half'	**hanner,** (hanerau, haneri), *n.m.*	**hanner,** *eg. ll.* hanerau, haneri	**hanner,** *eg. ll.* hanerau, haneri	**hanner** [...] *eg.* [...] *ll.* hanerau, haneri, a hefyd fel *adf.*	**half** *n., a. & adv.* **1.** *n.* (*a*) hanner (hanerau, haneri) *m* [noun]	**hanner** (hanerau, haneri) *nm, adj, adv*
traean (masc.) (-au), *n.m.* 'one-third'	**traean,** (-au), *n.m.*	**traean,** *eg.*	**traean,** *eg.*	**traean** [...] *egb. ll.* -au, a hefyd gyda grym ansoddeiriol[38]	traean(-au) *m*	**traean** *nm*

---

34   'The last of four'.

35   'One part of four'.

36   *d.n.* stands for 'dual noun'.

37   *nd* stands for 'noun dual'.

38   'And also with adjectival potency.'

digon (masc.) 'enough'	**digon,** n.m. e-nough, a-bundance a. & ad. sufficient-(ly)	**digon,** 1. eg. [...] enough, sufficiency [...] 2. a. ac adf. sufficient(ly)	**digon,** 1. eg. [...] enough, sufficiency [...] 2. a. ac adf. sufficient(ly)	digon [...] eg. a hefyd fel a. ac adf.	**enough** n. & adv. **1.** n. digon m **sufficience, sufficiency** n. digon m [**sufficient** a. & n. **1.** a. digonol **sufficiently** adv. yn ddigon [adv.]	**digon** nm, adj, adv
gormod (masc.) 'too much/many'	**gormod,** (-ion), n.m.	**gormod : gor-modd,** a. ac adf.	**gormod : gor-modd,** a. ac adf.	**gormod, gormodd** [...] eg. ll. -on	**too ~,** gormod (m) **excess** n. & attrib. **1.** n. (a) (= too much): gormod m **surplus** n. [...] **2.** (= too much): gormod	**gormod** (-ion) nm
llawer^-oedd (masc.) 'many'	**llawer,** (-oedd), n.m, a. & ad.	**llawer,** a. ac eg. ll. -oedd	**llawer,** a. ac eg. ll. -oedd	**llawer** [...] rh. ll. -oedd, -ion, a hefyd fel adf.[39]	**many** a. & n. **1.** a. lawer, llaweroedd [adj.]	**llawer** (-oedd) nm, adj, adv
tipyn (masc.) 'little'	**tipyn,** (-nau, tip-iau), n.m.	**tipyn,** eg. ll. -nau, tipiau	**tipyn,** eg. ll. -nau, tipiau	letter not yet reached	**bit²** n. **1.** (a) [...]: darn(-au) m, tipyn (tipiau) m **little** a., n. & adv. I. [...] II. n. **1.** ychydig m, tipyn m	**tipyn** (-nau, tip-iau) nm

The existence of feminine and masculine forms of cardinals is well displayed in the general-purpose and learners' dictionaries, although indicated in various ways. *Y Geiriadur Cyfoes*, for instance, exhibits inconsistencies in the presentation of the gender category as can be seen when comparing the entries of *dau/dwy*, *tri/tair* and *pedwar/pedair* (cf. above). Slightly inconsistent is also *Geiriadur yr Academi*, which indicates the gender before the numeral, such as in *f. pedair*, after, e.g. in *dwy(oedd) f.*, or before and after it, such as in *f. tair (f)*.

The gender inflection of the ordinals is less well represented. This becomes apparent when looking for *trydedd* or *pedwaredd* in the bi-directional dictionaries. In addition, the *Works-Dictionary* continues to separate morphological categories as is illustrated by the following examples:

---

39 'Pronoun, plural -oedd, -ion, and also as adverb.'

dau *num* **(deuoedd)** two.
[...]
dwy *num* (*f*) two.
[...]
pedair *num* (*f*) four.
[...]
pedwar *num* four.
[...]
tair *num* (*f*) three.
[...]
tri *num* three.

The bi-directional general-purpose dictionaries are, therefore, rather for native speakers who know about feminine ordinals.

The plural inflection of numerals is recognised somewhat individually in Welsh dictionaries. Whereas the historical dictionary *GPC* includes all gender and plural inflections as far as can be said from the headword list available so far, this is not the case in the other dictionaries. Only the uni-directional general-purpose dictionary *Geiriadur yr Academi* suggests plural inflection from the numeral 'two' onwards. *Y Geiriadur Cyfoes* provides the plural for *un*, *wyth*, *ten* and regularly from *cant* onwards. *Y Geiriadur Mawr* and *Y Geiriadur Bach* include plurals for *dau* and consistently from *ugain* onwards. The *Works-Dictionary* displays the plurals for *dau* and *deg* and then from *cant* onwards. *Spurrell* gives the number inflection for *wyth* and regularly from *deg* onwards. The learners' dictionaries do not take notice of any plural forms before the numeral *ugain* (Gruffudd) or *cant* (King).

It is apparent from the word class labels displayed for the lexical items in the above table that these items are not easy to classify. Whereas numerals are recognised as an individual word class in *Geiriadur yr Academi*, i.e. predominantly as 'numeral adjectives' or numeral, and in *GPC*, i.e. as numerals, *Y Geiriadur Mawr* and *Bach* do not continue the inclusion of a phrase with *rhifol* 'numeral' in the explanatory part of their entries from *ugain* onwards. The *Welsh Learner's Dictionary* even distinguishes between cardinals and ordinals (cf. also the word class labels in *Geiriadur yr Academi* above). The *Works-Dictionary* defines the numerals from *cant* onwards as nouns and the *Pocket Modern Welsh Dictionary* from *mil* onwards.

However, also in *Geiriadur yr Academi*, a considerable variety of word class labels is provided for lexical items classified as numerals in this investigation (cf. above table), that is, theoretical concepts for this word class seem to be somewhat unclear in Welsh.

Spurrell and *Y Geiriadur Cyfoes* do not seem to recognise this word class at all as if they followed English word class classification (cf. above). They rather attribute numerals to adjectives and from *cant* onwards, the definition as nouns predominate.

Comparing the word class labelling with the recognition of plural forms, a rough correspondence between them is noticable (cf. above). At this point the importance of well-defined word classes becomes apparent, when the registration and presentation of major morphological forms or other features of lexical items is aimed at.

In this case the very extensive explanations (direct information) on the complementation of *Geiriadur yr Academi* could be reduced to the indication of the actual mutation and illustrating examples (indirect information). Defining them as a subgroup of adjectives, however, additional explanations on the use of this subgroup, which normally does not follow the valency of adjectives (cf. above), remain necessary.

Unnecessary, however, in both *GPC* and *Geiriadur yr Academi* is the information that spirant mutation is suffered by *p, t, c* (cf. entries of *tri* and *chwech*), since other consonants cannot be changed by spirant mutation. In the entry of *pump* in *GPC*, however, the restriction of the nasal mutation to *b* and *d* is useful, since *c, g, p, t* can also suffer nasal mutation.

Too much information is also given for 'four' in *Geiriadur yr Academi* when writing that '*neither* pedwar *nor* pedair *mutate the noun following...*'. It does not seem to be sensible to include what complementation is not necessary.

Major mutations (cf. section 1.3.2.3.7. (C)) are also well indicated in the learners' dictionaries and in *GPC*. Both display direct and indirect information. For *dau*, however, only indirect information is given in *GPC*.

The complementation by a noun in the singular or by the partitive particle 'o + a noun in the plural' is clearly displayed (direct information) only in *Geiriadur yr Academi* and the *Pocket Modern Welsh dictionary*. The latter also includes direct information on the complementation of *digon, gormod*, and *llawer*. The other dictionaries offer here only indirect information.

Y Geiriadur Mawr and *Bach* indicate the complementation of *pump* and incompletely also of *chwe*. *Y Geiriadur Cyfoes, Spurrell* and the *Works-Dictionary* continue to neglect the complementation of their headwords (cf. sections 4.3.1.2., 4.3.3.4., 4.3.4., 4.3.5.2., and 4.3.6.).

To sum up: varying word class labels for Welsh numerals indicate that the word class numeral is not recognised in its own right by some general-purpose dictionaries. However, whereas the gender inflection of Welsh cardinals is well displayed in them, that of the ordinals is underrepresented.

The indication of the number inflection is almost absent from Welsh bi-directional general-purpose dictionaries. Except from some plural forms, this inflection is regularly provided only from the numerals from 'twenty' or 'hundred' onwards, when they are classified as nouns in most dictionaries.

Necessary information on gender and plural inflection is only included in entries of the historical dictionary *GPC* and in the uni-directional *Geiriadur yr Academi*.

The complementation of the numerals is in all bi-directional general-purpose dictionaries insufficiently displayed. In this respect, the learners' dictionaries, *GPC* and *Geiriadur yr Academi* cater well for dictionary users. With the recognition of a well-defined word class numeral, however, the entries of *Geiriadur yr Academi* could be more concise.

4.3.8. The Welsh particle

This section investigates the presentation of particles as introduced in section 1.3.2.3.8. in entries of Welsh bi-directional general-purpose dictionaries. *Geiriadur yr Academi* has not been consulted for this analysis, since sentence initial particles, which indicate the sentence type, do not exist in English. The negation, however, is well explained and exemplified in the uni-directional dictionary (Griffiths, B. & D.G. Jones 1995: 940f. and 946f.).

Par-ticles	Geiriadur Cyfoes	Geiriadur Mawr[1]	Geiriadur Bach	GPC	Works-Dict.	Spurrell
a^L	inter.part. rel.part.	inter. part.$^{(L)2}$ rel.part$^{(L)}$	inter. part.$^{(L)}$ rel.part$^{(L)}$	inter. part.^{L} rel.part.^{L}	rel.pron. inter. part.	inter.part. ♦ preverb.part ♦ rel.pron
ai	adv.	(inter.-)^3 part.	(inter.-) part.	inter.part.	conj.	adv.
fe^L	pron. [...] part. be-fore verbs	part. (be-fore verbs)$^{(L)}$	part. (be-fore verbs)$^{(L)}$	preverbal part.$^{(L)}$	pron.	pron. ♦ preverb. part.
mi^L	pron.	part.	part.	preverbal part.$^{(L)}$	pron.	pron.
na$^{L/S4}$(c)	adv.	neg.part.$^{(L)}$	neg.part.$^{(L)}$	neg. part.$^{L/S}$	**na** *conj* nor. • *adv.* no^5	**na** *conj* [...] ♦ adv. **nac** *adv*
na$^{L/S}$(d)	adv.	neg.rel.-pron. $^{(L)}$ neg.part.$^{(L)}$	neg.rel.-pron. $^{(L)}$	neg.-part.,$^{L/S}$ conj.	**nad** *adv* not	**nad** *adv* not
ni$^{L/S}$(d)	adv.	neg.part.$^{(L)}$	neg.part.$^{(L)}$	neg.part$^{L/S}$	neg.conj.	adv.
oni$^{L/S}$(d)	adv.	part. (for neg. ques-tion)$^{(L)}$	part. (for neg. ques-tion)$^{(L)}$	inter.part., neg.inter. part.$^{L/S}$	adv.	adv.
yn^L	*part.* (NO TRANSLA-TION)	part.$^{(L)}$	part.$^{(L)}$	letter not yet reached	prep.	**yn** *adj* particle^6

---

[1]   For reason of easy comparison, the *Metalanguage*, which is Welsh in *Y Geiriadur Mawr*, *Bach* and *GPC* is adapted to that of the other dictionaries.

[2]   When the indication of the government is put in brackets it can only be deduced from the context.

[3]   The specific word class is here defined by the context.

[4]   *L/S* indicates that the lexical item causes lenition in verbs beginning with *b, d, g, ll, m, rh* and spirant mutation in verbs commencing with *p, t, c.*

[5]   *Nac* is not contained in the headword list.

[6]   This entry looks incorrect and is, therefore, quoted. 'Particle' is certainly the word class label and 'adj' misplaced.

y(r)	preverbal, and rel. particle	part. for bod	part. for bod	letter not yet reached	art.	preverbal and relative particle

The above table corroborates what has already been said about pronouns (cf. section 4.3.4.), prepositions (cf. section 4.3.5.), and conjunction (cf. section 4.3.6.), namely that the word class definition of individual lexical items may vary considerably. In order to illustrate this phenomenon, some entries of the *Works-Dictionary*, *Spurrell* and *Y Geiriadur Cyfoes* have been copied into the table.

One reason for this variety may be different concepts of defining individual word classes. Another, however, may also be the ignorance of the comprehensive use of individual lexical items. Whatever the reason, the varying or indirect labelling of word classes can cause problems for dictionary users.

A is the only particle which is well classified in all dictionaries. In *Spurrell*, however, it is twice classified on the basis of its function, i.e. as an interrogative particle and relative pronoun, and once according to its position when defined as a preverbal particle (structural approach). This characterisation is somewhat misleading, since dictionary users may think of three functions this item has. However, the indication 'preverbal particle' rather provides syntactic information on its usage.

Different concepts of defining word classes may be reflected in the labelling of the particle *ai*, since its English equivalents suggest its major potential functions as is illustrated by examples from the *Works-Dictionary*, *Spurrell* and *Y Geiriadur Cyfoes*:

ai *conj* is it; either ... or
ai *adv* is it? what **a. e**? is it so?
ai, *ad.* IS IT? WHAT?

The particle function of *fe* is recognised by all except the *Works-Dictionary* and that of *mi* only by *Y Geiriadur Mawr*, *Bach* and the historical dictionary *GPC*.

The description of *na(c)* and *na(d)* seems to cause difficulties for the *Works-Dictionary*, *Spurrell* and *Y Geiriadur Cyfoes*. In particular the first does not include particles of negation, e.g. *nac* is omitted. In addition, it separates contextually varying forms from each other, e.g. *na*, *nad*. Indeed, *na* is the form before consonants for *nac*, *nad* and *nag* or

"may stand alone as a negative adverb answering a question introduced by *a* or *ai*. It is usually followed by a negative particle with a verb, noun, or pronoun &c" (Griffiths, B. & D.G. Jones 1995: 946f., cf. also 1459).

However, according to the entries in the *Works-Dictionary* its users are advocated to use *na* and *naddo*[7] for 'no' and *nad*, *ni*, *nid*, and *nis* (cf. section 1.3.2.3.8., Griffith 1995: 946) for 'not'. Checking in the English-to-Welsh section, dictionary users are told that they can use *heb*,[8] *na*, *nad*, *ni*, *nid* to express 'not'. In view of the regularities of negation in Welsh the minimum in-

---

[7] *Naddo* is an adverb which answers emphatic questions in the past.
[8] However, the English equivalent of *heb* is 'without' in the Welsh-to-English section.

formation in its regard is provided by *Y Geiriadur Bach*. The *Works-Dictionary* caters only for native speakers, who know how to use the words so long as they know that they exist.

The government of particles is only well explained in the historical dictionary *GPC*, mainly by direct information and context. *Y Geiriadur Mawr* and *Bach* give major information on mutations by the context. For the negative particles, however, the spirant mutation is not included. The other three dictionaries continue to neglect mutations caused by their headwords.

Further information on the syntactic use of particles is provided by the phrase 'preverbial particle', also in *Y Geiriadur Cyfoes* and *Spurrell*. This information, however, is not necessary, since apart from the emphatic use of *ni(d)* and *na(d)*, only *ai* and *yn* do not precede the verb. More user-friendly would be the information what function the particles have, e.g. *fe*, *mi* as affirmative particles and *y(r)* as affirmative particle and one which indicates the topicalisation of adverbials or prepositional complements (cf. section 1.3.2.3.8.). A label such as 'aff.part.' does not take more space than the label 'preverbal particle'. For *yn* the information 'yn^L+ adj.', 'yn^L + noun', 'yn^0 + verbal noun/verb' would contain all necessary information without additional context or functional explanations. The context provided in *Y Geiriadur Mawr* and *Bach* for *yn* takes more space, but remains incomplete as is shown in the next example:

> **yn**, *geir.* (mewn traethiad etc.).
> (PARTICLE).
> Yn mynd. GOING.
> Gwneud yn dda. DOING WELL.

The first phrase in the entry expresses action (cf. section 1.3.2.3.8.) and the second displays the adverbial particle, which causes lenition. The use of 'yn^L + noun' is not included.

To sum up: although the word class labelling for lexical items defined as particles differs widely in Welsh bi-directional general-purpose dictionaries, most information on their potential functions is provided. The only dictionary which does not give sufficient information in this respect is the *Works-Dictionary* as is illustrated by the following examples:

> **fe** *pron* he, him.
> **mi** *pron* I, me.
> **oni, onid** *adv* unless.[9]
> **yn, yng, ym** *prep* in.
> **y, yr, 'r** *art* the.

The government of particles is only well explained in the historical dictionary *GPC* and in the learners' dictionaries.

Consequently, whoever uses Welsh bi-directional general-purpose dictionaries will have difficulty in finding function words well explained (cf. also section 4.3.6.). Since these are of particular importance for the construction of sentences, i.e. basic units of speech acts, insufficiencies in their description may cause problems when communicating, or decoding and encoding texts (cf. section 1.3.2.3.). With a functional approach the description of particles could be more efficient.

---

[9]   *Onid* as introduced here is rather a conjunction.

4.3.9. Hyphenation

Hyphenation, as mentioned in section 1.3.2.3., does not belong to the type of information which has to be included in dictionary entries. In this section, however, reasons are given as to why the regular indication of where to hyphenate Welsh lexical items would be advantageous.

Whoever seeks to use space on paper efficiently - as done for instance in *GPC* in which lexical items are regularly hyphenated[1] - or to create special layouts will come across the question of where to hyphenate Welsh words. Words in Welsh can be as long as, for example, in German and tend to exceed the end of a line. This is due to the fact that both languages productively derive new words by prefixation and suffixation or form compound words (cf. sections 4.3.2.2.2. and 1.3.2.3.7., cf. also Pilch 1995, Zimmer 2000).

Trying to consult reference books for guidelines on Welsh hyphenation, Welsh language users will soon realise that there is not even agreement on the term for hyphenation in Welsh. The booklet *Termau Ieithyddiaeth* (E. Evans 1987), for instance, does not contain this term. Whereas the few reference books which do refer to hyphenation call it *rhannu geiriau*[2] 'dividing words', the staff of *GPC* prefers the phrase *hollti geiriau* 'splitting words'. *Heiffeneiddio* 'hyphenating', *cysylltnodi* 'hyphenating', or *trychu geiriau* 'cutting words' can also be heard.

If speakers of Welsh search for guidelines on hyphenation in reference books, they will first of all discover statements which suggest that they should not hyphenate, e.g. in P.W. Thomas' leading *Gramadeg y Gymraeg* (1996: 778) in which he writes: *Yn gyffredinol, dylid ceisio osgoi rhannu'r gair* 'In general, one should avoid hyphenation'. Similar suggestions are made by J. E. Hughes in *Canllawiau Ysgrifennu Cymraeg* (1998: 7.1.) and by E. Davies in *Rhannu Geiriau* (1954: 24):[3]

> "Mae'n well ceisio osgoi rhannu geiriau ar ddiwedd llinell o ysgrifen neu o deipio." 'It is better to avoid hyphenation at the end of a written or printed line.'
>
> "Ni ddylid rhannu geiriau ar ddiwedd llinell mewn teipysgrif na llawysgrif." 'It should not be hyphenated at the end of a line of a typescript nor a manuscript.'

Indeed, comparing old and new publications and present day statements on hyphenation (cf. above), it becomes apparent that hyphenation was more popular before the eighties. This trend is displayed in the following table.

---

[1] To hyphenate regularly means to split words at the end of the line when too long.

[2] In view of synchronic language use *rhannu geiriau* seems to be a problematic term, since the meaning 'share' goes strongly with the word *rhannu* 'divide, share, distribute'. It is very common, for instance, to say *rhannu meddyliau, syniadau* 'share thoughts, ideas', although it is not clear whether this is an anglicism.

[3] I would like to take this opportunity of thanking Siôn Williams, University of Cardiff, and William Ll. Griffith, Dinbych/Wales, for providing me with material and of thanking Dr Iwan Wmffre, Tregaron/Wales, for helpful discussion on this matter.

Name of publication[4]	hyphenating		irregular/rare hyphenation	regular hyphenation
	not at all	where there is a hyphen already		
Prichard, Rh., (1867), *Canwyll y Cymry*, Llanymddyfri.				x (including personal and place names)
Lewis, H., 1925 (1967), *Chwedlau Seith Doethon Rufein*, Caerdydd.			x (morphologically)	
Williams, I., 1930 (1982), *Pedeir Keinc y Mabinogi*, Caerdydd.				x (morphologically,[5] also personal names[6])
Lewis, H., 1931 (1974), *Hen Gerddi Crefyddol*, Caerdydd.				x (morphologically, also personal names and Middle Welsh)
Williams, I., 1935 (1978), *Canu Llywarch Hen*, Caerdydd.				x (morphologically, also personal names and Middle Welsh)
Williams, I., 1938 (1978), *Canu Aneirin*, Caerdydd.				x (morphologically, also personal names and Middle Welsh)
Lewis, H., 1942 (1974), *Brut Dingestow*, Llandysul.				x (morphologically, also personal names and Middle Welsh)
Richards, M., 1948 (1980), *Breudwyt Ronabwy*, Caerdydd.				x (morphologically, also personal names and Middle Welsh)
Jarman, A.O.H., 1951 (1967), *Ymddiddan Myrdin a Thaliesin*, Caerdydd.				x (including personal and place names)
Morgan, T.J., 1952 (1989), *Y Treigladau a'u cystrawen*, Caerdydd.				x (morphologically, also personal names and Middle Welsh)
Jarman, A.O.H., 1957 (1979), *Chwedlau Cymraeg Canol*, Caerdydd.				x (morphologically, also personal names and Middle Welsh)
Roberts, K., 1959 (1987), *Te yn y Grug*, Dinbych.				x (morphologically including personal and place names)

---

4   An attempt was made to compile a list which presents a wide range of publications.

5   Syllabic hyphenation seems to have been employed as well, e.g. in *tragwy-ddol* (T.J. Morgan 1952: 157), *cymera-dwyir* (A.O.H. Jarman 1979: xv).

6   Place names were also hyphenated.

Reference		
Williams, I., 1960 (1977), *Canu Taliesin*, Caerdydd.		x (morphologically, also personal names and Middle Welsh)
Rowland, W., 1961. *Straeon y Cymry*. Aberystwyth.		x (morphologically)
Owen, D., 1962. *Straeon y Pentan*, Wrecsam.		x (morphologically including personal and place names)
Parry-Williams, T.H., 1966, *Pedair Canc y Mabinogi*, Caerdydd.		x (morphologically)
Roberts, K., 1969 (1981), *Prynu Dol*, Dinbych.		x (morphologically including place names)
Elis, Islwyn Ffowc, 1971, *Eira Mawr*, Llandysul.		x (morphologically)
Roberts, K., 1976 (1983), *Yr Wylan Deg*, Dinbych.		x (morphologically including place names)
Goetnick, G.W., 1976, *Historia Peredur vab Efrawc*, Caerdydd.		x (morphologically, also personal names and Middle Welsh)
Evans, H.M., 1979, *Y Mabinogi Heddiw*, Abertawe.		x (morphologically)
Davies, P., 1979, *Mabinogi Mwys*, Abertawe.		x (morphologically)
Williams, P., 1982, *Kedymdeithyas Amlyn ac Amic*, Caerdydd.		x (morphologically, also personal names and Middle Welsh)
Ifans, A., 1983, *Macsen Wledig*, Llandysul.		x (morphologically)
Tomos, A., 1984 (1994), *Cyfres Rala Rwdins*, Talybont.		x (morphologically)
Meredith, S., 1987. *Prifio*, Aberystwyth.	x	
Hywyn, G., 1987, *Tydi Bywyd yn boen?*, Caernarfon (Series).	x	
Edwards, H.LL., 1987, *Dydaliadur Nant y Wrach*, Caernarfon	x	
Bromwich, R. & D.S. Evans, 1988, *Culhwch ac Olwen*, Caerdydd.		x (very rarely: morphologically and syllabic)
Huws, J.O., 1988. *Gawn ni Stori?*, Llanrwst.	x	
Johnston, D., 1989. *Iolo Goch*, Caernarfon.		x (morphologically)
1989, *Y Testament Newydd*, Glasgow.		x (morphologically)

Reference					
Davies, S., 1989, *Pedeir Keinc y Mabinogi*, Caernarfon.					x (morphologically)
1991, *Menter Cwm Gwendraeth*, Llandybïe.					x (morphologically and syllabic)
Tomos, A., 1991 (1992), *Si Hei Lwli*, Talybont (ac eraill).					x (morphologically)
1991, *Adroddiad Trydan De Cymru*, Caerdydd.		x			
1992, *Papurau gwaith Caerdydd*, Caerdydd.					x (morphologically)
Cyngor Celfyddydau Cymru, 1993, *Cynllun Iaith Gymraeg*, Caerfyrddin.		x			
Ackroyd, R., 1992, *Hanesion Ysbryd Traddodiadol o Gymru*, Llangeitho.				x (morphologically, syllabic and faulty: digwyd-diad)	
Thomas, G., 1992, *Chwedl Taliesin*, Caerdydd.				x (twice: ychwan-egodd, gor-gorhendaid)	
Roberts, M., 1994, *Dyddiadur Gwraig Ffermr*, Llanrwst.		x (one English and one Welsh word)			
Crockett, K., 1995, *Sïn Roc*, Talybont.		x			
Jones, D., 1997, *Cyflwyniad i Ddwyieithrwydd*, Caerfyrddin.				x (rarely; syllabic and morphologically: pwysi-grwydd, symu-doledd, dwyiei-thog ac anghywir: enghreiffti-au)	
Sefydliad Materion Cymreig a Chyngor Defnyddwyr Cymru, 1998, *Ansawdd Gwasanaeth, Dwyieithrwydd a'r Gwasanaeth Cyhoeddus yng Nghymru*, Caerdydd.			x (cyd-testun)		
Ifans, D. & Rh.,1998, *Hud yr hen chwedlau Celtaidd - Y Mabinogion*, Llanrwst.	x (apart from one exception)				

As can be seen from the table, hyphenating was less stigmatised before the eighties. Morphological hyphenation, including proper names, and even words in Middle Welsh, was the norm. Hyphenation was even employed when there was no need to save space; it was obviously also seen as a matter of aesthetics.

RHAGAIR.

GOLYGWYD y testun hwn yn y dull arferol trwy atalnodi a rhannu'n baragraffau. Dymunol yw gennyf ddiolch i'm cyfeillion parod am eu help a'u cefnogaeth : i'r Athro Henry Lewis am ddarllen y gwaith drwodd ac am liaws o awgrym-iadau ; i Stephen J. Williams am ddarllen rhan o'r proflenni; i'r Dr. Elwyn Davies am ym-gymryd o'i wirfodd â pharatoi map i egluro taith Rhonabwy, ac am ei ddiddordeb cyson ; i Fwrdd y Wasg am dderbyn y llyfr i'w gyhoeddi; i Wasg Gomer am ei gofal.

Rhagfyr, 1947.   M.R.

It remains a question, therefore, why Welsh language users are advised in recent reference books to avoid hyphenation, particularly in an age when everybody is looking for the best layout. Is the stigmatisation a long-term effect of seeking to introduce a simplified language (cf. section 4.1.1.)? Or is it because Latin - the knowledge of which supports morphological hyphenation (cf. below) - is no core subject in modern education?

Whatever the reason, in view of productive derivation (cf. sections 4.3.2.2.2., 4.3.3.2.1., and 4.3.3.3.1.) and composition patterns (cf. section 4.3.7.) of Welsh word formation, the suggestion not to hyphenate is somewhat incomprehensible. The consequences of such an approach are, first, a reduced prestige of the language if it is not used in a way similar to other languages. A second effect is an inefficient use of space.[7] In daily papers, e.g. in the *Western Mail*, however, space seems to be less important than quick production. The *Western Mail* could add whole additional adverts were its editors to make use of hyphenation. Non-daily papers, magazines, and books, on the other hand, have to calculate more cautiously.[8]

---

[7]   Examples which illustrate the situation can be found in *Gwaith Maes, Western Mail, Tivy Side, Y Faner Newydd, Y Cymro, Taliesin, Barn.*

[8]   Whoever writes creatively will certainly remember discussions with publishers on the number of words or even on punctuation in order to save space, pages and consequently ensure a more profitable sale.

A third effect of neglecting to hyphenate is the uncertainty of applying rules in its regard. This uncertainty becomes apparent when hyphenation does not occur in various publications, or when hyphenation occasionally takes place, or when this is predominantly used for English words. Such approaches are displayed in the following table:

Papers	hyphenation			
	not at all	occasionally	mostly of English words	always
Barn	x	(rarely and when there is a hyphen already)		
Cambria				x
Cambrian News				x
Daily Post				x
Golwg	x	(rarely and when there is a hyphen already)		
Gwaith Maes	x			
Lingo	x			
Lol	x			
Tafod y Ddraig	x			
Taliesin		(words which already have a hyphen)	x	
Cardigan and Tivy-side Advertiser		x		
Western Mail	x			
Y Cymro		x		
Y Faner Newydd	x			
Yr Herald Gymraeg	x			

Welsh words which already have a hyphen are, for instance, *ad-drefnu* 'to re-organise', or *di-baid* 'ceaseless'. The only papers in the above table which hyphenate regularly are the *Cambrian News*, *Daily Post*, and *Cambria*. The last, however, does not hyphenate in each Welsh article.

The way these papers hyphenate, nevertheless, is according to the guidelines introduced in *Orgraff yr Iaith* (Lewis 1987: 69), P.W. Thomas (1996: 778), E. Hughes (1998: 7.1.), and Hart (1998: 136, cf. below) erroneous. This fourth consequence of neglecting hyphenation becomes apparent when the digraph ⟨dd⟩ is regularly hyphenated in these papers just as the diphthong /ai/, presented as ⟨ae⟩, in the *Cambrian News* and in *Cambria*.

Apart from hyphenating morphologically and syllabically, *Y Cymro* also hyphenates incorrectly and leaves, for instance, the digraph ⟨dd⟩ alone on the next line (1.9.1999) or ⟨ch⟩ (8.9.2001).

However, hyphenation is not only a problem of papers and publishers, but also of those who teach Welsh as can be seen from a circular of the *Cymdeithas Broffesiynol i Diwtoriaid Cymraeg* 'Professional Association of Welsh Tutors'[9] (below), in which the diphthong /ai/ (⟨ae⟩)

CYLCHLYTHYR

CYMDEITHAS BROFFESIYNOL I DIWTORIAID CYMRAEG

Rhif 2.　　　　　　　　　　　　　　　　　　　　　　Chwefror 2001

'Y Tiwtor'

Fel y dywedwyd yn y rhifyn diwethaf, cafwyd £420 gan Fwrdd yr Iaith i dalu am gysodi ac argraffu'r cylchgrawn, eleni. Erbyn hyn, mae 130 copi o'r *Tiwtor* wedi eu dosbarthu. Can diolch i Uned Gymraeg i Oedolion Prifysgol Abertawe, ac yn enwedig i Mark Stonelake, am y gwaith cywrain a graenus a wnaethpwyd wrth lunio, cysodi ac argraffu'r rhifyn presennol.

Y Cyfarfod Cyffredinol
Trefnir y dyddiad a'r lleoliad yn y Penwythnos Hyfforddi Mewn Swydd yn Nant Gwrtheyrn

BYGYTHIAD I ARHOLIADAU CBAC

Yn sgil y newidiadau arfaethedig yn nhrefn cymwysterau Lefel 'A', anogodd Helen y Gymdeithas i gefnogi'r ymdrechion Pwyllgor Arholiadau CiO CBAC i gadw'r Arholiad Defnyddio'r Gymraeg Uwch. Fodd bynnag, rhybuddiodd Phyl y byddai'r cadw'r arholiad presennol fel tystysgrif fewnol CBAC yn unig yn golygu na fyddai'n cyfateb i'r cymwysterau UG ac U2 arfaethedig, ac efallai mai nawr yw'r amser i ddechrau ymgyrch dros sefydlu set o gymwysterau cyrhaeddiad yn y Gymraeg - yn debyg i'r hyn a geir yn Euskadi (Gwlad y Basg).

Ers y cyfarfod, clywyd bod Prif Weithredwr ACAC, John Valentine, wedi cytuno i ohirio dileu Arholiad Defnyddio'r Gymraeg Uwch am ddwy flynedd, gan roi inni amser i ymchwilio i'r posibilrwydd o gymhwyso cyrnwysterau ALTE (Ewropeaidd).

Bydd Canolfan Dysgu Cymraeg Prifysgol Caerdydd yn gyfrifol am y rhifyn nesaf ym mis Chwefror, a Chanolfan Addysg Barhaus Prifysgol Cymru, Aberystwyth ym mis Gorffennaf - oni phenodir golygydd parhaol ym y cyfamser.

NEWYDDION DA

Mae Bwrdd yr Iaith wedi cytuno i dalu rhyw £500 y flwyddyn i gyflogi golygydd.

PENWYTHNOS HYFFORDDIANT MEWN SWYDD NANT GWRTHEYRN

Ar ôl tipyn o amryfusedd, gellir nawr gadarnhau y cynhelir y Penwythnos Hyfforddi Mewn Swydd yn Nant Gwrtheyrn yn ystod y penwythnos 14-16 Ebrill, eleni. Gw. y rhaglen amgaeedig am fanylion.

Mae'r rhan fwyaf o ddarparwyr yn fodlon noddi tiwtoriaid rhan-amser i fynychu'r PHMS. Holwch am drefnydd lleol am fanylion.

★★
★　　　**CADW MEWN CYSYLLTIAD Â'R AELODAU**　　　★
★ Ar ôl pob cyfarfod o'r Pwyllgor Gwaith, cynhyrchir cylchlythyr - i'w anfon at bob ★
★ aelod o'r Gymdeithas.　　　　　　　　　　　　　　　★
★★

LOGO

Hyd yn hyn, dim ond un cynnig a ddaeth i law. Beth am ddod â'ch cynigion i'r Nant?

Y CYFANSODDIAD

Amgaeir copi o gyfansoddiad y Gymdeithas. Bydd angen ei dderbyn yn ffurfiol yn y Cyfarfod Cyffredinol.

is hyphenated and ⟨w⟩ left alone on the next line.

In the following table, major and most common mistakes in hyphenating Welsh words are displayed.[10]

9　　This is a translation by the author. It is has to be emphasised that an official translation into English does not exist. 'Tutors' here are Welsh language teachers for adults.

10　　The examples are taken from *Western Mail* (1996, 1999), *Barn* (1996, 1998), *Daily Post* (2000), *Y Cymro* 2001).

| digraph | | | | diphthong | | | | |
dd	ll	ff	ng	ae	ei	wy	yw	oe
agwed-dau	allweddel-lau	Bodf-fordd	cyfryn-gol	amaethyddia-eth	cymde-ithas	arw-ydd	lly-wydd	Tro-edrhiwllan
amaethyd-diaeth	cynl-lun	cynf-fonau	Llanfihan-gel	arfa-ethedig	gobe-ithir	camlw-yddiant	lly-wyddwyd	
amaethyd-dol	cynl-lunio	dif-fuant		barddonia-eth		llw-yddiannus	rhy-wbeth	
amgylched-dol	diwyl-liant	hof-fem		buddugolia-eth		llw-yddiant		
ard-derchog	diwyl-liannol	Minf-fordd		cadwra-eth		llw-yddo		
Bedyd-dwyr	enil-lion	perf-formiad		cystadleua-eth		new-ydd		
blynyd-dol	Llanel-li			da-eth				
blwyd-dyn	Dolgel-lau			gnwa-eth				
bud-dsoddiadau	gel-lir			gwasana-eth				
byd-dant	Gwenl-lian			marwola-eth				
byd-din				profediga-eth				
byd-dwn								
cadeiryd-des								
cerd-dwyr								
cyfarwyd-dwr								
cyhoed-dwyd								
did-danu								
did-dordeb								
did-dorol								
digwyd-diad								

diwed-dar					
diwed-daraf					
gwleidyd-dion					
hed-diw					
llwyd-dodd					
med-dai					
newyd-dion					
oed-dwn					
Penwed-dig					
rhinwed-dau					
rhod-dodd					
rhod-dwyd					
roed-dym					
sosialyd-dion					
swyd-dogion					

i-combinations			single letters		
ia	io	iau	w	dd	ch
cyfrani-adau	cynhyrchi-ol	eisi-au	cad-w	gwleidy-dd	hytra-ch
profi-ad	cynrychi-oli	enghreiffti-au		maesy-dd	
profi-adol	di-olch			ysgrifenny-dd	
syni-ad	pri-od				
syni-adaeth					

A look at the above table shows that hyphenating the digraph ⟨dd⟩ and the diphthong /ai/, presented as ⟨ae⟩, are generally the most frequent mistakes. Most of them are erroneous, whether the chosen way of hyphenating is morphological or syllabic or mixed. The hyphenation of Welsh digraphs, monosyllabic words and diphthongs can also be observed in the time of the Renaissance. In this time, however, different theories on orthography influenced spelling and the presentation of the vernacular language in comprehensive publications was still it its infancy (cf. section 2.2.2.).

After this short survey on present day common practise of hyphenation in Welsh in popular and wide spread publications, linguistic consequences of incorrect hyphenation are exemplified in the following.

First, when the digraphs ⟨dd⟩, ⟨ng⟩, ⟨ff⟩, ⟨ll⟩, ⟨ph⟩, or ⟨th⟩[11] are hyphenated the pronunciation of their individual letters changes, since digraphs are not double letters. Only the letters *n* and *r* can really double[12] in Modern Welsh spelling and that only under the influence of a suffix, e.g. *llythyren* 'letter' + plural ending -> *llythrennau*. To see digraphs separated may cause people pronounce /d/ instead of /ð/, /n/ + /g/ instead of /ŋ/, /v/ instead of /f/, or /l/ instead of /ɬ/. This is certainly true for learners. These, however, form a high percentage of Welsh speakers (cf. section 4.1.1.).

Second, not only is pronunciation itself a major problem, but mis-hyphenation can also lead to mis-understanding of the entire lexical items. Mis-understandings may occur when, for instance, *ar-wydd* is hyphenated like *arw-ydd* (cf. above table). In certain circumstances *arw-ydd*[13] could be interpreted as a 'person who is somewhat rough - *garw* - in character'. Something similar happens when *cadw* 'to keep' is hyphenated like *cad-w* (cf. above table). In this case an association with *cad* 'battle' is suggested to the readers before they reach the following line.

---

[11] I could not find the digraphs ⟨ph⟩ and ⟨th⟩ being (mis)hyphenated. This may be due to the fact that both can also be found in the English language, in which they are not hyphenated either (cf. further explanations).

[12] ⟨i⟩ doubles in exceptional circumstances, e.g. *sgii di* 'go skiing' (second person singular present).

[13] Both forms would have to occur in an environment in which they suffer mutation.

Although the context would mostly ensure the actual meaning of the hyphenated lexical items, the reading is disturbed.

In addition, the two individual elements of a digraphs exist also as single letters. As such, however, they perform different functions. For instance, they indicate the border between two constituents of derivated or compound lexical items. Derivations from a stem by prefixation are words such as *addysg* 'education', in which -dd- derives from *ad* + *disco* (Latin); or *dangos* 'to demonstrate, show', in which -ng- derives from *dan* + *cos*; or *arholi* 'to examine', in which -rh- derives from *ar* + *holi*. A compound word is, for instance, *Ponthir* (place name), in which -th- derives from *pont* + *hir* 'long' + 'bridge'.

Third, the hyphenation of diphthongs leads (a) to a situation in which they cannot be recognised as such any more and (b) since diphthongs often form part of morphemes the latter cannot be recognised either, and are thus diminished in their function as elements of word formation. The morpheme *-aeth*, for instance, which is used to form abstract nouns, e.g. in *antur* 'venture' + *-aeth* -> *anturiaeth* 'adventure, enterprise', is often hyphenated as is seen in *cystadleua-eth* 'competition' and other examples of the above table.

Another morpheme which suffers mis-hyphenation is *-iad*. It is also employed to derive abstract nouns, such as in *profi* 'prove' + *-iad* -> *profiad* 'experience'. A last example in this context is the morpheme *-iol*, which may be used to form adjectives, e.g. *cynhyrchu* 'to produce' + *-iol* -> *cynhyrchiol* 'productive'.

It is a similar matter to leave ⟨dd⟩ alone on the following line (cf. table), since it can also form part of morphemes. ⟨dd⟩ may be an element of the morpheme *-ydd*, which denotes the agent, e.g. in *ieith-ydd* 'linguist', *siarad-ydd* 'speaker', *ysgrifenn-ydd* 'writer' or a tool, as in *addas-ydd* 'adapter'.

When hyphenating syllabically, as for instance in German, morphemes are also split. For Welsh, however, a predominantly morphological hyphenation has been suggested by *Orgraff yr Iaith* (1987), P.W. Thomas (1996), J.E. Hughes (1998), and Hart (1998):

> "Wrth rannu gair ar ddiwedd llinell yr arferiad cyffredin yw dilyn rhaniad ei elfennau, fel *car-ed-ig*, yn hytrach na rhaniad seiniol y sillafau [*ca-re-dig*]" Ond i'r rheol hon y mae'r eithriadau a ganlyn: Y mae'n arferiad cyffredinol dodi'r cysylltnod rhwng dwy cytsain unrhyw, megis *can-nu*, *cor-rach*. Doder ef hefyd rhwng mud a llaes, fel *dl, dr, gl, gn*, etc., megis *cenhed-loedd, med-raf* [...] Ni all *mh, nh, ngh* fod yn seiniau diweddol; gwell *ng-h* nag *h-* ar ddiwedd llinell. Na thorfynygler sillaf, megis *gwr-aig* [...] er maint a fo o lythrennau ynddi.
> Wrth rannu geiriau'n sillafau i gyfateb i nodau miwsig fe ddylid dilyn y rhaniad seiniol, fel y canlyn: Doder cytsain sengl gyda llafariad yr ail sillaf, megis *ca-nu, gwe-nau* [...] Doder *p, t, c, m, ng, ll, s* gyda llafariad y sillaf acennog, megis *at-eb, cym-od* [...], ond *a-te-bodd, cy-mo-di* [...] Lle bo dwy gytsain ysgrifenedig doder y cysylltnod rhyngddynt, megis *ton-nau, plen-tyn* [...]; lle bo tair dilyner y ffurfiad: *car-tref, can-dryll* [...]."

'When hyphenating a word at the end of a line, the common usage is to follow the division of its elements, e.g. *car-ed-ig*, rather than the phonetic division of its syllables [*ca-re-dig*]. It is common usage to put the hyphen between any two consonants,[14] as in

---

At this point the user has to know that digraphs do not count as double consonants.

cor-rach. It is also placed between voiceless and voiced consonants, like *dl, dr, gl, gn,* etc, as in *cenhed-loedd, med-raf* [...]. *mh, nh, ngh* cannot be final sounds; it is better to have *ng-h* than *h-* at the end of the line. A syllable such as *gwr-aig* [...] is not to be headed off, regardless of how many letters it contains.

When dividing words in syllables to correspond to musical notes, one should follow the sound division, like in the following: the single consonant is given to the vowel of the second syllable, like *ca-nu, gwe-nau* [...]. *P, t, c, m, ng, ll, s* are given to the vowel of the accented syllable, like *at-eb, cym-od* [...], but *a-te-bodd, cy-mo-di* [...]. Where there are two written consonants, the hyphen is placed between them, as in *ton-nau, plen-tyn* [...]; where there are three, the form to be followed is as in *car-tref, can-dryll'* [...] *Orgraff yr Iaith Gymraeg* (1987: 69).

The guidelines on hyphenation provided by *Orgraff yr Iaith* reflect a somewhat mixed approach. Although morphological hyphenation dominates, syllabic and aesthetic principles are also included. P.W. Thomas (1996: 778) provides more simplified guidelines, which are clearly based on a morphological approach:

- "ni rennir geiriau unsill, na geiriau fel *chwaer* na *mawr*
- ni rennir deugraffau
- dim ond pan ceir ffiniau rhwng morffemau y goddefir rhannu geiriau lluosill
- yr unig eithriadau i'r rheol uchod yw geiriau sydd yn cynnwys clymau o ddwy gytsain"

- 'monosyllabic words, e.g. *chwaer* and *mawr*, are not to be hyphenated
- digraphs are not to be hyphenated
- it is only permitted to hyphenate at the border of morphemes of polysyllabic words
- the only exceptions to the rule above are words which contain clusters of two consonants'.

The subsequent guidelines which also suggest morphological hyphenation are given by J.E. Hughes (1998: 7.1.):

- "Peidiwch fyth â rhoi cysylltnod i wahanu *ch, dd, ng, ll, ph, rh, th,* gan mai UN llythyren yw pob un o'r rhain yn y Gymraeg. Mae'r un peth yn wir am *ng* (e.e. nid cywir fyddai *dian-gen*) ond os digwydd *n* ac *g* yn llythrennau ar wahân, byddai'n iawn i ni roi cysylltnod rhwng y ddwy lythyren (e.e. *Ban-gor*).
- Peidiwch fyth â rhannu gair drwy ddefnyddio dau gysylltnod (e.e. <u>ni</u> ddylid teipio *cyd-ddyn-ion*).
- Ceisiwch osgoi cael llai na thair llythyren y naill ochr neu'r llall i'r cysylltnod (h.y. peidiwch â theipio *am-gaeedig, en-webu, bendiged-ig* [...]
- Os dymunir rhannu gair yn cynnwys *-nn-* neu *-rr-*, gellir rhoi'r cysylltnod rhwng y ddwy gytsain (e.e. *pen-naeth, cyn-nwys* [...]
- Gellir rhannu o flaen rhagddodiaid megis y rhai a ganlyn: *arch-, cam- cyd-, cyf-,* [...]
- Gellir rhannu o flaen ôl-ddodiaid neu derfyniadau megis y rhai a ganlyn: *-adwy, -aeth, -aid, -aidd, -der, -dod* [...]
- ENWAU LLEFYDD AC ENWAU POBL: ceisiwch beidio â rhannu'r geirau hyn o gwbl os oes modd ond pan na ellir osgoi hynny:
    - ceisiwch rannu mewn lle synhwyrol (e.e., Aber-honddu, Llanfair-fechan)
    - peidiwch â gwahanu llythrennau blaen yn enw rhywun ar ddiwedd llinell (e.e., W.J. / Gruffydd <u>not</u> W./J. Gruffydd)

- Er mor hwylus yw'r ddyfais, peidiwch â defnyddio'r cylfeuster a geir ar brosyddion geiriau i gysylltnodi'n awtomatig gan nad yw'n gallu rhannu geiriau'n gywir yn y Gymraeg."

- 'Never put a hyphen in order to divide *ch, dd, ng, ll, ph, th*, since in Welsh each of them is ONE letter. The same is true for *ng* (e.g. dian-gen would be wrong) but when *n* and *g* occur as separate letters, it is possible to put a hyphen between them (i.e. *Ban-gor*).
- Never hyphenate a word by using two hyphens (e.g. *cyd-ddyn-ion* should not be typed).
- Try to avoid less than three letters left over on one or the other side of the hyphen (that is, do not type *am-gaeedig, en-webu, bendiged-ig* [...]
- If it is wished to divide a word which contains *-nn-* or *-rr-*, it is possible to put the hyphen between the two consonants (e.g. *pen-naeth, cyn-nwys* [...]
- One can hyphenate before prefixes like those which follow: *arch-, cam- cyd-, cyf-*, [...]
- One can hyphenate before suffixes or endings like those which follow: *-adwy, -aeth, -aid, -aidd, -der, -dod* [...]
- PERSONAL AND PLACE NAMES: try not to hyphenate such words at all if possible, but if it cannot be avoided:
  - try to hyphenate at a sensible place (e.g. Aber-honddu, Llanfair-fechan)
  - do not divide initials of any names at the end of a line (W.J. / Gruffydd nid W./J. Gruffydd)
- Despite the convenience do not use the facilities which are available on word processors to hyphenate automatically since they cannot hyphenate words correctly in Welsh.'

J.E. Hughes establishes some rather incomprehensible rules; not to hyphenate (a) when the words already contain a hyphen, (b) when less than three letters would be left on the next line, (c) when the words are place names and personal names. He also suggests not to use automatic hyphenation.

Why should a word not be hyphenated if it already contains a hyphen? Its understanding would not be impaired. In addition, why should never less than two letters be left alone on the next line? Morphological as well as syllabic hyphenation regularly produces morphemes and syllables which contain only two letters. In examples like the following, this claim does not make sense, since the letters form whole morphemes, e.g. in *am-gaeedig* 'en-closed', or *bendiged-ig* 'blessed' < *bendigo* 'to bless'. In words such as *gwleidy-dd* and *gad-w* (cf. table), however, the separated letters do not form a morpheme or syllable and must consequently not be left alone on the next line. Which letters can be left alone is, therefore, not a question of counting letters, but of recognising morphemes or syllables.

The next question is, why should Welsh personal and place names not be hyphenated? In particular, the latter are internationally known for being very long (cf. *Llanfair P.G.*). Since Welsh place names are often still understandable, it is even easier to hyphenate them *mewn lle synhwyrol* 'in a sensible place' (cf. J.E. Hughes above), e.g. *Aber-honddu, Llan-fair-fechan*, that is, morphologically.

In addition, it is discouraging to read that for the Welsh language the facilities on word processors should not be used, since they hyphenate incorrectly in Welsh. Such a claim may in extreme cases be taken to suggest that Welsh is not a language to be used on computers, a demand which undermines its prestige. It would be more correct to say that English-language software should not be used for the Welsh language, in the same way as English spellcheckers cannot be used for German, French or any other language. Welsh is not a dialect of English but a natural and fully developed language and should be recognised as such. Indeed, the need to develop appropriate software for Welsh is to be emphasised.

The most comprehensive guidelines on hyphenating Welsh words can be found in *Hart's Rules for Compositors and Readers at the University Oxford Press* (1998: 136f.), which also suggest morphological hyphenation:

–   Single letters, including the digraphs *ch, dd, ff, ll, ph, th* must not be divided: *ng* is indivisable when a single letter, but not when it represents *n + g* [...]
–   Dipthongs and triphthongs must not be divided: they are *ae, ai, au, aw, ayw, ei, eu, ew, ey, iw, oe, oi, ou, ow, oyw, wy, yw* (in earlier texts also *ay, oy*), and other combinations beginnning with *i* and *w*, in which these letters are consonants. The presence of a circumflex or an acute does not effect word-division, but it is legitim to divide after a diphthong or triphthong before another vowel. Thus *barddonï-aidd* 'bardic', *gloyw-ach* 'brighter', *ieu-anc* 'young'.
–   A suffix beginning with i + vowel must be broken off: *casgl-iad* 'collection'; here the *i* counts as a consonant; so too with *w* + vowel (but *an-nwyl, eg-lwys* and a few other words in which -*wy*- is not a suffix and the *w* is vocalic).
–   Otherwise the rule is to follow etymology rather than pronunciation. As a rough guide: take back a single consonant other than *h* except after a prefix (especially *di-, go-, tra-*), *g-l* but *s-gl* (and so similar groups), but suffixes should be broken off; [...] Particularly in narrow measure, two-letter suffixes may have to be taken over, above all the plural -*au*. However, it is always safe to divide *l-rh, ng-h, m-h, n-h (but n-mh), n-n, m-rh, r-r*, and after a vowel *r-h*. NB: Initial *gwl-, gwn-, gwr-*, and their mutated forms must not be divided, since the w is consonantal; *gwlad* 'country; *(hen) wlad* '(old) country' [...]

Morphological hyphenation would actually support productive Welsh word formation patterns and thus language acquisition. The understanding of words would be supported as well as the creation of vocabulary. In addition, the awareness of the patterns of Welsh word formation is basic in order to understand a language comprehensively and to enrich one's vocabulary in order to make full use of the lexical potential of the language.

However, the problem with morphological hyphenation in Welsh is that no systematic lexi-cological[15] research in its own right has been done in Wales. Lexicological investigations are, of course, part of the work of the compilers of the historical dictionary *GPC*. Nevertheless, apart from the book *Welsh Roots and Branches* (G. Jones 1994), there are no manuals[16] available which treat Welsh lexicology separately. Limited guidelines in its regard are predominantly provided by explanatory sections of dictionaries, e.g. in *Y Geiriadur Mawr* and *Y Geiriadur*

---

[15]   For a definition of lexicology, see section 1.3.1.
[16]   The book *Studies in Welsh Word-Formation* (Zimmer 2000) is a highly theoretical investigation and cannot be considered a manual. Pilch's publication (1995) is an article.

Cyfoes, or in some sections of grammar books, e.g. under *Morffoleg* 'Morphology'[17] in *Gramadeg y Gymraeg* by P.W. Thomas (1996).

The only book which tends to include etymological explanations of Welsh lexical items, which may indicate morphemes of word formation (cf. Hart above), is *GPC*. Further etymologies can be obtained from the *Etymological glossary of Old Welsh* by Falileyev (2000). Some morphemes, mostly grammatical ones, are indicated in *Orgraff yr Iaith Gymraeg* (cf. below). However, these reference books are neither etymological nor morphological dictionaries. As a result, lack of systematic lexicological research is reflected when etymological derivations are not consistently provided for the headwords in *GPC*. A large number of lexical items remains without etymology and consequently without any suggestions where to hyphenate them. This is true, for instance, for loan words, e.g. *posibl* 'possible', or for words for which no source is given, e.g. *cyhoedd* 'public', *bygwth* 'to threaten'. However, even if the etymology is given, hyphenation does not automatically become clear as can be seen from examples like *angen* 'need', *gobaith* 'hope' *aelod* 'member', *dymuniad* 'wish'. The need for unambiguous markers of hyphenation, therefore, remains.

This is confirmed by the fact that even if *GPC* contained the etymology of headwords, it would not reach enough people, since the dictionary is (a) a specialist, i.e. a historical dictionary, (b) a very comprehensive and (c) an expensive reference book which goes beyond the reach of a casual dictionary user.

Consequently, other solutions of popularising hyphenation are required. A good starting point is offered in *Orgraff yr Iaith Gymraeg*, but also in the dictionaries and computer software of other languages, such as English and German. Since it was originally not compiled as a guide to hyphenation, *Orgraff yr Iaith Gymraeg* has its disadvantages: (a) it comprises a rather restricted part of the lexicon, (b) grammatical comments are more frequent than those in relation to Welsh word formation, and (c) many words remain without any further information as is illustrated by the following examples from page II/16:[18]

---

17   For a definition of morphology, see section 1.3.2.2.2. Morphology as defined by P.W. Thomas would be assigned to lexicology in this investigation.

18   The numbers following the words refer to their pronunciation or to particuliarities in their spelling, all exemplified in the first part of *Orgraff yr Iaith Gymraeg*. Initials and numbers refer to other reference books, the comments in square brackets are mine.

D

d' dy 68
dadannudd
dad-ddysgu
dadlaith 7
dadlau 31, dadleu·af, ·odd [conjugation]
dadlen·nu, ·iad [derivation of noun]
dadluddedu
dadlwytho 7
dadmer 7
dadorchuddio
dadwneuthur, dad·wneud [infintive]
daear 29, -eg, -o, -yddiaeth, [derivations]
    gw. *dey-*
daeargryn, -fâu, ·feydd [plural]
daethpwyd 53, gw. *deu-*
dafaden, -nau, -nog [plural, adjective]
daint, dannedd § 66 (2) [plural]
daioni 9, daionus
dal, -a; -iaf, deli 25, deil [conjugation]
damcaniaeth, -au, -ol [plural, derivation of adjective]
dam·eg, ·hegion [plural]
dan danaf danat [inflection]
danad, dynad, danadl [variation]
danfon, -af [conjugation]
dangos [...] -af, -iad (nid
    danghosaf, etc) [conjugation, derivation of
    noun]
danhedd·og 62, 57, ·u [derivation of verb]
dannod (o dant)
dannoedd *toothache*
danodd *underneath*
dant 62, dannedd 67 [plural]
dâr b. (=derwen), ll. deri [plural]
dar·fod, ·fyddai, derfydd, dar·fûm,
    ·fu, ·fuasai [conjugation]
darlun, -iau, -io [plural and conjugation]
darllaw, -dy, -r, -ydd [derivation of nouns]
darllen -af 32, -wr, -iad, -ydd [conjugation, derivations]
darofun 38, -af [conjugation]
dar·paraf, ·peri, ·par, b.e. ·paru,
    ·par [conjugation]
datblyg·u, ·iad, ·af [derivation of noun, conjugation]
datgan 7, 52, -u
datgein·iad C.D. 212. ll. ·iaid [plural]
datgorffor·i, ·iad [derivation of noun]
datgudd·iad, ·io [derivation of verb]
datgymalu

datod 7
datroi, datrâf, detry [conjugation]
dau, deu, dwy. treiglir enwau gwr.
    a ben. yn feddal: dau fachgen, dau
    gyfaill, dwy ferch [... - grammatical explana-
    tion]
daufiniog 10, gw. *deu-*
dawn, doniau [plural]
deall, dyall 24, us, -gar, deellir 41,
    deellwch deall·wn 42, ·twriaeth [derivations,
    conjugations]
deau 31, 61, 62
decllath 54
decpunt 52
dechrau 31, G.R. 12, 18, 19
    dechrau·af, ·ad, ·asant, *neu*
    ·sant [conjugation]
dedfryd, -u [variation]
dedwydd *(w ŷ)*
defnydd, -iau, -io [plural, derivation of verb]
defnyn, -nau, -nu [plural, derivation of verb]
deffro 34, ·ad, deffroi, deffry,
    deffr·rôch, ·rônt 22,
    ·rowch 21 [conjugation]
deg; am sylwadau ar y treiglad ar ei
    ôl, gw. dan *naw* [grammatical explanation]
degfed; am sylwadau ar y treiglad [... - grammatical
    explanation]
deng 17, (tr.ar ôl) 58-9 [grammatical explanation]
deheu·barth, ·dir, ·bartheg 61; [derivations]
    deheuol
deheuig
deheulaw
dehongl·af, ·iad, deongliadau, b.e.
    dehongli [conjugation, derivation of noun,
    plural]
deigr, -yn, ll. dagrau § 66 (2) [plural]
deil 30
deilen, dalen, dail
deincod (o daint); *diddeincod*
    G.R. 195; llygriad yw *dincod* [...]

Dictionaries produced by Langenscheidt, e.g. *Langenscheidts Taschenwörterbuch Englisch* (1990), offer an efficient method of indicating hyphenation when providing the markers of hyphenation in the headword.

test Eignungsprüfung *f.* **2.** Neigung *f.* Hang *m (for* zu). **3.** Auffassungsgabe *f.*
aq·ua·ma·rine [ˌækwəmə'riːn] *s* **1.** *min.* Aquamarin *m.* **2.** Aquamarinblau *n.*
aq·ua·plan·ing ['ækwə,pleɪnɪŋ] *s mot.* Aquaplaning *n.*
aq·ua·relle [ˌækwə'rel] *s* **1.** Aquarell *n.* **2.** Aquarellmalerei *f.* ˌ**aq·ua'rel·list** *s* Aquarellmaler(in).
a·quar·i·um [ə'kwcərɪəm] *pl* **-i·ums, -i·a** [ˌɪə] *s* Aquarium *n.*
A·quar·i·us [ə'kwcərɪəs] *s ast.* Wassermann *m: be (an)* ~ Wassermann sein.
a·quat·ic [ə'kwætɪk] *adj* Wasser...: ~ *plants;* ~ *sports pl* Wassersport *m.*
aq·ue·duct ['ækwɪdʌkt] *s* Aquädukt *m, a. n.*
a·que·ous ['eɪkwɪəs] *adj* wäßrig, wässerig.
aq·ui·cul·ture ['ækwɪkʌltʃə] *s* Hydrokultur *f.*

This method is also used by German spelling dictionaries, e.g. the *Duden* (Dudenredaktion 1991) or *Die neue deutsche Rechtschreibung* (Hermann 1996, cf. below), by *Webster's Academic Dictionary. A Dictionary of the English Language* (G. & C. Merriam 1895, cf. below), and by the *American Heritage Dictionary* (Picket, J.P. & D.R. Pritchard et al. 2000, cf. below):

Betltag *m. 1;* Buß- und Bettag
Bettlbank *w. 2, österr.:* als Bett und Bank benutzbares Möbel;
Bettlcouch [-kautʃ] *w. 9;* **Bettdelcke** *w. 11*
Betltel *m. 5 nur Ez.* **1** das Betteln; **2** Gerümpel, alter Kram;
betltellarm; Betltellbrief *m. 1;* **Betltellei** *w. 10 nur Ez.;* **Betltelmönch** *m. 1;* **betltein** *intr. 1;* ich bettele, bettle; **Betltellorlden** *m. 7;* **Betltellstab** *m. 2, nur in der Wendung* jmdn. an den B. bringen: jmdn. arm machen
betlten *tr. 2;* **betllälgelrlg; Betllälgelrlglkeit** *w. 10 nur Ez.*
Betltler *m. 5*
Bettlnäslsen *s. Gen. -s nur Ez.;* **Bettlnäslser** *m. 5;* **betltlreif** *ugs.;* **Bettlrulhe** *w. 11 nur Ez.;* **Bettstatt** *w. Gen. - Mz.* -stätlten;
Bettuch ▶ Betltltuch *s. 4*
Bettlumlranldung *w. 10;* **Bet-**

Beultel *m. 5* **1** Säckchen; **2** ~ Beitel; **beulteln 1** *tr. 1* schütteln; ich beutele, beutle ihn; **2** *intr. 1* einen Beutel bilden, sich bauschen (Kleid); **Beultelschnellder** *m. 5* Gauner; **Beultellschnelldelrel** *w. 10 nur Ez.;* **Beultelltler** *s. 1* **beultellusltig**
beulten *tr. 2;* Bienen b.: in eine Beute einsetzen; **Beultenlholnig** *m. 1 nur Ez.* in Beuten gewonnener Honig von Waldbienen
Beultelstück *s. 1;* **Beultelzug** *m. 2*
Beutller *m. 5* **1** Beuteltier; **2** *früher:* Beutelmacher
Beutlner *m. 5* Züchter von Waldbienen; **Beutlnelrel** *w. 10 nur Ez.*
Belvaltron [engl.] *s. 1 oder s. 9* in Berkeley (CA) erbauter Teilchenbeschleuniger

A-base' (-bās'), *v. t.* [F. *abaisser*, fr. LL. *bassus* low. See Base, *a.*] To lower; to cast down; to humble; to degrade. — **A-base'ment**, *n.*

A-bash' (-băsh'), *v. t.* [OE. *abaissen*, OF. *esbahir*, fr. L. *ex* + interj. *bah*, expressing astonishment.] To destroy the self-possession of; to shame; to disconcert.

Syn. — To Abash; Confuse; Confound; disconcert; shame. — We are *abashed* when struck with shame or a sense of inferiority. We are *confused* when an unexpected occurrence destroys our self-possession. We are *confounded* when our minds are overwhelmed by something amazing, dreadful, etc., so that we have nothing to say.

A-bat'a-ble (-bāt'à-b'l), *a.* Capable of being abated.

A-bate' (-bāt'), *v. t.* [OF. *abatre* to beat down, L. *batuere* to beat.] To bring to a lower state or degree; to lessen; to moderate; to do away with (a nuisance, writ, or tax). — *v. i.* To decrease; to come to naught; to subside; to fail.

Syn. — To Abate; Subside; decrease; intermit; decline; diminish; lessen. — *Abate* implies diminution of

Ab'di-cate (-kāt), *v. t.* [L. *abdicare*; *ab* + *dicare* to proclaim. See Diction.] To surrender or relinquish. — *v. i.* To renounce (a throne, office, etc.). — **Ab'di-ca'tion**, *n.* — **Ab'di-ca'tor**, *n.*

Syn. — To Abdicate; Resign; give up; vacate; relinquish; renounce. — *Abdicate* expresses the act of a monarch who formally yields up sovereign authority. *Resign* is applied to the act of anyone who gives back a trust into the hands of him who conferred it.

Ab-do'men (ăb-dō'měn), *n.* [L.] 1. The belly, or that cavity of the body, which contains the stomach, bowels, and other viscera. 2. The posterior section of the body, behind the thorax, in insects, crustaceans, etc. Pertaining to the abdomen; ventral.

Ab-dom'i-nal (-dŏm'I-nal), *a.* Pertaining to the abdomen; ventral.

Ab-duct' (-dŭkt'), *v. t.* [L. *abductus*, p. p. of *abducere* to lead away; *ab* + *ducere* to lead.] 1. To take away (a human being) wrongfully; to kidnap. 2. To draw away (a limb or other part) from its ordinary position. — **Ab-duc'tion**, *n.*

ā, ē, I, ō, ū, long; ă, ĕ, I, ŏ, ŭ, ў, short; senāte, ĕvent, idea, ōbey, ūnite, cåre, ärm, ásk, ąll, final, fẽrn, recent, ōrb, rŭde, fŭll, ûrn, fōod, fŏot, out, oil, chair, go, sing, iŋk, then, thin.

---

ge•om•e•trize (jē-ŏm'ĭ-trīz') *v.* -trized, -triz•ing, -triz•es
—*intr.* 1. To study geometry. 2. To apply the methods of geometry. —*tr.* 1. To present in geometric form. 2. To bring into conformance with the laws and principles of geometry.

ge•om•e•try (jē-ŏm'ĭ-trē) *n., pl.* -tries 1a. The mathematics of the properties, measurement, and relationships of points, lines, angles, surfaces, and solids. b. A system of geometry: *Euclidean geometry.* c. A geometry restricted to a class of problems or objects: *solid geometry.* b. A book on geometry. 2a. Configuration; arrangement. b. A surface shape. 3. A physical arrangement suggesting geometric forms or lines. [Middle English *geometrie*, from Old French, from Latin *geōmetria*, from Greek *geōmetriā*, from *geōmetrein*, to measure land : *geō-*, geo- + *metron*, measure; see *mē-²* in Appendix I.] —**ge•om'e•tri'cian** (jē-ŏm'ĭ-trĭsh'ən, jē'ə-mĭ-), **ge•om'e•ter** *n.*

ge•o•mor•phic (jē'ə-môr'fĭk) *adj.* Of or resembling the earth or its shape or surface configuration.

ge•o•mor•phol•o•gy (jē'ō-môr-fŏl'ə-jē) *n.* The study of the evolution and configuration of landforms. —**ge'o•mor'pho•log'i•cal** (-môr'fə-lŏj'ĭk), **ge'o•mor'pho•log'i•cal** (-ĭ-kəl) *adj.* —**ge'o•mor'pho•log'i•cal•ly** *adv.* —**ge'o•mor•phol'o•gist** *n.*

ge•oph•a•gy (jē-ŏf'ə-jē) *n.* The eating of earthy substances, such as clay or chalk, practiced among various peoples as a custom or for dietary or subsistence reasons. —**ge•oph'a•gism** *n.* —**ge•oph'a•gist** *n.*

ge•o•phone (jē'ə-fōn') *n.* An electronic receiver designed to pick up seismic vibrations.

ă pat	oi boy
ā pay	ou out
âr care	ŏŏ took
ä father	ŏŏ boot
ĕ pet	ŭ cut
ē be	ûr urge
ĭ pit	th thin
ī pie	th this
îr pier	hw which
ŏ pot	zh vision
ō toe	ə about, item
ô paw	♦ regionalism

Stress marks: ' (primary);
' (secondary), as in
dictionary (dĭk'shə-nĕr'ē)

With the intention to show possibilities of the derivation of different word forms (Lewis 1997: 8), a similar approach can be seen in Lewis (1997). The indication of morphemes in his dictionary, however, remains limited as is demonstrated by the following examples:

    achub·wr, achub·ydd *m* (·wyr) saviour.

    adarydd *m* (·ion) ornithologist.

    adiol·yn *m* (·ion) additive.

If the method used by Lewis was adopted by other Welsh lexicographers and expanded in a manner similar to the method used by the aforementioned dictionaries, the problem of hyphenating Welsh lexical items would soon disappear at no extra cost.

434

To sum up: after demonstrating a situation in which hyphenation is treated as a matter of a somewhat idiosyncratic language use, a situation is thereby reached that was once described for the whole of Welsh orthography and which led to the compilation of *Orgraff yr Iaith Gymraeg* (Lewis 1987: I/6):

> "Ar fyr, nid heb reswm y dywedid bod gan bob ysgrifennydd a phob argraffwr Cymraeg ei orgraff ei hun [... a bod] y diffyg hwn yn taflu cryn ddirmyg ar ein hiaith."
> 'In short, it is not without reason that it is said that every writer and every Welsh language publisher has his own orthography [... and that] this deficiency shows quite a contempt for our language.'

Hyphenating incorrectly according to the guidelines provided by Hart (cf. above), particularly in daily newspapers and magazines which generally have a strong influence on any language (a) affects the *Sprachgefühl*, that is, the correct automatic application of language patterns and rules by native speakers, who do not have to learn rules by heart; (b) it undermines the efforts of learners to acquire the language systematically and according to the principles of the language; (c) continuous mis-hyphenation legalises the division of digraphs, diphthongs, and triphthongs into single letters and consequently undermines or ignores their functions, as done in the Welsh dictionary *CysGair*;[19](d) as a result, mis-hyphenation affects the productive patterns of Welsh word formation and weakens them, thus allowing the omnipresent English language with its own vocabulary, rules, and patterns to penetrate into Welsh easier.

In view of Wales' English neighbourhood, of an enforced convergence of features of the Welsh language with English (cf. sections 4.3.1. and 4.3.2.), and a high percentage of learners of Welsh (cf. section 4.1.1.), properties of the Welsh language are thus undermined and gradually being based on or adapted to the English language. The inclusion of markers of morphological hyphenation in general-purpose dictionaries, as seen in those dictionaries produced by Langenscheidt (cf. above), by Pons such as the *Kompaktwörterbuch Englisch-Deutsch/Deutsch-Englisch* (Weis, E. & H. Kaul 1996), or by G. & C. Merriam, such as the *Webster's Academic Dictionary. A Dictionary of the English Language*, or by Houghton, such as *The American Heritage Dictionary* is, therefore, strongly recommended as a useful and efficient tool in written communication. It would thus promote productive word formation patterns and a creative and flexible use of the language.

Irrespective of the impacts erroneous hyphenation has on the language, an efficient use of this tool also saves money and supports the creation of optimal formats and aesthetic layouts. The suggestion not to use hyphenation, however, can undermine the prestige of the language.

---

[19] In *CysGair*, the digraphs in the alphabet are ignored. The following sequences of headwords can, therefore, be found in this electronic dictionary: ... *ceunant, ceunant sych, ceunwyddau, cewyn, cewyn papur, chi, chwa, chwâl, chwaer ... chwythlamp, chwythu, chwythu eprom, chwythu gwydr, chwythu'n gryf, chwythlwm, chwythydd, chwythydd periannol, ci, ci bach, ci defaid, ci hela...*

4.4. Phonetic transcription[1]
4.4.1. Necessity for phonetic transcription

Not all dictionaries include information about pronunciation. There is little need for such information in a dictionary of Russian, for instance, although at least the word stress is mostly indicated. Given knowledge of the relevant rules which express the relationship between phoneme and grapheme as well as the indication of the word stress, in all except the rarest cases Russian pronunciation of a lexical item may be inferred from its spelling.

Some Welsh scholars claim that Welsh, too, is a language in which the pronunciation can be inferred from its spelling when saying:

> "[...] fortunately the orthography of Welsh is, with some exceptions, broadly phonemic,
> i.e. as a rule one letter or combination of letters (ch, ll, rh, ng) represents one phoneme.
> By following the rules of orthography, Welsh words may be pronounced at sight"
> (Griffith, B. & D.G. Jones 1995: xx, cf. also Brake 1994: 7, Rh.T.J. Jones 1992: xi).[2]

Although stress patterns can in no way be deduced from spelling conventions and the claim above presupposes a standard Welsh (cf. below, cf. also Griffith, B. & D.G. Jones 1995: ix), it has been used as the major argument for not including phonetic transcription in Welsh dictionaries. Of the bilingual and bi-directional Welsh general-purpose dictionaries under review (cf. section 4.2.), none contains phonetic transcription. Only *The Welsh Learner's Dictionary* by H. Gruffudd (1998) offers a transcription, in this case 'imitated pronunciation' (cf. section 4.4.2.).

The only bi-directional general-purpose dictionary which includes transcription in the *International Phonetic Alphabet* (IPA) is the German-Welsh dictionary by Greller et al. (1999). The transcription, however, provides - according to the purpose of this reference book - information on the pronunciation of the German words, not of the Welsh. This is interesting, since German, as Russian or Spanish, belongs to those languages whose pronunciation can be relatively regularly derived from the spelling. However, major lexicographers are aware of the fact that word stress and pronunciation may, particularly in German and Spanish, as well deviate from rules (cf. below) and consequently often include their phonetic transcription (cf. Axel Juncker Verlag 1999).

Considering the number of rules about accents, vowels and consonants presented in *Orgraff yr Iaith Gymraeg* (Lewis 1987), the need to include transcription also for Welsh lexical items becomes apparent. The reader of this book will find five pages devoted exclusively to explanations of how to pronounce stressed monosyllabic words in Welsh. In addition, the headwords in *Orgraff yr Iaith Gymraeg* are frequently followed by numbers (cf. examples below) which tell the users where to find guidelines on their pronunciation (Lewis 1987: II/10, 17).

[1] I would like to take this opportunity of thanking Dr Orin Gensler, Max Planck Institute for Evolutionary Anthropology/Leipzig, Dr Iwan Wmffre, Tregaron/Wales, and Siôn Williams, University of Cardiff, for helpful discussion on this subject.
[2] In a personal conversation with Bruce Griffiths, editor of the uni-directional *Geiriadur yr Academi*, in the Eisteddfod 1996, he also made the point that he would for the same reason not include any transcription in a Welsh-English dictionary.

carwden [ca-rw´-den], -ni
cas 17, -âf, -â, -ewch, -ânt, -âi, -aent
    -aodd, -áu 22, -eir, -eid, -awyd;
    -awr, -awyr

deon 23, -iaid
deor, deora (3 u. P.M.)
derbyn, -iaf -nid 27; -neb *receipt*
dernyn, -nau, -nach
derwen, ll. derw
deudroed 12
deuddeg; a. sylwadau ar y treiglad ar
    ei ôl, gw. dan naw; gw.
    hefyd dud. 29 yng nghorff y llyfr
deuddydd 12
deufin 10

Even the brief illustrations of pronunciation in other reference books generally comprise several pages. *Y Geiriadur Cyfoes* takes five pages to explain basic rules and *Geiriadur yr Academi* nine pages, that is, too much specific linguistic information for the casual dictionary user to remember and apply correctly when necessary.

In addition, there are many exceptions to the rules, e.g. for the word stress when this is described as in the following:

> "In polysyllables the main stress falls as a rule on the last syllable but one. If one or more syllables are suffixed, the rule still applies, i.e. the stress will automatically move forward to the last syllable but one, e.g. ffenestr, plural ffenestri" (Griffith, B. & D.G. Jones 1995: xxvi).[3]

Consequently, *Geiriadur yr Academi* provides comprehensive lists[4] of lexical items which are not pronounced according to the rules, such as the following words, which have the word stress on the final syllable (1995: xxvi, xxvii):

2. Classes of words accented on the final syllable are:

(a) the emphatic pronouns myfi, tydi, efe, efo, hyhi, nyni, chwychwi, hwynt-hwy;

(b) compound adverbs, adjectives and prepositions: heblaw, drachefn, gerllaw, erioed, ymhlith, ymhell, paham, ynghylch, ynghlwm, ngholl, ynghynn, ynghyd, ynglŷn, ynghlo, ymysg, ymhen, ymron, islaw, uwchlaw, cyfuwch, gogyhyd, gogyfuwch, goruwch, gorîs, yrhawg, ymlaen, ymhlith, cyhyd, gyhyd, i gyd, perhôn, diymdroi, ychwaith, ynghynt, yn unswydd, yn isgîl;

---

[3]   The exceptions would be reduced when accepting the stress system as introduced by Pilch (1975). He distinguishes between (a) bi-syllabic stress-groups which are stressed on the penultimate syllable, (b) monosyllabic stress-groups which have the stress on the ultimate syllable, and (c) double stress-groups which have a double stress (ibid.: 70).

[4]   Lists of exceptions are certainly of great value for everybody doing research in the Welsh language. However, they are not very helpful for ad hoc communication, since they can hardly be memorised by dictionary users. The need to be constantly looking up various details of properties of the Welsh language in different places in order to use lexical items is not user-friendly and makes communication difficult, when carried out in written form and nearly impossible orally.

(c) certain compound verbs beginning with ym-, e.g. ymhel, ymweld, ymwneud, ymdrin, ymlâdd = **exhaust oneself,** ymddẅyn = **conceive, bear;** third person forms such as ymgêl from ymgelu, ymwnêl, ymwnaeth, ymwnâi from ymwneud, ymlŷn from ymlynu, also atbrŷn from atbrynu;

(d) verb-nouns ending in -au, -oi, -eu-: ail-greu, ail-weu, atroi, datroi, amdroi, atgloi, camdroi, cildroi, cogordroi, cyfleu, cyfrdroi, cylchdroi, chwyldroi, dileu, dyheu, geirdroi, datgloi, datoi, osgoi, paratoi, ymbaratoi, cilgnoi, cyffroi, atgnoi, cydgrynhoi, cyfloi, gwrthdroi, nydd-droi, tindroi, tyndroi, ymdroi, crynhoi, ymroi, crasgnoi, amgáu, nesáu, dynesáu, amlhau, llesáu, glanhau, arwyddocáu, boddhau, breisgáu, dyfalbarhau, esmwytháu, gwacáu, hirbarhau, brochgáu, cwpláu, tecáu, brwysgáu, parhau, llesgáu, gwanhau, nacáu, gwastatáu, tristáu, iselhau, hwyhau, lleihau, mwyhau, mwynhau, caniatáu; coffáu, atgoffáu, iacháu, lladratau, liwfrhau, cyfiawnhau, dyfnhau, anufuddhau, edifarhau, meinhau, ymwacáu, ymnesau and their third person forms lladratâ, &c.;

(e) compounds of gwneud, gweld, ymweld, cyfweld, ail-wneud, ymwneud, dadwneud and their third person forms, ymwnâ, cyfwêl, &c.;

(f) nouns ending in -âd, -had (always long), usually formed from verbs ending in -au, -hau-, e.g. amlhad, arwyddocâd, byrhad, cadarnhad, caniatâd, coffâd, cwblhad, cyflawnhad, dyfalbarhad, dyfrhad, eginhad, eglurhad, esmwythâd, glanhad, gwacâd, gwanhad, gwellhad, hirbarhad, hwyhad, iachâd, iselhad, parhad, pellhad, perswâd, prinhâd, rhyddhad, sarhad, sicrhad, trugarhad, tynhad, ymfoddhad, ymwacâd, penllâd;

(g)[5] in compounds of -wr ending in -awr, -ewr, -iwr, -owr, -uwr, -ywr the endings are of two syllables, with the main stress regularly on the first, sometimes indicated by the diaeresis (¨), thus bwyt|awr, not b|wytawr, gwrand|awr, not gwr|andawr; e.g. casäwr, cyfiawnhawr, difawr, glanhawr, gwrandawr, iachawr, darlläwr, crëwr, cyflëwr, syrfëwr, crïwr, storïwr, comedïwr, copïwr, dyweddïwr, gweddïwr, marsiandïwr, mechnïwr, ysbïwr, ffrïwr, cnöwr, chwyldrowr, glöwr, osgowr, töwr, tröwr, düwr, plüwr, rhüwr, süwr, lletywr, gwestywr, &c.; however: awr, cawr, clawr, gwawr, llawr, mawr, nawr, pawr, sawr, dewr, piwr are monosyllables;

(h) nouns ending in -fa in the singular form plurals in -fâu (long) and/or -feydd (short). In these plurals the stress is always on the last syllable, e.g. athrofâu, berfâu, camfâu, cadwrfâu, canolfâu, crynfâu, curfâu, cuddfâu, cychwynfâu, cyfrinfâu, cylchfâu, deorfâu, drefâu, dychrynfâu, enynfâu, genfâu, gwahanfâu, gwalfâu, gwarchodfâu, gyrfâu, helfâu, llechfâu, llewygfâu, llethrfâu, maethfâu, magwrfâu, neithdarfâu, poenfâu, porfâu, taenfâu, trofâu, tyrfâu; angorfeydd, arosfeydd, atomfeydd, cerddorfeydd, cronfeydd, glofeydd, golygfeydd, porfeydd, rhegfeydd, ogofeydd, dychrynfeydd, gweithfeydd;

(j) some nouns ending in -a in the singular form a plural in -âu, which is stressed: berâu, bwâu, dramâu, sinemâu, themâu, plâu. The plural of gwely is often gwelâu; of beudy often beudái, and of gweithdy often gweith-dái;

(k) some proper names: Bartim|eus, Elis|eus, Zach|eus, Gwrtheyrn, Cyndeyrn; some names of places: Caerdydd, Caerweir, Caerlŷr, Llandaf, Llandẅ, Llandygái, Llandylẅyf, Tre-fin, Llan-giwg, Llangyndeyrn, Llanllŷr, Llan-soe, Llan-teg, Coed-llai and other hyphenated names of the type Bryn-coch, Rhyd-ddu, &c.;

---

5   This paragraph does not really belong here, since the word stress is regular in these examples.

(l) adjectives ending in -aus, -eus, -ous, -aig, -eig: boddhaus, bywiocaus, dyfalbarhaus, parhaus, sarhaus, trahaus, trofáus, anghyfleus, amheus, cyfleus, anghyfleus, chwareus, diamheus, cyffrous, hirymharhous, ymarhous, ymrous, cynhaig, bwyteig, Cymreig, Hebreig, also the nouns Cymraes, Cymraeg, Hebraeg, Almaeneg;

(m) loose compound adjectives and nouns formed with the prefixes di-, cyd-, cyn-, cam-, gor-, hunan-, e.g. di-âm, di-boen, di-lyth, di-feth, di-ffael, di-lun, di-siâp, di-rif, di-fref, di-les, di-nag, di-dâl, dichwaeth, di-oed, &c. (many have a more literary form stressed on the penult, e.g. dilyth, dirif, &c.);[...]

For immediate guidance on the usage of lexical items, such lists are of no help, since dictionary users must carry out a complete new search procedure in order to find the relevant rules or exceptions. Furthermore, in view of the fact that some dictionaries do not provide any guidelines on pronunciation, e.g. *Y Geiriadur Mawr* and *Y Geiriadur Bach*, it would be much easier to find the necessary information in the dictionary entry itself.

Indeed, these two dictionaries, present isolated references to the pronunciation of individual lexical items in the headword list, such as for *ei* 'his, her; him':

> **ei** (sain *i*), *rhag.* trydydd person unigol
> rhagenw personol blaen. HIS, HER
> ITS, OF HIM, OF HER, OF IT.

Other indications of pronunciation are included for words with the combination of the graphemes ⟨w⟩ and ⟨y⟩ whereby non-vocalic ⟨w⟩ is indicated by ⟨wỳ⟩ and vocalic ⟨w⟩ by ⟨ŵy⟩ as is illustrated by the following examples:

> **gwyll (wỳ),** *eg.* tywyllwch, caddug.
> GLOOM, DARKNESS

> **gwyrdroi (ŵy),** *eb. ll.* -iau. digwyddiad
> rhyfedd, rhywbeth goruwch-natur-
> iol. MIRACLE.

> **tywyll (wỳ),** *a.* 1. heb olau, heb fod yn
> olau, pŵl, aneglur, prudd, digalon.
> DARK, SAD.
> 2. dall. BLIND.

> **wy (ŵy),** *eg. ll.* wyau. yr hyn a ddodwyir
> gan aderyn o gynhyrchu aderyn bach.
> EGG.

This method was also used by Dr John Davies, Mallwyd during the Renaissance period. At this time, however, linguistics was still in its infancy (cf. sections 2.2.1.1. and 2.2.2.).

Despite the extensive explanatory section on pronunciation in *Geiriadur yr Academi* (cf. above), isolated comments on how to pronounce Welsh lexical items can also be found in entries of this dictionary as is exemplified in the following:

> **all** *a., pron. & adv.* **1.** *a. (a) before a proper n. or ~* **the** *before an (usually) uncountable n. = the whole of:* cyfan, oll, *F:* i gyd *(always pronounced as if* i gîd) *or* holl + *soft mut.* [...]

> **cringing** *a.* gwasaidd, cynffongar *(pronounced ng-g)*, ymgreiniol, taeogaidd.

> **place**[1] *n.* **1.** *(a)* lle(-oedd), *(often incorrectly;* -fydd)[[6]] *m*, man(-nau) *mf*, llecyn(-nau) *m, Lit:* mangre(-oedd) *f (pronounced* ng-g); [...]

> **straight** *a., n. & adv.* I. *a.* **1.** syth *(f.occ:* seth, *pl.occ:* sythion), union, unionsyth(-ion), diwyro, *S:* cymwys *(usu. pronounced* cwmws); [...]

> **your** *poss.a.* **1.** *(prefixed form): (sing. & familiar):* dy + *soft mut., occ: before vowel* d'; *(pl. & polite):* eich *(usu. pronounced* ych); [...]

In addition, word stress which is not on the penultimate syllable is often, but not always,[7] also indicated in entries of this dictionary, namely by ⟨|⟩ or ⟨′⟩, as is shown in the following examples:

> **enjoy** *v.t.* **1.** mwynh|au [...]
> **approach**[2] *v.i.&t.* **1.** *vt.* dynesu, nesu, nesáu, agosáu [...]
> **clean**[2] *n.* glanhad *m*,[... no indication that the stress is on the final syllable]
> **clean**[3] *v.t.* glan|hau [...] sychlan|au [...]

In view of the various and ample descriptions of how to pronounce Welsh lexical items it becomes clear that a phonetic transcription of Welsh headwords is advocated, since spelling conventions by nature do not offer safe guidance for pronunciation and no guidance for stress patterns. It would also be expecting too much from the casual dictionary user to understand Pilch's stress-system (cf. above), since the distinction between the three stress-groups are not clear, when defining, for instance *cwpaned* /ku'paned/ 'cupful' and *pentan* /'pentan/ 'place near the fire where waterkettles are placed for boiling' as words ending in a bi-syllabic stress-group (ibid.: 70).

The following paragraphs illustrate some of the difficulties in Welsh pronunciation, which cannot be cleared up by referring to spelling conventions. The system of phonetic transcription employed in this investigation is based on Thorne (1985: 116-154). It comprises the following vowels: /i, e, ɑ, o, u/, /ɪ, ɛ, a, ɒ, ʊ/ and /ə/. For South and Mid Walian pronunciation he adds the

---

6   This comment is wrong. *Llefydd* is the regular plural of *lle*.

7   At page xxvi in *Geiriadur yr Academi*, the following sentence can be found: "In this dictionary exceptions to this rule are indicated by a thin vertical line | before the stressed vowel".

440

medium long vowel /ɔ/ (/i, e, ɑ, ɔ, o, u/), as for instance in *coleg* /'kɔlɛg/ 'college' (ibid.: 140).[8] The clear qualitative differences between long and short vowels as well as medium long vowels found in South and Mid Walian pronunciation are far less marked in the North.

This distinction of long, medium long and short vowels in monosyllabic and other words (cf. Lewis 1987: I/15) is not easy to master, e.g. in *llên* /ɬeːn/ 'literature', *menyn* /'menɪn/ 'butter', *llen* /ɬɛn/ 'curtain', or *ysgol* /'əsgɒl/ 'school', *coleg* /'koˑlɛg/ (/'kɔlɛg/) 'college', *ôl* /oːl/ 'trace', or *can* /kan/ 'can', *canu* /'kaˑni/ 'to sing', *cân* /kɑːn/ 'song'. The length of a vowel can, for instance, even depend on etymological developments, that is, when a word ends in *l, n* and *r*, the length of the vowel depends on the original consonant of the word, e.g. the vowel is long when it was originally followed by a single consonant and long when followed by a double consonant (cf. ibid.: I/17; for further deatils, see also G.E. Jones 1984).

Griffiths, B. & D.J. Jones, the compilers of *Geiriadur yr Academi*, must have realised that vowel length may be unpredictable when occasionally including comments on their length in dictionary entries as was illustrated for *i gyd* 'all' (cf. dictionary entry of 'all' above). For other lexical items, however, such explanations would also be necessary. How, for instance, are learners to know the different vowel length which distinguishes *llun* 'photo, picture', *llyn* 'lake' and *llin* 'flax'[9] (cf. also below) in order to make themselves understood in oral communication when the written form is not available? Or how can they know that *byth* /bɪθ/ 'ever, never' is pronounced with an /ɪ/ and *syth* /siːθ/ 'straight' with an /iː/? Or how are the learners to know that *tu* 'side', *tŷ* 'house', *di* 'your', *du* 'black' may be pronounced with the same /iː/ under certain circumstances, that is, in South Walian pronunciation and when *di* is emphasised? The ⟨u⟩ notoriously causes irritation for learners, since ⟨u⟩ in other writing systems, except Russian, is almost always a grapheme for an /u/-sound.

How are dictionary users to know that the graphy ⟨ng⟩ can be (a) a digraph (cf. section 4.3.9.) where the ⟨g⟩ is simply there to velarise the /n/, as in *angen* /'aŋɛn/ 'need' and ⟨ng⟩ therefore a single letter, or (b) a sequence of consonants where ⟨g⟩ has its own full value, such as in *anger*[10] /'aŋgar/ 'smoke' or *dangos* /'daŋgɒs/ 'to show' (cf. section 4.3.9.). The only indication to correct pronunciation in such cases is the subtlety of alphabetic ordering, whereby, for instance, *anger*, having a sequence of two consonants, *n* and *g*, follows words such as *anffyniannus* 'unsuccessful' and *anffyrf* 'weak', or *dangos* words such as *danfon* 'to send', *danfoniad* 'sending'. *Angen*, on the other hand, with the single letter *ng*, which is alphabetised between *g* and *h* in Welsh, precedes words such as *aig* 'shoal', *ail* 'second', *anferth* 'huge', or *anffyrf*. Welsh alphabetisation, however, has in one example already been changed: in the electronic dictionary *CysGair* (cf. section 4.3.9.), the English alphabet is taken as a basis, so that there is no indication as regards pronunciation.

---

8 The system used by G.E. Jones (1984: 40-64) includes the following vowels: /i, e, ɑ, o, u/, /ɪ, ɛ, a, ɔ, ɒ/ and the unpaired /ə/.

9 In addition, the vowels of *llun* 'photo, picture' and *llin* 'flax' have a different quality.

10 This word is indicated an archaic word but chosen here to illustrate the different functions of ⟨ng⟩

Other difficulties in pronunciation may occur with loanwords, which can be difficult to pronounce for learners, but at times also for native speakers. They often maintain the orthography of the language of origin for a while, but follow rules of pronunciation of the language into which they were introduced. This is definitely the case with most loanwords containing simple vowels, since those are mostly pronounced as diphthongs in English but monophthongs in Welsh. The following examples illustrate words which maintain the same or a similar spelling in both languages, but exhibit differences in pronunciation: *actio* /'aktjo/[11] 'to act' /ækt/,[12] *angel* /'aŋgɛl/ 'angel' /'eɪndʒəl/, *brecwast* /'brɛkwasd/ 'breakfast' /'brekfəst/, *hast* /hasd/ 'haste' /heɪst/, *cario* /'karjo/ 'to carry' /'kærɪ/, *catholig* /ka'θɔːlɪg/ 'catholic' /'kæθəlɪk/, *coridor* /kɒ'ridɒr/ 'corridor' /'kɒrɪdɔː/, *doctor* /'dɒktɒr/ 'doctor' /'dɒktə/, *ffair* /fair/ 'fair' /feə/, *ffansïo* /fans'iːo/ 'fancy' /'fænsɪ/, *murmur* /'mɪrmɪr/ 'murmur' /'mɜːmə/.

Furthermore, there are Welsh lexical items which are spelt like English words but which both have a different meaning and a different pronunciation, e.g. *am* /am/ 'at, for, of; because; around' <-> am /æm/, *at* /at/ 'to' <-> at /æt/, *tan* /tan/ 'until' <-> tan /tæn/, *to* /toː/ 'roof' <-> to /tuː, tɔː, tə/, *sad* /sad/ 'firm, steady' <-> sad /sæd/, *mud* /miːd/ 'dumb' <-> mud /mʌd/, *gallant* /'gaɬan/ 'they can, they will be able' <-> gallant /'gælənt/, *gall* /gaɬ/ 'he, she, it can' <-> gall /gɔːl/, *hen* /heːn/ 'old' <-> hen /hen/. Given the English-speaking background of the vast majority of learners of Welsh insecurity in pronunciation in such cases is likely.

Another problem is the sound /ɬ/, e.g. in *llachar* /'ɬaxar/ 'brilliant, sparkling', a sound which does not exist in English, but whose graphematic presentation occurs in English, e.g. in *jolly* /'dʒɒlɪ/, *gallery* /'gælərɪ/, *all* /ɔːl/. Another sound which is unknown to English is /r̥/, e.g. in *rhin* /r̥in/ 'extract'. It does, however, exist as a grapheme ⟨rh⟩, e.g. in *rhino* /'raɪnəʊ/. Both sounds should, therefore, be clearly indicated as /ɬ/ and /r̥/ when occurring in Welsh lexical items in order to distinguish them from the sequence of consonants, as for instance in *ail-law* 'second-hand' or in *arholi* 'to examine' (cf. section 4.3.9.).

The other Welsh phonemes are also present in English. Problems arise where the grapheme-phoneme-realisation differs in the two languages; ⟨ch⟩ in English, for instance, is usually pronounced as /tʃ/ as in *chamber* /'tʃæmbə/, *bachelor* /'bætʃələ/, sometimes as /k/ as in *ache* /eɪk/, or /ʃ/ as in *chef* /ʃef/. Only rarely does the sound /x/ occur in English, e.g. in *loch* /lɒx/[13] and *ugh* /ʌx/ and most speakers have difficulty pronouncing it correctly in Welsh, e.g. in *diolch* /'diɔlx/ 'thank', *achlysur* /ax'ləsɪr/ 'occasion'.

The graphy ⟨ng⟩ as in *dangos* /'daŋgɒs/ 'to show' can also be realised as /ŋg/ in English, e.g. in *English* /'ɪŋglɪʃ/, *finger* /'fɪŋgə/. Very often, however, it is pronounced as /dʒ/, for instance, in *change* /'tʃeɪndʒ/. The graphy ⟨dd⟩, realised in Welsh as /ð/ as in *blaidd* 'wolf' /blaið/ or *brawddeg* /'brauðeg/, is pronounced as /d/ in English, e.g. in *add* /æd/, *toddle* /'tɒdl/. Finally, there is a difference between Welsh and English in the grapheme-phoneme-realisation of ⟨f⟩, which re-

---

[11]	Although the pronunciation of ⟨o⟩ in the ending of verbal nouns is mostly transcribed by /o/ (cf. A. Watkins 1993: 298, Ball, J.M & E.G. Jones 1984) it is rather pronounced /ɔ/.
[12]	The transcription of the English lexical items is taken from Langenscheidts Taschenwörterbuch (1999).
[13]	This is, however, frequently also pronounced /lɔk/.

presents the phoneme /v/ in Welsh, e.g. in *braf* 'agreeable' /brav/, but the phoneme /f/ in English, e.g. in *beef* /bi:f/.

Consequently, for immediate guidance on the pronunciation of lexical items which display particular features of Welsh orthography or phonology the inclusion of phonetic transcription in their dictionary entries is advocated.

Some scholars who refuse to include phonetic transcription in Welsh dictionaries do not emphasise the pronunciation according to the spelling, but rather stress the dialectal variation of the Welsh language in relation to pronunciation, which makes the language allegedly untranscribable.[14] This second argument, however, is not valid either, since dialectal variation is a phenomenon which is not confined to the Welsh language. Many English words, for instance, exhibit a multiplicity of spoken forms even within *Received Pronunciation*, e.g. *either* /'aɪðə/, /'i:ðə/; *often* /'ɒfn/, /'ɒftən/. Apart from these and a few other examples, however, variant pronunciations in English follow regular and statable rules (cf. Wells 1985: 46f.).

In German, dialects are very prominent, too. The Bavarian or Swiss pronunciation[15] is often un-intelligible even to other native German speakers. In other cases the Bavarians or Swiss may wish to exclude outsiders from their communication. When speakers of these or other dialects perform on television in Germany, subtitles are often provided. Indeed, the various dialects of German have also been shaped by the influence of the different languages which are spoken on the borders of Germany, Austria, and Switzerland. Despite this dialectal variation, the German language in dictionaries is presented in a form which can to some extent be shared by most German-speaking people, including those in Austria and Switzerland.[16]

Nevertheless, as said before Welsh scholars tend to either emphasise that Welsh ponunciation can easily be inferred from spelling or that it varies too much to be transcribed in a dictionary (cf. above). As with English, however, variant pronunciations in Welsh follow regular and statable rules, such as the monophthongising of diphthongs in southern pronunciation, as in *troed* /trɒid/ -> /tro:d/ 'foot' or *traed* /traid/-> /trɑ:d/ 'feet' (cf. Thomas B. & P.W. Thomas 1989). In addition, in view of dialectal variation in other countries, Welsh - which is nowadays predominantly influenced by English - would be an exception if it were not possible to find forms of pronunciation which can to some extend be shared by most Welsh-speaking people (cf. also the case of Irish, below). Indeed, Griffiths, B. & D.J. Jones suggest a kind of standard pronunciation when saying

> "By following the rules of orthography, Welsh words may be pronounced at sight, giving a standardized pronunciation intelligible to all educated Welsh speakers" (ibid.: xx).

According to both, there is a standard pronunciation in Welsh, that is, the language spoken by educated native speakers. In this case, it is useful to include a standard phonetic transcription in

---

14 This, for instance, was the result of a talk I had with Dr David Thorne in summer 1993 in Llanbedr Pont Steffan when discussing Welsh pronunciation.

15 Lexical and grammatical features, of course, augment this phenomenon.

16 An example is the recent reform of German orthography. In December 1994, Germany, Austria and Switzerland agreed on an orthographic reform, which in essence would hold equally in all three countries. On the first of August in 1998, Germany adopted this orthography offically.

dictionary entries. This not only supports the high percentage of learners among Welsh speakers, particularly in anglicised areas (cf. immersion schooling in section 4.1.1.). In addition, such a transcription is also beneficial for native speakers. First, it furthers the mutual intelligibility among native speakers of dialect or native speakers in isolated areas (cf. section 4.1.1. and below). Second, as there are English monolingual dictionaries which include phonetic transcription (cf. section 4.4.2.), although the language is well presented in omnipresent media, there is even more need to have a similar tool available for native Welsh speakers which have only recourse to Welsh media which are limited in quantity and quality (cf. below and section 4.1.1.). Third, since most native speakers still obtain education predominantly in English, they may have difficulties in using Welsh terminology, for instance, of science when necessary. Fourth, when looking for international recognition it is recommended to present the specific language of the country in a manner which is internationally standard in order to be taken seriously.

In the light of these facts, phonetic transcription should even be included when lexicographers see no chance to find a form of the language which is acceptable to a wide range of speakers. In this case, they can still choose one dominant variant and explain any major differences in the preface. Such an approach is often chosen for British English and American English and exemplified in Langenscheidts Taschenwörterbuch (1990).

Die Aussprache des amerikanischen Englisch

Einige Worte noch zur amerikanischen Aussprache:
Amerikaner sprechen viele Wörter anders aus als die Briten. In diesem Wörterbuch haben wir uns allerdings auf die britische Aussprache beschränkt, wie Sie sie auch in Ihren Lehrbüchern finden. Ein paar Regeln für die Abweichungen in der amerikanischen Aussprache wollen wir Ihnen hier aber doch geben.

Die Aussprache des amerikanischen Englisch weicht hauptsächlich in folgenden Punkten von der britischen ab:
1. ɑː wird zu (gedehntem) æ(ː) in Wörtern wie *ask* [æ(ː)sk = ɑːsk], *castle* ['k æ(ː)sl = 'k ɑːsl], *grass* [græ(ː)s = gr ɑːs], *past* [p æ(ː)st = p ɑː st] etc.; ebenso in *branch* [bræ(ː)ntʃ = brɑː ntʃ], *can't* [kæ(ː)nt = k ɑːt], *dance* [d æ(ː) ns = dɑːns] etc.
2. ɒ wird zu dem helleren ɑ in Wörtern wie *common* ['kɑmən = 'kɒmən], *not* [nɑt = nɒt], *on* [ɑn = ɒn], *rock* [rɑk = rɒk], *bond* [bɑnd = bɒnd] und vielen anderen.
3. juː wird zu uː, z. B. *due* [duː = djuː], *duke* [duːk = djuːk], *new* [nuː = njuː].
4. r zwischen vorhergehendem Vokal und folgendem Konsonanten wird stimmhaft gesprochen, indem die Zungenspitze gegen den harten Gaumen zurückgezogen wird, z. B. *clerk* [klɜːrk = klɑːk], *hard* [hɑːrd = hɑːd]; ebenso im Auslaut, z. B. *far* [fɑːr = fɑː], *her* [hɜːr = hɜː].
5. Anlautendes p, t, k in unbetonter Silbe (nach betonter Silbe) wird zu b, d, g abgeschwächt, z. B. in *property, water, second.*
6. Der Unterschied zwischen stark- und schwachbetonten Silben ist viel weniger ausgeprägt; längere Wörter haben einen deutlichen Nebenton, z. B. *dictionary* ['dɪkʃə,nerɪ = 'dɪkʃənrɪ], *ceremony* ['serə,məonɪ = 'serɪmənɪ], *inventory* ['ɪnvən-,tɔːrɪ = 'ɪnvəntrɪ], *secretary* ['sekrə,terɪ = 'sekrətrɪ].
7. Vor, oft auch nach nasalen Konsonanten (m, n, ŋ) sind Vokale und Diphthonge nasal gefärbt, z. B. *stand, time, small.*

In other dictionaries, difficult variations in the pronunciation of a lexical item are included all together in the corresponding dictionary entry (cf. Wells 1985: 46, Standop 1985: 94, or Broderick 1984 and below). In the *Longman Dictionary of Contemporary English* (1978), for instance, double pronunciation entries occur wherever *Received Pronunciation* and *General American* diverge.

In this regard, it is significant that *IPA* transcription is included in the pocket dictionary of Modern Irish, the *Foclóir Póca* (An Roinn Oideachais 1990), even though Irish is known for its dialectal variation, which is certainly more difficult to handle than Welsh dialectal variation. The mutual intelligibility of the Welsh dialects has increased since the installation of the Welsh television channel S4C in 1982 (cf. section 4.1.1.).

Foclóir Póca: **cluanaireacht** kluənər´əxt ʃ3 deceitful-
ness; flattery, coquetry
clúdaigh kluːdi: *vt* cover, wrap
cluichíocht kliχ´iː(ə)χt ʃ3 gaming, sport-
ing

IPA is also included in the *Elementary breton-english & english-breton dictionary* (Delaporte 1995) despite the broad level of dialectal variation found in Brittany, too:

erbediñ [erˈbeːdĩ] *v.* **1.** to
recommend; **2.** to register (letter,
parcel).
ergerzh*et* [erˈgɛrzɛt], ergerzh*out*
[erˈgɛrzut] v. to travel through (on
foot); to explore
erminig [erˈmĩːnik] *m.* **-ed** *Zool.*
stoat; **-où** *(Heraldry)* black spot on
ermine fur.

One need only follow the debates about different Breton orthographies in the twentieth century[17] in order to establish how difficult it is to deal with dialectal variation. The pronunciation given in a small Breton dictionary, therefore, can only reflect that of some of the people. Even under these conditions, however, dictionary users will acquire some knowledge of the language. On this basis, they can later add more knowledge and expand their language abilities.

A different solution as regards dialectal variation and its presentation is offered by Favereau (1993). In his dictionary entries, he presents *KLT* pronunciation followed by *Vannetais* pronunciation. In addition, he indicates variations existing in the three main orthographies (cf. above). The following examples illustrate his method:

BERJIN(ES) /-(EZ^{XO}) [bɛrˈʒiːnəz-s], [berʒin(ez-s)] str.
-enn *aubergines.*[18]
BERRANALEG,-ALANEG /&-K^{X} [bɛrãˈnaːləg-k],
[-alãːnəg-k] ad. G. -ion b. *asthmatique.*[19]
BERWIDIG^{+} /-V-^{XO}/&-K^{X} [bɛˈrwiːdig-k] [bɛrɥədig-c]
a-w. BIRV- [birˈviːdig-k] ad. *ardent effervescent. & exalte*
g. *pépie* (kmg. berwedig): gwad bɛrwidig dindan o iwinoù.[20]

---

[17] There are even political implications in the debate over the most appropriate Breton orthography. It remains a fact that *Vannetais* differs so remarkably from the other dialects that all attempts thus far failed to include this variant in a generally accepted common orthography.
The first reform of Breton orthography in the twentieth century was launched in 1908. It was taken up by writers grouped around François Vallée and initially popularised by the weekly *Kroaz ar Vretoned* and later by Roparz Hemon's literary journal *Gwalarn* after 1925 (cf. Sven-Myer 1999). Representing the dialects of Kerne, Leon and Treger, this reformed orthography was called *KLT* (cf. Le Dû & Le Berre 1996: 1257). A characteristic feature of the three dialects is that they exhibit a *z* at the end of a word where the Vannetais dialect shows an *h*, e.g. *Breiz* versus *Breih* 'Brittany'. *Vannetais* as a written dialect was popularised in the paper *Dihunamb* by Loeiz Herriau.
In 1941 Hemon and a number of writers, and Breton nationalists tried to include the Vannetais dialect as well. Thus the *KLTG* orthography was born, also known as *brezhoneg peurunvan* 'completely unified Breton' or *zh*-orthography, because it wrote *zh* instead of the *z* of the Kerne, Leon and Treger dialects and the *h* of Vannetais. Hemon had, unfortunately, closely collaborated with German occupying forces and was employed by the German Celtic scholar Leo Weisgerber, who was himself an agent of the occupying forces (cf. Calvez 1999). Although the *zh*-orthography is the one most frequently used today, e.g. in all Breton *Diwan* schools and in the University of Rennes, it is still rejected by some for being reactionary and nationalistic (cf. Le Dû 1999).
In 1955, François Falc'hun introduced an orthography called *Universitaire*, which is rather a system of teaching Breton spelling and seeks to promote the correlation between the literary standard and spoken Breton (cf. ibid.). In final position, it prefers voiced consonants to voiceless ones, gets rid of the grapheme ⟨c'h⟩ and preserves *Vannetais* as a secondary regional standard. It is frequently used by teachers in private schools and on television.
In the seventies, the orthography *Interdialectale* was developed which claims to unify all dialects whilst preserving dialectal variation at the same time. It has been popularised by the paper *Ar Falz*. At present, the three orthographies, apart from *KLT*, are in competition with each other.
[18] 'X' stands for the *KLT*-orthography, 'O' for the orthography called *Universitaire*.
[19] 'K' is the abbreviation for Kerne.
[20] A '+' indicates that the word is frequently used. 'V' is the abbreviation for Vannetais.

In the dictionary of *A Handbook of Late Spoken Manx* (Broderick 1984), *IPA* is used to transcribe all headwords and phrases.[21]

AALIN: ɛːlinˊ JW, NM, ɛːlən, öːlɪn, öːlən HK, ɑːlənˊ TT - fine, fair, beautiful. Ir. álainn.
  a. reayrt aalin - rɛːt 'ɛːlinˊ NM - a fine view.
  b. inneen aalin - ïˊNˊiːnˊ 'ɛːlinˊ NM - a beautiful girl.
  c. laa aalin - lɛː ɛːlinˊ JW - a fine day.

STRIPPIT: strɪpətˊ TC - stripped. E.

WHOOR: wuːr NM - boys, lads.
  a. ny whoor elly - nə 'wuːr 'elˊə NM - the other lads.

For Scottish-Gaelic a *Sprachführer Deutsch-Gälisch* (Fàilte 1995) has been published. It includes 'imitated pronunciation' (cf. infra) based on German in order to facilitate the pronunciation of Scottish-Gaelic. It is interesting in this context that there have been three pronouncing dictionaries for Scottish-Gaelic, more than in any other Celtic Language: *Pronouncing Gaelic Dictionary* by Neil M'Alpine (1831), *A Pronouncing and Etymological Dictionary of the Gaelic Language* by Malcolm MacLennan (1925), and *A Pronouncing Dictionary of Scottish Gaelic* by H.C. Dieckhoff (1932). In all these dictionaries, including the revised re-editions of MacLennan's, 'imitated pronunciation' (cf. section 4.4.2.) is employed, since they were originally compiled before the invention of *IPA*. The latest re-editions, however, provide some discussion of *IPA* in their introductions and emphasise the only 'approximately correct' reflection of pronunciation by a transcription system based on the English language (MacLennan 1992: xi).

Earlier scholars of Welsh saw the need to explain pronunciation, too. Three bilingual pronouncing dictionaries were produced in the nineteenth century: *An English-Welsh pronouncing dictionary* by Spurrell (1850-1886; cf. chapter III), *Geirlyfr seiniadol (neu gynaniaethol Saesoneg a Chymraeg* by E. Thomas (1850, cf. chapter III), and *An English and Welsh pronouncing dictionary* by R.J. Pryse (cf. Gweirydd ap Rhys 1857, 1888, 1899, cf. section 2.4. and chapter III). These, however, included pronunciation only for English lexical items, not for Welsh.

A third argument presented against phonetic transcription in Welsh dictionaries is that the *International Phonetic Alphabet* would not be understood by anybody. This problem can certainly be easily resolved. Either, as done in some Webster's dictionaries of English (cf. for instance F.C. Mish 1995), a standard list of words exemplifying the *IPA* symbols could be given at the bottom of every page (cf. section 4.3.9.), so that the reader would always have them visible present; or the *IPA*, as applicable to the language under discussion, could form part of the preface, as illustrated by Langenscheidts Taschenwörterbuch (cf. also dictionaries by Pons):

---

[21]   This handbook presents the lexicon used by the last native speakers of Manx. It can, however, also be used as a uni-directional dictionary.

Explanations of phonetic symbols as found in Langenscheidts Taschenwörterbuch.

[ʌ]	much [mʌʃ], come [kʌm]	kurzes *a* wie in *Matsch Kamm*, aber dunkler
[ɑː]	after ['ɑːftə], park [pɑːk]	langes *a*, etwa wie in *Bahn*
[æ]	flat [flæt], madam ['mædəm]	mehr zum *a* hin als ä in *Wäsche*
[ə]	after ['ɑːftə], arrival [ə'raɪvl]	wie das End-e in *Berge, mache, bitte*
[e]	let [let], men [men]	*ä* wie in *hätte, Mäntel*
[ɜː]	first [fɜːst], learn [lɜːn]	etwa wie *ir* in *flirten*, aber offener
[ɪ]	in [ɪn], city ['sɪtɪ]	kurzes *i* wie in *Mitte, billig*
[iː]	see [siː], evening ['iːvnɪŋ]	langes *i* wie in *nie, lieben*
[ɒ]	shop [ʃɒp], job [dʒɒb]	wie *o* in *Gott*, aber offener
[ɔː]	morning ['mɔːnɪŋ], course [kɔːs]	wie in *Lord*, aber ohne *r*
[ʊ]	good [gʊd], look [lʊk]	kurzes *u* wie in *Mutter*
[uː]	too [tuː], shoot [ʃuːt]	langes *u* wie in *Schuh*, aber offener
[aɪ]	my [maɪ], night [naɪt]	etwa wie in *Mai, Neid*
[aʊ]	now [naʊ], about [ə'baʊt]	etwa wie in *blau, Couch*
[əʊ]	home [həʊm], know [nəʊ]	von [ə] zu [ʊ] gleiten
[eə]	air [eə], square [skweə]	wie *är* in *Bär*, aber kein *r* sprechen
[eɪ]	eight [eɪt], stay [steɪ]	klingt wie *äi*
[ɪə]	near [nɪə], here [hɪə]	von [ɪ] zu [ə] gleiten
[ɔɪ]	join [dʒɔɪ n], choice [tʃɔɪ s]	etwa wie *eu* in *neu*
[ʊə]	you're [jʊə], tour [tʊə]	wie *ur* in *Kur*, aber kein *r* sprechen
[j]	yes [jes], tube [tjuːb]	wie *j* in *jetzt*
[w]	way [wei], one [wʌn], quick [kwɪk]	mit gerundeten Lippen ähnlich wie [uː] gebildet. Kein deutsches *w*!
[ŋ]	thing [θɪŋ], English ['ɪŋglɪʃ]	wie *ng* in *Ding*
[r]	room [ruːm], hurry ['hʌrɪ]	Zunge liegt, zurückgebogen, am Gaumen auf. Nicht gerollt und nicht im Rachen gebildet!
[s]	see [siː], famous ['feɪməs]	stimmloses *s* wie in *lassen, Liste*
[z]	zero ['zɪərəʊ], is [ɪz], runs [rʌnz]	stimmhaftes *s* wie in *lesen, Linsen*
[ʃ]	shop [ʃɒp], fish [fɪʃ]	wie *seh* in *Scholle, Fisch*
[tʃ]	cheap [tʃiːp], much [mʌtʃ]	wie *tsch* in *tschüs, Matsch*
[ʒ]	television ['telɪˌvɪʒn]	stimmhaftes *sch* wie in *Genie, Etage*
[dʒ]	just [dʒʌst], bridge [brɪdʒ]	wie in *Job, Gin*
[θ]	thanks [θæŋks], both [bəʊθ]	wie *ß* in *Faß*, aber gelispelt
[ð]	that [ðæt], with [wɪð]	wie *s* in *Sense*, aber gelispelt etwa wie deutsches *w*, Oberzähne auf Oberkante der Unterlippe
[v]	very ['verɪ], over ['əʊvə]	
[x]	loch [lɒx], ugh [ʌx]	wie *ch* in *ach*

[ː] bedeutet, daß der vorhergehende Vokal lang zu sprechen ist.

448

Lengthy explanations, such as in *Geiriadur yr Academi* (1995: xx-xxiii and xxxiv-xxxii) could thus be avoided and the acquisition of pronunciation skills would be facilitated.

An approach similar to that of Langenscheidt is often also used when introducing 'imitated pronunciation' (Brake 1994: 7-12, Gruffudd 1998: 6f., Picket, J.P. & D.R. Pritchard et al. 2000).

Those dictionary users who are in the process of acquiring another language or who have a good command of one, may already be familiar with the *IPA*, as this alphabet is widely used internationally in dictionaries. For instance, since the eighties the *IPA* forms regular part of major English and French[22] dictionaries thus providing interested dictionary users with a basis of comparison. In Germany and Russia, English-language transcription is even to be found on work sheets for eight- and nine-year-old children in Junior Schools (cf. Lauster 1999) as can be seen from the figure below:

🐱 Vokabeln in Bildern

Kennst du auch diese 20 Vokabeln? Ihre deutsche Bedeutung steht auf der Seite unten. Lies die Wörter laut vor.

car (kɑ:) 1

horse (hɔ:s) 10

doll (dɒl) 9

chair (tʃeə) 15

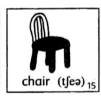

fly (flaɪ) 13

key (ki:) 8

sponge (spʌndʒ) 24

bear (beə) 15

---

[22]   French is the first foreign language in Great Britain.

🐾 Die Lautschrift

Damit du weißt, wie das englische Wort ausgesprochen wird, musst du die Lautschrift lesen können. Sie steht hinter jedem neuen Wort in einer eckigen Klammer. Auf den folgenden drei Seiten werden dir die Zeichen der Lautschrift mit Beispielen erklärt.

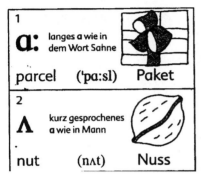

1		
a: langes a wie in dem Wort Sahne		
parcel	('pɑːsl)	Paket
2		
ʌ kurz gesprochenes a wie in Mann		
nut	(nʌt)	Nuss

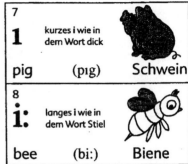

7		
ɪ kurzes i wie in dem Wort dick		
pig	(pɪg)	Schwein
8		
iː langes i wie in dem Wort Stiel		
bee	(biː)	Biene

In addition, the *IPA* has in fact been used for the transcription of Welsh sounds when describing various dialects (cf. Ball M.& G.E. Jones 1984) or when giving a survey of the language (cf. Watkins 1993, A.R. Thomas 1992, 2000). The first transcription of Welsh lexical items in a lexicographical work using the *IPA* was carried out by S. Heinz in 1994, based on the southern pronunciation. This approach, however, has not been taken up by others.

To sum up: as was illustrated in the preceding paragraphs the inclusion of phonetic transcription in Welsh general-purpose dictionaries is generally useful, predominantly, for the learner, but also for the native speaker. First, such a transcription furthers the mutual intelligibility among native speakers of dialect. Second, a situation has developed in Wales in which Welsh can often no longer be heard sufficiently to maintain and improve individual and general levels of communicative competence through daily usage, a fact also important for native speakers. Third, the Welsh language as heard in the media is deficient in quality and insufficient in quantity (cf. section 4.1.1.) and education cannot compensate for all these factors (cf. section 4.1.1.). Learners have thus only a limited scope for upgrading their Welsh language skills in a linguistic environment that is increasingly deprived of native speaker interaction.

In view of these facts, phonetic transcription is generally a safe guide for native speakers and learners. Consequently, it should form a regular part of dictionary entries, since detailed explanations in introductory sections of reference books are of little help for immediate guidance in communication and often include too much specific linguistic information for the casual dictionary user.

There are, however, also specific reasons which advocate the inclusion of phonetic transcription in dictionary entries. Indeed, the pronunciation of Welsh lexical items may be unpredictable for both learners and - considering loanwords, Welsh terminology, or dialect words - native speakers. First, Welsh orthography is not an unambiguous guide to pronunciation because of a sizable number of specific orthographic rules and exceptions. These can, in addition, be difficult to apply for the casual dictionary user, e.g. those which are based on etymology. Moreover, stress patterns cannot be inferred from spelling.

Second, dialectal variation may interfere with the rules of pronunciation. Third, there is interference from English because of the English-speaking background of the vast majority of Welsh language learners (cf. above and section 4.1.1.). Griffith, B. & D.G. Jones suggest, therefore, that

> "[t]he learner is advised to listen to Welsh radio and television broadcast, to practise conversation with a good native speaker" (ibid.: xx).

In light of the facts presented above and in section 4.1.1. the need of phonetic transcription is at this point clearly corroborated. As the discussion here has demonstrated it is indeed possible, as a practical matter, to include phonetic transcription of lexical items. In the following section, different kinds of transcription are discussed.

4.4.2. Choice of notation system

One basic decision a lexicographer must make after deciding that transcription of some kind is necessary is what sort of transcription system to use. One option is to resort to 're-spelling' or 'imitated pronunciation', that is, the Welsh lexical item is transcribed as if it were a word written in another language with that language's orthography. Invariably, in a Welsh language context the 'other language' is English. Alternatively, one can make use of proper phonetic symbols. Various hybrid systems are also possible (cf. Wells 1985: 48).

The need to include at least basic phonetic guidelines was apparently recognised by H. Gruffudd in *The Welsh Learner's Dictionary* (1998). In contrast to others, his publisher had no problem with the fact that his transcription is based specifically on the southern dialectal variant.[1] Gruffudd opted for the 'imitated pronunciation', based on the English language. This, however, is a problem since (a) the 'imitated pronunciation' is based on *Received Pronunciation* (*RP*, cf. Brake 1994: 7), which is the language of only a very few people in Great Britain, and (b) English is famous for having a spelling system which itself is very broadly interpretable. As stated in MacLennan (1992: xi) for the Gaelic transcription system:

> "[This] medium of expression is incomplete. The English alphabet can be so manipulated as to give a great range of sounds, but it has its embarrassments. There are certain sounds in Gaelic for which there are no equivalents in English. So often, too, the same symbol varies in sound, e.g. *ie* in f*ie*, f*ie*ld, f*ie*rce; or *u* in c*u*p, f*u*neral, s*u*re; or *ou* in r*ou*t, r*ou*te, r*ou*gh. Further, the same sound may be presented by different symbols, e.g. *i* in th*i*rst, e in h*e*r, u in c*u*r, *ou* in col*ou*r; *o* in the last syllable of mot*o*r and *a* in mot*a*r represent one and the same sound. For this reason one's choice of symbols is materially circumscribed in the endeavour to reproduce the sounds of unfamiliar words."

The point is as true for Welsh. Another problem reveals itself when comparing the transcription by 'imitated pronunciation' found in Gruffudd's dictionary with that presented in the Welsh manual *Welsh in Three Months* (Brake 1994). The two systems differ markedly from each other as can be seen from the following table:

---

[1]   As a consequence, the northern /ɨ/, for instance, is not included, or /ʃ/ in final position, such as in *mis* 'month'.

examples	Brake (1994)	Gruffudd (1998)
allan 'out, outside'	a<u>lh</u>-an	allan
clywed 'to hear'	kluw-ed	kluhooed
chwech 'six'	<u>ch</u>weh<u>ch</u>	chooech
gweithio 'to work'	gweyth-yoh	gwe-eethyo
gweld 'to see'	gweld	gooeld
gwlyb 'wet'	g(w)leeb	goo'leeb
llaeth 'milk'	<u>lh</u>yeth	llaeeth
llygad 'eye'	<u>lh</u>uh-gad	lluhgad
myfyriwr 'student'	muh-vurr-wirr[2]	muhvuhryoor
pabell 'tent'	pah-be<u>lh</u>	pabell
rhyw 'some'	rhiw	rhioo
ymwelydd 'visitor'	um-wel-i<u>dd</u>	uhmooelidd

Looking, first, at the variety of graphemes used to present the various phonemes, e.g. ⟨lh⟩, ⟨ll⟩ for /ɬ/; ⟨u⟩ and ⟨uh⟩ for /ə/; ⟨ey⟩ and ⟨e-ee⟩ for /əi/; or ⟨ye⟩ and ⟨aee⟩ for /ai/, it would seem much better to transcribe unfamiliar sounds with properly standardised, unmistakable, unchangeable and broadly recognised signs instead of somewhat idiosyncratically chosen graphemes of a particular language. Second, both systems neglect to include the word stress. Third, the transcriptions themselves allow a variety of interpretive pronunciations in both reference books. Fourth, it seems likely, that learners, who have chosen these two reference books because both are based on the same southern dialectal variant, may well be puzzled or irritated by the use of two such dissimilar-looking versions of 'imitated pronunciation'.

It can be stated quite generally that transcription systems which are based on 're-spelling' are rather chaotic (cf. Standop 1985: 93). This situation is not only due to the presence of competing systems, but to the fact that the systems are inconsistent in themselves (ibid.). Transcriptions based on 're-spelling' are particularly hard to apply to the indication of different vowel lengths. An opposition of two vowel lengths can be indicated by additional diacritics above the letters as, for instance, in *food* /fo͞od/ and *foot* /fo͝ot/; three different vowel lengths are even more difficult to handle. In Gruffudd (1998), however, not even short and long vowels are regularly distinguished, not to mention medium long vowels (cf. Lewis 1997: 15), as can be seen in the following table:

---

[2] This transcription looks rather like the plural of *myfyriwr*, i.e. *myfyrwyr*.

Lexical item	Gruffudd	IPA
llun 'picture'	*[lleen]*	/ɬiːn/
llyn 'lake'	*[llin]*	/ɬɪn/
llinell 'line'	*[lleenell]*	/ˈɬiˑnɛɬ/
ger 'near'	*[ger]*	/gɛr/
gêr 'gear'	*[ger]*	/geːr/
gorau 'best'	*[goraee]*	/ˈgoˑrai/
goleuo 'to lighten'	*[gole-eeo]*	/goˈləio/
golwg 'sight'	*[goloog]*	/ˈgoˑlʊg/
man 'place'	*[man]*	/man/
mân 'small'	*[man]*	/mɑːn/
math 'kind'	*[math]*	/mɑːθ/
mor 'so'	*[mor]*	/mɒr/
mo 'not, nothing of, from **dim o** [...]'	*[mo]*	/mo/[3]
môr 'sea'	*[mor]*	/moːr/
set 'set'	*[set]*	/sɛt/
sêt 'seat'	*[seht]*	/seːt/
rhemp 'excess'	*[rhemp]*	/r̥ɛmp/
rheoli 'to manage'	*[rheolee]*	/r̥eˈoˑli/
eang 'wide'	*[eang]*	/ˈeːaŋ/
tan 'until'	*[tan]*	/tan/
talu 'to pay'	*[talee]*	/ˈtɑˑli/
tân 'fire'	*[tan]*	/ˈtɑːn/
ton 'wave'	*[ton]*	/tɒn/
tôn 'tune'	*[ton]*	/toːn/
ymladd 'to fight'	*[uhmladd]*	/ˈəmlað/
ymlâdd 'to wear oneself out'	*[uhmlˈadd]*	/əmˈlɑːð/

---

[3]   According to its position *mo* can also be pronounced with an opener vowel.

454

Looking at the above table, it is apparent that the vowel length is only rarely indicated in the transcription, as in *set - sêt,* transcribed as *[set]* and *[seht].* It is a question, however, whether English based dictionary users will interpret ⟨eh⟩ as /eː/, a graphematic representation which is known in German, but not common in English and not explained in the introduction of *The Welsh Learner's Dictionary.* In addition /eː/ itself does not exist in *RP* pronunciation.

The *International Phonetic Association* claims itself to a notational standard for the phonetic representation of all languages,[4] that is, including Welsh. Whereas, therefore, the *IPA* provides specific signs for particular sounds for many languages, the 'imitated pronunciation' uses (a) graphemes of a particular language, in this case RP English, a language with (b) a different inventory of phonemes, and (c) a different grapheme-phoneme-realisation than the language to be transcribed, in this case Welsh. These three difficulties leave more room for divergent transcriptions of sounds than would occur with an alphabet which was invented deliberately to transcribe sounds of other languages, in order to make them accessible to a broader audience.

There is, unfortunately, no unique *IPA* way of representing the sounds of a given language. For English, for instance, there are several slightly different competing systems, with a recent tendency to favour the 'Gimson' system; that is, a standardisation process can be observed (cf. Wells 1985: 49ff., Standop 1985: 93).

To illustrate the differences, three major systems are exemplified in the following table:

---

[4]   On its website, the *International Phonetic Association* formulates the following goals:
"The aim of the Association is to promote the scientific study of phonetics and the various practical applications of that science. In furtherance of this aim, the Association provides the academic community world-wide with a notational standard for the phonetic representation of all languages - the International Alphabet (also IPA)" (http.//www2.arts.gla.ac.uk/IPA/ipa.html, 20.10.2001).

Jones	Windsor-Lewis	Gimson	Exemplificatory keywords
iː	i	iː	bead, fleece, knee
i	ɪ	ɪ	bid, kit
e	e	e	bed, dress
æ	æ	æ	bad, trap
ɑː	ɑ	ɑː	bard, bath, start, palm
ɔ	o	ɒ	cod, lot, cloth
ɔː	ɔ	ɔː	board, north, force, thought
u	ʊ	ʊ	could, foot
uː	u	uː	mood, goose, two
ʌ	ʌ	ʌ	bud, strut, love
əː	ɜ	ɜː	bird, nurse, fur
ə	ə	ə	letter, comma
ei	eɪ	eɪ	made, face, hay
ou	əʊ	əʊ	mode, goat, know
ai	ɑɪ	ʌɪ	bide, pride, high
au	ɑʊ	ɑʊ	loud, mouth, how
ɔɪ	ɔɪ	ɔɪ	boy, choice, joy
iə	ɪə	ɪə	beard, near, idea
ɛə	eə	eə	bared, square
uə	ʊə	ʊə	moored, cure

The 'Jones transcription' has a reduced number of special symbols but can be misleading in as much as the vowel distinctions are represented as resting primarily on quantity (length) rather than on quality (timbre). The 'Windsor-Lewis transcription' has not proved a success because of objections that it is easily misread. The 'Gimson notation' gets the best of both, at the expense of some redundancy (cf. Wells 1985: 50). Consonants are shown uniformly in all *IPA* transcriptions of English.

For Welsh there are two major transcription systems; one is based on Thorne and the other is presented in *Welsh Phonology* by Ball, M. & G.E. Jones (1984; cf. section 4.4.1.). In order to avoid a situation much deprecated by publishers, learners, and authors because of the variety of systems even within *IPA*, a list at the beginning of a dictionary explaining the *IPA* symbols used is necessary (cf. section 4.4.1.).

Another problem with the phonetic transcription as presented by H. Gruffudd and P. Brake is that neither author indicates the word stress in their imitated pronunciation. This was alredy included in very early dictionaries; in the dictionary of W. Evans (1771 and 1812), for instance, the stress is indicated for the lexical items of the language to be acquired (cf. The Preface), in this case the English language:

> ABE'TTOR, (f.) annogwr. - cynhaliwr [...]
> ABI'DING, (f.) prefwyliad, arhosiad [...]
> ABJE'CT, (adj.) diystyr, distadl [...]

The only dictionary which comes near such an approach is *Geiriadur yr Academi* when indicating anomalously stressed words by providing them with a mark of stress in the form of a vertical bar immediately before the stressed vowel, e.g. ac|ademi 'academy' (cf. section 4.4.1.).

In light of the already established use of *IPA* for the precise description of Welsh dialects and for general surveys of the language (cf. section 4.4.1., Watkins 1993, A.R. Thomas 2000) or in order to make differing pronunciations of lexical items comparable to each other, a serious question arises as to why it should not also be used for phonetic transcription in Welsh dictionaries. Why should Welsh dictionary users be offered less precise linguistic descriptions? Is the most widely spoken Celtic language considered by its scholars to be somehow less amenable to *IPA* description than Irish, Breton or even Manx? It is barely credible that it should take more time to get used to the *IPA* - which some dictionary users may, moreover, know already from the study of other languages (cf. section 4.4.1.) - as opposed to the time required to come to terms with the differing systems of 'imitated pronunciation', which also ask for some training in order to be followed. Indeed, both require an introductory section at the beginning of the dictionary. Wells stated in 1985:

> "Anyone seriously interested in pronunciation has to get grips with phonetic transcription. The use of IPA symbols in English monolingual dictionaries for the native speaker is gaining ground in Britain [...], and in the EFL [English as a Foreign Language] world the use of phonetic symbols has long been accepted as essential" (ibid.: 45).

All in all, it seems both advicable and necessary to employ *IPA* signs for the phonetic transcription of lexical items in Welsh dictionaries. It is the main function of a dictionary to provide necessary linguistic information for lexical items directly in the given entry and not in general terms in an introduction. Only such information enables dictionary users to apply lexical items both orally and in written form on demand. Consequently, pronunciation must be included in the entry for every headword. A transcription based on 're-spelling', however, should - if at all - be used only in monolingual dictionaries aimed at the native speaker, not for learners with a different mother tongue background (ibid.: 49).

4.5. Summary

In this section, a comparative survey of the individual presentation of different word classes is given thus summarising that which has been analysed in the preceding sections. Lexically relevant grammatical features and their presentation in entries of Welsh dictionaries, some lexicological and specific semantic problems closely connected to Welsh grammatical properties as well as the assistence in pronunciation given in dictionaries are the subjects of the following table:

Presentation of	Geiriadur Cyfoes	Geiriadur Mawr	Geiriadur Bach	Geiriadur Prifysgol Cymru	Geiriadur yr Academi	Works-Dictionary	Spurrell & Gem	Learners' dictionaries[1]
Verb inflection	not at all	not at all	not at all	verbs presented in first p. sing. pres./ fut., occ. an irreg. third p. sing. present	from *bod* 'be'; occasionally an infl. form in phrases	irregular verbs with reference to appendix	not at all	not at all//irregular verbs and some verb stems
government	not at all	very rarely stochastically included	very rarely stochastically included	word class label indicates regularly minimal synt. valency, actual government and collocations are undifferentiatedly listed together	actual government and collocations are undifferentiatedly listed together; basic syntactic government not guaranteed	not at all	not at all	very rarely stochastically included
collocations	not at all	very rarely stochastically included	very rarely stochastically included			not at all	not at all	very rarely stochastically included
Noun spec. gender inflection	partly	partly	barely	comprehensively	partly	comprehensively	partly	barely

---

[1] The comment before '//' refers to *The Welsh Learner's Dictionary*, that behind to the *Pocket Modern Welsh Dictionary*.

number inflection	mixed syst. (English/W.); some forms remain untraceable	mixed syst. (English/W.); some forms remain untraceable	mixed syst. (English/W.); some forms remain untraceable	well reflected; occasionally the singulative is part of the macrostructure with a reference to the basic word form	English system is presented	English system is presented; produces mistranslations	mixed syst. (Engl./W.); some forms remain untraceable	inconsistent presentation; traceability is guaranteed
Adjective gender inflection	a good half	nearly comprehensively	nearly comprehensively	comprehensively	comprehensively	nearly not at all within the entries but comprehensively as separate entries	nearly comprehensively	nearly a quarter//limited lexicon is nearly comprehensively reflected
number inflection	nearly a half	nearly a half	a half	comprehensively	comprehensively	nearly not at all	nearly a half	nearly a half// barely
de-adjectival nouns (-ion)	nearly a half is presented	nearly three quarters	a good quarter	nearly comprehensively	a good third	a good third	a good half	a third//a half of a very limited lexicon

degree	not at all	one adjective	one adjective	irregular comparisons	all irregular comparisons and most of those which cause changes in words	not at all within the entries but some irregular forms as separate entries	not at all within the entries but some irregular forms as separate entries	not at all// most irreg. comp. & most of those which cause changes in words within in limited lexicon
de-nominal adjectives (-af ...)	nearly a half	nearly a half	a good third	three quarters	three quarters	a good half	less than a half	nearly a quarter//less than a quarter
positionally dependent meaning	a good half	a good third	a third	nearly completely	two thirds	nearly not at all	nearly two thirds	a good third//a third within limited lexicon
government	nearly not at all	nearly a third	a good third	comprehensively	comprehensively	not at all	not at all	comprehensively
Pronoun: government	not at all	nearly not at all	more than two thirds	three quarters	nearly comprehensively	not at all	one lexical item	nearly comprehensively//comprehensively
recognition of the word class	nearly two thirds	three quarters	three quarters	more than three quarters	only two	less than a half	less than a half	nearly a half// one lexical item recognised as pronoun

Preposition: compound p. in headword list	very little	more than two thirds	more than two thirds	nearly all	[not applicable in English-Welsh dictionary]	very little	less than a fifth	nearly a half//a good half
inflection	not at all	more than a quarter	nearly a third	nearly three quarters	nearly comprehensively	less than a quarter	one lexical item	less than a half //comprehensively
government	not at all	nearly a half (indirectly)	nearly a half (indirectly)	comprehensively	comprehensively	not at all	not at all	comprehensively
Conjunction: recognition of the word class	less than a half; some remain untraceable	nearly a quarter	a quarter	good three quarters	most lexical items are well classified by their complementation	a good third within limited lexicon	less than a half within limited lexicon	a good third within limited lexicon//nearly two thirds
government	not at all	one lexical item	one lexical item	more than a third	most lexical items are presented with their government	not at all	not at all	more than three quarters//comprehensively
Numeral: recognition of the word class	as adjective or noun up to hundred, then as noun	as adjective or noun, up to twenty also numeral	as adjective or noun, up to twenty also numeral	cardinals and ordinals defined as numerals	mostly as numeral adjective and numeral, also as noun, ordinal adjective and ordinal conjunction	as numeral up to hundred, then as noun	as adjective or noun up to hundred, then as noun	as numerals apart from ordinals//as numerals apart from 'ail' up to thousand

fém./masc. forms	incompletely	completely[2]	completely	completely	completely	completely	completely	completely
plural	from hundred on consistently	from ten on consistently	from ten on consistently	consistently	consistently	from hundred on consistently	from ten on consistently	from twenty onwards
government	one lexical item	one lexical item	one lexical item	comprehensively	comprehensively	not at all	not at all	comprehensively
Particle: recognition of the word class	more than a third	comprehensively	comprehensively	comprehensively	--[3]	one lexical item	more than a third	comprehensively
government	not at all	more than two thirds	more than two thirds	comprehensively	--	not at all	not at all	comprehensively
Phonetic transcription	four pages of introduction	not at all, apart from isolated comments	not at all, apart from isolated comments	not at all[4]	isolated comments on pronunciation in dictionary entries and nine pages of introduction	not at all	one page and a half of introduction	imitated pronunciation// two pages of introduction

---

2   The attribute 'complete' can only be used when there is a strictly defined number of lexical items, which everybody agrees on.

3   Since sentence initial particles and particles indicating a deviation of the word order in the sentence do not exist in English, the English-Welsh dictionary has not been consulted for their analysis.

4   A historical dictionary is not a tool for ad hoc communication and, therefore, does not need to include phonetic transcription for this purpose.

From the twenty-six linguistic phenomena analysed in the dictionaries under review, nine are not described at all in the entries of the *Works-Dictionary*. In addition, it predominantly offers 1:1 equivalences. These, however, are insufficient in Welsh, since a number of its lexical items can vary its meaning according to the position, i.e. whether the words come before or after a referent (cf. adjectives in section 4.3.3.4.). Other lexical items change their meaning with the gender (cf. nouns in section 4.3.2.1.) or number (cf. nouns in section 4.3.2.2.), or with the word class (cf. conjunctions in section 4.3.6.). Considering also the fact that lexical items generally hardly express one semantic meaning only, the *Works-Dictionary* is far from being recommendable for anybody, and definitely not for learners (cf. below). The advert on its back cover claims:

"A fully up-to-date, comprehensive and clearly presented compact dictionary - the ideal reference aid for learners and speakers of Welsh.
• Over 20.000 headwords
• Irregular forms of the adjectives, verbs and plural nouns are given
• Appendix of irregular Welsh verbs"

The number of the headwords may be correct and an appendix of most of the irregular verbs does exist, too. It addition, it is user-friendly to find some selected irregular verb forms as separate entries in the headword list. The separation of individual morphological forms in other word classes, however, causes morphological obscuring, for instance, when feminine and masculine forms of adjectives mainly occur in different entries (cf. section 4.3.3.1.), or when the plural forms of adjectives form independent dictionary entries (cf. section 4.3.3.2.), or when the forms of adjective comparison (cf. section 4.3.3.3.) or inflected forms of prepositions (cf. section 4.5.5.3.) are separately included in the headword list. An approach which takes morphological features of lexcial items as criteria for separate dictionary entries makes it difficult to ascertain morphological paradigms and establish relations between varying forms of lexical items. If such links between morphological forms cannot be set up the usage of lexical items is impeded.

In short, the limited lexicon in the *Works-Dictionary* is introduced as a compilation of isolated lexical items. Adding the insufficient indications of their government and the lack of elementary usage notes, this dictionary resembles a word list, which is predominantly useful for native speakers who know how to use the words so long as they know of their existence.

In case one decides to use small dictionaries, the *Spurrell* and *Gem* dictionaries should be given preference, since they include slightly more linguistic description of their lexical items and cover a wider semantic range. In addition, both dictionaries include more morphological forms of lexical items and do not separate these consistently. The government of the various word classes, however, is almost totally absent from their dictionary entries, too.

A similar characteristic can be provided for *Y Geiriadur Cyfoes*, although it comprises more lexical items (cf. section 4.2.).

A step further ahead in quality is *Y Geiriadur Bach*, the macro- and microstructure of which is very similar to that of *Y Geiriadur Mawr*. Almost all linguistic phenomena analysed in this investigation are partly reflected in the entries of these dictionaries, although to different degrees of quality and quantity. Guidelines on pronunciation, for instance, are very rare (cf. section 4.4.).

In addition, the presentation of the government of lexical items (cf. in particular the sections on pronouns in 4.3.4., on conjunctions in 4.3.6., and on numerals in 4.3.7.), of properties of the verb (cf. section 4.3.1.), and of the category degree of adjectives (4.3.3.3.) is insufficient in both reference books.

Nearly all linguistic phenomena investigated here are also covered by the learners' dictionaries. The lexicon presented in them, however, is very limited, particularly in the *Pocket Modern Welsh Dictionary*. In addition, for the target group learners, the features of the Welsh verb are in no way sufficiently described in the entries of both dictionaries (cf. section 4.3.1.). Apart from the government of the verb, the complementation of the other word classes is much better indicated, particularly when it occurs in form of mutation which is imposed on the subsequent constituents of the sentence (cf. adjectives in section 4.3.3., pronouns in section 4.3.4., conjunctions in section 4.3.6., numerals in section 4.3.7., and particles in section 4.3.8.). The word classes are also relatively well defined.

The best description of the phenomena analysed in this investigation can be found in the historical dictionary *Geiriadur Prifysgol Cymru (GPC)*. It is the only reference book which regularly presents the system of Welsh nouns to a greater extent and, exclusively according to the Welsh system, that is, nouns the stem of which has plural meaning form part of the headword list and not their secondary singulative (cf. section 4.3.2.2.). *GPC* also provides the best definitions of word classes (cf. section 4.3.7.). As a result, the same lexical item may form more than one dictionary entry when being assigned to different word classes (cf. section 4.3.6., cf. the *Works-Dictionary* above which takes morphological features as criteria for different entries).

Insufficiently included is the category of degree of the adjectives (cf. section 4.3.3.3.) and the government of the conjunctions (cf. section 4.3.6.). However, as a whole this dictionary presents more features of individual lexical items than any other dictionary and thus provides to a great extent potential information which entries of bi-directional general-purpose dictionaries should contain (cf. prepositions in section 4.3.5., numerals in section 4.3.7., and word formation patterns in sections 4.3.2.2.2. and 4.3.3.2.1.), although in a more formulaic and concise manner (cf. section 4.3.2.2.2.).

It would be desirable, however, to have the third person singular present of verbs regularly included and syntactic valency separatedly listed from semantic valency in the entries of *GPC*. Indeed, the reflection of the government is a general problem of Welsh dictionaries. Although *Geiriadur yr Academi*, for instance, provides abundant exemplification for the application of its lexical items, the inclusion of the basic government of verbs, for example, is not guaranteed (cf. section 4.3.1.2.). Much better is the complementation of function words included and could - with a more formulaic and concise presentation - serve as a model for dictionary entries of, for instance, conjunctions (cf. section 4.3.6.) in bi-directional general-purpose dictionaries.

Well covered are also the features of the adjectives, numerals, and conjunctions in *Geiriadur yr Academi*, although not always completely in the respective dictionary entries. At times, several entries and the explanatory section have to be consulted in order to obtain the entire information for individual lexical items (cf. section 4.3.3.).

Since *Geiriadur yr Academi* has also encoding function for Welsh learners, the indication of verb stems and the inflection of irregular verbs in the dictionary entries - as done for the verb *bod* 'to be' - would seem recommendable, if not essential. Long lists of selected verbs in the explanatory sections as well as major inflection paradigms are of little help for immediate guidance on the usage of lexical items, since dictionary users must carry out a complete new search procedure in order to find the relevant rules or exceptions.

An improvement of the recognition of the Welsh morphology of the nouns is also urgently suggested (cf. section 4.3.2.), even more since *Geiriadur yr Academi* is together with *GPC* an important lexicographical source for the *Centre for Standardizing Terminology* at the University of Bangor (cf. http://www.netwales.co.uk/byig/adrodds.htm, 20.10.2001) as well as for other major institutions.

A general deficiency in the Welsh dictionaries analysed here, be it general-purpose or learners' dictionaries, is a non-codified *Metalanguage*. The lack of a standardised syntax of grammatical description becomes most clear in *Geiriadur yr Academi* which provides extensive context (cf. for example section 4.3.3.). The impression is that individual dictionary entries were written by various authors. Indeed, at times, *Geiriadur yr Academi* provides redundant information (cf. section 4.3.5.) and could be more concise when codifying abbreviations, syntax, and content of the *Metalanguage*. As said before, various information has to be gathered from several entries and the explanatory section (cf. above). In addition, particularly within long entries, there is a somewhat haphazard presentation of the linguistic material, that is, the access structure of the dictionary remains hidden.

Part of the problem *Metalanguage* is the lack of word class labels of the equivalents of the target language. Only in the *Works-Dictionary*, *Geiriadur yr Academi* and *CysGair*, there is the gender of the equivalent Welsh noun indicated.

Varying *Metalanguage* is, however, also evident in the learners' dictionaries as well as a differing structure of their dictionary entries. The *Pocket Modern Welsh Dictionary*, for instance, fails, at times, to give equivalents in the target language, e.g. for the compound prepositions *er mwyn* 'for the sake of' and *er gwaethaf* 'in spite of' (cf. section 4.3.5.).

A second general deficiency is the lack of guidance to pronunciation in the dictionary entries. Whereas it is not necessarily part of the task of a historical dictionary, it seems basically necessary for a modern bi-directional general-purpose dictionary. Such a transcription not only furthers the mutual intelligibility among native speakers of dialect. In view of increasing English immigration, a limited range of Welsh media, and dominating English-language education (cf. section 4.1.1.), phonetic transcription is generally a safe guide for native speakers and learners. It is demonstrated in some of the entries of *Geiriadur yr Academi* that explanations on pronunciation are indispensable (cf. section 4.4.). This necessity is also the result of, at times, unpredictable pronunciation of Welsh lexical items as is illustrated in section 4.4. Long explanations in introductory sections, as for instance in *Geiriadur yr Academi* (cf. section 4.4.), however, are of little help for immediate guidance in communication and often include too much specific linguistic information for the casual dictionary user.

The need to introduce at least basic phonetic guidelines was recognised by H. Gruffudd in *The Welsh Learner's Dictionary*, which transcribes each headword in 'imitated pronunciation'. This kind of re-spelling, however, presents Welsh lexical items as if they were words written in

English with that language's orthography. The apparent disadvantages of this notation system are described in section 4.4.

A third general deficiency found in Welsh dictionaries is the treatment of lexical units which consist of more than one constituent part. As can be seen from the compilation of compound prepositions (cf. section 4.3.5.), such lexical units are rarely found in the macrostructure of Welsh dictionaries. If they do occur in the microstructure, they are rather unsystematically listed together with idioms and phrases and are difficult to be distinguished from these.

A fourth general deficiency recognised in Welsh dictionaries is the omission of the government of lexical items in the general-purpose dictionaries (cf. sections 4.3.1.2., 4.3.3.4., 4.3.4., 4.3.5., 4.3.6., 4.3.7., and 4.3.8.). The government, however, is often unpredictable but essential for communication, since it is one of the phenomena which allows the connection of individual lexical items to larger units. The latter carry complex information which is offered and exchanged in the speech act. In addition, the government may also be a decisive criterion for assigning lexical items to different word classes (cf. sections 4.3.4., 4.3.6., and 4.3.7.). However, only in the specialised reference books, i.e. the two learners' dictionaries and the historical dictionary *GPC*, as well as in the uni-directional dictionary *Geiriadur yr Academi*, the government is better reflected.

A fifth deficiency is the lacking presentation of the inflection of the verbs, which is inadequately included (cf. section 4.3.1.). As said before, the *Works-Dictionary* lists some irregular forms as separate entries and provides an appendix in their regard. The learners' *Pocket Modern Welsh Dictionary* gives selected inflected forms of irregular verbs and some verbal stems. *Geiriadur yr Academi* offers an explanatory section in its introduction (cf. above) and *GPC* the first person singular present (cf. section 4.3.1.1.) in the headword list. Otherwise, neither are the stems of verbs indicated in Welsh bi-directional general-purpose dictionaries, nor irregular verb forms, nor inflection paradigms.

To this fifth deficiency the insufficient presentation of the category of degree of adjectives, which is only satisfactory included in *Geiriadur yr Academi*, has to be added (cf. section 4.3.3.3.) and the poor description of the morphology of the nouns (cf. section 4.3.2.2.), which is in part better treated by *Y Geiriadur Mawr* and *Y Geiriadur Bach* and well presented only in *GPC*. A system which presses Welsh nouns into English categories affects the linguistic identity of native speakers. Cultural identity may be spoiled considering that the number inflection of the Welsh noun belongs to those morphological devices which contribute to the construction of the culture-specific way of perceiving reality in Welsh culture (cf. section 4.1.2.).

A final deficiency is the limited presentation of definitions, collocations and idioms, particularly in the smaller dictionaries and in *Y Geiriadur Cyfoes*. On the back cover of *Y Geiriadur Cyfoes* dictionary users can read: "containing over 100.000[5] words and definitions, this is an essential reference book." However, the following examples illustrate that there are no regular definitions, but only 1:1 translations (cf. also section 4.2.):

---

[5]   The basis of the number of words provided remains hidden (cf. section 4.2.).

dirgroes, *a* OPPOSITE
dirgryn, *a* VIBRATE
dirgryniad, (-au), *n.m.* CONCRETENESS
dirgrynol, *a.* VIBRATING
dirgrynu, *v.* VIBRATE
diriaeth, (-au), *n.m.* CONCRETENESS
diriaethol, *a.* CONCRETE
diriant, (-nnau), *n.m.* STRESS
dirlawn, *a.* SATURATED
dirlawnder, (-au), *n.m.* SATURATION

Considering the limited range of Welsh dictionaries, the linguistic situation in Wales, that is, the high percentage of Welsh learners in an English-language context, Welsh media limited in quality and quantity (cf. section 4.1.1.), as well as problems of teaching Welsh (cf. section 4.1.1.) in the context of methodological deficiencies in language teaching in Great Britain and the tendency to minimise the teaching of languages (cf. *The Independent*, 11.2.2002), the systematic inclusion of definitions, collocations and idioms in Welsh dictionaries is to be highly recommended. In addition, the presentation of other features of the Welsh language (cf. above) need to be considerably improved in these reference books, too.

In view of the deficiencies analysed in the individual sections, there seem to be general theoretical problems which, at least, partly cause the weaknesses of Welsh general-purpose dictionaries. One of them are differing concepts of word class definitions. This is apparent when labelling pronouns and conjunctions defined as such by the leading grammar by P.W. Thomas (1996) as other word classes (cf. sections 4.3.4. and 4.3.6.). In particular with numerals the English classification seems to dominate the concepts of the lexicographers of, at least, *Y Geiriadur Cyfoes*, *Spurrell*, and *Gem* (cf. section 4.3.7.).

A feature of all Welsh general-purpose dictionaries which reflects English influence is the classification of nouns and verbs (cf. section 1.3.2.3.1.). Their presentation in Welsh general-purpose dictionaries reveals a description which ignores genuine properties of the Welsh language, such as the complementation of the Welsh verb as well as nouns the stem of which has plural meaning (cf. above and sections 4.3.1. and 4.3.2.2.).

A third reflex of English influence is the alphabetical order presented in *CysGair*. By ignoring the Welsh alphabet indications of how to pronounce Welsh lexical items are lost (cf. section 4.4.).

A fourth theoretical problem can be seen in the lack of support for Welsh word formation patterns in bi-directional general-purpose dictionaries. They could be introduced by including derivations and compound words of the headwords (cf. sections 4.3.2.2.2., 4.3.3.2.1., and 4.3.3.3.1.). Since dictionaries are those reference books which present the lexicon of a language, but always to a limited extent, they need to make word formation patterns perceptible in order to further creative language use and to maintain the vitality of the language. Indeed, the elucidating of word formation patterns could be assisted by morphological hyphenation (cf. section 4.3.9.). However, manuals on lexicology do not exist and make this task difficult to fulfill.

A fifth problem is the neglect of the category of degree in the dictionaries of this type. Although the equative does not exist in English, the Welsh learner does not learn anything about this category if relying on the dictionaries under review.

A sixth theoretical problem is the following; *Geiriadur yr Academi*, for instance,

> "is based, with kind permission of Messrs Harrap, on the English-French half of their *Shorter English and French Dictonary* (1975 and subsequent revisions) and in the main has adopted the format and conventions of that work, with necessary adaptions. The scope of the vocabulary has been immensely increased after consulting many other standard general dictionaries, British and American, as well as many specialized works of reference" (Griffiths, B. & D.G. Jones 1995: ix).

There is no explicit reference, however, to a Welsh dictionary or grammar book, or to a dictionary of another Celtic language, that is, a language of a more similar structure.

GPC is methodologically orientated on *The Oxford English Dictionary* and *Geiriadur Almaeneg* was aligned on a preceding French-Welsh dictionary. Methodologically, such an approach is perfectly justifiable. However, one does get the impression that the selection of vocabulary in *Geiriadur yr Academi* and *Geiriadur Almaeneg* was influenced by the French dictionaries, too, and that the presentation of the Welsh language as such loses out. The inclusion of borrowings into English, which are not yet naturalised and put in italics affirm this assumption. Some examples are the following entries:

> **Béchamel** *Pr.n. Cu:* ~ sauce, ymenyn *(m)* toddi, saws *(m)*
> Béchamel
> ***bêche-de-mer*** *n* **1.** *Coel:* = **trepang. 2.** *Ling:* = beach-la-mar.
> ***force majeure*** *n.* gorfodaeth *f.*
> ***choucroute*** *n. Cu:* bresych *(pl)* picl.

In a French context these words need to occur also in the English section, but not in a Welsh context, in which the items they denote are not common or are known under a different name. In the last example the lexicographers could also have chosen the German[6] word *Sauerkraut* which is known in English, too.[7]

A similar lexical influence is apparent in the *Metalanguage*, when French explanations are included, that is the *Metalanguage* is switched. This, however, could with the same right have been done in German, as is shown in the next example:

> **know²** *v.t.* **1.** *(a) (a person): (= Fr. connaître, reconnaître):*
> adnabod, F: 'nabod [...]
> **2.** *(a fact, how to do sth*
> *&c): (= Fr. savoir): usu.* gwybod, *F:* gwybod; to be in
> surroundings one knows; bod yn eich cynefin; [...]

---

[6] The reference to German is made in order to illustrate the influence of French on the selection of lexical items in *Geiriadur yr Academi*. It does not suggest to include German lexical items instead.

[7] French is traditionally the first foreign language to be learned in Great Britain. The question is, however, whether this justifies the inclusion of French words in Welsh dictionaries (cf. also section 4.2.).

To know a person could have been explained by German 'kennen' and to know something by 'wissen'.

The question arises as to why Welsh lexicographers do not seem to take the approaches of their Celtic language colleagues into account. Guidance in pronunciation in the *IPA* is provided in Breton, Irish and Manx dictionaries (cf. section 4.4.). Lexical units consisting of more than one constituent part are well included in the macrostructure of the small Gaelic-English dictionary by Buchanan (cf. section 4.3.5.1.). For the presentation of morphological categories some advice can also be obtained by looking into other Celtic language dictionaries.

Guidance from those dictionaries is strongly recommended, since the major problem of bi-directional Welsh general-purpose dictionaries is that they not only exclude grammatical description to a large extent, but compile their entries in such a way that particularly the morphology of the Welsh language is badly affected. The morphology of the Welsh language is undermined when (a) Welsh plural nouns are listed under their singulative (cf. section 4.3.2.2.); (b) the gender- and number-coupled semantic meaning is neglected (cf. sections 4.3.2.1. and 4.3.2.2.); (c) the plural form of an adjective is separated from its base word (cf. sections 4.3.3.2. and 4.3.3.2.1.); (d) lexical items expressing different degrees of adjectives are separated from their base words (cf. section 4.3.3.3.); (e) the de-adjectival noun formation by taking a plural ending is neglected (cf. section 4.3.3.2.1.); (f) the de-nominal adjective formation by taking suffixes of comparison is ignored (cf. section 4.3.3.3.1.); (g) the word class label is not provided or the word class is not recognised (cf. sections 4.3.4., 4.3.6., and 4.3.7.); (f) the inflection of prepositions is not indicated (cf. section 4.3.5.); (g) the inflection of verbs is not sufficiently provided (cf. above).

Since morphology is not the only lingusitic domain of the language which is inadequately described, the insufficiencies listed above become more severe. The syntax is affected, when (a) the word class label is not provided accurately, particularly that of function words (cf. above); (b) function words are under-represented; (c) positionally dependent semantic variation of adjectives is not inlcuded (cf. section 3.2.3.4.). Considering that the government of lexical items is generally neglected, basic syntactic information is excluded from Welsh general-purpose dictionaries. However, if features of lexical items are not sufficiently presented in popular reference books, they may in a linguistic situation as described for Wales (cf. above and section 4.1.1.) quickly get lost, e.g. mutations and inflections (cf. also Broderick 1999: 106), that is, properties which are not features of the respective dominating language.

Another domaine of the language directly affected is the field of semantics of the lexical items, particularly their semantic range. The latter is artificially limited when (a) gender- and number coupled semantic meaning is not indicated (cf. above); (b) the word classes are not re-cognised (cf. above); (c) lexical units consisting of more than one constituent part are not included in the macrostructure; (d) 1:1 equivalences form the standard structure of the dictionary (cf. the *Works-Dictionary*); (g) definitions and collocations (semantic valency) are not presented.

A consequence of omitting lexical items because of the number of their constituent parts is the encouragement of the transfer of English for native lexical items (cf. Broderick 1999: 144).

The omission of collocations and idioms furthers the intrusion of English idiom (cf. Broderick 1999: 155). English idiom can be observed in *Geiriadur yr Academi*, for instance, when translating 'benefit of the doubt' with *mantais yr amheuaeth* or 'play an instrument' with *chwarae offeryn* rather than *canu offeryn*.

Linguistic devices, such as morphological, syntactic, semantic, and discourse structures form a culture-specific way of perceiving reality, a process which is part of the construction of identity. With such devices, members of a specific society maximise the expression of their common experiences. As a result, particularly syntactic and semantic valency as well as idioms belong to what furnishes the language with a soul which makes it lovable to the native speakers and learners and distinct to foreigners (cf. section 4.1.2.).

As a result, deficiencies in linguistic descriptions of popular reference books as mentioned above may be of minor importance when seen in isolation. However, taking the Welsh features and linguistic devices mis-presented together and considering the linguistic situation in Wales, there is a real danger that Welsh turns into a kind of pidgin or even faces language death (cf. section 4.1.1. and Broderick 1999: 163); in particular when given up by native speakers because the identity-constructing function has been hollowed out (cf. section 4.1.1.).

In view of the influence of English linguistic concepts on the description of Welsh features in general-purpose dictionaries (cf. above), it can be concluded, that the Welsh language presented in them is to a great extent robbed of some of its particular properties which define it as such and as a language belonging to the Celtic group. A continuous transformation towards the English language system is thus being fostered which may turn the language, at least, into a pidgin (cf. above and section 4.1.1.). This, however, is a tendency which is unnecessary and can more easily be stopped than the migration of English people into Wales and the dominance of English language media.

The structure and content of a Welsh dictionary should first of all be established according to the needs of the Welsh language. It is necessary to compile a Welsh general-purpose dictionary which is orientated to the Welsh language and firmly based on Welsh linguistics (cf. above). This, however, is a problem since different branches of linguistics for the Welsh language have not yet been established as a subject in its own right, e.g. lexicology (cf. section 4.3.9., Fife 1990: 8ff.). There are, nevertheless, grammar books which well reflect the particular features of Welsh, e.g. *Gramadeg y Gymraeg* by P.W. Thomas (1995). As was outlined in section 1.3.2.2.6., English lexicography has well developed after coupling grammar and lexicographical work, since a thoroughly useful dictionary ought to give full information about those grammatical constructions which characterise individual words, and cannot be deduced with certainty and ease from a simple grammatical rule. For learners some lexicographers even demand a combined dictionary and grammar book:

> "Foreign learners should be offered a dictionary/grammar that does not only explain how indidvidual words and phrases are used in meaningful wholes, but also how these words and phrases can form structurally correct strings and how particular structures and forms recur in the grammar of the language. A transparent system of codes is needed that does not only provide self-explanatory abbreviations, but that is also supported by full exemplification. Furthermore, the dictionary should have a central grammar

component that allows users to have easy access to explanations of individual grammar codes used in the dictionary. These explanations should not stop short at the end of that particular code, but should also provide the learner with additional examples of the phenomenon" (Lemmen/Wekker 1986: 12f.).

We have to realise that in grammars, rules are presented for word classes. However, particular grammatical features of individual lexical items are not easily deducable from general rules of grammar books. Consequently, they have to be included in the respective dictionary entry in a formulaic manner (cf. discussion of the *Metalanguage* above).

The only Welsh dictionary which is indeed based on a grammar book is the *Pocket Modern Welsh Dictionary* by King (2000). His reference book *Modern Welsh. A Comprehensive Grammar*, published in 1993 (cf. review by S. Heinz 1995), provided the basis for King's dictionary. Some of the phenomena described in his work are clearly reflected in his dictionary, e.g. the definition of pronouns which can be employed as possessive pronouns or as possessive adjectives (King 1993: 80f.) or the description of the verbal system. Others, unfortunately, are partly ignored or obviously failed to be described in his lexicographical work. One example is the number system of nouns. Although he writes, for instance:

> "The number system for nouns in English is a simple singular/plural opposition, of which the singular is the base form. Any noun in English can be classified into one of three sub-classes within this two-way system:
> (a) nouns that can be used in either the singular or plural (the vast majority of non-abstract things - *cat, star, radiator*)
> (b)   nouns that can normally only be used in the singular (mainly abstract ideas and 'uncountable' *things - honesty, milk*)
> (c) nouns that can only be used in the plural (often denoting things that are or have two parts - *trousers, scissors*)
>
> Welsh has mutually exclusive twin systems:
> *system 1*: singular/plural
> *system 2*: collective/unit
>
> System 1 works on much the same lines as in English, with the same three sub-classes. The difference from English is that these do not account for all nouns in Welsh, because a certain number lie outside the singular/plural system and belong instead to the collective/unit (c/u) system, which has its own rules of operation. It should, however, be pointed out that most grammar books treat Welsh c/u nouns as anomalous singular/plurals, a misleading approach which distorts the logic of the Welsh system" (King 1993: 47f.),

this c/u system is not consequently reflected in his own dictionary (cf. section 4.3.2.2.1.). King affirms that the c/u system is treated as anomalous in grammar books. Maybe, it has for that reason been ignored in the dictionaries. King's grammar, however, was published in 1993 and *Gramadeg y Gymraeg*, which takes a similar view of this special sub-category of nouns, was launched in 1996, enough time for reference books, like the *Works-Dictionary, Geiriadur yr Academi* and re-editions of other dictionaries to change the presentation of the lexical items concerned.

In short, Welsh bi-directional general-purpose dictionaries not only ignore basic Welsh grammar and partly semantics but, even worse, undermine both at times. The principle deficiencies in these reference books may be summarised as follows: (a) the absence of direct information on the government of lexical items, (b) the virtual exclusion of the morphology of Welsh verbs, (c) the inadequate presentation of the morphology of Welsh nouns, and the limited reflection of the morphology of adjectives, (d) the restricted inclusion of the morphology of prepositions, (e) the inadequate labelling of the word classes of function words, (f) the absence of phonetic transcription, (g) the ignorance of lexical items consisting of more than one constituent part, (h) the presentation of limited semantic context of lexical items, (i) a non-codified *Metalanguage* and varying structures of entries.

The uni-directional general-purpose dictionary *Geiriadur yr Academi* offers some improvement as regards: the illustration of the government of lexical items except verbs, the presentation of the morphology of adjectives, and the inclusion of the morphology of prepositions, an adequate linguistic description of features of numerals and conjunctions, as well as the provision of semantic contexts of lexical items. In addition, an extensive explanatory section introduces the grammatical basis of the dictionary.

Nevertheless, it seems that Welsh lexicographers of bi-directional general-purpose dictionaries have neither taken dictionaries of the other Celtic languages into account, nor have they firmly based the description of the lexicon included on a grammatical analyses. Some reasons and consequences of this development are discussed in the final chapter (*Conclusions*).

V.   Conclusion

At the end of the twentieth century, Welsh lexicography reached a new quality with the compilation of *Geiriadur yr Academi* (Griffiths, B. & D.G. Jones 1995, cf. section 4.2. and 4.5.). This comprehensive dictionary was the Book of the Year 1995; nearly 10,000 copies were sold during the first months following its publication. Since then it has been a lexicographical source for the production of other dictionaries, such as *Geiriadur termau archaeoleg/A dictionary of archaeological terms in English and Welsh* (cf. Williams, J.Ll. & B. Griffiths et al. 1999), as well as for the work of institutions, such as the *Centre for Standardizing Terminology* at the University of Bangor.

In addition, *Geiriadur yr Academi* was warmly welcomed by various groups and individuals, such as native speakers, learners, translators and others concerned with Welsh language matters (cf. section 1.1.). The dictionary is used for professional translating and second language teaching, for the improvement of communication skills and linguistic research, but also as a self-instructional learning aid and for personal perfection. It has thus been accepted as a general-purpose dictionary.

Indeed, it is the first Welsh general-purpose dictionary which comes near international standards and presents Welsh as a language equal to others, that is, as a language which has all the resources of any modern language to denote new social contexts. In addition, it provides linguistic information which has not been included in any Welsh general-purpose dictionary before, such as:

- usage notes covering style and register,
- alternative regional variants,
- an extensive introduction to Welsh grammar and phonology,
- extensive context for individual lexical items,
- productive Welsh word formation patterns,
- the morphology and syntax of adjectives,
- the government of pronouns,
- the inflection and government of prepositions,
- the complementation of conjunctions,
- the inflection and government of numerals.

Moreover, *Geiriadur yr Academi* furthers linguistic confidence and identity by appealing to all sectors of the country.

In view of these features, the statement at the beginning of this study about *Geiriadur yr Academi* as the first Welsh dictionary (cf. section 1.1.) appears justified.

However, *Geiriadur yr Academi* could already rely on a substantial amount of lexicographical work previously carried out in Wales. On the one hand, one should consider the extensive terminological work that has gone on in Wales in recent years (cf. section 3.2.1. and appendix), and on the other, there is the historical dictionary *Geiriadur Prifysgol Cymru* (*GPC*, 1950-, cf. sections 4.2. and 4.5.). Since it comprises sixty parts, it is not within the reach of the casual dictionary user and is only affordable for a limited number of institutions and individuals with special interest in the Welsh language.

GPC forms an essential lexicographical and linguistic source. It contains most of the information general-purpose dictionaries need to present to the casual dictionary user, though, of course, this should be given in a more formulaic and concise manner. The following Welsh linguistic properties are more adequately presented in *GPC* than in *Geiriadur yr Academi* (cf. also section 4.5.):

- verb inflection (by including the first person singluar present of the verb, occasionally also the third person singular present),
- basic syntactic valency of the verb (by word class label),
- semantic valency of the verb,
- the Welsh system of the number inflection of the noun,
- Welsh word formation patterns,
- word class definitions.

The above facts indicate that *Geiriadur yr Academi* also suffers from deficiencies. The first is that it is a uni-directional English-Welsh dictionary. As a consequence, it looks at the Welsh lexicon from the viewpoint of an English database. Indeed, from an English-language perspective it is difficult at times to include Welsh phenomena which are structurally and semantically distinct from English, or which do not exist in English, such as particles used as markers of change in word order (cf. sections 1.3.2.3.8. and 4.3.8.) or the adverbial marker *yn*. Inadequacies in Welsh grammar and semantics undermine the construction of linguistic confidence and identity (cf. below and section 4.1.2.).

In addition, another function of dictionaries, that is, the construction of cultural identity (cf. sections 1.1. and 4.1.2.), is limited when the language appears not to deserve a general-purpose description from a Welsh perspective and the existing English-Welsh section is based on the dictionary of another culture (cf. sections 4.2. and 4.5. and below).

Further deficiencies of *Geiriadur yr Academi* can predominantly be found in the field of grammar, or concern user-friendliness. The following insufficiencies are apparent:

- the indication of the verb inflection does not form a regular part of dictionary entries,
- the basic government of the verb is not guaranteed,
- the presentation of the number inflection of Welsh nouns is based on the English system,
- collocations and idioms are partly influenced by English,
- the dictionary entries present a non-codified and non-standardised *Metalanguage*,
- the access structure in dictionary entries is unclear,
- the linguistic information on the same lexical item may vary in different entries,
- the entire information of individual lexical items needs to be gathered from different places,
- French lexis and explanations may occur.

In particular, the fact that *Geiriadur yr Academi* is a uni-directional dictionary forces for the casual dictionary user to refer to bi-directional general-purpose dictionaries. In oral and ad hoc communication, the size of *Geiriadur yr Academi* is also disadvantageous. The casual dictionary user will, therefore, still make frequent use of the smaller and bi-directional general-purpose dictionaries (cf. sections 1.2. and 4.2.). These, however, remain clearly behind international standards and predominantly fail to present the properties of the Welsh language.

The best among them are *Y Geiriadur Mawr* (Evans, H.M. & W.O. Thomas 1987) and *Y Geiriadur Bach* (Evans, H.M. & W.O. Thomas 1987, cf. section 4.2. and 4.5.). They are the only dictionaries under review which provide synonyms and definitions for the headwords, as well as some phrases which partly illustrate the usage of the headwords. *Y Geiriadur Mawr* also includes some usage notes, thus serving the purposes of advanced learners and native speakers. Although they present the number inflection of Welsh nouns better than *Geiriadur yr Academi*, they do not adequately illustrate the following properties of Welsh:

- the government of any word class,
- the verb inflection (totally absent),
- the category of degree of adjectives,
- differences in word classes.

Other bi-directional general-purpose dictionaries are *Y Geiriadur Cyfoes* (H.M. Evans 1992), *Collins Spurrell Welsh-English/English-Welsh Dictionary* (Thorne, D. & A. Convery 1991, henceforth *Spurrell*), its miniature version the *Collins Gem Welsh-English/English-Welsh Dictionary* (*Gem Dictionary*, Thorne, D. & A. Convery 1992) and the *Welsh-English/English-Welsh Dictionary* (D.G. Lewis 1997, henceforth the *Works-Dictionary*; for others, see section 3.2.1.). Only *Y Geiriadur Cyfoes* includes, as do *Y Geiriadur Mawr* and *Y Geiriadur Bach*, technical terms put into miscellaneous lists (cf. section 4.2.). The others do not contain any specialist lexis.

Whereas *Y Geiriadur Cyfoes* and *Spurrell* exhibit further deficiencies, e.g. no synonyms of the headwords are provided, no inflection of prepositions (cf. sections 1.3.2.2.7. and 4.3.5.) and nearly no government for any word class is indicated, the *Works-Dictionary* has additional shortcomings, which are listed in the following:

- the headword list is very limited,
- it predominantly presents 1:1 translations,
- the semantic range of the lexical items has been limited,
- morphological features of lexical items serve as criteria for separate dictionary entries,
- no context is included which indicates or exemplifies the usage of the headwords,
- no government is provided,
- nearly no headword is listed which consists of more than one constituent part,
- the description of particles is inadequate.

1:1 translations are generally insufficient, since lexical items rarely express only one semantic meaning. In addition, various lexical items in Welsh can vary their meaning according to the position, that is, whether the words come before or after a referent (cf. adjectives in section 4.3.3.4.). Other lexical items change their meaning with the gender (cf. nouns, sections 1.3.2.3.2. and 4.3.2.1.) or number (cf. nouns in section 4.3.2.2.), or with the word class (cf. conjunctions in section 4.3.6.).

An advantage in the *Works-Dictionary* is that some selected irregular verb forms are included as separate headwords with a reference to the verbal noun and to the appendix of paradigms of irregular verbs. When, however, separating feminine, plural and comparative forms of adjectives, as well as inflected forms of prepositions from their base words, the separation of different morphological forms of lexical items undermines the morphology of the language. Since, in addition, there are no further appendices or introductory explanations, no translations, e.g. of the inflected forms of prepositions, and no references to the base word, e.g. for feminine adjective forms, such an approach reduces the communicative potential and learner-friendly acquisition of Welsh.

However, the separation of different morphological forms of lexical items is in part also a feature of general-purpose dictionaries. Only *Geiriadur yr Academi* and *GPC* present these forms together, thus supporting Welsh grammar. In short, the *Works-Dictionary* which takes morphological features more consistently than other dictionaries as criteria for separate dictionary entries presents its limited lexicon rather as a compilation of isolated lexical items, predominantly useful for native speakers who know how to use the words so long as they know of their existence.

The deficiencies of the bi-directional general-purpose dictionaries, and partly also the inadequacies of *Geiriadur yr Academi*, appear somewhat suprising when considering the dictionaries produced by lexicographers of the Celtic sister languages, in particular Breton and Irish compilations. Comparing the *Collins Gem Welsh-English/English-Welsh Dictionary* with *The Collins Gem Irish Dictionary English-Irish/Irish-English* (Mac Mathúna, S. & A. Ó Corráin 1996), it becomes clear that the deficiencies of the smaller general-purpose dictionaries are not primarily owed to conditions or restrictions imposed on the lexicographer by the publisher. The Irish *Gem Dictionary*, for instance, is twice the size of the Welsh one and describes the features of the other Celtic language much better.

Breton dictionaries notably illustrate how the number system of the Brittonic noun as well as noun derivations can be well displayed in the type of dictionaries under review (cf. sections 4.3.2.2.1. and 4.3.2.2.2.). Basic information on verb inflection is indicated in Irish and Breton dictionaries (cf. section 4.3.1.1.) as well as basic syntactic valency of the verb (cf. section 4.3.1.2.).

In addition, the comparison of adjectives is better presented in dictionaries of other Celtic languages than in Welsh bi-directional general-purpose compilations. Irish dictionaries, for example, include the class of declension of the adjectives, thus indicating the different kinds of comparison. Further, they provide full paradigms of irregular forms on a far more regular basis than Welsh dictionaries. Breton dictionaries also include adjective comparisons, although this is more regular than in Welsh (cf. sections 1.3.2.3.3. and 4.3.3.). Whenever it induces the slightest change in given lexical items, the comparison is exemplified. Even the Scottish Gaelic *The illustrated Gaelic-English Dictionary* (E. Dwelly 1994, cf. section 3.2.6.) presents irregular comparisons and offers more information on the category of degree of adjectives than Welsh dictionaries (cf. section 4.3.3.3.).

The government of Breton pronouns is also consistently provided (cf. section 4.3.4.) as well as that of prepositions. The inflection of the latter is, at least, indicated by a reference to an appendix. The government of the other word classes is also well included.

Another example is the presentation of headwords which consist of more than one constituent part, such as compound prepositions. They are comprehensively listed in the small *Gaelic-English/English-Gaelic Dictionary* (Buchanan 1998), which is very similar to the *Works-Dictionary* (cf. section 4.3.5.1.).

Generally incomprehensible is the non-inclusion of phonetic transcription for Welsh headwords in bi-directional general-purpose dictionaries. Despite dialectal variation (cf. Irish and Breton, section 4.4.) or pronunciation which may be inferred from spelling (cf. Breton), space reasons in dictionaries, or assumed mis-comprehension of the *IPA*, this phonetic transcription is even used by smaller Irish and Breton dictionaries of the type under review, such as *Geriadur brezhoneg-alamaneg hag alamaneg-brezhoneg* (Cornillet 2000), *Elementary breton-english & english-breton dictionary* (Delaporte 1995, cf. section 3.2.2.), or *Foclóir Póca* (An Roinn Oideachais 1986, cf. section 3.1.).

In short, a look at dictionaries of the other Celtic languages, in particular of Breton, would provide some guidance on how to improve Welsh dictionaries. However, the achievements of Breton lexicography are not even sufficiently taken into consideration by Welsh lexicographers when compiling Welsh-Breton or Breton-Welsh dictionaries (cf. *Geiriadur Cymraeg-Llydaweg* by Rh. Hincks 1991, *Geiriadur Bach Llydaweg-Cymraeg* by R. Williams 1985, and *Geiriadur Cymraeg-Llydaweg: Geriadur Kembraeg-Brezhoneg* by R. Williams 1990, cf. section 3.2.1.). The comparison of adjectives, for instance, is not indicated in any of them nor is phonetic transcription provided. Nevertheless some improvements are apparent, for example:

- the presentation of the number inflection of Welsh nouns,
- the inclusion of basic syntactic government of the verb,
- the inflection of irregular verbs in both dictionaries,
- the inflection of prepositions (R. Williams),
- the government of lexical items (Rh. Hincks).

Since the linguistic description in Welsh bi-directional general-purpose dictionaries has been characterised as deficient in particular in comparison with Irish and Breton dictionaries, an investigation of the corpora produced in the Celtic countries was advocated (cf. chapter III). Results of such an investigation do not really explain the development of different approaches to compiling dictionaries as mentioned above. However, they do reveal which types of dictionaries were generated in the Celtic countries, thus illustrating different or similar trends in the respective lexicographical traditions, and indicating further lexicographical gaps.

The first dictionary of a Celtic country, the trilingual *Le Catholicon amoricain* (Français, Breton, Latin) was produced in Brittany by Jehan Lagadec (1499, cf. sections 3.2.2. and 3.3.). Wales came second with *A Dictionary in Englyshe and Welshe* compiled by William Salesbury (ca. 1520-1584?, cf. sections 2.2.1.1. and 2.2.2.) and published in 1547. However, Wales comes first in the number of dictionaries produced (97) in a Celtic country, although Brittany (80) and Ireland (79) follow closely.

A general trend for dictionary production in all Celtic countries is that they (a) make use of modern computer technology, (b) recognise the need to produce dictionaries for young learners, and (c) have produced only a limited range of specialist dictionaries featuring linguistic properties of the respective languages.

The language specific situations in lexicography, however, differ strongly. Breton lexicography, for instance, has predominantly concentrated on the provision of lexis and has, in addition, comprehensively recorded lexical items of former periods of its language. In view of the number of historical, etymological and monolingual general-purpose dictionaries produced in this country, monolingual lexicography is most advanced in Brittany. There is, however, a lack of learners' dictionaries.

Irish lexicographical works cover a comparatively broad range of specialist dictionaries with regard to the lexicon included in them.

Scottish Gaelic lexicography apparently pursues a different way of presenting the Scottish Gaelic lexicon in that it concentrates on re-editing older popular dictionaries. The number of dictionaries produced, therefore, is relatively small, and current works including terminology are underrepresented. As with Breton dictionaries, there seems to be a lack of learners' tools.

With regard to some particular dictionary types produced in the Celtic countries the following conclusions can be drawn:

- Monolingual general-purpose dictionaries are available in Brittany, Ireland and Scotland, but not in Wales, Cornwall, and the Isle of Man.
- Etymological dictionaries were produced for Breton, Irish and Scottish Gaelic, but not for Welsh, Cornish, and Manx.
- Pronouncing dictionaries have only been compiled for the q-Celtic languages, thereby suggesting that the pronunciation of the p-Celtic languages is strongly phonetic (cf. section 4.4.). Nevertheless, Breton lexicographers have produced general-purpose dictionaries, which include phonetic transcription. This is also common in Irish but not in Welsh dictionaries of this type.
- Dictionaries of syllables and of clusters of consonants have been generated in Wales. Such dictionaries do not exist for the other Celtic languages except an older and incomplete *Dictionnaire des rimes* (Berthou, 1933-39) for Breton. This situation reflects a peculiarity of Welsh literary production, that is, the production of strict metre poetry, incorporating the principle of *cynghanedd* (cf. section 2.2.1.2.2.). These complex metres based on principles of regulated consonance and assonance deriving from, at least, the Middle Ages are still in popular use and productive in Wales today, thereby indicating the vitality of bardic composition in modern Wales.
- Current work on terminology is predominantly done for the Welsh, Breton and Irish languages.
- The provision of lexicographical material for translation into languages other than the dominant language of the respective Celtic country is most advanced in Breton.
- A relatively large number of learners' dictionaries has been produced in Wales, particularly in recent times. The respective Irish works are on average a few decades older. However, in both countries, the production of

learners' dictionaries reflects the status of the languages (cf. sections 3.1.
and 4.1.1.), which is much greater here than in the other Celtic countries.
– School dictionaries are best represented in Irish, thereby reflecting the
status of the Irish language as the first official language of the country
and Irish as a core subject in Irish schools.

In short, although Wales has produced the highest number of dictionaries of any Celtic country, it has, unlike most of the others, not generated etymological and pronouncing dictionaries for the vernacular. It has no current monolingual general-purpose compilations either. However, learners' dictionaries are well developed, although there is only one current school dictionary. In addition, Wales is the only Celtic country which has generated dictionaries of syllables, clusters and synonyms. The pronunciation of the Welsh language is not adequately included in any of the existing dictionaries.

There are three other important conclusions which can be drawn from this investigation: First, the number of dictionaries produced in the individual Celtic regions seems roughly to correspond with the number of the speakers there. This is on the one hand somewhat surprising, since the range of lexicon needed in order to communicate in life is not dependent on the number of speakers. On the other hand, the correspondence of the number of dictionaries with the numbers of speakers gives apparently an idea of the actual status of the Celtic communities in their countries. Indeed, the second conlusion which can be drawn from the study of the corpora of Celtic dictionaries is that the production of dictionaries reflects the actual status and prestige of the respective language rather than official language policy. However, economic aspects also play a part in the correlation of dictionary production with the number of speakers (cf. section 4.1.1.).

Third, lexicographical production in Celtic regions has always increased when the languages were in decline. In Wales, for instance, the decline of the *Bardic Order* during the Renaissance and the rise of the humanists marked (a) an increase in lexicographical production and (b) a change of emphasis in lexicographical work away from monolingual vocabularies to bilingual dictionaries (cf. sections 2.2.1.1. and 2.2.3.). In particular after the publication of Dr John Davies', (also Siôn Dafydd, Mallwyd 1627-93, cf. sections 2.2.1.1. and 2.2.2.) *Antiquae Linguae Britannicae Dictionarium Duplex* in 1632, dictionary production in Wales became more continuous.

However, the first substantial general increase in the number of dictionaries produced in the Celtic countries occurred in the Romantic period when the languages were in decline (cf. also section 2.4.) and Cornish already declared dead (cf. sections 2.2.3. and 3.2.3.). In addition, the question of the language was now related to that of the nation, thereby turning the language into a political issue (cf. sections 2.4. and 2.5.).

Apart from Cornwall and the Isle of Man, a more intensive lexicographical production was noticable after the Second World War (cf. chapter III) when the Celtic languages were in an even weaker position. This is also true for Ireland, although Irish was granted the status of the first official language in 1937 (cf. section 3.1.). This new situation contributed to the rise in dictionary production, too, because of the subsequent demand of inventing new lexical items in order to cover communicational needs according to social developments.

In Wales the struggle for the language helped to establish a network of institutions working in its support (cf. section 4.1.1.). As a result the status of the language gradually improved. The *Welsh Language Act* of 1993 stated for the first time that Welsh and English were to be given equal status in the conduct of public business and administration of justice in Wales. However, despite increasing numbers of Welsh speakers, the language is in severe decline (cf. section 4.1.1. and below). Consequently, since 1997, the year of the successful referendum for a Welsh Assembly, the question of the language has again been related to that of the nation (cf. sections 4.1.1. and 2.5.). These developments instigated a third major increase of lexicographical activities in the nineties.

In search of reasons for insufficiencies in Welsh dictionaries as mentioned above, a look at the history of Welsh lexicography was also suggested.

An early and firm lexicographical basis developed in Wales from the habit of glossing and explaining difficult passages from the Bible and other religious and non-religious texts, while at the same time teaching languages and related subjects (cf. sections 2.1.-2.1.4.). The specific pre-conditions for dictionary production developed in Wales during the Renaissance, when education was no longer restricted to elitist groups, but was accepted as part of profound and comprehensive education for larger groups of people. Further social conditions were established by new scientific, economic and technical achievements, which laid the foundations for extensive book production, and by a new stage of intellectual and cultural exchange (cf. section 2.2.1.1.).

The new quality of dictionaries, in contrast to glossaries and vocabularies, can be characterised by the following features (cf. section 2.2.3. and below):

- they developed from being mainly supplementary tools into basic teaching aids (cf. in particular Thomas Jones), into tools for translation (cf. Thomas Jones) and, in addition, into compendia of the language to describe and to handle knowledge (cf. Thomas Wiliems, Dr John Davies, Henry Salesbury);
- dictionaries contained as many lexical items as were considered necessary to meet the needs of contemporary communication (cf. Thomas Wiliems, Dr John Davies, Henry Salesbury, Thomas Jones);
- they regularly included additional linguistic information, particularly about grammar, semantics, phonetics, stylistics, and/or (pseudo-)etymology in order to (a) display knowledge (cf. Dr John Davies), (b) enrich the language of the dictionary users (cf. Thomas Jones), (c) make the meaning of lexical items explicit, or (d) guide correctness in spelling (Thomas Jones) and pronunciation (cf. William Salesbury);
- they were aimed at a particular audience (cf. William Salesbury, Thomas Jones) and produced on the basis of concepts which were acquired by studying preceding dictionaries or other lexicographical material (cf. William Salesbury, Thomas Wiliems, Dr John Davies, Thomas Jones);
- they were intended to increase the prestige of the vernacular language and to develop it;
- in the case of languages of limited social influence, such as Welsh, they

were produced to maintain and purify, and thereby stabilise them (cf. Thomas Jones).

The earliest lexicographical works in Western Europe were predominantly compilations which presented the vernacular language together with the important or dominant language that was to be understood, that is, the first dictionaries were mainly bilingual and displayed the vernacular language first and then Latin. As is illustrated in the following, this was different in Wales (and also in Ireland):

- Monolingual lexicographical works dominated here first. Apart from a Latin-Welsh herbal list from the fourteenth century, they are attested for Wales at least from the fifteenth century (cf. sections 2.1.4. and 2.2.1.2.2.), that is, earlier than in England.
- Monolingual compilations, e.g. the vocabulary of Gruffudd Hiraethog (cf. section 2.2.1.2.2.), demonstrate an interest in mastering and developing the vernacular language at an early date in history. They were mainly compiled by bards, that is, by the feudal elite oriented towards literary scholarship. This phenomenon can also be observed in Ireland. The first dictionary produced in this country was the monolingual Irish dictionary *Foclóir no Sanasan Nua* published in 1643 by Mícheál Ó Cléirigh (cf. section 3.2.4.)
- In Wales, the change of emphasis in lexicographical work away from monolingual vocabularies to bilingual dictionaries during the Renaissance was introduced by a Welsh-English dictionary, thereby reflecting new political constellations in society.
- From then on a kind of labour division emerged, whereby the scholars predominantly dealt with bilingual and the bards with monolingual material useful for literary training and composition.

When dictionaries became popular Europe-wide and the first methods of compiling were established, the Welsh joined in with their own fund of knowledge, although somewhat delayed. When Welsh dictionary production began, the compilation of English dictionaries had already been flourishing for more than a century (cf. section 2.2.1.1.). Although the Welsh succeeded in keeping up with basic trends in European linguistics, they fell behind in the field of specialist lexicography. In addition, shortcomings in the description of the Welsh language became apparent as early as at that time.

Some of the reasons for this development can be found in Welsh history. Events in the wake of the incorporation of Wales into England after the *Acts of Union* in 1536/42 (cf. section 2.2.1.1.) caused more retardation for the development of Welsh society than inspiration for it (cf. section 2.2.1.1. and 2.2.3.). Since then Welsh lexicographers predominatly belonged to a region of minor social status within England, the people of which did not deserve to participate in all the achievements of the English mother country, but whose native developments had been dislocated. That intellectual potential was oppressed, is evidenced by the fact that the printing press was established in Wales as late as 1718, that is, after a delay of 242 years (cf. section 2.2.1.1.). University institutions were not founded before the Romantic period, that is, St. David's College

Llanbedr Pont Steffan in 1827, Aberystwyth College in 1872, Cardiff University in 1883, and Bangor University in 1884.

In addition, Welsh lexicographers described a language of limited social influence (cf. sections 1.1. and 4.1.1.). In such a social and linguistic situation economic and intellectual resources would of necessity be limited, and products generated under such circumstances liable to exhibit deficiencies. Some of the achievements in, and shortcomings of, early dictionary production are illustrated in the following:

The first Welsh dictionary, compiled by William Salesbury (cf. above and section 2.2.2.), provided synonyms as well as word families of headwords and word class labels on an irregular basis. However, it still displayed some features of a vocabulary. In addition, W. Salesbury left headwords untranslated and presented a very limited lexicon. He also hyphenated Welsh digraphs, monosyllabic words and diphthongs and displayed a varying *Metalanguage*. In his time, however, dictionary production was still in its infancy and different theories on orthography influenced spelling as well as the need to vary the writing of individual words for poetical reasons (cf. T. Jones 1688: 7).

Major improvements in information on word classes and the alphabetical arrangement of headwords were apparent in Thomas Wiliems' (1545/46-1622) dictionary *Thesaurus Linguæ Latinæ et Cambrobritannicæ siue Latinæ Linguæ et Britannicæ Veræ, Dictionarum Locupletissimum.* This, however, was never printed.

One of the most influential dictionaries was compiled by Dr John Davies, Mallwyd (cf. above and sections 2.2.2., 2.3., and 2.5.). Just as W. Salesbury had done, he included synonyms on an irregular basis. In addition, he defined meanings by Greek, Hebrew, and Breton equivalents and provided context for the usage of headwords on an irregular basis, thereby also illustrating mutations. In his headword list, arranged in second-letter order, Dr J. Davies included lexical items consisting of more than one constiutent part as well as mutated words. Moreover, he made use of cross-references to indicate orthographical and grammatical variation. Apart from including the plural, Dr J. Davies also commented on pronunciation where it strongly deviated from the written forms and provided a number of pseudo-etymologies. The *Metalanguage* used in his book was Latin. All in all, the achievements in the description of the Welsh language in his dictionary may perhaps be compared with those presented in *GPC* today (cf. above and sections 4.2. and 4.5.).

Henry Salesbury's (1561-1637?) dictionary *Geiria Tavod Comroig hoc est Vocabvlarivm Lingvæ Gomeritanæ*, compiled before the publication of Dr J. Davies' *Dictionarium Duplex*, displayed alphabetical order according to pronunciation and a thematically wide range of lexical items. He provided synonyms on an irregular basis and invented new lexical items. By making frequent use of derivations, for instance, by employing the prefix *ar-*, he also elucidated word formation patterns. A further achievement is that he included nouns in the headword list the stem of which has plural meaning, that is, he correctly displayed the number inflection of Welsh nouns.

The work of John Jones (1585-1657/58, cf. section 2.2.2.) remained unfinished and in manuscript form. However, he displayed morphological features and word formation patterns by including several plural forms of nouns and presenting diminutive derivations in the headword list.

He used both Latin and Welsh as *Metalanguages* and indicated the word class of each headword. Whereas the aforementioned lexicographers gradually presented the properties of Welsh to quite a considerable degree, a sudden reduction of the linguistic description can be noted in Thomas Jones' (1648-1713, cf. section 2.2.2.) dictionary *Y Gymraeg yn ei disgleirdeb, neu helaeth eirlyfr Cymraeg a Saesnaeg Yn Cynwys yr holl eiriau yng Eirlyfr Dr Davies*, published in 1688. He also provided synonyms of the headwords and offered a broad lexical basis including Breton words. However, he cut the grammatical description of Welsh lexical items back to the level of the most rudimentary information as provided by W. Salesbury (cf. above and section 2.2.2.). He even neglected the plural of nouns.

Major reasons for the neglect of the achievements in the description of properties of Welsh in his dictionary may perhaps be explained by reference to (a) the purpose of his book and (b) his educational background. The purpose of his book was primarily to contribute to the maintenance and the purification of the language and to provide a broad lexical basis for poets. Since he was neither copyist, genealogist, trained academic, cleric or bard as the other lexicographers were, and, therefore, not linguistically trained, he may deliberately have ignored Dr J. Davies' linguistic information. He perhaps did not feel the need to display his knowledge or take notice of works in manuscript, but was more keen on producing "inexpensive adequately printed reading matter for the common man" and to supply cheap Welsh-language books of good technical quality" (cf. section 2.2.2.).

To briefly turn to English dictionaries, it may be noted that their lexicon was being displayed in alphabetical order as early as the Renaissance period; that is, at a time when it was not yet international common practice (cf. section 2.2.3.). In addition, they indicated pronunciation by diacritical signs, exemplified contexts, presented idiomatic expressions, definitions of words, basic etymological explanations, grammatical classification, and elementary usage notes covering style and register.

Early Welsh dictionaries taken as a whole provided synonyms (cf. W. Salesbury, T. Wiliems, Dr J. Davies, J. Jones, T. Jones), exemplified lexical items in context, presented definitions of a number of words and to a varying degree lexical variation, introduced basic morphological categories to different degrees (cf. Dr J. Davies, H. Salesbury, J. Jones), and to a limited extent pseudo-etymological explanations (cf. Dr J. Davies). Appendices explaining rhetoric or artistic composition could also be found.

However, there were no indications of pronunciation by diacritical signs, although some Welsh scholars, including W. Salesbury (cf. section 2.2.2.), were familiar with phonetic descriptions (cf. Siôn Dafydd Rhys, 1534?-1621?, in section 2.2.1.2.1.). In addition, some of the achievements in the description of the Welsh lexicon subsequently vanished or were not further developed. In short, Welsh scholars did not reproduce European linguistic trends in the same complexity, quantity or of a comparatively high standard for their own language, thus generating a situation from which Wales has never fully recovered.

Alphabetical word order, for instance, first appeared in Welsh lexicographical works when they were modelled on Latin compilations, e.g. in the work of T. Wiliems (cf. above), that is, as early as the Renaissance period. However, up to the Romantic period, Welsh lexicographers predominantly arranged their lexicon in the second-letter order.

In addition, the comprehensive work of the Welsh lexicographers of the Renaissance had laid the foundation for specialisation in lexicography, which had developed in England in the sixteenth century (cf. section 2.2.3.). However, specialist Welsh dictionaries were another late development, appearing as late as the Romantic period, that is, in the nineteenth century (cf. section 2.4.), to be precise.

Apart from William Owen Pughe's (1759-1835) dictionary *Geiriadur Cynmraeg a Saesoneg: A Welsh and English Dictionary ... to which is prefixed a Welsh Grammar*, published between 1793 and 1803, which dominated the first half of the nineteenth century and remained important in its second half (cf. chapter III, cf. section 2.4.), monolingual dictionaries became popular in the Romantic period. The first was *Cyneirlyfr: neu eiriadur Cymraeg*, compiled by Edward Williams (1747-1826, cf. Iolo Morganwg in section 2.4.) and published in 1826. Two other Welsh-Welsh dictionaries followed.

Whereas pronunciation in English language dictionaries was indicated systematically from the seventeenth century, the first pronouncing dictionary in Wales *An English-Welsh pronouncing dictionary: Geiriadur cynaniaethol Seisoneg a Chymraeg* (sic) was published by William Spurrell (1813-1889) in 1850. Two others followed (cf. section 4.4.). However, they all provided the pronunciation of the English lexical items, thereby first of all promoting the acquisition of English (cf. section 2.3.).

Another type of dictionary was introduced by Robert Ellis (Cynddelw, 1812-1875, cf. section 2.4.) and Edward Williams with *Geiriadur y bardd : neu yr odlydd cyffredinol, at wasanaeth y beirdd, yn yr hwn y trenir y geiriau yn ol eu hodlau* in 1874. This rhyming dictionary, which helped the bards compose poetry in the traditional metres, was only produced a decade later than the first English dictionary of this kind. Relatively late, in 1892, *Cyfystyron y Gymraeg*, a dictionary of synonyms, was published by Griffith Jones (1836-1906).

In the context of growing specialisation in lexicography, a new function was attributed to Welsh vocabularies. After the first Welsh-Welsh dictionary had been published in 1826, the function of the vocabularies to provide monolingual material had ceased. Now, they became predominantly bilingual lexicographical works mainly restricted to special subjects and reduced in the grammatical description of their lexical items, quite similar to their function today (cf. section 1.3.2.1.1.).

In addition, from as early as the Classical period onwards, bardic literature no longer constituted the main lexical basis for the compilation of lexicographical works. Instead, other dictionaries and field work supplied lexical material. The Classical period is also the time in which firm etymological considerations became part of Welsh lexicography, included in the *Archaeologia Britannica* which was published by the enlightened scientist Edward Lhuyd (1660?-1709) in 1707. However, apart from Thomas Richards' (1710-1790) *Antiquæ linguæ Britannicæ thesaurus* (cf. chapter III) published in 1753, English-Welsh dictionaries dominated in this period. The four dictionaries of this type (cf. chapter III) produced in this period indicated the weak status of the Welsh language (cf. section 2.3.). William Evans (fl. 1768-1776) was the first Welsh lexicographer to make an attempt to indicate English pronunciation by diacritical signs and occasionally also by the spelling in his English-Welsh dictionary, published in 1771 (cf. sections 2.3. and 3.2.1.).

In short, the works of the lexicographers of the eighteenth and nineteenth centuries filled a number of gaps in Welsh lexicography. However, the range of specialisation reached altogether remained restricted. In addition, although Celtic linguistics had further advanced, its achievements were not comprehensively reproduced for the linguistic description of Welsh lexical items in dictionaries.

In view of the facts presented in the preceding paragraphs, it is apparent that gaps in the generated types of dictionaries and in the number of produced books may predominantly be explained by the limited resources of an incorporated country and social needs imposed on it. However, inadequacies in the linguistic description of the lexical items in dictionaries are also due to the theoretical concepts of the lexicographers. In view of an entirely insufficient promotion of the Welsh language by official institutions up to the nineteenth century (cf. above), most Welsh scholars were highly dependent on the education and research facilities English universities offered them. An orientation towards the achievements of English-language descriptions and the neglect of the properties of Welsh are, consequently, not surprising.

The first traces of an orientation on the English language can be found in the dictionary of W. Salesbury (cf. above and section 2.2.2.). He introduced a large number of English loanwords in order to facilitate the acquisition of English. In addition, he made frequent use of the suffix *-io* in order to cymricise English verbs. This word formation pattern remains productive up to the present day.

Although lexicographers after W. Salesbury, in particular Dr J. Davies, H. Salesbury, T. Jones, and W.O. Pughe, made serious attempts to strengthen the Welsh lexicon, the method of giving English preference or of facilitating language acquisition has since been employed (cf. below and section 4.1.1.).

The method of using diacritical signs was introduced in Welsh lexicography in the Classical and Romantic periods, but only for English lexical items. The description of Welsh in this field was neglected.

Despite further linguistic descriptions of Welsh, in particular in later works, such as by Syr John Morris-Jones (1894-1929, see first of all his publications from 1890, 1913, 1922, 1931 in section 6.2.2.1.), as well as in modern reference books, such as by Stephen Joseph Williams and Peter Wyn Thomas (cf. section 6.2.2.1.), and in the historical dictionary *GPC* (cf. above), an orientation towards English-language descriptions in some areas of Welsh is still apparent in this language's lexicography.

One feature which reflects English influence in all Welsh general-purpose dictionaries is the classification of nouns and verbs. Their presentation reveals a description which ignores genuine properties of the Welsh language, such as the complementation of the Welsh verb (cf. section 1.3.2.3.1.) and the number inflection of nouns with stems which have plural meaning (cf. above and sections 4.3.1. and 4.3.2.2.).

A second theoretical problem is the neglect of Welsh word formation patterns in bi-directional general-purpose dictionaries, for instance, of de-adjectival nouns and de-nominal adjectives. Particularly the derivation of adjectives by adding affixes of adjective comparison to nouns is not known to English.

A third problem is the neglect of the category of degree in the dictionaries of this type. Although the equative does not exist in English (cf. section 1.3.2.3.3.), the learner of Welsh does not learn anything about this category if relying on the dictionaries under review.

Influence of English-language description may also be the reason for differing word class definitions. In particular with numerals the English classification seems to dominate the concepts of the lexicographers of, at least, *Y Geiriadur Cyfoes*, *Spurrell*, and *Gem* when defining them as adjectives. In English, numerals form a word class on the basis of mainly lexical features. Syntactically, the individual members of this word class act as nouns, adjectives, pronouns, or adverbs and would consequently be dealt with under the respective word classes. In Welsh, however, numerals can be defined on the basis of semantic, morphological, and syntactic properties as has been the case in this investigation: Welsh numerals comprise cardinals, ordinals, fractions, and some quantifiers. They exhibit traces of gender inflection and to a greater extent number inflection. In addition, they regularly require complementation which is different from that of nouns, pronouns, and adjectives. Moreover, Welsh numerals predominantly precede their referent (cf. sections 1.3.2.2.7., 1.3.2.3.7., and 4.3.7.).

A fifth reflex of English influence is the alphabetical order presented in *CysGair*. By ignoring the Welsh alphabet indications of how to pronounce Welsh lexical items are lost (cf. section 4.4.).

A sixth theoretical problem is the use of non-Welsh data-bases for dictionaries, e.g. for *Geiriadur yr Academi* (cf. above and sections 4.2. and 4.5.). There is no explicit reference to a Welsh dictionary or grammar book, or to a dictionary of another Celtic language, that is, a language of a more similar structure, which may have provided conceptual ideas for the compilation of this dictionary. Only the English-French half of the *Shorter English and French Dictonary* (cf. section 4.2. and 4.5.) and "many other standard general dictionaries, British and American, as well as many specialized works of reference" (Griffiths, B. & D,G. Jones 1995: ix) are specifically mentioned.

However, if linguistic devices, such as morphological, syntactic, semantic and discourse structures become too strongly adapted to the structure of another language, they lose the force of their culture-specific way of perceiving reality, a process which is part of the construction of identity (cf. section 4.1.2.).

I hope to have demonstrated that achievements of, and shortcomings in, Welsh lexicography heavily depend on, at least, the following factors:

- the social status of the country,
- the social status of the language,
- the achievements of the general description of the language,
- the linguistic training of the lexicographers,
- the chosen concepts of linguistic descriptions, and
- the purpose of the dictionaries.

By the end of the twentieth century, the official status of the language and the social status of the country had improved (cf. above), as well as the description of the language. However, the indication of the pronunciation of lexical items in <u>bi-directional general-purpose</u> dictionaries has not much improved (cf. Dr J. Davies, Mallwyd), although Welsh dialects are well described by the *IPA* and *The Welsh Learner's Dictionary* (H. Gruffudd 1998) includes imitated pronunciation. The number inflection of Welsh nouns, first correctly presented by H. Salesbury (cf. above), is predominantly still presented according to the English system (cf. above). Headwords consisting of more than one constituent part are still insufficiently included in the headword lists (cf. Dr J. Davies). The government of lexical items in form of the mutations is nearly totally excluded from the dictionaries under review except indirect information provided by *Y Geiriadur Mawr* and *Y Geiriadur Bach* (cf. above); a method already employed by Dr J. Davies (cf. above; his method of including mutated words in the headword list has been employed in the dictionaries of Edwin C. Lewis 1992, 2001, cf. section 3.2.1.). In addition, the need for support for word formation patterns is something the lexicographers of the Renaissance realised, but which is still insufficiently presented in bi-directional general-purpose dictionaries. Referring back to the shortcomings of dictionaries of this type, as illustrated at the beginning of this chapter, support for the morphology of Welsh lexical items remains generally deficient (cf. above and section 4.3.3. and 4.3.5.), in particular that of the adjectives (cf. in contrast *GPC* and *Geiriadur yr Academi* as well as section 1.3.2.2.7.). Also necessary is the indication of verb inflection and the inclusion of syntactic and semantic valency of the verb in all Welsh general-purpose dictionaries, at least, to an extent as done in *GPC* (cf. sections 1.3.2.2.7. and 4.3.1.). In addition, it is of no help for the prestige of the language when its use is deliberately restricted. This is the case when suggesting not to hyphenate (cf. section 4.3.9.), when explaining why phonetic description is not necessary (cf. section 4.4.), when English-to-Welsh sections in dictionaries are more precise than the Welsh-to-English sections (cf. for example section 4.3.2.2.), or when a full range of dictionaries is not provided.

In view of the aforementioned facts it becomes apparent that a major knowledge of Welsh linguistics is available which could eliminate the insufficiencies in the type of dictionaries under review. Three major measures need to be taken to fully succeed in this task: first, the reduction of English-language description. The investigation has demonstrated that Welsh dictionaries gain quality as soon as a language other than English forms the target language. This becomes apparent when studying the works of T. Wiliems, Dr J. Davies Mallwyd (cf. section 2.2.2.), W. Evans, or the modern Welsh-Breton dictionaries (cf. above), and the German-Welsh *Geiriadur Almaeneg-Cymraeg/Cymraeg-Almaeneg* (Greller et al. 1999).

Second, Welsh lexicography needs to fully reproduce the achievements of research done in Welsh linguistics, such as in the phonetic description of dialects or the linguistic description of Welsh as illustrated in *GPC*.

Third, the description of Welsh lexical items needs to be based on a grammar which adequately describes the properties of the Welsh language. English dictionaries, for instance, improved considerably after being based on grammars; a method employed since 1942 (cf. section 1.3.2.2.6.). In a similar way the description of Welsh lexical items used to improve when Welsh grammarians

488

produced lexicographical works. This tendency becomes apparent when looking at the works of the bards Gruffudd Hiraethog and Simwnt Fychan (cf. sections 2.2.1.2.1. and 2.2.1.2.2.), the humanists Dr J. Davies and H. Salesbury (cf. section 2.2.2.), the enlightened scholars Siôn Rhydderch (1673-1735, cf. section 3.2.1.), and E. Lhuyd (cf. section 2.3.), or when investigating the compilations of William Gambold (1672-1728), John Walters (1721-1797), Thomas Richard (1710-1790), and W.O. Pughe (1759-1835), or in the twentieth century of Gareth King, i.e. the learners' *Pocket Modern Welsh Dictionary* (2000, cf. sections 4.2. and 4.5.). In this context, the insufficiencies of *Spurrell* and the *Works-Dictionary* (cf. above) are difficult to understand, since the compilers of both works have a long record in linguistic research in Welsh (cf. section 6.2.2.1.).

In short, a focus on the achievements of Welsh linguistics and the description of the properties of the Welsh language is highly recommended. If searching for external inspiration in order to improve the description of Welsh, a look at languages which display more inflection than English is advocated. In addition, it must be borne in mind that English is a dominant language in the world. Therefore, its acquisition is supported world-wide and furthered by trade, tourism and mass media. This is not the case with languages of limited social influence, such as Welsh. In order to master lesser used languages (cf. section 1.1.), an equivalent or greater extent of detailed grammatical information in dictionaries (and other reference books and in teaching material) is required.

Indeed, inspired by German a classification of Welsh verbs and nouns has been elaborated for this investigation. As a result, a basic categorisation of verbs on the basis of their obligatory complements is proposed. This is intended to help the presentation of their complementation in dictionaries. A categorisation of Welsh verbs based on their syntactic complementation may be presented as follows:

(a) intransitive verbs, which take no complement, e.g. *marw* 'to die',
(b) transitive verbs, which take a direct object, e.g. *adnabod* 'to know',
(c) prepositional verbs, which take prepositions as connectors to the complements, e.g. *mynd at* 'to go to somebody', *dal i* 'to keep',
(d) verbs 'to be complemented', which take *yn* as a connector; after taking *yn* they can be complemented in accordance with their base verb,
(e) verbs which take adverbials, e.g. *dodi yma* 'to place here',
(f) verbs which take verbs as a complement, e.g. *ymarfer nofio* 'to practise swimming',
(g) reflexive verbs, e.g. *ymolchi* 'to wash oneself'.

Apart from a syntactic categorisation, semantic subgroups of verbs have also been elaborated in this investigation (cf. 1.3.2.3.1.):

(a) idiomatic verbs, e.g. *bod am* 'to want',
(b) collocations based on verbs, e.g. *clywed arogl* 'to smell',
(c) idioms based on verbs, e.g. *canu ar ei fwyd ei hun* 'not behoven to any benefactor'.

The descriptive need for nouns in entries of general-purpose dictionaries may be served quite effectively by a categorisation of nouns which places emphasis on the morphology of the number category, as suggested in the following:

(a)   Nouns which exhibit plural inflection following the basic <u>singular-plural opposition</u>. They form the major part of the nouns, e.g. *drws - drysau* 'door', *byddin - byddinoedd* 'army'.

(b)   Nouns the stem of which has plural meaning. They are called <u>collective nouns</u>. Such nouns predominantly denote a group or a complex of realities and use singular inflection only when single individuals or realities have to be described, e.g. *mefus - mefusen* 'strawberry', *moch - mochyn* 'pig'; that is, they form singulatives. They tend to occur in special semantic fields, such as denotations for living things, creatures and weather phenomena.

Some of them can exhibit additional plural inflection, e.g. *coed* (ncoll) - *coeden* (nf) - *coedydd* (npl), thereby indicating different species or kinds of the denoted living things, creatures, or phenomena.

(c)   A limited number of nouns has no plural form, thus being called <u>singularia tantum</u>. They mostly denote abstracta, but also plants and other realities. They cannot be immediately combined with numerals and need a partitive, as in *llawer o fara* 'much bread'.

(d)   A limited number of nouns has no singular form, thus being called <u>pluralia tantum</u>. Only if they do not refer to a particular group they can be counted, otherwise they need a partitive, e.g. *llawer o wartheg* 'a lot of cattle'.

Further improvements of Welsh bi-directional general-purpose dictionaries may be achieved when the first and third person singular present of the verb form part of dictionary entries. Word formation patterns could be elucidated by including derivations and compound words in the entry of the headword (cf. sections 4.3.2.2.2., 4.3.3.2.1., and 4.3.3.3.1.). Since dictionaries are those reference books which present the lexicon of a language, but always to a limited extent, they need to make word formation patterns perceptible in order to further creative language use and to maintain the vitality of the language. Indeed, the elucidation of word formation patterns could be assisted by morphological hyphenation (cf. section 4.3.9.).

The inclusion of phonetic transcription is also highly recommended, since the pronunciation of Welsh lexical items may be unpredictable for both learners and native speakers. Apart from dialectal variation which may interfere with the rules of pronunciation, there is interference from English because of the English-speaking background of the vast majority of Welsh language learners, or new vocabulary unknown also to the native speaker. In addition, in a linguistic situation in which Welsh can often no longer be heard sufficiently to maintain and improve individual and general levels of communicative competence through daily usage and in which the Welsh language as heard in the media is deficient in quality and insufficient in quantity (cf. below and section 4.1.1.) phonetic transcription is generally a safe guide for native speakers and learners (cf. section 4.4.).

If possible, most of the linguistic information should be contained in the dictionary entry of the headword and predominantly be illustrated by formulaic direct information, i.e. abbreviations and codes (cf. section 1.3.2.2.6.). Although a full inventory of grammatical information should be given, this should not depend on highly abstract theories. A recognisable link to some commonly used comprehensive grammatical system is advocated (cf. sections 1.3.2.2.3. and 1.3.2.2.6.). Long explanatory sections are also of little help for immediate guidance on the usage of lexical items, since (a) they contain too much specific linguistic information to remember when necessary and (b) the dictionary user needs to carry out a totally new search procedure in order to find the relevant rules or explanations.

Considering Welsh lexicography as a whole, further measures should be taken to ensure that the dictionaries can altogether fulfill their functions as

- instructional,
- translational and
- research tools, but also as
- devices for language maintenance and
- the construction of cultural identity.

As stated previously, the range of dictionaries produced in Wales is limited. One of the types of dictionaries which has not yet been generated is a Standard Welsh-Welsh dictionary (cf. above and section 3.3.). Such a compilation is, first of all, intended for native speakers. It is the vehicle of their culture, since both its content and its organisation are strongly indicative of the values, judgements, and priorities of the society in which the dictionary is compiled (cf. section 4.1.2.2.). As a consequence, dictionaries of this kind contribute considerably to the construction of identity. In addition, the description of lexical items in the vernacular enhances the overall feeling of linguistic confidence (cf. section 4.1.2.3.).

Although other types of dictionaries are also desirable (cf. above and section 3.3.), a Welsh-English supplement to *Geiriadur yr Academi* seems to be most essential. Such a dictionary could include phonetic transcription (cf. above and section 4.4.) and would present all Welsh particles (cf. section 4.3.8.). In addition, it would already cater to some extent for the native speaker, thereby partly compensating the lack of a Standard Welsh-Welsh dictionary (cf. sections 3.3. and 4.1.1.).

Only if the situation in Welsh lexicography is going to be considerably improved, may it indeed contribute sufficiently to language acquisition, research, language maintenance and the construction of cultural identity. However, in view of current insufficiencies in popular reference books it may instead induce further pidginisation (cf. section 4.1.1.). This becomes apparent when considering the communicative situation in Wales, which can be briefly characterised as follows: Because of ongoing immigration into Wales, a linguistic situation has developed here in which Welsh can often no longer be heard sufficiently to maintain and improve individual and general levels of communicative competence through daily usage, a fact also important for native speakers. Consequently, even in areas with a higher percentage of Welsh speakers, school-based language acquisition has become the principle means of transmission of Welsh to the younger generation, that is, the school has to a large extent to compensate for the lack of home-based transmission. In addition, the fact that an increasing number of people learning Welsh comes from relatively anglicised backgrounds means that the language must be learnt formally and in a somewhat clinical environment, either in the nursery school, in Welsh- or English-medium education, or in courses for Welsh for adults.

Welsh in English-medium education has second-language status. As a consequence, Welsh has to be acquired here like a foreign language in other countries, that is, ideally with the help of manuals and dictionaries as the main instructional tools. In Wales, however, where manuals for second-language Welsh learners have not been in existence for the last few years (cf. section 4.1.1.), the reference books teachers and pupils have to rely on are older or self-introductory manuals, grammars and dictionaries available on the market and chosen rather individually.

In addition, a number of the teaching material for Welsh still suffers from the invention of *Cymraeg Byw* 'Living Welsh'. This was introduced in 1964 in order to simplify Welsh for second-language learners. The intention was to regulate the language and avoid any difficulties, an attitude which immediately lowered its prestige. Although *Cymraeg Byw* was intended as an oral standard for the whole of Wales, it was gradually also adopted as a medium for writing by Welsh native speakers (prescriptive power of language material, Knowles 1995: 321). Some of the results of its introduction were the enforced use of periphrastic constructions and a simplification of inflected verb forms, thereby reducing the morphology of the Welsh verb (cf. section 4.1.1.).

In addition, since the introduction of *Cymraeg Byw* it has often been argued that there is no standard for the Welsh language, and complicated explanations have been introduced in order to explain current registers of Welsh. As a result, the confusion on the part of Welsh speakers with regard to the choice of forms of the language increased, a phenomenon called 'linguistic in-security'. At this point, learners often give up using the language.

Moreover, *Cymraeg Byw* was felt by many Welsh speakers to be highly artificial. The kind of Welsh now produced also discourages native Welsh and, at times, tends to make them give up using their language. In the case of *Cymraeg Byw* the status of a construct with reduced mor-phology, idiom, and stylistic range was promoted instead of that of a living register of Welsh with full morphology, idiom, and stylistic range.

However, if the language is likely to be given up by its learners and native speakers, that is, all its potential users, it is in severe decline. Indeed, the predominant use of a reduced or anglicised morphology (cf. for example nouns, verbs, adjectives), the presentation of a reduced syntax (cf. for instance the government of words, particles), and the preference of an anglicised idiom (cf. verbs, one-word headwords, word formation) are elements of language death rather than language change (cf. section 4.1.1.). Investigating the decline of other languages, research has shown that, first,

> "[i]f a rule is optional with the older generation which has a full and varied command of a still vigorous language system, it is lost in the disintegrating language of a younger generation" (Dressler 1972: 425)

and, second, "[w]hen a language surrenders itself to foreign idiom [...] the penalty is death" (T.F. O'Rahilly 1988: 121). The reasons for such developments are clear; morphology and syntax form the structure of the language, that is, its skeleton. Collocations and idioms add lin-guistically to the unique component parts which make up the conception of the language, thereby arousing particular feelings and associations among its speakers. They are part of what furnishes the language with a soul which makes it cherished by native speakers and learners and distinct to foreigners.

In view of the communicative situation in Wales, the fact that the higher the percentage of Welsh learners the deeper is the impact of education on the language taught as well as the fact that about three quarters of Welsh speakers are learners, the trend to, at least, pidginisation becomes apparent. Research has shown that the language can change significantly when it is inadequately described and insufficiently and/or erroneously taught (cf. section 4.1.1.). Historically inappropriate forms become increasingly prevalent in situations when second-language learners dominate and societal monitoring is absent or only pursued by the limited resources of a pressure group (cf. section 4.1.1.).

In addition, the Welsh language as heard in the media is deficient in quality and insufficient in quantity (cf. section 4.1.1.). A first result of the developments as illustrated above is that the language spoken by children from immersion-schools in highly anglicised areas is often rather poor. In addition, people between 25 and 44 years of age, that is, the age group with the highest social impact, write and read less frequently and fluently than any other age group. This is to a considerable extent due to deficiencies in the area of describing and presenting the language, that is, in manuals and reference books such as dictionaries as well as in the media (cf. section 4.1.1.). Welsh learners have currently only a limited scope for upgrading their Welsh language skills in a linguistic environment that is increasingly deprived of native speaker interaction. Pidginisation can under the socio-linguistic circumstances as exemplified here also establish a stage before language death.

In light of the facts presented in the preceding paragraphs, it becomes apparent that the Welsh language despite an improved social status of the country and its language was at the end of the twentieth century in severe decline (cf. the situation of Irish in Ireland). Consequently, the struggle for Welsh has been enforced at the turn of the century (cf. section 4.1.1.).

In this process the availability of dictionaries provides the language with the prestige that it is worthy of being used and learned, a message important also for immigrants and non-Welsh speaking Welsh people. In addition, in a communicative situation as illustrated above, diction-aries have descriptive and creative tasks, as well as codifying, compensatory and supplementory functions. Therefore, the availability of popular reference books and an adequate presentation of the properties of the Welsh language in them as suggested above is essential to ensure that the language can be broadly made applicable to its potential speakers, thereby furthering the adoption of language schemes and the promotion of a permanent use of the language throughout society.

Presenting a wide range of dictionaries incorporating an improved description of Welsh lexical items, Welsh lexicography may well support the construction of linguistic confidence and linguistic identity as well as cultural identity. These are needed as widespread personal char-ac-teristics in Wales to make full use of the language and its potentials, to offer it to learners, and to present it self-confidently to people who neglect cultural integration.

VI. Appendix
6.1. List of Welsh vocabularies[1]

Date	Author	Vocabularies and other lexicographical work[2]	Location	Publisher
before 1564	Hiraethog, Gruffudd	A Welsh Dictionary	Pen. 230	
1567-74	Llŷn, William	Welsh-Welsh dictionary	Pen. 230, Cardiff Free Libr.	
no data	Llŷn, William	Geirlyfr	UCW 29	
1568-74	Salesbury, William	Llysieulyfr	LIGC 4581	edited by Edgar, Iwan Rhys, 1997, Gwasg Prif-ysgol Cymru, Caerdydd
1588	Morys, Roger (Thomas Wiliems)	(Welsh-Welsh vocabulary)	Pen. 169	
no data	Wiliems, Thomas	Sir Thomas Wiiems's Common-Place Book	Pen. 188	
no data	Wiliems, Thomas & John Edwards	Geirfa A Gramadeg	Puleston1	
no data	Lewis, Evan	English-Welsh dictionary	Llanwrin	
< 1632	no data	Hen Gymraec A Chymraec Newydd	Pen. 138	
1639	Jones, John	Llyfyr Geirydd om kyssefin gasgyl if o bob gair addas iw kynhwysso mewn llyfrau Geiryddion or rain y mae yn berthnassawl i bennodau neillituawl, megis am lyssieu, yn dau dryll yn y llyfr hwnn P. I (not consistently glossed; herbal names in Latin, English, Welsh)	Pen. 308	
no data	Maurice, William († 1680)	Geirfa Cymraeg a Lladin	Crosswood 39	
no data	no data	Welsh-English-Latin Dictionary	Jesus College 10	

---

[1] There are uncertainties about the completeness of unpublished vocabularies and also of some printed ones because:
  (a) The former are mostly early lexicographical works and are, at times, difficult to identify and date, since they remain partly in manuscript form. Some of them only comprise a few paragraphs. Others are listed without providing any data or author.
  (b) The staff from the *Welsh Book Council*, which is the marketing unit for Welsh books, told me that they would not know of books printed by various societies, e.g. *Cymdeithas Edward Llwyd*, which may contain vocabularies.
  (c) Periodicals and magazines, which may contain lists of vocabularies, i.e. the *Gwyddonydd*, have not been systematically consulted.
  The titles are listed as found on the cover of the publications.

[2]

Date	Author	Title	Place	Publisher
1707	Lhuyd, Edward	Some Welch Words Omitted in Dr Davies's Dictionary (in: Archaeologia Britannica)	Oxford	at theTheatre
no data	Gambold, William	Lexicon Cambro-Britannicum	Llanstephan 189	
1707-1722	Gambold, William	English-Welsh/Welsh-English	Llanstephan 190	
1719 (1733)	Baxter, William	Glossarium antiquitatum britannicarum : sive, Syllabus etymologicus antiquitatum veteris Britanniae atque Iberniae, temporibus Romanorum	London	J. Watts (T. Woodward)
1782	Milles, Jeremiah	An Archaeological epistle to the Reverend and Worshipful Jeremiah Milles, D.D. Dean of Exeter, to which is annexed a glossary extracted from that of the learned Dean	London	J. Nicholas
no data	Davies, Walter (1761-1849)	A Welsh-English Vocabulary	Crosswood 67	
later than 1794	Davies, Walter	An English-Welsh Dictionary based on John Walter's An English-Welsh Dictionary	Crosswood 260	
1804 (-16; -20)	Evans, Thomas (Tomos Glyn Cothi)	An English and Welsh vocabulary : or An easy guide to the ancient British language	Merthyr (Dolgelley)	W. Williams (Gomerian Press)
1828	Rowland, Jones	Geiriadur poblogaidd : yn cynnwys mwy nag wyth gant o eiriau a'nghyfiaith a arferir yn gyffredin yn lle geiriau Cymraeg, wedi eu hegluro a geiriau dealladwy dilediaith (sic)		
1832 (1837)	Williams, William	A vocabulary of familiar dialogues in English & Welsh : containing such questions as may be requisite to English travellers : to which is added a sketch of the history of the county of Caernarvon in both languages	Caernarvon	L.E. Jones
1845	no data	A Welsh-English vocabulary : containing an explanatory introduction to the Welsh language, a short list of the parts of speech, names of places, creatures, relatives, artisans, &c.: with familiar dialogues and other interesting instructions to understand and speak the language	Aberystwyth	D. Jenkins
1848 (1852)	Griffiths, Evan (Ieuan Ebblig)	An English and Welsh vocabulary : containing a list of words in common use, together with several familiar dialogues upon various subjects = Geiriadur Saesneg a Chymraeg : yn cynnwys rhes o eiriau mewn arferiad cyffredin, ynghyd ag ymddyddanion sathredig ar wahanol destunau	Swansea	E. Griffiths
1851	Williams, Rev. John	A Glossary of Terms used for the Articles of British Dress and Armour	London	W. Pickering

Date	Author	Title	Place	Publisher
18??	Humphreys, Hugh	The tourist's English-Welsh vocabulary : containing the exact mode of pronouncing the Welsh alphabet : with a collection of useful phrases and familiar dialogues	no data	no data
1911	Williams, David David	Geirfa prifeirdd	Lerpwl	Hugh Evans a'i feibion
1913 (1995)	Fynes-Clinton, Osbert Henry	Welsh Vocabulary of the Bangor District	Oxford (Llanerch)	Oxford University Press
1934	Harry, G. Ivor	Geiriadur o Enwau Blodau Gwyllt	no data	W. Spurrell & Son
1949	Ordnance Survey	Glossary of the most common Welsh words used on the Ordnance Survey	London	Ordnance Survey
1950	no data	Termau Technegol	Caerdydd	Gwasg Prifysgol Cymru
1954	Lewis, Evan & David Enwyn Morgan	Geirfa gweithfeydd glo carreg Deheudir Cymru	Caerdydd	Bwrdd Gwybodau Celtaidd
1955	Peate, Iorwerth (Cyfeiliog)	Geirfa'r saer	Caerdydd	Bwrdd Gwybodau Celtaidd
1955	Prifysgol Cymru	Termau crefft: gwaith saer, gwaith gof a pheirianneg y gweithdy	Caerdydd	Bwrdd Gwybodau Celtaidd
1955	Lloyd, Illtyd	Geirfa Mathemateg	no data	no data
1956	Peate, Iorwerth (Cyfeiliog)	Termau'r ffatrïoedd gwlân	no data	Bwrdd Gwybodau Celtaidd
1957	no data	Termau Mathemateg	Caerdydd	Gwasg Prifysgol Cymru
1957	Y Weinyddiaeth Addysg	Geirfa Natur	Caerdydd	Gwasg Prifysgol Cymru
1958	no data	Termau Egwyddorion Addysg	Caerdydd	Gwasg Prifysgol Cymru
1959 (1972)	no data	Termau Daerydiaeth	Caerdydd	Gwasg Prifysgol Cymru
1959	Prifysgol Cymru	Termau gorfforol a mabolgampiau	Caerdydd	
1959	Bwrdd Gwybodau Celtaidd	Termau Hanes	Caerdydd	Gwasg Prifysgol Cymru
1959	Ysgol Addysg Prifysgol Cymru	Termau Addysg Gorfforol A Mabolgampau	Caerdydd	Gwasg Prifysgol Cymru
1960 (1966)	no data	Termau Gwaith Coed	Caerdydd	Gwasg Prifysgol Cymru
1960	Ysgol Addysg Prifysgol Cymru	Termau Coginio	Caerdydd	Gwasg Prifysgol Cymru
1960-1963	Humphreys, Gwilym	Termau'r chwarel	no data	Y Caban
1962	Thomas, David	Geiriau'r môr	Caernarfon	Y Lleufer

Year	Author	Title	Place	Publisher
1962	Parry, Meirion	Casgliad o enwau adar	Caerdydd	Gwasg Prifysgol Cymru
1962/63	Jones, R. Emrys	Casgliad o dermau chwarel	Caerdydd	Bwrdd Gwybodau Celtaidd
1963 (1982)	no data	Termau gwyddor gwlad	no data (Caerdydd)	*Gwyddor Gwlad (WJEC)*
1963-1970	no data	Geirfa	no data	*Y Gwyddonydd*
1964	Jones, R. Emrys	Termau'r Theatr	Caerdydd	Gwasg Prifysgol Cymru
1964	Jones, R. Emrys	Casgliad o dermau'r theatr	Caerdydd	Gwasg Prifysgol Cymru
1964	no data	Termau Technegol - Gramadeg, Seineg, Moeseg, Metaffiseg, Estheteg, Rhesymeg	Caerdydd	Gwasg Prifysgol Cymru
1965 (1983)	Ysgol Addysg Prifysgol Cymru (WJEC)[3]	Termau Ffiseg A Mathemateg	Caerdydd	Gwasg Prifysgol Cymru
1965	Wiliam, Aled Rhys	Geirfa cyfoes	no data	*Arolwg*
1965	Ysgol Addysg Prifysgol Cymru	Termau Chwaraeon ac Adloniant	Caerdydd	Gwasg Prifysgol Cymru
1966	no data	Termau gwaith coed	Caerdydd	Gwasg Prifysgol Cymru
1967	Prifysgol Cymru	Termau Gwniadwaith, Brodwaith a Gwau a Golchwaith	Caerdydd	Gwasg Prifysgol Cymru
1967	no data	Termau bioleg	Caerdydd	Gwasg Prifysgol Cymru
1968	Ministry of Labour	Geirfa Weinyddu	no data	no data
1968	Prifysgol Cymru	Termau diwinyddiaeth gydag atodiad ar enwau priod	Caerdydd	Gwasg Prifysgol Cymru
1968	no data	Geirfa ffilatellol	Aberystwyth	Cymdeithas Ffilatelwyr
1968	no data	Termau diwinyddiaeth	Caerdydd	Gwasg Prifysgol Cymru
1969	Prifysgol Cymru	Enwau planhigion	Caerdydd	Gwasg Prifysgol Cymru
1969	Parry, Meirion	Casgliad o enwau blodau, llysiau a choed	Caerdydd	Gwasg Prifysgol Cymru
1970	Prifysgol Cymru	Termau Addysg	Caerdydd	Gwasg Prifysgol Cymru
1970	Prifysgol Cymru	Termau celfyddyd a chrefft - Celfyddyd Gain. Coed. Metel. Pensaerniaeth. Rhwymo Llyfrau.	Caerdydd	Gwasg Prifysgol Cymru
1970	Prifysgol Cymru	Termau Swyddfa a Busnes	Caerdydd	Gwasg Prifysgol Cymru
1971	Wiliam, Aled Rhys	Termau Technegol	no data	*Y Gwyddonydd*

[3] WJEC stands for *Welsh Joint Education Committee.*

Year	Author	Title	Place	Publisher
1971	Jones, Glyn E.	Geirfa saer cerrig	Caerdydd	Bwrdd Gwybodau Celtaidd
1971	no data	Termau Coginio	Caerdydd	Gwasg Prifysgol Cymru
1971 (-76, -88)	no data	Termau Cymdeithaseg	Caerdydd	Gwasg Prifysgol Cymru
1971	Prifysgol Cymru	Termau Llywodraeth Leol - Iechyd Cyhoeddus	Caerdydd	Bwrdd Gwybodau Celtaidd
1972	Lêwis, Robyn	Termau Cyfraith/Legal Terms	Llandysul	Gwasg Gomer
1972	no data	Termau Economeg ac Econometreg	Caerdydd	Gwasg Prifysgol Cymru
1972	no data	Termau Iaith a Llên	Llandysul	Gwasg Gomer
1973 (1993)	Jones, P. Hope	Rhestr o Adar Cymru	Caerdydd	Amgueddfa Genedlaethol Cymru
1975	Williams, D. Moclwyn	Geiradur y Gwerinwr	Dinbych	Gwasg Gee
1976	no data	Geirfa Gwaith Gweinyddiaeth Gymdeithasol	Caerdydd	Gwasg Prifysgol Cymru
1976	Davies, Lynn	Geirfa'r Glöwr	no data	Folk Museum
1976	no data	Termau Gwleidyddiaeth	Caerdydd	Gwasg Prifysgol Cymru
1978 (1992)	no data	Termau Cerddoriaeth	Caerdydd	Gwasg Prifysgol Cymru
1978	no data	Termau Llyfrgell a Byd Llyfrau		Welsh College of Librarianship
1980	no data	Nuclear Power - A Glossary of Technical Terms	no data	United Kingdom Atomic Energy Authority
1981	Owen, Gwilym B.	Llawlyfr Pwyllgorau a Chyrff Cyffelyb	no data	Gwas Gee
1981	no data	Termau Daeryddiaeth	Caerdydd	WJEC
1982	no data	Termau Astudiaethau Crefyddol	Caerdydd	WJEC
1983	Cyd-Bwyllgor Addysg	Termau Clasurol	Caerdydd	WJEC
1983	Tibbot, Minwel	Geirfa'r Gegin	no data	Folk Museum
1984	no data	Termau Gwniadwaith, Brodwaith a Gwau a Golchwaith	Caerdydd	WJEC
1985	Jones, Ann	Geirfa Tŷ'n y Pant	Caerdydd	*Cardiff Working Papers in Welsh Linguistics*
1985	no data	Termau y Teulu a'r Cartref	Caerdydd	WJEC
1986	Richards, Eluned	Geirfa arlwyaeth	Dolgellau	Coleg Meiryionnydd
1986	Willimas, Anne E.	Termau Archifau	no data	Gwynedd Archive Centre

Date	Author	Title	Place	Publisher
1986 (1993)	no data	Termau Meddygol	Caerdydd	Gwasg Prifysgol Cymru
1986	Cyd-Bwyllgor Addysg	Termau Cyfrifiadureg	Caerdydd	WJEC
1987	Evans, Emrys	Termau Ieithyddiaeth	Aberystwyth	Coleg Prifysgol Cymru
1987	no data	Geirfa gwaith cymdeithasol	Caerdydd	Gwasg Prifysgol Cymru
1987 (1990)	no data	Termau Hanes	Caerdydd	WJEC
1988/89	Hughes, Richard Elwyn	Termau technoleg a gwyddoniaeth Gymraeg	no data	Y Gyddonydd
1988-1990	Elias, Twm	Geirfa amaethyddol		Fferm a Thyddyn
1988	ap Owain, Steffan	Geirfa'r Mwynwyr	Llanrwst	Gwas Carreg Gwalch
1990	no data	Termau Gwaith Coed	Caerdydd	WJEC
1991	no data	Termau Gwaith Metel	Caerdydd	WJEC
1991	no data	Termau Addysg Arbennig	no data	Clwyd County Council
1991	Edwards, R. John	Termau Amaeth	no data	Language Studies Centre
1992	Dyfed County Council	Geirfa Cyngor a Phwyllgor	Caerfyrddin	Cydweithgor Dwyieithrwydd yn Nyfed
1992	Acen	Cymraeg newyddion: geirfa a thasgau i ddysgwyr	Caerdydd	Acen
1992	MEU,[4] WJEC	Geiriadur Termau Cyfrifiadureg	Caerdydd	MEU, WJEC
1992	Garrod, Neil	Termau Cyfrifeg	Caerdydd	Gwasg Prifysgol Cymru
1992	no data	Termau Busnes	Caerdydd	WJEC
1992	no data	Termau Economeg	Caerdydd	WJEC
1992	Williams, Hywel	Geirfa Gwaith Cymdeithasol	Caerdydd	Gwasg Prifysgol Cymru
1993	Prys, Delyth	Geirfa Gwaith Plant	Caerdydd	Gwasg Prifysgol Cymru
1993	Rees, David & Howard Alun Williams	Llawlyfr Technoleg	Caerdydd	Gwasg Prifysgol Cymru
1993	Griffiths, D.G.	Termau Adeiladu	Llangefni	Canolfan Astudiaethau Iaith
1994	Cymdeithas Edward Llwyd	Creaduriaid Asgwrn-Cefn	Talybont	Lolfa

[4] MEU stands for *Microelectronics in Education Unit Wales.*

Year	Author	Title	Place	Publisher
1994	Lewis, E.Dewi	Enwau Adar	Llanwst	Gwasg Carreg Gwalch
1994	Heinz, Sabine	Geirfa Cymraeg-Almaeneg	Lewiston	The Edwin Mellen Press
1994	Elias, Twm	Termau Amaethyddiaeth a Milfeddygaeth	Caerdydd	Gwasg Prifysgol
1994	Jones, Handel	Geirfa Cyfathrebu	Bangor	Normal College
1995 (1997)	Robert, Gwerfyl & Delyth Prys	Termau nyrsio a bydwreigiaeth/An English-Welsh Dictionary of Nursing and Midwifery Terms	Bangor	Ysgol Astudiaethau Nyrsio a Bydwreigiaeth
1995	Davies, D. & J. Arthur	Enwau Cymraeg ar Blanhigion	Caerdydd	Amgueddfa Genedlaethol Cymru
1996	Lewis, David Geraint	Termau Llywodraeth Leol	Llandysul	Gomer
1997	Hughes, J. Elwyn	Geiriau ac Ymadroddion 3, Geiriau'r newyddion	no data	no data
1997	Jones, Ceri	Six Thousand Welsh Words - A Comprehensive Basic Vocabulary	Llandysul	Gomer
1997	no data	Magu'r Babi	Caerdydd	Bwrdd yr Iaith
1998	Uned y Gymraeg	Geirfa Saesneg - Cymraeg Asiantaeth Budd-Daliadau	Caerdydd	Uned yr Iaith
1998	Prys, Delyth & J. Jones	Termau Deddfwriaeth Priffyrdd	Caerdydd	Bwrdd yr Iaith Gymraeg
1998	Tolau Cartref a Thramor	Glossary of Technical Terminology		
1999	Harper, Sally	Geirfa		*Hanes Cerddoriaeth Cymru*
1999	National Language Unit of Wales	Geirfa mathemateg	Caerdydd	Uned Iaith Genedlaethol Cymru (CBAC)
1999	Hayles, Leonard	Welsh Phrases for Learners	Talybont	Lolfa
2000	Bwrdd yr Iaith Gymraeg	Geirfa Saesneg-Cymraeg. English-Welsh Vocabulary (Highway terminology)	Caerdydd	http://www.netwales.co.uk/byig/rhestrs.htm
2000	Falileyev, Aleksandr I.	Etymological glossary of Old Welsh	Tübingen	Niemeyer
2000	Prys, Delyth	Termau Addysg y Cynulliad/Dictionary of Education Terms for the National Assembly Wales	Caerdydd	http://www.netwales.co.uk/byig/rhestrs.htm
2000	Prys, Delyth	Termau Cyllid y Cynulliad/Dictionary of Finance Terms for the National Assembly of Wales	Caerdydd	http://www.netwales.co.uk/byig/rhestrs.htm
2000	Prys, Delyth	Termau hybu iechyd	Bangor	Prifysgol Cymru
2000	Prys, Delyth	Termau Gwaith a Gofal Cymdeithasol	Caerdydd	Gwasg Prifysgol Cymru

2001	no data	Common Technical Terms	no data	no data
no data < 96	no data	Termau Coginio	Caerdydd	WJEC
no data < 97	no data	Termau Gramadeg	Caerdydd	Gwasg Prifysgol Cymru

6.2.   **References**[5]
6.2.1.   **Primary Sources**
6.2.1.1.   **Authors**

Alston, R.C., ed., 1968a, *John Davies. Antiquae Linguae Britannicae, nunc communiter dictae Cambro-Britannicae, à suis Cymraece vel Cambricae, ab alijs Wallicae, Rudimenta. Londini: Iohannem Billium, 1621*, in: *English Linguistics 1500-1800*, 70, Menston.

idem, ed., 1968b, *John Davies. Antiquae Linguae Britannicae Dictionarium Duplex, Londini, impress. in œdibus R Young, 1632*, in: *English Linguistics 1500-1800*, 99, Menston.

idem, ed., 1969a, *Henry Salesbury. Grammatica Britannica in usum ejus linguae studiosorum. Londini: Thomas Salesburius, 1593*, in: *English Linguistics 1500-1800*, 189, Menston.

idem, ed., 1969b, *William Salesbury. A briefe and playne introduction teachyng how to pronounce the letters in the British tong, Londini, 1550*, in: *English Linguistics 1500-1800*, 179, Menston.

Anfilowjewa, A.A., 1987, *Dictionnaire Français-Russe*, Moskau.

ap Rhys, Gweirydd, 1866, *An English-Welsh Dictionary, To Which Is Added, A List Of Proper Namens Of Places, &c., With Their Welsh Synonyms. Geiriadur Cymraeg A Saesneg, At Yr Hwn Yr Ychwanegwyd Enwadur Daearyddol, Hefyd Geiriau Cyffelyb Sain, Ond Yn Gwahaniaethau Mewn Ystyr, &c., Gan Gweirydd ap Rhys*, Caernarvon.

Barnhart, R.K.B., ed., 1988, *The Barnhart Dictionary of Etymology*, New York.

Benson, M. & E. Benson et al., 1986, *The BBI Combinatory Dictionary of English*, Amsterdam.

Boatner, M.T. & J.E. Gates, 1975, *A Dictionary of American Idioms*, Woodbury, New York.

Broderick, G., 1984, *A Handbook of Late Spoken Manx. Dictionary*, Bd. 2, Tübingen.

Bromwich, R., ed., 1978, *Trioedd Ynys Prydein*, Caerdydd.

Brown, L., 1993, *The New Shorter Oxford Dictionary*, Oxford

Buchanan, D., 1998, *Gaelic-English/English-Gaelic Dictionary*, Edinburgh.

Caldas, Th.F. & C. Schleicher, 1999, *Wörterbuch Irisch-Deutsch*, Hamburg.

Cownie, A.R., 2001, *A Dictionary of Welsh and English Idiomatic Phrases. Geiriadur Idiomau*, Caerdydd.

Davies, C(ennard), 1980, *Lluniau Llafar*, Llandysul.

idem, 1987, *Y Geiriau Bach*, Llandysul.

idem, 1990, *Darluniau Byw*, Llandysul.

idem, 1996, *Torri'r Garw. Idioms for Welsh Learners based on the verb-noun*, Llandysul.

Davies, D. & A. Jones, 1995, *Enwau Cymraeg ar Blanhigion*, Caerdydd.

Delaporte, R., 1995, *Elementary breton-english & english-breton dictionary*, Lesneven.

Desbordes, Y. & D. Kervella, 1994, *Geriadur bihan brezhoneg-gallek*, Lesneven.

Dieckhoff, H.C., 1932, *A Pronouncing Dictionary of Scottish Gaelic*, Edinburgh.

Dwelly, E., 1901-1911 (1994), *The illustrated Gaelic-English Dictionary*, Glasgow.

Edgar, I.Rh., ed., 1997, *Llysieulyfr Salesbury*, Caerdydd.

Evans, D.S., ed., 1977, *Historia Gruffudd vab Kenan*, Caerdydd.

Evans, E., 1987, *Termau Ieithyddiaeth*, Aberystwyth.

Evans, H.M., 1982, *Y Geiriadur Cyfoes. The Modern Welsh Dictionary* (sic), Abertawe.

idem, 1987, *Y Geiriadur Mawr*, Llandysul.

idem, 1953, *Y Geiriadur Newydd*, Llandybïe.

---

[5]   The titles are listed as found on the cover of the publications.

502

Evans, W., 1771, *English-Welsh Dictionary: containing All Words necessary for Reading an English Author; wherein not only the Corresponding British is given to the English, and the various Significations properly arranged; but also Every English Word is accented to prevent a bad Pronunciation, The Part of Speech added to which each Word respectively belongs, And proper Authorities subjoined where necessary*, Carmarthen.

idem, 1812, *A New English-Welsh Dictionary*, Carmarthen.

Falileyev, A.I., 2000, *Etymological Glossary of Old Welsh*, in: Buchreihe der *ZcP*, Bd. 18, Tübingen.

Favereau, F., 1993, *Dictionnaire du breton contemporain. Geriadur ar brezhoneg a-vremañ*, Morlaix.

Fynes-Clinton, O.H., 1913, *Welsh Vocabulary of the Bangor District*, Oxford.

Griffiths, B. & D.G. Jones, 1995, *Geiriadur y Academi. The Welsh Academy English-Welsh Dictionary*, Caerdydd.

Greenslade, D., 2000, *Cambrian Country*, Llanrwst.

Greller, W., 1996, *Geiriadur Almaeneg*, Aberystwyth.

idem et al., 1999, *Geiriadur Almaeneg-Cymraeg/Cymraeg-Almaeneg*, Aberystwyth.

Gruffudd, H., 1998, *The Welsh Learner's Dictionary*, Talybont.

Hermann, U., 1996, *Die neue deutsche Rechtschreibung*, Gütersloh.

Hill, E., 1988, *Llyfr Mawr Geiriau Smot*, Llandysul.

Hincks, Rh., 1991, *Geiriadur Kembraeg-Brezhoneg*. Lesneven.

Hornby, A.S. & E.V. Gatenby et al., 1963, *The Advanced Learners's Dictionary of Current English*, Oxford.

Hughes, G.H., 1976, *Rhagymadroddion 1547-1659*, Caerdydd.

Ifans, D. & R.L. Thomson, 1979/80, 'Edward Lhuyd's Geiriau Manaweg', in: *Studia Celtica* 1979/80, Caerdydd.

Jones, M., 1996, *Y Cleciadur*, Aberystwyth.

Jones, R.E., 1987, *Ail Lyfr o Idiomau Cymraeg*, Abertawe.

Jones, R.M., 1969, *Geiriadur Lluniau*, Llandybïe.

Jones, T., 1688 (1977), *Y Gymraeg yn ei disgleirdeb, neu helaeth eir-lyfr Cymraeg a Saesnaeg Yn Cynwys yr holl eiriau yng Eirlyfr Dr Davies*, London (Llanwrda).

Jones, T., ed., 1940, *Y Bibyl yng Nghymraec: sef Cyfieithiad Cymraeg Canol o'r 'Promptuarium Bibliae'*, Caerdydd.

King, G., 2000, *The Pocket Modern Welsh Dictionary*, Oxford.

Knox, W., 1998, *The Pan-Celtic Phrasebook*, Talybont.

Lange-Kowal, E.-E. & E. Weymuth, 1982, *Langenscheidts Taschenwörterbuch Französisch*, Berlin, Munich et al.

Lewis, C., 1987, *Orgraff yr Iaith Gymraeg*, Caerdydd.

Lewis, E.C, 1992, *Teach Yourself Welsh Dictionary*, London.

idem, 2001, *Y Geiriadur Cryno/The Concise Welsh Dictionary*, Llandybïe.

Lewis, D.G., 1994, *Geiriadur Gomer i'r Ifanc*, Llandysul.

idem, 1997, *(The Works) Welsh-English/English-Welsh Dictionary*, New Lanark.

Lewis, H., ed., 1925 (1967), *Chwedleu Seith Doethon Rufein*, Wrecsam (Caerdydd).

idem, ed., 1932, 'Glosau Rhydychen a Chaergrawnt', in: *BBCS* 6.

idem, ed., 1942 (1974), *Brut Dingestow*, Llandysul (Caerdydd).

Léwis, R., 1992, *Geiriadur y Gyfraith*, Llandysul.

Lhuyd, E., 1707 (1971), *Archaeologia Britannica*, Oxford (Shannon).

Lindsay, W.M., 1921, *The Corpus Épinal, Erfurt and Leiden Glossaries*, in: *Publications of the Philological Society* VIII, London.

Lloyd-Jones, J., 1988, *Geirfa barddoniaeth gynnar Cymraeg*, Caerdydd.

503

Loomis, R.M., ed., transl., 1982, *Dafydd ap Gwilym. The poems*, Binghamton.

MacAlpine, N., 1831, *Pronouncing Gaelic-English Dictionary*, Glasgow.

MacLennan, M., 1925 (1992), *A Pronouncing and Etymological Dictionary of the Gaelic Language*, Edinburgh.

Mac Mathúna, S. & A. Ó Corráin, 1996, *The Collins Gem Irish Dictionary English-Irish/Irish-English*, Glasgow.

Maund, K.L., 1996, *Handlist of the Acts of Native Welsh Rulers 1132-1283*, Caerdydd.

Meissinger, H. & G. Türck et al., 1990, *Langenscheidts Taschenwörterbuch Englisch*, Berlin, Munich et al.

Meyer, K., 1913, *Sanas Cormaic*, in: *Anecdota from the Irish manuscripts*, vol. v, Halle, Dublin.

Mish, F.C., 1995, *Merriam-Webster's Collegiate Dictionary*, Springfield/Massachusetts.

Morris, J., ed., tranls., 1980, *Nennius. British History and the Welsh Annals*, Phillimore.

Ó Dohartaigh, C., 1996, *CysGair*, Bangor.

Ó Duibhín, C., 1998, *GaelDict 98*, http://www.ceantar.org/Comp/GAELDI98.HTML (1.12.2000).

Orschel, H., 1991, *Langenscheidts Taschenwörterbuch Russisch*, Berlin, Munich et al.

Quin, E.G., 1976, *Dictionary Of The Irish Language Based Mainly On Old And Middle Irish Materials* (sic), Dublin.

Picket, J.P. & D.R. Pritchard et al., eds., 2000, *The American Heritage Dictionary*, Boston.

Rees, E.C., 1932, *Cymraeg i'r Werin. Welsh Simplified. A practical Modern Dictionary of Words and Phrases for Teachers and Students*, London.

Roberts, B.F., ed., 1961, *Gwassanaeth Meir*, Caerdydd.

Rowlands, E.I., ed., 1976, *Gwaith Rhys Brydydd a Rhisiart ap Rhys*, Caerdydd.

Salesbury, W., 1547 (1877), *A dictionary in Englyshe and Welshe: moche necessary to all such Welshemen as wil spedly learne the englyshe tõgue unto the kynges majestie very mete to be sette for the to the use of his graces subjectes in Wales: whereunto is pfixed a little treatys of the englyshe pronûnciation of the letters*, London, [Facsimile reprint for the Cymmrodorion society, 1877, London.]

Shaw, J.R. & S.J. Shaw, 1990, *The New Horizon Ladder Dictionary of the English Language*, New York.

Schlegelmilch, A., 1985, *Handwörterbuch Französisch-Deutsch*, Leipzig.

Sinclair, J., ed., 1987, *Collins COBUILD English Language Dictionary*, London.

Stephens, R., 1978, *Yr Odliadur*, Llandysul.

Stevenson, W.H., ed., 1929, *Early Scholastic Colloquies*, Oxford.

Summers, D., ed., 1978, *Longman Dictionary of Contemporary English*, London.

Terrel, P. & V. Schnorr et al., eds., 1997, *Pons Collins Großwörterbuch für Experten und Universität. Deutsch-Englisch, Englisch-Deutsch*, Stuttgart, Düsseldorf.

Thomas, J., ed., 1952, *Brut y Tywysogion or The Chronicle of the Princes. Peniarth MS. 20 version*, Caerdydd.

idem, ed., 1955, *Brut y Tywysogion or The Chronicle of the Princes. Red Book of Hergest version*, Caerdydd.

Thomas, R.J. et al., 1950-2002, *Geiriadur Prifysgol Cymru*, Caerdydd.

Thorne, D. & A. Convery, 1991, *Collins Spurrell Welsh-English/English-Welsh Dictionary*, Glasgow.

idem, 1996, *Collins Gem Welsh-English/English-Welsh Dictionary*, Glasgow.

Thorpe, L., ed., transl., 1983, *Geoffrey of Monmouth. The History of the Kings of Britain*, Harmondsworth.

504

Walters, J., 1771, *A dissertation on the Welsh language : pointing out it's antiquity, copious-ness, grammatical perfection, with remarks on it's poetry and other articles not foreign to the subject* (sic), Cowbridge.

Weis, E. & H. Kaul, 1996, *Pons Kompaktwörterbuch Englisch-Deutsch, Deutsch-Englisch*, Stuttgart.

Williams, G.A., ed., 1986, *Ymryson Edmwnd Prys a Wiliam Cynwal*, Caerdydd.

Williams, G.J. & E.J. Jones, eds., 1934, *Gramadegau'r Penceirddiaid*, Caerdydd.

Williams, G.J., ed., 1930, *Barddoniaeth neu Brydyddiaeth gan Wiliam Midleton*, Caerdydd.

idem, ed., 1939, *Gramadeg Cymraeg yn ôl yr argraffiad y dechreuwyd ei gyhoeddi ym Milan yn 1567*, Caerdydd.

Williams, I., ed., 1927, 'The Computus Fragment', in: *BBCS* 3.

idem, ed., 1929, 'Glosau Rhydychen', in: *BBCS* 5.

idem, ed., 1930, 'Glosau Rhydychen: Mesurau a Phwysau', in: *BBCS* 5.

idem, ed., 1932a, 'Tri englyn y Juvencus', in: *BBCS* 6.

idem, ed., 1932b, 'Naw englyn y Juvencus', in: *BBCS* 6.

idem, ed., 1932c, 'Glosau Rhydychen a Chaergrawnt', in: *BBCS* 6.

idem, ed., 1955, *Canu Llywarch Hen*, Caerdydd.

idem, ed., transl., 1972, *Armes Prydein*, Dublin.

Williams, J.L., 1973, *Y Geiriadur Termau*, Caerdydd.

Williams, P., ed., 1982, *Kedymdeithas Amlyn ac Amic*, Caerdydd.

Williams, R., 1985, *Geiriadur Bach Llydaweg-Cymraeg*, Aberystwyth.

idem, 1990, *Geiriadur Cymraeg-Llydaweg*, Aberystwyth.

Williams, S.J., ed., 1968, *Ystorya de Carlo Magno*, Caerdydd.

Zimmer, S., 1987, *Geiriadur Gwrthdroadol Cymraeg Diweddar*, Hamburg.

6.2.1.2. Institutions

Alex Juncker Verlag, 1999, *Großes Wörterbuch Französisch*, Munich.
Alex Juncker Verlag, 1999, *Großes Wörterbuch Englisch*, Munich.
Alex Juncker Verlag, 1999, *Großes Wörterbuch Spanisch*, Munich.
An Roinn Oideachais, 1990, *Foclóir Póca*, Dublin.
idem, 1981, *An Gearrfhoclóir Gaeilge-Béarla*, Dublin.
Awdurdod Addysg Morgannwg Ganol, 1979, *Y Geiriadur Lliwgar*, Caerdydd.
Bertelsmann, 1997, *Universalwörterbuch Englisch* (Compactdisc), Berlin.
Bwrdd yr Iaith Gymraeg, 1989, *National Curriculum: Welsh for ages 5 to 16*, Caerdydd.
Cambridge University Press, 2000, *Cambridge International Dictionary of English*, Cambridge.
Canolfan Dysgu Cymraeg, 1991, *Cwrs Wlpan*, Caerdydd.
Commission of the European Communities, 1983, *Faclair Eòrpach*, Bruxelles.
Cyfadran Addysg Coleg y Brifysgol Abertawe, 1964, *Cymraeg Byw: Rhifyn 1*, Abertawe.
Dudenredaktion, 1991, *Duden. Rechtschreibung der deutschen Sprache*, Mannheim.
Evangelische Haupt-Bibelgesellschaft zu Berlin, 1955, *Die Heilige Schrift*, Berlin.
Fàilte, 1995, *Facal: Sprachführer Deutsch-Gälisch*, Inverness.
idem, 1995, *Facal: recueil d'expressions francais-gaélique*, Inverness.
idem, 1995, *Facal: English-Gaelic Phrase book*, Inverness.
idem, 1996, *Facal: Espanol-Gaélico vocabulario*, Inverness.
idem, 1996, *Italiano-Gaelico vocabolarietto*, Inverness.
Gwasg Pobl Cymru, 1993, *Y Thesawrws Cymraeg*, Abertawe.
Koch Media, 1998, *Wörterbuch Französisch* (Compactdisc), Munich.
Langenscheidt, 1998, *Power Wörterbuch Englisch*, Berlin.
Merriam Co, G. & C., 1895, *Webster's Academic Dictionary. A Dictionary of the English Language*, Springfield.
Uned Iaith Genedlaethol Cymru, 1976, *Gramadeg Cymraeg Cyfoes. Contemporary Welsh Grammar*, Y Bontfaen.
University of Wales Press, 1993, *Termau Meddygol*, Caerdydd.

506

6.2.2. Secondary literature
6.2.2.1. Authors

Aarts, F., 1999, 'Syntactic information in OALD5, LDOCE3, COBUILD2 and CIDE', in: Herbst, Th. & K. Popp, eds., 1999, *The Perfect Learners' dictionary (?)*, in: *Lexicographica Series Maior* 95, Tübingen.

Aitchison, J.W. & H. Carter, 1985, *The Welsh Language 1961-1981*, Caerdydd.

idem, 1993, 'The Welsh Language in 1991. Analysis of Census Results', in: *Planet* 97.

idem, 2000, *Language, economy and society. The changing fortunes of the Welsh language in the twentieth century*, Caerdydd.

Alen, J.P.B. & S. P. Corder, 1975, *Papers in Applied Linguistics*, London.

Allerton, D.J., 1991, 'Language as form and pattern: Grammar and its categories', in: Collinge, N.E., ed., 1991, *An Encyclopedia of Language*, London, New York.

Arnold, R. & K. Hansen, 1982, *Englische Phonetik*, Leipzig.

Axford, W., 2000, 'Scotland the What?', in: *focus* 31 (1) 2000.

Ball, M. & G.E. Jones, eds., 1984, *Welsh Phonology. Selected Readings*, Caerdydd.

Baker, M., 1992, *In Other Words*, London, New York.

Barbier, A. & M. Barbier et al., 1822-27, *Dictionnaire des ouvrages anonymes et pseudonymes composés, traduits ou publiés en français et en latin, avec les noms des auteurs, traducteurs et éditeurs*, Paris.

Bartel, H. & D. Fricke et al., 1984, *Wörterbuch der Geschichte*, Berlin.

Bergenholtz, H. & J. Mugdan, eds., 1985, *Lexicographie und Grammatik*, in: *Lexicographica Series Maior* 3. Tübingen.

Bergenholtz, H. & S. Tarp, 1995, *Manual of Specialised Lexicography*, Amsterdam, Philadelphia.

Best, R.I., 1913, *Bibliography of Irish Philology and of Printed Irish Literature*, Dublin.

Bischoff, B. & G. Harlow et al., 1988, *The Épinal, Erfurt, Werden, and Corpus Glossaries*, Copenhagen.

Bono, B., 1984, *Literary transvaluation: from Vergilian epic to Shakespearean tragicomedy*, Berkely, London.

Bowen, G., 1997, 'Roman Catholic Prose and its background', in: Gruffydd, R.G., 1997, *A guide to Welsh literature c. 1530-1700*, Caerdydd.

Brake, Ph., 1994, *Welsh in Three Months*, Norwich.

Broderick, G., 1999, *Language death in the Isle of Man: an investigation into the decline and extinction of Manx Gaelic as a community language in the Isle of Man*, Tübingen.

Bronstein, A.J., 1986, 'The History of Pronunciation in English-Language Dictionaries', in: Hartmann, R.R.K., 1986, *The History of Lexicography*, Amsterdam, Philadelphia.

Brooks, Seimon, ed., 2001, *Llythyrau at Seimon Glyn*, Talybont.

Brown, A., 1988, *The Renaissance*, London.

Brown, M.P., 1991, *Anglo-Saxon Manuscripts*, London.

Buchholz, O. & A. Beyrer et al., 1977, *Syntaktische Kontexte des Verbs in den Balkansprachen*, in: *Linguistische Studien*, Reihe A, Berlin.

Bullock-Davies, C., 1966, *Professional Interpreters and the Matter of Britain*, Caerdydd.

Burgschmidt, E., 1984, 'Singularmarkiertheit im Walisischen und Englischen', in: *Anglistentag Konstanz 1983*, Giessen.

idem, 1990, 'Collectives and individualisation in German, English and Welsh', in: Bahner, W. & J. Schildt et al., eds., *Proceedings of the 14th International Congress of Linguistics*, Berlin.

Bussmann, H., 1996, *Dictionary of Language and Linguistics*, London, New York.

Calvez, R., 1999, 'Le réenchantement d'un monde. Mouvement breton, nazisme et émissions de radio en breton', in: Heinz, S., ed., 1999, *Die Deutsche Keltologie und ihre Berliner Gelehrten*, Berlin et al.

Carr, G., 1983, *William Owen Pughe*, Caerdydd.

Carstensen, B., 1985, 'Von *ja* bis *Jux* ohne *Tollerei*', in: Bergenholtz, H. & J. Mugdan, eds., 1985, *Lexikographie und Grammatik*, in: *Lexicographica Series Maior* 3, Tübingen.

Carter, R., 1987, *Vocabulary. Applied Linguistic Perspectives*, London.

Châtal, T., 1997, *Buhez hag oberoù Erwan Vertoù-Kaledvoulc'h*, Lesneven.

Chosmky, N., 1965, *Aspects of the theory of syntax*, Cambridge, MA.

Clarke, K., 1983, *The art of humanism*, London.

Cohen, W., 1985, *Drama of a nation: public theater in Renaissance England and Spain*. London.

Collins, S., 1989, *From divine cosmos to sovereign state: an intellectual history of consciousness and the idea of orders in Renaissance England*, New York, Oxford.

Cowie, A.P., 1990, 'Language as Words: Lexicography', in: Collinge, N.E., ed., 1990, *An Encyclopedia of Language*, London, New York.

idem, 1995, 'The Learner's Dictionary in a Changing Cultural Perspective', in: Kachru, B.B. & H. Kahane, eds., 1995, *Cultures, Ideologies, and the Dictionary*, in: *Lexicographica Series Maior* 64.

Cowley, F.G., 1977, *The Monastic Order in South Wales, 1066-1349*, Caerdydd.

Crystal, D., 1992, *An Encyclopedic Dictionary of Language and Languages*, Harmondsworth.

idem, 1999, 'Death sentence', in: *The Guardian*, 25.10.1999.

Cummins, J. & F. Genese, 1985, 'Bilingual Education Programmes in Wales and Canada', in: Dodsen, C.J., ed., *Bilingual Education: Evaluation, Assessment and Methodology*, Caerdydd.

Davies, C(ennard), 1975, *Gweld, dweud a gwneud: basic patterns in Welsh*, Llandysul.

Davies, C(eri), 1995, *Welsh Literature and the Classical Tradition*, Caerdydd.

Davies, E., 1954, 'Rhannu Geiriau', in: *Cyfarwyddiadau i Awduron*, Caerdydd.

Davies, J., 1990, *Hanes Cymru*, Caerdydd.

Davies, J., 1993, *The Welsh Language Today*, Caerydd.

Davies, V.E., 1959, *Gruffudd ap Cynan*, Caerdydd.

Davies, W., 1989, *Wales in the early Middle Ages*, Leicester.

Davies, W., 1990, *Patterns of Power in Early Wales*, Oxford.

De Bhaldraithe, 1981, 'Foclóir agus Foclóireacht na Gaeilge', in: *The Maynooth Review*. Revieú *Mhá Nuad*. A journal of the arts, vol. 6, no 1.

Délecourt, J., 1863, *Essai d'un dictionnaire des ouvrages anonymes et pseudonymes publiés en Belgique au XIX siècle*, Bruxelles.

Dixon, R.M.W., 1997, *The Rise and Fall of Languages*, Cambridge.

Dodd, W.St., 1998, 'Twentieth-Century Welsh Lexicography as a Context for the *Geiriadur yr Academi*', in: *International Journal of Lexicography*, Cowie, A.P., 1998, Oxford.

Dressler, W., 1972, *On the Phonology of Language Death. Papers from the Eighths Regional Meeting of the Chicago Linguistics Society*, Chicago.

Dressler, W. & R. Wodack-Leodolter, 1977, 'Language Preservation and Language Death in Brittany', in: *International Journal of Sociology of Language*, 12.

Edwards, H.T., 1976, *Yr Eisteddfod: cyfrol ddathlu wythganmlwyddiant yr Eisteddfod*, Llandysul.

Elis-Thomas, D., 1995, *The Panel for Official Welsh*, Caerdydd.

Elton, G.R., 1976, *Renaissance and Reformation, 1300-1648*, New York, London.

Emanuel, H., 1972, 'Geiriaduron Cymraeg 1547-1972', in: *Studia Celtica* 7.

508

Esteep, W.R., 1986, *Renaissance and Reformation*, Columbia.

Evans, D.S., 1992, *Gramadeg Cymraeg Canol*, Caerdydd.

Evans, J.G., 1898, *Report on Manuscripts in the Welsh Language vol 1.*, London.

Evans, J.J., 1960, *Gramadeg Cymraeg*, Llandysul.

Evans, J.W., 1991, *St. Davids Bishop's Palace*, Caerdydd.

Farina, D.M.T.C., 'Marrism and Soviet Lexicography', in: Kachru, B.B. & H. Kahane, eds., 1995, *Cultures, Ideologies, and the Dictionary*, in: *Lexicographica Series Maior* 64.

Fife, J., 1990, *The Semantics of the Welsh Verb*, Caerdydd.

Fife, J. & E. Poppe, 1991, *Studies in Brythonic Word Order*, Amsterdam, Philadelphia.

Fishman, J., 1991, *Reversing Language Shift*, in: *Multilingual Matters* 76, Clevedon, Philadelphia.

idem, 1995, 'Dictionaries as Culturally Constructed and as Culture-Constructing Artifacts: The Reciprocity View as Seen from Yiddish Sources', in: Kachru, B.B. & H. Kahane, eds., 1995, *Cultures, Ideologies, and the Dictionary*, in: *Lexicographica Series Maior* 64.

Foley, A., 1991, *The Yimas Language of New Guinea*, Stanford.

Franklin, A., *Dictionnaire des noms, surnomes et pseudonymes latins de l'histoire du moyan âge (1100 à 1530)*, Paris.

Gensler, O., 2002, 'Why should a demonstrative turn into a preposition? The evolution of Welsh predicate *yn*', in: *Language* 2002.

Giamatti, A.B., 1984, *Exile and change in Renaissance literature*, New Haven, London.

Gillies, W., 1993, *Scottish Gaelic*, in: Ball, J.M. & J. Fife, 1993, *The Celtic Languages*, London, New York.

Gneuss, H., 1992, "Bücher und Leser in England im zehnten Jahrhundert", in: Tristram, H.L.C., ed., *Medialität und mittelalterliche insulare Literatur*, Tübingen.

Gordon, D.J., 1975, *The Renaissance imagination: essays and lectures*, Berkely, London.

Görlach, M., 1997, 'Language and nation: the concept of linguistic identity in the history of English', in: Görlach, M, ed., 1997, *English World-Wide. A Journal of Varieties of English*, vol. 18, Amsterdam.

Graustein, G. & A. Hoffmann et al., 1982, *English Grammar*, Leipzig.

Green, J., 1977, *Chasing the Sun. Dictionary-makers and the Dictionaries They Made*, London.

Gruffudd, H., 1999a, *Cynllun Normaleiddio Addysg Gymraeg yn Abertawe*, Abertawe.

idem, 1999b, *Awdurdod Iaith i Gymru*, Talybont.

Gruffydd, R.G., 1972, *Argraffwyr Cyntaf Cymru. Gwasgau Dirgel Y Catholigion Adeg Elisabeth*, Caerdydd.

idem, 1989, *Llenyddiaeth Y Cymry. Cyfrol 2.* Llandysul.

Halliday, M.A.K., 1985, *Introduction to functional grammar*, London.

Halloran, J.A., 2002, *Sumerian Lexicon*, München.

Hansen, K., 1987, *Studien zur Sprachvariation (unter besonderer Berücksichtigung des Englischen)*, Berlin.

Hansen, K., Carls, U. & P. Lucko, 1996, *Die Differenzierung des Englischen in nationale Varianten. Eine Einführung*, Berlin.

Harrison, A., 1986, 'Nótaí faoi Ghraiméir agus Foclóirí Scuitbhéarla i mBaile Átha Cliath 1700-1740', in: Watson, S., 1986, *Féilscríbhinn Thomáis de Bhaldraithe*, Dundalk.

Hart, H., 1998, *Hart's Rules for Compositors and Readers at the University Press Oxford*, Oxford.

Hartmann, R.R.K. & G. James, 1998, *Dictionary of lexicography*, London.

Hartung, W., 1998, 'Sprachdiskurse und ihre Bedeutung für ethnische Zusammengehörigkeit und Abgrenzung', *Utopie Kreativ* 95 (September) 1998.

509

Hausmann, F.J., 1989, 'Wörterbuchtypologie', in: Hausmann, F.J. & H.E. Wiegand et al., 1989, *Wörterbücher. Dictionaries. Dictionnaires. Ein internationales Handbuch zur Lexikographie*, in: Steger, H. & E.H. Wiegand, eds., *Handbücher zur Sprach- und Kommunikationswissenschaft*, Berlin, New York.

Hausmann, F.J. & H.E. Wiegand et al., 1989, *Wörterbücher. Dictionaries. Dictionnaires. Ein internationales Handbuch zur Lexikographie*, in: Steger, H. & E.H. Wiegand, eds., *Handbücher zur Sprach- und Kommunikationswissenschaft*, Berlin, New York.

Heath, D., 1985, 'Grammatische Angaben in Lernerwörterbüchern des Englischen', in: Bergenholtz, Henning & Joachim Mugdan, eds., 1985, *Lexikographie und Grammatik*, in: *Lexicographica Series Maior* 3, Tübingen.

Heinz, M., 1993, *Ethnizität und ethnische Identität*, Bonn.

Heinz, S., 1994, *Eia Popeia*. (Translation of the novel *Si Hei Lwli* by Angharad Tomos, 1991, Talybont; including glossary 'Walisisch-Deutsch'), Lewiston.

idem, 1995, 'Gareth King Modern Welsh: A Comprehensive Grammar', review in: *ZcP* 47.

idem, 1998a, 'Gareth King Colloquial Welsh: A Complete Language Course', review in: *ZcP* 51.

idem, 1998b, 'Der Anschluß von Wales an England und seine Folgen', in: *Utopie Kreativ* 9/1998.

idem, 1999a, 'Study Visit to the Basque Community in France - *Iparralde*', to be published by The European Bureau for Lesser Used Languages.

idem, 1999b, 'Frühe walisische Sprachmittler und ihr Handwerkszeug im multikulturellen Spannungsfeld', in: Poppe, E. & H.L.C. Tristram, 1999, *Übersetzung, Adaption und Akkulturation im insularen Mittelalter*, Münster.

idem, 2000, 'Die keltischen Sprachen an den Rändern Großbritanniens', in: *Hard Times* 71.

idem, forthcoming, 'The Diminutive in the Modern Welsh Language', to be published by Celtic Forum/Japan.

Helbig, G. & J. Buscha, 1981, *Deutsche Grammatik. Ein Handbuch für den Ausländerunterricht*, Leipzig.

Helbig, G. & W. Schenkel, 1973, *Wörterbuch zur Valenz und Distribution deutscher Verben*, Leipzig.

Hemon, R., 1976, 'Diminutive Suffixes in Breton', in: *Celtica* 12/1976.

Herbst, T., 1983, 'Untersuchungen zur Valenz englischer Adjektive und ihrer Nominalisierungen', in: *Tübinger Beiträge zur Linguistik* 233.

idem, 1985, 'Das zweisprachige Wörterbuch als Schreibwörterbuch: Informationen zur Syntax in zweisprachigen Wörterbüchern Englisch-Deutsch/Deutsch-Englisch', in: Bergenholtz, H. & J. Mugdan, eds., 1985, *Lexikographie und Grammatik*, in: *Lexicographica Series Maior* 3, Tübingen.

Herder, J.G., 1772, *Über den Ursprung der Sprache*, Berlin.

Hincks, Rh., 1993, *Geiriau Llydaweg a fabwysiadwyd gan y geiriadurwyr Thomas Jones, Iolo Morganwg, William Owen Pughe ac eraill*, Aberystwyth.

Hindley, R., 1991, *The Death of the Irish Language*, London, New York.

Hofman, R., 1996, *The Sankt Gall Priscian commentary*, Münster.

Hugh, D., 2000, *Medieval Welsh Manuscripts*, Aberystwyth.

Hughes, J.E., 1998, *Canllawiau Ysgrifennu Cymraeg*, Llandysul.

Humphreys, H.Ll., 2000, 'Le pays de Galles tel qu'en lui-même...' in: Le Disez, J-Y., 2000, *Triade*, Brest.

Huws, D., 2000, *Medieval Welsh Manuscripts*, Caerdydd, Aberystwyth.

510

Ickler, T., 1985, 'Valenz und Bedeutung. Beobachtungen zur Lexikographie des Deutschen als Fremdsprache', in: Bergenholtz, H. & J. Mugdan, eds., 1985, *Lexikographie und Grammatik*, in: *Lexicographica Series Maior* 3, Tübingen.

Ilson, R.F., 1991, 'Lexicography', in: Malmkjær, K., ed., 1991, *The Linguistic Encyclopedia*, London, New York.

Isaac, G.R., 1994, 'The Progressive Aspect Marker: W. *yn*/OIr. *oc*', in: *Journal of Celtic Linguistics* 3.

idem, 1996, *The verb in the Book of Aneirin: studies in syntax, morphology, and etymology*, Tübingen.

Jackson, K.H., 1994, *Language and HIstory in Early Britain*, Dublin.

Jackson, H., 1985, 'Grammar in the Dictionary', in: Ilson, R., 1985, *Dictionaries, Lexicography and Language Learning*, Oxford.

Jarman, A.O.H. & G.R. Hughes, 1976, *A guide to Welsh literature. Volume 1*, Swansea.

Jarvis, B., 1997, 'Welsh Humanist Learning', in: Gruffydd, R.G., 1997, *A guide to Welsh literature c. 1530-1700*, Caerdydd.

Jenkins, D., 1970, *Cyfraith Hywel*, Llandysul.

Jenkins, G.H. & M.A. Williams, 2000, 'The Fortunes of the Welsh Language 1900-2000: Introduction', in: Jenkins, G.H. & M.A. Williams, eds., 2000, *Let's Do our Best for the Ancient Tongue. The Welsh Language in the Twentieth Century*, Caerdydd.

Jenkins, G.H., 1983, *Hanes Cymru yn y Cyfnod Modern Cynnar*, Caerdydd.

idem, ed., 1997, *The Welsh Language before the Industrial Revolution*, Caerdydd.

Jones, A. & A. Jones, 1967-1977, *Siarad Cymraeg 1*, Pontypridd.

idem, 1970 (1982), *Siarad Cymraeg 2*, Pontypridd.

Jones, B., 1965-68, *Cymraeg i Oedolion*, Caerdydd.

Jones, B.R., 1994, *William Salesbury*, Caerdydd.

Jones, D., 1997, *Cyflwyniad i Ddwyieithrwydd*, Aberystwyth.

Jones, D.L., 1974, 'Dehongli'r Dull Dwyieithog', in: Williams, J.L., 1974, *Ysgrifau ar Addysg*, Caerydd.

Jones, E., 1992, 'Economic Change and the Survival of a Minority Language: A Case Study of the Welsh Language', in: Dafis, Ll., 1992, *Lesser Used Languages - Assimilating Newcomers*, Carmarthen.

Jones, E.P. & D. Reynolds, 1998, 'Education', in: Osmond, J., ed., 1998, *The National Assembly Agenda. A Handbook for the First Four Years*, Caerdydd.

idem, no date, *Welsh Medium & Bilingual Education in Wales. Addysg Gymraeg a Dwyieithog yng Nghymru*, Caerdydd.

Jones, G., 1994, *Welsh Roots and Branches*, Powys.

Jones, G.E., 1984, *The Distinctive Vowels and Consonants of Welsh*, in: Ball, M.J. & G.E. Jones, 1984, *Welsh Phonology. Selected Readings*, Caerdydd.

Jones, J.G., 1994, *Hanes Cymru*, Caerdydd.

Jones, M., & A. R. Thomas, 1977, *The Welsh Language: studies in its syntax and semantics*, Caerdydd.

Jones, M.C., 1998, *Language Obsolescence and Revitalization*, Oxford.

Jones, Rh.T.J., 1992, *Teach Yourself Welsh*, London.

Jones, T., 1983, *Hanes Cymru yn oes y tywysogion*, Caerdydd.

Kabel, L., 1995, 'Pobal na Gaeilge - The Communicative Aspect of Irish in Belfast', unpublished paper.

Kibee, A.D., 1986, 'The Humanist Period in Renaissance Bilingual Lexicography', in: Hartmann, R.R.K., 1986, *The History of Lexicography*, Amsterdam, Philadelphia.

Keynes, S. & M. Lapidge, eds., 1983, *Alfred the Great*, Harmondsworth.

Kim, Ch.W., 1995, 'One Language, Two Ideologies, and Two Dictionaries: The Case of Korean', in: Kachru, B.B. & H. Kahane, eds., 1995, *Cultures, Ideologies, and the Dictionary*, in: *Lexicographica Series Maior* 64.

King, G., 1993, *Modern Welsh: A Comprehensive Grammar*, London.

idem, 1995, *Colloquial Welsh: A Complete Language Course*, London.

Klappenbach, R. & W. Steinitz, 1981, *Wörterbuch der deutschen Gegenwartssprache*, Bd. 4, Berlin.

Klaus, G. & M. Buhr, 1975, *Philosophisches Wörterbuch*, Leipzig.

Knowles, F.E., 1995, 'Dictionaries for the People or for People?', in: Kachru, B.B. & H. Kahane, eds., 1995, *Cultures, Ideologies, and the Dictionary*, in: *Lexicographica Series Maior* 64.

Koch, J.T., 1997, *The Gododdin of Aneurin: text and context from Dark-Age North Britain: historical introduction - reconstructed text - translation - notes*, Caerdydd.

Kromann, H.-P., 1985, 'Zur Selektion und Darbietung syntaktischer Informationen in einsprachigen Wörterbüchern des Deutschen aus der Sicht ausländischer Benutzer', in: Bergenholtz, H. & J. Mugdan, eds., 1985, *Lexikographie und Grammatik*, in: *Lexicographica Series Maior* 3, Tübingen.

Kühn, P., 1989, 'Typologie der Wörterbücher nach Benutzungsmöglichkeiten', in: Hausmann, F.J. & H.E. Wiegand et al., 1989, *Wörterbücher. Dictionaries. Dictionnaires. Ein internationales Handbuch zur Lexikographie*, in: Steger, H. & E.H. Wiegand, eds., *Handbücher zur Sprach- und Kommunikationswissenschaft*, Berlin, New York.

Lapidge, M, 1986, "Latin Learning in Dark Age Wales", in: *Proceedings of the Seventh International Congress of Celtic Studies*.

Lara, L.F., 1995, 'Towards a Theory of the Cultural Dictionary', in: Kachru, B.B. & H. Kahane, eds., 1995, *Cultures, Ideologies, and the Dictionary*, in: *Lexicographica Series Maior* 64.

Laugaa, M., 1986, *La Pensée du pseudonyme*, Paris.

Lauster, U., 1999, *Englischspiele*, Munich.

Le Dû, J. & Y. Le Berre, 1996, 'Français - Breton', in: Goeble, H. et al., eds., 1996, *Kontaktlinguistik*, Berlin.

Le Dû, J., 1999, 'Through the Breton Looking Glass', paper at the Humboldt-University on the 17th of June in 1999.

Le Menn, G., 1981, *Contribution à l'étude de l'histoire des dictionnaires Bretons, Thèse d'université Haute-Bretagne Rennes II*, Part I-VIII, Rennes.

Lehnert, M., 1956, 'Das englische Wörterbuch in Vergangenheit und Gegenwart', in: *Zeitschrift für Anglistik und Amerikanistik* 4 (1956) 3, Berlin.

Lemmens, M. & H. Wekker, 1986, *Grammar in English Learners' Dictionaries*, in: *Lexicographica Series Maior* 16, Tübingen.

Lepschy, A.L. & J. Took et al., 1986, *Book production and Letters in the Western European Renaissance*, London.

Letts, R.M., 1981, *The Renaissance*, Cambridge.

Lewandowska-Tomaszczyk, B., 1995, 'Worldview and Verbal Senses', in: Kachru, B.B. & H. Kahane, eds., 1995, *Cultures, Ideologies, and the Dictionary*, in: *Lexicographica Series Maior* 64.

Lewis, C.W., 1997, 'The Decline of Professional Poetry', in: Gruffydd, R.G., 1997, *A guide to Welsh literature*, Caerdydd.

Lewis, D.G., 1993, *Y Treigladur*, Llandysul.

idem, 1995, *Y Llyfr Berfau*, Llandysul.

Lewis, S., 1932, *Braslun ar Hanes Llenyddiaeth Gymraeg*, Caerdydd.

Lindsay, D., 1971, *From darkness to light: Renaissance science*, Harlow.

512

Lindsay, W.M., 1929, 'Introduction', in: Stevenson, W.H., 1929, *Early Welsh Scholastic Colloquies*, Oxford.

Lloyd, J.E., 1937, *The Story of Ceredigion*, Caerdydd.

Lloyd, N., 1970, *A history of Welsh scholarship in the first half of the seventeenth century, with special reference to the writings of John Jones, Gellilyfdy. D.Phil.*, Oxford.

idem, 1997, 'Late Free-Metre Poetry', in: Gruffydd, R.G., 1997, *A guide to Welsh literature c. 1530-1700*, Caerdydd.

Lowson, N., 1991, *A new Geography of Wales*, Cambridge.

MacGiolla Chríost, 2000a, 'The Irish Language and Current Policy in Northern Ireland', in: *Irish Studies Review* 8 (2000) 1.

idem, 2000b, 'Civic and ethnic nationalism in the Celtic UK: the linguistic context', unpublished paper.

Malo, R.J., 1994, *Les pseudonymes des Bretons*, Brest.

Matonis, A.T.E., 1981, 'The Welsh Bardic Grammars and the Western Grammatical Tradition', in: *Modern Philology* 79.

idem, 1990, 'Problems Relating to the Composition of the Welsh Bardic Grammars', in: Matonis, A.T.E. & D.F. Melia, 1990, *Celtic Language, Celtic Culture: A Festschrift for Eric P. Hamp*, California.

McCorduck, E.S., 1993, *Grammatical Information in ESL Dictionaries*, in: *Lexicographica Series Maior* 48, Tübingen.

McKee, 2000, *Juvencus: Codex Cantabrigiensis*, in: Sims-Williams, 2000, *Cambridge Medieval Celtic Studies*, Cambridge.

Merser, A., 1980, 'Les Graphies du Breton', in: *Ar Helenner* 15.

Meyer, K., 1907, 'The Sources of some Middle-Irish Glossaries', in: *Archiv für Celtische Lexikographie* III., Halle.

idem, ed., 1914, *Sanas Cormaic. An Old Irish Glossary*. Dublin.

Mirollo, J.V., 1984, *Mannerism and Renaissance poetry: concept, mode and inner design*, New Haven, London.

Moon, R., 1998, *Fixed Expressions and Idioms in English*, Oxford.

Morgan, T.J., 1989, *Y Treigladau a'u Cystrawen*, Caerdydd.

Morris, D., 1992, 'The Effect of Economic Changes on Gwynedd Society', in: Dafis, Ll., 1992, *Lesser Used Languages - Assimilating Newcomers*, Carmarthen.

Morris-Jones, J., 1890, *Yr Orgraff*, Caernarfon.

idem, 1913 (1970), *A Welsh Grammar. Historical and Comparative*, Oxford.

idem, 1922, *An elementary Welsh grammar*, Oxford.

idem, 1925, *Cerdd dafod sef celfyddyd barddoniaeth Gymraeg*, Oxford.

idem, 1931, *Welsh syntax: an unfinished draft*, Caerdydd.

Mugdan, J. 1985, 'Pläne für ein grammatisches Wörterbuch. Ein Werkstattbericht', in: Bergenholtz, H. & J. Mugdan, 1985, *Lexikographie und Grammatik*, in: *Lexicographica Series Maior* 3, Tübingen.

Mungham, G. & K. Williams, 1998, 'The Press and Media', in: Osmond, J., ed., 1998, *National Assembly Agenda. A Handbook for the first four years*, Caerdydd.

Murray, J.A.H., 1900, *The Evolution of English lexicography*, Oxford.

Ó Cuív, B., ed., 1961, *Seven Centuries of Irish Learning 1000-1700*, Radio Éireann.

idem, 1973, *The Linguistic Training of the Medieval Irish Poet*, Dublin.

O'Rahilly, C., 1924, *Ireland and Wales. Their Historical and Literary Relations*, New York.

O'Rahilly, T.F., 1988, *Irish Dialects. Past and Present*, Dublin.

Osmond, J., ed., 1998, *The National Assembly Agenda. A Handbook for the First Four Years*, Caerdydd.

513

Osselton, N.E., 1986, 'The First English Dictionary? A sixteenth-century compiler at work', in: Hartmann, R.R.K., 1986, *The History of Lexicography*, Amsterdam, Philadelphia.

Pagel, W., 1986, *From Paracelsus to Van Helmot: studies in Renaissance medicine and science*, London.

Palisca, C., 1986, *Humanism in Renaissance Musical Thought*, Yale.

Palmer, H.E., 1938, *A Grammar of English Words*, London.

idem, 1938, *A Grammar of spoken English*, Cambridge.

Parry, Ch., 1997, 'From Manuscript to Print - II. Printed Books', in: Gruffydd, R.G., 1997, *A guide to Welsh literature c. 1530-1700*, Caerdydd.

Parry, Th., 1979, *Gwaith Dafydd ap Gwilym*, Caerydd.

Pheifer, J.D., 1988, 'Épinal and Erfurt I', in: Bischoff, B. & G. Harlow et al., 1988, *The Épinal, Erfurt, Werden, and Corpus Glossaries*, Copenhagen.

Phillips, D., 2000, *The History of the Welsh Language Society 1962-1998*, in: Jenkins, G.H. & M.A. Williams, eds., 2000, *Let's Do our Best for the Ancient Tongue. The Welsh Language in the Twentieth Century*, Caerdydd.

idem, 1998, *Trwy ddulliau chwyldro...? Hanes Cymdeithas yr Iaith Gymraeg*, Llandysul.

Pilch, H., 1975, 'Advanced Welsh Phonemics', in: *ZcP* 34.

idem, 1995, 'Word Formation in Welsh and Breton: A Comparative Study', in: *ZcP* 48.

Pohling, H., 1971, 'Zur Geschichte der Übersetzung', in: *Beihefte zur Zeitschrift Fremdsprachen* III/IV, Leipzig, 125-162.

Poppe, E., 1991, 'The figures of speech in *Gramadegau 'r Penceirddiaid*', in: *BBCS* 38.

idem, 1997, 'Henry Salesbury's Grammatica Britannica (1593) and Ramist Linguistic Method', in: *Studia Celtica Japonica* 9.

Powell, Th., 1887, 'Notes on William Salesbury's Dictionary', in: *Y Cymmrodor*, vol. 8.

Quirk, R. & S. Greenbaum et al., 1972, *A Grammar of Contemporary English*, London.

Read, A.W., 1976, 'Dictionary', in: *The New Encyclopedia Britannica. Macropaedia*, Vol. 5., Chicago etc.

Rees, W., 1959, *Historical Atlas of Wales*, Caerdydd.

Reese, G., 1959, *Music in the Renaissance*, New York.

Reid, John, 1832 (1968), *Bibliotheca Scoto-Celtica*, Glasgow, Edinburgh, London.

Roberts, M.E. & R.M. Jones, 1974, 'Cyfeiriadur i'r Athro Iaith', in: Williams, J.L., 1974, *Ysgrifau ar Addysg*, Caerdydd.

Ross, B., 1996, *Britannica et Hibernia: nationale und kulturelle Identitäten in Irland des 17. Jahrhunderts*, Heidelberg.

Rowland, T., 1872, *A Grammar of the Welsh Language*, Wrexham.

Russell, P., 1988, 'The Sounds of a Silence: The Growth of Cormac's Glossary', in: Sims-Williams, P., ed., *Cambridge Medieval Studies* 15 (Summer 1988), Cambridge.

Russell, P., 1999, 'Laws, Glossaries and Legal Glossaries in Early Ireland', in: *ZcP* 51.

Schaeder, B., 1985, 'Die Beschreibung der Präpositionen im einsprachigen deutschen Wörterbuch', in: Bergenholtz, Henning & Joachim Mugdan, eds., 1985, *Lexikographie und Grammatik*, in: *Lexicographica Series Maior* 3, Tübingen.

Schmidt, K.H., 1991, 'Altirische Lexicographie', in: *Wörterbücher. Dictionaries. Dictionnaires*, Berlin, New York.

Schmitt, Ch.B., 1984, *The Aristotelian tradition and Renaissance universities*, London.

Schmitt, Ch.B. & Q. Skinner et al., 1988, *The Cambridge History of Renaissance philosophy*, Cambridge.

Schumacher, H., 1985, 'Grammatik im semantisch orientierten Valenzwörterbuch', in: Bergenholtz, H. & J. Mugdan, 1985, *Lexikographie und Grammatik*, in: *Lexicographica Series Maior* 3, Tübingen.

514

Scott, M., 1982, *Renaissance drama and a modern audience*, Basingstoke.

Sintenis, F., 'Die Pseudonyme der neueren deutschen Literatur, Vortrag gehalten zu Dorpat am 29.11.1896', Hamburg.

Skidmore, I., 1996, *Owain Glyndŵr*, Abertawe.

Slover, C.H., 1926, *Early Literary Channels between Britain and Ireland*, Texas.

Sorlin, E., 1999, 'Geiriadur yr Academi: The Welsh Academy English-Welsh dictionary', in: *ZcP* 51.

Standop, E., 1985, *Englische Wörterbücher unter der Lupe*, in: *Lexicographica Series Maior* 2, Tübingen.

Stassen, L., 1985, *Comparison and Universal Grammar*, Oxford.

Stein, Gabriele, 1986, 'Sixteenth-Century English-Vernacular Dictionaries', in: Hartmann, R.R.K., 1986, *The History of Lexicography*, Amsterdam, Philadelphia.

Stephens, M., ed., 1997, *Cydymaith i Lenyddiaeth Cymru*, Caerdydd.

Stephens, R., 1983, *Gwaith William Llŷn*, Aberystwyth.

Strachan, J., 1900, 'The notes and glosses in the Lebor na hUidre', in: *Archiv für Celtische Lexikographie* I., Halle.

Sven-Myer, G., 1999, 'The response of the Breton journal Gwalarn to the Second World War', in: Heinz, S., ed., 1999, *Die Deutsche Keltologie und ihre Berliner Gelehrten bis 1945*, Berlin et al.

Ternes, E., 1991a, 'Die Lexikographie der neukeltischen Sprachen', in: *Wörterbücher. Dictionaries. Dictionnaires. Ein internationales Handbuch zur Lexikographie*, in: Steger, H. & E.H. Wiegand, eds., *Handbücher zur Sprach- und Kommunikationswissenschaft*, Berlin, New York.

idem, 1991b, 'Neue Überlegungen zur Wörterbuchtypologie: Segmentierung als Klassifikationsmerkmal', in: *Lexicographica* 7/1991, Tübingen.

Thomas, A.R., 1992, 'The Welsh language', in: Macaulay, D., 1992, *The Celtic Languages*. Cambridge.

idem, 2000, *The Welsh Dialect Survey*, Caerdydd.

Thomas, B. & P.W. Thomas, 1989, *Cymraeg, Cymrâg, Cymrêg... Cyflwyno'r Tafodieithoedd*, Caerdydd.

Thomas, G.C.G., 1997, 'From Manuscript to Print - I. Manuscript', in: Gruffydd, R.G., 1997, *A guide to Welsh literature c. 1530-1700*, Caerdydd.

Thomas, H., 1972, *A History of Wales 1485-1660*, Caerdydd.

Thomas, I., 1997, 'Translating the Bible', in: Gruffydd, R.G., 1997, *A guide to Welsh literature c. 1530-1700*, Caerdydd.

Thomas, P.W., 1995, *Gramadeg y Gymraeg*, Caerdydd.

Thomson, D., 1993, *The Companion to Gaelic Scotland*, Glasgow.

Thorne, D., 1985, *Cyflwyniad i Astudio'r Iaith Gymraeg*, Caerdydd.

idem, 1991, 'Cymreigyddion y Fenni a Dechreuadau Ieitheg Gymharol yng Nghymru', in: *Cylchgrawn Llyfrgell Genedlaethol Cymru* 27.

idem, 1993, *A Comprehensive Welsh Grammar*, Oxford.

Tovey, H. & D. Hannan et al., 1989, *Cad Chuige An Ghaeilge? Why Irish?*, Dublin.

Tristram, H.L.C, 1997, *The Celtic Englishes I*, Heidelberg.

idem, 2000, *The Celtic Englishes II*, Heidelberg.

idem, 2002, *The Celtic Englishes III*, Heidelberg.

Trubetzkoy, N., 1939, *Grundzüge der Phonologie*, Göttingen.

Vetter, E., 1997, *Nicht mehr Bretonisch?*, Berlin, Bern et al.

Watkins, T.A., 1961, *Ieithyddiaeth. Agweddau ar Astudio Iaith*, Caerdydd.

515

idem, 1992, *Kurze Beschreibung des Kymrischen*, in: Meid, W., ed., 1992, *Innsbrucker Beiträge zur Sprachwissenschaft* 71.

idem, 1993, 'Welsh', in: Ball, M. J. & J. Fife, eds., 1993, *The Celtic Languages*, London, New York.

Wells, J.C, 1985, 'English Pronunciation And Its Dictionary Representation', in: Ilson, R., ed. 1985, *Dictionaries, Lexicography and Language Learning*, Oxford.

Wiegand, H.F., 1989a, 'Aspekte der Makrostruktur im allgemeinen einsprachigen Wörterbuch: alphabetische Anordnungsformen und ihre Probleme', in: Hausmann, F.J. & H.E. Wiegand et al., 1989, *Wörterbücher. Dictionaries. Dictionnaires. Ein internationales Handbuch zur Lexikographie*, in: Steger, H. & E.H. Wiegand, eds., *Handbücher zur Sprach- und Kommunikationswissenschaft*, Berlin, New York.

idem, 1989b, 'Der Begriff der Mikrostruktur: Geschichte, Probleme, Perspektiven', in: Hausmann, F.J. & H.E. Wiegand et al., 1989, *Wörterbücher. Dictionaries. Dictionnaires. Ein internationales Handbuch zur Lexikographie*, in: Steger, H. & E.H. Wiegand, eds., *Handbücher zur Sprach- und Kommunikationswissenschaft*, Berlin, New York.

idem, 1989c, 'Formen von Mikrostrukturen im allgemeinen einsprachigen Wörterbuch', in: Hausmann, F.J. & H.E. Wiegand et al., 1989, *Wörterbücher. Dictionaries. Dictionnaires. Ein internationales Handbuch zur Lexikographie*, in: Steger, H. & E.H. Wiegand, eds., *Handbücher zur Sprach- und Kommunikationswissenschaft*, Berlin, New York.

idem., 1998, *Wörterbuchforschung*, Berlin, New York.

Wight, A.D., 1896, *The Warfare of Science with Theology*, New York.

Williams, C., 1999, *Cymraeg Clir*, Bangor.

Williams, C.H., 1998, 'Operating through two languages', in: Osmond, J., ed., 1998, *The National Assembly Agenda*, Caerdydd.

idem, 2000, 'Restoring the Language', in: Jenkins, G.H. & M.A. Williams, eds., 2000, *Let's Do our Best for the Ancient Tongue. The Welsh Language in the Twentieth Century*, Caerdydd.

Williams, G., 1996, 'Nodiadau Golygyddol' in: *Taliesin*, vol. 93, Spring 1996, Caerdydd.

Williams, G., 1997a, 'Unity of Religion or Unitiy of Language? Protestants and Catholics and the Welsh Language 1536-1660', in: Jenkins, G., 1997, *The Welsh Language before the Industrial Revolution*, Caerdydd.

idem, 1997b, *Wales and the Reformation*, Caerdydd.

Williams, G. & D. Morris, 2000, *Language Planning and Language Use. Welsh in a Global Age*, Caerdydd.

Williams, I., 1941, "Vocabularium Cornicum", in: *BBCS* 11.

Williams, J.E. Caerwyn, 1983, *Geiriadurwyr y Gymraeg yng Nghyfnod y Dadeni*, Caerdydd.

idem, 1988, *Llyfryddiaeth yr iaith Gymraeg*, Caerdydd.

idem, 1995, 'Preface', in: Griffiths, B. & D.G. Jones, 1995, *Geiriadur yr Academi. The Welsh Academy English-Welsh Dictionary*, Caerdydd.

Williams, S.J., 1990, *Elfennau Gramadeg Cymraeg*, Caerdydd.

Wolski, W., 1989, 'Das Lemma und die verschiedenen Lemmatypen, in: Hausmann, F.J. & H.E. Wiegand et al., 1989, *Wörterbücher. Dictionaries. Dictionnaires. Ein internationales Handbuch zur Lexikographie*, in: Steger, H. & E.H. Wiegand, eds., *Handbücher zur Sprach- und Kommunikationswissenschaft*, Berlin, New York.

Zimmer, S., 2000, *Studies in Welsh Word-Formation*, Dublin.

Zorc, R.D., 1995, 'Philippine Regionalism versus Nationalism and the Lexicographer', in: Kachru, B.B. & H. Kahane, eds., 1995, *Cultures, Ideologies, and the Dictionary*, in: *Lexicographica Series Maior* 64.

6.2.2.2.   Institutions

Canolfan Dysgu Cymraeg, 1991, *Cwrs Wlpan*, Caerdydd.

Uned Iaith Genedlaethol Cymru, 1976, *Gramadeg Cymraeg Cyfoes*, Y Bontfaen.

Welsh Joint Education Committee, 1991, *Canllawiau Ysgrifenedig Cymraeg Llafar*, Caerdydd.

Welsh Office, 1995, *1992 Welsh Social Survey: Report on the Welsh Language*, Caerdydd.

6.2.3. Documents and Manuscripts

Bwrdd yr Iaith Gymraeg, 1997, Data Ynghylch Addysg Cyfrwng Cymraeg.
Bwrdd yr Iaith Gymraeg, 1998, Data Regarding Welsh Medium Education.
Bwrdd yr Iaith Gymraeg, 1999, *Y Ffeil-o-Iaith Gymraeg*, Caerdydd.
Bwrdd yr Iaith Gymraeg, 2001, *Gwyddoniaeth a Mathemateg Trwy Gyfrwng y Gymraeg - Y Ffeithiau!* (flyer)
Council of Europe/Conseil de l'Europe, 1992, *European Charter for Regional or Minority Languages. Charte européene des langues régionales ou minoritaires*, in: *European Treaty Series. Série des traités européen*/148, Strasbourg.
Cylch yr Iaith, 2001, *Arolwg Cylch yr Iaith o Rhaglenni Radio Cymru Wythnos 1.7.01-7.7.01*.
Cymdeithas yr Iaith, *Y Tafod dyddiol* (flyer from 11.8.2000).
Cymuned, *Poeni fod eich iaith yn marw?* (flyer from August 2001)
Education Reform Act 1988, Chapter 40, pp. 2039-2041.
House of Commons, 1996, *Bovine Spongiform Encephalopathy in Great Britain. A Progress Report*, London.
Peniarth 169: Geirfa Roger Morris, ca. 1588, Aberystwyth.
Peniarth 230: Geirfa Gruffudd Hiraethog, ca. 1560, Aberystwyth.
Peniarth 228: Geiriadur Thomas Wiliems, ca. 1607/08, Aberystwyth.
Peniarth 309: Geiriadur John Jones, ca. 1623, Aberysthwyth.
Plaid Cymru Newsletter, Spring 1996.
Welsh Language Act 1993, 1993 Chapter 38, pp. 1765-1783.

Leaflet by the staff of *Geiriadur Prifysgol Cymru*, 2000.

6.2.4. Personal correspondence

Brake, Ph., personal correspondence, July 1996.
Brooks, S., personal correspondence, 25.7.1996.
Falileyev, A.I., personal correspondence, 18.5.1998.
Griffith, W.Ll., personal correspondence, 7.11.2000.
Gruffudd, R., personal correspondence, 24.5. and 30.5.2000.
Hincks, R., personal correspondence, 18.7.1996.
Lacey, R. Personal correspondence, 13.9.2000.
Robertson, H., personal correspondence, 16.8.2000.
Thomas, W., personal correspondence, 20.6.1996.
Thomson, D., personal correspondence, 25.7.2000.

6.2.5. Papers

Barn (Nr. 314-316 1996, 318/319 1996, 398/399 1996, 426/427 1998)
Cambria (Autumn 1997, 1999)
Cambria News (24.5.1996, 31.5.1996, 3./17.10.1996)
Daily Post (21.3.2000, 18.8.1999, 18.8.1999, 21.3.2000, 1.4. 2000, 17.8.2000, 29.12.2001)
Der Standard (19.11.2001)
Golwg (continuously)
Gwaith Maes (Autumn 1995)
Lingo (March/April 1999)
Lol (Nr. 37, Summer 1999)
Sbec (18.1.-24.1.1997)
South Wales Echo (28.11.2000)
Tafod (Eisteddfod 1994)
Taliesin (Volume 93, 1996)
The Independent (3.2.2002, 11.2.2002)
Tivy-Side (1.9.1999)
Y Faner Newydd (12, Summer 1999)
Y Cymro (1.9.1999, 31.12.2000, 8.9.2001)
Yr Herald (5.8.1997, 4.8.2001)
Y Tir & Welsh Farmer (3/1989)
Wales on Sunday (21.9.1997)
Western Mail (24.5.1996, 31.5.1996, 7.6.1996, 15.9.1999)
Lili 7/1999

6.2.6. Internet Resources

Dictionaries:

(Breton)	http://www.francenet.fr/~perrot/breizh/dico.html (20.10.2001)
	http://www.bretons.org/dico.cgi (20.10.2001)
	http://www.notam.uio.no/~hcholm/altlang/ht/Breton.html (20.10.2001)
	http://www.breizh.net/saozg/mahtmls.htm (20.10.2001)
	http://www.compling.hu-berlin.de/~johannes/dict/brezhoneg/ (20.10.2001)
	http://www.mavicanet.com/directory/eng/22297.html (20.10.2001)
(Cornish)	http://www.summerlands.com/marketplace...ore2/amazon_store/language/cornish.htm, 20.10.2001)
	http://www.clas.demon.co.uk/html/body_lexicon.htm (20.10.2001)
(Irish)	http://www.csis.ul.ie/focloir/ (20.10.2001)
	http://www.smo.uhi.ac.uk/gaeilge/foclora/ (20.10.2001)
	http://www.smo.uhi.ac.uk/~smacsuib/bng/tobar/ (20.10.2001)
	http://www.foreignword.com/Tools/dictsrch.asp?p=files/f_40_87.htm (20.10.2001)
	http://gofree.indigo.ie/~cocaomh/English-Irish%20Dictionary.htm (20.10.2001)
	http://gofree.indigo.ie/~cocaomh/EnglishLatinIrish.htm (20.10.2001)
	http://irelandman.de/curgail/kurs-dic.pdf (20.10.2001)
	http://www.mavicanet.com/directory/eng/13428.html (20.10.2001)
	http://www.his.com/~rory/idicts.html (20.102001)
(Manx)	http://smo.uhi.ac.uk/~kelly/LIST/DICTIONARY/dict/index.html (20.10.2001)
	http://www.ceantar.org/Dicts/search.html (20.10.2001)
	http://homepages.enterprise.net/kelly/LIST/LESSONS/LESSONS.html (20.10.2001)
	http://www.embedded-systems.ltd.uk/ManxStart.html (20.10.2001)
(Sc. Gaelic)	http://www.ceantar.org/Dicts/search.html (20.10.2001)
	http://www.cs.vu.nl/dick/Summaries/Misc/NatLang.html (20.10.2001)
	http://www.electronicscotland.com/history/literat/dictiona.htm (10.10.2000)
	http://www.ceantar.org/Dicts/MB2/index.html (20.10.2001)
	http://psst-heyn.com/dictionarydownloads/slanguages.html (20.10.2001)
	http://www.ceantar.org/Dicts/MF2/index.html (20.10.2001)
	http://www.smo.uhi.ac.uk/cgi-bin/sbg (20.10.2001)
	http://www.smo.uhi.ac.uk/gaidhlig/ga-ge/gluais.html (20.10.2001)
	http://www.smo.uhi.ac.uk/gaidhlig/ga-ge/faclair.html (20.10.2001)
	http://www.smo.uhi.ac.uk/gaidhlig/ga-ge/coimeashtml (20.10.2001)
	http://www.smo.uhi.ac.uk/~smacsuib/focloir/gaelic-l/ (20.10.2001)
	http://www.sst.ph.ic.ac.uk/angus/Faclair (20.10.2001)
	http://www.estelnet.com/catalunyacymru/catala/dicgae_a.htm (20.10.2001)

520

(Welsh): http://members.tripod.com/gwybodiadur/dicts.1.htm (20.10.2001)
http://www.linguru.com/product/index.html (20.10.2001)
www.aber.ac.uk/~gpcwww/ (Geiriadur Prifysgol Cymru, 20.10.2001)
http://www.estelnet.com./catala/gbssampl.htm (20.10.2001)
http://perso.wanadoo.fr/heinecke/dict/cymraeg/ (20.10.2001)
http://www.cs.brown.edu/fun/welsh/LexiconForms.html (20.20.2001)
http://www.cyberphile.co.uk/~taff/taffnet/pages/xlate.htm (20.20.2001)
http://www.dragontechnology.com/geiriadur/ (20.10.2001)
http://cymraeg.lamp.ac.uk/geiriadur/ (20.10.2001 pass word necesary)
http://www.estelnet.com./catala/gbssampl.htm (20.20.2001)
http://pssst-heyu.com/dictionarydownloads/wlanguages.html
(20.20.2001)
http://www.melin.bangor.ac.uk/ga/ga.asp (temporarily available)

IPA: http://www2.arts.gla.ac.uk/IPA/ipa.html (20.10.2001)

Institutions:
Centre for Standardizing Terminology:
http://www.netwales.co.uk/byig/adrodds.htm (1.11.2000)
Libraries: www.ib.hu-berlin.de (Berlin/FR Germany)
www.library.nuigalway.ie (Galway/Ireland)
www.tcd.ie/library (Trinity College Dublin/Ireland)
http://www.nli.ie/bookscatalogue.html (National Library of Ireland)
http://booleweb.ucc.ie (Cork/Ireland)
www.llgc.org.uk (Aberystwyth/Wales)
www.nls.ac.uk (Edinburgh/Scotland)
http://catalogue.bnf.fr./ (Paris/France)
http://www.univ-brest.fr/S_Commun/Biblio/Catalogue.html
(Brest/France)
http://blpc.bl.uk/ (British Library)
Book shops: www.gwales.com
www.vlb.de
http://www.arbedkeltiek.com/galleg/livres.htm
http://www.addall.com/Browse/Author/2363662-1 (20.10.2001)
http://arbedkeltiek.com/galleg/rec_livres.asp/ (20.10.2001)

http://webbo.enst-bretagne.fr/Brezhonet/LevraBzh/savia-fr.htm (20.10.2001)
http://jade.ccccd.edu/grooms/llgrgh.htm (20.5.2000)
http://www.acad.bg/echo/eu92.html (15.11.2000)
http://www.netwales.co.uk/byig/adrodds.htm (1.11.2000)
http://www.eape.es/publications/RLD/rld29abs.htm (4.6.2001)
http://www.irlgov.ie/taoiseach/publication/english (1.1.2002)
TESTUNAU@JISCMAIL.AC.UK (20.10.2001)
http://www.aber.ac.uk/~merwww/papurdyddiol/PapCefn.htm (20.10.2001)
http://www.statistics.gov.uk/census2001/censuslatest.asp (24.10.2001)
http://www.cymdeithas.com/gwybodaeth/deddfiaith/canrifnewydd/ (20.10.2001)
http://bangor.ac.uk/addysg/cyrsiau/cstc.html (20.10.2001)
www.cymuned.org (20.10.2001)
http://www.penllyn.com/cymuned/papurau/cym1.html (7.11.2001)

http://www.bwrdd-yr-iaith.org.uk/ (20.10.2001)
http://wings.buffalo.edu/soc-sci/linguistics/dryer/dryer.hmt (20.10.2001)
http://www.aclu.org/library/pbp6.html (20.10.2001)
http://ourworld.compuserve.com/homepages/JWCRAWFORD (20.10.2001)

522

6.3. Index

524